THE AMY VANDERBILT
COMPLETE BOOK OF ETIQUETTE

To Joan & Hilary
Merry Christmas 1986

The Juckelands

Other Books by Letitia Baldrige

ROMAN CANDLE

TIFFANY TABLE SETTINGS

DIAMONDS AND DIPLOMATS

HOME

JUGGLING

THE AMY VANDERBILT COMPLETE BOOK OF ETIQUETTE

A Guide to Contemporary Living

Revised and Expanded by

LETITIA BALDRIGE

Drawings by Mona Marks

DOUBLEDAY & COMPANY, INC., GARDEN CITY, NEW YORK

I have used a variety of names and addresses for the sake of illustration. Any similarity to those of actual people, living or dead, is coincidental.

L.B.

Drawings on How to Eat a Maine Lobster, courtesy of the Maine Development Commission

ISBN: 0-385-13375-8 TRADE
      0-385-14238-2 THUMB INDEX
Library of Congress Catalog Card Number 77–16896

ACKNOWLEDGMENTS

During the two years of writing and revising this book, I talked to so many people about what is happening to human behavior and the manners which frame it that it would require another book to include them all. They all gave freely of their time and knowledge, but ultimately the finished material and the viewpoints the book reflect are mine alone. The following are but a few names of individuals and organizations who helped in this project.

The charts designating the correct forms of address for domestic and foreign officials were compiled after consulting at length with Elizabeth Denham of the Department of State; Ambassador Pedro de Churruca, the Chief of Protocol to the United Nations; Sarah Jack of the British Information Service; Gretchen E. Stewart; Dorothy Stewart; Joan Gudefin; the Social Office of the White House; the Protocol Division of the Department of State; and the Italian Mission to the United Nations. Advice on military protocol was obtained from the United States Military Academy, the United States Naval Academy, the United States Air Force Academy, and the United States Coast Guard Academy. Jean Schmidt of the United States Conference for the World Council of Churches, Inc., New York City, was of immeasurable help in advising on the proper address for the Protestant clergy. Also assisting with material on their own denominations were the Right Reverend James G. Wilders, St. Thomas More's Church, New York City, and the Reverend James B. Simpson, Christ Church, Middletown, New Jersey.

Gary Roberts of the New England Historic Genealogical Society, Boston, reviewed the material on heraldic devices, and Hope Skillman Schary of the National Council of Women of the United States, Inc., reviewed parliamentary procedure. Charles M. Forbes of the Memorial Sloan-Kettering Cancer Center provided valuable guidelines for hospital patients and their visitors; likewise, Claire G. Berman of the North American Center on Adoption, Loyce W. Bynum of the Spence-Chapin Services to Families and Children, New York City, and Jane Dunne and Evelyn Stein proved invaluable in advising me on the current situation in adoption. I wish to thank Eunice Kennedy Shriver of the Joseph P. Kennedy, Jr., Foundation, Washington, D.C., for her valuable suggestions regarding the handicapped person, as well as the New York Association for the Blind, the Rehabilitation Institute of Chicago, and the Lexington School for the Deaf, New York City. Information pertaining to drugs was obtained from Odyssey House, Inc.,

New York City; the American Lung Association; the National Council on Alcoholism; Freedom Institute and the National Clearing House for Drug Abuse, Rockville, Maryland. Circuit Judge Walter J. Cummings of Chicago, Gertrude S. Broker, and Olive A. Sullivan provided suggestions on courtroom behavior for prospective jurors. Barbara Tober, editor of *Bride's* and *Seventeen* magazine were helpful on a variety of subjects. Mary Lois Vann of the American Formalwear Association and Bob Pressman of Barney's provided assistance on the subject of men's wear. Tiffany & Company was extremely helpful pointing out current stationery trends and styles on monogramming. Among the stores assisting in many areas relating to the home were Léron, Inc.; Baccarat, Inc.; Bloomingdale's; and B. Altman & Company. Ely Callaway, Temecula, California, and Gateway Wine & Spirits Company, Inc., New York City, helped me to a great extent in the preparation of the section on wines. The subject of catering was researched through Hough Caterers, Inc., Cleveland; Gaper's Catering, Inc., Chicago; Charles Wilson Caterers, New York City; and Donald Bruce-White Caterers, Inc., New York City. Much of my information regarding travel was obtained from Frances Koltun; Peter Hahn of the Automobile Club of America, Inc.; Brian Duff, Director News Services, AMTRAK, Washington, D.C.; Lola Conrad, AMTRAK, New York City; Frew Hall Travel, Inc., New York City; Prudential Lines, Inc.; Avis Rent-a-Car; and Trailways Bus System. Michael Schweiger of New York's St. Regis-Sheraton helped me on hotels. In the area of sports, many people gave graciously of their time and knowledge, Laura L. Ault; Charlene S. Cruson of *Golf Digest;* Reese E. Howard; Lynn Jacox; Harry Platt; B. Blair Vedder, Jr.; William Wisner; the National Parks Service; National Ski Patrol Systems, Inc., Denver; and the U. S. Department of the Interior, Washington, D.C. Arthur Quinn, Chairman, New York Bank for Savings, and Roger Horchow were enormously helpful to me in many ways, as were the following people with whom I consulted on a variety of subjects: Thomas Almy; Alice Baldridge; Megan Baldrige; Molly Baldrige; Mally Cox-Chapman; Rosemary Falbee of the Family Court, Westbury, New York; Martha Langmann; Ellen LaNicca; Robert A. Mansur; Per Mohn; Nancy and Camilla Rees; Linda Richardson; Alexandra Tanner; B. J. Trumpbour; Betty Tuckerman; and Gail Wofford.

This new edition is lovingly dedicated
to the memory of the late Amy Vanderbilt

PUBLISHER'S NOTE

Doubleday has had the privilege of publishing *Amy Vanderbilt's Etiquette* since 1952. In Letitia Baldrige we and Miss Vanderbilt's heirs feel we have found an author eminently qualified to carry on this work. Ms. Baldrige served as Social Secretary in the American Embassies in Paris and Rome and was Social Secretary at the White House in the John F. Kennedy administration. She heads her own public relations firm and has a first-hand knowledge of manners, customs, and problems in everyday relationships for executives, including women, in business and the professions. As a wife and mother of two, Ms. Baldrige also has personal experience of the problems and needs of the family in a dynamic time. Today's world is an ever-changing one, offering innumerable options in the way we live and deal with one another. Letitia Baldrige brings to this book and to the complex world of contemporary manners a background in, and current knowledge of, the world of diplomacy, business, society, and the family.

PREFACE

When Doubleday asked me to carry on the work of the late Amy Vanderbilt, I was immensely pleased and felt not a little honored. Miss Vanderbilt (she wouldn't have liked my referring to her as "Ms. Vanderbilt") had spent twenty-five years observing and reporting on our society's mores with an expert eye. She had assisted literally millions of people through the years, answering their questions, and helping them feel better, live better, and relate to each other more easily. People sought her advice whether they were living in mansions or in efficiency apartments, in skyscrapers or in tract homes. Everyone at some time needs help in dealing with other people, whether a child is being christened or a daughter married, a woman is taking a trip alone, a man is organizing a party by himself, or a couple is moving to a new community.

I felt qualified to carry on for Miss Vanderbilt, having spent so much time in diplomatic life abroad and at the White House, as well as writing frequently on the subject of manners. Like hers, my philosophy of manners is that they are based on efficiency, yes, but even more on a superb trait of character called kindness. "Etiquette" is a starchy word, but manners are not starchy. Etiquette has to do with when you wear white gloves and how you unfold the napkin on your lap; *real manners* are being thoughtful toward others, being creative in doing nice things for others, or sympathizing with others' problems. There is nothing formal or stiff about that!

As our population grows and we are forced to live ever more closely together, never have manners been more desperately needed. But as daily life becomes more complicated, we also have more options than ever before on where we can go, what we can do with our leisure time, what kind of friends we can make, and how we choose to entertain them.

Having good manners gives one a feeling of security in dealing with people, so that teaching a child manners must still have top priority in family life. I will be pleased if a parent finds some helpful information and clear guidance in what follows. I hope men will use this book, because their roles are changing, too. Traditionally women handled the social obligations for a family, but in today's world social tasks must be shared by men and women, whether it is planning a party or writing thank-you notes. And along with a man's assumption of a greater role in social planning comes his need for "knowing how to do things right"—which is synonymous with doing them efficiently and in the best possible manner for all concerned.

As a long-time president of my own company and a corporate director, I have addressed the problem of manners in the office at some length in this edition. Women in positions of authority in the business world have greatly multiplied. Never before have men and women competed so avidly with each other in the business and professional worlds. A double standard has quite logically evolved. Men and women are free to treat each other in the traditional male-female patterns in their social lives outside the office, but in the office a very different form of behavior is seen. The successful woman executive treats the male executive like a colleague to whom every consideration should be shown. Additionally, she shows by her friendly but no nonsense manner that she can hang up her own coat, push in her own chair, and, in general, take care of herself!

When I began the task of revising this book, I had no idea of the scope of it or the seriousness of the mission I was assuming. Life had changed so much in the late sixties and in the seventies that it was a fast foot race to keep up with it. If how to fly the flag or march in a wedding procession had not changed, most everything else had. It was clear I had no right to pass moral judgments on anyone who had adopted any particular life-style, including the unwed live-togethers; society must adjust to these new social entities because just in sheer numbers they are a factor.

Without my Doubleday editor, Karen Van Westering, and my Doubleday project assistant, Nancy Tuckerman, there would have been no book. I shall miss our early morning work conferences greatly now that the book is finished. In Karen, Doubleday gave me a sharp, endlessly patient young editor and a cool professional. And in Nancy, I had the wisdom and supporting comfort of a long-time friend, who, like me, had been swimming in official waters for years. We puzzled a lot over this project, talked a lot, and, thank heavens, *laughed* a lot. Dealing with every aspect of human behavior *requires* one to keep a sense of humor.

I owe a vote of thanks to my office staff, who patiently put up with the constant interruptions of calls and retyping drafts, which kept them from getting their own work done. They were also a continuous source of good information on what was "really" happening out there. As for my patient husband, Bob, and our children, Clare and Malcolm, they deserve medals for putting up with my weekends of work. The children assured me, in firm now ten- and thirteen-year-old voices, that whenever I was wearing my Amy Vanderbilt chapeau, I was not to expect them to behave any better than usual!

This book is really an "exercise in options," because fortunately the hide-bound rules of behavior have relaxed. One may do "this" or perhaps "that" and be correct. What has not changed is the need for consideration of others. For this, there are no options.

I really hope that Amy Vanderbilt herself would approve of what is written on the pages that follow. Much is different from what she wrote, but her spirit is here; and if I have captured her compassion for people, then the changes will be legitimate and truly helpful. My goal, after all, is the same as hers: to help people make it through life just a little more easily and be a little more sure of themselves.

LETITIA BALDRIGE
New York City
1978

INTRODUCTION TO THE ORIGINAL
1952 EDITION

Who needs a book of etiquette? Everyone does. The simplest family, if it hopes to move just a little into a wider world, needs to know at least the elementary rules. Even the most sophisticated man or woman used to a great variety of social demands cannot hope to remember every single aspect of etiquette applying to even one possible social contingency. The human mind is so constructed that even if a person were to read through a book such as this from cover to cover he could retain only that information that had interest for him at the time of reading. Consciously, at least, the rest would be discarded as irrelevant to his way of life. But let some new way of living open up for him—a move from city to country, a trip to a new part of the world—and his etiquette becomes his *reference* book, ready to piece out his own store of information.

You might imagine that the writer of an etiquette book would certainly know everything in it and therefore have no need for it as reference or guide. But even this is not the case. After ten years as an etiquette adviser, five years of writing this book—five years of interviewing dozens of authorities in their own fields for material to be incorporated here—I, too, can remember only those details that have or have had relevance to my own way of living. If you asked me, for example, some detail of a wedding in a faith other than my own, I might have to refer to my own book. The information is here—the result of my research—but in the writing of such sections I made no attempt to memorize all these details. However, in this book, I, like you, have such information in simple, complete form all in one place, and it can be readily found if needed.

The word "etiquette" for all the things I have tried to discuss is really inadequate, yet no other will do. It covers much more than "manners," the way in which we *do* things. It is considerably more than a treatise on a code of social behavior, although all the traditional information still of value has, I feel, been included in a way that is simple and concise, shorn of mumbo-jumbo and clearly learnable. For we must all learn the socially acceptable ways of living with others in no matter what society we move. Even in primitive societies there are such rules, some of them as complex and inexplicable as many of our own. Their original *raison d'être* or purpose is lost, but their acceptance is still unquestioned.

Change in etiquette usually comes slowly, just as changes come slowly in the dictionary. The analogy applies, too, in that it is not necessarily social leaders who bring about such changes, but rather the people themselves who, through slighting certain forms for a long enough period, finally bring about their abolishment or at least their modification.

Inventions, wars, political upheavals, legislation, all, of course, have repercussions, sometimes immediate, in the field of etiquette. In certain Moslem countries *purdah,* the centuries-old veiling of women in public, was abolished by law overnight. Think of the social adjustment that was required! What had been rigorous social custom now became *illegal.*

Etiquette, too, is obviously geographically influenced. In cities thousands of families live under one roof, yet most never speak to one another on meeting. In the country not to speak to one's neighbor on encountering him would be very rude. In some parts of the South girls are quite accustomed to young men asking for late dates, a date—usually with an old beau—following one that may end at about eleven. Elsewhere such behavior might be considered questionable.

In young countries—and ours is certainly one when you think in terms of Paris's two thousand years—etiquette books have an important place. The physical and economic changes the country undergoes inevitably bring about fairly rapid social changes. The people who first come to virgin country usually arrive as workers, for every hand is needed, living facilities are at a premium, and there is little if any of the leisure or money necessary for the immediate development of an aristocracy. That is why all old American families such as mine have strong and simple roots here. Some of them may have brought with them the drawing-room manners of older civilizations, but they found that many of the niceties of living required adaptation—or else had to be discarded—in this vigorous, busy young land.

My great-great-grandfather, who "read law," was one of the founders of the Bank of Manhattan Company and a man of parts, as they used to say in those days. But in the tradition of his father and grandfather, Hollanders both, he was manually proficient and he had a proper respect for whatever work he did. He seems to have owned a number of "shoe manufactories," and I do not doubt that he could apply a sole with the same expertness that he used in some of the fine mahogany furniture he made for his family and which I still use. On the facing page is his advertisement in the *Diary; or Evening Register* of Wednesday, April 9, 1794.

My own line of descent from the first Vanderbilt to settle in America— Jan Aoertsen van der Bilt, who had a farm near Flatbush, Long Island—has been strongly Dutch, but I have a good admixture of Irish, English, and French blood. That and my partly European education, my fairly extensive traveling here and abroad, my years as a writer, as an etiquette adviser, and in business have given me a flexible attitude toward etiquette which is reflected, I am sure, in everything I have written on the subject.

WEDNESDAY, APRIL 9, 1794.

OLIVER VANDERBILT,

At his Boot and Shoe Manufactory No. 7, the corner of Smith and Princefs-Streets,

TAKES this method, to return his thanks to his cuftomers, for their generous encouragement in the line of his bufinefs, and hopes by his fteady attention and abilities to ferve, to merit the fame. He has lately difcovered a method, which effectually prevents the prevailing evils fo common in the prefent mode of making boots which are thefe, the folding or running down behind and breaking above the counter and in the tongue, which frequently caufes almoft new boots not only to look bad, by caufing pieces to be put in them, but by running down wears very uncomfortably He continues to make, and has for fale, the following articles, wholefale and retail. viz.

	£.	s.	d.
Finifhed boots of Englifh ftuff	3	0	0
Do. tanned, brain and oil dreffed buck fkin legs	3	0	0
Do. American calf fkin, or cordiwan legs	2	16	0
Second quality do. do. do.	2	10	0
Stout ftrong boots.	2	4	0
Bootees of Englifh legs	2	5	0
Do. of American do	1	18	0

I have a respect for people who do things with their brains and with their hands, who are not afraid of hard physical and mental work. I respect, too, people who are unpretentious yet mannerly, considerate and honest, forthright yet kind and tactful. I dislike display and foolish expenditure in the sense of what Veblen called "conspicuous waste," that is, spending to impress those who have less, as well as to impress associates. I dislike *chichi.*

I believe that knowledge of the rules of living in our society makes us more comfortable even though our particular circumstances may permit us to elide them somewhat. Some of the rudest and most objectionable people I have ever known have been technically the most "correct." Some of the warmest, most lovable, have had little more than an innate feeling of what is right toward others. But, at the same time, they have had the intelligence to inform themselves, as necessary, on the rules of social intercourse as related to their own experiences. Only a great fool or a great genius is likely to flout all social grace with impunity, and neither one, doing so, makes the most comfortable companion.

It is my hope that this book answers as fully and simply as possible all the major questions of etiquette and most of the minor ones too. It is the largest and most complete book of etiquette ever written. Like a dictionary, it will have few cover-to-cover readers aside from my meticulous editor, Marion Patton, the copy editors, and the proofreaders. But this undoubted fact does not in the least disturb me, for a reference book such as this has a long and much-thumbed existence. It can become a reliable friend to whom one may turn many a questioning glance over the years and get a helpful answer. It can put down roots and become an integral part of the family, even be an objective counselor to the children as they enter their teens.

It is axiomatic that as we mature and grow in years and experience we must be able to meet more demanding social situations with confidence and ease. This book contains, I believe, explicit information on every possible social problem one is likely to encounter in modern social living.

Westport, Connecticut   AMY VANDERBILT
1952

CONTENTS

PREFACE   xi

INTRODUCTION TO THE ORIGINAL 1952 EDITION   xv

Part One: THE IMPORTANCE OF FAMILY AND HOME

1. Family Relationships   5

Is It a Child's World? • We Shoot Too High • Respect for Authority • Teaching a Child Self-control • Communication • Children Want Rules • People with Special Problems • The In-laws and Grandparents

2. Manners in the Family   17

The Social Behavior of Children • Children's Manners at Table • Manners Around the Home • Clothes for Your Child • About Allowances

3. The Teen-ager and Young Adult   37

Courtesy Begins at Home • Manners • Allowances and Teaching Financial Responsibility • Jobs • Grooming, Shaving, and Make-up for the Teen-ager • Teen Dates • Teen Car Manners • Check List of Common Courtesies and Discourtesies

4. Drugs, Alcohol, and Tobacco: Major Problems   52

Why Drugs Are Abused • Parents Should Be Alert to Changes in Their Children • Preventing Drug Abuse • Socially Acceptable Drugs • Marijuana and Hashish: Marginally Socially Acceptable • The Major Categories of Drugs • Alcohol • Tobacco • Where to Go for Help

5. The Adopted Child   **62**

Showers and Presents • Announcing an Adoption • Talking to an
Adoptive Child and His Parents • Explaining Another Child's
Adoption to Your Child • The Adoptive Parents' Attitude

6. The Single Life   **66**

A Single Person's Options Are Extensive • Personal Business •
The Widow and Widower • Divorce • Single Parents • Going to
Work • Volunteer Work • New Stationery Is Called For • A
Divorced Woman and Her Name • The Importance of Entertain-
ing • The Newly Single Person's Home • Travel

7. Household Management in a Servantless Society   **80**

The "Household Staff" • Today's World • Hiring Domestic Help •
Workmen's Compensation • Social Security Deductions and Withholding Tax • State Unemployment Insurance Tax • Handling
the Telephone • Firing a Household Employee • The Baby- or
Child-sitter • A Routine for Managing Your Household

Part Two: CEREMONIES OF LIFE

8. Christenings and Confirmations   **105**

The Birth of a Baby • When the Baby Is Christened • First
Communion • Confirmation • Jewish Traditions

9. Graduations and Debuts   **115**

High School and College Graduation • Debutantes

10. Engagements   **121**

Telling the Family • Engagement Parties • Announcing the En-
gagement in the Newspapers • When an Engagement Is Not
Announced • Complicated Relationships • Legally Changed Name
• Bride on Her Own • The Engagement Ring • Behavior of an
Engaged Couple • Breaking an Engagement • Premarital Living
Together

11. Wedding Invitations and Announcements   **132**

Preparing the List • Invitations to Those in Mourning • When
Should Invitations and Announcements Be Sent? • Engraving and
Stationery • How to Address the Envelopes • Wording of Formal
Invitations • Combining Invitation to Church Ceremony and Re-
ception • The Separate Reception Invitation • The Late Reception

Invitation • Foreign Wedding Procedures • Enclosure Cards • Recalling Wedding Invitations • Postponing Weddings • Replying to Formal Wedding Invitations • Recalling a Formal Acceptance • Invitations to Informal Weddings • Replies to an Informal Wedding Invitation • Wedding Announcements • Variations of the Usual Wording • Military and Naval Forms for Wedding Invitations and Announcements

12. Wedding Gifts 163

The Bridal Registry • Wedding Gift Register • Gifts at Receptions • Wedding Gift Display • The Bride's Thank-you Letters • When a Gift Is Exchanged • Returning Wedding Gifts • Gifts for the Attendants from the Bride and Groom • Gifts to the Bride and Groom from Their Wedding Party • The Bridal Couple's Gifts to Each Other

13. Today's Trousseau 169

Bed and Bath Linens • Linens for the Table • China Services for Today • Serving Containers • Tea Service • Silver • Fine Glassware • Basic Household Needs

14. Preparations for the Wedding 179

Arrangements with the Clergyman • Special Problems • Choosing a Place for the Wedding • Choosing a Time for the Wedding • Church Preparations • Wedding Photographs • Wedding Guest Book • Wedding Reception Music • Putting Up Guests • Expenses of the Bride's Parents • Groom's Expenses • Ex-husband's Responsibility Concerning the Wedding • The Expense of the Home

15. The Wedding Attendants and Their Duties 187

Maids and Matrons of Honor • Bridesmaids • The Best Man • Ushers • Going to the Church • If an Attendant Drops Out

16. Pre-wedding Parties 195

The Bridesmaids' Party • Parties for Out-of-town Guests • Bridal Teas • Bridal Showers • The Bachelor Dinner • The Rehearsal Dinner

17. Dress for the Wedding 200

The Bride's Dress • The Wedding Ring • Superstitions • The Mature Bride • Women's Wedding Attire • The Bride's Formal Wedding Pictures • Wedding Publicity in the Papers • Dress of Groom

and Best Man • Ushers • Men's Wedding Dress • Bridal Attendants • Flowers for the Wedding Party • What the Parents and
Guests Wear

18. The Rehearsal   212

Which Arm Does the Bride Take? • The Processional • The Recessional • When There Are Two Main Aisles

19. The Wedding Ceremony   217

Procedure During the Ceremony • Giving Away the Bride • The
Double-ring Ceremony • The Double Wedding • Wedding Guests
at the Church • Differences in Religious Ceremonies • The Home
Wedding • The Clergyman's Wedding • Driving to the Reception •
If There Is No Reception • Elopements and Civil Ceremonies

20. The Wedding Reception   238

The Receiving Line • Photographs at the Reception • Flowers at
the Reception • The Wedding Guest Book • Gratuities at the Re-
ception • The Wedding Breakfast • The Table for the Parents •
The Bride's Table • Food at the Reception • The Wedding Toasts
• The Wedding Cake • Music at the Reception • Throwing the
Bride's Bouquet • Problems of the Divided House • Guests at the
Reception • Giving Your Own Wedding Reception • Second or
Delayed Wedding Receptions

21. Second and Subsequent Marriages   251

What Constitutes a Second Marriage • Engagements Before Second
Marriages • Invitations for Second Marriages • Reception Invi-
tations • Wedding Announcements • Gifts for Second Marriages •
Preparations for a Second Wedding • Attendants at Second Wed-
dings • Children as Guests and as Attendants at Second Weddings
• Entertaining Before Second Weddings • Dress for the Second
Wedding • Second-wedding Ceremony • Reception for the Second
Wedding • Paying for the Second Wedding • Remarriage of Di-
vorced Persons to Each Other

22. After the Wedding   259

The Honeymoon • Upon Arrival at One's Honeymoon Destination
• The Newly Marrieds in a New Neighborhood • Behavior of the
Newlyweds

23. Wedding Anniversaries   262

An Anniversary Celebration • Formal Engraved or Printed Invitations to a Wedding Anniversary • Replies to Formal Wedding

Anniversary Invitations • Anniversary Gifts • Anniversary Photographs • Reaffirmation of Marriage Vows

24. Funerals   266

What to Do when Death Comes • Choosing Someone to Be in Charge • Dealing with the Mortician • Clothing for Burial • Hanging the Bell • Where the Funeral Takes Place • Death Notices • Obituaries for Prominent People • Attending a Funeral • Sending Flowers • Mass Cards • Funeral Calls • The Funeral Service • Cremation • Interment and Grave Marking • Fees to the Clergyman, Sexton, Organist, Vocalist • Acknowledgments for Flowers, Donations to Charity • Acknowledgments to Clergy, Pallbearers, Ushers • Letters of Condolence • Contributions to Charity • Food After the Funeral • Distributing Family Possessions • Mourning Dress • The Concept of Mourning • Christmas and Greeting Cards After Bereavement

Part Three: ENTERTAINING

25. Informal Entertaining   287

Invitations • Greeting the Arriving Guests • Seating at Dinner • Protocol • Toasting • Dinner Service with One Maid • The Buffet Supper • A Sit-down Dinner Without a Maid • After-dinner Activities

26. Menu Inspiration   310

Dinner Menus • Cocktail Buffet Menu • Lunch Menus • Menu for an Easy Sunday Brunch • The Least-expensive Menu Possible • When Disaster Strikes in Cooking • How Many Courses Do You Serve? • Special Needs of Guests • The Kinds of Wine to Serve • The Wine Cellar • Wineglasses • The Wine Service

27. Setting Your Table   327

The Design Revolution • Praising Your Hosts • The Logistics of Table Settings • Menu Cards

28. Cocktail Parties   337

Party Logistics • The Bartender • The Cocktail Menu • The Party's Over • The Problem Drinkers • Special Kinds of Cocktail Parties

29. Informal Luncheons and Teas   347

The Informal Luncheon • The Informal Tea • Coffees • Playing Bridge

30. Formal Entertaining   355

The Formal Dinner • The Formal Dinner Table • The Formal Luncheon • The Formal Tea • The Guest at Formal Meals • Caterers

31. Entertaining Out of Doors   371

Dinner on a City Apartment Balcony • An Outdoor Buffet • Patio Entertaining • Picnics • Poolside Entertaining • Barbecues

32. The Weekend Guest   381

Invitations • The Guest Room • The Guest Bathroom • Breakfast for Guests • Organizing the Day • For the Guest to Remember • The Overnight Guest in Cramped Quarters • Saying Thank You After Being Entertained

33. Special Types of Entertaining   391

Children's Birthday Parties • A Teen-age Party • College Entertaining • Post-college Entertaining • Special-event Parties

34. At Ease at Table   405

Who Is Served First? • When to Begin Eating • The Use of the Knife and Fork • The Dessert Silver • Drinking Beverages at the Table • The Napkin • If Silverware Is Lacking • Tipping of Dishes • The Handled Soup or Bouillon Cup • Testing Liquids • How to Hold Cups • How to Hold Glasses • The Use of Chopsticks • Token Portions • Taking Portions from a Serving Dish • Adding Gravies and Sauces • Seasoning • Additional Butter • Jellies and Sauces • Bread as a Food-pusher and Sauce-sopper • The Left-handed Person • Rearranging the Seating • Getting Something Out of the Mouth • Accidents at the Table • Swallowing the Wrong Way and Choking • Sneezing • Speaking with Food in the Mouth • Food in the Teeth • Burping • Foreign Matter in Food • Leaving the Table • Reaching Across the Table • Smoking at Table • Conversational Flow at Table • Posture at the Table • Saying Grace • How to Eat Various Foods

Part Four: MANNERS IN BUSINESS

35. Getting a Job   437

Writing a Résumé • Job Application Forms • Going on a Job Interview • Employer's Responsibility Toward Job Applicants • Writing a Letter of Reference • Letters of Resignation

36. Men and Women as Colleagues in the Office   447

Women's Raised Consciousness • The Use of "Ms." • A Woman
Picks Up the Tab • Lighting and Offering Cigarettes • Business
Travel • Dress in the Office • Special Executive Facilities

37. Business Entertaining   455

Invitations • How to Extend an Invitation • When There Is No
R.S.V.P. Card Enclosed • Thank-yous for a Business Social Event
• Business Hosts and the Receiving Line • Badges • Invitations
from Business Associates

38. Telephone Manners   465

Answering the Telephone • Messages • Executives Answering
Their Own Telephones • Telephone Conversations • Long-distance
Telephoning • Business Calls at Home • Dealing with an Answer-
ing Service • The Telephone Answering Machine • Recorded
Music

39. General Office Manners   474

The Secretary • The Well-written Note: An Important Factor in
Executive Relationships • Handling Executive Visitors and Appointments • Office Gifts • Office Party Behavior • Smoking in
the Office • Some Office Do's and Don'ts

40. Opening Your Own Business   485

Budget Check List • Announcing You Are Open for Business •
Gifts to Send for the Opening of a New Business • Stationery •
Deciding the Office Image • Free Advice About Jobs and Business
Opportunities

Part Five: STATIONERY: AN IMPORTANT COMMUNICATION
TOOL

41. A Stationery Wardrobe   495

The Proper Form of Stationery • Women's Personal Stationery •
Men's Personal Stationery • A Married Couple's Personal Station-
ery • Children's Stationery • The House Stationery • Official
Paper • Signatures • Addressing Social Envelopes • The Use of
"Personal," "Please Forward," and "Opened by Mistake" • The
Use of "Mesdames" • The Use of "Messrs."

42. **Letter Writing: the Ultimate in Human Communication**   513

The Form of Your Letters • The Age to Begin Note Writing • The Thank-you Letter • The Congratulatory Letter • Writing After Hearing Bad News • Condolence Letters • The Impulse Note • The Recorded Message • Letters of Apology • Letters of Social Reference and Introduction • Sending Tourists to Friends Living Abroad • Letters to Public Figures • Writing Personal Business Letters • Using Postcards • Greeting Cards • Christmas Cards

43. **Invitations, Acceptances, and Regrets**   533

When to Invite • Formal Invitations • Accepting Formal Invitations • Regrets to a Formal Invitation • Map Enclosure • Extending Informal Invitations • Accepting Informal Invitations • Postage Considerations • Reminders • Telling Your Guests What to Wear • Bringing a Friend • Bringing Along One's House Guests • Canceling a Party • Breaking an Engagement

44. **The Etiquette of Calling Cards**   547

How Names Are Used on Social and Business Cards • Joint Social Card • Cards as Gift Enclosures • Making and Receiving Calls

45. **Heraldic Devices**   553

The Lozenge • How Are Heraldic Devices Used?

Part Six: YOUR OFFICIAL SELF

46. **Correct Forms of Address**   563

United States Government Officials and Individuals • United States Military Personnel • Religious Officials • Foreign Government Officials and Nobility

47. **Parliamentary Procedure**   630

48. **Jury Duty**   633

49. **The White House**   635

White House Invitations • A State Dinner • Business Calls at the White House • Gifts to the White House • Letters to the President and First Lady • Taking a White House Tour

50. The Flag and Our National Anthem   **640**

Regulations for Displaying the Flag • Invocation and Salute to the
Flag • The Singing of Our National Anthem • "The Star-Spangled
Banner" • Anthems of Other Nations

51. Visiting a Naval Vessel   **645**

Aboard Ship • Prohibitions Concerning Naval Vessels • Officers'
Staterooms • Nautical Terms

52. An Audience with the Pope   **649**

Having a General Audience • Semiprivate Audiences • Private
Audiences • How to Dress for an Audience • The Pope in
St. Peter's Basilica

Part Seven: YOU ON PUBLIC VIEW

53. You, Your Wardrobe, and Your Accessories   **657**

Organizing a Woman's Wardrobe • Dressing Well and Following Fashion • Style • Grooming • How You Move in Your
Clothes • Pants • Skirts • Furs • Accessories

54. Men's Apparel   **669**

Business   Suits • Shirts • Ties • Shoes • Socks • Hats • Leisure
Wear • Jacket and Tie Code at Restaurants • Formal Wear

55. Dining in Restaurants   **679**

The Fine Restaurant • Ordering • Tipping and Paying the Check
• Entertaining a Large Party at a Restaurant • Restaurant Manners • Complaints and Compliments • Informal Restaurant Dining

56. Private Clubs   **694**

Joining a Club • Staying Overnight • Using Club Facilities for
Entertaining when You Are Not a Member • Christmas Fund for
Employees • Other Clubs and Organizations

57. The Considerate Sportsperson   **699**

Yachting and Sailing • Tennis and Racket Sports • Golf • Riding and Fox Hunting • Swimming and Water Sports • Winter
Sports

58. The Importance of Introductions   723

Who Is Introduced to Whom • The Importance of the Handshake
• Husbands and Wives Introducing Each Other • When a Woman
Keeps her Maiden Name After Marriage • Introducing Strangers
at Parties • Forgetting Names • People Greeting Each Other •
Acknowledging Compliments • Receiving Lines • The Use of
"Ma'am" and "Sir" • The Use of "Lady" and "Gentleman" Versus
"Woman" and "Man"

59. Public Speaking   729

Your Voice • The Microphone • Stage Lighting • Introducing a
Speaker • Master of Ceremonies • If You Are the Major Speaker
• Taking Care of the Celebrity Speaker • Handling Press Relations

60. Conversation: the Great Social Tool   742

The Way You Talk • The Basis of Good Conversation • Appropriateness of Subject • Talking to a Celebrity

61. Hospitals and Doctors   748

Visiting the Patient • Tips for the Patient • How a Woman Registers • Services in the Hospital • Your Hospital Roommates •
Your Nurse • Your Doctor • The Psychiatric Patient

Part Eight: GIFT GIVING: AN ACT OF HUMAN KINDNESS

62. The Philosophy of Giving   759

The Universally Accepted Gift: Money • Gift Certificates • Gifts
Made to Charitable Organizations • The Unexpected Gift •
Flowers • Gifts of Fine Jewelry • The Don't-give Gifts

63. Gift Ideas for All Occasions   766

Christening or Baby Presents • Classic Presents for Children Ten
and Under • First Communion Presents • Classic Gifts for Teen-
agers • Christian Confirmation Presents • Gifts for Bar and Bat
Mitzvah • High School Graduation Gifts • Gifts for a Debutante
• Gifts for the College Graduate • Gifts for Priests, Ministers,
and Rabbis • Gifts for a Nun • Teachers' Presents • Kitchen
Shower • Linen Shower • Lingerie Shower • Christmas Gift
Giving • Wedding Gifts • Anniversary Presents • Birthdays •
Housewarming Gifts • House Guest Presents • Gifts to Send
Someone in the Hospital • Gifts for the Traveler • Gifts for Spe-
cial Interests

Part Nine: THE ETIQUETTE OF TRAVEL

64. Basic Travel: Public Transportation   **799**

By Airplane • By Train • By Bus

65. Travel by Motor Vehicle   **814**

Taking Taxis • The Sensible Driver • Car Travel with Children •
Rental Cars • Recreational Vehicles

66. Planning Your Vacation Trip   **822**

Travel Agents • Before You Go • Travel Preparations • Travel
Check List • Packing Your Suitcase • Hotels and Motels

67. Taking a Cruise   **834**

Booking Passage • When You Leave • On the Ship • The Captain's Table • Dress • On-shore Excursions • Tipping • Travel
by Freighter

INDEX   843

Part One

THE IMPORTANCE OF FAMILY
AND HOME

Family Relationships   5

Manners in the Family   17

The Teen-ager and Young Adult   37

Drugs, Alcohol, and Tobacco: Major Problems   52

The Adopted Child   62

The Single Life   66

Household Management in a Servantless Society   80

A graduate student sat in a crowded lounge at the feet of a famous visiting professor of philosophy. He asked his idol in awed tones, "And what, sir, was the hardest thing you ever had to overcome philosophically in your life?" "Growing up" was the reply.

When you reflect on that for a minute, it's probably true for most of us. Growing up is a tremendous task, something that continues throughout our lives, because, as customs change, mores shift, and personal disappointments multiply, we must continue growing and adjusting right along with them.

How often does a parent look at his newborn baby and vow with all his heart and soul, "I'm going to make it easy for you, little one. I'm going to help you grow into a strong, fine human being with as little pain as possible"?

Life just doesn't work that way. Even if a child is born with good looks, wealth, a keen intelligence, and a good measure of talent, it's still a long road between childhood and maturity. A parent can't make it easy for his child. He can only equip him with the tools to grow up more easily. If he takes with him from childhood a firm, ingrained set of manners, these will help to give him the security of knowing how to act, and they will have molded his character so that kindness and consideration of others are instinctive acts. His parents will have fortified him with the greatest possible tools for achieving a successful voyage.

Children grow up to mirror their parents. If their parents have good manners and try to pass them on, almost inevitably the children assimilate them. If there was ever a justification of the importance of the family as a unit and of the need for parents' giving time and thought to the teaching of manners in the home, it is in the results of recent research carried on by the Institute of Human Development at the University of California at Berkeley. Psychologists there have found that a child's pro-social behavior is for the most part the result of his parents' training, and that the most powerful teachers for good or evil are indeed his mother and father.

A child's character is mainly formed not at school but at home. He won't learn how to get along with others unless he receives guidance and support in his human relationships at home. Whether "home" means a big, loving, scrappy family or a rather quiet existence with a single parent, the responsibility rests right there. If parents set standards of behavior that are reasonable and attainable, most children eventually will conform to them. They may pass through more than one stage of rebellion in their lives, but if their parents "stay cool" children stand a good chance of keeping their ship on an even course. A child who is undisciplined will not be able to steer a steady course; one cannot demand it of him, because he has no code by which to behave, no standards by which to measure himself. For him, life will be much more difficult than for the child who knows what he has to do, when he has to do it, and why he has to do it.

Chapter 1

FAMILY RELATIONSHIPS

Is It a Child's World?

Some modern parents have the mistaken idea that adults no longer count. Parents, too, do have their rights and should assert them. No child should be permitted to make the adults around him miserable or to deprive them of all peace, quiet, and privacy. There are—and should be—limits to all adults' patience with children. A child who has discovered that he can ride roughshod over the adults in his family is far from contented with his tyrannical role. Consideration of others comes slowly to the young and must certainly be regularly imposed within the child's ability to understand. And that understanding can be absorbed very early indeed if the handling of the child is relaxed and loving.

Habits are fixed through doing the same thing over and over again. If you pick up after your children—scolding as you do so—and expect them to become neat as a result, you are making a sad mistake. A child must go back and do the routine things over and over before they become habits. He needs to be reminded—patiently and firmly reminded—to do the things expected of him. But don't nag. Use charts, stars, rewards of various kinds, praise when he remembers, pleasant reminders when he forgets. Don't get his back up. You didn't learn to brush your teeth, comb your hair, scrub your nails, tie your shoelaces, and wash your face automatically merely by being asked to do so once or twice.

We Shoot Too High

If our children were always spotlessly clean, never made any noise, were always pleasant when spoken to, jumped up at every request, and never talked back, there would be something very much the matter with them. They aren't born that way, and it is a very long time before they come to believe there is some virtue in what we ask of them.

Healthy children must get dirty. It is part of the business of playing, and the dirtier they get the better they like it. When a child is afraid to get dirty, to put his hands in mud pies, to yell and run with the other children, he's not normal. Adult standards have been imposed upon him with too great an effect and to the detriment of his whole life.

There are times when it is better if a child manages to keep reasonably clean—if he's in his Sunday best, for example—but if he does, by accident of course, splash into puddles or slide into home plate in the back yard while he's waiting for you, the world is not going to collapse even if you may feel it is going to!

Respect for Authority

When a child is very young, the only authority he or she knows is the parent, or perhaps an older sibling or a nurse. As the child grows, many new figures of authority cross his path—the Sunday school teacher, the day nursery teacher, the day camp counselor, the librarian. As his social and school contacts grow, so do his opportunities to learn that it is within the structure of authority that things work. One has to respect the policeman on his beat, the safety patrol student guarding the street crossing, the theater manager organizing the waiting lines outside the movie house. A child must learn to respect a particular person who is in charge of a job that entails giving orders to others, for the good of everyone.

The parents' own attitude toward people in authority determines the mindset of their children. If the child's father belittles a high official, if he cheats on his income taxes and brags about it, if he lies to a state trooper, his child will probably grow up to be just like him. If, however, a child sees his parents always obeying authority, whether by not running a traffic light or by moving quickly to the rear of the bus, that child will grow up to do likewise. His parents will have taught him that obeying an authority is for the good of the public as a whole, and that not obeying it is pure selfishness.

Consideration for Those Who Serve Us   Side by side with respect for those in authority should go respect for those who serve us. A child should be made to realize that even if the cleaning woman is in his parents' employ or the store clerk's salary is paid for by his father's purchasing power, these individuals are worthy of his respect. The responsibility of instilling this in a child lies squarely with his parents. If a child hears Daddy calling a garage mechanic "an idiot," he will grow up feeling he may address a mechanic in the future in the same manner. If he hears his mother yelling at the cleaning woman, he will feel he can do what he pleases in her presence. A child should be taught to obey a domestic employee in the home who, after all, may be the one to stop the child from hurting himself in the home.

The way in which a child sees and hears his parents relate to all of the people who serve them in any way (the waiter, the cleaning woman, the grocer, the laundry deliveryman, the taxi driver) makes an impression on him. He will most likely mirror their behavior when he himself is an adult. A parent should be constantly aware of this and learn to control his temper and show consideration of those who serve him.

Teaching a Child Self-control

Since babies are born totally selfish, self-control is something that comes much later in their development. In order to develop self-control a child has to be old enough to understand why he should have it. Just telling him that self-control is the basis of manners is not a good enough explanation. It's much more fun to do as one pleases, if one can get away with it.

I heard an eight-year-old give her definition of self-control to her mother: "It's not blowing your stack." Along with not blowing your stack, self-control is the acceptance of "no" from someone else without fighting back; it's the applying of the brakes to oneself quite independently of anyone else, in order not to hurt someone else or not to hurt oneself. The six-year-old who lets his birthday party guest take the best piece of cake is using self-control; the eighth-grade girl who intensely dislikes another girl for good cause but who speaks well of her in talking to classmates is using self-control; the high school football player who is taunted unfairly for his team's loss that day but who does not answer his attacker as he would like to is using self-control. In every case, there is an immediate or eventual reward for this social behavior. The little boy gains the beaming approval of his mother for having given up his piece of cake; the eighth grader knows that if she spoke badly of her classmate her own reputation might suffer; and the football player was too proud of his team to stoop to answer his critic in the angry manner he would have liked to use. He therefore reinforced his own position as a man of merit.

A parent should articulate to a child that others will like him better and that he will get ahead faster in life if he thinks and checks himself before he acts. This is how the foundations of his character are laid.

Communication

Communication between parents and child and between parents themselves is the key to the successful raising of a son or daughter. From early childhood the parent talks to his child, helping him explore the world and learn to verbalize what he sees and feels around him. Many parents drop their responsibilities for this later in life; they become too busy with their own activities, and the child's preoccupation with television or with his friends comes almost as a welcome relief to a parent who has too much else on his mind. This is when the lines of communication break down. The two generations do not tell each other what is important to them, what is happening to them, whether it is good or bad. When a parent tells his teen-aged child that he is really worried about the possibility of losing his business, the child is taken into his world and becomes an important source of consolation and support. Likewise, when a child misses out on being chosen for the team, or doesn't have a date to the prom, or was unfairly graded on an important exam—these are deep emotions that must be communicated to the parents; handling the emotions involved should be worked out in a joint effort.

One often hears a question asked, "How are the kids coming along?" If the parent answers, "Well, at least we're still talking to each other," it is meant as a half-joke. But a parent who can honestly make that statement is fortunate indeed—and so is the child who lives in that family. No matter what happens in the way of conflict between the two generations, those talk lines *must* be kept open. If the parent says at a certain point, "I see your side of that," then at a certain moment the child will feel more ready to say, "You know, I see your side of that particular point." It is in the give-and-take, the necessary compromise, and the ability to empathize with someone else that the communication lines are kept from breaking. It takes time on the parents' part. They have to show their children they really do consider them a priority in their lives.

The quality of the communication usually depends on the parents. They are the ones who set the pace. If they lavish sympathy on a four-year-old girl who breaks her arm, then they must give her the same sympathy when she is kept out of a girls' high school club because she wouldn't smoke pot with the others, or is rejected for admission to the college of her choice. As a child grows up, his disappointments and sorrows grow up with him. Each is as serious and as desperate as the last one; everything is relative, and no parent should laugh at or belittle a hurt of any kind. Otherwise, the child will withdraw into himself, and when real trouble comes, the parent will not be able to break through the barrier to help.

Parents also have to communicate with each other. If a child learns he can play one parent off against the other, the temptation to do so is irresistible. If a boy knows his mother is a softer touch than his father and gets a "yes" from her when his father had already given him a "no," the ship steers off course. It is imperative that parents back each other up on their directions and disciplinary actions, even if it is a question of relative unimportance. This is particularly true for a stepparent in residence—or for divorced parents when the child leaves the home of one to visit the other. An intelligent mother informs her former husband of a potential problem concerning their child. "Mary was asked by a high school senior to his prom. There's going to be a lot of drinking, and I told her that at fourteen she is much too young to go. I'd appreciate your holding to that line, because she's extremely upset and I know she'll try to gain your sympathy when she sees you this weekend. She thinks she can talk you into saying she should go."

One cannot overemphasize the potential for good in a family a stepparent possesses. If a child says, "I can talk to her, and she talks to me, too," the child is paying her a supreme compliment. Quite often the stepparent living at home, instead of being a divisive element in the household, is the saving grace of the family, as far as the child is concerned.

Your Tone of Voice   There is nothing so catching as the sharp manner. Have you noticed that children whose parents speak to them in a petulant, annoyed tone of voice speak to others in the same way? Conversely, if a child, right from the beginning, is spoken to with the same politeness and consideration one would give an adult, even when he is a tiny baby and can understand only the tone, not the words, he is usually a gently spoken child. Harping parents make harping children who grow into harping parents.

Take time and effort, if possible, before any necessary admonition of a child to control your irritation toward other people or with irrelevant things. The smallest child is quick to resent anger unjustly taken out on him for trivial transgressions. To vent one's irritation on the handiest person, especially on a child who does need correction, is human enough. If it happens, your relationship with your child will be better if you can apologize. No child thinks his parents are infallible creatures. Children know that parents are often wrong, sometimes make mistakes. It improves our stature as parents if we can say, even to the youngest child, "Johnny, I'm sorry I was cross just now. You know how it is when people get too tired. They sometimes get cross without much reason." This isn't spoiling Johnny. This is treating him like a real human being and teaching him that the quickest way to dispel another's anger is to admit you're wrong—sometimes even when you aren't completely convinced that you really are.

Are Threats Effective?   Never make a threat to a child that you don't intend to or cannot carry out if infraction does occur. It is cruel and stupid to say, "If you do that, Mommy won't love you," or "If you get out of that bed once more, Mommy will leave and never come back." Quite intelligent parents often resort to such threats in desperation, so increasing the anxiety and unmanageability of their children. Parents' love must be inviolable. They cannot always love the *behavior* of their children, and they have every right to take prompt steps to correct it, but they must never withdraw love itself as a means of punishment. To damage a child's love-security is to open the way to his becoming a neurotic.

It is certainly better to use the pleasure principle than the punishment principle when dealing with a child. How much more sensible—and effective —to say to a child who keeps jumping out of bed, "Now settle down, darling, and get your sleep. Tomorrow, if the weather is nice, we'll go on a picnic," than to threaten, "If you don't go to sleep immediately, I won't take you on that picnic tomorrow even if it is a nice day." Did *you* ever try to go to sleep promptly, on order?

Children Want Rules

It is much more comfortable to conform to a set of generally accepted standards than to be in a constant state of rebellion. Children want and need rules. They want to know what is expected of them in their particular role in the family. They don't want to live by the rules by which their little sisters must live, or their older brothers. Each child wants to know what is expected of *him*. Wishy-washy parents who backtrack on a rule laid down are very discomforting to a child. There is tremendous comfort in knowing you may *not* do a certain thing, and in knowing why your parent feels it is dangerous or ill-advised for you. A little child will say proudly, "I'm not allowed to go to anyone's house after school without my mother's permission." The older teen-ager will say in exaggerated disgust, "My mother won't let me go to that kind of place. She's a pill about it, but she absolutely refuses to let me." (Meanwhile, she is greatly relieved she will not be placed in the position of having to decide whether to go to that place with her friends.) A child who is allowed to do anything he pleases becomes insecure and will always show it in his behavior.

An overly strict parent who is totally out of tune with what other children of the same age are allowed to do is harmful to the child, but even more harmful is one who shows neglect of his child by having no rules at all.

People with Special Problems

A Child's View   When a young child sees someone else who is "different" in any way, he tends to stare, point, and ask questions in a loud voice. It is embarrassing for everyone involved, yet it is quite natural. He may be afraid that the difference he sees in someone else could also "happen" to him. A parent should quiet a child who says, "Look at the funny man," gently and reassuringly and explain, "I will tell you about it later." The parent should then remember *to discuss it later* with his child, and explain about people who have handicaps and physical difficulties in life. A parent should teach a child that the person with the thick glasses guiding himself with a white cane is a very brave person, that he is like anyone else except for not being able to see well, and that when the child grows up he can do something to help the people in this world who have problems like that. Then end the discussion. Do not dwell at such length on any of these problems that they become a fixation in the child's mind.

Individual school districts are now required by law to provide education within their own schools for handicapped youngsters of normal intelligence. Many handicapped and non-handicapped children, therefore, now share the same schools, sometimes with help from specialized teachers in addition to the regular teaching staff. You should explain to your child in private that some children are deaf and some have eye problems, and that these problems occur in degrees. Some will be more handicapped than others.

If a child comes home from school saying there is a deaf boy in his class, explain how deaf children sometimes communicate with each other in American Sign Language—a fully developed language, complete with verb tenses, phraseology, and idioms. If a television station in your community offers the news broadcast in American Sign Language, watch the program with your child. You should teach him there are various degrees of being deaf, and you should tell him that when deaf children begin to learn how to talk, at first their speech may sound gruff and distorted. Above all, your child and his friends should never mock in fun the deaf child's efforts, for he is trying to perfect one of the hardest tasks ever tackled by a human—learning normal speech and language without having heard the spoken word.

If your child refers to another wearing braces on his legs, explain how difficult life is for that person, how courageous the child is to try to lead a normal life in school, and how adept and skilled he is to be able to operate with those heavy braces and possibly crutches or a wheel chair. Teach your child to have compassion for someone not as fortunate as he, but above all instill in him the necessity to act with the child in braces as with any other friend—and not to draw attention to him, or shower him with pity.

There may be a child in your neighborhood who is retarded. You should explain to your children that this child learns more slowly than they do, and you should encourage them to be enthusiastic about what such a child can do. They should include him in their play as often as possible and praise his small accomplishments. Emphasize the positive experiences, all the things that he and your children can try to do together. Teach your children to ask what games the child enjoys and already knows, or to pick a simple game like tag or ball that gives him an opportunity to succeed and show how well he can do.

Normal children gain all kinds of understanding and tolerance from contact with the retarded, and the retarded gain from acceptance by their peers. Your children will be learning a very important part of life—patience, compassion, and understanding—in relating properly to the retarded child.

The Hard of Hearing For most of us, it is the everyday situations that are the most perplexing in knowing how to act with someone who has difficulty hearing. Consider the dearly loved but progressively deafer parent. When talking to such an older person, we often grow impatient at having to repeat trivial information or answers. But put yourself in the place of the person whose hearing is impaired and who feels cut off from the mainstream. To help such a person, speak slowly and clearly; this eliminates much of the confusion of sounds in his ear. Try to get him into a quiet corner when you talk with him, so that distracting noises are minimal. Don't try to hold a conversation near a loud television set, or while the stereo is playing or the children are shouting. When older people begin to lose some of their hearing.

they are losing part of the sounds of words; they aren't being stubborn or trying to irritate you.

If someone is wearing a hearing aid, don't shout at him, for the sound will probably be distorted. The hearing aid works most effectively when you speak in a normal modulation.

Perhaps a younger friend suffers from a progressive hearing loss. She may interrupt conversations and seem to monopolize them, but actually she is frightened by the fact that when she listens to others, she hears very little. You can help such a person in a social situation. If you invite her to dinner place her next to someone she would enjoy talking to, for that person will probably be the only one she will be able to understand. Try to keep surrounding noise to a minimum. If there is entertainment, seat her away from it. (Place her away from the stereo speakers, for example, or from the piano if someone is playing.) Be sure she is seated where her conversational partners are well lit; it will help her understand them if she sees their faces clearly. For someone trained in lip reading, good lighting is essential in being able to function properly.

If you accompany a deaf person to a lecture or church, be sure to take seats right up front, so he will have the best conditions for lip reading or translating signs.

At times you may encounter a deaf person who uses American Sign Language (Ameslan) or finger-spelling as the primary mode of communication. Unless you also have a good working knowledge of Ameslan, communication through it will be extremely difficult. Don't be afraid to communicate through writing; this is never out of place, even at a dinner party. Be aware of the body language and facial expressions of the person, too, to help you understand the tone and importance of his message. The feelings and the enthusiasm of ideas of the deaf are as intense and as exciting as anyone else's.

The Sight-impaired Person   With the advent of Seeing Eye dogs, commonly referred to as guide dogs, visually impaired and blind people have become more active in the business world, as well as leading more normal social or leisure lives. The dog means they can travel, eat in a restaurant, and attend church, the theater, or a lecture.

If a blind person needs directions in finding a new place, don't use yourself as a reference point, use *him.* "You are now facing west; you're on Third Avenue and Fifty-fourth. To reach Park Avenue and Fifty-fourth, just keep walking in this direction two more blocks, west, and you'll be there." When you're guiding a blind person, *offer the elbow of your arm. Don't take his arm,* which is one's natural inclination. Walk half a step ahead of him. As your body moves even slightly to change direction, he will be sensitive to that movement and change with you.

If a blind person is your guest at home or in a restaurant, guide him to his place at the table and put his hand on the back of his chair. Describe the elements of the table setting briefly; when the food is served, describe the location of the side dishes. But do not overwhelm a blind person with information he doesn't need or want.

When a blind person comes to visit in your home, describe the furniture as you are passing through the rooms so he will feel comfortable walking back through them again. Be sure all the drawers in desks and bureaus are closed and all doors you walk through are wide open and not ajar. Accidents often occur when the visually handicapped encounter the unexpectedly sharp edges of doors and drawers.

If your visually handicapped friend has his guide dog with him, don't feed or pet the dog. Ask if the dog needs anything—perhaps water—but remember that he is a working animal and must not be treated like a pet.

How We Can Help   If you see a handicapped person having difficulty, perhaps in going through a heavy door or across a busy intersection, go up and quietly ask, "May I help you?" Ask before you rush into action, and don't be conspicuous with your assistance if he accepts it. All too often, tactless people treat the handicapped like children. A man confined to a wheel chair suffers humiliation when a thoughtless waiter taking the order turns to his wife, asking, "And what does *he* want?"

We frequently encounter slightly retarded adults, socially or in business. We should be on the alert to give them a helping hand when they need it. And we should work hard in our communities to support the programs that find jobs for these people, as well as creating new ones so they can perform simple tasks for money. The wages they earn may be small, but the self-respect they earn is enormous.

We should support legislation that makes things easier for the physically handicapped, too, such as the law that requires that new buildings erected with federal money be barrier-free. All newly constructed government buildings, some new commercial malls, and many public facilities such as libraries, schools, and museums now have ramps and rest rooms to accommodate wheel chairs. Not only public buildings should be built this way, but all future buildings.

Seeing Eye dogs for the blind or near-blind are now the only animals allowed to travel anywhere unconfined, including on public conveyances. Television stations are utilizing more and more American Sign Language minutes on certain programs. These acts should be encouraged by the public. We must educate our children to develop a sincere understanding of the special problems of other people—and resolve to work toward making their lives easier, freer, and more like our own.

The In-laws and Grandparents

With longevity increasing by decades, the possibility of a young couple having mothers- and fathers-in-law with whom they must interact is much greater than it was in years past. A mother-in-law, particularly when she is a widow or a divorcée with her children grown and gone from her home, can be either a source of great love and respect or a source of friction to her children and their spouses. When a man says, "My mother-in-law is great," it usually translates to "My mother-in-law is supportive of what I'm doing, loving to our children, and helpful when we need her." When a woman says, "My mother-in-law is great," she usually means that her mother-in-law is noninterfering, uncritical, and a marvelous baby-sitter.

The "in-law" problem must be looked at from both sides. Consideration of one's in-laws should be shown by the couple and their children, and consideration of one's married children and grandchildren should be shown by the in-laws. A mother-in-law must remember that if she fed her son "a good nourishing dinner every night at home" and she considers him ill fed now, she should keep quiet. It is up to her son to arrange better food in his house, or perhaps *he* might learn how to cook. A mother-in-law should not tell her daughter-in-law to take better care of her son. Nor should a father-in-law criticize the economic planning of his son-in-law. If he feels his daughter's husband is shirking his financial obligations and not planning wisely for the future, he must remember that he, too, had to learn by his own mistakes. One cannot run the life of anybody else, particularly not in the next generation. One can only "suggest" certain things and then spend the rest of the time keeping quiet and hoping that one's advice will be asked for again.

I remember hearing some sage advice from a woman who was telling her friend to cease interfering in her only child's marriage. "The next time you want to criticize Michael for not taking proper care of your daughter," she warned, "close your mouth as though you had just drawn a fast zipper across it; then take three deep, slow breaths, exhaling slowly each time, and change the subject. The oxygen intake will give you the courage *not* to say what never should be said.

One should never criticize a grandparent in front of a child; husband and wife should vent their frustrations on the subject privately to each other, so that the children will grow up respecting their grandparents, regardless of the closeness or lack of warmth of the relationship.

Despite drastic changes in life-styles, the family as a unit is still the source of our greatest strength, and the happiest families today are those where the various generations are in close touch with each other, learning from each other, respecting each other and *needing* each other.

Treatment of Aged Parents   If one's parents are in a nursing home, the children and grandchildren should write to them and visit them as a matter of course, not as an exceptional act. To place one's parents in a home and leave them there unattended, neglected, unvisited, is a tragedy for them and a crime for those responsible for doing it. If there is an ounce of compassion in the younger generation, the aged person in a home will be regularly visited, telephoned, written to, with little thoughtful presents sent every so often. After all, the younger generation will be the older one someday, and it doesn't hurt to start thinking of the Golden Rule at a very early age.

When a Parent Requires Financial Support Many young married people have to support one or more parents or at least contribute to their support. A married couple should, if possible, live by themselves. Any couple needs privacy. It is better for parents to live separately, no matter how simply, to ensure their own independence and that of their children. Whether the dependent parents live with their children or not, their bills should not be paid for them if they are at all capable of managing their own affairs. Unless they are senile, they should be treated like responsible people and permitted to handle their own expenditures for rent, clothes, food, and spending money. Unless they ask to be relieved of the responsibility, they should have their own checking or savings accounts to which their children contribute at stated intervals. They should know how much money they can count on and when. Even if the income is small and they must keep strictly within it, most old people feel more self-respect managing it themselves.

The very aged are seldom willing to consider that their remaining days are limited. They often have the fantasy that they will outlive those who care for them and then, without means, will be dependent on "charity."

Money in their own name helps them to feel that they have a little more time. And they need to make their own decisions on how to spend it.

When an Older Grandparent Comes to Live with You In most cases today when a parent lives with a daughter or a son, that person is elderly; and while the situation may create problems for a younger family, it is a kind and happy alternative to a beloved relative's having to live in a home for the elderly.

Many children who have a grandparent living at home have grown to adulthood much the better for that close relationship. The young have so much to learn from the old, and when there is a give-and-take in the home between generations, the outcome can be affirmative, wholesome, and important to a child's growth.

When a grandparent comes to live with a family, he (or she) should be given a cheerful room of his own with some of his own furnishings, including a television set and radio. A very little in kindness goes a very long way for an older person in residence, who may feel as though he is imposing on the others (which he sometimes is) or who may feel as though he is inferior (which he is not) because he cannot keep up with the lingo and trends of the two younger generations.

Along with providing a comfortable private room and attractive surroundings for the grandparent, one should involve him in family chores so he will be able to feel useful in some way. Perhaps the grandparent could be in charge of the family marketing, the care of the dog, or the garden. A grandmother might take over the family mending and sewing chores, while a grandfather might be in charge of the children when they come home from school, seeing that they do their homework before the parents return from work. An older person usually has a lot of energy left for certain tasks, and he should be made to feel that in your house he is both loved *and* needed. At the same time, one should not take advantage of grandparents. Taking care of small children is a strenuous activity, and the older generation should not be overutilized. An older person who has been out of practice for many years can be exhausted quite easily after spending one hour with an active three-year-old.

When a grandparent comes to live with a family, all members should be reminded of certain universal factors:

1. *Privacy.* No one has the right to open anyone else's mail or to listen in on anyone else's conversation. Teen-agers have no right to be noisy and boisterous when Grandma is entertaining some of her friends in the living room; Grandma has no right to be around when the teen-agers are having their party in the living room; no one should intrude when the parents are having a dinner party of their friends. The living room or the family room or wherever entertaining is done should be considered "private turf" for whoever is entertaining on any particular day or evening.

2. *Everyone's possessions remain his or her own.* A grandparent, for example, should not refer to possessions around the house as "our things," but rather as "my daughter and son-in-law's furniture, car," and so on. "What is yours is yours and what is mine is mine" is an old axiom but a true one.

3. *Contain your criticism.* Living at close quarters causes considerable tension between generations. It's bad enough with two generations, but when a third is added, it can cause harsh words and hostile accusations. I have one friend who used to go up to her bedroom and write down her outpouring of anger against her mother-in-law, who lived with them for twenty years. She would let it all out on paper, but never vocally, and she was, I might add, always careful to destroy the paper afterward! She said it was her solution to "flipping her lid" at times.

4. *Remember the enormous good* that is derived from an exchange between the generations. The younger ones should love and respect the grandparent and realize they are what they are because of the upbringing and sacrifices of that generation; and the grandparent should realize his or her good fortune in being surrounded by family members who care and who have plenty of love to go around.

Chapter 2

MANNERS IN THE FAMILY

The Social Behavior of Children

"Making" Children Mind Their Manners There are certain accepted manners that children should be continually encouraged to cultivate. Their attention should be drawn to the fact that on various occasions Mother and Father do certain things to be socially agreeable and these courtesies will be expected of them, too, as soon as they are able to cope with them.

The mother who makes a scene with her child because he won't shake hands with Mrs. Smith or thank a small hostess for a party he didn't in all honesty enjoy does little but make everyone uncomfortable. It is far better to say, "Helen, Johnny would like to tell you what a nice time he had at your party. And he hopes to see you soon again," the minute one senses that a child is going to balk at the expected amenities. Most children eventually rise to the social graces in their own good time. In the meantime, they should hear us deliver the courteous phrases for them, without irritation.

If necessary, a mother should prepare her young son with whom she is walking on the street to greet another person properly. "Here comes Johnny's mother, Mrs. Anderson. When she stops to speak, put out your hand and say, 'Hello, Mrs. Anderson, how is Johnny?'"

A little friendly review at home of manners before and after parties and social events attended by your children is a must. Self-reliance in manners is, of course, mostly acquired away from the parents, but without the base laid by the parents there is no self-reliance and there are no manners! Children need plenty of opportunity to practice what they have been taught at home in the company of other children who are going through the same social exercises. At the age of eight and up, dancing class may be helpful. In a city like New York it is still a social force, but in some cities dancing classes are regarded as "old-hat."

Taking your child to museums, concerts, the theater, ballet, or opera and encouraging him to join the Boy or Girl Scouts, Camp Fire Girls, Boys Clubs, 4-H Club, and other extracurricular activities where co-operation and social ease are fostered among one's peers are very valuable. The lessons learned there, in a spirit of fun and co-operation, do not come from over-harping parents, and they are therefore often more easily learned.

Children and Adults in Introductions and Good-bys   Except for dancing classes still given in certain parts of the country, little girls are rarely exposed any more to the art of curtsying. (The early grades of the Convents of the Sacred Heart still teach curtsying, but it is becoming a rarity.) Little boys may learn how to bow at dancing school, but they never use it again. (An exception is the boy who grows up to be a businessman who travels often to Japan.) The disappearance of such charming customs does not imply any lessening of the need for respect of one another, or the need of a child to greet an adult with civility.

When an adult, either a relative or a friend of his parents, comes into his home, the child should turn away from the TV or stop playing with his friends and greet the adult by standing up, putting out his hand, and saying, "Hello, Mrs. Stevens." If he does not know who the lady is who has come to visit his mother, he puts out his hand and says, "Hello." The lady will come forth automatically with her name. Both boys and girls should be taught to greet adults, men as well as women, in this manner. Once that formality has been dispensed with, the child can return to whatever he was engaged in; he does not have to rise again should Mrs. Stevens come in and out of the room several times during the visit. He should, however, rise once more to say "Good-by" when Mrs. Stevens leaves. (It is unfortunate when parents permit their children to ignore completely the presence of an adult who comes into the room where the children are playing.)

If an older child or even someone of his own age comes into the house, the child does not have to go through this formal greeting procedure, but he should look up from whatever he is doing and call out, "Hello, George," as a way of acknowledging that someone outside the family has entered the room. (If the person entering the room is his own friend coming to play with him, he should rise to say hello.)

When a child is introduced to an adult, the parent says, "Mary, this is Johnny, our son. Say hello to Mrs. Jenkins, Johnny." The child is always presented *to the adult,* not the other way around, and Johnny should always put out his hand in greeting and say, "Hello, Mrs. Jenkins."

When a child has another child over, whether it's for a birthday party or just informal play, he should learn to escort the child to the door when it's time to leave, and say, "Thank you for coming to my house."

Learning to Say Thank You   The first word of real politeness that a child usually learns to utter is "Please," even if it comes out first as "Pease." If an adult says "Please" to a child often enough when the latter asks for something, the little one will begin to mimic and associate the word with requesting and with having the request fulfilled. As he begins to form words and sticks out his cup for more milk, whoever is feeding him should ask him,

"Say 'Please'?" and eventually back will come the word "Please" when the learning process is really taking hold.

"Thank you" is harder to say, but it follows along right after "Please." When the baby bangs his empty mug in glee while giving it back to Mommy, who will wash it, she says in mock gratitude, "Oh, thank you, thank you *very* much." The baby grins with delight. Mommy has just thanked him and he recognizes those "Thank you" sounds, even if he can't say them yet.

As the child develops verbally, his parents should teach him to say "Thank you" for each meal, car ride, toy, or cookie offered to him. When the Christmases and birthdays roll around, his mother or some relative should write a short thank-you note on his behalf for every present received and every birthday party attended. He will become so used to seeing the written thank-you sent after a special act of kindness, a gift received, or a special occasion that with little fuss he will assume the task himself when he is able to write well enough. By the time he is nine years old, a "reminder" note from his mother, giving the name and address of the person to whom he is writing, should be enough. He should be able to write the thank-you note and give it to her to mail without any more prompting.

By this time he should also have learned to say thank you automatically to people who hold open a door for him, who picked up his dropped book, who place food before him at the lunch counter, or who pay him a compliment. The child who learns to say, "Please may I get down?" when he wants to descend from his high chair soon becomes a socialized human being—with an ingrained sense of good manners that he will most likely carry through life.

Paying and Receiving Compliments One of the most gracious forms of communication is the paying of a compliment. It is an art. Children learn how to pay compliments by living in a household where the parents compliment other members of the family, their friends, and the people with whom they come in daily contact. Sons and daughters are influenced by the way in which their parents receive a compliment or automatically react to a situation by giving a compliment. A child who grows up in an environment where one is not afraid to express praise, where one does it to please others, but also to encourage and help them, will probably emulate his elders when he grows up.

Extending Invitations from Child to Child When children are very little their mothers make their social engagements for them, either by telephone calls—"Can Johnny come over to play with Harry one afternoon this week?"—or by written birthday party invitations.

When the children are old enough to handle the telephone themselves, they begin to extend invitations in their own way: "Pamela, will you come to my house this Saturday?" If Pamela says yes, it is up to the mother of the little girl extending the invitation to talk to Pamela's mother and assure her the invitation was made with her knowledge and consent. The mothers should straighten out on the telephone all the logistics of time, transportation, whether a meal is involved, and whether pocket money or any extra clothes will be needed.

Not too much changes until the high school years. High school students are on their own in extending invitations to peers to attend parties in their homes. If, however, a teen-ager invites a friend from another town to visit overnight or for the weekend, the mother of the would-be host or hostess should talk to one of the parents of the invited guest, so that the parents will realize it is a legitimate invitation and will know that there will be adults present in the house.

A Child's Party Manners No young child can remember all his party manners at once. This is particularly true if he is host at his own birthday party. He should not be goaded and pushed and corrected by an overanxious parent all during the proceedings. He can probably handle the basics well enough: he shakes hands with all as they come in the door; he tells them he's glad they came; he thanks them for their presents (even for the ones he doesn't like—and he never tells anyone if he already has what they brought him); he gives them first crack at the games and prizes; he sees them to the door and says good-by to each guest.

All of this is trying to a young person, particularly as the honoree is probably embarrassed at having so much attention showered on him. So if he greets a friend from school, "Hi, Horseface! I was hoping you wouldn't come," the parent must not be upset. "Horseface" is probably flattered to be the object of the joke. Children should be allowed to joke with their friends without parental interference.

After the party is over, if your child did something glaringly bad—an act of real unkindness—bring it up when things are calm and people are less tired. Otherwise, congratulate him on the way he behaved himself, and tell him "he's coming right along in his manners." Children need encouragement and praise far more than they need censure.

Dancing Class Social etiquette is traditionally taught in young people's dancing classes along with basic steps such as the waltz and fox trot, and the much more popular disco dance steps. Until about the tenth grade, the girls are usually taller than the boys and more poised socially, but conversation between the sexes and knowing what to do and how to behave is a strained situation at best. When children in grade school go to dancing class or school dances, there is a lot of the sexes standing around in groups by themselves, combined with silly "horsing around." Nevertheless, it's a beginning. The dancing schools mostly have given up on the girls wearing white gloves and such formal niceties; instead they work on teaching the boys and girls to say something to each other on the dance floor, and not just giggle and blush.

The ability really to dance is a tremendous asset for any young person, whether he learns it in a dancing school in the seventh and eighth grades or by sneaking a few lessons in at a professional ballroom dancing school for adults. It is also helpful for parents to encourage their children to put their new knowledge to practice by dancing with them or older siblings at home whenever the occasion arises. It is not only the moving of the bodies in time to the music and the graceful movement of the feet that is involved; it is a young man's knowing how to approach a young woman and say, "I'd like to have the next dance with you." It's a mother teaching her daughter to coax a shy, recalcitrant boy to dance. "Just smile a lot at him and say, 'Why don't you try it with me—that's one of my favorite songs.' " The best way to become a good dancer is to master the art at a young age so it becomes as natural as walking and a delightful exercise to be enjoyed the rest of one's life.

Bad Language   No matter how careful you are with your language at home, and no matter how exclusive the private school your children may attend, most children come home from school at some point in their young lives uttering obscenities and swear words. While still very young our two children listened to the "street talk" and mimicked it, delighted at our initial reaction of shock—"What? What did I just hear you say?"

If you are initially shocked that your very own flesh and blood could be using foul language, change your attitude quickly to a matter-of-fact one. Say calmly to your child, "You know, that's an unattractive way to speak. Do you know what those words really mean?" Chances are your child will not. "Well, don't use words you don't understand." You don't need to say more. There is no reason to make a court case out of the episode, for if you do, the child will decide to use such words to gain attention or to fight back when he's displeased about something.

If a child's language becomes studded with obscenities, it may indicate a disturbed child, and professional help should be sought. But most children, thanks to their peers, will pass through—perhaps at several points in their lives—periods of using bad language. If the parents' attitude upon hearing this language is, "You know, only an insecure person has to talk like that, and we never considered you one of those," the young person will not wish to keep those words in his vocabulary.

If parents use foul language themselves around the home, their children will become leaders in spreading the habit in their schools. One has to practice what one preaches in bringing up a child. If you have a daughter who emerges from college and into the job market using four-letter words with equanimity, you might remind her it will be a serious handicap for her in most jobs—whether in a business, in a profession, or in the arts. But it may require something as serious as a job loss to make a young person realize the truth.

I remember one of my godchildren going through a period in her college years when she couldn't utter a sentence that didn't sound like locker-room lingo. Her family, rather than applying punitive measures, applied affirmative ones. They had been planning the first family trip to Europe for several years and decided to base their departure date on their daughter's conquering of her bad language habits. She was helped along immeasurably by her brother and sisters, because they stood to be rewarded as well by her conquering of the habit. She did the job, of course, and the family finally took their trip abroad.

Teaching Respect for Others' Property The public libraries each year report thousands and thousands of dollars' worth of damage to books. The damage is not all done by children, of course, but the damage done by adults —tearing out pages, dog-earing pages, doodling and scribbling, and breaking the back of books—results from the lack of training during childhood.

A small child cannot be controlled with a constant stream of prohibitions. When he reaches the crawling and toddling stage, breakables like ash trays and ornaments must be put out of his reach wherever possible and his activities confined to areas he can't seriously damage. He should not be allowed to play with such things as phonograph records, which he is bound to break. He will squall when he is removed from such enticing playthings with the words, "Those are Mother's, you mustn't touch," but in time he will find it not worth his while to turn in their direction, especially if acceptable articles are given him immediately as a substitute. It accomplishes nothing to give him cracked or damaged records to break, for he cannot distinguish between the records he may treat with impunity and those he will be punished for breaking.

A baby should have his own books—with the first ones the undamageable cloth kind. Later, when paper books are introduced, they should be looked at only under parental supervision at first. An infant's span of interest is very short, and in minutes the new book that was so bright and arresting may pall. The baby will throw it on the floor or start tearing out the pages, particularly the pop-up kind. This should not be permitted. The mother should say, "We don't hurt books. I'll let you see the book later." And the book should disappear until the next supervised reading. If this procedure is followed every time, eventually even a child of one or two will not destroy his books and won't harm those of his parents, should any be within reach. To give a baby old magazines to mutilate, or permit him to harm his own books, is inviting trouble. He can't know the difference between old and new magazines, between his books and his parents'.

When the child gets his first pencils and crayons he should be allowed to use them only under supervision until he learns how they are used and where. The minute interest lags and the crayon starts straying off the paper or coloring book, the little artist's equipment should be gently put away until the next time.

Children's Manners at Table

Playing with Food A happy, year-and-a-half-old child may make efforts to feed himself with his spoon. If so, let him do as much as he can in some easily cleanable place, but don't expect him to take over the function immediately and don't let fussy grownups annoy him with their admonitions to keep his hands out of his food. A baby who puts his hands in his cereal or dabbles his fingers in his mug of milk is experimenting with self-feeding—not exhibiting bad manners. If he spills some on the tray before him—an inevitable result—don't be in too much of a hurry to clean up the mess, because to him it is delightful. He slides his fingers around in it, and it makes an interesting squishy sound. He likes the feel of it and needs this kind of play whether with mud pies, water or, under such circumstances, his food. A child who dawdles over food once he is competent to feed himself may want to attract his mother's attention so she'll sit with him or perhaps give him a hand with some of the less tractable items, like custard (and why not?), or else he's not hungry. In the latter instance the food should be pleasantly removed.

Some of us were taught always to clean up our plates (because there are people starving in the world). Others of us were taught always to leave some food on a plate, because otherwise we would be considered gluttonous and uncultured. I am of the school that believes that a waste of food is a crime and that adults should serve themselves smaller portions of food and eat every bit of it. But since babies and small children are not really tuned in to the problems of either etiquette or feeding the world's population, we should approach the food that goes on their plates in a different manner.

Each baby is born with a built-in, well-functioning hunger mechanism. It tells him when he should eat and when he should stop eating. If this mechanism is respected by parents and baby, normal growth and appetite usually follow right along. But interference with this delicate adjustment can cause serious emotional difficulties in a young child that may continue into his adulthood in a very complex manner. Constantly coaxing a child or forcing him to eat beyond his capacity, beyond what his hunger dictates at the moment, puts this mechanism out of commission. It often results in an overweight child or one tense and thin, prone to car sickness and frequent digestive upsets.

Should a Child Choose His Own Food? Suppose someone with quite different tastes from yours dictated every morsel you put into your mouth. Would you enjoy your food or would you feel frustrated and angry? Anger causes digestion to stop dead in its tracks. A chronic state of tension at mealtimes is the cause of many of our modern ills, especially ulcers. Unpleasant mealtimes must be avoided for the sake of the whole family and especially that of the children, whose attitudes concerning food are being set at this time. Insisting that a child eat food he doesn't like (and usually the dislike will pass) is bad for the child-parent relationship.

But if you let a child dictate what he'll eat and when, won't he fill up on sweets and never eat the things his body needs? There are many modern children for whom no problem about feeding has ever arisen—they are under the "permissive" or "self-regulating" system. Such children are not fussy eaters unless there is some particular reason for the fussiness—teething, oncoming illness, overfatigue—which is respected by the adult in charge. The child is excused from his meal with no comment one way or the other. Conversely, when he eats well he is not praised for eating. Why should he be? It is important that the whole issue of eating to please a parent (or of not eating to displease) never arise and that happy mealtimes geared to the child's food preferences be the rule.

Where a child has experienced tension over meals and has been subjected to rigid rules of manners even in the nursery, he may, when introduced to the self-regulating system of feeding, start eating his dessert first or refuse to eat anything but sweets. This is because a premium has always been placed on these things—"If you don't eat your meat, you may not have your ice cream!" This puts good, sound meat into the class of something unpleasant but necessary, to be bolted quickly so the "good" child can have the "delicious" dessert.

Psychologists and psychiatrists working with children have found that children who have been exposed to this kind of handling may, once the given opportunity to choose what they want to eat, eat their dessert first. If they do, it's not important, not worth making an issue of, because shortly they will want to be like other people who eat their meat and potatoes first and finish with dessert. In experiments with very young children it was shown over a period of time that children have selective appetites—one day a child may want nothing but string beans for lunch and won't touch his milk; another day he'll want the meat but not the vegetable on his plate—but careful graphing of such food intake over a period of a week will show that the normal child, allowed to select his food according to his preference, will instinctively consume a properly balanced diet if he has been offered, each day, the various elements in it. If he skips lettuce one day and eats twice as much of it the next, he is getting what he needs, isn't he? The body, given the chance, dictates what is required for adequate nutrition.

A Young Child at the Family Table   When a child is old enough to eat with the "big people" at their Sunday lunch or dinner table, he learns that he may not come to the table unless his hands are washed, his hair combed, and his clothes neat. It is to be hoped that this is a habit he will carry with him through life.

Using implements gracefully at table requires a lot of practice; in time he will become more agile. He learns which things are used for certain types of food; he learns after many reminders to chew his food quietly, with his mouth closed. Instead of reaching across the table for something, he learns to ask for it with a "Please" attached, and to say "Thank you" when he gets it.

He learns not to play with his food on the plate, and to be careful so that the milk glass and water glass don't spill over. A child gradually learns to listen to other people's conversation around the table, and to await his turn before blurting out what's on his mind. When he does not wish to eat any more or is just plain longing to leave the adult world at the table and return to his own world, he knows he must first utter the password, "Please may I be excused?" Eating with the adults is a tremendous responsibility for a young one, and everyone should try to make the occasion as pleasant as possible for him. He is, after all, undergoing the strain of a tremendous learning experience. The grownups must show patience and not laugh at his mistakes or punish him when accidents happen. Awkwardness at the dinner table is only increased by nagging. Children learn better table manners if they learn them slowly, and with a very clear edict to the older children in the family that no one is allowed to make fun of the younger one's errors. Otherwise the meal experience, which should be one of the most pleasant hours of the day, will become associated in his mind with everything bad.

What do you do with your hands? If you teach your child to eat continental-style, both hands will be busy holding an eating utensil (fork in the left hand, knife in the right). If your child eats American-style, he will have a fork in his right hand and his left hand idle. Teach him to rest it casually on the table next to his plate, rather than holding it stiffly in his lap. Many well-mannered adults do the same thing.

Learning How to Converse at the Family Dinner Table   The family dinner table provides one of the greatest learning situations there is. The child who graduates from his high chair to his rightful place at the table in an adult chair, eating by himself, knows he has made a major step in his own life. Along with the polishing of his table manners, he understands that he shares in the responsibility of partaking in the family conversation.

Wise parents use the family dinner hour as a time to find out what is going on in their children's lives and to expose them to the things of life that they cannot possibly get at school. The dinner hour should be a no-nonsense, no-interference, very sacred tradition. If the mother or father comes home late from the office, the family should wait.

Everyone should come to the table well groomed, hair combed, fingernails clean. And *everyone* should be asked to give an accounting of his or her day. "What kind of a day did you have?" should be asked around the table, with each child contributing, as well as both parents. If Mary got a gold star on her drawing in kindergarten class, this is important news, and time must be made to enable her to relay it. She should be listened to with the same respect as is her father when he describes how he landed an important piece of new business, or her mother who has news about the hospital wing her board of trustees voted on today, or her big brother who shares his disgust with the school's basketball team performance.

There should be no telephone interruptions allowed; no one should be able to leave the table early because "there's a great TV program starting tonight." In the give-and-take of this family situation, a child learns the art of conversation, a skill that will serve him all his life. He begins to learn what is of universal interest to all people; he feels the joy of wit when someone says something that makes everyone laugh. He hears his mother say, "That's enough, Peter. That story has gone on far too long," and he realizes why. He hears his father say, "That was very well put, Suzanne," and he begins to analyze why his sister earned that compliment.

When we were children my brothers and I not only had to contribute to the general conversation with each of our own "important" activities, but also had our own "evening news" as our parents discussed the lead stories of that day from the Omaha *World Herald*. It made us feel we were "in the know" at school the next day. Our conversation often became so spirited that our parents had to call a firm "Table Silence"—five-minute periods when only they could speak and we children had to remain silent. Then the time out ended and we could once again resume conversation, hopefully in a more orderly, noninterrupting way, and with less sibling rivalry expressing itself!

A Knowledgeable Teen-ager's Table Manners   A child should have fairly good table manners by the time he is in high school. He will learn more polish and dexterity later, particularly as he attends more parties, as he eats more exotic foods, and as he matures in general. By the age of fourteen he should be familiar with the following eating and party situations.

At a buffet party, he should instinctively step back and let adults go ahead of him in line. A boy should step back for any girl, too, unless he is well ahead in the line. When he reaches his place at the table, he should stand until the other adults begin to sit down. A boy should push in the chair of the girl next to him, a disappearing custom, as a natural result of our "equalizing world." But it is *still* nice for a boy to learn how to help seat the lady on his right at the table, and the lady on his left, too, if she is still standing before he sits down.

A child should sit up straight in his chair, and not tilt back (which is a great way to break one's hostess' chair).

He should know how to cope with a napkin. If it is luncheon-size he should unfold the whole napkin; a large dinner napkin may be unfolded in half or three quarters. It is the first thing he does when he sits down. If he is eating a boiled lobster or a spaghetti dinner, he may tuck his napkin up under his chin, to protect his clothes, but not otherwise. His napkin-tucking days are over.

He should know to serve himself *small* portions of everything he takes from a platter on the buffet table or one that is passed to him by a waitress; there are usually second helpings. Things like chocolate sauce should be poured sparingly over the ice cream when it is passed, even though his natural inclination may be to let it pour torrentially.

He should know how to replace the serving fork and spoon face down on the side of the platter and to put the serving spoon back into the serving bowl.

He should not begin eating at the table until he sees his hosts or other adults begin. If food is passed that he dislikes, he should take a small portion of it anyway and say nothing, for to keep refusing platters of food will upset his hostess. He can always pretend he is eating something, and move the food around the plate a bit. (If his hostess notices he is not eating and offers to have someone in the kitchen make him a peanut butter and jelly sandwich he should say, "Oh no, but thank you very much anyway.")

He should learn the order of courses. Show him the logic of starting with his eating utensils, both left and right, from the outside and working toward the middle (or toward the plate). For soup he would take the large soup spoon on his right and tip it away from himself as he fills it with soup. If, when most of the soup is gone, he would like the remaining liquid, he has only to tip the plate away from himself and continue to spoon up the soup. It should be sipped silently and not slurped. If the soup is served in a two-handled cup, there will be a smaller, round-bowl spoon on the far outside right of the flatware. When he tires of spooning the soup from the cup, he may lift the cup and drink from it in small sips. When crackers or celery and olives are passed during the soup course, he may take whatever he would like (that is, up to two pieces of anything) and put them on his butter plate, if there is one, or else on the side of the plate under the soup cup or soup bowl.

If fish is served, be sure he can recognize the fish fork and knife on the outside left and right sides of the plate respectively. They are smaller than the regular forks and knives; the fish knife often has a wide blade ending in a point. The same rule holds for eating with a fish fork and knife as for any fork and knife. The knife is often there to look pretty, because most fish can be cut with a fork, although it is useful if there are bones to contend with.

He should recognize the largest knife and fork, the dinner knife and fork. These he will find lying inside the fish fork and knife. I feel it is much easier to eat in the "continental manner" and would encourage you to teach your child this style. He should grasp the fork in his left hand with the tines pointing down, the knife in his right, his forefinger bracing the top of the handle, near the blade, for good leverage. Only one or two small pieces of meat should be cut at a time, and these should be eaten before cutting again.

If he feels the urge to spear a bit of potato or vegetable on top of the small piece of meat already on his fork, it's all right to do it. In other words, the fork acts as a catalyst for combining bits of food and sauces into one delicious mouthful, aided and abetted by the knife in the right hand that pushes the food onto the fork's tines. When he raises his fork to his mouth, he should raise his arm vertically, instead of sticking out his elbow in a triangular sweep.

If he is resting from eating or deep in conversation, he should learn to rest his fork and knife on the plate in the mid-section, with the fork, tines down, crossed over the knife. This is the "rest" position, and a well-trained serving person will know not to remove his plate. When he has finished eating, however, he should inform the waiter of this fact simply by putting his knife, its sharp blade facing left, alongside the fork with its tines down. If he is eating a piece of cake or pie, which requires a fork only, the rule changes. When he is finished, he simply leaves his fork, tines up, on the plate. (Also see page 407.)

He should learn to lay down his eating implements first if he is going to wipe his mouth or drink some water. He should never gesticulate with his knife and fork, no matter how vital a conversational point he is making. (My son almost stabbed me in the eye once when I brought him a plate and he was telling his father with energetic motions about the St. David's soccer game that day.)

A young man should be taught not to daydream and slowpoke his way through a meal, holding up everyone else who has long since finished, but he should not race, either. The sight and sounds of someone speeding through his meal are hardly appetizing.

Even though butter plates are not seen much these days, he should know how to use one. If he has a roll or piece of bread on his butter plate, he should halve it with his fingers, not with the butter knife.

When salad is served to him as a separate course, he may find a salad knife and fork among his implements. If he does not have to cut his lettuce in order to eat it easily, he may leave the knife right where it is, unused. If a platter of different cheeses is passed with the salad, he should cut himself a small portion of one or two or even three of the cheeses, if he would like them; otherwise he does not have to take any cheese. (It is not something over which the hostess has slaved for hours in the kitchen!) He should use his salad knife to spread some of the cheese on a cracker (crackers are also passed with the cheese course). He may also eat his cheese with a fork if he does not wish bread or crackers. Sometimes he will find the salad is not served as a separate course, but will be placed right on his dinner plate or on a small plate to the left of his dinner plate. He may eat this salad with his regular dinner fork, while he is eating his meat or main course.

When it's time for dessert, he should take the spoon and fork lying horizontally at the top of his place setting; or else, if there is a maid serving, the fork and spoon might be served on the dessert plate. He should simply remove the fork and spoon from the plate and place them on the table (fork to the left of his plate and spoon to the right) until the dessert is served. Sometimes at dessert time the plate is brought in under a finger bowl on a small doily. He should remove the bowl and the doily and place them to the upper left, near his plate. (Our daughter was eight when she very gracefully drank from the side of the finger bowl before I caught her in the act. The sedate dining room at the Williamsburg Inn in Virginia will not soon forget her.)

If the dessert is something delightfully gooey, like a mousse or a crème brûlée, a guest may either eat it alone with a spoon or should know enough to hold the spoon in his right hand and push some of the dessert onto the spoon with the fork, held in his left hand. When he is finished, the fork should be in the center of the plate, tines down, next to the spoon, which is face up. If he forgets the latter niceties, he can learn them later.

He may run into the European custom of serving fresh fruit as a final course. A small plate with a small fruit knife and fork will be placed in front of him. If he likes fresh fruit, he may choose a piece from the big bowl usually placed on the table. Again, if he does not wish any, he will not offend the hostess. He should use his knife to core, peel, and quarter the fruit he takes. He can also serve himself grapes from the bowl, taking some grapes with his fingers or snipping some off a large stalk by using the grape shears attached to the bowl. If he chooses a banana, teach him how to remove the skin with his fingers, then take the fruit fork and knife and cut off small pieces, eating each piece as he goes. (When he's older, if he goes to Europe to study, he will learn how to eat a banana as the Europeans do, their fingers never touching the fruit, their knives and forks doing the peeling, sectioning, and everything but the eating.)

Don't make him feel uptight about his table manners. Adults who have been going to fancy dinner parties all their lives make mistakes about the silverware they're supposed to use with certain courses. They may end up a knife short because they used a knife when they weren't supposed to, or the table may have been set improperly in the first place. If your child makes a mistake with the flatware, he should learn to make a joke about it and laugh at himself. No one gets a perfect record on this subject, even after living a long and full life!

Manners Around the Home

The Responsibility for Keeping Things Tidy When one works hard to keep a house clean and presentable, it is more than annoying when a child's room is continuously and completely messy. Shouting and showing aggravation are not going to help. If a mother cleans up the mess herself, meanwhile berating her child, the problem will continue. He will see someone else picking up after him. The best way is for a parent to say, "Let's clean this up together, right this minute," and the child will feel compelled to work along with the parent to put the room to rights again. He will most likely feel a sense of accomplishment for having co-operated with his mother or father and for having his room look nice again.

A parent should help a child become orderly by giving him enough bureau drawers for his things, enough hooks and closet rod space, and enough attractively labeled boxes and other storage facilities to inspire the child to keep collections of this and that in their proper places. It is also up to a parent to clean out a child's closets of outgrown clothes and discarded toys, to make room for the new.

Strict rules can be laid down about a child's not leaving his things lying around the rest of the house, but they are not always obeyed. Many is the time that upon entering our apartment, I have had to run an obstacle course of volleyballs, footballs, hockey sticks, baseball mitts, and the like, in order to get into the living room. We have our own system of demerits when this happens, and so many demerits for one child means one less baseball or football game attended. Each parent must find his own key for what will motivate his child to pick up after himself.

Bathroom Manners   The most potentially irritating situation in any family is a lack of sufficient bathrooms. Parents who establish strict laws governing the time and length of usage and the way in which each child keeps the bathroom are sage parents. During "rush hours" everyone wants to be in the bathroom at once. Even if only two people are vying for it in the morning, problems are created.

In whatever manner the parents work out the family bathroom laws, the plan must be communicated effectively to each child. Each person should have his own rack with his own towels and facecloths, as well as his own glass for toothbrushing materials, and perhaps a shelf of the medicine cabinet for each male's shaving needs and each female's make-up needs. Each should be held responsible for hanging up his wet towels, removing any clothes that were thrown on the floor, putting away razor blades, recapping bottles, and cleaning hair, toothpaste, shaving cream, or spilled make-up from the washbasin. And if someone is responsible for creating a flood of water on the floor, he or she should mop it up, not leave it for the next person to cope with. Boys should be taught to leave the toilet seat down, too, before leaving the bathroom.

If a bar of soap on the washbasin washed extra-dirty hands, those same hands should wash out the dirty soap dish afterward. The bathroom should be well supplied with a detergent, sponges, and a brush, so that anyone can easily clean the bathtub or shower stall if it needs it. Everyone should wipe clean a steamed-up or spotted over-the-basin mirror, too. The bath mat should be hung neatly over the side of the tub to dry; the shower curtain should be spread wide to dry, and the window should be opened to air out the room if it is needed. If shampoo, soap, toilet paper, or facial tissue has run out, the last person to use it should go to the supply closet and immediately replace it.

Telephone Manners   The first thing a child should learn about the telephone is how to answer it properly. He should learn to pick up the receiver and answer in clearly spoken tones. He should not answer the telephone in a series of Neanderthal grunts: "Huoh. Yeh. Huh? Dunno." End of conversation.

A child should learn to start with a well-enunciated "Hello. . . . No, my mother is not at home. Who's calling, please? . . . May I take a message?" I discovered the secret of one family's good telephone manners when I saw a chart by the telephone depicting a sunny face, with the scenario written out, complete with all the "pleases" and "thank you for callings." Don't expect a child to take good messages if the parents don't leave pads and pencils by every extension.

By the time a child is about nine, the telephone calls to and from peers begin in earnest. Some of the conversations are an honest exchange of home work assignments or a clarification of school events. Children should be encouraged to talk correctly to their friends on the telephone, including ending a conversation with something like "Well, I'm sorry you can't come to my party," instead of just hanging up when the response on the other end is negative. But there is no reason a child should completely take over the telephone when he is home from school, which often happens by the time he is twelve or thirteen. There are several avenues of action open to parents whose children are afflicted with "telephonitis":

1. Give up completely and give the child his own extension in his bedroom. At least the noise level in the family rooms will be lowered.
2. Give the children their own private telephone number and extensions. To some people this is tantamount to giving them a Cadillac when they are sixteen, but to others it is not an act that will spoil the child, only a way to allow the parents to survive in the same house with them.
3. Give the children specific hours of the day or night when they may receive and make calls from their friends. The children should communicate these hours to their friends, so that everyone will have an understanding of the rules.

Adults should follow some rules, too. It is rude to call anyone in a busy family early in the morning, when the household is trying to get off to school and work. No one should call anyone after nine-thirty at night. It is an imposition to call later, unless it is a matter of urgency and you know the person you are calling will not have retired.

By the time your child grows into the high school years, the telephone will probably become even more important in his life. He will want privacy in making his calls, and if he gets his own instrument and private telephone number, preferably he should pay for it himself out of his earnings or allowance. If this is not feasible, he might be given it as a major annual Christmas present. He should keep the ring low so that it will not disturb other members of the family. No one else should have to answer it when it rings and he is not in his room. It should also be made clear that all long-distance calls will be paid for by him, and that his friends may not have free use of the instrument, since that will escalate the bill.

Pets If there is a family pet, you and your children should be conscious of the possibility that your visiting guests may feel uneasy with animals around. It's simple enough to put a pet in a bedroom or outdoors during a visit or a party. Small children are often seriously frightened by animals, and some people really loathe being jumped upon by a dog or a cat. Some people are allergic to animal fur, so your leaping, jumping pet may upset your guest very much. When a guest arrives, start to remove the pet from the room, which will give your guest the opportunity to say, "Don't be silly. I love dogs [or cats]." If the guest says nothing, he is probably speechless with gratitude over your kind gesture in removing the pet.

Likewise, it is important that a guest never take along a pet unless it is explicitly invited. Your host or hostess may have an animal who gets very upset and agitated when another animal is introduced into the household. Your hosts may smile tightly, saying "Oh, it's perfectly all right of you to have brought along Spot," but in reality they may be furious.

Bedtime Every preschool and school child should have a fixed bedtime, for which he should be pleasantly but firmly prepared. Give children plenty of advance warning of bedtime—or mealtime. Children's play is their "work," from which they can't be suddenly separated without warning. They have little sense of time, even after they can tell time. It is better to say, "You have just enough time to put your blocks away—see, I'll help—before bathtime," than to say, arbitrarily, "In twenty minutes, have these blocks put away and be ready for your bath!"

You may be relieved that the end of the day has come and the children will be soon in bed. But if you show it you are in for trouble—dawdling trouble and "drink-of-water" trouble. Children hate to give up, even when they are dog-tired. They are afraid they'll miss something and that all fun really begins when they are out of the way. So they refuse to get out of the way, using all kinds of legitimate and illegitimate pretexts to keep you with them or to rejoin the adult world.

If bedtime trouble regularly crops up in your household, examine your manner with your children at the end of the day, to see if it is polite and unhurried. Be sure you make them feel you still have adequate time for them—again within reason. Keep in mind the bedtime deadline—and have *them* keep it in mind—but be relaxed about it. When the deadline comes, see that they are in bed and arrange your household affairs so that you do have time to hear prayers, tell a bedtime story, or sing a lullaby. It is nice for a parent to sit down on the edge of the bed and have a short chat with the child after the latter is all tucked in. It's a time when a small worry might be voiced by the child that can be calmed with a measure of love and reassurance.

When, occasionally, you can't keep this bedtime date with your children, realize their disappointment and substitute a little treat of some kind to make up for it.

Clothes for Your Child

Your motive in dressing your baby is to keep it warm and comfortable. When your child begins to attend school, however, another very important factor enters the picture. Your child should dress in the same style as the other children of your neighborhood for school and for party occasions. Feeling the same as, not different from, everyone else is important for healthy emotional growth. If you make a little Lord Fauntleroy of your son, refusing to crop his charming little curls, or if your daughter wears velvet and taffeta to Sunday school when the other children wear clean, pretty cotton dresses, then you are handicapping them. Children have a psychological necessity to be exactly like the others in their group. If they are made to be different by strong-minded, often highly individual parents, they miss something very important in their development.

This does not mean that you can't mention an eventual goal of tidiness and quality of dress to your growing son when he is at the interminably long stage where he won't wear anything but blue jeans, T shirts, and dirty sneakers, or worn topsiders. All children at times are expected to wear "Sunday clothes," with ties, shined shoes, clean nails, and combed hair, so he won't feel too discriminated against if you insist on his conforming to adult custom on these occasions, too.

From six on—sometimes earlier—he should have something to say about the clothes he wears. If he detests certain colors and textures or styles, try to avoid them. If he wants his hair long and you prefer it reasonably short, try to effect a compromise.

Little girls are likely to be more clothes-conscious than boys, and at an earlier age, but not necessarily so. Boys, if they get a chance to express them, have strong opinions on what is "the thing" to wear, and, within reason, parents should shut their eyes to the ridiculousness of current boy and girl clothing fads. Each generation has had its own fads, and to prohibit a child from following what is probably a quite harmless fashion, even if it offends your own and your friends' sensibilities, is to make the child "not belong" with his crowd, a hurtful thing.

Hand-me-downs and Made-overs   Even the last child—indeed, particularly the last child—in a family deserves a few clothes bought just for her. If one's life is a constant series of hand-me-downs from older sisters, it is a just cause for a complex about the situation. A child needs to develop a pride of possession, and when a family's economics do not permit the purchase of new clothes for a child, efforts should be made to give her *something* of her own. Swapping clothes with other mothers may be the answer, or a visit to a thrift shop, where used clothes in good condition are often on sale. Schools often hold their own clothes sales. A mother should be very tuned in to how her child feels about his or her hand-me-downs and try to arrange something every season that is truly that child's own, and a first in his or her family.

When Do Children Choose Their Own Clothes?   Children should be at least consulted on their clothes preferences almost from the time they are able to state an opinion. Where a child is making an obvious mistake, he should be guided, but within reason he should not be forced to wear clothes he patently dislikes. He has his own, sometimes quite peculiar to us, ideas of what's becoming to him. And consideration of any strong opinions he may have on the subject is only fair if we wish to follow the ideal of considering the child as a person right from the start, not just a possession to jump at our superior commands.

His taste in clothes and in other things develops slowly, partly through example and partly through his own character growth, through enthusiasms passionately embraced, then quickly or gradually abandoned to be replaced by others. We can help children find their style by letting them, wherever possible, make their own choice if they seem ready to make one—velvet corduroy pants instead of more practical wool flannel ones, or a flowered challis skirt instead of a more useful solid-colored one. Mistakes will be made, but they won't be made a second time if they have caused the child any discomfort.

Children's tastes in good clothes are usually conservative, perhaps because it takes an individuality they haven't yet achieved to choose something which, while still in good taste, is not just like everybody else's. The teen-age girl who, despite gentle advice to the contrary, selects a dress that is too old for her or too impractical for the purpose will, after having worn it, learn the valuable lesson that something that looks fine in the shop under the salesperson's blandishments may look all wrong viewed against her existing wardrobe or next to the party dress of her best friend. The development of taste by a teen-ager is often aided by a parent's gift of a subscription to a fashion magazine for the younger market.

About Allowances

How Much Allowance Should the Child Have? The amount of a child's allowance should depend on what he is expected to do with it and, when he's very young, on what others his own age in his community normally get. A child of wealthy parents should not have more pocket money than the children with whom he regularly associates. But neither are children expected to "keep up with the Joneses" if a large family, heavy responsibilities, or other circumstances make it necessary to give a child less spending money than is customary in the neighborhood. Children are much more realistic than we believe. They can accept all kinds of economics and deprivations if they are told quietly and sympathetically why they are necessary.

Whatever the allowance is, its entire use should not be dictated by the parents, because a child learns to use money intelligently only through handling it himself. If a seven-year-old gets a quarter a week allowance and is made to put it all in his piggy bank, he gets no idea that the real use for money is as a medium of exchange. He gets the shiny coins and they promptly disappear. The idea of a bank account is much too abstract for so small a child, although he can be made to understand and enjoy saving his pennies —not all of them, only a part of what he receives—to buy something he especially wants. By the time he is eight he is old enough to participate in the opening of his own savings account. Take him to the bank, open a savings account for him, and then encourage him to put a certain amount of any checks he receives as gifts into the bank and watch his balance grow as entry by entry is made. He should be saving, earning, and spending suitable amounts all along in order to learn how to manage money and to keep him in a favorable status with his friends. The boy who never can "treat," who can't join the kids in a candy store occasionally, because he has to save every cent he gets or earns for some big dim project his parents have chosen for him, is a sorry child and likely to be left out of things.

Give the child a chance to earn some money around his home or in the neighborhood to develop his initiative. Give him a set allowance, expect certain not-too-difficult or time-consuming chores from him, and pay him for extra work you ask him to do that is definitely not part of his regular household chores. A child should not expect to be paid for everything he does to help his parents. But let him spend his own money as he pleases after he and you have agreed to some saving and spending plan that leaves him leeway to move in his own little world as a sufficiently moneyed individual.

Children treated with this kind of understanding don't squander their money. They nearly always save and nearly always are solvent. They don't attach undue value to money, because it is not used as a weapon against them and they are not told what to do with each penny supposedly freely given them. Taking away some privilege is safer punishment for a serious infraction of discipline than withdrawal of the child's allowance, because a child's "social obligations" go right on and having no spending money might encourage a resentful child to pilfer or to impose on others in his desire to get the things "all the other kids have." A child wants to be able to depend on his allowance being given to him on a set day and to have nothing interfere with it, if that is humanly possible. To him it is a pay check, and what he has planned to do with it is as important to him as the family income is to his father.

Withholding Allowances   The only time an allowance should be withheld, if you want your child to have an understanding of money, is when he himself wishes to borrow in advance for an immediate purchase. Explain that loans must be promptly returned and that his allowance will be withheld until his contemplated loan is paid up. Usually he will prefer to save for the purchase, instead—a very good practice to encourage.

If allowances are withheld for the sake of punishment, his share of the family income ceases to be in the proper perspective for the child—instead, it is something he can't count on, which can be given or withheld according to what he thinks of as his parents' whims. An allowance riddled by fines, which are often levied at moments of parental anger, ceases to be the inviolate thing it should be.

There are other ways of punishing a child that are more effective than by using his allowance as a club. When he handles the money that he receives on schedule, money restitutions are often valuable in developing a sense of his obligation. Suppose a child habitually rises late, misses the school bus, and has to be driven to school by a harassed mother or father, thus upsetting their daily schedules. Sometimes the way to cure that is to give warning that the next time it happens the child must go by taxi and the fare must be returned to his mother, out of his allowance—no matter how long it takes. His actual handing over of that money until the debt is paid is more valuable educationally than the complete withholding of the allowance by the parents for the same period. And there is more dignity in such an arrangement for the child, especially if it is all done on a quiet, businesslike basis devoid of scolding and moralizing about promptness. He will get the point very well.

Keeping an Allowance Record   There are spending and saving record booklets for children available in bookstores and stationery stores that help teach the value of planning, saving, sharing, and analyzing their spending habits. This can be a first step in helping a child develop the ability to manage his own money. While a parent might initially want to oversee the child's use of this simple record, once the child understands, he should not ask to see it again. One's financial records, at any age, should be private.

Chapter 3

THE TEEN-AGER AND YOUNG ADULT

Today's teen-ager is a young adult, more mature and responsible, sociologists tell us, than many generations of previous teen-agers. He is nevertheless beset with the customary trials and tribulations natural to his age group—disconcerting periods of indecision, self-doubt, other periods of self-sufficiency and superiority. His character and personality are not set but are in the process of being molded. It is a stage where he is not quite on his own, not altogether sure he wants to be on his own, yet resentful of too much parental pressure and old-fogyness. Much of this attitude and feeling will change as he learns how to live with the world, especially with his parents, siblings, and teachers.

Strictness, in itself, is not the perfect answer to the teen-ager's social problems. Any smart teen-ager can circumvent an overly strict parent who thinks in terms of the discipline he or she received as a child, rather than of the effectiveness of it. Along with the firm rules about home-coming and frequent reporting of activities must go an understanding heart and a real friendliness with the teen-ager. It's a wonderful, creative, often troubling time.

Most adults, thinking back, would never wish to go through it again.

Courtesy Begins at Home

Everyone is more or less under compulsion in the outside world to follow certain accepted social rules, whether it be in school or business. It is human, and especially so to the pubescent, to let down a little at home. Parents who are relatively lenient about small courtesies, who don't crack down at every small infraction within the household, often find that they get reports from the community that their teen-agers are indeed courteous away from home. On the other hand, each household needs to have a code of basic courtesies that the adults practice toward the children and the children should practice toward each other and toward their parents. Parents are wise to overlook seemingly disrespectful outbursts from time to time. The teen-ager who, in a fit of anger, screams at his mother or father "I hate you" may really be reflecting serious doubt as to whether at that moment he is himself loved. As with little children, we need to make it clear that it is certain behavior we dislike or even hate, but that these feelings in no way disturb the essential loving relationship between parent and child. The parent must get across the idea that "I love you always but sometimes I do not love your behavior."

Manners

Teen-agers, especially in recent years, feel that they inhabit a world of their own in which they can make their own rules. Parents who can break through this fallacy in a gentle fashion can make their teen sons and daughters realize the essential discourtesy to other people, who also have rights, when teen-agers are noisy in public, or monopolize the telephone, the family car, or any other convenience or possession meant for general sharing.

Every teen-ager needs to be reminded about many of the things that careful adults take for granted, such as the need to answer all invitations promptly, to acknowledge gifts graciously and quickly, to show respect and courtesy toward adults, to be protective and kindly toward the younger and weaker.

Teen-agers rightly complain that parents nag. Nagging is irritating and virtually useless at any age, but particularly ineffective between parents and teens. Similarly, accusations call for automatic denial. Rather than nag, it is far better first to get a teen-ager's full attention, to tell him once, and then perhaps to leave written reminders of what you want him to do. It is more effective to tell a teen-ager that you know he has done something of which you disapprove than to ask him if he has done so. It is good psychology to teach children that they avert your irritation if they freely confess their misdeeds. After all, what can you do when a courteous, repentant teen-ager says, "I did it and I am sorry." The biblical injunction to agree with an adversary quickly is very sound, and if it were more generally followed, especially between parents and teens, a great deal of dissension would be avoided.

Allowances and Teaching Financial Responsibility

When the child grows into his teens, allowances usually need to be increased to allow for transportation costs, lunch money, movies, magazines, records and cassettes, teen club spending, and dating money. It is up to the parents to decide when a child is mature enough to be given an even larger allowance that will encompass his clothes, purchase of sports and hobby equipment, entertainment, travel, and other large-ticket items. With some young people it is a wise gesture to put them on an all-inclusive monthly allowance. With others it would not work. As a parent, you must decide, but if you can teach a child to make a detailed ledger of all his expenses and to keep an accounting of it against his allowance when he is in high school, you will have accomplished a great step forward in his education. If you explain that he must "stick within his budget" and you give him the money for a one-month period, you can easily tell by going over his ledger with him at the end of the month whether he is mature enough to handle his own money yet. Some parents give their children allowance money for the necessities (carfare, lunch money, books), but insist that their children earn the luxuries themselves through odd jobs like tutoring, baby-sitting, dog-walking, party cleanups, part-time jobs at the grocery store, and so on.

Teen-agers are capable of learning how the stock market works and frequently become quite interested in it, particularly if they are encouraged to buy some shares of low-priced stock that can be followed every day on the financial page. The growth of teen investment clubs is a healthy development, too. By participating in such projects, a young person will learn some important basic facts about the economy of this country and will become a much more sophisticated manager and planner of his own money. It is very important that the girls in the family be given every bit as much encouragement and stimulus to understand the money market and to deal in it as their brothers.

Jobs

There comes a day when every teen-ager rebels against having to take every cent he needs from his parents even when parental giving is generous and understanding of teen needs and obligations. Holding down a job and earning money are fun even when what you are doing won't necessarily lead to your life work. If a teen-ager knows where he is heading and is able to get summer or after-school jobs that will lead naturally to his eventual goal, that is fortunate, but all productive work well performed is valuable discipline.

How does a boy or girl get a job while still a student? First, he or she must evaluate the amount of time available for such a job without neglecting school work. For most, a Saturday or Sunday job or one for Friday night may be all that can be comfortably managed. The range of possibilities is wide. Teen boys and girls clerk in supermarkets or in banks, drive delivery trucks, run errands, work in libraries, baby-sit, paint houses, tutor, act as file clerks and stenographers, model, work in restaurants, hotels, and hospitals, and sell door-to-door or by appointment a wide range of products and services. Many teen girls are relief operators for the telephone company, a job that is well paid and highly disciplinary in that it requires discretion, strict concentration, and unfailing courtesy to the public.

Once the teen-ager has evaluated his time and assayed his talents (the latter with the help of family, friends, and guidance counselors) he may find that the fastest route to a job is to ask everyone he knows if there is some opportunity for him. If his school maintains an employment office, he should use its services or apply to the state employment office. Newspaper ads should be thoroughly checked. Job openings for teen-agers are usually available on a part-time basis in most communities, but the summer plums in camps and resorts must be applied for in a businesslike way months, sometimes years, in advance. Today everyone wants a job, not just needy students. Every teen-ager should have the opportunity to earn money and handle a job at some time during these important years in preparation for a lifetime of work ahead, whether or not he actually requires such earnings for his education and maintenance.

The working world is a serious place even for a teen-ager working part time. He will need to conform to the standards exacted of older workers in regard to dress, behavior, performance, and punctuality. It should be a matter of pride on the part of the teen worker that he need never be chided on these things, and generally it seems true that the current and coming teen-age groups are more serious-minded and stable in this regard than were many such in the past. Teen earnings are at an all-time high and climbing further. Teen spending is an essential pillar of our economy.

Sometimes, however, a teen-ager may be offered a position that affords an excellent training experience, but with no pay. He should take it, if there are obvious learning benefits to be derived from such an apprenticeship. Experience is worth anything when one begins to climb the career ladder.

Applying for a Summer Job   The letter of application and the job interview are both extremely important for the job-seeking teen-ager. Each presents a different aspect of your personality to your prospective employer. Your letter of application should be written clearly and correctly, and typed (if possible) in the usual business style. Here is an example:

> 45 Maple Street
> Larchmont, New York   zip code
> March 15, 19—

Mr. David Parnes
The Parnes Corporation
116 Laurel Avenue
Larchmont, New York   zip code

Dear Mr. Parnes,

In June I will complete my sophomore year at Larchmont High School. I am sixteen years old and I am preparing for a career as a legal secretary. My scholastic average is a B. I am interested in working for your company during the summer and would like to do any type of secretarial work. I type 60 words per minute and take shorthand at the rate of 100 words per minute.

I would appreciate meeting you and talking to you about job possibilities. I am available for an interview any weekday after 3 P.M. and all day on Saturday. My telephone number is 623–0162.

> Sincerely,
> [*your signature in ink*]
> Ann Morse [*typewritten*]

Note that your signature is never preceded by your title, Miss or Ms., except parenthetically where necessary (if your name could be mistaken for a man's).

For the job interview be sure you arrive on time. Your clothes should be simple, clean, neat—a jacket and tie for a boy and a dress or suit and non-gimmicky shoes for a girl. Speak clearly, and answer the interviewer's questions directly. Don't be embarrassed about letting your interviewer know that you are very much interested in working for his or her company. If you do so with enthusiasm and sincerity, the interviewer will appreciate your interest and attitude. When the interview is over, rise and thank the interviewer.

Don't smoke during an interview even if the interviewer is smoking. Gum chewing, of course, is definitely out.

Appreciation A teen-ager should be careful when he gets a job to thank those who helped him land it. Ambitious people sometimes forget the necessity of looking back to see how they effected their progress. The prompt note of appreciation, the telephone call to report the result of interviews, the continuing contact with advisers and helpful friends of the family all build toward a sound future. These are necessary courtesies in life but also good business. You can never know when you will need someone again. Only you can leave the right impression.

Grooming, Shaving, and Make-up for the Teen-ager

Hair and hands are the two most conspicuous elements of bad grooming among teen-agers. The gift of a hair dryer helps home grooming, and a really good hairbrush is an excellent investment. When a boy's beard grows, he should shave every morning, for there is nothing that will ruin his looks more quickly than a stubble, however blond or thin. If he wears a beard in his late teens, he will have to watch his grooming even more meticulously.

Most adolescent girls are unimpressed with their mothers' logical reasons why heavy make-up is inadvisable for them. They are even unimpressed with the obvious argument that if at thirteen they get themselves up to look twenty, when they *are* twenty no one will believe it. The natural look is the prettiest and the most appropriate for any young girl to strive for, and if this takes a bit of foundation, a light dusting of powder, a very light touch of blusher and a natural-colored lipstick or lip gloss to accomplish, then it's all right to use those items. Eye shadow should really not be worn until a girl is sixteen, and then only in the evening. Eyeliner should wait until she is about eighteen, but mascara brushed lightly on her eyelashes is acceptable at sixteen. A young girl's nails should be nicely shaped, with cuticles that are soft and carefully pressed down after each bath; her fingers should be free of hangnails, hands should be unchapped, and nail polish that is colorless is by far the best. Young girls are impatient with bright-colored polish and tend to chip it, bite it off, or peel it into a most unappetizing state.

I remember so well listening to a first-class argument between one of my goddaughters and her mother. My goddaughter was going to a dance given by her sophomore class, and she was made up so heavily she looked, as her brother suggested, "like a hooker." Her mother was desperate. "I don't know what I'm going to do with her." The girl looked over at me for help, because I was usually on her side. "What do *you* think? This is perfectly okay, isn't it? It's what everyone else will be wearing." "No," I said, "If I were you, I'd take a bit off—just a bit."

"But why?" she asked, obviously deflated by my lack of support.

"Simply because it makes you look tough."

She went into the bathroom and took half of it off. No one was going to call *her* tough tonight.

Teen Dates

When does dating begin? Earlier and earlier, it seems. It is often difficult these days to distinguish a twelve-year-old girl from her seventeen-year-old sister if a misguided or overpressured mother permits the younger one to dress and wear make-up as her sister does. Physically, each generation's girls are bigger, and this physical bigness often deceives parents into believing that emotional development necessarily follows size.

Boy-and-girl dating really should not begin until thirteen or fourteen, on a limited basis—early movies, dates at home of course, various sports, days at the beach, bicycle trips that bring the two home before dark, and so on. Steady dating should be firmly discouraged throughout the early teens, for many reasons, including the fact that tastes are formed through a variety of contacts.

In a young girl's life there are periods when one boy seems to be more in evidence than others. When this becomes quite obvious the family often undertakes to reduce him in status in various ways. Such passing attachments always do seem more of a menace than they usually are and should be accepted with a certain amount of humor untinged with ridicule. Puppy love is serious to the lovers, if a little ludicrous to parents, brothers, and sisters, but it should be respected, for it has its painful aspects. Very few daughters really wish to settle their affections for life on a teen-age boy when it comes right down to it, though the fantasy of undying devotion is very evident for a time.

In large cities where many children must necessarily achieve independence early, boys and girls in their early teens are allowed to go unaccompanied to lunch, the movies, the theater, rock concerts, and sporting events (if in the evening, transportation must be provided, however, or taxis must be taken). The kind of entertainment the young couple goes to must be approved of by both sets of parents. They should not go to discos and night clubs, of course, and they should be thoroughly aware of the penalties for breaking the laws governing the legal age for drinking.

Many parents feel safe in permitting their teen-age children to go places at night with a group of other boys and girls. This is fallacious reasoning, for the group, once out of sight of parents, may break up into twosomes immediately, with the rules of behavior determined by the boldest. This independent course should be permitted only if the group is going to a specific, approved place and will return at an exact, agreed-upon time. Its whereabouts should be known by the parents at all times, and no unaccountable junketing around the countryside in some boy's car should be allowed. Remember, adolescents want rules and need them. They do not respect the too "easy" parent.

How Does a Boy Ask for a Date? At what age a boy dates depends very much on the boy himself. And again physical size bears no relation to emotional readiness. Anywhere from thirteen or fourteen on, a boy may be ready to leave the teasing group of boys and go on his first date. His family should be well prepared for the metamorphosis that may occur.

The first sign, of course, is cleanliness. He will suddenly begin bathing without reminders, lengthily combing his hair before setting out for school instead of merely running the comb—or more likely, his fingers—through it. Suddenly his shoes may seem to take on a polish, and he will stop biting his fingernails. He will require two or three times his usual number of clean shirts, and he may even take an unusual interest in ties, socks, and handkerchiefs, hitherto items of no interest at all. He will also begin to agitate about his inadequate allowance and start wondering out loud how he can augment it by a little manual labor. He constantly asks if anyone notices how deep his voice is getting. Of course, none of these things may happen—but if they do, you are lucky parents.

It is usually Mother who sees the signs first. She knows instinctively that her son is about to take his first steps away from her apron strings. Most of what she can do for him she has already done. Soon he will probably turn more and more to his father for counsel, or to some father substitute.

Boys usually don't need advice on how to ask a girl for a date. They bungle through somehow in the early years of dating, eventually acquiring a certain polished technique only experience can bring. Parents can help by showing that they expect their children to date whenever they are ready. They should never force the issue or make the choices for the children.

Boys usually begin by going to games and school dances stag. They yearn from the sidelines, while pretending a vast lack of interest in the equally cohesive girls. After a certain amount of this, mothers often suggest, "Joe, why don't you take Mary to the game this afternoon?" This is usually met with a derisive snort, but soon, sure enough, Mary and Joe are eating popcorn together in the bleachers. As a result of the motherly approval he needed, Joe has probably blurted, "You want to go to the game tomorrow,

Mary?" and Mary has said, "Sure." From then on, making dates is easy enough.

Embarrassing Moments   Running short of money can be a possible source of embarrassment but really shouldn't be. Everybody miscalculates from time to time. A girl should always have some money with her on a date, if only "mad money." If a boy finds he doesn't have quite enough money, say for a taxi tip, he can always say to the girl, "Can you lend me some change?" Sometimes he doesn't have enough for dinner. The girl should be ready to chip in and forget about the repayment.

What if you arrive at a party in exactly the wrong clothes? Don't let it spoil the evening—or the day. If you hold your head up and are obviously having a good time, people may even think that they are wrong and you are right and starting a new style. If you do make any comment about it, make it once and let it go. This kind of thing happens to everybody else, too. What if you have forgotten to respond to an invitation promptly, or worse still, forgotten the date? The best way is to admit your error and apologize quickly—and thoroughly. Sometimes you can't really make amends for these things, which can be great slights, but at least you have done the best you can do. You can promise yourself to be more considerate of others in the future.

In fact, one of the greatest protections for anybody is to be able to say, "I did it. I was wrong. I am sorry." Hardly anyone can continue berating you once you have made this statement.

Dates and Money   Dating, for boys, does bring with it increased financial responsibilities. While Dutch treating is more common that it once was, especially in group entertainment, a boy often pays for the entertainment of his special date. If his allowance is not adequate for his participation in the social activities of his high school group and if his parents cannot comfortably increase it, then after-school jobs must provide the difference. And boys should learn early to be unembarrassedly frank with girls about what entertainment they can afford to offer. Pretending to have more money than one actually has is an acutely uncomfortable business, and usually no one is deceived by the pretension.

A boy might say, "Jane, I can take you to either dinner or the movies. Which shall it be?" Jane will probably answer, "I'll ask Mother if I may ask you here to dinner. Then we can go to the movies afterward." And, of course, it's perfectly proper for parents to furnish theater, concert, or opera tickets and permit their daughters to ask boys to escort them or for a father or mother to go along occasionally, and to pay for everything for both young people.

Even if the parents are not along, if a girl invites a boy to the theater or a sports event she should pay not only for the tickets but also for the bus or taxis, the soda and hot dogs consumed, and any other expenses. She may wish to give her date a sum of money from which he can pay for things as they go along, if he would be embarrassed to have her pay directly.

Parents and Dates The girl's parents should meet, if possible, any boy who is going to take their daughter on an evening date. This does not forecast an inquisition. It means that when the boy calls, he should meet the girl's parents or some responsible adult in the family. He should be able to exchange a few graceful words with them, and they in turn should realize that such moments can be acutely embarrassing for the boy. Conversation should be light and casual and not admonitory. Few daughters are so desperate for dates that they accept them injudiciously. And after all, the boy has been willing to show his face at the door.

Returning Home from a Date A boy should not just drop his date off but should see her to the front door when returning after dark. It is important for the boy to be particularly alert in apartment house lobbies if there is no doorman in attendance. He should not let his date go upstairs alone in an elevator at night. He should see her to her apartment door, using the same care as he did entering the building. A man always goes first into a darkened room and lights a light if none has been left on. Whether a boy is invited in after a date depends on the hour and a girl's understanding with her parents in the matter, and whether or not someone is home. After midnight she should say good night at the door, adding, "I'm sorry I can't ask you in." She should say something of the kind at any hour if no one is at home.

Refusing a Date It is always a woman's prerogative to refuse an invitation from a man. Suppose there is a country club dance. Mary, like every other girl in her group, is dying to go and waiting impatiently for the telephone to ring. The wrong boy calls up. Must she accept, or can she wait for the right boy to ask her? One cannot pick and choose one's dates in this fashion. It is the same in adult life. One cannot pick and choose one's party invitations, delaying a response while waiting for a better offer to come along, or accepting something and then regretting later in order to go to a different party.

If a shy, insecure young man asks a girl for a date, she should be extra-careful and compassionate about the way in which she refuses it. She should sound genuinely sorry about having already accepted another invitation first, or "having to go somewhere with the family." If he persists in inviting her and she does not wish to go out on a date with him, the kind thing for a girl to do is to invite him to a gathering of several people at her home.

Going Steady It is very difficult to dissuade young people from going steady in high school. Yet everything that can be done to discourage teenagers from tying themselves closely to each other *should* be done. Leaving aside the complicated questions of the sexual relationship that may develop, such a relationship limits their social development in many ways: they should be learning how to step forward in a social situation, meet new people, get along by oneself at a party, observe the social play being acted on the stage and taking a role in it. Going steady is an emotional crutch. Two young people have each other as the answer to all social situations. There is no question mark in their lives, and solving the question mark is an important part of learning how to cope with life. Neither has to worry about the availability of anyone else for after-school activities. While going steady, the couple may miss the deep friendships with members of their own sex that develop in the teen years. The person who dates freely learns how to conquer shyness in meeting new people, gets to know the good and the bad in everyone, learns to judge human nature, and even develops compassion for his fellow human beings. Young people going steady have no opportunity to know anyone but each other. Their horizons, instead of expanding, remain very limited.

Adult Supervision   The word "chaperon" has an onerous sound to teen-agers, but no teen party should be given at home, or in a club or at school without the restraining presence of some adults in the background. At home, the parents do not have to show their faces once they have met all the guests. But everyone should know they are there, and if one parent has to waft through to the kitchen to get something, the teen-agers should consider that quite normal and not a spying operation (which it may very well be!). The presence of an adult somewhere in the house is a restraining influence on the introduction of hard liquor and hard drugs to the party. If a particular group in school has been getting into trouble at its gatherings, a smart parent will introduce a respected college student into the group (perhaps a popular athlete) who, when asked by the young people why he's there, will say frankly, "Just to keep you kids in line." A well-liked college student is a role model to high school students, so they will accept this presence as a chaperon gracefully, whereas they would find the constant presence of an adult at the party an intrusion. The college student must, of course, be paid for his services that evening.

In more than one city there are nightly radio and TV reminders to parents at 10 P.M.: "Do you know where your children are tonight?" Teen-agers may give lip service to the idea of complete freedom, but at the same time it frightens them, especially the girls. Reasonable requirements and regulations are reassuring and show them that their parents do care about what happens. Teen-agers of both sexes need protection against themselves and against vicious gossip.

When we insist on protection for our children, it is to guard them from possible physical harm in the streets at night, from possible foolishness, or from involving themselves in situations from which they are not mature enough to extract themselves.

Just how much adult supervision is necessary for a teen-ager depends on the community and the customs of the child's group. This does not mean that if some parents are dangerously careless, all parents should follow along in their footsteps. But a golden mean can be achieved. Too much protection where other children have relative freedom can set a child off too much from his group.

Proms After a period of disfavor senior proms are once again being held in most parts of the country. Some are informal, but the black-tie-for-boys, long-dress-for-girls type is increasingly in vogue, although the customs differ according to the region and the traditions of the school—public, boarding, or private day school. Boys often rent their tuxedos locally for proms.

If the boy invites the girl, he generally pays. If the girl invites the boy, she generally pays—and that means tickets to the dance and any expenses relating to the dinner beforehand or the breakfast following what is usually an all-night affair. A date should be invited at least a month ahead of time. Boys or girls who attend a prom in another town pay for their own transportation, but they are "put up" by the parents or by the boarding school. If they have to stay in an inn or motel, the one who issues the invitation should pay.

In some areas the boys buy corsages for their dates (to be worn on either the dress or the wrist). If the girl finds the flowers sent absolutely ruin the look or color of her dress, she should pin the corsage to her evening bag. It is the custom in some communities for the girl to buy a boutonniere for her date; some schools have an arrangement where they purchase the same boutonniere for all the boys, and the girls contribute toward the cost.

A girl or boy should write a warm thank-you note to the date and to the date's parents, too, if the latter were involved in housing, transporting, or feeding guests for the prom festivities.

Duty Dances When a young man first begins attending dances at school or a family club, he learns from his parents to watch out for his date, if he has one, and to make sure that she is danced with and has a soft drink when she wants it. As he grows older and goes to debutante dances, college proms, and even private parties where there's dancing, he learns he must dance with the guest of honor and with his hostess at least once. He should also dance with other older women involved in the party—such as the debutante's sister or aunt.

The easiest way to ask someone to dance is "Would you like to dance?" If the young woman says, "I promised this one to someone else," or "I have to make a telephone call," the man can ask her again later in the evening. If she keeps refusing his offer to dance, he should forget about asking her.

Each area has its own rules about how and when a man can "cut in" on another couple dancing. One should find out what the rules are—or at least observe them from the sidelines—and follow suit. Women do not yet cut in on men, unless the dance is announced as a "women cut-in," or unless wives and husbands who are all close friends cut in on each other.

Teen Car Manners

A boy picking up a date when his parents are driving goes to the girl's door, steps in and greets her parents, then escorts the girl to the car. If necessary, he introduces her to his parents by saying, "Mother and Dad, this is Judy." When they return, he takes her to her door and thanks her for the evening, saying good night to her parents if they are still up.

If the boy is doing the driving, he should, if he can, go to the girl's door to pick her up. If he knows that parking will be impossible, he phones ahead and tells her exactly when he will be outside, warning her that he will not be able to leave the car. She should not keep him waiting. As she approaches the car, he should lean over and open the door for her. The traditional courtesy of a boy exiting first and rushing around to assist the girl from her side of the car is not often practiced today, although girls still enjoy the extra attention, especially on a special occasion like a prom. Otherwise, girls usually leave and enter cars without waiting for special courtesies.

A young driver must take very seriously his responsibility for his passenger or passengers. He must not crowd the car beyond the legal limit or drive while under the influence of liquor or drugs. He may not permit an unlicensed driver to take the wheel. A boy should not drive with one arm around a girl, because both hands should be on the wheel. A car is a potentially lethal machine. Psychologically, it is said to represent an extension of the masculine personality and thus many teen-agers use it aggressively, causing accidents and deaths to such a degree that insurance for young men under the age of twenty-five is routinely uprated. Not so with girls, who, thanks to the same driver instruction the boys get plus natural conservatism, are adjudged safer drivers.

Parents' Permission   In many a family there is constant friction about the use of the car by junior family members. Driving a parental car should be considered a privilege rather than a right. Family conferences can establish ground rules that should be respected by all. If a young son or daughter is to be permitted the use of the car, his or her needs should always be subsidiary to those of the parents. Once permission is granted, it should not be capriciously withdrawn. Parents should be able to make adjustments, too.

A Girl and Her Car   Sometimes a girl has her own car and the boy she dates does not. He may certainly drive in the car with her, but he should not be permitted to take the wheel if the car is registered in her parents' name without specific permission from them, because it is possible the insurance might be invalidated in case of an accident. If she is the owner of the car, she may permit any licensed driver to take the wheel, however. She should certainly be very careful not to let her date drive if he has been drinking or is under the influence of drugs. She should be ready to take the wheel back at the first sign of subversive driving, and without apology. She can always say, "We are not permitted to speed. Please stop the car. I'll drive now." Better to be square than dead or injured.

Check List of Common Courtesies and Discourtesies

Almost every parent has a conscious or unconscious check list of good behavior that he hopes his children will follow as they grow and mature into adulthood. Even George Washington used a set of fifty-four maxims, probably translated from the French, to which he referred often, covering everything from *not* picking one's teeth in public to *not* opening other people's letters. If he were alive today, he would probably have a list of a thousand maxims of good behavior to cover the wide range of life-styles today.

From the time a child can reason, a parent should call his attention to manners, in a positive way rather than in the "Do Not" way. Point out something that someone else did that was nice and kind. Praise your child for doing something thoughtful, however small and insignificant an act. Even a three-year-old can understand the Golden Rule. An eight-year-old can understand very well, too, that manners are an efficient way of behaving that enables the group to operate more easily.

It is the little things that make life easier and more pleasant for all of us. "Good manners" are not something to be turned on for special occasions, but should become an integral part of our daily lives, no matter what our age. The attached list could be expanded into a book in itself, but it suggests some of the most common examples of small actions that make daily life more enjoyable for all family members and those around us.

Being Considerate of Relatives and Friends

Write a note or call a friend when you hear he or she has just received bad news or good news; make a special effort to console or rejoice with a member of your family over their special news.

Invite the least popular member of your class to your party, because he or she rarely gets invited anywhere and it would mean so much.

Have good bathroom manners, which means no dawdling unnecessarily and also careful tidying up.

Think up imaginative things to do for someone who is home sick or in the hospital.

Always knock and ask permission before entering someone's room.

Return borrowed possessions on time; lend your own things graciously and without hesitation.

Arrive punctually at friends' parties; don't overstay your welcome; help clean up.

Learn how to compliment. Praise the food you have been served; comment on your mother's new dress, your father's haircut, your brother's performance at the ice hockey rink.

Be attentive to your date, even if there's someone much more exciting nearby to talk to.

Don't sound like a lumbering elephant going up and down stairs; close doors softly rather than bang them shut.

Never "leave it for the next person," whether it's unloading the dishwasher, cleaning the lint from the washing machine trap, putting air in the bicycle tires, or cleaning up the mess left by the family dog. Learn to do it yourself—and *now*.

Be considerate of the family telephone and other people who want to use it.

Learn and follow good table manners.

"Good English" is something we all should strive to speak; remember it is spoken without swear words or "dirty talk."

Don't jeopardize other people's safety and pleasure with your playtime pursuits. Use your skateboard carefully; don't throw snowballs at anyone but your friends who are prepared for it; ride your bicycle with care and consideration.

Write a thank-you note for every present received.

Don't put your feet up on the furniture.

Help your parents around the house *willingly and quickly*. Learning how to take orders well is one of the first great lessons in learning how to be a successful adult.

Becoming a Valued Member of Your Community

Obey the signs (Keep off the grass. Close the fence behind you. No dogs allowed. Quiet Zone.)

Work with the land, whether it's growing vegetables in a community garden project, working as a volunteer in a neighborhood beautification project, or just helping pick up the litter in your residential area.

Work for your house of worship, whether it's baby-sitting with the toddlers at services, acting as a runner at the church fair, or helping make Christmas or Hanukkah decorations.

Offer your services when help is needed, everything from licking stamps for a politician's mailing campaign to putting up posters in your school for the local community fund-raising drive.

Behaving in Public

Keep your feet out of public passageways, so you won't trip people.

Never point out or make fun of someone who is handicapped, slow, overly thin or overly fat, or unusual in any way.

Don't pull your finger joints, drum your fingers on the table, pull at your hair constantly, or exhibit any other nervous mannerisms.

If someone near you, even a stranger, drops something, pick it up and hand it back.

Don't dawdle over a telephone call if someone is waiting behind you in line.

Always answer your invitations; never accept one and then later say you can't come because you want to accept a better offer; and always write a short thank-you note after the party.

Learn to greet people nicely; answer in words ("Yes, thank you") instead of grunts ("Uh-huh").

Play your radio or cassette player so softly that no one around you on the bus, on the beach or in the park will be bothered.

Be considerate of the performers in a theater or concert hall as well as of those sitting around you. No chewing-gum-smacking, rustling of programs, and rattling of gum and candy wrappers!

Give your seat on the bus to someone who needs it.

When you sneeze or cough, especially in close quarters on a crowded bus or in an elevator, do it into your handkerchief, with your face turned away from those closest to you. Always say "Excuse me please" afterward.

Don't try to cheat in a line.

Treat books with the greatest of respect; never mark them, and always return them promptly.

Never spit, pick your teeth, comb your hair, or fiddle with your nails in public.

Move through crowds carefully, paying attention not to bump anyone; apologize if you do bump someone.

Don't be boisterous with your friends; polite people are inconspicuous.

Don't write graffiti or deface public property.

Always place all your litter in the trash receptacles; never throw anything on the streets or leave it in cabs or on public transport.

Hold open the postbox lid for someone approaching who does not have two hands free; hold open the doors for someone rushing to get on your elevator (by pushing the OPEN button).

When you dial the wrong number, say "I'm very sorry" before hanging up.

Let someone with only one or two items go ahead of you in the supermarket checkout line if you have many items.

Move over a seat at a counter, when your place would otherwise separate two friends who wish to sit together.

Chapter 4

DRUGS, ALCOHOL, AND TOBACCO:
MAJOR PROBLEMS

We live in a society seemingly dedicated to pleasure and relief from pain or discomfort. Drugs, including pills, alcohol, and tobacco, surround the lives of our children from the time they reach the upper levels of grade school. It is time to emphasize the *prevention of drug abuse*. Parents must teach their children what drugs do to their bodies and minds; they must give them alternatives to seeking relief in the drug world; and they must make them strong enough to withstand the peer pressure that says, "If you don't join us, you're chicken."

Why Drugs Are Abused

The reasons why people use drugs are affirmative ones as far as they are concerned. People want to change the way they feel. They want to feel happy, or different, or maybe they want to feel absolutely nothing. They want to remember or to forget, to be popular and loved, to be at ease with others, to be anything different from what they are. Drugs suddenly become the easiest way to change one's mood, so that one can become self-assured, know one is attractive to others, or stop feeling mental or physical distress. The sad thing is that, although people on drugs feel momentarily different about themselves, the effects are fleeting. Afterward one's self-esteem is lowered, one's problems increase, and the frequency of drug use escalates. That is how one becomes trapped.

Children copy their parents' weaknesses every bit as much as their strengths. If a mother or a father drinks to excess on occasion, then the child instinctively feels it is all right for him to get some "kicks," too, in alcohol or other drugs. Children also copy their peers, and sometimes the peers' influence is much stronger than the parents'. If he does not go along with "what they're into," they may freeze him out of their group. The family at home must be aware, sympathetic, and ready to understand in order to help the child cope with this rejection. By the time the child is an adolescent, the need to be liked by one's peers is even more important.

Additionally, the mind and body changes of adolescence can be disorienting. The young person begins to question old values; there is a secret joy in experimenting with the forbidden; he feels strong and independent as he pushes against the boundaries of what his parents allow him to do.

Parents Should Be Alert to Changes in Their Children

Drugs users may be difficult to discern in the early stages. Only a few drugs, such as barbiturates and narcotics, can cause physical dependence (addiction), but almost any drug, when used regularly or misused, can make someone feel he must have that drug to function properly. The family must stand ready to cope with the reality of the situation. The parents must first of all be alert to their children and know them well enough to catch the behavior changes. Is their son cutting classes? Does he seem slightly dreamy? Is he trying to find amounts of money all the time, perhaps borrowing or even stealing from members of the family? Is he becoming secretive, withdrawing from the family group?

Parents should give priority to keeping the lines of communication open with their children, in order to know what their children are feeling and *why* they may be seeking relief from their problem in drugs. They should find out what the problem is. The family is the place where the education of the child in drug abuse should take place; it is also the place where love and support for the child come through. School cannot perform these functions; only the family can.

Sometimes, when a family encounters drug abuse, the problem seems larger than it can handle, so it tends to withdraw from the very friends and relatives who could help. A family in trouble needs to talk about it among themselves, to friends, the children's teachers, their clergyman. There are other people having similar experiences, so the family should seek help and comfort, rather than feel ashamed and secretive about its problem.

Preventing Drug Abuse

If parents help their children grow in personal strength, it will be unlikely that they will hurt themselves or others through the misuse of chemical substances. *This is prevention of drug abuse in its best form.* If a child grows up in a family that loves him, with parents who are always available to listen to, encourage, and understand him, that child will have no reason to abuse drugs. *Parents have to give time to their children,* doing things with them that they enjoy doing. This requires conscious planning, but can be handled just as easily by working parents. Time spent with one's children should be quality time; time not spent with one's children should be well supervised, so that the parents know what is happening in that young person's life. This is where senior citizens could be so useful; retired older people need jobs, and working or single parents need *them*—to be home when the child returns from school. If a student is not coming home after school, shouldn't the parents know? Many people do not seem to care where their children are—and they include mothers who do not work.

Many parents think that because they supply all the material benefits their child could want, they are being "good parents." Understanding and companionship are far more important. Letting a child know what he may or may not do is also more important, as is disciplining him with wisdom and love instead of a heavy hand. If two adults are going to have a child, they should continue to be responsible for him until that child is full grown. If the home is beset by the hostility of constantly bickering parents, the child will often resort to alcohol or drugs in order to escape reality, for in the drugs the child will receive a momentary sense of well-being and self-assurance he does not otherwise have.

Prevention of drug abuse starts in the home. "Parents," "protection," and "prevention" all start with a *P!*

Socially Acceptable Drugs

Coffee, tobacco, alcohol, and aspirin are socially acceptable and are looked upon, under certain circumstances, as useful substances. Some adults abuse these drugs daily, with little thought to the terrible influence this has on their children.

Alcohol and tobacco are often referred to as the "gateway drugs," since they are the first drugs one comes across in most societies. They introduce a person to the drug culture; if that person has any wisdom, he goes no further.

Marijuana and Hashish: Marginally Socially Acceptable

Drugs with marginal social acceptance, such as marijuana and hashish, are illegal but are used by more and more people every year. Well over 30 million Americans have tried marijuana (also called pot, grass, and weed), which comes from the chopped-up leaves of the *Cannabis sativa* plant. Hashish is the dark brown resin from the tops of the same plant. While actually using these drugs, one's ability to drive or work complex machinery or perform complicated tasks is impaired. Their long-term use is still being studied, but these drugs are by no means harmless. There are three strong reasons, in my opinion, against a young person's smoking marijuana. First, he may become secretive and isolated from his family, because he's telling lies to cover up his smoking. Then, by virtue of the fact that he's already taking one drug, it's very easy for him to start taking other drugs (which can cause a highly dangerous interaction between those drugs). Third, when a young person's personality is still being shaped in his teens, he may not be able to handle the disorientation that may result from smoking marijuana, whereas an adult would be better able to cope with it.

The Major Categories of Drugs

There are five major categories of drugs: stimulants, depressants, narcotics, hallucinogens, and inhalants.

Stimulants The most popular of the stimulants (or "uppers") is caffeine, which is found in coffee, tea, and cola drinks (the cola nut is a source of caffeine). Stimulants relieve the effects of exhaustion or drowsiness; a strong one like Methedrine may produce euphoric effects. If stimulants are used too often and too long, one may become hyperactive, irritable, and dependent upon them. Amphetamines ("speed"), sometimes prescribed for diet pills, are a legal drug, but they are being studied further. Cocaine, however, is illegal and is smuggled in from South America in large quantities. A very expensive drug, it makes a person feel very "up" and is thought of as a luxury drug. When overused, it may cause sleeplessness and anxiety and may also damage the sinuses.

Depressants Depressants (or "downers") are sedatives that depress the central nervous system. The most prescribed drugs in the world, they calm a person and make him feel sleepy and, if overused, may be very dangerous. Alcohol is a depressant; so are Valium, Librium, and the addictive barbiturates. (Someone coming off "barbs" may enter a state of medical emergency, so no one should suddenly abandon them without seeing a physician first.) Barbiturates and alcohol taken together, of course, make each other more potent and more dangerous.

Narcotics Narcotics are all very addictive; they are used as painkillers in medicine. Codeine, Demerol, heroin (the latter an illegal drug), and morphine are all narcotics. They are derived from opium or made synthetically.

Hallucinogens The hallucinatory drugs are called perceptual drugs because they seem to change the way the world looks and sounds to the person who takes them. LSD and PCP (or "angel dust") are two of the better known. PCP is perhaps the most dangerous and can cause temporary psychosis and violent behavior. PCP is unfortunately sometimes sprinkled on the tobacco or marijuana of someone's cigarette, without that person's knowledge. Parents must warn their children against this possibility.

There are natural hallucinogens that grow in nature, like the "magic mushrooms" (Psylotybin) of Mexico and mescaline.

Inhalants The category of inhalants includes common chemical solvents such as deodorants, hair spray, and gasoline. Inhaling something like hair spray or airplane glue can give a child a dizzying high, and so it is popular with children from eight to ten years old who enjoy "feeling funny." It is not addictive but can be very dangerous and poisonous.

Alcohol

It is bad enough that today there are more than 10 million problem drinkers in the United States alone. An even more horrifying statistic is that a quarter of all seventh graders reported recently that they were drunk one or more times during the school year.

One hears parents of children who are caught drinking rationalizing about it: "Oh well, at least she's not on drugs." Alcohol *is* a drug, one of the oldest in human history, and certainly one of the most destructive of the addictive drugs.

How does a seventh grader have access to "booze"? They manage to obtain an older brother's legitimate I.D. card. Or they pool their allowances and ask an older friend to buy it for them. Or they take it from the liquor closet in their own home.

Parents Need to Educate Their Children on Drinking Parents should never panic when they discover that their teen-ager has had too much to drink for the first time. As with experimentation in other drugs, he may have felt the strength of peer pressure and "had to do it once."

A parent, smelling alcohol on the breath of his son or daughter, might say to the child in a calm, sympathetic voice, "I think I smell alcohol on your breath. Did you have something just now with your friends? Let's talk about it." If the child admits it, and he should, because he has been caught with the evidence on his breath, then talk with him calmly. Ask him how much was served, how he felt about it, how the others felt about it. Keep him talking and communicating with you—for this is your life line to help him all through his growing years. Then you might say, "Well, now you've done it. You know what it's like. You can say to your friends you'd like to wait until you're older, because you didn't really like the taste of it all that much."

If your child keeps repeating the episode, you should find out why he has the need to turn away from reality. Spend more time with him; this is the time for parents "to really go to work" in a family sense.

An education on the basic facts of drinking is advisable for children, because almost all of them are going to try drinking. They should know about alcohol. For example, parents might explain the following to their children:

1. Drinking in moderation does the body little permanent harm, but, when taken continuously in large doses, alcohol may prove disastrous to the heart or other major organs.
2. Even mild social drinking dulls the reflexes; in any given year many *thousands* of deaths from traffic accidents are caused by heavy drinkers and also by people who have been drinking only moderately.
3. Just as people aren't alike, alcohol affects people differently. The effects of the drug on people depends on how much they weigh, how fast they

imbibe their drinks, the amount of food eaten with their drinks, the general atmosphere in which they are drinking, and their expectations and feelings about the particular group they are with at that particular time.

4. Alcohol taken in moderate amounts is said to have benefits for certain people, but no one is anything but harmed by too much.

5. There are other ways to help one feel relaxed or good or happy, the main reason young people begin to drink. The "life of the party" who's high on alcohol becomes a terrible bore rather quickly; the life of the party who has natural energy and good humor is the real mover of any group.

6. It is preferable to eat while drinking; one should sip one's drink slowly.

7. It is impossible to perform a very concentrated activity, such as take an exam or figure out an exacting problem or use one's athletic skills, if one has been drinking. To drink is *not* to be in top shape.

8. Young women who look forward to having babies should realize that alcohol in their systems may seriously harm the baby they carry.

9. Anyone who cares about danger of brain damage or damage to one's liver does not drink except in moderation. When alcohol enters the bloodstream, it is immediately carried to the brain.

10. Beer is 4 to 6 per cent alcohol, wine is 12 to 20 per cent, and most hard liquor is 40 to 50 per cent. The rest of beer, wine, and hard liquor is mostly water.

11. There is the same amount of alcohol in a 5-ounce glass of wine, in a 12-ounce glass of beer, and in a 1½-ounce "shot" of hard liquor. People making their own drinks, however, often double the size of a shot.

12. There are four kinds of drinkers: abstainers (those who never touch alcohol; recovering alcoholics are among these); social drinkers, who drink occasionally for fun, but who do not need alcohol to get along and who have no dependency on the drug; problem drinkers, who cannot drink without becoming belligerent; and alcoholics, who drink too much because they are addicted to the drug and feel extreme physical or mental discomfort without it.

13. Being able to "hold one's liquor" is not a sign of valor and strength, but a sign of tolerance for the drug, slowly acquired through constant use; dependency is often the next step.

14. Dependency on alcohol is debilitating to one's looks as well as to one's system.

15. Lastly, but perhaps most important, it is essential that every young person understand the legal aspects of drinking even before he has reached the legal drinking age in his state. Show your children what happens to young people who are arrested for drunken driving who were under the legal age limit.

The Example at Home If a child's parents return home at night gasping, "I had such a terrible day—where *is* that drink? God, how I need a drink!"

the chances are very good that the child will grow up to drink for relief from his troubles. Many alcoholic children are those born to alcoholic parents, not because of heredity but because of the atmosphere in the home. Parents who control their drinking or who do not drink at all set a compelling example for their offspring. When a young person can say to his friend, "Well, *my* parents don't need alcohol to get their kicks. My parents don't have to get drunk to have a good time," that child has excellent insurance on his future.

Supportive parents who are sympathetic to peer pressures on their child are responding to an urgent need. Parents should work out a good "defense program" their children will be able to use against the taunts from friends who accuse them of being "goody-goodies."

When a Child Starts to Drink at Home   When the parents serve wine or champagne at important family celebrations, if their child at age twelve or so asks for a glass, too, he should be permitted to have it. When a high school student tells his parents "all the kids are trying out different things" in the alcoholic line, his parents should arrange for him to do *his* experimenting at home under their supervision. They should satisfy his curiosity at home, letting him taste different cocktails, rather than having him sneak away from the home to do his experimenting in public. If he keeps insisting on the fact that "everyone in my class is drinking," the parents should find out through the teachers just how many "everyone" is. It is certainly not "everyone"; make your child proud to be in the other percentile. And perhaps it's time for your child to give an alcohol-free party at home, full of so much fun and activity it will prove to the class that you don't have to have alcohol to have a good time.

Driving Under the Influence   If you do not accomplish anything else with your child in alcohol education, impress on him never to take the wheel when he has been drinking, and never to drive with anyone else who has been. Sometimes it's the promise that "I'll come and get you quickly and without a fuss if you'll just make a telephone call" that will do it. I know of parents who responded to such a call from a child and drove quickly to a "roadside joint" at two in the morning. One parent drove seven of the young people to their homes; the other parent drove the young drinker and his car to his home. A terrible tragedy was possibly avoided. No sermons were given by the parents to anyone; no reference was made to anyone's drinking too much. The next day each of the seven friends of their child called his home to say a simple "thank you" to those parents.

Tobacco

Tobacco, one of the "gateway drugs," is a "socially acceptable drug," although logically it should not be. Cigarette smoking can kill; it can cause death by cancer of the throat and lungs, emphysema, and heart attacks. Yet America's teen-agers are swelling the ranks of smokers at an alarming rate, particularly very young girls. They start smoking at an early age to "feel grown-up," to "look sophisticated," to "have something cool to do with their hands."

The time for parents to educate a child on the hazards of smoking is *before* he is even exposed to it. Studies are under way on the possible harmful effects of smoking on the unborn fetus; young women should be made aware of these. But there are more frivolous reasons for young females not to smoke: the acrid smell of tobacco smoke stays in their hair, in their clothes, and on their fingers; their handbags have loose tobacco in them; their nails and teeth become stained by yellow nicotine.

Once again, the best education is the example of one's own parents' *not smoking*. This is the most compelling reason for a young child's not smoking. If you smoke and your child follows logically along behind you in the habit, you should teach him to obey and respect the laws prohibiting smoking in public places, such as on elevators, on public transport, and in department stores.

Teach your child to dispose of his smoking litter (empty cigarette packs and used match books) instead of leaving it on the table or throwing it on the floor. He should also empty any ash tray in his own home or in a friend's house when he has finished using it.

Smoking etiquette at meals is important, because so many people are ill-mannered in this respect. No one should light up a cigarette at someone's dinner party (or at home, for that matter) until after dessert is finished. If there is no ash tray at his place, he should ask his hostess for permission to smoke, and, if it is granted, he should then go into the living room and find himself an ash tray. He should not use his dessert plate with the remnants of food on it; the black ashes floating in the melted ice cream form an unattractive sight.

Young people should learn not to smoke on the street. It looks tough. Unfortunately, a woman smoking on the street looks even less attractive than a man does. And anyone who keeps a cigarette dangling from the lips deserves every bit of the inevitable stinging smoke that hits the eyes. It looked all right on Humphrey Bogart, but no one has been able to get away with it since.

Young smokers should also be taught never to smoke in bed. This is a primary cause of death from fire. And while you, the parents, are trying to teach proper smoking etiquette to your children, are you following the rules yourself?

The best solution for anyone dogged by the problem of what to do about smoking manners is simply to give up the habit. The American Cancer Society will help you and will give you many reasons why you should.

Where to Go for Help

Drugs

1. National Clearing House for Drug Abuse Information
P.O. Box 1635
Rockville, Md. 20857
The government agency clearing houses will send you free upon your written request the latest information booklets and materials pertinent to your particular problem, as well as a list of all the programs nearest to your address.
2. Write to the Department of Mental Health in your state, or call them. (In the telephone book, there is usually a subheading for "Drug Abuse" or something similar in the state listings.)

Alcohol

1. National Clearing House on Alcohol Information
P.O. Box 2345
Rockville, Md. 20852
2. National Council on Alcoholism
733 Third Avenue
New York, N.Y. 10017
Before you write the national headquarters, however, contact your local state affiliate, which is listed in the telephone book.
3. Alcoholics Anonymous
Contact the local chapter directly. The local chapter can also, in most cases, refer you the nearest Alateen (for children of alcoholics) or Alanon (for spouses of alcoholics).
4. Women for Sobriety, Inc.
P.O. Box 618
Quakertown, Pa. 18951
This new organization is directed at women alcoholics and has local chapters throughout the country.

For a particularly good pamphlet, *Kids and Alcohol,* which is free, write to the National Council on Alcoholism, at the address given above. This booklet was originally developed for the U. S. Department of Health, Education, and Welfare. Every child, thirteen and up, could benefit from reading it.

Tobacco

1. The American Cancer Society puts out excellent pamphlets on the subject of smoking. For help in kicking your own habit, that of your teenager, or that of an expectant mother or an adult friend, contact your local state division of the American Cancer Society. There is one in every state. Or write to the national headquarters:

American Cancer Society, Inc.
777 Third Avenue
New York, N.Y. 10017

2. Your local lung association also has excellent material on the subject of smoking. Call or write them, or write to the national headquarters:
The American Lung Association
1740 Broadway
New York, N.Y. 10019
They also have some excellent material on non-smokers' rights, including the right to be assertive rather than aggressive in asking people not to smoke.

Chapter 5

THE ADOPTED CHILD

The adoption of a child is one of the most exciting, momentous occasions in one's life. It is a time of great anticipation and joy. Having a baby is a wonderfully creative event; so is having a child come to one's home through adoption. Friends of people who have adopted a child should congratulate the parents and rejoice and share in their happiness.

Adoption has become a more flexible, open process than in the past. It is no longer true that children have to be "matched" to their adoptive parents, partly because there are so few babies available for adoption today. Many people are actively seeking to adopt children of other racial or cultural groups, as well as older children or children with physical or mental handicaps, who previously might never have had an opportunity for adoption. At the same time, agencies have become more flexible about age and religious and marital status of applicants who wish to become adoptive parents. More and more single parents are adopting children. Religious background is no longer a determining factor in many adoptions, and the age of the adopting couple is not a barrier as it once was. If you would like further information about adoption today, you can write to the North American Center on Adoption, 67 Irving Place, New York, N.Y. 10003. This center acts as a source of information and action to find families for waiting children throughout North America. There is also a national organization of adoptive parents and concerned citizens, the North American Council on Adoptable Children, located at 250 East Blaine, Riverside, Calif. 92507.

Showers and Presents

Showers are as appropriate for a newly arrived adopted child as for any baby. When you know that a close friend's adopted child has finally "come home," or if you receive an announcement of an adoption from a good friend in another city, it is a gracious gesture to send a present—something appropriate for the age and sex of the child, whether something in silver (for all engraving or lettering, use the child's actual birth date, not his adoption date) or a gift of clothing, a toy, or money. A warm letter congratulating the new parents on the arrival of the child is sometimes the most appreciated gift of all.

A Party of Welcome for the Adopted Child   If the newly adopted child is older, perhaps already in school, it is a nice idea to give a party for the child's own age group or classmates. This is a particularly good idea if the child is entering a strange school for the first time and knows no one in his class. Many parents wait until their child's birthday before holding a party in his honor. In this way, they can celebrate the child's adoption and his birthday at the same time. The child's birthday is, after all, the date that should be observed ceremonially.

Announcing an Adoption

After the child has come home, it is a nice gesture for the parents to send out announcements of the glad tidings to all their friends and relatives, and even close business associates. It may be a very formal announcement, engraved in black on a traditional white or ivory card:

Mr. and Mrs. Allan Ingalls Fisher
announce that their son
John David Fisher,
Born June 30, 1978,
Arrived on September 15

In several states, a child is not legally adopted until at least six months beyond the day the child was placed with the family, so one cannot say in an announcement "has been adopted" until the six-month period has passed.

It may be an informal printed announcement:

The James Connells
Take pleasure in announcing that
Anne Clare Connell,
Born on August 30, 1978,
has joined their family

When a relative, whether stepparent, grandparent, or aunt and uncle, adopts a child, an announcement such as this one, engraved or printed, may be sent out:

Mr. and Mrs. George McKay
take great pleasure in announcing that
he has adopted his stepdaughter Alane Adams
and she will hereafter be known as Alane McKay

Home address

One of the nicest informal announcements I ever saw consisted of a folded card. On the front it said:

> To welcome a child is to affirm life
> Celebrate with Us

Inside:

> Kathryn Anne Clarke, born October 12, 1971,
> Has joined our family.
> Name of the parents and children already in the family
> Home Address

Newspaper Announcements Large metropolitan dailies usually do not carry adoption announcements, but smaller newspapers—suburban papers and weeklies—often do carry them. One should type the information with one's address and telephone number and send it to the "Announcements" department of the newspaper. It is better not to give the age or the birth date of the child, particularly in small communities, as there is always the possibility that the child's identity will thus be revealed to his or her biological parents.

An announcement like this one would be appropriate:

> Mr. and Mrs. Joseph Infante of Rice Lake
> announce the arrival of a son, Bernard Giacomo

Talking to an Adoptive Child and His Parents

A great deal of sensitivity surrounds the use of adoptive terminology. One does not refer to the child's first parents as "the real mother" or the "true father." The "true parents," it is felt, are those who are truly involved in the continuing act of parenting. However, the original parents should be acknowledged. Such terms as "birth parent," "biological parent," and a composite form, "bio-parent," are increasingly being used. Similarly, in referring to a child born to them, the parents' "natural child" has been replaced by "biological child," since all children are "natural children."

The friends of a person who adopts should be sensitive to the parents' feelings on the subject. Such comments as "What wonderful people you are" and "Isn't the child lucky to have you" are inappropriate. People who adopt are not being altruistic, but are fulfilling a wish to have a child to love, and care for, whether the adopted child is their first or their tenth. Both child *and* parent are lucky. When talking with adoptive parents, ask about their child within the normal context of the family. Parents dislike their adopted child's being treated as though he were an oddity. Parents of several children note that they are uncomfortable when too much attention is paid to the adopted child. He should not be singled out, but should be treated as are all the other children in the family. Equally inappropriate is to comment that the adopted child "looks so much like you, he could have been your own." This suggests that "matching" is desirable.

When parents adopt a child of another race, rather than plying them with curious questions about why they did it, or praising them for "doing such a courageous thing," friends should be supportive of the adoption action. However, the adopting parents will probably welcome questions that help their friends understand why they took their action, as long as questions are well intentioned. The same is true for the adoption of a child with any problems that require special care.

Explaining Another Child's Adoption to Your Child

If your child comes home from school and suddenly asks questions about what exactly "being adopted" means, you should answer him succinctly, but do not dwell on the subject. How much you tell the child depends on his age and how much you feel he can understand. You should explain adoption to your child in such a way that he will consider it an act of love, not an unusual thing. Be sure your child understands that an adopted child is loved and cared for by a new mother and father who now become his "real parents" in every important sense of the word. Explain that adoption means that the child was born to two other parents, but is being loved and raised by parents other than those to whom he was born.

The Adoptive Parents' Attitude

When the adoptive parents should tell their child he is adopted is up to them. But the trend in recent years has been to start relating the child to his adoptive situation as soon as normal questions about origins are raised. The earlier the child is exposed to the word, "adoption," the more comfortable he will be with it. And since there is no guarantee against a child's inadvertently learning of his adoption from playmates or other adults, the earlier he is told, the less likely it is that such problems will arise.

When the questions do start to come, as with questions of sex, give the amount of information you think the child can handle at that time. Open discussion of adoption should continue as the child grows up, as frequently and with as much detail as is required to answer the child's immediate questions. Although such queries may lead to some discomfort, clear answers, given to the best of the parents' ability, are more effective in the long run than half-responses or innuendos.

Chapter 6

THE SINGLE LIFE

In the last half of this century, our attitudes toward singleness have changed greatly, just as the opportunities for a single people to lead completely full lives have greatly increased. In spite of the new attitudes toward the single person, nothing can change the initial shock when one loses a spouse or a lover through death or rejection. The unaccustomed solitude for most people is momentarily debilitating. The change of pace and even of the sound level in one's life can be depressing; the sudden lack of someone with whom to share decisions and responsibilities can be disorienting. One's ego, always fragile, may be battered, and it can be a time when self-pity flourishes to the detriment of one's energies.

The goal of most people in life is *to be happy*. That is just as true for the newly single person as for anyone else. This change in life pattern should be looked upon as an opportunity for positive action, a time for special fulfillments. Hobbies and interests that have been dormant for years can be nurtured anew; further education can open doors to new experiences; and new interests can be pursued, perfected, and just plain enjoyed.

It's a time to feel proud of oneself, a time to "get one's act together." It's a question of being well organized, of having an affirmative attitude, and of keeping the eyes wide open, so that one will not miss the new directions and opportunities that lie ahead.

A Single Person's Options Are Extensive

The list of things a newly single person can undertake is a lengthy one, but you should not make the mistake of attempting everything simultaneously. You must establish priorities and not become overwhelmed by trying too many new things at once. You should refer to your list every so often to see how you are doing and check off the items you have successfully achieved. Even one accomplishment reinforces the affirmative outlook for a newly single person. Everyone's list will be different, depending on individual interests, but possible options could be:

1. *Get a job.* For some women, this is the most important option of all, and preparation should begin at once. It is also one of the most difficult to accomplish quickly.
2. *Increase your volunteer work.* Either move into new areas or intensify your efforts in your present field.
3. *Travel,* trying new places rather than going to familiar old places.
4. *Further your education* by taking courses you always wanted to, but never had time for. A great many museums have evening lecture series. Attending one of these series serves as an opportunity to increase one's knowledge of the arts as well as providing an opportunity to meet new people. Courses that enhance one's chances for employment are, naturally, a priority for someone returning to the job market.
5. *Follow an intensive physical-improvement plan,* which should involve health (diet and exercise) and good looks (more exercise, new hair style and make-up, plastic surgery, and so on).
6. *Enter politics* by becoming visible in a local organization, helping candidates, and possibly laying the groundwork for running for office yourself, whether it's for the local school board or the United States Senate!
7. *Read more* and keep yourself better informed so that your conversation takes on added sparkle.
8. *Seek psychological counseling,* if you need it. Don't be ashamed to get help, but first be a good consumer and shop around for the right person, who will truly understand your needs.
9. *Become an expert at something,* whether it's Chinese export porcelain or ice skating, chess or gardening or playing the options market.
10. *Make new friends* of both sexes, which should be easy because of all the new facets of your life you are busily polishing. People will want to be around you.
11. *Rediscover your talents* in the performing and creative arts. Take up your career in singing again, go back to art classes, or re-enroll in ballet school.
12. *Fix up your home environment.* If your home is badly in need of a total redecoration and you can't afford it, then redesign certain elements, which will make the interior look fresh, warm, and inviting.
13. *Entertain.* Do it well, often, and imaginatively.
14. *Buy a pet.* The right one will become your best friend and provide company at all times, as well as make living noises to break the stillness at home.
15. *Remember the house of worship of your choice.* It's the great healer of loneliness, for when you're in church, you're part of the greatest "coming together" there is.

Personal Business

First things first: a woman must get her personal business in order. She needs *a good lawyer*, who may not necessarily be her divorce lawyer, to call upon for help—just as she needs the name of a good doctor to call in emergencies. She should not, however, bombard her lawyer with telephone calls, but be businesslike in her approach to legal matters. When she makes an appointment to see him or her, she should have an agenda of matters to discuss. If she sees her lawyer socially at parties, she should never address a question on her legal affairs. Professional people, even good friends, should be seen in their offices, not queried on the golf course for free advice.

Finances and Credit   The next thing the newly single woman must learn, if she does not already know it, is how to handle her finances. There are excellent courses offered at colleges, as well as seminars sponsored by local banks and business concerns on the subject of finance. She should make it a point to attend some and to read books on the subject. As a result of the Equal Credit Opportunity Act passed by Congress in 1974, all creditors are now required to record family accounts in the names of both spouses. The result is that women now have credit identities just as their husbands do, even if the accounts are in their husband's name. Nonetheless, a newly single woman should establish credit in her own name immediately. This can be done through store charge cards, a national credit card, or a bank loan. Each organization has its own requirements for granting credit, but may not deny credit to a woman on the basis of her sex.

A newly single woman should establish good relations with her *banker*. He can give her good advice and assistance, but she will also need a good *investment counselor*, who will make a complete financial plan, tailored to her situation. He will help her with such matters as a retirement plan and will look at her income, expenses, investments, insurance, and estate planning with an eye on current tax legislation and the problems of inflation.

A single woman should have a good *accountant* to file her taxes and save her money, even if her business investments are small, by finding every legal tax deduction that applies.

After the death of a spouse, or a divorce, insurance is one of the first concerns to be dealt with. A woman should look around for a reliable insurance agent, one who is sympathetic to her needs and who comes up with the most comprehensive and least expensive plan. One skillful agent can handle her household, health, life, and automobile insurance, keep her premiums as low as possible, and, above all, *prove* that she is not being discriminated against in obtaining insurance because she is a woman.

In her marriage she may have been unwisely "sheltered" from having to cope with financial matters. Understanding money used to be the prerogative of the husband; it is no more.

The Widow and Widower

Grief is such an intensely personal thing that no one can presume to lay down rules that will apply to everyone following the death of a beloved spouse. Anyone touched so harshly by sadness has to forge a new life with his or her own resources, following an individual timetable. Some people are able to begin the healing process earlier than others. If young children are left, it is sometimes easier to start the healing, because concern for their feelings helps one forget about one's own.

This is a time when friends are most needed and when they should push to the maximum their capacity to be thoughtful and imaginative in helping a bereaved friend. By the time the realization of the loss finally hits the person left behind, friends sometimes tend to overlook "how long it's been since we called to say hello and see how everything's coming along." Real friendship manifests itself in actions long after the death. Friends should be particularly solicitous of a friend who is alone and may need help in the raising of children. A child who grieves very hard for a deceased parent puts a terrible burden on the remaining parent's shoulders. Friends who help shoulder this burden are really proving the meaning of friendship.

Entertaining Even though it is not in good taste for a widow or widower to throw a large, raucous party right after the spouse's death, entertaining should begin again as soon as the person feels up to it. Perhaps the first events should be quiet evenings with a very few friends to enjoy a meal or the activities the group used to do together—whether it's going to a movie or a baseball game or playing backgammon by the fire. It's a healthy sign when a recent widow or widower starts to invite friends over again. It's a way of announcing, "Look, I'm fine; I'm standing on my own two feet."

Dating The widow or widower can begin dating another of the opposite sex whenever he or she feels like it. The set period of mourning, as well as the custom of wearing black for a certain length of time, has ended. There is, however, as always, a question of good or bad taste. A widower can invite a woman of any age to dinner, and a widow can certainly accept invitations from a man when she wishes to. This should not be looked upon by others as attempts to seek a possible sexual encounter, but rather as a nice gesture of a friend lending a helping hand and providing comfort.

When a recently widowed parent begins to date one person seriously, the situation must be explained carefully to the children, for a daughter may have a hard time understanding why "Daddy took the pretty lady out to dinner instead of staying home with me," or the son resents the fact that "there's a man who comes to dinner all the time now and sits in Daddy's chair." These are strong emotions with which all members of the family must deal, and the parent should tackle them with understanding and tact. Some children feel a deep-seated resentment of any substitute for their late father or mother; others try to push too hard to make a new relationship happen when their own parent is not ready for it.

Continual Consideration for the Late Spouse's Family A widow or widower should continue through the years to show consideration for the immediate family of the late spouse, even after remarriage. The children should be kept in close touch with the spouse's family, too. One considerate woman I know in Baltimore who happily remarried after her husband's death telephones her former in-laws every Christmas and Easter, and writes them a note around the date of her late husband's birthday each year. Although it's a financial sacrifice, she pays for the children's trip to see their grandparents once a year on the West Coast, for her late husband's family does not have the funds to pay for it themselves.

Consideration of the New Spouse A widow or widower who remarries should show consideration, too, to the new spouse. If there is an enormous portrait of the late husband dominating the library over the fireplace, it should come down; no man wants to have his predecessor constantly reminding him of his presence. Framed photos of the deceased should be relegated to the children's rooms or to family photo albums. If a man is unable to give his wife jewelry as elaborate as that she received from her late husband, she should wear her new husband's more modest pieces, and save the elaborate ones to give to a daughter or to reset sometime into something else. If her engagement ring given to her by her first husband is something she loves very much, she should have the ring reset and wear it on her right hand, or perhaps turn it into a necklace clasp.

And every woman or man who remarries should make a silent but serious pact with herself or himself never, no matter how heated the argument with the new spouse, to accuse the new spouse of doing things "Jim would *never* have done," or to claim that "Nancy would never *ever* have behaved like that!"

Divorce

Divorce rates unfortunately continue to rise, and at some point in our lives most of us will have to face and cope with divorce—whether as one of the spouses, or as a child, parent, or good friend.

A divorced person finds that suddenly he or she has to know himself or herself very well, and that outlets will have to be found for the inevitable feelings of hostility that occur at this time. Sometimes one partner feels very wronged, particularly if the ex-spouse immediately remarries. It is a time to react affirmatively and to go outward, rather than turn inward to too much self-introspection.

The Number One Consideration: The Children The children should be considered first in this situation, and put ahead of one's own possibly battered feelings. They must be told before other people know about the split, and they must be told in a situation where both parents pledge that the love that surrounds them will continue as before. They must be made to understand that, although their parents are going separate ways, their attitudes toward their children will not change.

The secret of success in raising children after a divorce lies in the intelligence, restraint, and self-control of the parents. The children's visitation rights must be vigorously respected by both, and the bitterness and recrimination either feels must not be transmitted to the children. No child should be put in the position of having to take sides.

If at all logistically and humanly possible, the family social traditions should continue as long as possible after the divorce. The opening of the stockings on Christmas Eve, the Easter egg hunt for the children and their friends, the family lunch at a restaurant after Confirmation—these are occasions that should continue in the presence of both parents for as long as possible. If a woman has remarried, it is gracious of the new husband to spend Sunday golfing with his friends when her daughter has her sixteenth birthday party and wants her father present. If a man remarries, it is considerate of his new wife to have "other things to do" when his children get dressed up in their Halloween costumes and invite him to dinner "at home" before he takes them out trick-or-treating. No matter how much rancor and bitterness and jealousy exist beneath the surface, family traditions should continue for young children until they are old enough to accept intellectually the separate lives of their parents.

The Divorced Person's Handling of the Subject in Conversation The biggest bore in the world, in the opinion of many, is not the person who talks incessantly about his operation but the one who talks nonstop about his divorce complications. Everyone has his own problems with which to contend, and social situations should not be used as a search for compassion toward oneself. Real support from friends usually comes when they notice that the divorced person is brave and unselfish about troubles. Friends are eager to help those who help themselves.

Invitations Sent to Divorced People When people send out invitations to a large party, such as an annual Christmas open house, or a wedding reception, they may not know that a couple has been recently separated or divorced. The spouse remaining in the home should handle invitations addressed to the married couple. If you are the one who receives the mail, and if the invitation does not involve an R.S.V.P. or seating at a meal, you should accept for yourself but mention in a note or telephone call, "You probably don't know that Ron and I are getting a divorce; I will forward your invitation to him, because I'm sure he'll want to come, too." If the invitation is to a dinner (and you would *not* like to be at close quarters with him under any circumstances), you should write a note immediately to your hostess: "I'm sure you did not know that Ron and I are only recently divorced. Knowing what a problem it can be to have an extra woman at a dinner, I will regret and hope you will give me a rain check. I have not forwarded your invitation to Ron, feeling this is something you might want to discuss separately with him."

If your hostess knows the proper way to react to all this, she will make every effort to have you attend her dinner and to find a man to balance the table. (If she cannot, she should have you, anyway.) She would then invite your ex-husband to another party soon after, if she and her husband considered you both friends. If she was close only to you and not to your husband, there would be no reason for her to invite him on another occasion.

Inviting Divorced People on Alternate Occasions   For the first six months or so after the divorce of two people you like, it is kind and generous to alternate your invitations to them, and let them know you are doing just that. Jealousy regarding mutual friends is one of the most bitter aftermaths of a divorce, and the couple's friends should be very sensitive to the situation, treat both fairly, and not allow one to gloat, "They like *me* much better than him [or her]!"

Single Parents

For divorced or widowed single parents, there is help all around today, in the form of workshops with child-care facilities; social, athletic, and physical activities; excellent books to read on the subject; and organizations whose sole purpose is to help single parents help their children and themselves at the same time. Most such programs are financed through public or private grants, so there is no charge for services. The Parents Without Partners organization, with headquarters at 7910 Woodmont Avenue, Washington, D.C. 20014, has many local chapters nationwide.

The problems of single parents are not necessarily different from those of other parents; the responsibilities are merely doubled. Much can be gained by talking to others who are in the same boat, both in the way of support and in imaginative new ideas for confronting the future.

Going to Work

The greatest antidote (next to a new, loving partner) for grief, despair, and loneliness is work. For many women who have been married since they finished their schooling, a job commensurate with their intellectual abilities may be difficult to find. Such women are considered "unqualified." They may have low self-esteem and be unable to present themselves in a proper light at job interviews.

For many women today who are widowed or divorced, there is no choice about going to work or not; they must, for compelling financial reasons. If they must, they might as well pep themselves up and approach working as an exciting project, where they will make new friends, and take on and *succeed at* new challenges.

Getting a job today is no easy matter, even for a young, qualified person. A woman should locate the Resource Center for Women nearest her and seek its help in learning how to go on a job interview and in preparing a résumé that will properly focus on her education and years of experience—even as a volunteer—so that she will present herself in an affirmative professional manner. (See Chapter 35, "Getting a Job.")

If a woman really wants to qualify herself for an interesting job, she may have to educate herself further. There are organizations ready to help, with job referral programs, placement services, and job counseling, advice to the woman entrepreneur, and so forth. Many of these services are free; some charge fees. Do a good research job on the avenues of assistance and counseling open to you in your area. Ask the reference librarian at your public library to help you find periodicals on the various employment services; write also to the Women's Bureau, U. S. Department of Labor, Washington, D.C. 20210, for recommended pamphlets.

Volunteer Work

Being a volunteer has many compensations: you will be helping your community and its institutions, all of which badly need help; you will meet new people and make new friends; you can gain excellent experience that may be of help if in the future you want a paying job. You will also learn a lot about your community, how its services function, and how it needs improvement.

If you decide to add volunteerism to your schedule, first research the institution and the kind of work you like to do. If you like people, maybe an out-patient clinic needs a receptionist; social services caring for the elderly are always looking for people to talk to the lonely ones, who never have family visiting them. If you are an art history buff, maybe the museum needs a docent to lead groups of children through the galleries. If you have secretarial or accounting skills, maybe the drug rehabilitation house in your neighborhood is in desperate need of such help in their office on Saturdays. There are urgent calls for patient people to help children learn how to read after school hours, or for volunteers to read textbooks to the blind. Whether it's for the handicapped or the recovering alcoholic, there is work to be done, and people with the proper attitude are needed. It is an easy way for a person who might have cause to feel self-pity to turn outward.

It doesn't matter how lowly the task. I remember one night at a victory rally, the candidate who had just won thanked all his workers as the band played, confetti and balloons peppered the air, and people cried from exhaustion and joy. "I want to thank some of the most important people in my campaign—those who licked stamps and sealed envelopes," he said. "They did a dirty job that isn't exactly the most stimulating activity in the world. But I owe them special gratitude," he added, smiling, "because without them there simply would have been no mailings, no money, no campaign, and no victory here tonight!"

A newly single person might think seriously about adding the advantages of volunteer work to his or her schedule, even if working full time. The satisfactions and new friends that result from volunteer work are one of the greatest therapies that exist.

New Stationery Is Called For

A widow does not have to change her stationery after her husband's death, except for informals, enclosure cards, or correspondence cards that may have been jointly engraved with her and her husband's names. It is bad taste for her to use engraved stationery with her late husband's name in view or crossed out. She should destroy that stationery, or preferably use it for scratch paper and use only her own paper ("Mrs. Garrett Ackerman" or ("Betty Ackerman"). The same applies to a widower; he should not use stationery engraved with his wife's name.

The divorcée must immediately cease using stationery and cards that call her by her husband's first name. She is no longer "Mrs. Denton Walker." She should have new die cuts made for engraving, or use new printed or plain stationery.

A single, divorced, or widowed woman is wise to list her name in the telephone book by last name and first initials, and not by an obviously female first name, if she lives in a large urban center where crime is prevalent.

A Divorced Woman and Her Name

The custom of a woman using her maiden name in front of her husband's last name is passé. In other words, Alice Canning who marries Denton Walker becomes after a divorce Mrs. Alice Walker, and not Mrs. Canning Walker. On calling cards and stationery she should be just "Alice Walker." On mailing address labels or when she hand-writes a return address to someone who does not know her, she should use "Mrs. Alice Walker," so that the recipient will know how to address her in reply.

If she wishes a three-letter monogram for her stationery, she should use *ACW*.

Some divorced women without young children prefer to take back their maiden names entirely. This is becoming more common, particularly if the woman bears a good family name. In this case she would become "Alice Canning" once again on all stationery, credit cards, bank accounts, passport, and so on. I have seen very handsome printed postcards that women have sent out to their entire mailing list of friends, Christmas card recipients, and people with whom they do business, stating:

The former Mrs. Denton Walker will be known as Alice Canning.
(The address is listed below.)

Some women take back their maiden names after a divorce even when there are children—because the latter are young adults and would understand why their mother has dropped their father's last name. Sometimes when the former husband and his new wife live in the same town, it is easier for the divorcée not to be known by her former husband's name or to be confused with his present wife.

It sometimes happens that a woman who has been divorced several times will revert to the name of a husband who was more famous or social than her other husbands or her present husband whom she is divorcing. This is improper and a misuse of a name, and it is certainly in conflict with the principles of women's moving toward equality and independence. However, reverting to the name of a former husband is justified if one's minor child bears that name.

If a woman and a man who hyphenated their last names divorce, each drops the half of the name that pertains to the other person. In other words, if John Smith marries Alice Jones and they call themselves "Mrs. and Mrs. John Smith-Jones," it is preferable for them to return to the names of John Smith and Alice Jones if they divorce. Any new wife, for example, would certainly not want to be saddled with a hyphenated name, part of which belonged to neither her new husband nor herself!

The Importance of Entertaining

Regardless of one's marital status, the ability to entertain well is the major tool of social success—and for many people, it is a major tool of happiness. When one entertains well, one is fulfilling a creative urge *and* giving pleasure to others at the same time. The best way for a person who lives alone to be invited to other people's parties is to give good parties himself.

For example, a thirty-year-old divorcée was transferred by her company to a city where she knew no one. She managed to solve the loneliness problem very easily. Two different executives in the company had been instructed to "be nice" to her, so they invited her home with their families for dinner. (To share a meal with a family in a new city is a special treat for a person alone.) She reciprocated by arranging a dinner party in a restaurant to which she invited those two couples from her firm, plus a bachelor she had met only briefly two nights previously at a political volunteer rally, and the young minister and his wife from the church she now attended. As a result of that one dinner in a restaurant, her social life took off. The minister and his wife introduced her to other young people of the congregation at a party in the church hall. A young man she met there took her to two cocktail parties, where she met others in her age and interests bracket. In the meantime, the senior members of her firm and their wives kept a parental eye on her and put her on their special entertaining lists. Soon she was "at home" in her new town. Once the pebble is tossed into the social waters, the concentric circles of new acquaintances overlap and extend indefinitely.

Another example: a woman who had not worked during the years she raised her children wanted to meet new friends after her divorce (partly to avoid the social circles where she would continue to meet her ex-husband and his new young wife). She used a different approach. She enrolled in a training course in occupational therapy, a subject that had interested her for years. She also joined the Foreign Policy Association, to attend their meetings and lectures on foreign affairs. Then she invited a mixture of both new groups to several Sunday brunches at her home—the kind of party she could do easily and well. She was asked back by almost everyone she entertained. Within a year, she had an entirely new set of friends, including men, who had nothing to do with her former life as a married woman. She continued to see on a selective basis old friends from her "other life," but she was no longer dependent on them for her social life.

The Host and Hostess in One Person   If the single woman becomes an accomplished hostess on her own, she will not have to lean on a male guest at her parties "to act as host." If she was used to her husband's taking over certain responsibilities in entertaining the guests, she must fulfill these now herself. She can manage them, whether greeting her guests, getting them their cocktails, or passing the men their cigars. If she is a man short at her table, she should sit at the head of the table with her male guest of honor on her right and a woman guest on her left. She should make sure that the woman on her left has a man on her other side.

The "Extra Woman"   It is time that women who live alone let their hosts realize that it is not the "end of the world" if they do not have a man supplied for them. It is better to spend a cozy evening in good company, enjoying good conversation, than to have an extra man brought in (or an extra woman, for a single man) who detracts from the group harmony.

If a divorced woman knows a suitable escort of whom her hosts may not be aware, it is up to her to communicate this to good friends. Let the word get around. All she has to say is, "There's a man named Mike Brent whom I see once in a while. He's no great love in my life, just a friend who contributes nicely to a party." If the woman's friends use Mike Brent as her escort too often and it becomes a bore for either of them, she should say the next time she is asked to bring him, "Why don't I just come by myself? Mike and I have decided to give this joint partygoing a rest for a while."

Men Should Entertain   Just because a man is a bachelor or divorced or widowed and is in demand for parties because of his singleness, it does not mean that he is excused from paying back his obligations to his hosts and hostesses. The easiest way for him to do it is to give a cocktail party; the nicest is for him to give a big dinner party or two or three small ones during the year—either by having a caterer come to his home, or by taking his guests to a restaurant or a club. Some of the best cooks are men, of course, and so some of the best "little dinners" are given by bachelors.

Some bachelors become truly bored by having to attend parties every night and always having to take care of whichever single woman is present. If this is the case, the man should be frank with his friends. "Look, I'd love to come over some night to have a hamburger with you and the kids and to relax a bit, but I'm tired of parties." Frankness in social relationships never has to be rude; well-stated frankness is always for the best.

Transportation Home for the Single Woman   A woman dinner guest who arrives by taxi or public transportation may feel perfectly at ease returning home in the same manner. Today many women prefer to be independent rather than to rely on another guest to escort them home. If this is not the case, then the woman should bring up the subject with her host or hostess at the time the invitation is extended. One should not be reticent about asking: "I'd love to come but am frankly nervous traveling home alone at night. Is there another guest living in my direction who could drop me home?"

When a single woman chooses to leave before the other dinner guests, the host or hostess should offer to call or see her to a taxi. Should she say this is not necessary, then respect her wishes and do not draw attention to the subject of her departure, which might only cause her embarrassment. After all, chances are the woman has been a dinner guest on other occasions and knows how she wants to deal with the situation.

The Newly Single Person's Home

Many people who are suddenly alone also find their home is no longer right for them. If a woman's husband has died and the children are grown, she may have to sell a big house for reasons of finances—or perhaps just plain loneliness. If a man's wife has divorced him and taken all the furniture, he will probably be moving into smaller quarters and need to furnish them from scratch. I ran into a recently divorced friend on the Fifth Avenue bus early one morning and he said, "You used to see me with my *Wall Street Journal* every morning; now it's Macy's home furnishings sale catalogue!"

Whatever happens, the necessity of "getting one's house in order" is one of the first steps in any rehabilitation of the psyche after it has suffered the blow of death or divorce. One's surroundings must be comfortable before any other step forward is possible, and delaying too long in reaching a decision about one's living quarters is a luxury few can afford.

I know one widow, financially strapped after the death of her husband, who sold her entire house with its traditional and antique furnishings, including a set of very fine oriental rugs. She kept eight of everything for her table (good glasses, dinner plates, dessert plates, sterling flatware), sold the rest, and moved into a typical small studio apartment. She purchased all contemporary and inexpensive furnishings for that one room. She finished unpainted wood furniture in bright blue or yellow lacquer paint, and put down inexpensive machine-washable blue and yellow throw rugs on the polished parquet floor, a far cry from the orientals. Her apartment sang with fresh color and with the gleam of shiny chrome and glass; her walls, which formerly had been hung with nineteenth-century French pictures, were now accented with modern framed graphics. She completed all of this—the sale of her home, the move, and the decoration of the new apartment—within five months of her husband's death. She had always entertained beautifully throughout her married life—she did not stop in her "new life." Instead of moving her dinner guests into the lovely Louis XV–furnished dining room of her former home, she now moved them from one end of her room to the other, where they dined at a small round card table, covered with a beautiful cloth to the floor. The same excellent food was served; the hostess lavished the same loving care on her guests. Although her husband was gone, his spirit permeated her entertaining, because they had enjoyed it together when he was alive. There was no sadness transmitted to her guests, only enthusiasm and delight with her new dollhouse, as she called the apartment.

In contrast, I know a woman in Georgia who with her husband had been living for several years in a modern high-rise apartment in Atlanta. They had put all her family's very fine antiques in storage at the time they had left their big house. Two weeks after her husband died, this woman, well into her late sixties, called in an architect, and together they executed the plans for remodeling the old barn on her family's farm. She pulled some of the biggest pieces of furniture and all her favorite antiques from storage—from velvet armchairs to crystal chandeliers. She moved back to the country, permanently, and there she began a wonderful new life, once again in big spaces, able to spend her remaining days with all the possessions she loved and had been surrounded with in her younger days. It took money to do this, but it also took courage and imagination.

The Single Man Keeps House   A man who has had his home life taken care of by his wife—his meals, his social schedule, the laundry, the household bills—is as disoriented by her loss as a woman is dioriented by the loss of her husband when she knew nothing of their financial affairs. A man who is financially comfortable can move into his club or an apartment hotel with daily maid service. But the vast majority of men have to begin coping with the chores of housekeeping, laundry, cooking, and soaking the scrambled eggs out of the frying pan. For those who have never had to think of these seriously, they are a real challenge, an exercise not only of patience but of intellect. If a man can afford to hire someone to come in to clean once or twice a week, he still has to know how to interview, hire, pay, and give orders to her. He has to be able to articulate what he wants her to do, and at first a good female friend may be needed to answer his cry for help. I saw one man sheepishly follow his sister-in-law around his new apartment while she explained to him the electrical gadgets he had never had to know how to use before. She taught him the "mysteries" of his new vacuum cleaner and how to clean the vinyl tile kitchen floor. As soon as she reached her own home the telephone was ringing. It was her brother-in-law. "But you didn't tell me how to open the ironing board" was his lament. This particular widower was remarried a year and a half later. His bride smilingly toasted him at the wedding dinner and said, "The real reason I married him is because he's so good around the house!"

Travel

Travel is one of the greatest mind stretchers there is, because while it opens new doors, it allows one at the same time to accumulate good memories.

A good travel agent with a broad knowledge of what's going on in this country and around the world is invaluable to anyone planning a trip specially adapted to particular interests. Whether someone enjoys wandering through the great gardens of Italy, poking through the archaeological excavations in Central America, playing tennis all day at a New Hampshire tennis camp, or examining the unusual marine life in the Philippines, there is no longer any stigma attached to pursuing these interests *alone*. No longer need a woman alone fear others will view her as someone who's available.

Naturally, a woman who has a friend traveling with her enjoys the company of someone close at hand with whom she can share and discuss each experience. However, if she is alone, what she lacks in sharing experiences she more than compensates for in a more acute perception of each experience. (See also Chapter 66, "Planning Your Vacation Trip.")

Chapter 7

HOUSEHOLD MANAGEMENT IN A SERVANTLESS SOCIETY

Our world today is one in which "domestic help" is becoming rarer every year. Ours has become an age of the superorganized person who lives in a small, efficient space, utilizing every mechanical gadget on the market that will help make life easier.

If running a household is more difficult than it used to be, because of a lack of domestic help, then there are also endless sources of assistance and advice that were never available before. Home economists and consumer specialists are teaching us how to shop, how to organize, how to live. Our magazines and newspapers are chock-full of useful information and ideas —all to make us live better, more easily, and therefore more happily. Fortunately, new inventions and remarkable products are constantly being introduced to support this do-everything-ourselves state of existence. If recent predictions come true (and they are less farfetched than many that have already come true), the household work of tomorrow will be accomplished via pushed buttons. Everything will be done electronically on a computerized basis. That friendly robot may not be too far away.

Until that glorious day, however, we must continue to cope with the household ourselves—in a shrinking space with an expanding population. It is not really surprising that manners reach into the science of household management.

The "Household Staff"

Let us dream a little.

Let us turn back the clocks for a minute to another era, when people of wealth and station had "household staffs." King of the household was the butler—well trained, often English-schooled although sometimes oriental, and always of impeccable grooming, with a superb manner and an unchallengeable way of giving orders to others. He was often better dressed and more distinguished-looking than the "master," and people the world over have mistaken the butler at the front door as their party host. I remember so well the night that Capitani (our butler at the Ambassador's residence in Rome, when I was a member of Ambassador Clare Boothe Luce's staff) was at the front door for a very important diplomatic dinner. He was resplendent in his white tie and tails, helping direct the traffic of arriving guests and ordering the staff to move quickly and well. A famous *principessa*, wearing, it seemed, all the family jewels, alighted from her limousine. She swept into the villa in her ball gown, eyed Capitani, and came over to him, her jeweled right hand thrust imperiously into his face. He had no choice. He kissed her hand with great aplomb, and then muttered, *Buona sera, Principessa.*" A moment later the princess came up to her hostess, Ambassador Luce. "I had no idea, Madame Ambassador," she said in halting English, "that Signor Henry Luce spoke Italian so perfectly."

"But he doesn't speak it yet," Clare Luce replied. It was then that the princess discovered her error in identity.

The housekeeper came next in status. She did the buying, the hiring of the staff, the meal planning, in conjunction with the cook, and even the bookkeeping. She wore her own clothes, had her own apartment in the house or on the estate, and was given her own car. Like the butler, she was a Person of Power.

The housemen (or footmen) assisted the butler. There would be two or three of them. They were dressed in black trousers with linen or cotton jackets, and black bow ties. For great dinners, they wore the fancy house livery and served the dinner, one standing behind every two chairs. They were usually joined for these dinners by "extras" hired from the outside. The housemen wore khaki pants and shirts for work clothes.

The family chauffeur (sometimes there were two or three, one for him, one for her, and one for the children) wore an expensively tailored uniform (chosen by the head housekeeper, but approved by the employers), sometimes with black leather "puttees" and always with handsome gloves and a visored cap. A fur lap robe in wintertime was a necessary accessory in the back seat, and part of the chauffeur's job each day was to shake it out and fluff it up.

The housemaids wore white or pastel uniforms with lacy aprons and matching caps by day, and black serving uniforms with white aprons, collar, and cuffs for the evening.

The cook dressed in a white uniform, and she had a pantry maid or two to assist her. If her house was blessed with a chef (instead of a cook) he always wore his tall hat in the kitchen, his white scarf tied around his neck, and a white cotton tunic apron over his black-and-white-checked cotton trousers—the symbol of his station in life. He usually had one or two pantry boys to assist him, and on important party occasions a pastry chef would come in to work with him for two days before the party.

"Nanny," the children's nurse, held reign over the nursery quarters and was always dressed in a white uniform or a striped cotton one with a big white apron. Outdoors, she wore a gray coat and matching "nanny's" gray felt hat, and, of course, white gloves were *de rigueur* when she pushed her well-dressed charge in his pram. She was also assisted by one or two nursery maids, whose job was to clean the children's rooms to absolute perfection, and to mop up after a typical late afternoon nursery tea of jelly or egg salad sandwiches, fresh strawberries and cream, and cookies.

There was a laundress who came every day and worked long, hard hours on the master's shirts, Madame's pleated silk nightgowns, the children's hand-smocked Liberty lawn dresses, and the white damask napkins and forty-foot-long banquet cloth used at last night's dinner party.

A social secretary, who often lived grandly on the estate, took care of issuing invitations, co-ordinating R.S.V.P.s, and working with the butler and chef on party details.

The gardens were cared for by a head gardener who lived with his family on the estate and by his assistants. The head gardener was often from Japan or from one of the Mediterranean countries; these men were frequently artful landscape architects even without the formal education of a landscape architect. They took care of the great number of plantings in the house, fresh flowers for the tables, and the rotating of delicate trees, flowering plants, and other greenery from the house to the greenhouse, to the garden, and back to the house again.

It was a whole world of its own, of very professional people who did their jobs with great pride. Everyone, from the butler organizing his wine cellar to the pantry maid vigorously polishing the silver, knew what his or her job was and did it well. It was a world that will probably never exist again.

Today's World

Today the magic word is "service industry." Housekeeping chores are done by service agencies, many of them franchised, which do everything from keeping our houses clean to throwing our parties and watering our lawns. While it is not as personal as the household staffs of the past, we are still fortunate to have this service industry because it takes care of our basic needs, according to our means. When we entertain, the butler, bartender, housemen, or waitresses can all be supplied by a catering service, along with the food and the plates. A cleaning woman comes in by the day—or by the hour—to handle what a full-time "upstairs maid" used to do.

Private social secretaries are rare today. However, a woman who entertains frequently, particularly in benefit work, sometimes retains a woman with secretarial skills to work at home with her on lists and invitations, as well as other logistical details involved with a charity affair. There are also public social secretaries today who "free-lance." They have their own offices, sometimes with assistants, and plan such events as debuts, weddings, private dances—and benefits, too.

If there is a chauffeur today, the chances are that he is paid by the husband's or wife's business corporation. He is usually a business driver, not one formally assigned to the family for their private pursuits.

Service agencies have supplanted the gardeners. Their employees truck to the various houses who are clients; they water your lawn, cut the grass, trim the hedges, tend the plants, and even plant your garden seeds for you.

The English or Irish nanny has all but disappeared, and the baby nurse is a rarity. If a woman is lucky, she has a professional baby nurse spend the first two weeks after the baby comes home from the hospital living in her home, getting the baby on schedule and generally helping with the new infant. Such a baby nurse does not, however, do the family cooking and housework; her job is to take care of the baby and the mother. The diaper service then comes into play for those who do not want paper diapers all the time; and then the cultural phenomenon called "the baby-sitter" becomes a part of the young family's life.

There is no laundress any more. Instead, one sends out the laundry to a commercial establishment if one does not do it oneself at home or at a laundromat. Synthetic blouses and shirts are worn so that they can dry wrinkle-less over the bathtub, and the baby is dressed in easy-care clothes instead of the pure cotton and Viyella smocked dresses and suits that required hand laundering and pressing. Even the table has changed. Plastic place mats and polyester no-iron napkins are seen everywhere. If a young hostess today were to be shown a forty-foot-long white damask banquet cloth, she would probably ask incredulously, "What's *that?*"

Times have changed, but we still have the same opportunity in our entertaining for warm hospitality—and an even greater opportunity for creativity. We are put to the task when we entertain far more than our rich forebears ever were, but, on the other hand, we don't have to be rich today to entertain well. So let us not lament the past, except for some of its niceties. And let us definitely celebrate the present.

Hiring Domestic Help

Whether you are hiring a chauffeur, butler, or lady's maid (which in these days is highly unlikely) or a baby-sitter, housekeeper, or cleaning person, the surest way of finding the right person is through word-of-mouth references. Good references from a former employer are the best insurance you have in finding a good potential employee. Failing that, a reputable employment agency is the place to go. The agency will tell you what the going wages are and what kind of benefits the employee must be provided, and it will carefully screen any applicants it sends you, checking on their references and so on. The agency usually charges you a fee for its services if you actually employ the person it sends you. Sometimes the fee is a month's salary.

The Interview If you live in an apartment, the person who comes to be interviewed should enter through the front door and use the front elevator, and not be ushered through the service entrance. Take the person's coat and have her sit down for a few minutes' conversation in some comfortable place in your home, during which time you should put that person at ease. Ask about the last job, for example. Before the prospective employee comes for the interview, you should have carefully written or typed a general list of duties you would expect her to perform. Have that list with you as you talk, and then take her on a thorough tour of your home. If she is going to be cleaning your home, or if she is going to be a live-in housekeeper, state what has to be done in each room of the house as you pass through it. "This is the dining room; it should be vacuumed at least once a week, but more often if it needs it. . . . All of this silver hollow ware has been lacquered, so it is not supposed to need polishing, but I like the sterling flatware done every two weeks and put away very carefully. I am very particular about well-polished silver."

One of the first things you ask her is how she prefers to be called. "Do you like to be called Mary or Mrs. Wright?" If she answers, "Mrs. Wright," you should always use that name. Be sure to introduce her to any children you come across in the course of the tour of your home. "This is Jeremy's room. He's our youngest. Jeremy—this is Mrs. Wright, who might be coming to work in our house." (Jeremy should come over to her and shake her hand.)

If she is to live in, her quarters should be shown and discussed. If you happen not to smoke and she smokes, tell her that you prefer her to confine her in-house smoking to her quarters, and that you hope she will "air out her room regularly."

Show her everything about the house or apartment, and keep referring to your check list of her duties. Give her a copy of the list; it will spell everything out in black and white, so she cannot say later she was "deceived about the scope of the work."

If you like her and you sit down to discuss the job further, tell her what you would offer in wages, and how you would pay (weekly, biweekly, or monthly), and explain that you will pay one half of her Social Security payments and deduct the other half from her wages. Explain about how much vacation she will receive and how her weekly time off will be allocated.

If you do not like the person you are interviewing, don't give her a long tour. Show her to the door, saying, "Thank you for coming. I am interviewing several people, and I should know in a week or so. I will get in touch with you."

If you like her and if there are others competing for the services of this person, you might have to do a bit of "selling" of yourself. Tell the applicant as much as you can about your family, the "sane" hours you keep, how much entertaining you do, perhaps how much you are away from home and need a good strong hand at home for the children's sake. Relate how long your past employees stayed with you (and left only because they got married or retired). Most people prefer to work for someone who has a reputation for being kind than for someone who pays higher wages but who has a record of a rapid turnover in help.

If you have checked out her references, if you have liked her very much during the interview and if she likes you, and if your children reacted affirmatively to her, offer her the job. Select the date she is to begin, but first make her have a physical examination by your family doctor, for which you pay. (You do not want to take on the responsibility of hiring someone to do a demanding job who is in poor health.)

Helping a New Employee Start Off on the Right Foot Although you gave your prospective employee a list of over-all duties during the interview, you should now give her an even more detailed schedule of what you wish her to do day by day, room by room. Ask her which products she particularly likes to use for cleaning (or cooking), and let her purchase those at the store. Give her cash in a weekly account, for which she gives you back all receipts. (If she can charge at the store, it is easier for everyone.) Give her a list each day of what is needed for the house; gradually she will learn how to plan ahead and will buy it automatically. If the household needs new equipment like a mop or broom—even a vacuum cleaner—try to purchase those items. She will do her work with more enthusiasm and efficiency if she has the proper tools, in good condition.

Make Sure Her Living Quarters Are Nice They should be not just satisfactory but pleasant. She should have a decent room, or a bedroom with a sitting room, however small. She should have a television set and a clock. She should have towels and bedding awaiting her; the bed should be comfortable, not with a bumpy, antiquated mattress. The room should be clean (don't let it have accumulated dirt for her to clean); the walls should not be in dire need of a coat of paint. The closet and bureau drawers should be empty, awaiting her unpacking.

If she is being hired as a baby nurse and she has to sleep in the same room with the baby, show her some other room in the house where on occasion, with permission, she may receive a friend or relative in privacy. Show her where she can smoke (no smoking should be allowed in the nursery). Be sure she has bureau drawer and closet space in the baby's room, her own comfortable chair, and a table and lamp for reading and writing.

If she does not live in but works all day every day for you, you should provide her with a place to sit and rest in your home, plus a small part of a closet in which to store her things, and also a room in which to change into her uniform—even if it's a bathroom or the room of a child away at school.

Uniforms A housekeeper, maid, baby nurse, or cleaning woman looks neater in a uniform, and she should have one if she works full or part time every day for you. Women usually welcome the chance to wear it, because it saves their own clothes. Discuss with her the kind you want her to get, but let her make the final selection at the store. After all, even though you pay for it, she's the one who has to wear it all day. She may hate white uniforms and like pastel ones very much; you may much prefer white. A solution for a housekeeper would be to have her buy one white and two pastel (and she can wear white on the days you request her to). She will need at least three uniforms for the week. For winter, have her buy a matching colored cardigan for each. She can wear either white or black working oxfords with these uniforms. If you have someone living in who is financially strapped, you may have to buy her work shoes for her—and her winter coat, too.

Time Off Be sure always to give your household employee the proper time off, which is usually one and a half days per week. (Some employers give their household help the entire weekend off.) If you ask her to stay in during one of her days off to help you out in an emergency, you should repay her either in compensatory time or with money. You should not expect her to donate her time to you, out of loyalty.

And when you give time off to someone like the baby nurse, let us say, from Saturday noon to Sunday night, don't have two whole days of the baby's laundry facing her when she comes home. Try to wash the baby's things as you go along during the weekend.

Always let an employee off to go to church on Sunday or to temple on the weekend if he or she is a religious person. That should not be counted as time off. Don't feel you have to lend your car to an employee; but if you live in the country and there is no bus transportation to your home, you should provide transportation for your employee to and from the train station. Your maid or housekeeper obviously cannot afford to shuttle back and forth from the station by taxi.

Training Is a Continuous Process If an employee is to be truly useful in your home to every member of your family, you must train her, and continue to train her. You cannot expect her to be psychic about what you want done and how you want it to be done. This does not mean that you should be continuously behind her, criticizing and recommending further action. It does mean that the order should be issued pleasantly and intelligently, and that you should follow up later to see how it was carried out. That is the time for recommending "a little something to make it better," but it is also the time for praise if a job has been well done.

An employee does not train herself. You have to be there to show her. When she comes to work the first day for you, you should arrange to take a day's leave from your job, if you work, in order to be there to explain and demonstrate. It may mean her switching around her time off one weekend and staying home to have you show her how you like things done. Don't criticize a new employee to whom you have not given time in training. If your help is foreign, you have a further problem: one of communication. (I had a South American cleaning woman for seven years who did not speak one word of English; don't ask me how we managed, but we managed.) When there is a language problem, one must be extra-patient, be expert at sign language, and retain a sense of humor.

It helps if you leave explicit notes—about your schedule, how to reach you, what to do in case of emergency, and so forth. Teach her what to do in case of fire, and how to call the police.

Do Not Overwork Your Employee Some people do not realize how over-burdened their domestic help is. Some people think their employee is almost machine-like, devoid of feelings, and always full of energy and good health. But everyone has "blue" days, and everyone can be pushed to the extent of a breakdown by being overworked. Do a time study on your housekeeper or whoever is working for you, if she says she is overworked. She may need help. Perhaps someone else in the household can do the marketing; perhaps the sheets and your husband's shirts should go out to a commercial laundry. You cannot expect one person to do all the cleaning, marketing, cooking, sewing, laundry, and child supervision for one family. Remove some of her load, or you will lose her necessary, wonderful services.

Workmen's Compensation

By all means carry insurance to cover the possible injury of employees in your household. And check with your insurance broker on what other insurance may be necessary or advisable.

There are personal liability policies issued by major companies that protect the householder against what might be financially crippling liabilities incurred through bodily injuries, sickness, disease, or death to employees, guests, or even casual visitors such as delivery boys on your property. If a housemaid falls from a stepladder, her injuries, under such a policy, are covered by the medical clause. If she sues, the employer is covered by the liability clause.

Social Security Deductions and Withholding Tax

Domestic employees are specifically exempted from the withholding tax but any employee who is paid cash wages of $50.00 or more in a calendar quarter comes under the Social Security law. A calendar quarter is a three-month period ending March 31, June 30, September 30, or December 31. Disregard the value of food, lodgings, clothing, car tokens, and other non-cash items furnished to household employees. A cleaning woman, for example, who has been paid cash wages of $50.00 within a calendar quarter on one job must have Social Security payments deducted by her employer, who of course pays an equivalent amount to the Social Security fund on a quarterly basis. Since both you and the employee are liable under the law for noncompliance, you should obtain the employee's Social Security number before he or she starts to work. It is best to deduct the tax weekly if the employee is on a weekly basis, and by check, noting the amount of deduction on the face of the check. If wages are paid in cash, the amount of the tax must be taken out and entered in the household books, together with the employee's Social Security number and home address.

Beginning with the first calendar quarter in which you pay taxable wages to one or more household employees, you must file quarterly returns reporting the employees' taxable wages and remit the Social Security tax due for the quarter. The tax return and payment must be submitted no later than the last day of the month following the end of the quarter.

The law requires each employer to furnish to each employee a written statement of wages and employee tax for each calendar year on or before Janurary 31 of the next year. If a household worker's employment ends before December 31, the employer's statement should cover the part of the year through the last day of employment, and should be furnished within thirty days after the day on which the last payment of wages is made to the employee. Form SS-14, provided by the Internal Revenue Service, may be used as the statement.

Permanent workers in a household who are not domestics or independent contractors—social secretaries, secretaries—are subject to withholding tax as well as to Social Security tax and these deductions must be taken from pay checks and reported quarterly.

State Unemployment Insurance Tax

This is another tax paid by a household employer for the privilege of hiring domestic employees (the same tax is paid by business employers for their employees). No part of this tax is paid by the employee. The employer is assessed a certain tax percentage by the state based on the total amount of all the wages earned by his employees during that calendar quarter. (The tax rate rises according to the amount of money the employer's former employees who were let go are collecting in unemployment insurance and for the length of time they continue to receive it.)

Handling the Telephone

You should instruct your housekeeper, maid, baby nurse, cleaning lady, or whoever to answer your telephone in this manner: "The Johnson residence." You should see to it that there is a notepad and pencil by every telephone extension in your home, so that messages can be properly taken by everyone. Teach your domestic staff member always to take both the name and telephone number of anyone who calls, so that if one thing is wrong, you can still find out who it was who called you. A foreign language problem makes telephone message taking difficult—and an employer would do well to invest in English lessons for a live-in foreign employee who does not know the language well enough to handle the telephone.

You should spell out the rules of incoming and outgoing personal telephone calls to your domestic employee. When people return home at night after working all day, they do not want to be disturbed by having to answer the telephone constantly, only to have the calls for someone who works in the house. Perhaps the rule that all personal calls must be transacted during certain daytime hours could be put into effect. Any long-distance calls made by a member of the domestic staff should, of course, be reimbursed by her to her employer.

Firing a Household Employee

A member of your household staff, no matter how hopeless she seems, deserves a second chance—at least one. You should talk to her and say what has displeased you so greatly; tell her the truth. Then say, "Do you want another chance?" If she answers affirmatively with enthusiasm, give her that other chance—whether she was found drinking, or neglecting her duties, or cheating on the grocery accounts, or entertaining her boy friend in her bed. It is very difficult to find loyal, trained domestic help these days, but even if there were plenty around, one should still give any human being a second chance.

If you have given that chance, and the person still does not live up to your standards, dismiss her calmly and kindly. Give her two weeks' notice, and when she leaves, give her an extra week's salary, if you can, to be kind. If you wish her, however, for certain reasons, out of the house at once, ask her to pack up and leave immediately. Inform her you are giving her three weeks' salary; then she won't be able to accuse you of "gross unfairness."

The Letter of Reference Withholding a letter of reference is a very serious matter, because it means that person may find it impossible to get another job. Whether a domestic employee left of her own accord or was fired, you should write a reference letter. Another employer, in many instances, may find your ex-employee satisfactory because her own demands are simpler than your household's. You can always write a letter in which you state the dates of employment of the employee, and say a few nice things while omitting the unpleasant ones. A prospective employer of that person can call you to check out the details, but if you can, you should never keep a person from getting another job.

When you write or type a letter of reference for a domestic employee, do it on your own personal stationery. Here is a typical one:

Your address
Today's date

To Whom It May Concern:

Mary Davison was in my employ for the summer of 19—. [Even if she worked for you for only two or three weeks, you can stretch it a little.] She is cheerful and carried out my orders promptly and well. She was very kind and patient with my children and was a good cleaner. She is leaving me because, as a working mother who travels a good deal, I need to have in charge of the house someone who has had a great deal of experience and who knows how to initiate tasks by herself and without direct supervision. We all liked Mary very much and are sad to have her leave us.

Sincerely,

Giving References over the Telephone   If someone calls you to obtain additional information concerning a written reference you have given, you can be somewhat more frank than you were in the letter, but you should try not to be damning.

If you omitted "honesty" from your list of adjectives, you might say, "We were all careless about leaving loose money around, but I think that if you are careful about that, Henrietta will work out well for you." If the problem was drinking, be kind in what you say. "Melanie has a drinking problem, but she assured me she was going to seek help, and I think that in a quieter, less demanding household than ours, she would work out and stay on top of her problem." In other words, you should not withhold important information, but give your former employee every benefit of the doubt.

The Baby- or Child-sitter

Most parents are not totally at ease when they close the door to their home, leaving their children in the care of a sitter. Whether they leave for their jobs, or go out for a social evening, or go away for the weekend, there's usually a "clutching" feeling (really quite common to anyone leaving a child behind) and a wondering if the children will be all right. Davy may have missed earning a place on the school team and is as despairing, relatively speaking, as he ever will be again in his life. . . . Barbara may have a bad sore throat, but she can't go to the pediatrician before tomorrow morning. . . . Johnny may have fussed more than usual tonight, but that could be because he doesn't really like that sitter, or is it just because he didn't want his parents to go out? The list of possible things that could go wrong, whether one has one child or several and regardless of their ages, is endless. It is the responsibility of the parents to leave their small children with someone mature enough to handle emergencies. A pre-teen without any judgment does not fit the description.

The same sitter should be used as often as possible; young children are upset by constant changes and new adjustments. Parents should not go away leaving a sitter in charge who has not proven herself—or himself—to be excellent in every aspect. The person left in authority with your children is exceedingly important. Your children are, after all, your most precious assets. There are three major things to remember:

1. Find an appropriate, mature sitter and sign her up far in advance, if possible.
2. Clearly spell out her duties (intelligent training, in other words).
3. Give her proper working conditions and compensate her properly. (After all, you want her back.)

Ways to Locate a Good Sitter
1. The best way is by word of mouth—recommendations from other parents who think a particular sitter is excellent.
2. A well-run high school or college baby-sitters' registry exists in many communities. However, ask for a reference, and check it out before finalizing the arrangement.
3. Post a notice at your local grocery or drugstore, if the store has a "Help Wanted" bulletin board. If it doesn't, you might suggest they have one as a service to their customers. A notice might read:

WANTED: EXPERIENCED BABY-SITTER
For a four-month-old and a two-year-old.
Friday, September 13, from 6 P.M. until 1 A.M.
Pay: $2 an hour. References required.
Call 356-4715

4. Ask for recommended sitters from your church or synagogue.
5. Inquire of directors of senior-citizen programs near you about likely qualified people. Older people present a tremendous reservoir of experienced talent for this activity, particularly for long-term jobs. They have so much to give. They might work five afternoons a week after school, for example, in order to be at home to receive children returning from school (when both parents are at work). They could give the children a snack, supervise their homework, and prepare their dinner, leaving when a parent arrives home from work to take over.

Spelling Out the Sitter's Duties If the sitter has to prepare the baby's food, write out explicit instructions. Write down exact feeding times, even when a baby, for example, should be given a bottle of water. Give her little tips like how to make the baby "burp" most easily (a sitter cannot be a mind reader about a baby's idiosyncrasies!). If the baby is suffering from any minor ailment, inform the sitter, so she won't be unduly alarmed. If the children are used to a night light in the room when they go to sleep, write it down—even things such as how high to raise the window in the bedroom or how to raise or lower the crib rails. Good communication means the sitter will do a good job for you. Type your instructions and post them on a bulletin board (they may be used for any sitter any time).

Be sure to have on that bulletin board a list of all emergency numbers, such as the pediatrician's office and home emergency numbers, and the telephone of the nearby hospital that is used by the pediatrician. The sitter should take the child there if there has been an accident and she cannot get the pediatrician on the telephone immediately. The smart parent explains emergency procedures in detail.

"Look, this is not going to happen. But let's say it does. Let's say Johnny burns himself with matches. You call the pediatrician at once, not us; but his answering service might say it will take a while to contact him. Tell the answering service that Johnny Lewis has burned himself and that you are taking him to the Emergency Clinic of the Lenox Hill Hospital. The service will locate the pediatrician. Then call us. We'll leave at once for the hospital from our party, but you must go direct, by taxi, because time can't be wasted. If the Stevensons (our neighbors) are home, they'll provide transportation. Remember, if the Stevensons aren't home, report an emergency to the cab company, and if they can't send a cab immediately, call the police."

It sounds like a fairy tale, but I know of too many cases where parents have told a baby-sitter exactly what to do, and it has saved lives—maybe not on that job, maybe on another sitting job—because that young person had been taught how to react calmly in an emergency.

One must always tell a sitter what to do in case of fire in one's home, too. Make sure she knows all the exits (and fire stairway if the home is in an apartment building).

If the sitter is to serve the children's dinner you prepared earlier, leave out the heating or serving dishes on the kitchen table or counters. Be sure she knows the menu.

Leave specific written instructions on homework, lights-out time, how much TV and what can be viewed, and so on. If the child is a baby, leave out its nightgown—don't expect the sitter to know the drawers well enough to find any of the proper garments.

And, of course, leave the telephone number and the name of the people at whose home you will be. If you are going to be at a stadium watching a football game, for example, leave instructions about the number to call and how to have you paged.

Giving the Sitter Proper Working Conditions Don't expect the sitter to do housework and cleanup work for you, unless it is specifically understood between you that that will be part of her labors. Perhaps you wish to pay her a higher fee per hour to have her do some additional housework when the children are asleep.

You should have something for her to eat and drink, if it is a mealtime job or if you will be gone a long time. Be sure to tell her what it is she can take, so she won't be consuming the children's lunch for the next day, or one of the four lemon mousses you prepared for tomorrow's bridge foursome.

Tell her she may use the TV, but lay down the law: "Don't play it so loudly you can't hear Jane's coughing spasms."

If she asks if she can "have her boy friend over" to do homework together, be firm with your negative if you do not want her to. She has no right to ask, because she has a job to do from which she should not be distracted. However, if you know her well, and her young man, too, and you have no objections, then you might grant permission. You are not expected to provide food for him, nor may he under *any* circumstances help himself to your liquor supply.

Payment to baby-sitters is by the hour, by the day, or perhaps by a flat fee for a weekend of work. If you are coming back later than you said you would, you should call her to warn her you will be late, and pay her for all extra time beyond your original understanding.

A proper relationship between sitter and parent is a two-way street of efficiency and consideration for each other.

A Routine for Managing Your Household

I know many women who can afford full-time help who forgo it in these days of high wages and often quite inferior performance. They have faced the fact that the whole domestic employment situation has changed because the live-in worker is rare. Daily workers, instead, work in four- or eight-hour shifts, where full staffing is maintained. Outside professional cleaning services with bonded workers are the answer for many households, but no one is going to clean your home the way you can—for the simple reason that you probably *care*.

With such electric equipment as dishwashers, automatic washing machines, power vacuums, home freezers, electric waxers, and modern clock-watching stoves, with easy-care fabrics, and no-iron bed linen, an intelligent, organized person can do the work of even a fairly large household quite quickly and efficiently—just as long as there's no power blackout!

Every household has its own specific requirements and thus its own schedule; but unless some daily plan is followed, good housekeeping is almost impossible. The well-organized person at home, male or female, has a distinct advantage over the unorganized. The former spends much less time running the home, so that getting organized is well worth whatever investment in time and trouble.

Anything that helps avoid the morning rush is advisable. It is important for everyone to start the day without hurry and tension. It may seem like extra effort at the end of a long day, but it really does help if the breakfast table is set the night before and the next day's menus decided upon, so that, in the sleepy early morning, preparation of the breakfast and the children's school lunches can be more or less automatic. Most important is to avoid the last-minute search for mittens, schoolbooks, rubbers, Mother's briefcase, or Father's keys. These articles can be assembled the night before, or at least their whereabouts checked upon. Of course, they should all have their special places, but it is certainly not a good idea to count on everything being where it should be. Despite your best efforts, it takes years of training to get children (and adults, too) to "put things back."

Cleaning Routine Many people today do their general house cleaning on weekends if husband and wife both work. As the kitchen is the heart of the house, it should never be left untidy while other chores get prior attention in the morning. The best plan is to finish the kitchen first, then proceed to bedmaking, if it is not possible for each member of the family to air and straighten his own room and make his bed before reporting to breakfast.

After beds are made and bedrooms tidied, bathrooms should be cleaned and put in order, then the living room tidied (if this was not done the night before—and certainly the family should help). Now, with everything in order, dishes washed, and beds made, dusting and floors come last. The objective is, of course, to set the entire house to rights as soon as possible, so that if further housework must be abandoned for the day, as so often happens, or unexpected visitors arrive, there is at least order, if not perfect cleanliness.

When all the work is done by a woman at home, one room each day or at least once a week should be chosen for thorough cleaning. The room chosen should be disassembled as much as is practicable. Furniture should be pulled away from the walls, scatter rugs or carpets rolled up, ornaments removed from shelves, pictures taken down, draperies folded back.

All walls and woodwork should be cleaned first. Modern vacuum attachments are good at getting at dusty surfaces, cornices, cobwebs in corners or on the ceiling. Everything washable should be washed as time allows—window sills, shelves, even furniture finishes benefit from careful going-over with a clean, soapy, not-too-wet cloth or nylon sponge occasionally, followed by thorough drying and waxing. Since all dirt falls onto the floor as one proceeds, the floor is done last, whether washed, waxed, or vacuumed. Floors to be swept are done before the dusting, obviously. Whether the floor is to be washed depends on its surfacing, but waxed wooden floors respond well to an occasional thorough cleaning with one of the modern cleaning waxes or a solvent such as turpentine (after sweeping). The waxer is used only after the freshly applied wax is quite dry. Old wax should be removed from time to time anyhow, even from linoleum or vinyl tile, either with soap and water, a detergent, or a recommended liquid cleaner. (Windows should be open if the mixture is combustible!) In corners and inaccessible spots the floor should be lightly scraped with a paint scraper, steel wool, or a dull knife.

When the cleaning is finished, the room should be put in perfect order, not left for later reassembling. Too often schedules can't be completely adhered to in busy households, and it is dismaying to think of cleaning things to be put away, pictures to be rehung, and rugs to be relaid at the end of a long day.

Basic Information: Making the Bed Some basic information might be useful on household tasks that face us every day: for example, making the bed.

Any man with military training knows how to miter sheets, even if he pretends to have forgotten. There are people who loathe having their sheets tucked in and prefer to tear apart any bed so made before trying to settle down for the night. But for the most part, sheets mitered at the corners, all the way around for the bottom sheet if it's big enough, and at the bottom of the top sheet make the best-made bed. The easiest sheet to cover the mattress is, of course, a fitted one. If, however, you have only flat ones, look at the hems of a sheet before putting it on. The bottom sheet should be placed with the hemmed side next to the mattress. The top sheet should be the reverse, so that when the top of the sheet is folded over the blankets—to keep them from scratching, of course—the patterned or smooth side of the sheet will show. Your hostess will grit her teeth if you make up a bed with a designer sheet and turn down the sheet so the pattern is on the wrong side—now, what's the use of a colorful design that can't be seen in all its glory?

Pillows should be placed so that the hems of the slips are on the outside. To make a bolsterlike effect with the pillows, push them tightly against the headboard, put the bedspread on the bed, turn down a top fold just at the edge of the pillows, tuck this folded edge under the tightly placed pillows, then fold the edge of the spread back over them, tucking the fold in to give an unwrinkled appearance. The bedspread should hang evenly on the sides and on a bed without a footboard is usually best left hanging loose to cover the springs. The quilt, if any, is either put away for the day or folded attractively at the foot of the bed. Don't ever put a quilt under the bedspread—that gives a lumpy, unmade look to the bed.

Center top sheet lengthwise. Allow for folding back over blanket. Leave loose at foot. Place blankets on bed lengthwise at shoulder height. Allow blankets to hang over foot of bed. Provide toe space by making a box pleat at foot of bed, upper sheet and blankets together. Tuck sheet and blankets loosely under mattress at foot of bed. Retain pleat. Then add blanket cover, if desired, and finally the pillow and spread.

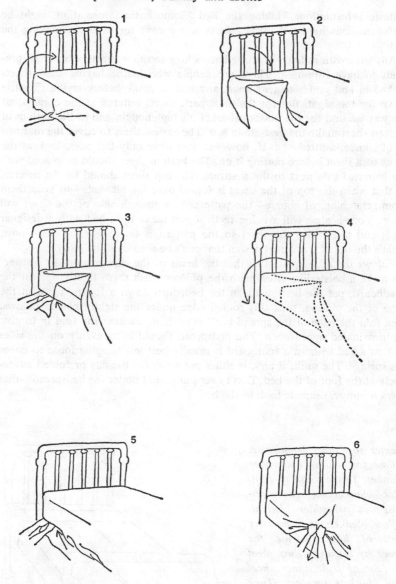

MAKING A BED, PLACING A BOTTOM SHEET THAT IS NOT FITTED. *1. Grasp sheet as shown, raise. 2. Let fall on top of mattress. 3. Tuck in hanging part of sheet smoothly. 4. Drop corner of sheet. 5. Tuck under, being sure to catch fold coming down over head of mattress. 6. With fists uppermost, hands together, pull diagonally and tuck under, holding on to roll as far as it will go. Repeat this along entire length of bed.*

Washing Dishes   The onus was taken off dishwashing by the electric dishwasher. Scrape the plate scraps into a garbage can or automatic disposal unit or onto several folds of newspaper (which you later roll up and discard). Save all food from the serving plates, putting it whenever possible into covered refrigerator dishes. Don't store it on the plate in which it was served unless the dish is plastic, Pyrex, or pottery, and then only if there is enough food left over to make the use of so much storage space sensible. Save leftovers from butter plates for cooking use. Clean bits of butter can go in a refrigerator dish or in a piece of wax paper. The smart dishwasher operator rinses everything well before putting it into the machine. Stubborn egg spots and lipstick marks on glasses should be removed by hand before the items are put into the machine.

Hand-washing Dishes   For the much disliked hand dishwashing there is only one correct, really sanitary method. If you have only one sink to work with, rinse each dish in running hot water, then stack before beginning the real washing. Remove any garbage from the sink, and clean the porcelain if it has absorbed grease from the rinsing. Now run in the hottest water your hands can stand (rubber gloves are a good idea) with enough soap powder or detergent to do a good cleaning job. Never put pots, pans, glasses, silver, and dishes in together! Do the dishes first, rinsing each as it emerges. Place them in the dish rack to dry by themselves or pour scalding water over the washed but unrinsed dishes once they have been stacked in the dish rack. This is really more sanitary than towel drying, according to the American Medical Association, in case anyone objects. You will need to dry the silver well, otherwise it will spot or rust.

Unless there is some limitation on the hot water—and if it is heated by a separate heating unit there may be—wash the glassware in fresh, clean hot water with a good detergent, then rinse in hot water. Washing it in with the dishes will often streak glassware, and no amount of rubbing with the towel will improve the situation. Let it dry itself. This prevents lint sticking to the glass. To test your efficiency, hold the glass up to the light. Be particularly careful to remove any lipstick from the rims. If you are working with hard water it may be particularly difficult to produce sparkling glassware. A bit of automatic dishwater detergent—or ammonia—my aid you in your hand-washing.

The greasy pots and pans are the worst of the operation. Pots are washed last, first rinsed of any food that may be sticking to them. They should be scoured inside and out wherever necessary. A good dishwasher leaves the bottom of the pot as shining as its sides. Pots should be rinsed and dried, with paper toweling, not with the best glass toweling. They should be put away, if possible, nesting if they are meant to nest.

The dish towel should be placed over the draining dishes, when you have finished, to keep dust from settling on them. In putting away kitchen cutlery, be sure it's perfectly dry or it will spot or rust. Leave the kitchen like the laboratory it should be—garbage disposed of, drawers and cupboards closed, dishcloth hung on a rack or neatly folded over the sink, broiler pan back in the oven, all counters wiped up (with the dishcloth or a sponge, not the dish towel!), the stove shining and with all the burners turned off. A really good housekeeper sweeps the kitchen floor after each main meal to repel rodents or bugs and just to be neat and clean. Sweepings should go into the trash can, not out the window or into the yard.

Laundry   It takes approximately twenty-five minutes for one load of wash to run through an automatic washer. Be sure, however, that you read the labels of all new purchases for proper washing instructions. Various fabrics require different lengths of time for washing. And if laundry is done at home, it is easier to do some laundry each day than to allow it to collect so that a whole morning must be devoted to the laundry project. If there is no dryer and there are hanging facilities in the cellar or elsewhere, it is not necessary to wait for sunshine. Where much laundry is done at home, however, an electric or gas clothes dryer is a virtual necessity in many households, at least for winter weather in the North.

In a large household with little or no help, ironing tends to collect, so easy-care fabrics, especially in children's wear and underclothes, have become increasingly necessary.

Daily sorting of laundry is another timesaver. This means that as the soiled laundry goes to the laundry area it is immediately put in separate hampers. Hampers are labeled "Woolens," "Lingerie," "White," "Colored," "Baby," and so on, according to requirements. First chore of the morning, after breakfast is over, is to load and start the washing machine. If it is loaded the night before, it can be started before breakfast so that clothes to be sun-dried—weather permitting—can be put out early.

Division of Household Tasks   The woman who stays at home is the traditional keeper of the house, with her husband and children helping her as much as their schedules permit. Today it is sometimes the man who stays at home (an artist or a writer, perhaps) while his wife goes off to an office all day. The roles reverse here, and he should assume the management of the home, with his wife and children helping him, whenever possible, and with the family working as a group on weekends to keep the home clean and well maintained.

When both husband and wife work, the division of labor quite logically splits into who does what best. Sometimes the man is a better cook than his wife; sometimes she is a better cleaner than he. He may enjoy cleaning the kitchen but despise cleaning the bathrooms; she may enjoy cooking but adamantly dislike cleaning up afterward. Somehow, in a good marriage, the division of labor is made on an equitable basis, so that cleaning, marketing, cooking, and maintenance chores are divided efficiently.

One has not fulfilled one's parental responsibilities if one has not taught the children—boys as well as girls—how to become good housekeepers. Any child who grows up without having had to master any of the daily tasks of living will have a difficult time at college and in marriage.

It is a happy development that work in the home is no longer classified as "woman's work" or work that is sissified for a man to do. The objective for everyone should be to get the work done, as easily and as quickly as possible. One of the things I wish I had learned as a girl was how to be an electrician and a plumber, too. It would have saved me a fortune through the years.

Part Two

CEREMONIES OF LIFE

Christenings and Confirmations 105

Graduations and Debuts 115

Engagements 121

Wedding Invitations and Announcements 132

Wedding Gifts 163

Today's Trousseau 169

Preparations for the Wedding 179

The Wedding Attendants and Their Duties 187

Pre-wedding Parties 195

Dress for the Wedding 200

The Rehearsal 212

The Wedding Ceremony 217

The Wedding Reception 238

Second and Subsequent Marriages 251

After the Wedding 259

Wedding Anniversaries 262

Funerals 266

Ritual is as old as civilization itself. It began when people, fearing the unknown, tried to cope with the reality around them and at the same time to appease some mysterious force far more powerful than themselves.

Today's rituals revolve around essentially the same important phases of life that were meaningful in ancient times: birth, puberty, marriage, and death. Many of the essentials of the ancient ceremonies, like feasting and presenting gifts, are just as basic to today's ceremonies of life as they were in earlier times, but all have been molded and shaped by the evolution of civilizations. The importance of knowing what actually occurs at any ceremony of life, knowing how to act and how to cope gracefully with the unexpected, is nothing new. Traditional ceremony is also a protection for us, particularly in times of emotional involvement such as death. We handle such situations far better if there is a customary framework within which we can act.

The mother of the bride in Gary, Indiana, goes through the same nervous tensions over her daughter's wedding that the Egyptian mother of the bride did in Pharaoh's court. And the guest at the wedding who blunders is as embarrassed in any country, in any century. "To do the right thing" must be an eternal longing for mankind.

Chapter 8

CHRISTENINGS AND CONFIRMATIONS

The Birth of a Baby

Baby Shower When news of the expected baby is known, someone may offer to give you a baby shower. Although this type of shower is held less often than it used to be, it is a delightful custom. There should be only one baby shower, not several, and it should not be scheduled until one month before the expected delivery date. The reasons for this are logical and humane, since miscarriages are rare toward the end of pregnancy. Some women are superstitious and won't allow a baby shower to be given for them until after the baby is born and home from the hospital.

Traditionally, the baby shower was held for close female friends and relatives at lunch or during the afternoon on a weekday. When the shower was held midafternoon, tea food was served. Since so many women work today, more and more showers are held on weekends. Of course, if the shower is given for a mother-to-be by her friends at her place of business, it is usually given at lunchtime, and often on her last day of work.

We are seeing the same thing happening to baby showers that has been happening to bridal showers. They are held more often in the evening, at the cocktail hour, with both men and women guests. Couples bring joint gifts, which are usually not opened during the party to minimize the number of oohs and aahs from the women when the tiny booties and such emerge from the gift paper.

Baby showers are usually held only for the first baby, since subsequent children are the "beneficiaries" of the hand-me-downs.

If you are giving a baby shower for a friend, it is a good idea to organize what the guests should bring, so that the parents aren't left with fourteen baby bibs, sixteen rattles, and nothing else. Gifts do not need to be elaborate, but should be truly useful. (For specific suggestions, see page 766.) If the new parents are financially strapped, you might suggest that three or four individuals join together in purchasing expensive items, such as a "pram" that converts to a stroller, or a high chair. If you give a friend a nice baby shower present, you do not have to send another gift at the time of the baby's birth or christening.

If the tragedy of a stillborn baby or an early infant death should occur, the parents' natural reaction will be to return the shower gifts to their friends. The latter should vehemently resist such an action. The friend should say, "Don't send it back. That sweater will do for the next baby, who'll be along soon. Put it away—it's not going to go out of style." When a couple's friends act so affirmatively about the "next one coming along soon," it will make things wonderfully hopeful for them. And that, after all, is what friends are for.

Choosing Baby's Name   What's in a name? Everything. Usually, long before the baby is born, its name has been chosen, argued over, changed, argued over again, and finally agreed upon through compromise. There are certain things to remember about names—first, that naming a boy after his father or a girl after her mother is an honorable tradition. It is best, however, to decide on a nickname right then that differs from the parent's, so that there will be less confusion about the house. Giving the child a different middle name can help to avoid this problem, too.

Naming a child after a grandparent brings enormous pleasure to that grandparent, but it may also contribute to a little jealous friction with the other set of grandparents.

Giving a child a family name as a first name like Crawford, Cameron, Bryant is a nice tradition, but it is best not to give a girl too masculine a family name (Hamilton, for instance) or a boy too feminine a name.

Parents should think twice before giving their child a first name used by both men and women: Duane, Marion, Beverly, Evelyn, or Carol. The child is teased in his or her early years, and in adult life constantly has to prefix an explanatory "Mr.," "Ms.," or "Miss" to the signature.

It is nice to combine a long, complicated last name with a short first name. Or if your last name is a one-syllable common one, give your child a rather exotic first name with more than one syllable, such as Evangeline, Nathaniel, Jeremy, or Marika.

Be sure to check how the initials read when you have decided upon the first and middle names. Don't saddle the child with initials that read, for example, S.E.X,. L.S.D., or D.D.T.

Catholic children often receive multiple names, one of which is that of a saint, perhaps that of the saint on whose day they were born. These names are not always all utilized when the child grows up but they are officially his, even though he may use a shorter form of his name for legal and social purposes. Greek Orthodox children have just one given name. A Jewish child of traditional background is rarely given a "Jr.," "Second," or "Third" because it is not customary for Jews to be named for living people. If any meaningful name is used, it is usually that of someone recently dead, although biblical names are popular, too.

Choosing a child's first and middle name to go with your last name is an enjoyable project. It's fun to research the meaning of names and delve into great literature for good name suggestions.

Announcing the Birth of a Baby Close friends and relatives, of course, usually hear the happy news by telephone. All of one's friends, however, would like to hear of the event, so one should send some kind of announcement, even if it's a note dashed off by hand. One's wedding or Christmas card list is an easy place to find the names and addresses of people who would be interested in hearing about the new arrival.

One of the most traditional and formal baby announcements is the affixing of the baby's engraved card (by means of a pink or blue ribbon bow) to the parents' engraved informal. One can also write on the bottom the baby's weight and the name of the hospital where he or she was born—but only to someone who is close.

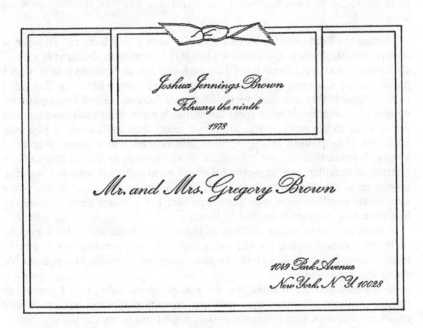

Joshua Jennings Brown
February the ninth
1978

Mr. and Mrs. Gregory Brown

1049 Park Avenue
New York, N.Y. 10028

There are other cards that can be ordered from the stationer's:

Mr. and Mrs. Garrett Eckerman
announce with double joy
the birth of their twin daughters
Annemarie and Denise
on the fourteenth of July, 19—

Many clever and amusing greeting cards are available in card shops ready to be filled in. Another popular custom is to have copies made of baby's first photo (the official hospital portrait made shortly after birth), and to incorporate the picture into a printed announcement card.

Those who receive announcement cards are not obliged to send a gift to the baby, but they should certainly send a note of congratulations or a Mailgram, or make a telephone call to rejoice in the good news.

And no matter how many children you may already have, each new arrival deserves an announcement by mail. Remember to put a copy of it in the baby book, too. How many of us today have a copy of our parents' announcement of our arrival? Very few, I would imagine, but how nice it would be to have it. Along with the newspaper announcement of that day's records of births, the announcement is the first time we see our name in print. In fact, it is a good idea for the proud parents to save the entire newspaper the day their child is born, to keep along with the baby book. Each of us is interested in knowing "what the world was like" on the day we were born.

Visiting the Baby   Going to visit a family with a tiny baby in residence is always a treat. There is something undeniably beautiful in the sight of one of God's marvelous creations, lying benignly (or not so benignly) in a sea of pastel coverlets, accepting the admiration of those around him. The first thing to remember is that you may very well startle him, so do not force yourself on him or take him suddenly from his mother's arms. Wait until the baby has gotten used to the sight of you and your voice; then ask quietly if you may hold him. If he protests in the slightest, give him back to someone whom he knows. It is not that you can't handle a baby, but that he is at a stage where a stranger handling him removes his sense of security. If you are wearing glasses or a hat, that may upset him, too. He may not react in the same manner to small children who approach him for the first time; perhaps he looks on them as friends instead of threats.

If there are other young siblings in the family, bring the baby a present with some remembrance for the other children, too, whether it's a box of sweets, some funny pencils from the dime store, or a puzzle. The reasons for doing this are obvious.

Be a smart consumer about the toy you bring the baby, too. I remember having to throw out more than half the presents that were brought to our children—the toys, that is—because they were frankly unsafe.

When the Baby Is Christened

Babies are baptized in the Protestant faith usually between two and six months of age, although in some faiths children are not baptized until they are eight or nine years old and can read the service with the member of clergy and be active participants in their own baptismal ceremony.

Catholic infants are baptized as soon as possible, usually from two to six weeks after birth, and earlier in some Mediterranean countries. When someone who is unbaptized converts to Catholicism, he goes through a baptism ceremony, too, under the supervision of two godparents he chooses himself.

Godparents and Their Responsibilities Catholic godparents must be of the Catholic religion. One may have co-godparents who are not. It is preferred but not mandatory in most Protestant denominations that the godparents be of the same faith in which the baby will be raised. Godparents are chosen from among close friends and relatives of the baby's parents. Traditionally, there are two godparents, one male and one female, although parents may ask another close friend, perhaps even of another religion, to serve as a kind of "honorary" one. It is a great honor to be asked to be a godparent, for it implies that you are an intimate friend of the baby's parents and that they hold you in high esteem and trust. The real responsibility of the godparent is to oversee the spiritual education of the child and to see that he is confirmed at the proper time. If one or both of the godparents cannot be present at the baptismal ceremony, the parents may choose proxy godparents to stand in for the missing ones at the ceremony.

It is nice if the godparents make a separate or a joint gift to the baby— perhaps a sterling silver engraved mug that will always remind the child as he grows toward adulthood of his godparents. The godparents should remember this child every Christmas (and at birthdays, too, if it is possible, until he is an adult). They should make him feel he always has a very special place in their hearts.

It used to be a tradition that, if both parents died, the godparents had the responsibility of taking care of their godchild. This is not the case today, however, for there is always a legally appointed guardian if such a tragedy occurs. When the child grows up, the godparent's duties cease to exist. The friendship between them should not, however.

Some people are asked to be godparents over and over again. They should not accept such responsibilities lightly. If they have three godchildren, perhaps they should tactfully turn down another one: "I do take the responsibilities seriously and feel I could not do your child justice, so please understand why I must say no."

Invitations to the Christening Party Invitations to a christening party are handled informally, usually by brief note, by telephone, by Mailgram, or in person. Only those really interested in the event through a very close friendship with the parents would be invited to the ceremony itself. A sample invitation:

Dear Abby,

Jessica is being christened this coming Sunday at St. George's Church at 1 P.M., after the twelve o'clock services. We're coming home afterward to drink a glass of champagne to her and have a little lunch. John and I hope you and Henry will join us.

Love,

If you plan to have a large cocktail reception after an afternoon christening, you should send printed invitations. Only the family and a coterie of very close friends would be invited to the ceremony itself.

Dressing the Baby for the Occasion   The long white lace-trimmed christening dress, puffing out over layers of long white organdy petticoats, exquisitely pleated, embroidered, and beribboned, is another of those lovely traditions that has all but disappeared. If you do not have access to one of the few remaining old ones, a lovely short all-white dress for the baby will do perfectly well. The baby can wear white booties to the church, or white silk shoes, or even white socks. If it's chilly, he should be brought to the church in his bonnet and coat; both of these will be removed before the ceremony. A Catholic child would wear his saint's medal pinned to his dress or on a chain around his neck, if he has already been given such a gold or silver medal. An older girl being christened would wear an all-white dress, and little boys would wear a dark blue jacket, white shirt, and dark blue or gray shorts.

The mother of the baby dresses as she would for church, in a nice dress (not black, however), and the father would wear a business suit.

Church Christenings   If the christening is to take place during a regular church service, arrangements must be made well in advance. As babies are not always too happy about this event, it is best to bring them to church just before the christening is to take place. The baby's outer wraps are removed; if the church is chilly, the baby should be wrapped in a white blanket and handed to its godmother. The godparents arrive with the family party or just in advance of it and take their places near the font. The other friends and relatives stand nearby. As the clergyman takes his place, the congregation stands. At a certain moment in the Protestant ceremony, the godmother hands the baby to the clergyman and, when asked the baby's name, pronounces it very carefully. Only baptismal names are given: for example, "Stephen John," not the surname. In the Catholic ceremony, the godmother holds the baby over the font to receive the holy water. If other than a godparent holds the baby, spiritual contact is established by the godparents as they touch the child during the ceremony. If the name is at all complicated, it should be written down for the minister and given to him just before the ceremony, for the baby's baptismal name pronounced during this ceremony legally becomes his name.

After the services the clergyman signs the baptismal certificate. It is a good idea for a Catholic to have several duplicate copies made and filed away in safe places, for the child will need his baptismal certificate later in order to receive Holy Communion, for confirmation, and in order to be married.

The Clergyman's Fee   As with other church sacraments, there is never any required fee. Parents usually give the clergyman an envelope containing an appropriate amount, anywhere from ten to fifty dollars. If there is a party afterward the officiating minister and his wife or the priest should certainly be invited.

The Christening at Home   Certain Protestant denominations permit home christenings; Catholics do not, except in case of dire emergency when the last rites are administered.

If the baby is christened at home, place flowers in a room large enough for assembled guests, and a small, waist-high table on which is set a silver bowl to be used as the font. The table, if it has a beautiful surface, may be left bare; otherwise, it should be covered to the floor with a formal cloth such as damask. It is nice to encircle the base of the silver bowl with tiny white fresh flowers. The clergyman is not necessarily in vestments in a home ceremony; but if he has to dress, he should be shown to a special room. He would change back again into his street clothes for the reception following the christening. The baby should not remain through the entire reception, for it will make him tired and fussy. Bring him back into the room once in a while for admiring glances, but don't expect him to enjoy—or to behave particularly well—at this, his first social occasion!

Refreshments After the Ceremony   A late morning christening is usually followed by a luncheon, often buffet. A late afternoon ceremony may be followed either by a formal tea or by a cocktail party. The food is more or less the kind served at wedding receptions, but an important ingredient of the party is a festive beverage with which to toast the baby's health: champagne, or a champagne punch, or even white wine. Either the godfather or the godmother should propose the first toast, and this is followed by toasts from the parents, guests, or even siblings, if they are present. Making a special fuss over children who are close to the baby in age is a thoughtful gesture. The nicest thing that happened at our son's christening was that an uncle of the baby noticed the two-year-old sister's nose was decidedly out of joint with all this attention being paid to her brother. So her uncle's first toast was to her, with the statement that her baby brother "couldn't go wrong having a terrific sister like that to teach him what it's all about."

There should always be a supply of soft drinks on hand at the christening party for the young children present, so that they can "toast" too.

It's nice to have a christening cake, white, with white icing, perhaps bearing the baby's initials and the christening date. Both parents cut the first piece together, reminiscent of their cutting the wedding cake. One of my favorite memories of a christening concerned a party where I saw a friend tucking a piece of christening cake into napkins, and then stowing it in her handbag. She saw me watching her and explained that if the old superstition held true about unmarried girls sleeping on wedding cake and dreaming that night of their intended, then she was going to sleep on the christening cake and dream that night about the baby she and her husband hoped to have.

(She had been married for nine years and had just about given up on having a baby.) Her baby was born nine months later.

The nicest thing about christening parties for some people is that they are healers of family rifts. Time and time again an estranged member of a family will accept a christening invitation when he or she would accept no other. There is something about a small baby that brings families together and heals all wounds.

First Communion

This is an event of great importance in a Catholic child's life. When he reaches seven or "the age of reason," usually in the second grade, he goes through a course of instruction in Catholic doctrine. Then his class makes its first Holy Communion together (either his entire class in a Catholic school, or his catechism class that he attends outside, if he goes to a non-Catholic school). Since this is such an important sacrament to the child, his close relatives should try to attend that mass, as should his godparents. If his godparents cannot be present, they should send him a gift or a card.

When it comes time to receive Holy Communion during this mass, the young children go up to the altar first, the adults afterward. Usually the homily given by the priest is directed to the young ones. Non-Catholics present are not supposed to join in with the other Catholic adults receiving Holy Communion with the children, because the Catholics make special preparations for their communion, which they hold to be the actual Body and Blood of Christ.

The little girls wear white dresses and veils; the little boys dark suits or white suits, according to the climate.

Usually a simple breakfast or luncheon is organized afterward by the children's mothers, and gifts are given to the children. Traditionally, these gifts all had to be religious in nature, like a sterling silver rosary (see page 768 on First Communion gifts), but today the children receive anything. The godparents, however, should give them something religious.

Confirmation

Confirmation, which means the day on which one is "confirmed" in one's faith, symbolizes in most churches the day when one officially becomes a member of the church congregation. Children are confirmed in the Catholic faith and in most Protestant denominations when they are in seventh or eighth grade. The Eastern Orthodox confirm a child at the same time he is baptized in infancy.

In both Catholic and Protestant practice, the restrictions on girls wearing all white at confirmation has relaxed. Now they may wear modest pastel dresses, even pastel prints, and the boys wear their best suits. It is a religious rather than a social occasion, so usually only one's family and godparents attend. It is a time when a godparent may rally around to take the child to a meal in a restaurant in celebration of the event, and there are some presents given (for suggestions, see page 769), but the event is otherwise celebrated quietly.

Jewish Traditions

Brith Milah   Jewish tradition has special celebrations related to the birth of a baby. A son, for example, is initiated into the Jewish covenant between God and man eight days after he is born, in the traditional Brith Milah ceremony. The boy is circumcised, given his name, and, like many Christian children, given godparents. This ceremony usually takes place at home or in a special room in the hospital. Guests gather and toast the baby and his relatives. Only close friends and relations are invited—by letter or by telephone. Guests wear the same clothes they would wear to the synagogue. A small party may be held afterward and often gifts are brought for the baby.

Girls receive their names in the synagogue on the first Sabbath after they are born. Their father is called up to the Torah (often the mother is present, too). He recites a little prayer at the altar and states his daughter's name, and the rabbi gives a special blessing. Close friends and relatives are invited to this service and to the reception following, hostessed by the baby's mother.

In Reform congregations, it is customary to offer a prayer and state the name of a child, whether male or female, at the earliest service of worship that both parents can attend after the child's birth. This is done regardless of whether the boy may have been officially named during the circumcision rite.

Confirmation in the Jewish Faith   In Reform synagogues, confirmation for boys and girls takes place at about the age of sixteen. Usually on the Feast of Weeks, Shavuoth (seven weeks after the second day of Passover), children attending Hebrew school are confirmed as a group in a solemn and meaningful ceremony. There are variations in Conservative congregations, according to the views of the individual rabbis; some confirm both boys and girls, and others Bar Mitzvah boys of thirteen and confirm girls only, at sixteen.

Bar and Bat Mitzvah   The "coming of age" for a Jewish boy of thirteen is a very important milestone in his life. The Bar Mitzvah is usually celebrated on the first Sabbath after he turns thirteen. He is expected to prepare conscientiously for this occasion, and from this day on he participates as an adult member of the congregation. Today we are seeing more and more girls of thirteen celebrating Bat Mitzvah, the ceremony corresponding to the Bar Mitzvah for boys. In most Conservative and Reform congregations, the Bat Mitzvah takes place on Sabbath eve. After the Sabbath worship service, the Bar or Bat Mitzvah child and the immediate family may gather in the social room of the synagogue to receive any members of the congregation who wish to congratulate them. This is often followed by a luncheon, dinner, or reception to which close friends and relatives are invited. "Black tie" is specified on the invitation if the afternoon or evening affair is to be formal; otherwise a dark business suit for a man and a dressy but modest dress for the woman are in order. The Bar Mitzvah boy or Bat Mitzvah girl dresses in clothes appropriate for the synagogue for the worship service, but may choose dressier clothing for the reception if it is formal.

A gift or check is presented to the young person from each family invited (for suggestions, see page 769). One can bring or send it; however, if the synagogue is Orthodox, the gift should be brought not to the ceremony but to the reception, which begins after the close of Sabbath; if no reception is held, the gift should be sent. The recipient should write thank-you notes promptly. Some of the most elegant dinner-dances given in America today, in hotels, clubs, or synagogue reception rooms, are Bar and Bat Mitzvah parties. The occasion is one for which parents save and is a time of great rejoicing for all generations of the child's family.

Chapter 9

GRADUATIONS AND DEBUTS

High School and College Graduation

High school and college graduations are taken very seriously in some communities, particularly small ones, and very casually in others. A high school graduation is a good reason for the parents to give their child a party, for example, but the parents should be observant and watchful that no liquor is served. Some of the guests will not have reached the legal drinking age, and others who have may not necessarily handle liquor properly.

Invitations or announcements may be sent for either high school or college graduations. One sends these only to close personal friends and relatives. Many educational institutions have nice ones already printed or engraved, which they distribute to the students in a limited number. The student has only to fill in his or her name or enclose a visiting card and mail them. The recipient is not obliged to send a gift to the graduate; however, if he is particularly close to the person or his family, he probably will. One should give the college-bound high school graduate something useful to take to college (for suggestions, see page 770), and the college graduate something he can use in his apartment as he begins life either working or in graduate school. Students should send thank-you notes promptly for these gifts.

College graduations are often held the same weekend as Alumni Day. Since the campus is so crowded, the student should reserve rooms for his family well ahead of time. Graduation weekend is a signal for a very full schedule of activities on many campuses; family visitors should therefore ask exactly what the schedule will be, so they can properly pack for anything from a dance requiring evening clothes to a father-daughter tennis tournament or a baseball game.

If a graduate invites a date as well as family members, the date should remain with the family and be included in all activities. (The senior class dance is usually attended by graduates and their dates only.)

Parents afflicted with "cameraitis" can upset the enjoyment of others at the graduation ceremonies. Some seem to spend their entire time in the aisle, buzzing away with movie cameras and candid cameras, distracting from the speeches and from the dignified look of the ceremonies.

Debutantes

A debutante traditionally signified a young woman who at eighteen or nineteen was ready to make her debut into society, and to put herself firmly on the marriage market. It was an open announcement to the world that these "jeunes filles de bonne famille" were ready to be courted. By the 1960s, however, "coming out" had lost its luster, in the wake of flower children and anti-Vietnam War feeling among the young. Many young women who would have been America's leading debutantes refused to have anything to do with it.

Now, in the late 1970s, debuts are enjoying an upswing in popularity once again. But it's a new young woman who is making her debut. She's still eighteen or nineteen, but she arranges her party scheduling around her scholastic commitments. She often makes her debut along with several other young women at a "mass ball," which is frequently sponsored by a local charity to which her family gives a large contribution. Perhaps her parents will give a joint dinner with the parents of two or threee other debutantes beforehand, but the lavish party given for one girl has all but disapppeared. If someone gives a party for a deb, the invitation reads "A Small Dance," and not "A Debutante Ball," or it can merely state there will be dancing.

The debutante season is during Thanksgiving and Christmas holidays—obviously to coincide with school vacation schedules. Some private parties are, however, given for the debutante the summer before her big season.

Invitations   The invitations to these summer parties may be engraved or they may be informal printed ones, such as:

In honour of
Alice Susan Einstadt
Mr. and Mrs. Robert Bain Einstadt
cordially invite you to
Dinner and a Square Dance
Saturday, the nineteenth of August
Eight o'clock until any time
The Bryant Barn on Round Hill Road

R.S.V.P.   Dress: Absolutely Anything
1320 Cranbrook Road

For private parties at the holiday season more formal, engraved invitations would be appropriate:

Mrs. Louis Warner
requests the pleasure
of your company
at dinner
in honour of her nieces
Miss Julie Warner
Miss Maria Warner
on Friday, the twenty-second of December
at seven o'clock
Bellevue
1000 North Ocean Boulevard
Palm Beach

R.S.V.P.   Dancing

Group Debuts Most of the famous debutante balls around the country where several girls come out at the same time have been in existence for many years. The Passavant Cotillion in Chicago; the Cotillion in Boston; the Junior Assemblies in New York; the Delta Debutante Ball in Greenville, Mississippi; the Harvest Ball at the Piedmont Driving Club in Atlanta; the Beaux Arts Ball in Oklahoma City; the Fiesta Ball in San Antonio, the Idlewild Ball in Dallas, and the Ak-Sar-Ben Ball in Omaha are examples of such long-established cotillions.

In many cities, it is necessary for a mother to apply several years ahead to have her daughter become eligible for the list of debutantes. At the proper time after the committee has made its selection and notifies the young women, the debutantes-to-be send in a list of their male escorts to the committee. The latter takes the responsibility for sending out invitations to the young men. The girls and their families are expected to pay for all the expenses of their escorts' tickets, however. If a young man who is new in town wishes to be on the list of extra men for the group debutante parties, he may write a letter to the head of the debutante committee. If there is room and someone on the committee recommends him, he will be invited.

Today, along with the well-established debutante presentations, there is a wide variety of presentations around the country made possible through one's church, civic association, or social club. In many urban areas, blacks have established their own debutante cotillions, too, a reflection of the growing black society.

Even with joint parties, coming out still costs the parents a substantial sum, because of expenditures for two or three evening dresses, accessories, and party costs, including flowers, invitations (and food, wine, liquor, and music if there is any kind of private party given before the main ball). To some fathers, having a debutante daughter is a status symbol of which they can be proud in their business community; to some wives, it is a necessary proof that they are socially acceptable in their communities. To most of the debutantes themselves, coming out is merely a lot of fun, a period of great gaiety and an active social life, an opportunity to meet lots of men, and a time of their lives to remember forever.

Attire   The young woman for whom her parents held a country dance in August may wear a country gingham skirt that night, but, like the other debutantes, on her presentation night at Thanksgiving or at Christmastime she will wear the prettiest white dress she can find, with long gloves. If she attends other dances connected with the debutante season, she will probably have one or two other evening dresses in her wardrobe, not white (but not black, either).

The man who presents her (usually her father, but if he is not there that night, then her grandfather, uncle, or older brother) wears white tie and tails. He also wears white kid or bleached chamois gloves. Her escorts should be in white tie and tails, too, but many young men have no access to such attire today. In this case, they come in black tie (but in a black dinner jacket, not a colored one, and in a plain white evening shirt).

Flowers for the Debutante   If the debutante is being entertained in the home of her parents, her grandparents, or another relative or friend, it is a nice gesture for the parents' friends to send the young woman flowers on the morning of or the evening before the party. At these private parties all flower arrangements are usually "banked" behind the place where the debutante will stand in a receiving line. The cards are, of course, removed, with names and addresses of donors carefully noted for later thank-you notes from the debutante. In some cities like Dallas, it is customary to inundate a debutante with flowers, both at her home and at the place of her private party.

Corsages have grown out of fashion with many debutantes, but on her "big night" her escort should ask if she wants a corsage, and act accordingly. Sometimes the girls are supplied with a uniform bouquet of flowers to hold, in which case a corsage would definitely be superfluous. An escort can send flowers to the debutante or her mother at her home before the party or mass debut, or he can send flowers to them after the party.

The nicest flower gift I have heard of was made to a debutante by a favorite uncle. The year she came out, he left a small, standing order at the local florist in her college town. Every week, a few fresh flowers would arrive in her dorm suite; her uncle knew she would never appreciate all the flowers sent the week of her big party, but he knew that this gesture would help keep him positioned as her "favorite uncle." (For additional gift ideas, see page 771.)

Debutante Teas   In some parts of the South the "debutante tea" is still given, usually by the debutante's mother, grandmother, or aunt. Only women are invited, usually of the parents' generation and older. The debutante invites some of her friends to assist her, and they all wear long pastel dresses. The debutante stands in a receiving line with her mother or whichever female relative is giving the party.

A more usual debutante tea today is the tea-dance, with young men invited. The tea table, therefore, makes way for a bar. If the debutante has her tea dansant in a club or a hotel, waiters pass glasses of champagne or cocktails. There may also be a punch table set up.

The receiving line for this party is once again the debutante and her mother or whoever is hosting the party. Sometimes her father stands in line for a short time at the beginning, but generally he circulates around to make sure everyone is having a good time. The honoree holds her father's bouquet; she wears a white or a pastel bouffant dress; she may wear long white gloves and a flower in her hair.

The debutante invites more men than young women to this party. She asks some of her best friends to "assist" her, but they do not have to stand in the receiving line or do anything except have a good time on the dance floor. After all the guests have passed through the receiving line, the debutante joins the dancing—the first dance, of course, goes to her father. Every young man present should ask her to dance before the evening is over; her mother should also be asked (or "cut in on"). Usually a deb's brothers, cousins, and uncles cut in on her while she's dancing with her father, and then it's up to the other young men to keep her dancing her feet off all night.

Small Private Dance   If the debutante is honored at a small private dance given for her in someone's home, she stands in a receiving line for at least an hour with her mother, or grandmother, or whoever is giving the party. If there is a long queue waiting to go through the receiving line, everyone should move through it quickly, giving just his or her name and smilingly passing on. "Good evening, Mrs. Jenkins, I'm Sally Poirot, one of Sarah's classmates at college." One can stop and chat for a while with the debutante if no one is going through the receiving line at that moment.

The father remains nearby during this receiving line, helping greet and taking care of those friends who arrive late. When the debutante leaves the receiving line, he escorts her to the room where there's dancing and dances the first dance with her. (Usually people smilingly applaud around the dance floor when this takes place.) Afterward the young men take over the honor of keeping her dancing. Her father then dances with his wife, other female members of the family, and finally anyone he would really like to!

Responsibilities of the Male Escorts of the Debutante   The debutante usually has two or three escorts at her own party. One of these might be an older brother. Their only real function is to get her to the events on time and see to it that she is danced off her feet and has a glorious time.

The escort does not have to pay for his ball ticket, which sometimes includes dinner. (If it does not include dinner, he will be invited to another dinner party before the dance.) He may have to pay for taxis, if he does not have a car.

He may be called upon to pay for drinks at a mass debut if the bar is not an open bar, with drinks on the house, so he should be prepared. Most debutantes' fathers, if the bar is not open, slip money to the male escorts to pay for these drinks.

An escort may feel like organizing a group to go on afterward to a night club or a breakfast place, so he should have money on his person for such emergencies. This is one night the debutante should not be made to go dutch treat.

Bad Manners at Debutante Parties   It is lamentable that a major report on the changes in the debutante world over the past thirty years shows a decline in the manners of the young men invited to these parties, whether they are invited as escorts or simply as guests. A majority of them do not bother to reply to their invitations; others show up uninvited at the parties, feeling it is their right and privilege to attend if some of their friends were invited. As a result, often the debutantes and their mothers do not really know who is coming to their party until they walk in the door.

Every invitation to a meal or to a dance requires a prompt response. Only parents can teach their children this fact of life, and it should be taught to a young man before he goes off to college and to debutante parties. The almost universal lack of response from college-aged men to invitations creates a nerve-racking situation for those giving the party. They don't know what to tell the kitchen; they don't know how many tables to set up; they don't know if there will be enough men to dance with the girls who have accepted. An expensive party can become a shambles under such circumstances.

One exasperated mother sent a Mailgram to each of the four men on her daughter's list of personal escorts to her debut dinner-dance, none of whom had replied one week before the party:

> Since you have been discourteous enough to reply neither to our engraved invitations, nor to our follow-up mailing, nor to our telephone messages, you are being disinvited from this party.

The debutante was mortified over her mother's action, but it worked. All four men immediately called on the telephone to accept and to offer their apologies. After the party each of the four sent flowers and wrote a thank-you note to the mother. They obviously knew they should have sent an R.S.V.P. They had just been too lazy to make this simple gesture. No doubt they now reply very promptly to all invitations.

Chapter 10

ENGAGEMENTS

Telling the Family

When a couple decide to marry, they should naturally first inform both sets of parents and stepparents (if there are any) before having a party planned or telling all their friends. If either the bride-to-be or groom-to-be has not met the other's parents, a visit should be made to the parents before the news officially breaks. It is inconsiderate to one's parents if they have to say to their friends, "Yes, we're very happy over the news, of course. We haven't met her yet, but we're sure she's lovely." A short visit is all that's necessary, even if the parents are far away. (One can always save the money by giving up other things.)

The days are long gone of the young man going trembling into the presence of the girl's father and saying, "Sir, may I have the honor of the hand of your daughter in matrimony?" However, a wise couple will always discuss their plans for marriage with their respective families, and a young man should suggest a "financial talk" with his future father-in-law before the latter is faced with the embarrassment of asking him for one. Even if a young woman has supported herself and lives away from home, her parents have the right to know just how her fiancé proposes to handle the long-range financing of their family and home. There might be years during which she is bearing and raising young children when she cannot work and will be unable to contribute financially. There should be plans made for such events. The fiancé should state his income, his savings, and his future expectations, without exaggerating any of them.

Many a young pair vastly overestimates their ability to get along on the income available to them once they leave their parents' homes and begin a new family. A businesslike talk with the bride's father or the groom's father can help start a young marriage along the right path, particularly if the couple are still in school and frankly dependent on one or both families for support. If, for example, the bride's father knows that his daughter's fiancé has only five hundred dollars in the bank, he may be able to augment that amount with a nice cash gift in lieu of an elaborate wedding. Or he might plan a very practical present, such as the rent for the first year on their apartment.

It is good insurance for the success of a marriage to start it on a sound, even if modest, financial footing. It is better to be practical if your budget is small. Tell your friends what you really need in the way of wedding presents, if they ask; sign up intelligently in the bridal registry of your store or stores. Don't encourage people to give fads and fripperies for wedding presents when you need a toaster and a vacuum cleaner.

Traditionally it is the bride's family that is responsible for the major cost of the wedding and reception. It is essential before making any wedding plans to know what kind of wedding is desired and what, if any, expenses will be borne by the groom's family. If the groom's family is wealthy and the bride's is not, then his family should be gracious enough to offer to pay for the wedding.

Engagement Parties

Engagement parties are given by the parents of the bride-to-be or by a relative of the bride acting for her parents, usually just before the newspaper announcement of the engagement. If the bride-to-be and her fiancé live in a city other than her parents', it is probably better for her parents to come to her city than for her to go home to them for the engagement party. She and her fiancé will, after all, be partied in her parents' home town during the wedding festivities. However, if the family home is not far away, it is proper for the engaged couple to travel there for the announcement party. The young man's family should be invited, too. If the bride's parents are no longer living, then a relative or a close friend can give the party. It is usually a simple cocktail party, with champagne served for toasts to the engaged couple. If the hosts do not serve alcohol in their home, a fruit punch is proper.

Since the announcement is usually meant to be a surprise, invitations should not give away the secret. If the groom is a stranger to the community, the invitation may read on the top "To meet Mr. Richard Hoffman." The occasion offers a host and hostess many possibilities for clever and creative ways to make the announcement, once all the guests are assembled. I remember one party where no one knew the secret until slides of both the man and the woman were suddenly flashed on two screens—slides of them as babies taking their first steps. Nice mementos of the party can be given as favors—match covers with the couple's initials and the date of the announcement, copies of poems dedicated to them, and so forth. This type of party can be held at home, or a club, or in a private room of a hotel.

If the party is essentially a family reunion dinner, the father of the young woman can rise and say, "This is such a happy occasion for my wife and me. We wish to announce the engagement of our daughter, Lucinda, to the nicest young man in an entire generation, Robert McIntyre." If a minister, a priest, or a rabbi is present, he should rise next to bless the couple.

If the party is very large, the engaged couple and the girl's parents might form a receiving line—but they do not have to. The bride-to-be usually wears her engagement ring officially for the first time on this occasion. If she has a gift for the groom-to-be, she gives it to him right before or after the engagement party.

Announcing the Engagement in the Newspapers

To ensure that an announcement sent to the local newspaper is published accurately, it is best to type it as you would like it to appear. Here is a typical engagement announcement:

CYNTHIA ANN RIVKIN
TO WED LAWRENCE C. DEVOE

Mr. and Mrs. Richard Rivkin of Eastfield Road announce the engagement of their daughter, Cynthia Ann, to Lawrence C. DeVoe, also of Waterbury. The couple will be married January 21.

Miss Rivkin was graduated from Kennedy High School and from the University of Connecticut with a B.A. in French. She is a French teacher at the Sacred Heart High School.

Mr. DeVoe, son of Mr. and Mrs. Stuart DeVoe, was graduated from the Taft School in Watertown and from the College of Wooster in Ohio. He is an executive with the Scovill Company.

In this example, Eastfield Road is in Waterbury, so it is not necessary to mention the town in which the newspaper is published. Some society editors have a form asking for the appropriate information that can be used.

If the time of the wedding is within one to three months of the engagement, the month the wedding will take place is mentioned. Otherwise the announcement should read: "No date has been set for the wedding."

Engagement Announcement of Prominent Families If an engagement is between very prominent people in a community the announcement may carry all the family information about the couple. If you think the papers are going to run a full story on your engagement, arrange to have them furnished with the proper facts. Send in the full report on your background, that of your fiancé, and that of any celebrity in the family. ("Dr. Hutchins is the grandson of the former Governor of Texas, John Hooper.")

If a woman is announcing her engagement for a second marriage, she does not send in an announcement to the newspaper unless she is very prominent in that city, in which case it becomes a news event.

When Should the Release Date Be? The newspaper announcement of your engagement should appear the day after your engagement party. To be most effective, this requires giving the announcement to the society editor of your local paper or papers (if there is more than one) anywhere from one to four weeks in advance. Check with the society editor about the lead time needed. If your engagement party is Monday night, February 5, put "HOLD FOR RELEASE UNTIL TUESDAY, FEBRUARY 6" in the upper left-hand corner of the typed release. Be sure to include the name, address, and telephone number of your mother, or some close relative, or a secretary of your parents in the upper right-hand corner of the release, so the editor will know whom to contact if she is in need of further information or verification.

Accompanying the Release with a Photograph   Almost every engaged girl enjoys seeing her photograph in the newspaper when the big news is announced. (Her fiancé's photograph will not be included at this time; it may be included in the wedding announcement, however.) A posed studio portrait (black and white, glossy, $8'' \times 10''$) is best. Head shots are preferred by most editors. Type a photo caption on a piece of paper, and tape it to the back of the photo. Include the engaged girl's name and the name of her fiancé in the photo caption; then send the photograph to the society editor in a photo mailer with a stiffener to protect it, along with your typed release.

When an Engagement Is Not Announced

You can't be engaged while you're married to someone else. If you are in the middle of divorce or annulment proceedings, it would be very bad taste to announce your engagement to the person you plan to marry, or wear his ring, until the legal proceedings on the former marriage are finished.

Complicated Relationships

Deceased Parent or Parents   If both parents of the bride are deceased, the engagement may be announced by a close relative, a guardian, or a friend. The word "late" should precede any reference made to either of the parents. If one parent has died and the remaining parent is not close to the child, or is one who prefers to ignore their relationship, the anouncement may be issued by another relative, but mention of the living parent should be made in any newspaper releases.

If the father or mother is deceased, and the other parent has not remarried, the announcement might be worded:

Mr. [or Mrs.] Eldon Hartwell Crosby announces the engagement of his [or her] daughter, Ellen Ragland, to Gordon Allen Dayton. Miss Crosby is also the daughter of the late Mrs. [or Mr.] Crosby, etc.

An announcement that gives the deceased some identification of his or her own is the following:

Mr. James Muncie announces the engagement of his daughter, Julia, to Edgar Allen Finley. Miss Muncie's late mother was the former Geraldine Pew, descendant of General Custis Pew, one-time business associate of Abraham Lincoln, etc.

If the father is deceased and the mother has remarried, the announcement reads:

Mr. and Mrs. Paul Johnston of Columbia Heights, Brooklyn, announce the the engagement of Mrs. Johnston's daughter, Althea Frances Warren, to Alfred Martin Otis. Miss Warren is also the daughter of the late Clarence Edward Warren, etc.

If the mother is deceased and the father has remarried, one method of handling the announcement is as follows:

Mr. and Mrs. Ralph Eggleston announce the engagement of Mr. Eggleston's daughter, Judith Anne, to Thomas Randolph Turner, etc.

If the daughter has never known her real mother, the announcement might be:

Mr. and Mrs. Ralph Eggleston of Sutton Place South announce the engagement of their daughter, etc.

Divorced Parents When parents are divorced, the mother usually makes the announcement, but the father *must* be mentioned in the story. Even in the case of the second marriage of a divorced or widowed daughter it is appropriate for the mother (if she is also divorced) to make the announcement if she so desires. In the case of a second marriage however, the woman (particularly if she is older) always has the option of announcing her own engagement, if it is announced at all, jointly with her new fiancé. A typical announcement by a divorced mother who has not remarried should read:

Mrs. Anne Weeks of 14 Sutton Avenue announces the engagement of her daughter, Pamela, etc. Miss Weeks is also the daughter of Mr. George Ranson Weeks of Asheville, North Carolina.

If this form is used, no mention of the word "divorce" is necessary, as it is clear that the parents are divorced and it is assumed, unless otherwise noted, that Miss Weeks lives with her mother.

If parents are divorced and the mother has remarried, the announcement reads:

Mr. and Mrs. Clifford Jones Stoddard announce the engagement of Mrs. Stoddard's daughter, Miss Pamela Weeks, etc. Miss Weeks is also the daughter of Mr. George Ranson Weeks of Asheville, North Carolina.

If it is the parents of the groom who have been divorced, a similar formula is followed in both the engagement and wedding announcements for the newspapers.

Mr. Rank is the son of Mrs. Alston Rank of Nashville, Tennessee, and Mr. Morris Seale Rank of Atlanta, Georgia.

In rare cases when the father makes the announcement of his daughter's engagement or marriage, it is worded the same as when announced by the mother.

If the mother is remarried and her daughter has known only her stepfather, the announcement might be:

Mr. and Mrs. Clifford Jones Stoddard announce the engagement of their daughter, Miss Pamela Weeks, etc.

If a girl whose parents were divorced and whose mother has subsequently died has been brought up by her aunt and uncle, the announcement of her engagement reads like this:

Mr. and Mrs. Seth McClure of 7 Hershey Drive announce the engagement of their niece, Miss Sally Guthrie, to Penn Snyder, Jr., son of Mr. and Mrs. Penn Snyder, also of this city [often the fiancé's complete address is omitted from the engagement announcement]. Miss Guthrie is the daughter of Mrs. McClure's late sister, Mrs. Marian Guthrie, and of Mr. Joseph Guthrie. [This indicates that Sally's father was divorced from her mother at the time of her mother's death.]

If a girl has a stepmother to whom she feels closer than to her real mother and the announcement is being made by her father and stepmother, her own mother should accept the fact that she should be merely an invited guest at an engagement party at which the stepmother is the hostess. Her real mother has the option of giving a separate party to announce the news to her friends.

Separated Parents   When parents are legally separated, engagement announcements are made in the name of the parent (or relative) with whom the bride lives. This is usually the mother, who must still use her husband's name, i.e., Mrs. Allen Smithton, *not* Mrs. Joan Smithton.

Adopted Children   When a child has been adopted by a couple, taken their name, and been brought up as one of their own children, there is no reason why the adoptive relationship need be mentioned in the engagement or marriage announcement, even if the fact is generally known. But if the child bears another name it is necessary.

Under special circumstances, sometimes a bachelor or an older unmarried woman adopts a daughter who may or may not have taken her adoptive parent's name. In such cases the engagement notice reads:

Miss Wilhelmina Bosworth announces the engagement of her adopted daughter, Miss Sybil Frank, etc.

or:

Dr. Orrin Metcalf announces the engagement of his adopted daughter, Florence, etc.

Legally Changed Name

Occasionally you see an engagement announcement or a notice of a marriage where some mention is made of a legally changed name. For example:

Mr. and Mrs. Josef Greenberg of 50 Riverview Drive announce the engagement of their daughter, Dorothy, to Robert Harris, son of Mr. and Mrs. Chaim Hirsh, also of this city. Mr. Harris changed his name legally.

This clears up Mr. Harris's status but is not strictly necessary so long as the notice states that he is the Hirshes' son. The reader will assume he changed his name, something he has a right to do with or without legal recourse.

Bride on Her Own

When a woman has reached a mature age, she has the choice of letting her parents or other relative (if both parents are dead) announce her engagement at a party. If she has been married before, she does not send an announcement to the newspaper (only for her wedding). If her fiancé has been married before, but she has not, she should send in an announcement of their engagement. If either she or her groom-to-be are extremely prominent in their community, and if both have been previously married, she should have the announcement of their engagement sent in to the society editor.

The Engagement Ring

The traditional engagement ring is a diamond solitaire. However, today anything goes—a ring with many colored stones, a ring with a large semiprecious stone, an heirloom ring reset in a modern design, or even a stone in the bride's family, simply reset in a Tiffany setting. The wedding ring should be of the same metal (platinum, yellow gold, or white gold) as the engagement ring. It is worn inside the engagement ring. Some women prefer no engagement ring but choose a wedding band that is studded with stones instead. No one has to have an engagement ring. A girl may want her fiancé to give her a pearl necklace instead, or a jeweled watch. Jeweled rings can be given as gifts on many occasions during their married lives—such as wedding anniversaries, the birth of a child, or an important job promotion.

Behavior of an Engaged Couple

Whether an engaged couple is living together or not, an old rule still prevails: people should be restrained in demonstrating their physical feelings toward each other in public. Kissing, touching each other, the woman sitting in the man's lap—all of this should be done on the couple's own time, and not on their friends' or strangers'. It is far better to think how much they must be bursting with physical desire for each other than to see them actually demonstrating it.

Breaking an Engagement

If you have just become engaged, assume that the engagement will lead to marriage. However, if things do not go right, look honestly at your future chances for success in marriage. If the troubles are mounting already in the rosy glow of an engagement, they will probably magnify many times over in the hard reality of daily married life. An engagement should never be entered into lightly or lightly broken. But if "things are not going well between us," it is far better to terminate the relationship at this point. Breaking an engagement is not an admission of failure. Give back the ring, or any other jewelry, return any wedding presents you have already received, and close the chapter in the book. There will be many brighter new ones.

If your engagement is broken, do not send out printed or engraved announcements of the fact. Simply call your friends and announce the fact, without giving gossipy reasons or criticizing your fiancé in any way. In fact, each should praise the other. Don't elaborate, but state simply, "It isn't working out, so we decided to part."

Premarital Living Together

When a person begins to see something rather special and wonderful in someone else—and the feeling is reciprocated and sustained—that couple will want to establish a more permanent relationship with each other. Often today that relationship may mean living together. If they begin to live together without benefit of marriage, it is not for others to approve or disapprove. If they are breaking a moral law, it is their business and no one else's. It used to be called living in sin, and to many Americans it still is, but it has become, by weight of sheer statistics, a way of life. We must therefore cope with it as such. If we love the separate members of such a union, we should not chastise them or exclude them from the hospitality of our home.

Parents' Attitude Parents should adjust to the moral codes of their children when visiting them in their homes. Adjusting to a "live-in" couple does not necessarily imply acceptance. It means that the lines of communication are being kept open between parents and child; it means that the parents are learning to cope with their personal feelings about their child's relationship. If they have done everything possible to train their child in their own feelings of morality, religion, and character, at a certain moment they must stand back and say, "We did all we could. Now it's up to our child. He's on his own." Pressing a son or daughter into a marriage that is unwanted could be counterproductive. Once the parents have made clear their disapproval of the living arrangement, they should accept the situation, and not discuss it ad infinitum. They should visit their child and his partner; they should welcome them to their own home. However, the child has responsibilities too, particularly when he is an overnight guest in his parents' home. He should make it clear that if his parents would prefer, he and his friend will be happy to sleep in separate bedrooms while they are under that roof. A dogged, stubborn insistence on sharing the same room while visiting is selfish, inconsiderate, and petty at the same time. The parents have every right to say at this point, "Look, this is our house. You can both go to the hotel nearby and pay for your own room if you refuse to accept the moral code of this house." Any couple should be willing to conform to such a request in order to promote a harmonious, pleasant visit for everyone concerned. After all, a separation for 2 or 3 nights out of 365 should be a statistic with which they can live!

A Social Entity A couple living together must be considered as a social entity. Even if you do not know one of the couple, an evening or a weekend invitation must be extended to them both (unlike a business lunch invitation). If you want to invite someone and you are not sure he or she has a "permanent" relationship at the moment, simply ask if you should invite a date for the one to whom you are speaking. Back will come the name of the person you should invite, and when you ask for his or her address, your friend will reply, "Same address as mine," and you have your answer.

In my opinion, all social acceptance, understanding, and supportiveness of the relationship ceases if one of the partners openly living with someone else is still married to another. Whether or not the divorce is pending, this kind of act removes any need for accepting the couple as a social entity.

Addressing the Envelope Send one invitation only to a couple living together, just as to a married couple. Two unmarried people are listed on separate lines in alphabetical order, as follows:

Ms. Anne Balcolm
Mr. James Tighesman
4314 Farnam Street
Omaha, Nebraska   zip code

The couple's names should be listed on their mailbox in the same manner. Each of them should have a separate listing in the telephone book, in the proper alphabetical place (this listing will probably cost extra).

What Do You Call Your Partner? A couple living together outside marriage have to reach a decision about how to refer to each other. It is difficult to find a term that does not sound flip or even sarcastic (among the latter: "my companionable; my apartment-mate; my live-in; my share-mate; my love-mate"). Most people use the long explanation "I'm one of a couple," or they refer to "the person with whom I live," or "the one with whom I share an apartment." "My lover" is too strong and intimate a term for everyday usage. A man may not refer to "my mistress," either, since in most of these relationships each person works and shares in the financial burdens as well as in the housekeeping.

Most couples do not approach living together as a casual, flip arrangement. They do a lot of planning and thinking out before they move in with each other. Some find it a good alternative to making a mistake in marriage (which they see all around them) and having to suffer through a divorce; others are far more positive in their attitude, believing they are maturing, working out their problems, learning to recognize their faults, with time to reflect, reason, and "predict the direction a relationship is taking."

Most of the older generations do not accept their reasoning. "It's a cop-out" is the attitude of many opponents of cohabitation. As one psychological counselor commented, "It's coming through the hard knocks of everyday life that is so satisfying, and people who make the commitment to marriage seem to survive them much better than couples who don't."

Fortunately, many of these relationships do grow into marriage. If we accept the philosophy that every person has the right to lead his own life, then we can also accept the fact that something else can remove that right, and that is when a baby is born. A person is leading more than just his own life at that point—and a good marriage is the best structure, emotionally, socially, and legally, in which to cope with the wonderful business at hand: the raising of a child.

A Word to the Wise for a Woman A woman who is living with someone to whom she is not married needs two professionals in her life that a man does not. She needs a good gynecologist to prescribe the proper birth control methods if she does not want a child, and she needs a good lawyer to protect her rights, which are quite limited in these circumstances. If the woman has a child she needs legal advice on the financial responsibilities her partner should assume. Unmarried couples may be refused the opportunity to rent or buy apartments or houses, and they may have to face other forms of discrimination. Life insurance is an important matter to settle between them, too.

Announcing the Engagement of Two People Living Together Couples who live together may, like everyone else, have their engagement formally announced by the girl's parents at a party, with a story and captioned photograph released to the newspapers, and with the usual showers, prenuptial parties, and so on. The engagement period should last no longer than six to eight weeks, however, according to the size of the wedding and how much time is needed to plan it. A girl who gets out of bed the morning of the wedding with the man with whom she has been living for a year or two may not want to put on a full, long white dress with cathedral train, long veil, et al. She may prefer a small church ceremony with a minimum number of attendants and may feel it is more appropriate for her to wear a less formal white or pastel dress. But if her parents want the big formal wedding, she should acquiesce. Many brides and grooms in history have gone through large weddings just to please their parents, which may be reason enough, if they love their parents.

Chapter 11

WEDDING INVITATIONS AND ANNOUNCEMENTS

Preparing the List

For very small or informal weddings, engraved invitations are not necessary. The bride may call, send a Mailgram, or write personal invitational notes in these cases. If, however, a large wedding is decided upon, the necessary invitation lists must be started almost as soon as the engagement is announced or this vital clerical chore will still be hanging fire during the complicated arrangements for such a wedding. You should always order a dozen more invitations than you think you can possible use. They will be needed for last-minute emergencies and family scrapbooks.

The groom and his family must co-operate by furnishing their typed invitation and announcement lists as early as possible, so the bride may combine them with her own usually larger lists, remove duplications, and, if necessary, shorten the lists with the help of both families. The groom's family should be allowed one half the total number of invitations, unless the majority of his relatives and friends live at a considerable distance, in which case a smaller proportion of the invitations may suffice and a larger list for announcements substituted. In either case, the proportion should be agreed upon by the groom and his family.

When the groom's family supplies its list, the complete names and addresses of all those to receive invitations should be clearly spelled out, just as they will appear on the envelope. For instance, the list should read "Mr. and Mrs. John David Cates," and *not* "Mr. and Mrs. J. D. Cates." Zip codes should be furnished with all addresses.

For a large formal wedding many more people receive invitations than can possibly accept. Even close friends and relatives at a great distance are informed by means of the invitation that the wedding is taking place. The list should include all relatives of the bride and groom, all close friends of both families, neighbors, old family retainers, business associates of the two fathers and of the groom and, of course, of the bride, if she is a career woman. But wedding invitations should never be sent indiscriminately to casual acquaintances of either a business or social nature. These people often feel obligated to send a gift, which is an imposition. If one wishes to invite nonintimate business associates to the ceremony only, this may be done verbally or through the posting of the invitation to the ceremony. Invitations should be sent through the mails to the parents of the groom, members of the wedding party, and the minister and his wife, as these are treasured mementos of the occasion. The bride's mother might wish to enclose a short note in the invitations or announcements to the groom's immediate family, saying they might wish to have them for sentimental reasons, and "didn't they turn out nicely?" Parents of members of the wedding party should receive invitations along with the spouses of any of the attendants, but do not have to be invited to a sit-down meal reception. It is customary to invite the spouse of a member of the wedding party, but he or she should not expect to be seated at the bridal table for any of the festivities. Young children of any attendants should not come to the reception; any children present should be related to the bride and groom.

One does not have to invite a date for each unmarried person invited to the reception. If you do wish unmarried persons to bring a date of their choice, you should either ascertain the names and addresses, and send them separate invitations, or include a personal note in your friends' invitations (written, of course, in black ink) saying, "Please bring Miss Anne Brown" or "please bring an escort." An engaged woman or man can ask to have his or her fiancé included, as can a person who is unmarried but living with someone of the opposite sex and as can one of a homosexual couple.

Dividing the List The full list is broken down into (1) those who will receive invitations to the wedding and reception; (2) those who will be invited to the ceremony only; and (3) those who will receive wedding announcement and At Home cards, if any.

Ordinary 3″×5″ file cards with two sets of alphabetical indexes and two convenient boxes provide the best method of compiling a working list. As names and addresses are placed on cards and alphabetized, duplicates can be weeded out. The cards can be coded in the upper left-hand corner with *CR* (ceremony and reception), *C* (ceremony only), or *A* (announcement); or different colored cards can be used for each.

The second file box should hold "Acceptances" and "Regrets" so that when the reception preparations are made a fairly accurate count may be had, with some allowance made for last-minute changes. Both acceptances and regrets should be filed alphabetically, too.

Invitations to Those in Mourning

People who have lost someone in the immediate family should certainly be included on the wedding invitation list, and should accept. It is even possible for one in mourning to be in the bridal party. All the attendants are considered to be in wedding uniform, their own problems and personalities subjugated for the day they are in the service of the bride and groom. This is understood by everyone, and only if bereavement has been very recent and very close is it sometimes necessary for an attendant to ask to be excused, not because of possible criticism, but because his own emotional state might cast a shadow on the happy day.

When Should Invitations and Announcements Be Sent?

Wedding invitations, unlike ordinary social invitations, are sent as much as four to six weeks in advance of the wedding. Engraved invitations take time and should be ordered at least eight weeks before they are to be sent out, with consideration given the time it will take to address outer and inner envelopes. One may, of course, pick up the envelopes in advance so that the addressing can be completed before the invitations arrive. Announcements, ordered at the same time, are not, of course, sent out until after the marriage has taken place, but, if possible, they should be stamped and ready for mailing *immediately* after the ceremony, so that news of the marriage in the papers does not too much predate friends' receipt of the announcements.

Engraving and Stationery

It is far better to write personal letters or inform your friends of your marriage by telephone than to have your invitations and announcements printed. They should always be engraved. Of the various types of lettering available, the least expensive, and the most used, is graceful script. It costs no more to go to a really good, reputable stationer for your announcements or invitations than it costs to go to an unknown one. There you will see styles of engraving such as the shaded, or shaded antique, roman currently in vogue. There are slight variations from time to time, but essentially the engraving procedure is rigidly conventional. Do it right, or don't do it at all.

Paper and Envelopes Use the best stock you can afford for announcements or invitations. People do look at the quality of paper, and many inspect the envelopes to see the name of the stationer from whom you ordered. The name of a good stationer embossed under the flap of the envelope lends a certain cachet and costs nothing extra.

The most distinguished wedding paper is the traditional ivory or ecru. Pure white is now seldom used. Symptomatic of the rebellion of the young versus the Establishment, and simultaneously with the barefoot bride and groom of the sixties being married in the cornfield, there was a rash of "poetic" wedding invitations. These were invitations often with drawings and the message charmingly written in personal tones. However, with the return to more formality, this kind of invitation is disappearing. Weddings are one time that calls for the traditional, formal kind of invitation.

The engraving is always in black and on the first page of the double sheet. If the bride's family has a coat of arms, a small crest, shield, and motto may be embossed—not die-stamped—in color as on ordinary stationery at the top of the first page. However, this is not done if a woman, *alone,* makes the announcement or issues the invitation. If the bride's family has no coat of arms, she may not use the crest of her husband-to-be until they are actually married, but even then, if her family issues announcements, the husband's device may not be used on them, although the bride's family's may be (see under "Heraldic Devices," page 557). If the couple themselves make announcement, the husband's full coat of arms may be embossed.

Two envelopes are usually used for wedding invitations and announcements, although only one is necessary. Where two envelopes are used, the inside one is unsealed (and must not be gummed), and is placed in the outer envelope so that it faces the flap. Stationers urge customers to include half-tissues with large invitations that must be folded to be inserted in the envelope. This is to prevent smudging. On small invitations that do not require folding, tissues may be dispensed with.

The length of the names, the style of lettering, and, in this case, whether or not plate-marked paper will be used have much to do with the size of the paper you choose. There are many acceptable variations, but a fairly standard size is 7½"×5½" for a folded invitation or announcement. Smaller announcements or invitations that may be inserted into the envelopes unfolded are also correctly used, but if reception or At Home cards are to be enclosed, it is possible they may never be seen if the unfolded style is used.

It is of course possible for a bride, especially one with an attractive or exceptional handwriting, to choose to write all of her own invitations for a small wedding. In cases where this is done, one should use only the highest-quality fold-over stationery, preferably white or ecru. Black ink should be used.

How to Address the Envelopes

The addressing of wedding invitations and announcements is rigidly prescribed. Abbreviations are not permitted except in "Dr.," "Mr.," "Mrs.," and "Jr." (or "Lt." when combined with "Colonel," etc.) or in an initial of a name if you don't know it in full. The names of cities and states are written out. When an invitation or announcement is being mailed in the same city as that in which the wedding is taking or has taken place, it has been customary to omit the name of the state. However, in expanding America, where mail delivery is difficult, it is a matter of necessity for the state to be included as well as the zip code in the address. For instance:

Mr. and Mrs. Cedric Moore McIntosh
1886 Shore Road
Chicago, Illinois   zip code

Where there are several members of a family to be invited, avoid the phrase "and family." On the inside envelope is written:

Mr. and Mrs. McIntosh
[NO FIRST NAME]
Belinda and Gordon
[IF THE CHILDREN ARE UNDER AGE]

But if there is an adult daughter or son or other woman or man in the household you wish to invite, she or he must receive a separate invitation. Anyone over eighteen should receive a separate invitation:

Miss [or Ms.] Margaret McIntosh
1886 Shore Road
Chicago, Illinois   zip code

The inside envelope reads:

Miss [or Ms.] McIntosh

If there are two sisters, write:

The Misses Agnes and Ann McIntosh (or Misses Agnes and Ann McIntosh), and on the inside envelope The Misses McIntosh (or Misses McIntosh) with no address, of course, on the inner one. There is no plural for "Ms." If you want to use the Ms. form for two sisters, address the envelope to Ms. Agnes and Ms. Ann McIntosh. On the inside envelope write: Ms. McIntosh and Ms. McIntosh.

Two grown sons (over eighteen) receive one invitation if they live at the same address. They are addressed as:

The Messrs. Keith and Ian McIntosh (or Messrs. Keith and Ian McIntosh) with simply The Messrs. McIntosh (or Messrs. McIntosh) inside.

In the case of a person who possesses a doctorate (a Ph.D.) and who usually uses his title, the envelope should be addressed to Doctor, or Dr., depending on the length of his name.

If you are sending an invitation to two persons of the same last name both of whom are medical doctors, you address it to The Doctors Smith. The same form is used if they are both Ph.D.s and use the title.

Women who are widows or are separated are addressed as Mrs. George Hart.

Two unmarried people who live together receive only one invitation, like a married couple. Their names are written on separate lines in alphabetical order:

Miss [or Ms., according to preference] Mary Andrews
Mr. Richard Bonhorne
14 Grover Place
Oklahoma City, Oklahoma   zip code

The inside envelope would read:

Miss [or Ms.] Andrews and Mr. Bonhorne

Return Addresses It is now essential to have a return address on *the front* of the envelope bearing a wedding announcement or invitation. This should either be engraved in the same style as the invitation, or embossed, or written by hand (by the same person who addresses the envelope) in black ink (not a ballpoint pen). One may also use printed address stickers with black printing on white, although that is the least attractive way to do it.

Stamps First-class postage should be used, or course, and the stamps should be put on carefully and neatly. Using a meter is not proper for formal invitations.

Penmanship Invitation addresses should never be typed, but should be handwritten in black ink by someone with as neat and as beautiful a handwriting as can be found. I have found people at senior citizen centers, nuns in convents, and good calligraphers in local colleges and universities who are delighted to have the opportunity to earn some extra money in addressing such invitations. If the bride's family calls in friends and family to help address the invitations, the handwriting should be as similar as possible. The envelopes usually are available upon request two or more weeks before the engraved invitations are ready, so one should begin the job of organizing the addressing immediately.

Wording of Formal Invitations

Invitation to Church Ceremony

Dr. and Mrs. Grant Kingsley
request the honour of your presence
at the marriage of their daughter
Penelope
to
Mr. George Frank Carpenter
on Friday, the ninth of June
One thousand nine hundred and seventy-eight
at twelve o'clock
St. Mary's Church
San Francisco

If the girl's father has a title he should use it on the invitation. For instance, a judge would probably issue an invitation as "Justice and Mrs. Thomas Ward Preston," although a judge in a lower court may optionally use "Mr."

Mention of the year is optional bordering on unnecessary on an invitation but obligatory on the announcement of the marriage. When the year is mentioned, I prefer to see it in the form "One thousand nine hundred and seventy-eight," but it is possible to include it as "Nineteen hundred and seventy-eight." The word "honour" is always spelled in the old way. The phrase "honour of your presence" is always used for invitations to a church ceremony. If the ceremony takes place other than in a church or synagogue one should use the phrase "the pleasure of your company." No R.S.V.P. (optional abbreviation R.s.v.p.) is used when the invitation is for the church ceremony alone.

In a large city where there are many churches, the address is engraved under the name of the church in this way:

Emmanuel Church
1122 South Moore Street
Denver, Colorado

The time of the ceremony, traditionally on the hour or on the half hour, is usually written out. If it is to be on the half hour the wording reads "at half after four" or sometimes "at half-past four." If the ceremony is on the quarter hour, the wording is "at quarter before four" or "at quarter-past four."

The word "junior" is written without a capital, but it now is abbreviated more often than not, just as "Doctor" is. But then it is "Jr." with a capital *J*.

Sometimes the "On" is omitted so that an invitation may read "Friday, the ninth of June," but simplification of the form reduces its dignity. The invitation may also read, as another option, "Friday, June ninth."

In the wedding of Catholics it is optional to include the information that the ceremony will be a nuptial mass. If you do include this information (in order to inform friends who might not know from the name of the church if it is Episcopal or Roman Catholic), you may either phrase the invitation, "at the nuptial mass in which their daughter," or include the phrase at the end of the invitation above the mention of the church.

Change in Date   If wedding invitations have already been engraved (but not mailed) and the date must be changed, an engraved card may be added to the invitation, or a printed card if there is not time for engraving, reading along these lines: "The date of the wedding has been changed to Saturday, the twenty-sixth of August at four o'clock due to the change in the groom's Foreign Service post departure date." The same information may be sent by Mailgram, of course, if necessary, and friends of the bride can help her telephone wedding guests if the change comes too late to inform people by mail.

The Woman with a Title If the bride is a doctor of medicine or of dentistry, she does not use her title in an invitation issued by her parents. Such an invitation reads:

Mr. and Mrs. George Frank Carpenter
request the honour of your presence
at the marriage of their daughter
Helena

If, however, the wedding invitation is issued by friends or perhaps a guardian, then the bride's name is given as Doctor Helena Carpenter. This is done also when the bride and groom, perhaps both doctors, issue invitations or announcements. The latter would read:

Doctor Helena Carpenter
and
Doctor James Howard Patterson
announce their marriage, etc.

If a woman has a doctorate in a field outside of medicine or dentistry, and uses her title professionally, she may choose to use it socially as well. However, it is somewhat pretentious for people who are not medical doctors or dentists to use "Doctor" in their wedding invitations or announcements. If the bride-to-be is accustomed to using her title and she is issuing her own invitations, then she has the option of calling herself Doctor or Miss or Ms., as she prefers. In the invitation and announcement the title is spelled out as "Doctor," but it appears in its abbreviated form, "Dr.," in any newspaper reports.

The Girl with the Same Name as Her Mother If a girl has the same name as her mother and has for convenience' sake been known as Helen Preston, second, she does not use this appellation in her wedding invitations or announcements, since her mother's name, as it must be used in the form, could not possibly be confused with her daughter's, unless the mother is divorced. In this case, the invitation would read:

Mrs. Helen Preston
requests the honour of your presence
at the marriage of her daughter
Helen

When the Parents Are Legally Separated Invitations and announcements are in the name of the parent (or relative) with whom the bride lives—usually the mother, who must use her husband's name, i.e., Mrs. John Kingsley, or her own professional name, if she has one, Ada Kingsley.

The Remarried Mother's Invitation If the bride's mother, widowed or divorced, has remarried, the invitation may read:

Mr. and Mrs. Roderick Merrill
request the honour of your presence
at the marriage of Mrs. Merrill's daughter
Penelope Kingsley

Sometimes a remarried woman issues the invitation to her daughter's wedding in her name alone, as:

Mrs. Roderick Merrill
requests the honour of your presence
at the marriage of her daughter
etc.

When the mother has remarried and divorced again, she issues the invitation using her first name plus her last married name, e.g., Mrs. Alicia Browning. The girl's father's name does not appear on such an invitation except in the case where he is giving the reception. Then he may enclose a separate reception card with his name (and that of his present wife, if he is remarried) and R.S.V.P. with his address.

The Foster Parent If a child has lived a long time with people who have not adopted her, but who wish to give her a wedding and make the announcement, the invitation best reads:

Mr. and Mrs. Joseph Post
request the honour of your presence
at the marriage of their foster daughter
[OR, OPTIONALLY, DAUGHTER]
Miss Alice Lamb
[OBSERVE INCLUSION OF THE TITLE "MISS," OR "MS.," BEFORE HER NAME.]

The Adopted Child The wedding invitation of an adopted daughter makes no mention of that fact. It follows the traditional wording.

When the Father or Others Issue the Invitation If the daughter after her parents' divorce has made her home with her father, her grandparents, her aunt, brother, or other relative or guardian, the person whose home it is makes the announcement jointly with his or her spouse. For example:

Commander and Mrs. Charles Simonson
request the honour of your presence
at the marriage of their granddaughter
etc.

or:

> The Reverend and Mrs. Myron Cyrus Kingsley
> request the honour of your presence
> at the marriage of his sister
> Penelope

If the bride's father is a widower, he issues the invitation. Also, if he is a divorcé and his daughter has lived with him, he issues the invitation, although he may choose to do the more graceful thing and permit the bride's mother to do so for the sake of convention, even if she and her daughter rarely see each other. An invitation from a father alone reads:

> Dr. Grant Kingsley   [OR DOCTOR]
> requests the honour of your presence
> at the marriage of his daughter
> Penelope
> etc.

An invitation from the bride's father who has remarried reads:

> Dr. and Mrs. Grant Kingsley
> request the honour of your presence
> at the marriage of Dr. Kingsley's daughter
> Penelope
> etc.

If the bride's sister is issuing the invitation, it reads:

> Miss Cordelia Kingsley
> requests the honour of your presence
> at the marriage of her sister
> Penelope

Only if the wedding is being given by a close relative is the relationship shown in the invitation. If cousins, friends, or a guardian issue the invitation, the connection is not shown.

EXCEPTION: The stepmother issuing an invitation for her stepdaughter uses that term in the invitation and announcement, whether or not she has remarried. In this last instance, the lines would read:

> Mr. and Mrs. Roland Campbell Potter
> request the honour of your presence
> at the marriage of Mrs. Potter's stepdaughter
> Marcia Rhodes, etc.

The announcement in the paper should include, "Miss Rhodes is also the daughter of the late Mr. Herbert Jackson Rhodes and the late Gwendolyn Morris Rhodes" (no "Mrs.").

Double Wedding of Sisters   In a double wedding if the brides are sisters the elder sister is mentioned first and the invitation reads:

Dr. and Mrs. Grant Kingsley
request the honour of your presence
at the marriage of their daughters
Penelope
to
Mr. George Frank Carpenter
and
Felicia
to
Mr. Amos Reynolds
etc.

Double Wedding of Cousins or Friends   If the brides are cousins or just friends, the invitation could read:

Dr. and Mrs. Grant Kingsley
and
Mr. and Mrs. Claude Roen
request the honour of your presence
at the marriage of their daughters
Penelope Kingsley
to
Mr. George Frank Carpenter
and
Marie Rose Roen
to
Mr. Gregory Pardee

Here the older bride is mentioned first, with her parents, but when the brides are more or less the same age the order is alphabetical. However, when there is a great difference in age between the two groups of parents or if, for example, one bride's invitations are issued by her grandparents, it is the older sponsors who take the precedence. While such an announcement as this is possible, it is more probable that each bride would prefer to have her own invitation, even for a double wedding. Separate invitations also make reception acceptances simple to handle. It is possible to indicate a double wedding by engraving the two separate invitations vis-à-vis on the inside of the double sheet.

When the Names of the Bride's Parents and the Groom's Parents Appear on the Wedding Invitations   Many couples today want both sets of parents to have equal participation in the wedding ceremony. The groom's parents, for example, are now sometimes seen in the processional at Christian weddings, a custom once seen only at Jewish weddings in this country.

Mr. and Mrs. Andrew Brown
request the honour of your presence
at the marriage of their daughter
Marianne
to
Mr. John Preston
son of
Mr. and Mrs. Robert Preston
etc.

Optional form

Mr. and Mrs. Andrew Brown
Mr. and Mrs. Robert Preston
request the honour of your presence
at the marriage of
Marianne Brown
to
Mr. John Preston
etc.

The Bride on Her Own Occasionally a young bride has no close relatives or friends to issue her invitation for her or make her wedding announcement. In this case, as with the older bride who wishes to make her own announcement or issue her own wedding invitation, the form reads:

The honour of your presence
is requested at the marriage of
[OR "WEDDING RECEPTION OF"]
Miss Cordelia Kingsley
[NOTE "MISS" OR "MS."]
to
[OR "AND"]
Mr. Winthrop Cass Bowers
etc.

The bride who has established herself in a career or profession under a different name may have her invitation engraved with her professional name beneath her real name:

The honour of your presence
is requested at the marriage of
Miss Cordelia Kingsley
(Delia King)
to
Mr. Winthrop Cass Bowers
etc.

The bride with her own resources may perhaps choose to issue her own invitations, or if she and her husband-to-be are sharing the cost of the wedding between them, they may issue invitations and announcements jointly.

Wedding Given by the Groom's Family

Mr. and Mrs. Perry Coates
request the honour of your presence
at the marriage of
Miss Laura Lee Mercer*
to their son
Mr. Trimble Coates
etc.

The circumstances would have to be very special indeed for the wedding to be given by the groom's family—and those circumstances very well understood by intimate friends of both the bride and the groom. To give remote examples, if the bride's parents were dead and there were no mature relatives, or if the families had been old friends or distantly related, or if the bride's home was far from the city in which the wedding was to take place and her own parents could not be with her, then she might properly accept her future mother-in-law's invitation that the wedding be given at the groom's home.

Invitation to a House Wedding   An invitation to a house wedding carries the R.S.V.P.[1] because food will be served after the ceremony and the number of guests needs to be known. Otherwise the house wedding invitation reads the same as one to the church except for the second line, which is changed to "the pleasure of your company." The house address is given in place of the name of the church:

Mr. and Mrs. Antonio Zompano
request the pleasure of your company
at the marriage of their daughter
Luisa
to
Mr. Herbert Stevens
on Thursday, the sixth of July
at twelve o'clock
1439 Lakeside Drive
Lake Placid, New York   zip code

R.S.V.P.

* The "Miss" is used when the givers of the wedding are not relatives. Also, "Ms." may be used instead of "Miss" on all invitations, according to the bride's wishes.

[1] R.S.V.P.: or, less usually, "The favour [note spelling] of a reply is requested," or, if preferred, the Anglicized verisions, "Please respond," or "Kindly respond."

If the wedding and reception take place in a club or hotel, it is noted that the R.S.V.P. is sent to the bride's home:

Mr. and Mrs. Theodore Stern
request the pleasure of your company
at the marriage of their daughter
Rebecca
to
Mr. Charles Philip Adler
on Sunday, the fifth of March
at half after five o'clock
The Plaza
New York

R.S.V.P.
1066 Fernway Road
Brooklyn, New York   zip code

Different Styles of Layout If a bride wants a very contemporary look to her engraved invitations, she may do so with a more tailored typeface and she may even line up her text against the left margin, if she wishes. The invitation above would look like this:

Mr. and Mrs. Theodore Stern
request the pleasure of your company
at the marriage of their daughter
Rebecca
to
Mr. Charles Philip Adler
etc.

The Divorcée A divorced woman does not send out engraved wedding invitations, but she may send out engraved reception invitations. Those who attend the church ceremony are invited by telephone or by personal note. She may send out engraved wedding announcements if she and her husband or her parents wish to.

The Young Widow A young widow who remarries may send out engraved invitations to the wedding ceremony as well as to the reception. If her family issues them, they read:

Mr. and Mrs. Sydney Myers
request the honour of your presence
at the marriage of their daughter
Sylvia Myers Kiser
to
etc.

(Optionally, but less preferred, the invitation may read "at the marriage of their daughter Sylvia Ann Kiser.")

If the young widow is issuing her own wedding invitation, it may read:

> The honour of your presence
> is requested at the marriage of
> Mrs. Maximilian George Kiser
> to
> etc.

The Older Widow   Many an older widow becomes used to being called by her first name in her later years (Catherine Jones) instead of Mrs. John Jones. She should still be known by her late husband's name on all formal invitations, including her wedding invitation:

> The pleasure of your company
> is requested at the marriage of
> Mrs. John Jones
> to
> etc.

If she is married at home or in a club, "The pleasure of yoour company" is used. If she is married in a church, or synagogue, "The honour of your presence" is used.

A widow should send an invitation to the wedding, or at least a wedding announcement, to the family of her late husband.

Outdoor Wedding Provisions   If you have planned an outdoor or garden wedding ceremony, there is always a chance it may rain, so alternate arrangements should be made, and the invitation should have engraved in the lower right-hand corner:

> In case of rain
> the wedding will be held
> in
> St. John's Church
> on Hillwood Lane

Wedding at Friend's Home   When the wedding itself is held, for some reason, in the home of friends, the invitation is in the name of the bride's parents, even though they cannot be present. If the parents are not living, the bride may either issue the invitation herself or have her friends as sponsors do so. In the latter case the form is:

> Mr. and Mrs. Angus Work
> request the pleasure of your company
> at the marriage of
> Miss Penelope Kingsley
> to
> Mr. George Frank Carpenter
> on Friday, the ninth of June
> One thousand nine hundred and seventy-eight
> at four o'clock
> 600 Rose Lane
> Waco, Texas   zip code

Combining Invitation to Church Ceremony and Reception

If all those at the ceremony are to be invited to the reception the wedding invitation may read as follows and no reception card is necessary:

> Dr. and Mrs. Grant Kingsley
> request the honour of your presence
> at the marriage of their daughter
> Penelope
> to
> Mr. George Frank Carpenter
> on Friday, the ninth of June
> One thousand nine hundred and seventy-eight
> at twelve o'clock
> Saint Mary's Church
> San Francisco
> and afterward at
> "The Gulls"
> Belvedere

R.S.V.P.
421 Taylor Drive
San Francisco, California   zip code

If there are to be two receptions, one at the church for all the guests and another following for family and close friends at the bride's home or at a restaurant or club, the wedding invitation should read as the above with the following after the name of the church:

And afterward at the reception
in the parlors of the church

Appropriately, a separate engraved card would be included for those invited to the more intimate reception, and it would contain an R.S.V.P.

The Separate Reception Invitation

Sometimes an invitation to the wedding reception is engraved on the same kind of double sheet usually used for the wedding invitation. This is useful where there may be only an intimate wedding ceremony, for which no engraved invitations may be issued, followed by a large reception. Such an invitation reads:

Dr. and Mrs. Grant Kingsley
request the pleasure of your company
at the wedding breakfast of their daughter
Penelope
and   [NOTE THE "AND"]
Mr. George Frank Carpenter
on Friday, the ninth of June
at one o'clock
"The Gulls"
Belvedere

R.S.V.P.
421 Taylor Drive
San Francisco, California   zip code

The Late Reception Invitation

Occasionally a wedding reception is given some time after the fact of the wedding by the bride's family, often by the family of the groom, or by both together. It is awkward, and not advisable, to give an evening reception on the same day as a formal morning or noon ceremony. But a young couple might be married in one city away from their parents and their friends and return to their parents' community for a reception after the honeymoon. The following form is often used on an engraved separate reception card for a reception that will take place when the bride and groom have returned from their wedding trip. It may be issued either by the parents of the groom or by the parents of the bride, or, as the following, by the bride and groom's families jointly:

In honour of
Mr. and Mrs. George Frank Carpenter
Dr. and Mrs. Grant Kingsley
Mr. and Mrs. John Price Carpenter
request the pleasure of your company
Saturday, the fourth of November
at eight o'clock
Four Sprucewood Lane
Lakewood, Illinois

R.S.V.P.
Mrs. Kingsley
Ten Toddy Hill
Morristown, Illinois   zip code

A reply to this invitation would be:

Mr. and Mrs. David Roy Sturgis
accept with pleasure
the kind invitation of
Dr. and Mrs. Kingsley
and Mr. and Mrs. Carpenter
for Saturday, the fourth of November
at eight o'clock

An informal alternative particularly good for the case in which much of the groom's family cannot attend the wedding because of distance, but where the couple will make a visit to his family's home some time after the wedding, is for his parents to send out their joint engraved informal with the phrase "To meet Mr. and Mrs. George Frank Carpenter" written in ink on the face of it. They should then write the day and time below their names and, if they wish, an R.S.V.P. This should all be done in black ink.

Foreign Wedding Procedures

It would of course be quite impossible here to go into the full details of the national customs concerning weddings in every country. There is, however, one important factor that should be made clear. If the wedding is being given by the bride's family in another country where English is not spoken, and you, as the groom's family, have supplied them with the names of people whom you would like to receive invitations, do not expect the bride's family to have a separate set of invitations printed in English to go to your friends. Since in most other countries wedding announcements are not used, you should provide the bride's family with a list of those to receive invitations that includes your friends who would normally receive only announcements in this country. The likelihood of any of these people attending such a wedding is almost nonexistent.

If the groom and his foreign bride are to return to this country after the ceremony to live, you might breach custom to the extent of including an At Home card with the wedding invitation. These cards could either be mailed to the bride's family to be put in with the invitation or sent separately by you.

In any situation where your son or daughter will be married in a foreign country and you feel inadequately versed in the country's customs, by all means do not hesitate to question your future son- or daughter-in-law's parents about your role. It is far better to appear a little overanxious about acquainting yourself with their procedures than to risk a serious breach of etiquette because you are embarrassed to admit that you are ignoring them.

Enclosure Cards

The Reception Card When not all those attending the wedding are to be invited to the reception a reception card of the same stock as the invitation and about half the size is included with its tissue. In the case where children are welcome at the ceremony but not at the reception, one may put only the parents' names on the inner envelope containing the reception card, thus indicating that the children are not to be brought to the later event. The reception card should not bear a crest, shield, or motto, and may read:

Dr. and Mrs. Grant Kingsley
request the pleasure of your company
at the wedding breakfast
following the ceremony
at
"The Gulls"
Belvedere

R.S.V.P.

Note "pleasure of your company," as this is now a social occasion. When the reception is to be held in the home of friends, the card reads:

Dr. and Mrs. Grant Kingsley
request the pleasure of your company
at the wedding breakfast
following the ceremony
at the home of
Mr. and Mrs. Curtis Platt
Turkey Hill Road
Belvedere

The favour of a reply is requested to
"The Gulls," Belvedere, Michigan zip code   [THE BRIDE'S HOME]

If a mother or father alone issues the wedding invitation, the reception card must include the name of the spouse if the divorced or widowed parent has remarried. A reception card bears the name of host and hostess.

In the difficult situation where the divorced mother issues the invitation, but the father who has remarried is giving the reception, a reception card can save much unnecessary embarrassment. Let it be handled this way. The invitation itself reads:

Mrs. Gertrude Green
requests the honour of your presence
at the marriage of her daughter, etc.

The card to the reception given by the bride's father and new wife reads:

Mr. and Mrs. James Oliver Green
request the pleasure of your company
immediately following the ceremony
in the Terrace Room of the Plaza Hotel
Fifty-ninth Street and Fifth Avenue [ADDRESS OPTIONAL]
R.S.V.P
1070 Park Avenue
New York, New York   zip code

Dinner Following Reception When a wedding reception after a four o'clock wedding is to be followed by dinner, it is advisable to say so on the wedding invitation. Otherwise those not understanding that dinner will be given, too, make other plans and the bride may find that she has half the number of dinner guests that she expected. The way this is done is to use the phrase either on the invitation itself or on the enclosed reception card: "Reception and dinner immediately following the ceremony."

Pew Cards The bride's mother and the groom's mother may send their visiting cards along with the wedding invitation to those special friends and relatives they wish to seat in reserved sections "Within the Ribbons"—bride's section (one or two pews) to the *left*, groom's to the *right*. Such a card should read:

Groom's Reserved Section   [HANDWRITING—BLACK INK]
Mrs. Norman Snowden Carpenter

Maps For a country or suburban wedding, when there's a possibility that people not knowing the area will become lost, it is wise to include a simple map card. This can be a sketch, reproduced on good-quality paper and tucked inside the invitation before it is mailed out.

Response Cards Printed response cards with a blank for checking "Will Attend" or "Will Not Attend," and with an accompanying envelope, are now sometimes used for weddings. I feel they are too impersonal, implying that the sender thinks the recipients are too lazy to sit down and write a note longhand. Response cards to be filled out were designed for business entertaining, and they should really stay in that field. However, if you receive one in a wedding invitation, fill it out and send it in, instead of writing your acceptance.

When there has been no reply to a wedding invitation within ten days before the wedding, it is proper, if you wish, to send a Mailgram or a postcard, handwritten or printed, that states that you have received no reply to the wedding invitation of (give the engaged couples names) which will take place on such and such a date (give time and place, too). Ask the recipient to telephone you or write you at once (give number and address in your message). I myself would never send out such a message, unless it was to a favorite relative or someone I really cared about who might not have received the invitation.

At Home Cards At Home cards are often included in wedding announcements, less often in invitations to weddings and receptions. If they are in the invitations, they may never bear the name of the couple, for the bride has not yet taken her new name. They give the new address of the couple and the telephone number. Smaller than the reception card, they are, however, of the same style and carry the correct postal address in detail:

At Home [OR THIS MAY BE OMITTED]
after the first of August
[CAPITAL "A" FOR "AFTER" IF FIRST LINE IS OMITTED]
Ten Washington Square South
New York, New York   zip code

Telephone: (000) 000-0000

Or:

Will be at home
after the third of November
Thirty-two Morgan Avenue
Bethlehem, Pennsylvania   zip code

Telephone: (000) 000-0000

When the couple will be moving to a very distant place to which it is difficult to send presents, or for which no definite address is yet known, the At Home card can read:

At Home
after the tenth of May
Calcutta, India
c/o The International Division
Forbes-Magnuson
500 Park Avenue
New York, New York   zip code

When At Home cards go out in the announcements, they may optionally read:

Mr. and Mrs. Kurt Samuels
after the third of November
Ten Washington Square South
New York, New York   zip code

Telephone: (000) 000-0000

When the Bride Keeps Her Maiden Name If the bride plans to retain her maiden name after marriage, it is very important that this be communicated properly to the couple's friends and associates. One of the best ways of doing it is with an At Home card, which can be included either in the wedding invitation or in the wedding announcement mailing. The wording might be as follows:

Marian Howell Smith
George Ramsay Wellington
at home
after the first of September
etc.

A couple living together without benefit of matrimony, however, should not mail out an engraved or printed card giving their joint address in such a formal way.

Recalling Wedding Invitations

If after wedding invitations have been sent out the wedding is called off, guests must be informed as soon as possible. They may be sent notes, Mailgrams, or printed or engraved cards (when there is time for the engraving):

Dr. and Mrs. Grant Kingsley
announce the marriage of their daughter
Penelope
to
Mr. George Knapp Carpenter
will not take place

A Mailgram, signed by those who issued the invitation, would read, "The marriage of our daughter Penelope to Mr. George Knapp Carpenter will not take place. Dr. and Mrs. Grant Kingsley." A message to a close relative would be less formally worded and would carry the familiar signature.

Telephone calls may also be made in this case. These calls are made in the name of the bride's mother by any friend or members of the family willing to do so. Everyone will be curious; the person making the call for the bride should be brief and refrain from any personal gossip.

Death in the Family When a death occurs in a family that has issued formal invitations, is it necessary to cancel the wedding? It certainly used to be, but our ideas have changed very radically on the subject of mourning. Certainly no bride would want to go through an elaborate wedding ceremony followed by the festivity of a large reception within a few days of her mother's or father's death or of the sudden death of the groom's mother, father, or a sister, or brother. The death of a very old person, a grandmother or grandfather, rarely calls for the postponement of a wedding these days, but it all very much depends on the feelings of all involved.

If after a family conference it is decided to recall a wedding invitation because of a death, the guests are notified by telephone, by Mailgram, or, if there is time, by printed cards in the same style as the invitation. They may read:

Mrs. Grant Kingsley
regrets that the death of
Dr. Kingsley
obliges her to recall the invitations
to the wedding of her daughter
[THE NAMES ARE OPTIONAL]
Friday, the ninth of June

This custom of sending cards, however, is infrequently followed today.

Such notification does not mean that the marriage won't take place. It may, instead, be a quiet family ceremony on the original day planned. The bride may even wear her bridal gown and have one attendant, but without a crowded church the full panoply of bridesmaids and ushers would be illogical.

Postponing Weddings

If a wedding is postponed and a new date has been set, guests may be informed by Mailgram or sent a new *printed* invitation done in the style of the original engraved one. It reads:

Dr. and Mrs. Grant Kingsley
announce that the marriage of their daughter
Penelope
to
Mr. George Frank Carpenter
has been postponed from
Friday, the ninth of June
until
Friday, the eighth of September
at noon
St. Mary's Church
San Francisco

Replying to Formal Wedding Invitations

Formal, engraved invitations to a church wedding do not require answering. But if a reception card is included or if a separate invitation to the reception is received, then one answers in the traditional form in response to the R.S.V.P. on the lower left of the card or invitation. If you receive a formal invitation to any party when there is no R.S.V.P. it means technically that the hosts are ready to entertain all who come. No reply is expected. However, if you cannot attend, you should send a note to thank those who invited you and to explain why you cannot attend. A telephone call the day afterward will also suffice, but a note is stronger, more pleasing, and less disruptive.

The reply to an invitation that includes an R.S.V.P. should be written in longhand on one's best notepaper in blue or black ink with the wording and its spacing taking the form of engraving. An acceptance reads (as it does for any engraved invitation):

Mr. and Mrs. Morrow Truitt
accept with pleasure
Dr. and Mrs. Kingsley's
kind invitation for
Friday, the ninth of June
at noon

A regret follows the same form (but see acceptable alternative below). It reads:

Mr. and Mrs. Morrow Truitt
regret that they are unable to accept
Dr. and Mrs. Kingsley's
kind invitation for
Friday, the ninth of June

A more detailed regret states "why" in this way:

Mr. and Mrs. Morrow Truitt
regret [OR REGRET EXCEEDINGLY, OR SINCERELY REGRET] that
their absence from the city
[OR A PREVIOUS ENGAGEMENT]
prevents their accepting
Dr. and Mrs. Kingsley's
etc.

In each case, of course, the envelope is addressed, for the reply to Dr. and Mrs. Grant Kingsley, using the names and address exactly as they appear in the invitation. For other kinds of invitations it is acceptable ordinarily to address a reply to the hostess only.

The wedding may be that of your most intimate friend or of your closest relative, but if you have received an engraved invitation you answer it in formal style. If one is going to decline an invitation and the third-person response seems too limited for the expression of sincere regret, it is best to enclose a personal note more fully explaining the circumstances. The format of the formal reply should also be followed.

In an acceptance it is well to repeat the hour but optional to repeat the full details of the invitation. If a joint ceremony and reception invitation is received and no separate time is given for the reception beyond "following the ceremony," it is acceptable to use that phrase in your reply instead of the time of the ceremony. If the full form is used in an acceptance, most of the wording in the invitation is repeated:

Mr. and Mrs. Morrow Truitt
accept with pleasure
Dr. and Mrs. Kingsley's
[OR DR. AND MRS. GRANT KINGSLEY'S]
kind invitation to
the wedding breakfast of their daughter
Penelope
to
Mr. George Frank Carpenter
at one o'clock
"The Gulls," Belvedere

A fully written out regret does not repeat the hour or the place, merely the date.

When one of a couple accepts the invitation and the other regrets, the form is as follows:

Mrs. Robert Allen Whittemore
accepts with pleasure
Mr. and Mrs. Josephson's
kind invitation for
Saturday, the tenth of June
Mr. Robert Allen Whittemore   [OPTIONAL]
regrets exceedingly
that he will be unable to accept

When one wishes to substitute a different family member for the one specified in the invitation (because, for instance, the husband is ill, and a grown son can attend in his place), telephone first to explain the circumstances and to see if it is agreeable to the hosts; then write a reply as follows:

Mrs. Gordon Ashley and Mr. Gordon Ashley, Jr.
accept with pleasure
the kind invitation of
etc.

If younger, or teen-age, children receive invitations to a formal wedding in the same envelope as their parents, the reply should indicate either the acceptance of all parties, or the acceptance by either the children or the parents.

If everyone can attend, the reply reads:

Mr. and Mrs. Robert Jones
and their children
[OR, OPTIONALLY, Brenda and William]
accept with pleasure
the kind invitation
of Mr. and Mrs. Jackson Brown
for
Saturday, the fourteenth of October
at four o'clock

If only some members of the family can attend, the reply reads:

Brenda Jones
William Jones
accept with pleasure
the kind invitation
of Mr. and Mrs. Jackson Brown
for
Saturday, the fourteenth of October
at four o'clock
Mr. and Mrs. Robert Jones
regret that they are unable to attend

It is always a great compliment to receive a wedding invitation. As I have said, it never requires an answer unless it includes an invitation to the reception, but it is a gracious thing for the recipient to write the person to whom he feels indebted for the invitation—the bride's mother, father, the bride herself, or the groom or his family—about his happiness at the forthcoming event. Such a letter, as it is not in direct reply to the invitation, which needs none, is couched in the usual social form, not in the third person. It might read:

Dear Jack [TO THE GROOM],

The news of the forthcoming wedding is *great*. I'd give anything to be there, as you and Alice must know, but I shall drink a toast to your happiness on that day and hope for a quick trip home soon, so I can enjoy the sight of both of you *married*. How about that! My love to the beautiful bride,

An alternative to sending a letter is to send a Mailgram to the couple (by telephoning it at least one full day before the wedding, so it can be delivered to the wedding reception on the appropriate day). The Mailgram can be sentimental or witty or however you want it to be. It should be addressed to the couple, with the date of the wedding and the place of the reception carefully noted:

Mr. and Mrs. John Austin
Wedding Reception—Afternoon of March 18
The Metropolitan Club
60th and Fifth Avenue
New York, N.Y. 10022

Responding to a Foreign Wedding Invitation   Formal invitations to weddings abroad in another language are increasingly common. In many other countries it is customary for a wedding invitation to have two panels, one side an invitation from the bride's family, one side an invitation from the groom's family. When responding to such an invitation, reply only to the family from whom one presumes one has received the invitation. You should reply in English, using the proper formal reply for either an acceptance or a regret.

Recalling a Formal Acceptance

If you have accepted an engraved wedding invitation and then something occurs that makes it impossible for you to attend, you may write a formal regret, send a Mailgram, or telephone your excuses, but a valid excuse must be given. You certainly may not back out of an accepted invitation because a more attractive one has arrived. Illness, death in the family, or a sudden business trip are acceptable excuses. A regret, following a previous acceptance, may take this form:

Mr. and Mrs. Morrow Truitt
regret that the sudden illness
of Mrs. Truitt
prevents their attending
the wedding on
Friday, the ninth of June

Invitations to Informal Weddings

A small wedding does not require engraved invitations—in fact, they may seem pretentious. Instead, the mother of the bride may write short notes or Mailgram the invitation or telephone the relatives and friends who are to be invited to the ceremony or the reception or both.

If the bride's mother is dead, her father or some close relative, preferably an aunt or grandmother, issues the invitations. Or she may even issue them herself if she has no close relatives. Often, after such informal weddings, engraved announcements are sent to friends and relatives at a distance, but never to those who have been invited to the ceremony or the reception. An informal invitation to a wedding may be telephoned—or it may be written on the household's conservative notepaper, in dark ink, in this way:

> "The Sea Lane"
> Madison, Connecticut   zip code
> April 1st

Dear Jane,

Clare is being married here at home to Ronald Ward on Saturday, April 15, at four-thirty. We do hope you will be with us and can stay for a glass of champagne to toast the newlyweds afterward.

> Affectionately,
> Helen

A short note, giving the time and place of the ceremony, or, if the invitation is being issued only for the reception, the time and place of the reception, is all that is necessary. Informal invitations may be sent on short notice, but no shorter than two weeks beforehand, if possible.

Replies to an Informal Wedding Invitation

A reply to an informal wedding invitation can be sent either by note, by Mailgram, or by telephone call, but it should be done promptly. In telephoning an acceptance, the recipient asks to speak to the sender of the invitation, or, if someone responsible answers, one may leave the message. "Please tell Mrs. Samuel that Mr. and Mrs. Wainwright accept her invitation with great pleasure to her daughter's wedding on the fourth." A note in reply might read:

> November 20

Dear Lenore,

We are so happy about Consuelo's forthcoming marriage and are delighted and honored to be included. We'll drive over and spend the night at the Inn. I have already made reservations. We look forward to seeing you on the fourth!

> Love,

A Mailgram might read:

Mrs. Lenore Samuels
1402 Eaton Road
Shaker Heights, Ohio   zip code

We are thrilled about Consuelo's marriage and will be there on the fourth with great joy. We have already made our reservations at the Inn. Our love to you all.

Wedding Announcements

Wedding announcements, which are mailed the day of the wedding so that they are received within two days' time, as previously noted, are sent only to those not invited to the wedding. It is possible to send an announcement to a large group, such as a faculty or the staff of an office, by addressing it the organization and asking that it be posted on a bulletin board. Announcements read:

Dr. and Mrs. Grant Kingsley
have the honour of announcing
[OR HAVE THE HONOUR TO ANNOUNCE]
the marriage of their daughter
Penelope
to
Mr. George Frank Carpenter
on Friday, the ninth of June
One thousand nine hundred and seventy-eight
[MUST GIVE YEAR]
Saint Mary's Church [OPTIONAL TO MENTION]
San Francisco

Sometimes an At Home card is included in the announcement. It contains the couple's new address and telephone number (if theirs will be an unlisted number and if they wish only friends to have it).

Variations of the Usual Wording

The Mature Bride   The mature bride may issue her own announcement. For example:

Miss [OR "MS."] Jane Charlotte Spencer
and
Dr. Elliot Squires Jackson
announce their marriage
on Friday, the ninth of June
One thousand nine hundred and seventy-eight
New York

Remarriage of Divorced Persons to Each Other Occasionally people who have been divorced eventually remarry each other. When this occurs, no formal announcements are sent out, but friends are informed of the good news by word of mouth, by letter, and by Mailgram. No formal announcements are released to the press unless the couple is very well known, in which case it becomes a news story. Often children are involved, so the reunion of the couple should be made almost as if the schism had never existed.

Military and Naval Forms for Wedding Invitations and Announcements

Noncommissioned Officers and Enlisted Men often prefer to use only their names with the branch of service immediately below. For example:

Dr. and Mrs. Grant Kingsley
request the honour of your presence
at the marriage of their daughter
Cordelia
to
Winthrop Cass Bowers [NOTE, NOT "MR."]
United States Marine Corps

but

Winthrop Cass Bowers
Staff Sergeant, United States Marine Corps

is correct, too.

Regular Officer, U. S. Armed Forces Only where the officer's rank is Captain or above in the Army, Air Force, or Marines (or Commander or above in the Navy, Merchant Marine, and Coast Guard) does the title appear first:

Capt. [OR CAPTAIN] Winthrop Cass Bowers
United States Navy

In either case it is optional to mention the branch of service, though the regiment is omitted. It may read:

Captain Winthrop Cass Bowers
Artillery, United States Army

The rank of a junior officer is placed below his name.

Winthrop Cass Bowers
Lieutenant, United States Army

Reserve Officers on Active Duty If officers are in the Reserves it is only when they are *on active duty* that they use their ranks on wedding invitations and announcements. Otherwise, they are "Mr."

For a Reserve Officer on active duty the phrase "United States Army" changes to "Army of the United States."

Retired Regular Army and Navy Officers   High-ranking Army and Navy officers retired from regular service keep their ranks in civilian life. Their names in wedding invitations, announcements, and engraved forms read:

Commodore Vincent Ludlow Bird
United States Navy, Retired   [NOTE COMMA]

or

Lt. General Packard Deems
United States Marine Corps, Retired

Retired or Inactive Reserve Officers (*Colonels or below*)   Do not use their former titles, socially or otherwise.

The Bride in Military Service   uses her military title in wedding invitations and announcements with the identifying branch of the service as does a man in service. When she is marrying a man in the armed forces, the service appears beneath each title.

Chapter 12

WEDDING GIFTS*

The Bridal Registry

There is no question but that the counseling of a good bridal consultant and an intelligent registering of one's gifts with a local department store or jewelry store is a tremendous help to someone who is not quite sure of her choices. The bridal registry also avoids the possibilities of many gift duplications and assures the couple of receiving things they want, in their taste. A good bridal consultant helps a bride color-co-ordinate her choices for her table, and sees to it that she is properly registered in the store's book and in all the proper departments. Choosing silver, china, and crystal patterns should, however, be a joint venture of both the bride and groom.

It is less confusing for all concerned if a bride registers with only one store of a kind. She should name some larger, expensive items, too, in case some of her friends or relatives prefer to give her a present jointly—for example, a pair of delicate crystal candelabra, a large silver bowl, or a set of expensive dessert plates. Another virtue of registering wedding gift preferences in a store is that people will be able to judge the bride's taste, which can guide them in buying a present elsewhere, or in giving something from their own "treasure closet" at home.

No girl should allow the store at which she is registered to send out notices to her friends and wedding guest list that she is registered there. That is rank commercialism and the height of bad taste. If the girl has registered, she must trust family and friends to spread the word. Most people like to have suggestions on what to buy as a wedding gift, and appreciate the chance to purchase something they know the bride and groom actually want and will use.

Wedding Gift Register

Every bride should have her own wedding gift register, a handsome book with empty pages or else one specially printed for this occasion, in which to

* For suggestions for wedding gifts to give, see pages 779–83.

record her gifts. As each wedding gift arrives and is unpacked, the bride or her mother should enter the name and address of the person who sent the gift, the store from which it came (in case it has to be returned as a duplication), a description of the item, and the date the thank-you note was mailed out. This book is fun to look at later in life, but it is also useful in helping the couple personally thank people again in the future when they come to visit. "Remember you sent us this salad bowl as a wedding present?" Aunt Mary is bound to be impressed.

Gifts at Receptions

In some country areas where parcel-post packages must be picked up at the post office, it is customary for guests to take wedding gifts to receptions. A gift table is set up and gifts noted in the bride's book by a friend or member of the family. It is improper to open any gifts at the reception. This prevents misplacement of cards, possible breakage in retransportation, and hurt feelings on the part of guests who may have brought something modest.

Wedding Gift Display

The custom of displaying the wedding gifts in a separate room at the wedding reception is seen less and less often. If such a display is set up at home (one should not attempt it at a club or hotel, for the danger of theft and breakage is too great), the gift cards should not be attached. Nor should any checks or money be in evidence. I feel it is easier and less pretentious for both the bride and groom to invite their closest friends over to see the gifts informally during the festivities. One of my nieces invited me over to see her wedding presents the week of her wedding, but, as she put it, "just for a look-see, Aunt Tish, no big deal." This seems to be the trend of the times, and it's a good one.

The Bride's Thank-you Letters

Even if the bride does not know the senders of the gift, who may be particular friends of her husband's, or even if she has thanked them verbally, she should write a thank-you note just as soon as she possibly can—certainly within two or three weeks of the receipt of the gift. Thank-you notes should never be written on cards that say "thank-you" on the top fold. They should be on good-quality note paper or correspondence cards. If the groom helps his bride with the thank-you note chores, he can use his own personal engraved letterheads, or he can write on the inside of engraved "Mr. and Mrs." joint informals or correspondence cards.

If the wedding is extremely large, with several hundred wedding gifts to thank for, an engraved card should be mailed out immediately upon receipt of the gift:

Miss [OR MS.] Penelope Kingsley
wishes to acknowledge the receipt
of your lovely wedding gift
and will write a personal note of thanks
at an early date.

When writing thank-you notes, no matter how tired you may be with the entire project, make each one a personal statement and an enthusiastic one. When a gift has been received from a couple, you can write either to Mr. and Mrs. Brown, or to Mrs. Brown and refer to Mr. Brown in the body of the note. One never addresses a couple as "the Browns" or writes "Dear Browns." Sign your thank-you note according to how well you know the person—"Sincerely," "Cordially," "With love," or "Affectionately."

If the engaged woman writes her thank-you notes before the wedding, she uses on the return address her maiden name and present address not her future married name and address. If she knows what her address will be after her marriage, however, it is a good idea to include it in her thank-you note.

Thank-you Notes for Gifts of Money When you are acknowledging gifts of money, it is better not to mention the sum. What *is* a good idea to include is how you are going to use the money, as the donor is usually interested.

Dear Aunt Mary,
What a beautiful, wonderful, generous, marvelous check! We've been having an argument every night over what to use it for, so we finally agreed that it will be used for much-needed furniture in our apartment—which at this point might be described, design-wise, as "early barren."
Thank you *so* much from us both. You're a *wonderful aunt.*
Affectionately,

Husbands Can Write Thank-you Notes It has been a firm tradition that thank-you notes are written by the female partner in the marriage. Along with everything else, this strict protocol of letter writing is changing. A woman who is under as much pressure as her husband—whether they are graduate students together or both working—has the right to ask her husband to assist in the job of writing the many thank-you notes for their wedding presents (and to help in all thank-you notes thereafter). Here is the kind of note a man could write:

Dear Eleanor,
Cynthia and I are really laboring at full steam with our daytime jobs and night school. We're both getting our master's, as you probably know. She's at the library tonight and joins me in thanking you and Jim and wanting you to know that your martini pitcher is an integral part of our household. In

fact, we sometimes think our friends love us only for the quality of our martinis, served in *your* shaker. It is a multi-purpose one, for we use it for a flower vase and a bread stick holder, too. Many thanks from us both,

Sincerely,

In years to come it will become traditional for husbands and wives to interchange in the task of writing thank-you notes, and who writes the note will depend on who writes better letters or who has more time. Social responsibility is meant to be shared in marriage, like everything else. The question of who does the writing is irrelevant; what is important is that the note is written, written well, and written promptly. It is a tool of good manners and an act of kindness extended in return for another act of kindness.

When a Gift Is Exchanged

Gifts from the immediate family of either the bride or groom should never be returned to a store in exchange for something else, as feelings could be easily hurt by such an action. The couple may certainly exchange duplicate gifts, however, for something else they want or need. They do not have to inform the donor they have done this. I remember two large weddings of friends when one bride received eleven of the same ice bucket and the other managed to receive twenty-three of the same crystal salad bowl. Whoever writes the thank-you note for such a present thanks for the ice bucket or the salad bowl, and not for the item for which it was exchanged.

Returning Wedding Gifts

When an engagement is broken or a wedding does not take place, the gifts must be returned to all senders with brief and tactful notes of explanation. The bride-to-be should enclose a note with the gift, written in her own hand, saying something like: "We decided to call it off and are both glad we managed to do it in time. Thank you again for the lovely present but I'm sure you can understand why I feel I should return it rather than keep it." If the gift came from friends or relatives of the groom, then he should write the note of explanation with the package. Each should take the responsibility for their own friends' gifts; in the case of joint friends, the bride and her family would take care of it. When an annulment takes place almost immediately after the marriage, any unused gifts should be returned to the donor, but never directly to the stores.

Only when the prospective groom has died is it proper for the girl to keep wedding gifts—and then only if she is strongly urged to do so, in some cases, by a donor whose gift may have a sentimental rather than monetary value. She should not keep gifts intended for a joint household that will never be. If a wedding has been postponed for any reason, gifts are not returned unless after a reasonable length of time the marriage still does not take place. In the event that the marriage lasts a brief time, the gifts legally belong equally to both. Traditionally, it has been customary to allot all wedding gifts to the bride except those explicitly given to the groom, but this is not fair. An equitable division of the gifts from mutual friends is far better. It is, of course, proper to return to the donors any jewelry or heirlooms received from the groom's family. Other gifts are not returned to the senders unless, perhaps, the gifts have not been opened and used.

Gifts for the Attendants from the Bride and Groom

Both bride and groom give their attendants some lasting memento of the occasion—the groom at his bachelor dinner, the bride at any convenient time before the wedding (usually a week in advance when all her attendants are together). If they wish to do so, it is appropriate for the bride and groom to give their honor attendants slightly more elaborate presents than they give the other members of the wedding party. For example, a bride might give each of her attendants a small gold heart, and her maid or matron of honor a gold chain, too, for the heart pendant.

The groom might give his ushers gold tie clips and his best man a gold belt buckle. It is nice to personalize these items with the initials of the bride and groom and the wedding date.

A present liked by everyone is a picture frame (it does not have to silver), sent to each member of the wedding party by the couple after the photographs have been printed and completed. A good photo of the entire wedding party, or of just the bride and groom, would be inside each frame, of course. Other ideas for presents, many of which are suitable for engraving, are:

Bridesmaids	Ushers
Silver key chain	Silver key chain
Gold bangle bracelet	Pocket flask
Pendant on necklace chain	Tie clip
Zodiac charm	Cuff links
Silver compact	Letter opener
Silver pocket mirror	Bar knife
Silver pin tray	Silver jigger
Lighter	Lighter
Leather earring box (with initials in gold)	Leather stud box (with initials in gold)
Gold brooch	Gold belt buckle
Gold hair ornament	Monogrammed bar glasses

Gifts to the Bride and Groom from Their Wedding Party

Toasting goblet in silver, pewter, or crystal—engraved or etched with couple's initials and wedding date

Sterling silver or good leather or inlaid wood or damask-covered photo
    frame to contain large photograph of the bride, of the bride and groom
    together, or of the entire wedding party
Silver tray for serving cocktails (engraved with wedding date and initials)
Silver box, the lid of which is engraved with a facsimile of the wedding invi-
    tation or of all the wedding party's signatures
Silver cocktail shaker or martini mixer, engraved
Set of four silver or pewter mugs, engraved—to put on library shelf or to
    use for cocktails or to use as flower holders for dinner table decorations
His and her matching wristwatches, with wedding date engraved on back
Mantelpiece clock—with brass plaque engraved with wedding date
Large leather photo box, embossed in gold and with wedding party's signa-
    tures written in gold on it

The Bridal Couple's Gifts to Each Other

The groom usually gives his bride a personal gift just before the wedding,
something sentimental and preferably of permanent value, such as a piece of
jewelry (an engraved gold heart on a chain, a string of pearls, a wristwatch
with the wedding date engraved on the back). If the man has no budget
problems, he might give his bride-to-be a diamond brooch, a new car, or a
fur coat. If he has great budget problems, he can give her something that
costs very little but has great meaning.

The bride in turn gives something to the groom—an engraved silver hair
or clothes brush, her wedding photograph in a silver frame, a handsome
monogrammed desk set for his office, or anything that is meaningful for his
personal use.

Today there is much more imagination used in choosing these personal
gifts than ever before. The bride may receive a sporty fur coat from the
groom, and he may receive from her a black leather wing chair and a black
leather-topped desk for his "den."

If one of the pair is far richer than the other, the one with the more
money should "tone down" his or her present. There will be plenty of time
for lavish presents later, on other occasions.

Chapter 13

TODAY'S TROUSSEAU

Traditionally, the bride brought to the marriage all the household linens and kitchen equipment, plus a wardrobe for all seasons of the first year of her married life. But no longer does a bride's family have to scrimp and save for years, borrowing money and selling treasured possessions in order to send a daughter forth with a proper dowry and trousseau. Today's bride brings what she can for her new home. If her groom is well fixed fiancially and she is not, *he* pays for the household furnishings. What usually happens is that they select them together, and share the expenses of buying them, if both are of similar means.

The trousseau today consists of pretty lingerie the bride-to-be may have received at a lingerie shower, several nice dresses, some casual clothes, and whatever linens and kitchen equipment she may have received at her shower. It is hardly what the bride of yesteryear moved into the closets of her first home. But our way of life has changed, and along with it the trousseau. Pure linen sheets used to be part of every proper bride's household trousseau. Today's bride would not even know how to launder and press them; she lives in a drip-dry world. The traditional hope chest has disappeared from view, unless one can call an old trunk that has been repainted and is used both for storage and as a coffee table today's hope chest.

Bed and Bath Linens

If the couple know where they will be living, and the color schemes of their new home, it is fairly easy to color-co-ordinate their linens. But if, when they begin purchasing linens, they do not know these things, it might be smart for the bride to choose white. It would be sad for her to choose bold Roman-striped colored towels and accessories, only to discover that the bathroom in the new apartment is a bower of delicate pink roses. If she chooses good white percale or fine cotton sheets, the top one may be monogrammed, either in white or in a color to match the blankets. The linens may be monogrammed with a woman's maiden name initials or her

maiden name combined with her husband's last name. We see less monogramming of linen, including towels, today, of course, because of the high-
fashion patterns and textures. It is best to purchase the bedspread last of all,
so that it will co-ordinate well with the final design scheme of the bedroom.
If one has not yet decided on the decoration scheme of one's bedroom-to-be,
one should not try to buy a bedspread for it, and usually it is better to
purchase window curtains or draperies and the bedspread at the same time.

Linens for the Table

Here again, one should have the measurements of the dining table and the
color and pattern schemes of the dining area before making purchases.
Every couple should have one very good tablecloth of damask, lace, or
embroidered linen that fits their table, with matching napkins. It does not
have to be an early purchase. It will be used for special entertaining only,
and while it will be either an inconvenience or an expense or both to
launder, it will still be worth it!

For regular use, every couple should have: two sets (four to six in each)
of plastic everyday place mats, with which they can use paper napkins, and
two sets (six to eight) of nicer ones, with color-co-ordinating fabric napkins,
for special occasions. These mats can be made of pure cotton or linen, or of
a natural material, such as braided straw, hemp, mother of-pearl, or cork.

China Services for Today

Many brides buy starter sets of four place settings in their patterns of fine
china, but more and more of them are turning away from buying place settings and buying instead eight to twelve of one type of plate at a time—
dinner size, luncheon size, then dessert, then demitasses and tea cups and
saucers. Many never buy butter plates or soup plates. The service does not
have to match, course by course. All of the plates for any one course at a
formal dinner should match, except that at demitasse time the coffee cups
may be a collection of antique cups, all different. Serving platters and items
like sugar bowls and creamers and sauceboats can be of silver, crystal, or
porcelain. They do not have to match the good china service.

Everyday china can be an inexpensive earthenware or plastic (if you like
plastic). It is better to buy this in separate pieces, too, according to what one
needs, rather than in the place setting or in an entire set form. If you don't
eat boiled eggs, don't buy eggcups. If you like your morning coffee in mugs,
buy mugs instead of coffee cups, and saucers (as long as you have your good
porcelain ones for entertaining). People on budgets should get along with
the minimum of everyday china but invest in really fine and beautiful things
to enjoy on special occasions.

Serving Containers

Serving containers do not have to match your china pattern. Buy only the containers that will be useful for what you eat. If you are in the habit of serving small portions of several vegetables for dinner, then buy several small serving bowls; if you normally have only one vegetable for dinner, then buy only one or two. Most newlyweds need only one large oval serving platter; those who entertain constantly for buffets and cocktail parties will need more. Some people need only one salad bowl; others need several, because they have a salad every night and they also use this type of bowl to serve desserts or fruit. Buy according to how you live and don't stock your shelves with unused dust catchers.

Almost everyone needs a water pitcher, a few small condiment dishes, and salt and pepper sets: good ones for guests, everyday ones for your own regular table, plus another pair for the kitchen stove. If you are a great saucemaker, then you will need a pair of sauce servers, with small ladles. Others who never make sauces simply do not need to stock their shelves with sauce boats; when they have a sauce, they can put it in a small serving bowl and use a ladle.

If one has a spacious kitchen, one should furnish it with a proper balance of useful objects and aesthetic ones that are more for appreciation's sake than for function. If one has a small kitchen, forget aesthetic objects and concentrate on an aesthetic arrangement of necessary items.

Tea Service

Until the middle of the twentieth century, a bride "had" to have a tea service, preferably in sterling silver, if not in very fine china. Today the tea service looks beautiful on the dining room sideboard, but young marrieds have little time for the daytime social act of serving tea. That does not mean that the drinking of tea is not popular in America today, for it is more popular than ever. But it is made more often "behind the scenes" in the kitchen than out front with the ritual of using the lovely tea service. A good earthenware teapot is an essential of any tea drinker's household.

Silver

Regardless of the informaility of many of today's households, the reason for having sterling silver flatware is as relevant today as it was when silver wedding presents were given in ancient Greece. Almost everyone has stainless-steel flatware for everyday use; but when it comes time for a dinner party, or a special occasion of any kind, including a birthday in the family, the visual and tactile joys derived from good heavy sterling flatware are undeniable.

Many girls begin collecting their own flat silver during their unmarried working years. There is no reason to assume they should wait to entertain graciously until they're married. Young women are entertaining more often and more creatively than ever before, and they care about a beautifully set table with good china, crystal, and silver. Sterling flatware is being purchased by the item, too, like good china, rather than always in the traditional place setting form.

Silver styles do not change quickly. Heavy, elaborate embossed or repoussé silver is hard to clean; but the contemporary-design silver is easier to scratch. One can combine elaborate silver and plain china with ease in any table setting; likewise, elaborate table linens and china patterns with modern, unadorned crystal and silver. Design-wise, a balance is best, which should be kept in mind when buying china, crystal, and silver patterns.

A dozen of everything in all-sterling flatware is ideal, but a young bride can do very well with six dinner knives, dinner forks, salad forks, teaspoons, and dessert spoons. The teaspoon will be used for consommé and cream soup, for desserts in small containers, and for grapefruit or fruit cup, as well as for tea or coffee. The dessert spoon will do for soups in soup plates and for desserts served on flat plates. She will need two pairs of serving spoons and forks, a butter server, a cheese knife, a carving set, a cake knife, and, of course, after-dinner coffee spoons.

If her budget is limited she should avoid purchasing flat silver that is used only occasionally—fruit knives and forks, oyster forks, iced-tea spoons, fish forks and knives, cheese scoops, and the like. If ancestral silver is to be used, it is probable that some of these things will be missing anyhow and substitutes will have to be found.

A word of warning to the bride who rejects offers of sterling silver when she marries in favor of household furnishings she feels she needs more. *If you don't get your sterling now, you may never get it.* Once a family starts growing, its constant needs too often absorb funds we thought would be available for something so basic as sterling. So we "make do" over the years with ill-assorted cutlery, deceptively inexpensive because it wears out.

Never again in her lifetime will a girl find her family and friends in such a giving and sentimental mood as they are at the time of her wedding. If she and her husband begin their married life with very little in worldly goods, they should at least be able to set their table with enough silver flatware for four people to dine. The rest of the silver can be added to the set in the future. The beginnings of a bride's silver should be in her possession—on her wedding day.

The Monogramming of Silver   The bride chooses her monogram style in the silver department of the store where she has registered. If she is unsure of what monogram she wants, she should consult the store experts about the most appropriate kind for the design of flatware she has chosen. Since she has registered the desired number of flatware and hollow ware pieces, the store will be able to monogram any pieces bought for her as wedding presents. It is preferable not to engrave hollow ware pieces and trays that are not listed in the bride's registry, in case they are duplicates or unwanted items. Once monogrammed, they cannot be returned or exchanged.

Today's bride has several options for her silver monogramming. She may have her silver marked either with the first initial of her given name or with the initials of her given name and surname, or with her maiden name initials and her husband's last name initial. The initials can be monogrammed straight across or vertically on the front or the back of the flatware pieces. Often an asterisk is included in the design. If Louise Swanson were marrying John Minton, her silver might be engraved thus:

$$L \quad or \quad L*S \quad or \quad L*S*M$$

She may wish to use her husband's and her first-name initials, in combination with the initial of his last name (Europeans have done this for many centuries), engraved on the underside of the flatware handles, in an inverted triangle or a triangle, with an asterisk. The monogram done in this manner would be:

$$\begin{matrix} L \ J & & M \\ * & or & * \\ M & & L \ J \end{matrix}$$

If a couple buys their silver flatware together after they are married, a combination of his and her initials should be on the pieces, so the monogramming immediately above would be correct. If a woman retains her maiden name after her marriage, a double monogram may be used, as, for example, with Louise Swanson and John Minton:

$$\begin{matrix} L \ J & & LS \\ * & or & * \\ S \ M & & JM \end{matrix}$$

Remember, however, that silver engraving is frightfully expensive—the more so, the more letters you use.

Fine Glassware

Of all a young bride's household possessions, the most fragile and therefore the fastest-disappearing is her fine crystal. She should not only keep it out of her dishwasher, but she should wash every glass by hand herself. Broken sets seldom get filled out again. That is why it is very wise to buy more than what you need in your pattern. If you want a dozen wineglasses, buy sixteen of them so that you have a good chance of lasting quite a few years with enough for dinner for twelve. Do the same with your good water goblets, champagne glasses, and liqueur glasses. Often a patter will be discontinued by the time you go to the store to order more pieces of it.

Glassware   (All shapes are optional)

1. *Water goblet. For entertaining.*
2. *Water tumbler. For everyday family use.*
3. *Juice glass. 3 to 4 oz.*
4. *Old-fashioned glass. 10 to 14 oz. are the most popular today. Fill close to the top, but with a lot of ice. Use for all kinds of on-the-rocks drinks.*
5. *Highball glass. Fill close to the top, including water and ice.*
6. *Shot glass. 1½ oz. For whiskey.*
7. *Red wine glass. 6 to 9 oz. Fill ½ full.*
8. *White wine glass. 4 to 6 oz. Fill ½ full.*
9. *All-purpose wineglass, tulip-shaped. Fill ½ full.*
10. *All-purpose wineglass, bowl-shaped. Fill ½ full.*
11. *Hock or Rhine wine glass. Often made of colored glass or decorated. Fill ¾ full.*

12. *Saucer-shaped champagne glass. Solid stems are preferred. Used for champagne cocktails, too. Fill close to top.*
13. *Tulip-shaped champagne glass. Fill ¾ full.*
14. *Traditional sherry glass. Around 4 oz. Fill ⅔ full.*
15. *Brandy snifter. 8 to 12 oz. Fill only ¼ full; for larger glasses, use even less.*
16. *Sweet liqueur or cordial glass. 2 oz. Fill ¾ full.*
17. *Martini glass. 3 oz. May also be used for other cocktails not served on the rocks. Fill close to top.*
18. *Punch glass. Fill ¾ full.*
19. *Iced-tea glass.*
20. *Pilsner glass.*
21. *Beer mug.*
22. *Ice-cream parfait glass.*
23. *Irish coffee glass.*

If you have a set of fine bar glasses, have a larger set of not so fine bar glasses to use for every day, but which may be used for a big party, too. If you care about your fine crystal, you should wash it after a party, dry it, and put it away, no matter how late the hour.

If you need more fine crystal, haunt the auctions and antique shops. Sometimes the values are extraordinarily good. If you attend an auction, go ahead to inspect the condition of the crystal closely. Do not buy any pieces with chips or cracks in them.

If your good crystal is chipped in the rim, take it to a specialist who grinds down glass. He might be able to salvage the glass for you. You will find the names and addresses of these repairers of porcelain and glass in antique magazines, and they are sometimes listed in classified directories.

Basic Household Needs

Linen List   When the couple begins to organize their household furnishings seriously, their first decision should be the kind of bed they want. Until this decision is made, no bed linens naturally should be purchased. (Nor should a hostess plan a bed and bath shower for an engaged girl without knowing this in advance.)

FOR THE BEDROOM (each item is per bed):
Bedspread and dust ruffle (last to be purchased)
Quilted mattress cover
3 sets of sheets (fitted bottom and top sheet in each set) and matching pillowcases
Thermal blanket (lightweight, for summer)
Heavy blanket (or electric blanket)
Quilt (not needed if there is an electric blanket)
Blanket cover
2 pillows per person
2 pillow covers

FOR THE BATH:
In matching towel sets:
    3 bath mats, one for each pattern of towels
    3 complete sets of 2 each of the following
    Large bath towels
    Face towels
    Facecloths
Shower curtain (with plastic liner, if necessary)
6 pretty guest towels (in terry, embroidered linen, printed cotton, etc.)
Bathroom rug

For the Kitchen

Basic Necessities:

3 sizes of saucepans (one should be a double boiler)
2 sizes of frying pans (larger one should have lid)
2 sizes of aluminum or Pyrex baking pans
Coffee pot
Meat broiling pan (two-piece)
Roasting pan with lid
Colander
Large strainer
2 sizes of oven-to-table covered casseroles
Set of sharp kitchen knives (chopping, carving, bread, etc.)
Carving fork
Cutting board
Mixing spoons
Set of canisters
Teakettle
Egg beater
Wire whisk
Large kitchen wastebasket
Set of mixing bowls
Can and bottle openers
Tongs
Slotted spoon
Corkscrew
Step-on garbage can
Salad bowl with salad servers
Grater
Peeler
Juicer
Small strainer
Set of measuring spoons
Pair of measuring cups
Set of plastic food storage containers
Cookie sheet
Pie plate
Flour sifter
Electric toaster-oven or toaster
Set of pot holders and oven mitts
Kitchen apron
Rubber spatula
Rolling pin
Cake pan
Wire racks
Spice rack

Muffin tin
Set of 4 linen dish towels
Dispenser for paper towels, plastic wrap and foil
Ladle
Set of wooden stirring spoons
Cookbook

Niceties

Electric items: can opener, juicer, blender, mixer, food processor, pop-corn maker, knife, crock pot, yogurt maker, ice-cream maker, coffee bean grinder, etc.
Rotisserie grill (indoors or outdoors)
Molds
Skewers
Funnel
Pastry brush
Vegetable brush
Wall-mounted library shelf for cookbook collection
Handsome cookie jar
Covered cake plate
Serving trays of different sizes—electric hot tray
Large dutch oven
Bacon cooker
Metric scale

For the Kitchen Closet

Dust rags (clean) in a laundry bag
Sponges
Dustpan and brush
Broom
Wet mop—dry mop
Rubber draining mat with stacking unit (if there is no dishwasher)
Stool or fold-up stepladder
Vacuum cleaner
Scrub pail full of cleaning supplies, scrub brush, detergents, etc.
Iron and ironing board.

(See also kitchen shower and linen shower gifts, pages 774–75.)

Chapter 14

PREPARATIONS FOR THE WEDDING

It is the bride's family that sets the size and style of the wedding, according to the wishes of the bride herself, unless these seem totally unreasonable. No family should go into debt over an extravagant wedding not in keeping with their daily life-style.

There are relatively few "musts" in planning your wedding today, but I believe strongly that there was never a successful wedding that did not contain at least a momentary understanding of the importance, seriousness, and solemnity surrounding the joining of two people in the eyes of God. It is a time for respecting tradition and sacred institutions, not for making a mockery of them. It should not be an occasion for merely attracting publicity or for breaking records for being amusing, daring, or outrageous.

In the 1960s the advent of both the youth revolution and the ecumenical movement saw great changes in the wedding ceremony. Some of the youth movement's experimentation was beautiful—the selection of a couple's own prayers and scriptural readings, and special music, for example, and the turning of natural outdoor settings into the most solemn of chapels. Too many, however, of these services degenerated into folksy undignified "happenings" with young people dressed almost in caricature. The ecumenical development, on the other hand, saw weddings being performed by clergy of two different faiths, each bestowing his blessing of one God on the new union.

Happily, the good influence of the 1960s has stayed and the bad has more or less evaporated. Formal weddings are once again popular; freakishness is not. The personal touch—the addition of personal pledges written by the couple themselves—is often present in today's ceremonies, combined with the traditional formal ceremony. The ecumenical spirit has grown even stronger in the uniting of two people of different professed faiths. Most couples today look upon their wedding as something they very much want to be beautiful, dignified, and meaningful.

Arrangements with the Clergyman

The bride chooses the officiator at her wedding (minister, priest, rabbi, judge). She is usually married by her own clergyman in her own church (or other place of worship), unless the groom himself is a clergyman or the son of one, in which case he usually selects the officiator. When the time comes to make the actual arrangements for the religious ceremony, both bride and groom should visit the clergyman together to decide upon a service that has personal meaning for them. The couple should have several alternate dates and more than one specific hour in mind, in case there is a conflict with other weddings and events previously scheduled in the church. At this time, the clergyman will discuss church regulations that must be followed, but basically he will work out with the couple the kind of wedding ceremony they really want. The clergyman prefers to see the couple before the ceremony to assure himself that there is no impediment to the union about to take place. When both principals are well known to the clergyman, sometimes the bride's mother makes the arrangements with the family's clergyman.

Special Problems

Catholics may not marry divorced people, except under very special circumstances and with special permission from the Sacred Rota in Rome.

Protestants who have been divorced may have some difficulty marrying in a church, especially if they have been divorced more than once. Some ministers make the distinction that they will remarry only the "injured party" in a divorce. They require that divorced persons present the credentials permitting their marriage.

Choosing a Place for the Wedding

If the bride feels that she wants a wedding that is too large or too formal for her parish church, she should investigate the possibility of availing herself of the facilities of a nearby cathedral of her own denomination, or of a cathedral in a city where she may be living at the time of her engagement. The girl's home town is usually chosen because it means that more of her friends and relatives will be able to attend and that her mother will be able to share with her the burden of wedding planning.

If the wedding is to be held in a public place such as a hotel, restaurant, or club, it is best to have several comparable places in mind that fit your budget and other requirements.

If the home towns of the bride and groom are widely separated, one should consider having the wedding in the home town of the bride and a later reception in the home town of the groom given by his parents or other relatives or possibly even by friends.

Choosing a Time for the Wedding

The time of day considered fashionable for weddings differs in different parts of the country. In New York many fashionable Protestant weddings take place at four, four-thirty, or five in the afternoon. Evening weddings are relatively rare in the East but fashionable in many other parts of the country (see below). Their own Sabbath, Christian or Jewish, is usually not chosen for a wedding day by brides of these faiths (religious Jews may not be married on the Sabbath—Friday sundown through Saturday sundown—or on High Holy Days and major festivals), nor is Lent by Catholics. It is not considered good taste for any Christians to have large weddings during Lent, though, of course, simple marriages with or without a clergyman do take place during these forty days of penitence.

Formal and informal Catholic weddings usually take place in church at a nuptial mass, which may be said at any hour a mass is permitted. Early morning weddings are frequently followed by a wedding breakfast. Weddings that take place later, at eleven or twelve, are also followed by wedding breakfasts—really lunch. No Catholic wedding takes place after seven at night, except in the case of an emergency such as a grave illness.

Protestant morning weddings are usually simple and informal, with the bride wearing a dress or suit, not a wedding gown. Wedding breakfasts—again, really lunch—may follow. In some parts of the country, Protestant weddings sometimes do take place at noon, that is, truly formal weddings with a bride in full bridal array and the groom and his attendants in cutaways.

The Evening Wedding Evening weddings take place mainly in the South and West. They may be formal or informal and may take place in church or at home. The preparations and procedures follow those of the daytime wedding. See Chapter 17, "Dress for the Wedding."

Church Preparations

Decorations Decorations in the church may be limited to suitable altar flowers—where decorating of the alter is permitted—for a small wedding or may be extensive and expensive, despite the desired simplicity of effect. Sometimes only the aisle posts on the *reserved* pews are decorated, even for very formal weddings. But a clever florist can do impressive things with boxwood, palms, ferns, and various available greenery, with or without flowers —which, if used, need not be white.

You will be wise to speak to a florist very soon after you have chosen the date and place of your wedding. For a florist to do his best work he needs ample time to prepare, and besides, there are just so many weddings he can do on any given day, and it would be unfortunate for you to be disappointed in this respect. When you speak with him, be specific about how much money you are willing to spend for floral decorations both at the ceremony and at the reception. With this information firmly in his mind he will be better able to create a floral design in keeping with your budget and you will not be unpleasantly surprised with a bill for which you are unprepared.

In general, it is wise to remember that churches are often dimly lit and that very subtle shades of flowers will go unappreciated in this setting. Blues and lavenders are particularly to be avoided unless they gather support from contrasting colors used in the arrangement. Often there is more than one wedding held in a church on the same day. In such a case the mothers of the brides should meet, confer, agree on one florist, compromise on their flower designs, and split the cost for decorating the church.

An effort should be made to co-ordinate the reception flowers with those used at the ceremony. And of course it should be remembered that flowers play a purely supporting role in a wedding, so they should never be wildly elaborate.

Who Pays for the Flowers?   In some parts of the country the groom pays for his own, his best man's, and the ushers' boutonnieres, and that of his father. He also pays for the bride's bouquet and the corsages (if they wish to wear them) of his mother and the grandmothers. However, this complicated division of fiscal responsibility is losing favor, and most florists now bill the bride's family for all the wedding flowers. If they wish, the family may collect from the groom's family for a portion of it. The florist needs to be told, of course, where to send the corsages and the men's boutonnieres.

The bride and her mother select the flowers for the church, in conference with a florist, and also those for the bridesmaids' bouquets or headpieces and for the reception. Most brides today select their own bouquet and their family pays for it, unlike the old tradition.

Canopy and Carpet   The canopy from the curb to the church door for formal weddings is not used much today, but the church aisle is often carpeted by the florist when he decorates the church. Or immediately before the procession starts and after the bride's mother is seated (and no one should be admitted after she starts down the aisle), two ushers starting in either direction roll the canvas covering, if one is to be used, down the aisle. The canvas is not centered. If the bride is to go down the aisle on her father's right arm, the canvas is slightly to the right. If she is to go down on his left arm, the canvas is placed slightly to the left. This serves as a protection to the bride's train and is left down until all the guests have left. The florist, or whoever furnished the canvas, removes it.

Wedding Music   It is necessary to discuss the wedding music with the officiating clergyman and the church's music director or organist, as various rules apply. In some churches soloists are not permitted, in others only rigidly prescribed music may be played by the organist. It is never in good taste for a bride or groom to sing at her or his own wedding. The *Lohengrin* "Wedding March" is traditional in Protestant processionals, while the Mendelssohn "Wedding March" from *A Midsummer Night's Dream* is popular as the recessional. Many brides prefer music that is not so expected. The organist should be conferred with, both as to the appropriateness of the suggested music and as to its suitability to the cadence of the processional and recessional. There is a fee of twenty-five to a hundred dollars for the organist, depending on the community and church, with an additional fee for soloists or a choir, if they are used, too. The bride and her family should ask the church officials about these details beforehand. If a member of the bridal couple's family is an accomplished organist and wishes to play as his or her gift to the couple, special permission must be otained from the clergyman, and the regular organist should still receive his fee, even if he is not allowed to play.

Wedding Photographs

Although there are more detailed instructions for the formal bridal portrait later on, this is a good time to remember that candid pictures and formal group pictures of the wedding party must be arranged well ahead of time. Compare the service and prices of local wedding photographers, but the best recommendation is from other brides and their parents. The photographer will give you advance advice on how to organize things so that the right pictures will be taken and the important pictures not missed. Color candids are now reasonable in price; remember to protect them in your wedding book, however, with some kind of plastic cover, so they won't fade in time.

The bride's family usually pays for this photographic coverage. It is a nice gesture if her family also pays for six or eight wedding pictures to present to the groom's family; his family can then order more from the proofs and pay for these extras themselves. It is best not to let a friend who is a "good photographer" take the wedding candids. It is a tough, demanding job; one has to know how to pose people and when to diplomatically intervene to get a good shot. It is also an imposition on any guest if he is asked to take pictures at a wedding, since his pleasure as a guest and duty as a photographer are bound to conflict at times.

Wedding Guest Book

As soon as possible after preparations for the wedding are begun, someone should be commissioned to purchase the album that you will use for your Wedding Guest Book (it can, of course, be a shower gift). Any attractive album with sufficient space for all of your guests to sign would be suitable, although albums designed specifically for this purpose are available.

Wedding Reception Music

While the actual day is relatively far away and things are still in the planning stages, you should make inquiries about the inclusion of music at your reception. Unless you are having a large dance after your ceremony, a two- or three-piece combo should be all that is necessary for dancing and incidental music. Consult with friends and family to see what musicians they may have used whom they would recommend, as good bands or combos are usually booked far in advance, especially during the popular wedding seasons.

Such details dealt with early are easily resolved. Left until the last minute they can be tension-provoking.

Putting Up Guests

In the days of larger houses and more commodious apartments, it was usual to put out-of-town members of the wedding, the groom's parents, and close relatives at the bride's own house, with neighbors, and with friends. Today hotels and motels mostly must take over this function. In the case of the groom's parents, if they are coming from out of town, the bride's mother writes or phones and offers to make a reservation at the hotel or motel of their choice—or she suggests one if they don't know the community. It is then usual for them to take care of their own hotel bills, but the bride's parents may assume them if they wish and are able to do so. Of course, it is still acceptable to find them quarters with relatives or friends or put them up in their own home if they have the room. Out-of-town bridal atttendants are accommodated the same way, but where hotel expenses are involved, it is usual for the groom to assume those of his attendants and for the bride's family to assume those of hers, if they can manage this financially. The arrangements should be perfectly clear to the attendants at the time they are asked to participate, and whether the bride's family or the groom's family will pay should be discussed and decided upon *well* in advance of the wedding.

Expenses of the Bride's Parents

Often today the groom and his family offer to share some of the costs that have traditionally been the burden of the bride's parents. For instance, in most parts of the country the groom's family now gives the rehearsal dinner or supper the night before the wedding. If the groom's family does not offer to contribute, the bride's family should not ask. It must be volunteered. Otherwise, the bride's family should give the kind of wedding that is commensurate with their means. If the bride and groom are both working, sometimes they pay the entire cost of the wedding. Customs are meant to change in an intelligent fashion, and this bridal custom is doing just that.

These are the traditional expenses borne by the bride's family:

Engraved invitations and announcements, and mailing costs
Bridal outfit, and the bridal attendants' dresses, if they cannot afford to pay for them
Bridal and wedding photographs
Bridal consultant and social secretary, if needed
Bride's trousseau
Household trousseau
Cost of bride's premarital blood test for wedding license
Wedding reception
Flowers for the church and reception, as well as for wedding attendants
Gifts for bridal attendants
Groom's wedding ring, if any
Music at the church (including organist and choir) and at the reception
Sexton's fee (church fee)
Carpets, ribbons, awnings, tents—anything rented for the wedding or reception
Gratuities for off-duty policemen or others directing traffic and parking at either the church or reception
Transportation for the bridal party from house to ceremony and from ceremony to reception
A wedding gift of substance or a honeymoon trip
Hotel bills for out-of-town attendants when they can't be accommodated in friends' homes

Groom's Expenses

The groom presumably provides transportation from the place of the reception to the locale of the honeymoon. Sometimes, of course, the bride's family does this, especially if the honeymoon is their gift to the couple.

Other expenses:

The bride's rings, both engagement and wedding
The marriage license and the cost of the groom's premarital blood test
The bride's bouquet and boutonnieres for the men in the wedding party
The ushers' wedding ties and gloves
The ushers' gifts
The clergyman's fee; tips to the altar boys, if there are any
A wedding gift for his bride (usually a piece of jewelry or something personal)
His bachelor dinner, if any

The wedding trip (unless this is a gift from the bride's parents or jointly expensed)

Hotel accommodations for his best man and ushers if they cannot be housed in others' homes

Ex-husband's Responsibility Concerning the Wedding

The question as to whether the girl's divorced father has a financial responsibility in the wedding is a matter for individual discussion and individual solution. Much depends upon whether the father has been paying alimony, or made a substantial settlement to the mother at the time of the divorce, and on the warmth of the relationships among him, his ex-wife, and his daughter at the time of the wedding. He may feel he is under no obligation to pay for the wedding, and yet he may very well feel inclined to do so, or at least a part of it. Often a remarried father offers to give the wedding reception whether or not the daughter still lives with her mother or has her own apartment. Sometimes the remarried father will pay for the honeymoon. Again, it is an individual matter to be talked out in the open, well before the wedding.

The Expense of the Home

Traditionally, the man was supposed to pay for the house and everything in it that his bride did not bring in her trousseau and in the joint wedding presents. Today, it's you-pay-for-this and I'll-pay-for-that. If either set of parents is wealthier than the other, they help out more. If the bride and groom are both working, they share the expenses themselves.

Chapter 15

THE WEDDING ATTENDANTS AND
THEIR DUTIES

The very simplest wedding must have at least one attendant for the bride, but an elaborate wedding may have as many as eight or more bridesmaids, a flower girl, perhaps a junior bridesmaid, a ring bearer, two pages, a maid *and* a matron of honor. No bride or groom should ever feel duty-bound to choose as an attendant any person in whose wedding he or she may have served in a similar capacity. Friends should understand that relatives should first be chosen for these honors, and beyond that, it is the bride or groom's preference, and never a tit-for-tat obligation, that determines this choice. No explanations ever need be given.

In the management of complex weddings one thing is most vital—the bridal attendants must be on time for the fittings for their gowns, for their appointments with the photographer if photographs are going to be taken prior to the wedding (a sound idea), to the showers and prenuptial parties for the bride alone and for the bride and groom. Being a bridesmaid entails definite responsibilities.

Maids and Matrons of Honor

The bride usually chooses a sister as maid or matron of honor, or, if she has none, a close friend. Although a groom may, under some circumstances, choose his father as his best man, the bride never chooses her mother as her matron of honor since the bride's mother already has her own complicated function in the wedding party. A matron of honor may be a widow or a divorcée, but it is preferable that she not be considerably older than the bride—at least not in a large formal wedding.

Both maid and matron of honor have specific parts in the ceremony. In the processional the matron of honor walks down the aisle just before the bride. The maid of honor usually precedes the matron. The bride may ask one or the other to hold her bouquet during the ceremony. Or the matron of honor, who will be next to the bride, may take it from her and pass it to the maid, who at the end of the ceremony passes it back to the matron to return to the bride. The matron of honor may lift the bride's veil just before the "Kiss of Peace" part of the mass in a Roman Catholic ceremony, and she also replaces it afterward. The bride decides whether the matron or the maid of honor will assume the duties of chief attendant at her wedding. Generally, if one is her sister, it is her sister who performs these duties. Before the recessional begins, the maid and matron of honor together straighten the bride's train and follow the bride and groom down the aisle, the best man escorting the matron of honor and the head usher escorting the maid of honor.

The two honor attendants aid the bride and her mother in any way they can during preparations for the wedding. They may help compile the guest list, address invitations, and run any last-minute errands, and help the bride dress and change into her going-away costume on her wedding day. They make sure she is properly packed, and do all they can to calm her nerves and the nerves of everyone else!

Bridesmaids

Bridesmaids, who may be young matrons, are chosen from among the bride's close friends and usually are not noticeably older than she. They are sometimes much younger than the bride, often children, especially in Canada, Britain, and Europe. If the groom has a sister of suitable age, it is customary to ask her to be a bridesmaid although not necessarily an honor attendant. Bridesmaids are expected to supply their own transportation to the wedding if they are from out of town. However, the parents of the bride arrange transportation of the bridesmaids, who frequently dress together at the bride's house, to the ceremony and the reception. They see that each bridesmaid has a safe way to get home (or at least to where she is staying) from the reception.

The "Junior Bridesmaid" or "Maiden of Honor"   There is occasionally a place in the wedding party for a girl between the ages of ten and fourteen. As junior bridesmaid in the procession she walks in front of the bridesmaids. If she is to be maiden of honor she precedes the bride is there is no maid of honor or matron of honor. If there is either of these, then she precedes the maid or matron of honor. If the bridesmaids are paired with ushers in the recessional, the junior bridesmaid may either walk alone or be paired with an usher who is not too tall (if she is short). A great discrepancy in age is not important and she would undoubtedly be very thrilled to be escorted if the other girls are (this is optional) in the recessional.

The Best Man

The groom chooses his ushers and best man. The best man is usually a brother, if he has one. If a brother does not serve, the groom's closest friend usually does, although sometimes his father (or stepfather, if he was raised by him) does the honors. If it is to be a large formal wedding, the best man has a great responsibility in co-ordinating arrangements from the male side. The groom should have his best man and ushers invited and prepared at least two months prior to the ceremony. This permits men who live at a distance to make necessary arrangements. A large wedding usually requires the attendants' taking at least one day off from work, which also requires advance planning.

In most cases the ushers and best man, like the groom, rent their wedding apparel. (They pay for the rental themselves, unless the groom is in a position to and wishes to pay for it.) The groom usually buys the ties and gloves (if gloves are to be worn) for his ushers, so either the groom or the best man should find out the proper sizes well in advance of the wedding, so the items can be purchased and ready on time.

Duties of the Best Man   The best man has always had an important role in weddings. In ancient times, when marriage was by seizure of some girl outside the tribe, the best man was chosen for his brawn and bravery, as he was needed to fend off the bride's male relatives and, later, to prevent the bride's escape from the groom. Today, his duties are less hazardous, but they are very extensive at a large formal wedding. His primary duty is to "organize the groom." He makes sure all the male attendants have their proper instructions about when and where to come, when and where to be fitted for their outfits, and so on. He helps the groom organize his bachelor's dinner, if there is one. He sees to it that the groom has the ties and gloves, as well as the ushers' gifts. He makes sure that the boutonnieres are ordered for the men, and that the bridal bouquet is being sent where it should be—and on time.

He rounds up the ushers for the rehearsal and sees that it goes off according to schedule. He co-ordinates with the bride's mother the logistics of the cars taking everyone to and from the church and the reception. The day of the ceremony, he helps the groom get dressed and sees to it that the marriage license is in the groom's inside pocket and that the wedding ring is safely on his own little finger or in his vest pocket. He is also one of the witnesses, along with the matron or maid of honor, of the signing of the wedding certificate.

He makes sure that he himself has the clergyman's fee and the church fee in envelopes in a pocket. Most clergymen depend upon these honoraria as necessary supplements to their incomes, so the groom should ask beforehand how much to give the clergyman and the organist, how much to leave for the church, and how much to tip the altar boys, if there are any.

The best man sees to it that the ushers are at the church, fully briefed as to their duties, at the appointed hour—usually an hour before the ceremony. He sees to it that the groom and he are in the vestry a good half hour before. No bride should ever be kept waiting at the church!

After the ceremony, the best man joins in the recessional, escorting the maid or matron of honor, then hurries to the place of the reception, perhaps driving some of the bridal party. He should also take charge of the couple's luggage—which he either places in the going-away car or hides in a spot where pranksters will not find it. He gives the car and baggage keys, sometimes even the hotel key, to the groom after he has changed into his traveling clothes. He may have helped make honeymoon reservations and often arranges to have wine or flowers waiting in the couple's room when they arrive.

If the reception is a seated one, the best man is placed to the bride's right, proposes the first toast to the couple, and reads any congratulatory telegrams. He should practice his toast; he should speak in loud, clear tones so all can hear, if there is no microphone. If there is dancing, he dances with the bride, both mothers, and as many bridal attendants and guests as possible.

When the bride and groom are ready to dress for their departure, the best man again valets the groom and sees that nothing has been forgotten. He fetches both sets of parents and any other close relatives for the private farewell. Then he clears the way through the guests for the bride and groom, who, all good-bys to their families said, race through a rain of confetti or rose petals (rather than rice, let's hope) to the waiting car or cab (also scheduled to be there at the exact moment by the best man).

Ushers

The groom's ushers should be chosen from among his intimate friends and close relatives. They may be married or single. He is not obliged to ask his brother or brothers to serve, but it is usual. He frequently asks at least one brother of the bride. Once asked, a man cannot refuse such an honor except for a serious reason.

In a big church it is necessary to have enough ushers—more than bridesmaids—to seat the expected guests. The rule of thumb is to have one usher for every fifty guests to be seated. When calculating this figure, assume that only three quarters of the invited guests will attend. In the processional and recessional the extra ushers walk together. However, if a big church is chosen, it is not necessary to invite enough guests to fill it, as part of the body of the church near the altar may be enclosed with boxwood or other greens to make a small chapel for the ceremony. It is possible to have a church wedding without ushers, but it would be difficult to manage in any but a small church or chapel.

Occasionally a relative of either bride or groom is chosen to be a junior usher. This is certainly all right, but it is preferable for him to be in his midteens so that he is able to perform the duties of a regular usher. A young boy looks rather ridiculous escorting adults down the aisle unless he is exceptionally tall and mature for his age.

Duties of Ushers   The duties of ushers at a church wedding are quite definite, but ushers at a home wedding serve in a more or less honorary capacity as there is little, if any, formal seating to do. Usually, standards, flower-decorated or not, are placed so they will mark off with white ribbon the areas where guests are to stand. Immediately after the ceremony it is the ushers' work to remove the ribbons and standards, so guests may leave.

Ushers should arrive at the church an hour before the ceremony, leaving their hats and outer coats, if any, in the vestry but donning the gloves, if worn, which they wear in the performance of their duties within the church. In the vestry they receive their boutonnieres—furnished by the groom— which are their badge of office and should be in place before the ushers enter the church. One usher may be designated by the groom to notify him of the bridal party's arrival.

Ushers group themselves to the left of the door inside the church, preferably in the vestibule if it is large enough. The "head usher," usually a brother or other relative designated by the groom, tells them of any special seating instructions he has received from the bride's mother. Each of them should be armed with a list of guests to be seated in reserved pews, but as guests rarely forget they have been honored by being assigned seats, these lists are rarely referred to unless, if pew cards were issued, a guest forgets to bring his. Unrecognized guests are asked their names and should themselves say "friend of the bride" or "friend of the groom," or the usher may ask the question so that they may be correctly seated—on the left of the church for the bride, on the right for the groom. If, as the church fills up, it seems likely that the seating will not be balanced, the ushers seat later-arriving guests on the side that has fewer filled seats, regardless of the guest's status. The head usher should watch to see that seating remains uniform.

Ushers should be gracious and seem unhurried even when, at a big wedding, they must seat a great many people. The groom should choose his attendants from among his most socially at ease friends.

An usher does not allow a lady to find her seat unescorted. If several guests arrive in a group, he offers his right arm to the eldest lady, and the others in the group follow singly, women first, and are seated together by the usher. If two women arrive at the same time, the younger steps back and permits the elder to take the usher's arm while she awaits his return or accepts the services of the next available usher or walks down the aisle behind the older woman and her escorting usher. If a lady arrives with an escort, an usher still takes her to her seat while her escort follows a few steps behind.

A male guest entering alone is seated by the usher, who naturally does not offer his arm unless the man is very aged and might have trouble negotiating the aisle alone. If two men arrive at the same time, the usher walks down the aisle with the elder and the younger man follows so that he may be seated at the same time.

Children—that is, girls and boys under fifteen or sixteen—follow along as their parents are ushered up the aisle. If there is time for such extra courtesy, an usher may escort a girl slightly under this age—to her obvious delight, or embarrassment!

Seating the Mother of the Bride and the Mother of the Groom   Five minutes before the mother of the bride is seated, one of the ushers seats the groom's mother, who should be at the church in ample time before the start of the ceremony. Since she is escorted to her seat by an usher, her husband, if he is with her, follows her down the aisle. The groom's parents are seated in the first pew on the right—not necessarily alone.

Their other children or perhaps their own parents may be with them. The groom's mother, however, must have the end seat on the aisle. When there are no ushers, the groom's father escorts his wife to her seat.

The head usher escorts the bride's mother to her seat, and her entrance, always carefully timed, is the signal that the processional is about to start. When there are no ushers, some male member of the family should escort the mother of the bride to her seat. It is after she is seated that the church doors are closed and the canvas, if any (necessary, actually, only if the bride wears a long train), is laid. The head usher and one other have the honor of rolling down the canvas.

After the bride's mother is in place no one else may be seated by ushers. The bride's mother, too, need not sit alone. She may well choose to share her honored pew with the bride's grandparents or close friends or relatives. Here too, however, the mother of the bride should be near the aisle, and space should be left so her husband, or whoever escorts the bride, may join her after his part in the ceremony. Any late-comers must wait outside until after the ceremony is over or quickly seat themselves on aisle seats in the back of the church if the doors have not been closed.

After the bride's mother is seated and the canvas, if there is one, is down, two designated ushers, starting with their left feet first, walk together up the aisle to the last reserved pews, where white satin ribbons have been carefully folded and laid alongside of the decorated aisle posts. They pick up the entire bundle and, again in step, walk the length of the pews, as rehearsed, drawing the ribbons behind the aisle posts in a straight line, placing the loop at the end of each ribbon over the last aisle post.

The ushers are then ready to take their places at the beginning of the procession. Ushers always go up the aisle in pairs, but in the recessional it is optional for them to pair with the bridesmaids, if there is an equal number. The procedure is decided by the bride and the clergyman in the rehearsal.

After the recessional the ribbons are left in place until the mothers of the bride and groom and at least some of the reserved pew guests have been escorted out. After the first few have gone down the aisle, ushers often take out groups in order to clear the church more quickly. It is bad manners to leave from the far side of the church before the reserved-pew guests have been escorted out and the ribbons removed.

Complications in the Seating of Couples' Families   When divorces among the bride's family make the traditional seating procedure inappropriate, here are some suggestions to follow. If the bride's parents are divorced, but neither has remarried, it is best for the father, after escorting his daughter, to return to the mother's pew, if they are friendly. Otherwise he returns to the second or third pew behind her. This is where a remarried father's wife is seated, if she attends. This is the appropriate seat, too, for a girl's mother and her new husband, if any, when a girl lives with her father and a stepmother who has assumed the mother's role in the planning of the wedding.

In the event that a brother or uncle is giving away the bride, he should return to sit with the mother of the bride in the first pew. It is always the bride's mother, or whoever is acting for her, who is first escorted out by the head usher.

If the groom's parents are divorced they may be seated together, if willing, in the first right pew, or the mother may be in the first alone or with her new husband. Her former husband is seated alone or with his new wife in the second or third pew. In these honored pews may also be seated children of the family, grandparents, or intimate friends, if desired.

If one of these solutions seems to fit your situation, it is recommended that you discuss the matter with all those involved and settle upon whatever is least disturbing to all.

At the Reception   Ushers' duties are not over once they have completed their schedules at the church. They must see to it that the bridal party is transported to the reception, if there is one, well in advance of the first guests' arrival, and they should arrange transportation for any reception guests who may not have it. They have limited time to attend to these details, because, although they do not stand in the receiving line, they should be on hand as soon as possible for the wedding group pictures, which should be taken while everyone is still relatively fresh and can be accounted for. And as no guest should arrive and have to wait to be received, you can see that there is split-second timing even here.

At the reception the ushers, at last, may relax and enjoy themselves. At a large formal reception caterers take charge of refreshments, but at a small one the ushers may help serve guests. They aid and abet the couple in a smooth getaway as the reception draws to a close, after the bride has thrown her bouquet to the waiting bridesmaids when she goes to change to her street clothes.

Gifts   Ushers, as members of the wedding party, always make gifts to the bride, individually, before the wedding or together give the couple some major gift from them all, with contributions to the fund tactfully geared to the circumstances of the least affluent usher. A silver bar pitcher, engraved box, or frame is appropriate and better than separate gifts from each usher, as they may be uncertain as to what constitutes a suitable wedding gift. A delightful personalized gift they might consider is a small silver tray bearing their facsimile signatures and the initials of the couple.

Going to the Church

Transportation of attendants to and from the wedding and reception is provided for and paid for by the bride's family. Bridesmaids always meet at the home of the bride before going to the church. They may dress there, if that seems advisable, or arrive dressed.

At the bride's home the attendants receive their bouquets. Attendants should all be assembled a full hour before the ceremony and able, if necessary, to aid the bride in her dressing.

The mother of the bride leaves the house first. She rides alone or with one or two bridesmaids, making sure she keeps room in the car for her husband to ride to the reception with her. The bride, alone with her father, always rides in a special car, whose driver, or chauffeur, might wear a white boutonniere as a festive note. The bride should be very careful in the way she sits on her wedding gown and handles her veil. In some new churches there is a bridal dressing room, where the bride puts on her gown. In this case, she arrives at the church, ready except for her gown and veil, at least an hour in advance of the ceremony, in this case so guests will not see her. The wedding consultant, if any, assists her, as do the bridal attendants, who also may prefer to complete their dressing at the church.

At a large wedding where the traffic will be heavy, the bride's family notifies the local police precinct, which may be able to send additional traffic patrolmen. If they cannot, or even if they can, the family frequently hires off-duty policemen or regular uniformed men to park cars and direct traffic. Rates for this work, of course, vary in different communities. The same procedure is used at debuts and other large functions, private and public. With the help of these men, as each car arrives it moves on to a designated parking space. The bride's car, however, remains in front of the church just where it delivered her and her father, until she re-enters it with the groom.

If an Attendant Drops Out

No attendant asks to be excused from the bridal party except for some very good reason—illness or such a recent death in his or her immediate family that burial does not take place before the wedding day. Sometimes, of course, factors such as bad weather intervene and a member of the wedding may not make it. In any case, the bride or groom is faced with a difficult problem in trying to replace the missing attendant. It is easier for them to leave the bridal party as it is and let the uneven usher walk alone, if it's a man who's missing, or the extra bridesmaid precede the maid or matron of honor alone in the processional. The friend who is asked at the very last minute to fill in at anything so formal as a bridal procession would be accepting at considerable inconvenience, while wondering why he was not asked to be a member of the wedding from the beginning.

Chapter 16

PRE-WEDDING PARTIES

There are several customary parties given before a wedding in many sections of the country. If the groom cannot be present during any one of these evening festivities, an escort from the family or wedding party should be provided. The bride should write a thank-you note the day after any wedding party given for her, and it is particularly nice if she sends flowers to her hosts (but only if she can really afford it). Too many parties preceding the wedding, or parties too closely scheduled, can be exhausting and physically harmful to everyone concerned. If too many suggest giving parties, the wise couple urges them either to join forces with each other or to give them a party after they return from their honeymoon.

The Bridesmaids' Party

In some communities the bridesmaids band together to give some kind of special party for the bride a week or more before the wedding—aside from the usual showers. This may be a luncheon, a dinner, or in some cases even a cocktail party. The guest list may include only the bridesmaids and honor attendants, or the groom, best man, and ushers may be included along with their respective wives and husbands. As a matter of fact, the party may be extended, if the hostess or hostesses wish, to include friends and relatives.

Parties for Out-of-town Guests

At big weddings where a number of out-of-town guests are expected, some kind of party is often planned by the bride's friends. For example, if the wedding is to be held in the late afternoon or evening, friends of the bride's parents might hold a festive lunch that day for all the wedding party and out-of-town guests. In former days the groom only would attend this lunch; the bride would be left nervously at her home, usually furious that she was not supposed to see the groom on her wedding day until church time. Today that old superstition has disappeared. Sometimes, if the wedding is in the morning, followed by a reception lunch, the time to entertain the out-of-town guests is at dinner that evening, before they return home.

Bridal Teas

Bridal teas, given by some close friend of the bride's family, have declined in popularity, although they are still held in some parts of the country. The main reason for their decline is that today's young woman usually works and cannot get off work to attend a tea, either for herself or for her friends. Sometimes they are held on Saturdays for a feminine guest list. Close friends of the bride pour, as well as relatives. Such a tea is a good way if the groom's mother is present from out of town, to introduce her to the bride's family friends. This kind of party is obviously for the pleasure of the bride's older female relatives, and she should act with graciousness and enthusiasm about the event.

Bridal Showers

Showers are held less often today, mainly because everyone is too busy to attend them, especially those who work. However, a shower is still a practical and attractive way to help a bride set up housekeeping—but senseless if she comes from a family that "has everything." For the basic idea of a shower *is* practicality—the bride's closest friends give her utilitarian things: kitchen supplies, linens, cooking equipment, staple groceries, pantyhose, all to form a little nest egg of needed articles with which to start off her new life.

It is possible, if the bride is going to be living far away from the site of the shower, to specify a "greenback" or "Money Tree" shower. In this case the money should be affixed to the branches of a tree or plant to make it more festive. Each bill may be twisted in such a way that the denomination is not visible. Showers are usually given a month before the wedding. It is nice for those planning showers to consult others who may want to do the same. It is usually a financial hardship on friends who are invited to four or five showers for the same girl. It is more considerate for the sponsors to join forces in one or two showers instead. One or two showers should be the limit, and the bride should discourage friends who wish to do more than this. Showers are not given for second marriages.

Showers, if any, may be given by any close friend, usually a member of the bridal party. Often they are given by the maid or matron of honor, if she isn't a sister or other relative and if she lives in the community and has the facilities for entertaining. She should also know the bride's clothing sizes in case anyone asks. This type of information cannot gracefully appear anywhere on the invitation.

Showers are never given by members of the bride's or groom's immediate families, but a cousin may give a shower. It is, however, acceptable for

members of the bride's or groom's families to offer financial aid to those giving showers, and they may even offer the facilities of their homes, so long as
the showers are not given in their names.

The bride is usually quietly consulted before the shower about what she
really needs, so that the gifts are appropriate.

It is necessary, of course, for shower-givers and guests to get together on
themes, colors, and the bride's needs. If she is to have a kitchen with red
accessories, a kitchen shower should have all gifts geared to the theme—
even to a red step-on garbage can or folding stepladder.

If either bride or groom is to receive things to wear, exact sizes should be
ascertained. The kind of shower should be chosen that permits even the most
short-of-money bridesmaid, who is involved with her own expenses of the
wedding, to make her own contribution, if only a pot holder or a handkerchief. Gifts should all be assembled, wrapped, and perhaps screened off, before the bride arrives. Any later-arriving guests present theirs personally.

The bride opens all gifts at the designated time—usually before the refreshments, which are simple. She should write a brief thank-you note to everyone who brought her a gift, however small, as well as a long thank-you to
the hostess.

You are never expected to send a gift to a shower to which you are not invited. Shower guests should be at least invited to the wedding if not the reception, unless the wedding is to be very intimate, including only attendants
and the immediate families of the couple. But perhaps it is a better idea, if
you wish to give a party to introduce a bride to people who cannot possibly
be invited to the wedding, not to make this type of party a shower. You cannot expect a bride to invite members of your family to her wedding just because you have given her a shower at which they were present.

If the wedding is called off, the bride should return each gift received at
the shower or showers unless it was a very trivial item.

Gifts for Showers   Shower gifts should be inexpensive, as the bride's
close friends usually give her wedding gifts as well—though in some cases it
is perfectly possible that the shower gift and wedding gift will be combined,
as in the gift of a food processor at a kitchen shower. Guests at a shower always take a gift (for suggestions, see lists on pages 774–76). As only the
closest friends of the bride are asked, it is usual—but not obligatory—for invited guests to send a little gift when they cannot attend. This means that
showers are somewhat limited in size. No bride has one hundred intimate
friends. People from out of town, other than grandmothers or close relatives
who might be flattered to receive the invitation, are rarely invited to
showers. Of course, if the hostess has erred in asking a mere acquaintance of
the bride to attend a shower for her, then the recipient of the invitation is
under no obligation either to attend or to send a gift. She must, though, in
all courtesy, reply to the invitation. It is usual to invite the mothers of the

bride and of the groom, although not obligatory. If they are invited, they, too, should bring little gifts.

Joint Showers In many bigger cities, joint evening showers for both bride and groom are often the only ones held. Such a shower might be an evening cocktail party, or a picnic or a buffet supper, often with a theme, like "Bar Shower" or "Gourmet Cooking Shower." Several couples usually band together and organize the party. Very informal handwritten invitations are the rule and sometimes all invitations are extended by telephone. Single friends attend with or without dates, but only the people who know the couple to be married bring a present.

The Bachelor Dinner

Preferably three or more nights before the wedding day, the groom may hold a bachelor dinner to which he invites his best man, ushers, favorite young male relatives, and a few close male friends. The dinner is usually held in a private room in a restaurant or a club. Many a groom has wished he never held the party. It is the night on which the groom usually presents his best man and ushers with their gifts "to say thank you for being in the wedding." (He gives them their wedding ties or gloves on this occasion, or at the wedding rehearsal, or at the rehearsal dinner the night before the ceremony.) The original purpose of this dinner was to "bolster the courage" of the reluctant, frightened bridegroom, but the party often only served to bolster the capacities of the guests to overextend their liquor intake. Today's life-styles have changed so much a man about to be married no longer needs to have "one last fling" before his marriage. He can hold a quiet, reasonably dignified dinner in the company of old friends that is sentimental and fun, not a blatant attempt at universal drunkenness. The men should be innovative in their toasts, in champagne, to the bride, but there is no longer any need to smash the champagne glasses.

Today's bride often holds her "maiden dinner" the same night her fiancé is holding his bachelor dinner. She may choose this time to present her honor attendants with their gifts. With her best friends around her, wishing her happiness and blessings, it may well be one of the most sentimental occasions in her life.

Neither a man nor a woman marrying for the second time would hold a bachelor or maiden dinner.

The Rehearsal Dinner

The wedding rehearsal is often held late in the afternoon the day before the wedding, followed by cocktails and a dinner, which is scheduled for seven or seven-thirty o'clock. It is now customary for the groom's parents to give this dinner, but if they are unable to do it, a close friend or a relative or godparent, or even the bride's family, may offer to entertain. The dinner may be a stand-up buffet supper in someone's home with little fuss, or it can be an elaborate black-tie dinner at a club or a restaurant. The hostess determines the size of the invitation list, but all members of the wedding party, including spouses if any and both sets of parents, must be included. The clergyman and his wife should also be invited if they are close family friends. Place cards are necessary, and this is one time the bride and groom should sit together. (After they are married, they will always be separated at formal dinner parties.) They might sit in the center on one side; the matron of honor would be on the groom's right (or the maid of honor if there is no matron), and the best man would be on the bride's left. The clergyman, if invited, would be seated on the hostess' right; the father of the bride, on her left. The bride's mother would be on the clergyman's right. The groom's father would be seated on her right. The wedding party should be interspersed (husbands and wives not sitting next to each other).

If the dinner is large enough to include them, relatives or close friends who have arrived from out of town might enjoy participating in some of the pre-wedding festivities. A very large party, however, should be avoided, as the rehearsal is tiring and it is difficult to know exactly when it will be over. The wise parents of the bride also make an announcement at the beginning of the dinner party (or have the best man make it for them) stating that "everything will be over tonight by such and such an hour, so that everyone will look rested and wonderful tomorrow and do what they're supposed to!"

Often at a really large reception there will be no chance for the guests (but only for the wedding party) to toast the bride and groom, so they are toasted by a larger group at the rehearsal dinner the night before. The best man should begin the toasting, admonishing everyone else to make their toasts "short and sweet," for sometimes they can be overdone and drag interminably. He should be the "moderator" of the toasting. When the bride and groom are being toasted, they do not sip from their glasses themselves along with everyone else but wait until after the others have sipped. An engaged girl or bride should always return her fiancé's or husband's toast.

It has been customary at weddings and rehearsal dinners in this country for the men to do the toasting, but now women toast, if they want to. The mother of the bride, the maid and/or matron of honor, and any other best friend could appropriately make a short toast. Some of the best wedding toasts come from the distaff side these days. If the bride is ill at ease on her feet, all she has to do is say something like, "I'm not very good at speeches, but I would like all of you to join me in raising a toast to the most wonderful man in the world, my future husband."

A wonderful wedding present for the couple is to have someone move a tape recorder around the table to catch the various toasts all evening, and to present the couple with a recording of a very important evening in their lives.

Chapter 17

DRESS FOR THE WEDDING

The Bride's Dress

For a formal winter wedding in church or at home, the bride wears a full-length bridal gown in a variety of possible materials—satin, velvet, taffeta, organza, chiffon, tulle, or lace. All, except velvet and heavy satin, can be worn for a summer wedding, plus a wide variety of summer cottons, from organdy to dimity. The formal wedding gown is usually white or off-white (champagne, ivory, oyster), with or without a full-length veil of tulle, lace, or other sheer material. A fingertip veil is often used on even the most formal gown, but a veil may be dispensed with entirely by the bride in favor of flowers or some other ornamentation in her hair.

For a traditional formal wedding, a wedding gown should follow a certain decorum: conservative neckline, and sleeves preferably long. The bride's shoes are white silk or satin; she should be sure to wear them around the house for a few days before the wedding so they will be comfortable when it counts most.

At an informal church or home wedding, the bride may wear a wedding gown of any length—and with a short veil, if she wishes. If she wishes to be less formal, she may wear a simple dress (not very décolleté) or suit. When they have an informal wedding, most brides choose a dress they will be able to wear often later.

If there is a lovely bridal gown that has come down through the family, even the bride's mother's dress, it is a sentimental gesture if she wears it—but only if it looks marvelous on her and if she truly likes it. No bride should be pressured into wearing a family heirloom, no matter how much it would please everyone. Sometimes there is an antique veil in the family, and this can always be combined with a new bridal gown.

The best way to store the gown, veil, or train is the traditional method of folding tissue paper between the folds of the material and storing in a cool, dry place. There are companies that specialize in the preservation of histori-

cal costumes and that can supply detailed information about properly storing
old dresses.

Gloves and Jewelry If the wedding dress has short sleeves or is sleeveless,
the bride may prefer to wear long white gloves. She no longer *has* to. If her
dress is long-sleeved, she would not wear gloves. If long gloves are worn,
they are not removed during the ceremony. Instead, the gloves are rolled
back to the wrists or the underseam of the ring finger is ripped, so the bride
can bare her finger to receive the ring. Her jewelry should be minimal and
real, such as a pearl necklace and pearl or diamond earrings. If she wears
her engagement ring to the altar, it should be on her right hand to leave her
ring finger free to receive the wedding band. She may wish to borrow an antique pin of pearls or diamonds, to take care of the "something old" and
"something borrowed" at one time.

The Wedding Ring

Although the bride helps select her wedding ring and has her finger size
taken at the jeweler, she does not see the ring again until the groom slips it
on her finger at the ceremony.

While the engagement ring is not engraved on the inside, the wedding ring
is, usually with the date and with the groom's initials followed by the
bride's: "J.W.M. to A.P." If the band is wide, further engraving may be
done. The superstition is gone about a bride's never being able to remove her
wedding ring. If she wears a jeweled one, she can remove it for activities
that would injure it (like rock climbing!), and she removes it for cleaning
the ring.

If the groom wears a wedding ring, he should select one in plain gold,
without decoration. His may be engraved inside in the same manner as hers.
The bride pays for it. He wears it on the same finger as his wife wears hers.

Guard Rings Guard rings are bands of precious or semiprecious stones,
either in one color or in a combination of colors. If a woman has long
fingers, a pair of guard rings flanking her engagement ring looks lovely, or
she may wear one only, between her wedding and engagement rings. If a
woman wears two guard rings with her engagement ring, the order is: wedding ring, guard ring, engagement ring, guard ring. Guard rings are sometimes anniversary presents from a husband to his wife, but many women buy
their own.

Superstitions

Many of the old superstitions relating to weddings have disappeared, but
"something old, something new, something borrowed, and something blue"
is still very much followed. Some brides still walk down the aisle with a
shiny dime in one shoe (in place of the traditional sixpence). One super-

WOMEN'S WEDDING ATTIRE

	Bride	Mothers of the Couple	Wedding Guests
Formal Daytime (up to 6 P.M.)	Floor-length simple or elaborate dress and veil. Short or long train. Long or short sleeves. If sleeves are short, long white gloves are optional. Bridal bouquet.	Simple floor-length or ¾-length costume, covered up. Evening footwear and bag. Matching hat or headpiece optional. Simple jewelry.	Simple daytime dress or soft tailored blouse and suit. Dress should not be décolleté. Simple jewelry.
Formal Evening (after 6 P.M.)	Floor length, long-sleeved, elaborate gown with veil and chapel (sweep) train. Bridal bouquet.	Floor-length evening gown (not too décolleté), furs, and full regalia of jewels. Evening bag and slippers. Long white gloves optional if dress is short-sleeved.	Evening gown of any length, furs, evening slippers and bag, one's best evening jewelry. Long white gloves optional.
Informal Morning or Afternoon	Street-length dress or suit with matching shoes and bag (of one's usual accessory color). Hat or headpiece, white Bible or prayer book with streamer or small bouquet.	Covered-up street-length dress or suit in simple fabric. Dressy daytime accessories. Short white gloves.	Same as for Formal Daytime.
Informal Evening	Long trainless wedding dress, or ¾- or street-length in a dress fabric. Shoes to match costume. Bouquet, white Bible or prayer book with streamers.	Late afternoon or ¾-length in a dressy fabric, not too décolleté. Short white gloves. Dressy shoes and bag.	Late afternoon or ¾-length (crepe, silk, lamé, velvet, etc.). Furs, simple jewelry.

Notes on Wedding Apparel

Women wedding guests look more "finished" if they wear gloves to and from the ceremony and reception. (A washable leather like doeskin is dressier than cotton or synthetic fabric gloves.) White is always correct at a wedding, but beige, pale gray, and other neutral tones are also dressy enough.

Wedding guests should not wear glittery fabrics (lamé, sequins, beaded dresses) except for an evening wedding.

Mothers of the bridal couple should co-ordinate their costumes as to color, style, and length.

Guests should not wear all-white to the reception, nor black before evening.

Hats (fur and otherwise) are optional and are appropriate for any wedding except a formal evening one.

stition that has flown out the window is that which says the bride may not see her groom on her wedding day until she sees him at the altar. Another dropped superstition is that the bride should never rehearse for her own wedding. Fortunately, the custom of tying tin cans or old shoes on the couple's getaway car is also outdated.

The Mature Bride

A woman in her mid-thirties or older who marries for the first time has the right to wear a long formal white gown and a long veil if she chooses, but she may feel more comfortable in a white or pastel costume that is *not* floor-length. She might also forgo the veil to wear flowers in her hair or a pretty hat, and find it more appropriate to have a simple ceremony with one attendant for herself and one for the groom. Her bridesmaid would wear a dress that co-ordinates in feeling with the bride's, rather than wearing a typical bridesmaid dress. But even if the mature bride has a simple ceremony, her wedding reception can be as big as she could possibly want it to be.

The Bride's Formal Wedding Pictures

The formal photographs of the bride in her bridal costume are taken after the final fitting of her gown, as many weeks before the hectic schedule of the wedding as she can manage, and when her hair has been done just as she wants it for the wedding. Bridal shops often arrange for the formal pictures to be taken there, or she may go to the photographer's studio, or even be photographed at home. Often the photographer arranges to send an 8″ × 10″ black and white glossy photo of the bride's choice to the local newspapers.

A bride should avoid heavy make-up for her formal portrait. She should be cautious with eye shadow, mascara, and too-dark lipstick. Very light make-up produces the loveliest bridal pictures. A wise bride will work with her hairdresser well in advance of the ceremony to achieve the best coiffure to wear at her wedding and for her bridal pictures. To do this, she needs to have her headpiece well in advance of her dress.

The cost of the wedding pictures is borne by the bride's family in most cases. In some Jewish circles the groom's family is expected to pay for half the photographs. The bride usually presents a formal wedding photograph to the groom's parents. Her own parents order pictures for the bride and groom's photo album, and for relatives and close friends. The groom's family should be presented, as I have stated before, with several candids; then it is up to them to order any extra or other candids themselves, and to pay for them.

Wedding Publicity in the Papers

Many large-city newspapers will not even publish coverage of the wedding, much less a picture of the bride, unless she has some kind of news value. In smaller cities, however, the day after the wedding the society department may publish a head-and-shoulders formal portrait of the bride, or sometimes a picture of both bride and groom. One should therefore provide the society editor with the details in advance, to make everything easier, more efficient, and more accurate. The name of the bride before her marriage, the name of her parents, the names of the groom and his parents are usually the first information. This is followed by the place of the marriage, the officiating clergyman, and the place where the reception was held. Then come the names of the wedding party, followed by the bride's college and any graduate work and the groom's college and graduate work. Next come notes on the bride's parents, then on the groom's parents, and the final information is usually the couple's places of employment and job titles.

The bride's family should call the society editor at least three weeks in advance to ask for space to be held for the wedding item on whichever day the coverage should appear. The photographer of the bride's formal portrait should arrange to get the glossy picture to the newspaper, and the bride or her parents can mail in the wedding details—leaving enough time for the editor to check for further information or verification.

If the bride comes from a famous family or is marrying into one, the news desk might send a news photographer to take a picture of the bride and groom coming out of the church, so that it becomes that paper's exclusive candid shot of the pair.

Dress of Groom and Best Man

The degree of formality of the men's dress at a wedding is determined by the type of dress worn by the bride. She sets the keynote for the entire wedding. All men in the wedding party, including the fathers of the bride and groom, dress in the same manner. Fathers no longer have to rent cutaways, however, if the ushers wear them; in this case they simply do not stand in the receiving line if they are not in cutaways.

Formal wedding clothes today are usually rented, right down to the cuff links and the shoes. Arrangements should be made for this at least a month in advance, so any temporary alterations may be made. Trousers should break slightly above the shoe tops, the jacket collar should hug the neck, and for a well-turned-out appearance, at least a half inch of white cuff should show below the sleeve of the jacket.

Ushers

All ushers should be dressed identically in terms of style, although variations in fabric are permissible. The lapel facing, type of fabric, and stripe on the trousers may differ slightly between that worn by the groom and that worn by the ushers and best man. The groom and best man's ties should differ slightly from one another; the ushers' ties should be different still. The groom should provide new ties for the men, if he is able to. The gray four-in-hand ties are worn with a turned-down collar usually attached to the shirt. (The separate collar is starched and more formal.)

Colorful wedding attire is popular for grooms and their ushers in many parts of the country. I feel that the traditional black and grays are much more appropriate than colored tuxedos and cutaways. And that goes for any season. White pants look well with dark blazers for summer weddings; all-white tuxedos do not; nor do frilly, ruffly shirts.

Gloves If the men in a formal wedding party wear gloves, the ushers may keep theirs on during the entire ceremony. The best man, however, removes his right glove once the bride and groom are together at the altar, so he can successfully pass the wedding ring to the groom at the proper moment without dropping it. The groom also removes his right glove to accept the ring and subsequently to slip it on his bride's finger. Each man holds the right glove in his left hand during this procedure, or he may place it in his inside breast pocket or hand it to an usher. The clergyman or sexton will instruct the two men during the wedding rehearsal on these details. The entire wedding party may go gloveless to simplify matters, but it does not look as "finished."

If the men do wear gloves, they have to remove them during the reception to shake hands, smoke, eat, drink, or dance. They should wear their gloves for the formal wedding portrait.

Summer Weddings Men do not wear very formal clothes such as cutaways for summer weddings. A black tie is the most formal—worn with a white dinner jacket and black trousers, or a tropical-weight all-black suit. When men are dressed less formally, they wear an all-white suit or a dark blazer with gray flannels or white trousers. The bride may be in full regalia, except for long white gloves.

In any case, the groom and his ushers should be dressed alike, including the shirts and ties. If it is a black-tie after-six wedding, the ties and cummerbunds should be black. If it is a daytime wedding, four-in-hand ties are worn.

MEN'S WEDDING DRESS

	Suit	Shirt	Tie
Formal Daytime[1] (up to 6 P.M.)	Black or Oxford gray cutaway or long jacket (most formal) with gray vest, gray striped trousers[2]	Any wing-collar shirt with an ascot Starched fold collar or the usual broadcloth shirt with cuffs with the four-in-hand	Ascot (gray in checks, stripes, solid) with wing collar. Four-in-hand (styled or check) with fold collar
Formal Evening (after 6 P.M.)	Tail coat (full dress), white piqué or waffle-weave waistcoat	Starched shirt, wing collar	White piqué or waffle-weave
Informal Morning or Afternoon	Single-breasted gray or black stroller, striped trousers, gray vest or Business suit in blue, black, Oxford gray	White shirt, fold collar, french cuffs White shirt, white fold collar	Gray tie or gray-and-white-striped Tie in a conservative color
Informal Evening	White or black (preferably) dinner jacket, single- or double-breasted black vest or cummerbund (If bride wears street-length dress—groom wears dark business suit.)	White pleated shirt, turned-down collar White town shirt	Black Conservative dark-colored

[1] In cold weather the groom should wear a dark dress coat, such as a black Chesterfield with a velvet collar, to his wedding, regardless of the hour. He would also wear gray gloves in winter. In former days, a formal wedding saw the groom in a silk top hat; a less formal wedding, in a black Homburg or derby. When men's hats come back into full popularity, we may see those styles again.

[2] *Note:* Fathers of the bride and groom dress as groom or ushers do, but may substitute dark suits for cutaways if they do not stand in the receiving line.

Shoes and Socks	Jewelry	Male Guests[8]
Black (plain—not wing-tipped or perforated) Black socks	Black or white pearl or onyx. Gold or silver cuff links—no colored stones	Dark business suits
Black patent-leather shoes Black socks	White pearl or really fine old or antique gold studs	Black tie (or white tie, if relative of couple)
Black (plain) shoes Black socks Black shoes Black socks	Black pearl or onyx Black or gold	Dark business suit
Black patent-leather Black socks Black shoes Black socks	Black or gold	Dark business suit

[8] Male guests should not wear boutonnieres. They are the prerogative of the men in the wedding party.

Bridal Attendants

The maid or matron of honor may be dressed in slightly different fashion from the bridesmaids, although that trend is not so prevalent as it used to be. If there are to be both a maid and matron of honor, they may be dressed alike, or within the proposed slight variations that follow. The honor attendant's dress may be of the same design but of a different color, or of the same color but of a slightly different design. Or all attendants' dresses may be alike with different flowers or headdresses distinguishing the maid or matron of honor. Attendants' dresses are chosen in fabrics to complement that of the bride's dress. For example, if the bride's dress is white satin, the attendants' dresses would not be piqué. Unusual but beautiful is the wedding in which all the bride's attendants wear white. Attendants' dresses should be the same length as the bride's or shorter. The attendants either go hatless or wear velvet or flowered headdresses or anything appropriate that might be designed by a milliner to complete the fashion statement of the wedding. Usually the pumps or sandals of the bridesmaids match their dresses.

Junior Bridesmaids   The junior bridesmaid should wear a dress that goes well with those of the other attendants, yet is suited to her age. It can be one of similar style, color and perhaps shorter in length, but it should not be décolleté. Her headdress need not to be too much like that of the bridesmaids, especially if theirs is relatively sophisticated. Often a wreath of flowers seems most suitable for a girl of this age. Her shoes should be flat-heeled, in a color to co-ordinate with her dress. Some of the prettiest weddings I have ever attended have been those in Europe, where all the attendants are junior bridesmaids and small children, the girls dressed alike in long garden dresses, with big satin sashes, the boys in velvet shorts, white satin shirts with Peter Pan collars, white knee socks, and black patent shoes with silver buckles.

Flower Girls, Page Boys, and Ring Bearers   The page boy or ring bearer in American weddings usually wears a dark blue Eton suit or, if it is a summer wedding, a white linen suit with shorts, and Oxfords. The flower girl wears either a long dress, similar to the bridesmaids', or a short, pretty party dress that co-ordinates with what the bridesmaids are wearing. Her dress does not have to be of exactly the same fabric as theirs. She should wear, according to the colors and length of her dress, ballet slippers to match her dress or black patent or white Mary Janes. If the bridal attendants wear white gloves, she should wear short white cotton ones, too. The flower girl often wears a small floral wreath on her head. She carries a tiny floral bouquet or a basket of flower petals, which she scatters in the aisle as she precedes the bride in the processional. It is permissible to have two flower girls. The flower girls precede the bride in the processional; they walk right behind the bride and groom in the recessional.

The ring bearer (chosen by the bride, as he is part of her entourage) carries the bride's wedding ring—for safety's sake, not the real one—on a little white satin pillow. The real ring is usually snug in the best man's pocket— and many a cautious clergyman wears a spare on *his* finger for emergency use. The ring is fastened to the cushion with light silken stitches, especially if precaution has been thrown to the winds and the real ring is borne by the child. If the ring bearer carries the actual ring, then he will necessarily have to remain with the wedding party during the ceremony. If he has been used merely for effect, however, it is quite simple for him to leave the procession as it reaches the pew of the mother of the bride. As the small attendants are usually under seven, it is sometimes hard for them to stand still at the altar throughout the ceremony, so it is safer if they join the bride's mother and are not in the recessional.

In the processional the ring bearer precedes the flower girl if there is one or otherwise walks directly in front of the bride and her father. If he is in the recessional, he pairs with the flower girl and they come down the aisle together. If the attendants are not paired, the ring bearer precedes the flower girl or girls immediately following after the bride and groom.

Pages, who may be boys or girls or one of each, are usually under seven, too, and about the same size. They must be big enough to carry the bride's formal train and, of course, if she is not in such formal dress, pages are not needed, nor are they always used even when the long train is worn. They appear in both processional and recessional, unless they are too small and restless, in which case, just before reaching the altar, they step into the bride's mother's pew and take no further part in the ceremony. Pages and ring bearers, as well as the flower girls, are considered the bride's attendants. She therefore presents them each with some small suitable token of the occasion —perhaps a tiny bracelet for the flower girls, small, engraved silver picture frames for the pages and ring bearer.

Parents of flower girls and parents of pages and the ring bearer are invited to parties preceding the wedding and to the rehearsal dinner and the reception. Mothers of these attendants should be included in pre-bridal parties.

Pages and very young flower girls appear briefly at the reception, if at all, and then firmly in the charge of their parents. The bride and groom should make a special effort to thank them before going on to the reception if they are not to be included at all in the festivities.

Candle Lighters Usually the candles to be used during the ceremony are lit by some member of the church staff. In some sections of the country and in some churches, however, young boys who are members of either the bride's or the groom's family perform this service. Generally the candles are lit just before the mother of the bride is seated. This custom varies from church to church, and it is well to check with your clergyman beforehand.

The boys wear what they would wear to church or Sunday school (a suit or pants and jacket, with a tie).

Flowers for the Wedding Party

The groom's boutonniere is traditionally a spray from the bridal bouquet, often a lily of the valley, if it is available. The ushers and best man wear another kind of boutonniere, just as the bridesmaids carry bouquets different from the bride's

The bridal bouquet traditionally is all-white, but pale flowers are often introduced into the mix of today's bouquets. The bride may choose to carry a white Bible or prayer book with a white satin streamer encircled with white flowers (such as orchids). Bridal attendants may carry either bouquets (equipped with a hand holder); or they may carry a sheaf of flowers, cradled in their arms, tied with ribbon; or they may wear wrist bouquets. The flowers should be anything seasonal and attractively combined with the colors of the dresses.

Corsages may be worn by the mothers of the bride and groom, but many women do not like to wear them and should not feel compelled to.

Artificial flowers are wrong from every point of view for a wedding. If budget is a problem, an attendant can always carry a bouquet of trailing ivy, or even one beautiful flower such as a lily or a long-stemmed rose.

What the Parents and Guests Wear

The bride's mother has first choice of color in her dress for her daughter's wedding; the groom's mother should wait to buy her own dress afterward, so that she can co-ordinate in color and length of dress. The dresses of the mothers do not have to match; they should simply be of the same feeling. At a daytime wedding a very low-cut dress is in bad taste; at an evening wedding a dress of simple cut of an informal fabric does not look right, either.

It is not correct for the mothers of the bride and groom to wear black; white usually is not a good color, either, particularly if the bride is all in white. However, I have seen some mothers in lovely off-white dresses at their children's weddings; somehow that does not seem to compete with the bridal white. White kid or washable leather gloves should be worn to and from the church and reception in cold weather, but they are seldom worn by mothers of the bridal couple in the receiving line any more.

Women guests should not wear white dresses, which would make them look as though they are competing with the bride. They may wear black to evening or late afternoon weddings. If they wish to wear hats, they should wear them. Long dresses should not be worn to morning or afternoon weddings by the guests (although in some Jewish daytime weddings it is customary for the women to wear long dresses; one should ask the mother of the bride).

When the groom wears formal day or evening wear, his father and his bride's father dress as he does, as do all the male members of the wedding party. Men guests at a formal or informal daytime wedding would wear dark business suits. At a formal evening wedding, where the men in the party are in white tie, the fathers of the bride and groom should be, too; other male relatives may also wear white tie on this occasion. Men guests at this rare kind of formal evening wedding would wear their dinner jackets and black ties. In warm climates, the black dinner jackets are of tropical weight.

Chapter 18

THE REHEARSAL

It would be preferable if weddings with more than two attendants could be rehearsed two or three days before the events. In most cases, however, the rehearsal takes place the afternoon before the wedding at the convenience of the clergyman, or in large churches the sexton, who must be present with the organist and any other participants.

Which Arm Does the Bride Take?

This is always settled at the rehearsal and depends on the preference of the minister. It is more convenient at a formal wedding for the bride to go up the aisle on her father's right arm, so that when his role is completed and he must return to the left front pew to stand with her mother he does not have to cross over the bride's train but will be already on the convenient side. However, some ministers prefer the other procedure in which the bride comes down the aisle on her father's left arm. (In all recessionals the bride takes the groom's arm and ushers offer their arms to bridesmaids if this pairing procedure is followed.) The clergyman's ruling is the deciding one.

The Processional

Ushers are paired, as are bridesmaids, so that the shorter ones precede the taller. They learn that they do not actually "march" but walk in time, slowly, left foot first down the aisle, keeping four pews apart, and after a little coaching they manage to deliver the bride to the chancel steps at the moment the music stops playing. The bride, no longer afraid to rehearse at her own wedding, counts eight beats of the music before she follows the attendants on her father's arm (preferably the right one).

No words of the service are spoken during the rehearsal, although the minister (or the sexton) indicates at what point each member of the party plays his role. The best man learns just when he must produce the ring from his vest pocket or, better, his little finger. The maid or matron of honor

ALTAR

PROCESSIONAL, CHRISTIAN CEREMONY
Reading from top down: *Bride and her father.*

Flower girl or ring bearer, if any, or ring bearer and flower girl, ring bearer preceding flower girl.

Maid or matron of honor. If there are both, they may walk together or the younger may precede the elder.

Bridesmaids. Shorters ones precede taller and they are paired according to height.

Ushers. Shorter ones precede taller and are paired according to height.

At the chancel steps: best man, groom, clergyman.

If there is a junior bridesmaid, her place is between the flower girl (or girls) if any, and the maid or matron of honor.

If there are pages, they follow the bride and carry her train.

notes at what point she takes the bride's bouquet or prayer book. The bride's father—or in some cases her mother—learns when the bride is to be "given away" if this is to be part of the ceremony.

The Recessional

Most rehearsed of all will be the ushers, who, if it is to be a large wedding, will have real work to do. Two ushers, chosen for the honor, will be shown how to handle the ribbons and, if there is to be one, how to lay the canvas runner* at the right moment. It is at the rehearsal that bride and clergyman, or sexton, decide how the recessional is to go. Bride and groom always lead in the recessional, but it is optional whether or not the ushers and bridesmaids pair up or return as they were in the processional, but this time with the bride's attendants immediately following the couple, in the proper order, then the ushers walking together. If there is an uneven number of ushers the extra man may walk in the middle (*see illustration*) and the second variation of the recessional is preferred.

In the recessional the father is missing—he has joined the mother in the first pew as soon as he has given the bride away.

When There Are Two Main Aisles

When a church has two main aisles one may be used for the processional, one for the recessional. When each is given the same importance the pew posts are decorated exactly alike. If it is decided that one aisle is to be used for both processional and recessional, the other aisle is used only for seating of guests and is not specially decorated. If one aisle is chosen, the grouping at the chancel is on the side of that aisle. When both aisles are given equal importance the grouping at the chancel is as it is for a church with a center aisle. If it can be arranged, the parents of the bride and groom should sit in the choir stalls on either side of the altar, with the bride's family on the left and the groom's family on the right. If this cannot be managed, however, the bride's family may either be seated in the pews on the far left or a dividing ribbon may be placed down the middle of the center pew and the bride's and groom's families may share the center front row.

* The runner is used only at formal weddings. Its purpose is to keep the bride's skirt hem clean, a mostly symbolic gesture.

ALTAR

RECESSIONAL, CHRISTIAN CEREMONY, OPTIONAL ARRANGEMENT

LEFT PANEL, Reading from top down: *Groom and bride.*

Flower girl or page, or pages, if any, or second honor attendant, if any. Best man and maid or matron of honor. Ushers and bridesmaids paired.

ALTAR

LEFT PANEL, Reading from top down: *Groom and bride.*

Flower girl or second honor attendant, if any.

Maid of honor and best man. If there are two attendants, the matron of honor is escorted by the best man, the maid of honor by the head usher. Bridesmaids, followed by ushers. If there is an extra usher he is placed somewhere in the center of the recessional so that he is not the "tail on the kite."

Chapter 19

THE WEDDING CEREMONY

Procedure During the Ceremony

In Christian wedding ceremonies the left side is the bride's, as one enters; the right, the groom's. The family and friends of the bride are, therefore, on the left of the church, and the groom's are on the right. When the wedding is held at a great distance from the groom's hometown and he will be having significantly fewer guests, the ushers should arrange the seating evenly.

As the bride approaches the chancel the clergyman stands at the entrance to the altar and the groom, facing slightly into the nave, is on the right, ready to step forward to assist the bride up the chancel step or steps. Below and behind him a little to the right is the best man. On the left of the chancel as the bride approaches stands her maid or matron of honor in the same position as the best man. Ushers, if any, are lined up below the choir stalls on each side of the chancel with the maids of honor usually in front of them and on a slanting line. In a small church it may be necessary to place only two ushers on the chancel steps, one left, one right, the rest on the floor of the church, flanking the chancel, but many variations of these groupings are used.

Giving Away the Bride

In Protestant ceremonies the father stays at the chancel until the question is posed as to who gives away the bride. He then places the bride's right hand in the hand of the clergyman and responds, "I do." Just as it is the right of a girl's real mother to announce her marriage, so it is the right of her real father to give her away, if he is capable. Stepfathers should not be afforded this honor if a girl's real father is alive and willing and able to take part. There is no graceful way for both a father and a stepfather to participate in the ceremony.

If the girl's father is too ill or infirm to walk down the aisle, but well enough to wish to participate in the ceremony, he can be brought in from

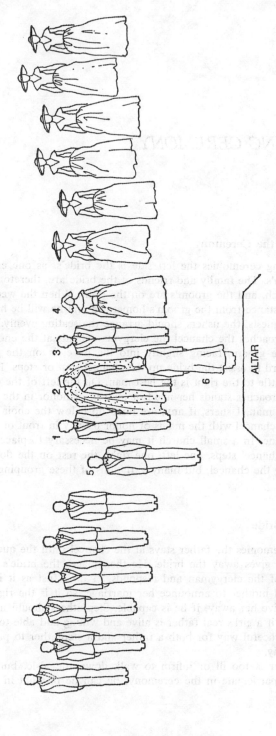

GROUPING AT THE ALTAR, PROTESTANT CEREMONY: (1) Groom, (2) bride, (3) bride's father, (4) maid or matron of honor, (5) best man, (6) clergyman. Figures far left and right, ushers, bridesmaids. NOTE: In the Roman Catholic ceremony the bride's father joins her mother in the first pew as he reaches it. He does not give the bride away. Otherwise the grouping at the chancel is the same, with the addition of an acolyte (see text). The flower girl would stand behind the maid of honor; if she is too young, she would return to her parents in their pew.

the vestry in a wheel chair just before the seating of the mother of the bride. The bride in such a case may go down the aisle either accompanied by her mother or by a male member of the family, or even alone, and join her father, who would be waiting in the group at the altar or seated in the first pew, to give her away. Any situation this irregular should be discussed with your clergyman. He may have valuable suggestions to make regarding a specific situation.

If a male relative (a grandfather, an uncle, an older brother, a close mature family friend) has the responsibility of giving the bride away, he merely stands in his appointed place with the bride and at the moment of "giving away" answers, "I do," or he may answer, "on behalf of her mother, I do."

If the bride's father is dead the bride's mother may give her away—if some male relative hasn't been selected for the honor. There are several ways this may be done. Either the bride's mother may walk down the aisle with her daughter—but not, of course, with the bride on her arm—or the bride may walk in the processional with her brother or other male relative, her mother joining her as the bride reaches the left front pew. Sometimes the bride walks alone in the processional and her mother joins her as she reaches her mother's pew. Still again, a male relative will escort the bride to the chancel steps and when the clergyman asks who is to give the bride away the mother nods from her traditional place or, just before the words are to be spoken, is escorted to the chancel by the best man, who steps down for the gesture, and she then places the bride's right hand in the hand of the clergyman. She may stand to the right of the bride's escort until the ceremony is concluded, and then be escorted by him back to her pew before the recessional begins or be escorted by him directly after the "giving away" to her pew. The ceremony then continues with the vows, the ring, and so on.

If a bride is marrying far from her home and none of her relatives will be able to attend to give her away, there are several alternatives. The bride may arrange with the minister to dispense with this portion of the ceremony altogether. On the other hand, if she is marrying where members of the groom's family will be present, she may ask her future in-laws to suggest some close male relative of their family to whom the honor of giving away the bride would be appropriate.

Another modern departure at Congregational wedding ceremonies that might be—with the clergyman's permission—inserted in any Protestant ceremony is as follows. The bride's father, when asked who gave away the bride, replied, "Her mother and I do."

These procedures are necessary only in those ceremonies—the Episcopal, for example—where the one who "gives the bride away" actually places her hand in the minister's. In the Episcopal Church there are alternatives now open to the bride that allow her to choose either a member of the wedding party (the father of the groom, perhaps), or some other person she wishes to honor, to read the scripture lesson. Also, if it is to be a Communion service, someone may be invited to bring the bread and wine to the altar.

Giving Away the Mature Bride In the weddings of previously married brides—widows or divorcées—it is not necessary that they be "given away," and this portion of the ceremony is often omitted, just as it is in civil ceremonies when there may well be no designated attendants, merely legal witnesses.

But the older woman who has a church wedding usually chooses to be escorted to the church by some male relative or close family friend, also male, although she may arrive with the best man, the groom, and her own attendant. She does not walk up the church aisle, but waits with the groom, best man, and maid of honor in the vestry until the clergyman is ready, then is escorted to her place at the chancel by the best man, while the groom escorts the maid or matron of honor.

At the Altar Rail In some ceremonies—namely, the Catholic and the Episcopal—the bride and groom follow the clergyman to the altar and may kneel at an indicated point in the ceremony. They are followed by the maid and matron of honor, if there are both in attendance, with the maid on the immediate left of the bride and the matron on the far left of the bride, so that it is the maid who assists with the bouquet and veil. The best man, on the immediate right of the groom, is followed by the ring bearer, if any, at far right, a few feet behind. When the clergyman asks for the ring, the best man produces it from his vest pocket or, better, his little finger. In the Catholic service he proffers it to the groom, who hands it to the acolyte, who in turn gives it to the priest, who blesses it. In the Protestant ceremony—and the Episcopal service or some variation of it is often used in Presbyterian and Congregational churches, too—he hands the ring to the groom, who gives it to the minister for the blessing.

During the blessing of the ring—or, if preferred, as soon as maid and matron of honor (or just the one attendant) are in place—the bride hands her bouquet or prayer book to the attendant chosen for the honor, so that her left hand will be free to receive the wedding ring.

As soon as the marriage service is completed, the bride turns first to the maid or matron of honor for her bouquet and to have her face veil, if she has one, lifted. If the maid or matron of honor finds that holding the bride's bouquet and her own becomes too confusing, especially when the veil must be lifted, a small table may be placed to the left of the altar to hold the maid or matron of honor's bouquet. Or the bride may hand her flowers to the junior bridesmaid before ascending with the groom into the chancel, and then, as the bride descends for the recessional, the flowers may be handed back. She then turns, and, although this is not part of the ceremony, receives the groom's kiss if they have decided to kiss at the altar, and the good wishes of the clergyman, who usually shakes hands with both bride and groom.

The bride then turns and takes the groom's right arm, and—after the maid of honor has adjusted her train—together they lead off in the recessional.

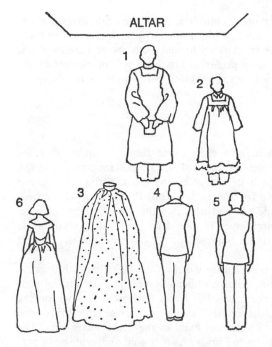

AT THE ALTAR RAIL, EPISCOPAL AND ROMAN CATHOLIC CEREMONY, OPTIONAL ARRANGEMENTS: (*1*) *Priest,* (*2*) *acolyte* (ROMAN CATHOLIC SERVICE), (*3*) *bride,* (*4*) *groom,* (*5*) *best man,* (*6*) *maid or matron of honor.*

When Does the Bride Take the Groom's Arm? In the wedding ceremony, although the groom takes a step or two forward to meet the bride and may take her arm to assist her to kneel, if that is part of the ceremony, optionally, the bride does or does not take the groom's arm or place her hand in his until the moment in the ceremony at which this is indicated. In some ceremonies the clergyman places the bride's hand in the groom's, in others the father—or sometimes the mother—makes this symbolic gesture. At other times the bride needs her hands free to arrange her gown for kneeling, to hand her prayer book or bouquet to her attendant. The groom may assist her to rise from a kneeling position.

When Does the Groom Kiss the Bride? At large formal church weddings it is not usual for the groom to kiss the bride at the altar after the clergyman has congratulated the couple at the end of the ceremony. However, at most weddings the kiss takes place. At an informal wedding, or at a wedding at home, the groom always kisses the bride immediately following the clergyman's congratulations. In the receiving line at the reception, everyone and anyone may kiss the bride; a light brush of a man's lips on her mouth or cheek is all that is really in good taste.

Kissing of Parents During the Ceremony In a Catholic ceremony, during the "Kiss of Peace" part of the service, the bride and groom kiss each other and may, if they wish proceed to the front pews and kiss both sets of parents or other close relatives. In other churches, when the bride arrives at the altar on her father's arm, she may kiss him as he steps back to give her away —and she may also go to the front pews to kiss both set of parents if she wishes. The bride and groom may prefer to kiss both sets of parents at the conclusion of the ceremony, before the wedding party marches out in recessional order from the church.

The Double-ring Ceremony

When both bride and groom give each other rings the question often arises as to who holds the groom's ring until the proper moment. It is the maid or matron of honor who is in charge of the groom's ring, just as the best man is always responsible for the bride's until the moment the groom slips it on her finger. The bride's attendant wears the groom's ring for safekeeping. If it won't stay on any finger it should be tied with a small white satin ribbon to her sash or belt, her bouquet, or her left wrist, so she can get it off easily.

A man's wedding ring was customarily worn on the right hand, but in recent years, when the double-ring ceremony became very popular during wartime, the ring was placed on the man's left hand. So now it is worn on the third finger of either the right or left hand, whichever the bride and bridegroom prefer but usually on the left hand as the bride wears hers. The groom's ring is always a gift from the bride. As it is gold and preferably perfectly plain, it may not necessarily match hers, as it used to. Most weddings are double-ring ceremonies, but the husbands do not necessarily wear the rings they receive.

The Double Wedding

Double weddings with the brides in formal wedding gowns are most impressive. Sometimes the brides are sisters who wish to marry at the same time, occasionally cousins, or just close friends, although in some denominations the brides must be related. The double wedding does not, of course, have to be formal, and the brides, whether in formal attire or in simple daytime costumes, need not be dressed alike.

In a formal double wedding, if each bride and groom have separate attendants it is necessary that they have the same number and that the costumes of the brides' attendants at least harmonize with each other. Sometimes sisters have the same attendants. The brides may act as maid and matron of honor for each other, or each may have separate honor attendants. The grooms, too, may act as best man for each other, or each have his own best man.

In a double wedding all the ushers are paired according to height in the processional. They are followed by the elder's bridesmaids, then her maid or matron of honor, then comes the senior bride on her father's arm, followed

PROCESSIONAL AT DOUBLE WEDDING, CHRISTIAN CEREMONY, OPTIONAL ARRANGEMENT

Reading from top down: *Younger bride with male family member.*

Maid or matron of honor of younger bride.

Bridesmaids of younger bride.

Elder bride and father.

Maid or matron of honor of elder bride.

Bridesmaids of elder bride.

Ushers paired according to height.

RECESSIONAL AT DOUBLE WEDDING, CHRISTIAN CEREMONY, OPTIONAL ARRANGEMENT

Reading from top down: *Elder bride and groom.*

Younger bride and groom.

Maids or matrons of honor of both brides, paired.

Ushers of elder bride paired with bridesmaids of elder bride.

Ushers of younger bride paired with bridesmaids of younger bride; or they may go out as they came in.

ALTAR

by the bridesmaids of the younger bride. After them comes the maid or matron of honor of the younger bride, then the bride herself on her father's arm, unless she is a sister of the elder bride. In that case a brother or other male relative escorts her. In the case of twins, the twin who was born first receives the privileges of the elder sister and is escorted by her father first and married first. However, it is possible for the father to escort both girls down the aisle, if he does so one at a time.

In the recessional the elder bride, who was married first, leads down the chancel steps with her groom and is followed by the younger bride with her groom. The attendants follow in the proper order—those of the first bride first, or paired with those of the second bride if an equal number makes it possible. Otherwise, they leave as they arrived.

If a church has two aisles, each bridal party may have its own, timing the entrance and exit together.

All the ushers of both groups must be identically dressed, even when the bridesmaids' costumes differ for each bride. The only time, by the way, ushers may ever be dressed differently is when civilians and military men serve together.

The mothers of the brides are escorted up the aisle by ushers in the usual way just before the ceremony begins, with the mother of the elder bride coming first. In entering the first pew they leave room between them for the fathers.

It is advisable, by the way, even if the brides are sisters, for each to have her own wedding cake so that no conflict arises over which couple should cut the cake.

Wedding Guests at the Church

The guest aids the work of the ushers by arriving at the church fifteen to twenty minutes before the ceremony or, at a large wedding, even earlier if pew cards are not issued. The early arrivals take the outside pew seats with the best view of the altar. The late arrivals do not deserve those seats. Therefore, those on the aisle should step out into the aisle and let late arrivals take the seats on the inside.

Each guest, man or woman, is met in the church vestibule by an usher who seats each in turn or in groups where all are to sit together (see "Duties of Ushers," page 191). As each guest joins an usher he says, "Friend of the bride" or "Friend of the groom," as the case may be, so that he may be seated on the left or the right side of the church. If he has a reserved seat, he presents the card that has been sent to him to the usher, or tells him his name if he is not recognized. At a formal wedding with ushers on duty, no invited guest seats himself.

After the guests are seated in the pews to which they have been escorted they may talk briefly in low tones suitable to church. They should not move about among their friends, wave, or turn around to talk to friends in rear pews. After the bride's mother is escorted to the front left pew no other guests are seated and the church doors are closed.

As the wedding march begins, all guests rise and turn toward the rear of the church to await the beginning of the procession. During the service one should stand, sit, or kneel when the rest of the congregation does. If it is not the custom of someone in his own church to kneel, he can at least bow his head over the back of the pew in front of him and stand and sit when others do the same. A Protestant at a Catholic wedding is not expected to make the sign of the cross, but a Christian man at an Orthodox or Conservative Jewish wedding would be considered irreverent if he did not wear a hat. For the same reason, non-Jewish married woman whose own churches do not require head covering in church do cover their heads in an Orthodox or Conservative synagogue, so as not to offend.

After the ribbons are in place no one may leave his pew, even if there is possible egress to a side aisle. Ushers escort the bride's mother and honored guests immediately following the recessional, before the ribbons are removed.

Differences in Religious Ceremonies

It is interesting to see how essentially alike the marriage services of different religions are. Most Christian ceremonies are similar, with but minor differences. As the Christian ceremony developed from that of the ancient Jews, there is between Jewish and Christian ceremonies a definite similarity. Increasing numbers of Reform rabbis and ministers are now recognizing these similarities and are agreeing to officiate in the joint blessing of interfaith marriages.

The Roman Catholic Ceremony   There have been so many changes in the Roman Catholic ceremony, and such a variety of options are now available, that it would be impossible to list them. The options incorporated in the new Rite of Marriage are up to each individual priest and can vary from one part of the country to another, as well as from one parish to the next. Civil marriage involving a Catholic is not recognized by the Catholic Church, but in an interfaith marriage, which may take place in a Roman Catholic church under certain circumstances, a Protestant clergyman (or a rabbi) may participate as an assisting celebrant, or a priest may participate as a guest in another faith's church, with the consent of the local bishop.

There are options on where the wedding party stands and kneels during the ceremony. Sometimes they are grouped in front of the altar rail; in larger churches, sometimes in the sanctuary area on the other side of the rail.

Music plays a prominent part in the wedding ceremony and selections are made with participation by the congregation kept well in mind. Songs from both traditions are permitted in an interfaith marriage. The couple may select the readings and the people to read them, who could be the maid of honor and best man. Altar boys are no longer usual. A guest at a nuptial mass ceremony should follow the instructions for the congregation in regard to sitting and standing. When wedding plans are first made, the bride and groom should visit the priest-celebrant to discuss all the options open to them in the order of Mass and the Rite of Marriage.

Jewish Ceremonies   There are three major interpretations of Jewish tradition practiced in the United States: Orthodox, Conservative, and Reform, Orthodox Judaism follows the most traditional approach in a rather strict interpretation of the legal standards of the Bible and later sources. Reform Judaism, on the other hand, follows a more liberal approach based on a progressive interpretation of the Jewish legal standards. Conservative Judaism very much falls within these two parameters, more liberal than Orthodox and yet more traditional in its practice than Reform.

A rabbi of an Orthodox or Conservative synagogue will not marry divorced persons who have received only civil decrees. A religious divorce decree is also necessary. Reform Judaism gives religious recognition to a civil divorce and therefore does not require, in addition, a religious divorce.

Before the ceremony the bride usually receives the wedding guests in an anteroom of the place where she is to be married. Seated with her attendants, she sees all but the groom before the ceremony. In liberal temples, however, she may even see him.

At Jewish weddings—Orthodox, Conservative, and Reform—music for the processional and, briefly, for the recessional is usual. Selection of the music depends on the couple's taste. Frequently, it is traditional Israeli or Hebrew music. A cantor is not necessary at a Jewish wedding but he frequently does take part in the wedding ceremony, especially in big weddings, chanting, not singing. There are no vocal solos at Jewish weddings. Instruments may vary from the organ to the violin or woodwinds. Sometimes the music is on tape. The cantor's fees for participation in the ceremony run from $25 to $100 or more depending upon the elaborateness of the ceremony. The organist—or other musicians—is compensated according to individual arrangements.

When the Orthodox ceremony is held in a synagogue, the bride stands to the groom's right before the Holy Ark, which corresponds to the altar with its cross or crucifix of most Christian faiths. The bride wears the traditional wedding gown and veil in a formal ceremony—exactly like that of the Christian bride. She has the same attendants, too—maid or matron of honor and bridesmaids if she wishes. Sometimes both fathers and both mothers take part in the ceremony and in the processional accompany the bride and groom. Grandparents may participate in the ceremony in this way, as well. In fact there is no prescribed limit in the Jewish faith on the number or nature of attendants a bride may choose to have. In the recessional both mothers and fathers may walk together side by side (*see illustration*). However, a girl contemplating having an extraordinary number of attendants should remember that they will only serve ultimately to distract attention from her own position of prominence.

ORTHODOX JEWISH CEREMONY AT ALTAR, OPTIONAL ARRANGE-MENT: *(1) Rabbi, (2) groom, (3) bride, (4) best man, (5) maid or ma-tron of honor, (6) groom's father and mother, (7) bride's father and mother, (8) bridesmaids, in aisle, (9) ushers.* NOTE: *The arrangement of the wedding party is not a matter of rabbinical law but of social custom; hence it varies. For example, parents may be under the canopy if there is room. Sometimes only the fathers take part, and their placement is optional.*

In the Jewish ceremony it is usually the right side of the synagogue or temple, as one enters, that is the bride's; the left, the groom's. However, this varies according to custom. In Reform practice, the right side of the syna-gogue, as one enters, is reserved for the groom's family and the left side for the family of the bride. The couple is wed beneath a canopy supported on standards and symbolizing home. Under the canopy with them stand the rabbi and, usually, their two principal attendants. If the canopy, or *chupah*, is large enough, the four parents stand beneath it, too; otherwise they stand

ORTHODOX JEWISH PROCESSIONAL AND RECESSIONAL, OPTIONAL ARRANGEMENTS

PROCESSIONAL Reading from top down, left: *Bride's mother, bride, bride's father.*
Flower girl or page, if any.
Maid or matron of honor.
Groom's mother, groom, groom's father.
Best man.
Rabbi, not in processional or recessional if ceremony takes place in a temple or synagogue.

RECESSIONAL Reading from top down, left: *Bride and groom.*

Bride's parents.
Groom's parents.
(Flower girl or page not necessarily in recessional.)
Maid or matron of honor and best man.
Rabbi. NOTE: *In Jewish ceremony the left (many rabbis prefer the right) side is the bride's. Attendants, if any, come up the aisle, paired, before the rabbi and may form a guard of honor through which the procession walks.*

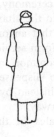

outside the fringe. Next to the rabbi, who faces the bride and groom, is a small covered table containing two cups of ritual wine and one glass wrapped in a snowy napkin. The service is in Hebrew and Aramaic in the Orthodox and Conservative synagogues. In the Reform practice the service is in both Hebrew and English.

The ceremony begins with an Invocation, which is followed by the two Betrothal Benedictions. After the first, the rabbi passes one glass of wine to the groom, who takes a sip and gives it to the bride. Then comes the ring ceremony with the ring, in the Orthodox ceremony, always plain gold. The best man hands it to the rabbi, who, in those states that require it, says in English, "Dost thou take this woman to be thy wedded wife?" receiving the usual responses in English. Then, in the Orthodox and Conservative services, the ring is placed on the bride's right index finger directly by the groom, though any time after the ceremony she may remove it and place it on what our Western society considers the proper wedding ring finger. In the Reform service the ring is placed on the bride's left ring finger.

The ring ceremony is followed by the reading of the marriage contract, "Kesubah," which is in Aramaic. The rabbi then delivers a short address in English (or the language of the congregation) to the couple on the sancity of marriage and his own personal concern for their future welfare.

Next the Seven Blessings are recited, or chanted, at the end of which comes the ceremonial drinking of the second glass of wine by both bride and groom. This is followed in the Orthodox and Conservative services with the crushing of a glass beneath the foot of the bridegroom, which symbolizes the sacking of the Temple of Jerusalem and is an admonition to the congregation that despite the happiness of the occasion all should remember and work for the rebuilding of Zion.

In the Reform service the wedding canopy is not required, the breaking of the glass is usually optional, and the rabbi does not read the marriage certificate in Aramaic.

The reception-with-collation that follows Jewish weddings is exactly like other receptions except that a special nuptial grace is always offered after food.

As in the Catholic ceremony, the Jewish does not require the father to give his daughter in marriage. In the Reform service, the father escorts his daughter on his right arm up the aisle to the groom who, with his best man, awaits her at the altar. In the Orthodox and Conservative ceremony, both sets of parents accompany the bride and groom respectively to the altar, taking their places under or near the *chupah*. It is not required that anyone except the bride and groom stand under the canopy. In the Reform service the parents do not stand up with their children. It is becoming common in both the Reform and Conservative ceremony for the groom to dispense with walking up the aisle and to come onto the pulpit platform instead by stepping out with the rabbi and best man from the platform doorway.

In Orthodox and Conservative Jewish weddings all males in the assemblage must cover their heads. They wear the traditional skullcaps or their own hats. Synagogues have skullcaps available in the vestibule for men who arrive without their hats. In Orthodox synagogues men and women do not sit together, and in the Reform temples the wearing of skullcaps is usually optional. Single women in Orthodox synagogues optionally wear a headcovering, but the heads of married women are covered by hat, shawl, or wig. In most Conservative synagogues all women, regardless of marital status, are urged to wear hats and in all cases to dress in a manner appropriate to a religious sanctuary.

No Orthodox or Conservative rabbi ever officiates at a mixed marriage and many Reform rabbis will not. However, though Jews do not seek converts, the non-Jewish partner in a proposed mixed marriage may go through a period of instruction and then be taken into the Congregation as a Jew. Any rabbi may then perform the marriage. Questions of conversion and intermarriage must be discussed with the rabbi before any plans may be made.

As I stated earlier, particularly among Orthodox Jews recently of European origin, the groom's family often pays for the liquor at the reception and shares the cost of bridal photographs. (Most rabbis will discourage the taking of photographs during the service.) Otherwise, the distribution of costs remains the same for both Jewish and Christian weddings.

The Christian Science Ceremony As Christian Science readers are not ordained ministers of the church, merely elected officers, they may not perform the marriage ceremony. When members of the Christian Science faith are married, the ceremony is performed by an ordained minister of the gospel, legally authorized to perform such a duty, or by the proper legal authority. Christian Scientists oppose the use of alcoholic beverages. Many do not serve them in any form, even the mildest, at wedding receptions, despite the presence of non-Christian Scientists.

Eastern Orthodox Weddings The Eastern Orthodox Church—the Holy Eastern Orthodox Catholic Apostolic Church—has numerous followers among Greeks, Russians, Rumanians, and other Mediterranean groups in this country. It has many ceremonial forms similar to those of the Roman Catholic Church but does not acknowledge the Pope as its spiritual leader.

Traditionally before their wedding the bride and groom must fast, make their confessions, and take Communion. The ceremony is celebrated without Mass and always takes place in either the afternoon or the evening.

In the Eastern Orthodox Church the ceremony does not take place at the altar but before a table placed in front of the sanctuary toward the center of the church. Many of these churches now have pews, a modern development, but in churches where there are no pews guests must stand or kneel before and throughout the hour-long service. In some churches only vocal music is permitted. In others, when the bride enters, special wedding hymns are sung by the choir, accompanied by an organ. The procession is like that in other

Christian services. The father of the bride gives the bride away, then returns to the pew with her mother.

In the Eastern Orthodox service the mystical number three, representing the Trinity, has great significance. The double-ring ceremony is used—with both rings placed on the right hands of the groom and bride. The priest blesses the rings three times at the altar, then places each ring first on the groom's finger, then on the bride's. Then the best man exchanges the rings three times on the fingers of the groom and bride. Just before the final vows are taken, the priest binds the hands of the groom and bride together and leads them, along with the members of the wedding party, three times around the table, which holds the Bible, or Scripture, a cross, a chalice of wine, candles, and flowers. Throughout the ceremony the bride and groom hold lighted candles symbolizing the light of the Lord. During the ceremony the priest places white wreaths made of imitation lemon flowers on their heads. In some churches they place gold-plated crowns on their heads, in accordance with the ancient tradition.

These are only the highlights of this richly impressive ceremony, usual in all Eastern Orthodox unions.

The Church makes divorce difficult and insists on a religious decree. Remarriage of divorced persons is permitted.

The Quaker Ceremony   Today a Quaker marriage ceremony may see the bride gowned traditionally and veiled, but these simple, unpretentious people believe in the renunciation of worldly display. Their ceremony is as plain as their meeting houses and impressive in its quiet sincerity.

A Quaker wedding may take place in the meeting house or in a private home, but notice of intention to wed is made by the couple at least one monthly meeting in advance of the date they have set. It is necessary for at least one of them to be a member of the Society of Friends. It is usual for the parents' permission to be appended to the letter of request, even when the couple is of age. After the letter has been read at the meeting, a committee of two women and two men is appointed to discuss with the bride and groom, respectively, the "clearness to proceed with marriage." The committee may discuss marriage and its obligations with the couple just as a minister would, for originally the Quakers had no appointed ministers but instead gathered together in Quaker silence, speaking up in meeting as the inner spirit moved them to express themselves. (In some meetings there is now a regularly appointed minister, especially in the West.)

The committee submits a report on its conferences with the couple to the monthly meeting. Overseers are then appointed to attend the wedding and to advise the couple on the marriage procedure.

On the wedding day bride and groom come down the aisle together—or there may be the usual wedding procession—and take the "facing seats," the benches that face the meeting. After the Quaker silence the couple rise and take hands. The groom says words to the effect that "in the presence of God

I take thee . . . to be my wedded wife promising with divine assistance to be unto thee a loving and faithful husband as long as we both shall live." The bride repeats the answering vow. The couple is then seated again, and the ushers bring forward a table containing the Quaker marriage certificate. This is then read aloud, signed by the bride, groom, and overseers, and later officially registered. The regular Quaker meeting follows.

At the next monthly meeting the overseers report that the marriage "was carried out to the good order of friends." Divorce among Quakers is rare.

The Mormon Ceremony   There are two kinds of marriages among the Mormons (members of the Church of Jesus Christ of Latter-day Saints). The first are those that are performed in temples of the Church by those holding the holy priesthood. In pronouncing the couple man and wife, the priest declares them wed "for time and for all eternity," instead of "until death do you part." Children born to parents so married are believed by the Mormons to belong to them in the eternal world by virtue of such marriages. These marriages are always referred to as temple marriages. All brides married in the temple dress in white and wear veils, although they may have previously been married.

There are also civil marriages performed by bishops of the Church or any other accredited person. Later, if the couple has complied with the requirements of the Church in their daily living, they may enter the temples of the Church and be married for time and for all eternity despite previous civil marriages.

Following temple or civil marriages, receptions for bride and groom with family and invited guests are usually held in the cultural hall of the church, or in the home of the bride's parents. In some communities there are special reception centers where such receptions are held.

Mixed marriage, although not encouraged, is permitted. Civil divorce is recognized but divorce is rare among those married in the temples. The Mormon Church takes no stand against remarriage.

The Home Wedding

If space permits, the home wedding can be lovely. The largest room, usually the living room, is selected and cleared for the ceremony, and an altar improvised before a fireplace or at some other focal point in the room, preferably at the greatest distance from the entrance or entrances. Seats are provided or not. (If the ceremony lasts more than ten minutes, there should be seats.)

If the room is large and the company numerous, "ribbons" are put in place just before the entrance of the bride's mother and the groom's mother to preserve an aisle. At large weddings a small section for the parents and immediate relatives is roped off on either side of the altar, bride's family to the left, groom's to the right.

Where there is a staircase the bride descends it at the first strains of the wedding march; otherwise she and the bridal party congregate outside the entrance to the main room before the music begins. This is only, of course, if the guests are numerous enough and the house large enough to permit a formal wedding if she wants it. Otherwise the bride wears a street-length or floor-length wedding gown and a short veil or a simple dress (never black or true red) or suit at noon, a covered-up cocktail dress or a soft suit later in the day. Her attendants dress similarly.

At a very small wedding there may be no music at all and the bride may be dressed informally. She need not make the usual dramatic entrance but, after the clergyman has taken his place, merely step before him for the ceremony. A collation or light meal is always served at a home wedding. It may be in the same room as that in which the wedding took place or in the garden or on a porch. A large table is usually moved against a wall and set with the wedding cake as a central theme.

A wedding, of course, may take place out of doors if the climate is sufficiently dependable or if alternative arrangements have been made. Sometimes the witness to the ceremony are limited and the reception is large and, often in summer, out of doors.

Receiving at a Home Wedding   At a home wedding there is no recessional unless a formal receiving line is to form elsewhere in the house or in the garden. Where there are many guests and space is limited, the receiving line, if there is to be one, is best located in a small room such as a hall or dining room with both exit and entrance to facilitate the flow of traffic. Guests should be able to pass on into a larger area where they may congregate and have refreshments. In simple home weddings it is usual for the bride and groom merely to turn around at the altar, *after* the groom has kissed the bride, and receive informally with the bridal attendants.

The Clergyman's Wedding

There are a number of circumstances related to the wedding of a clergyman that differ from those of the usual wedding. If he has his own church, synagogue, or temple the bride may wonder whether the entire congregation must be invited to the wedding and, if so, how the invitation should be presented. And where does the marriage take place, in his place of worship or hers? There is also the question of the wedding of the son or daughter of a clergyman. Where and when do such weddings take place, and who officiates? Who gives a clergyman's daughter away if her father performs the ceremony? What does a clergyman wear to his own wedding?

First, a clergyman, like any other groom, is usually married in the church, temple, or synagogue of his bride. The bride may prefer, however, to be married at the groom's place of worship, or in her own home or the home of friends. It may be that her place of worship is the same as the clergyman's in which case they may be married there by some other clergyman of their faith, his superior, a friend, or a clergyman from a neighboring parish or congregation.

A clergyman may choose to wear his clericals at his own wedding or, which seems to be more customary these days, dress in the same style as the ushers in his wedding. It depends on the feelings of the individual, as there is no specific form of attire that is considered correct.

A clergyman-father performing the marriage for his daughter cannot give her away, as is customary in the wedding ceremony. Instead, she is escorted by an older brother, a brother-in-law, a godfather, an uncle, a grandfather, or a family friend. After delivering her to the groom, her escort may remain to give her away or take his place in the first pew on the bride's side. When the clergyman asks who gives the bride in marriage, it is a matter of preference which person answers. The bride's mother may step forward and place the hand of the bride in that of the clergyman or in that of the groom, depending on the denominational custom, or the bride's escort may be chosen to give the bride away. The bride may feel that she would like to be given in marriage in the traditional manner by her father; in this case, the clergyman-father would also conduct this part of the ceremony.

In a very small community and in a church or synagogue that is unusually well attended, a clergyman might announce his forthcoming marriage from the pulpit and invite the congregation to attend the ceremony in his own house of worship. However, so informal a procedure, though it seems to be followed occasionally, risks the exclusion of those members who did not attend services on the day the announcement was made. More correct is the sending of individual invitations of some kind (see "Wedding Invitations," in Chapter 11) to the entire church membership. The reception, of course, could be and is expected to be limited to close friends, associates, and relatives of the bride and groom. In a small community where a bride, for extenuating reasons (no relatives of her own, for example), might come from a distance to be married in her husband's own church or synagogue, the people of the congregation might give the reception, especially if the couple's joint circumstances are modest.

A clergyman whose son is marrying is very often given the honor of conducting the ceremony in the bride's place of worship with the bride's clergyman assisting. If the bride's home is at considerable distance from his own, the father's congregation should not expect to be invited en masse, although various active members of the congregation might well be included in the invitation list.

A clergyman's wife should feel free to give a shower for any member of the congregation to whom she feels especially close. A clergyman, by the way, is not expected to proffer a gift to every couple over whose wedding he officiates.

Driving to the Reception

It must be remembered that after the wedding ceremony and before the reception the bride and groom should ride alone—no bridesmaids, no parents—in the car.

If There Is No Reception

At a small church wedding not followed by a reception the bride often receives with the groom, her mother, the groom's mother, and the bridesmaids in the vestibule of the church or on the porch—if there is one in a country church. The father of the bride may or may not stand in line, but the groom's father rarely does.

Elopements and Civil Ceremonies

"Elopement" is a word that is going out of style, as young people today are so independent they sometimes feel they do not need parental consent for their marriage. As one young woman told me, "We didn't 'run away.' We simply didn't feel like asking our parents to the wedding." It's a sad way to begin a marriage. Where parents have not become reconciled to the marriage and the couple marry in defiance of them, they should all work very hard to re-establish lines of communication and a good relationship afterward. It takes compromising on both sides. A marriage where there has been family bitterness at the onset is not the easiest thing to handle in mutual relationships.

Gifts for Elopers?   Sometimes formal announcements of the wedding are omitted after elopements, but more usually they are sent, even if as much time as six months or a year has elapsed since the ceremony, with the place of the marriage always stated and the date and year. If a civil ceremony has been performed, only the name of the city or town appears. If the couple was married in church, it is optional whether the church is mentioned.

If, as happens, a baby is very much on the way, announcement of the wedding is perhaps better made informally. Very early first babies happen these days with not-surprising regularity with the "situation" openly and unapologetically accepted by most good parents, relatives, and friends.

Strictly speaking, any couple for whom wedding invitations were not issued should not expect wedding gifts, even if they send formal announcements of the marriage. But of course close friends who receive the announcements and many relatives will want to send gifts. If an elopement is a second—or third—marriage for bride or groom, no gifts at all should be expected, although again there will be friends—usually of the less-married or not previously married partner—who may wish to send gifts. But once you have given a wedding gift, even to your dearest friend, you are not under an obligation to give one for a second marriage, too.

Parties for Elopers? If the bride's parents or some close relatives or friends would like to give a party for a couple who has eloped, some time after the news of the marriage has been made public, this is a nice gesture. Any friendly, informal gathering is in order. One would dress appropriately for the time of day. A receiving line would not be necessary.

Civil Marriage For a civil marriage in a registrar's office or in a judge's chambers the groom wears a dark business suit and the bride wears a simple street-length suit or dress, never a wedding gown. She may carry flowers if she wishes, or carry a white Bible or prayer book, with a flowered ribbon marker. Before the brief ceremony begins she removes her gloves (if she is wearing any) and places them with her handbag. The couple does not kneel during such a ceremony. They should limit themselves to one attendant each, with their attendants acting as witnesses. Where there is no best man and witnesses are garnered from the office staff, the groom, before the ceremony, quietly hands the officiating person a sealed envelope containing the fee—anywhere from ten to twenty-five dollars or more, depending on the circumstances. Where a high-ranking official—a mayor, governor, or Supreme Court judge—has performed the rite as a special favor to the families involved, no fee is offered but a gift is sent after the ceremony, again depending on the circumstances. Anything from a case of liquor to a humidor of good cigars or good seats to the football game might be appropriate.

It is also preferable to give a gift, not money, if the judge performs the ceremony in your home. It is also a nice gesture to invite the judge and his wife to any reception held after such a ceremony, just as you would the minister and his wife. If you have a sufficient number of guests to warrant it, a receiving line could be held at such a reception.

Chapter 20

THE WEDDING RECEPTION

There is sometimes an unavoidable delay of two to three hours between the
end of the wedding ceremony and the start of the reception, especially during the popular wedding months when churches, restaurants, clubs, or caterers' halls are booked to capacity. When this happens, the parents of the
bride or groom, or a relative or friend with a large home, should entertain
the entire wedding party, close relatives, and out-of-town guests at home.
The bridesmaids can kick off their shoes and relax; the bride can remove her
veil in order to be comfortable, and champagne and sandwiches might be
passed.

The Receiving Line

Guests go through the receiving line after the formal wedding pictures
have been taken. The bride's mother always stands first in line as the hostess. Should the wedding take place in the groom's mother's home territory
(where she will know substantially more of the guests), she should stand first
in line and help introduce.

Next to the bride's mother stands the groom's mother, and then, optionally, the bride's father. Next come the bride, the groom, the matron or
maid of honor, and the bridesmaids. The bridesmaids may also be divided so
that half are on one side of the bride with the matron of honor, and the
other half are alongside the groom. Very junior bridesmaids, flower girls,
ring bearers, and pages do not stand in line. They are just supposed to have
a good time for a very short while at the reception. There should be arrangements to have them taken home after the wedding pictures plus a short
time at the party. Ushers and the best man do not stand in the receiving line.
The bride's father may as well as the groom's father at very formal weddings. Sometimes the bride's father stands in line for the first half of the reception.

RECEIVING LINE WITHOUT FATHERS

This is an informal grouping for an inside or outdoor wedding, usually a small one. The mother of the bride usually receives guests first (1); next come mother of groom (2), bride (3), groom (4), matron of honor (5), maid of honor (6), and bridesmaids, oldest first (7 and on).

FORMAL RECEIVING LINE (WITH FATHERS)

Sometimes the pair's fathers like to stand in the receiving line. One is first received by the bride's mother (1). Then come father of groom (2), mother of groom (3), father of bride (4), bride (5), groom (6), matron of honor (7), maid of honor (8), and bridesmaids in order of age (9 and on).

It is nice for friends to slip glasses of champagne to the attendants and the bride and groom, provided there is a table or window sill behind them to hide their glasses. No one is supposed to be seen drinking in the receiving line, except for an occasional sip. Guests are not supposed to go through the line either with a glass in their hands.

If a very large reception is being held and the wedding party is being detained too long by the formal pictures, the parents of the bride and groom might start an informal receiving line, just to unclog the traffic in the entry hall. The guests who do not see the bride and groom can always come back later and pay their respects. If there is a large jam-up of the receiving line, an usher or the best man should help move people along, sending some guests directly into the room where refreshments and dancing are taking place, and urging them to "come back when the receiving line isn't so long."

If a small reception is being held in the church, permission from the clergyman might be obtained to hold a receiving line in the back of the church. This kind of receiving line is also used for the bride and groom to greet friends who came to the ceremony but who are not invited to the very small reception after.

In Place of the Bride's Mother   If the bride has no mother to receive for her, her father may receive just inside the door as the host, or a female relative (an aunt, cousin, grandmother, anyone who is close to the bride) may receive with him. The father in this case may be first in line, acting as host and introducing guests to the honorary hostess as they file past, "Aunt Mary, this is Bob Jones, one of my business associates. Bob, this is Mrs. John Beckwirth, the bride's great-aunt."

Divorced Parents in the Line   For the sake of their daughter, divorced parents may choose to stand together on a receiving line, but the father's place in line is not mandatory. If the stepmother is giving the reception, she receives, but otherwise a new spouse of a parent of the bride attends as a guest and does not stand in the line.

Conversation and the Receiving Line   No one really listens to what you say on the receiving line, as a friend of mine once dramatically proved by muttering something utterly incongruous as he made his way. You must seem cordial and happy to be where you are. As a couple proceeds through the receiving line, the woman preceding the man, the woman's name is given to the announcer first. The bride's mother—if she doesn't know you—has received your name from the announcer. On repeating their own names in the course of going through the line, all of the guests give their full names without a title. You then pass on to the groom's father, or mother, or whoever is next in line, mentioning your name and, if you are a relative, your relationship. To each you say, during the brief handclasp, "How do you do," or "Lovely wedding," or "So happy to meet you." To the bride you offer "my very best wishes" and to the groom "congratulations." (Don't *congratulate* the bride if you can help it; rather, comment on how beautiful she looks.) Your pause before the bridal couple may be perceptibly longer, but you must never hold up the receiving line with long-drawn-out dissertations. You may be able to get the couple's ear sometime during the reception—but even then remember that you are only one of many who deem it their privilege to have a word with the bride or groom.

If no one announces you as you approach the line, announce yourself. Don't assume that the bride's mother, who has perhaps seen you only a few times, is going to remember your name at a time like this. Help her out by saying, "Peter Gossett, Mrs. Kingsley. Such a beautiful wedding!"

What Does the Bride Say? The bride tries to make each acknowledgment of a guest's greeting sound warm and personal. She repeats the name, if possible, "Mrs. Osborn—so very nice of you to come so far for our wedding," or "Cousin Hattie, the coffee table is exactly what I needed!" Unless she is unusually poised and calm, however, she is safer not trying to remember who gave her what or where strangers to her have come from. She will have to write her thank-you notes anyhow, but the clever bride will contrive to make everyone imagine that she remembers each gift, in detail, and that she has been waiting impatiently to receive this particular felicitation and present the guest to her new husband.

What Does the Groom Say? The groom, usually less happy than the bride over the necessity of the receiving line, is often less than verbose. He says, "Thank you so much," or "Lovely, isn't she?" or "So glad you could come" before he introduces the guest to his wife, if introduction is needed—otherwise he passes him along with a "Here is Tom, Angela," or "Darling, you know Mrs. Osborn."

But the groom, no matter how uncomfortable he may feel at this last necessary formality of his wedding, must look happy at having to greet even a seemingly endless line of guests, when what he needs after all he's been through is a tall drink and his bride to himself. He is at this moment as much on display as the bride—in some ways more so, as the guests had a better chance to see the bride during the ceremony than they did him.

Photographs at the Reception

If photographs are to be taken of the bridal party standing together, they are usually taken right before the receiving line is formed, the minute the wedding party arrives from the church. The best man and the maid or matron of honor should help round up everyone quickly so that the photographer can take his pictures and the receiving line can start.

The photographer taking candids of the wedding reception should have a list of out-of-town guests and relatives of both bride and groom. He should be instructed to take a picture of everyone on his list at some point during the festivities. He should also be alerted about rituals such as the bride's dance with her husband, the cake-cutting time, the tossing of the bride's bouquet, and so on. Most wedding candid photographers know exactly which shots to get, but someone should help them with the cast of characters.

The bride will obviously want extra copies of the best photographs to send to her and the groom's attendants, as well as to relatives and close friends. If a guest requests a duplicate of a picture, he should deal directly with the photographer once he has the couple's permission and pay for the picture himself. The pictures are, after all, expensive.

Flowers at the Reception

Flowers at the reception are part of the bride's budget. They may be simply green plant arrangements or elaborately arranged flowers in any colors—perhaps to match the bridal bouquet. Sometimes the bride and her attendants place their bouquets in the center of their table. The table on which a wedding cake is placed may be decorated with ferns or other leaves. Tall plants in planter tubs make a nice background for the receiving line, especially in a hotel or club. The entire area where the reception is held can be brightened considerably by vases of tall flowering branches (dogwood, lilacs, forsythia, or anything in bloom) or even leafy branches.

The Wedding Guest Book

Stationers, department stores, gift shops all sell wedding guest books. They are not a requirement at weddings, but they certainly make a very nice and sentimental souvenir of the occasion. An ordinary guest book will, of course, do as well with someone to preside over it to see that as many guests as possible sign. Signatures are the proper social names, not "Bill and Betty Smith." Such a record of the wedding calls for proper formality, so "Mr. and Mrs. Joseph Sterling Smith," is the expected and definitive thing, written of course legibly. Years later would the bride necessarily remember "Helen and Joe?" These books are often used as a source of addresses as well, so you should co-operate and provide your complete address if it is requested. The person presiding over the guest book may be a young sister or friend perhaps too young to be in the wedding party, or it may be an older family friend, or even a young brother who enjoys the importance of such a position. It is perfectly acceptable to ask people to sign the book, not wait for them to notice its presence.

Gratuities at the Reception

It is customary that at any reception held in a club or hotel the bride's father's costs per head include gratuities for waiters, waitresses, and all others connected with serving the guests. Consequently, guests should never have to tip anyone at a wedding. In addition, the bride's father usually arranges to take care of gratuities for cloakroom and restroom attendants in advance, and a sign to this effect is placed by the management in the cloakroom. If you have made such an arrangement, check to see that the sign is in plain sight, so that guests will not feel that you have overlooked this nicety of wedding-reception etiquette.

The Wedding Breakfast

The wedding breakfast is actually lunch—three courses. When guests are seated, it includes a soup course, such at hot clam broth with whipped cream or possibly fruit cup or seafood cocktail, and a main dish, such as beef Stroganoff with green peas, small biscuits, and lettuce salad. For dessert, ice cream in fancy molds, petits fours, or tiny petits fours glacés, demitasses, and, of course, the bridal champagne or at least a fine wine to be served with the luncheon, sometimes both.

When the wedding breakfast is served buffet and there is no way of seating guests, even at small tables, the first course is usually omitted and the collation limited to two courses. There may be something like stuffed crepes in a creamed sauce, green salad, hot baked fruit with whipped cream, demitasses, and a good white wine or champagne, or both.

The Table for the Parents

At a wedding buffet, breakfast, or supper there may be a table for the bride's parents if there is a special bride's table, but not otherwise. It is larger than the guests' tables and is the same except for place cards. Placement of guests is as follows: father of groom to right of bride's mother, who is the table's hostess; opposite the bride's mother sits the bride's father, with the groom's mother to his right. The other guests at the table may include the grandparents of the bride and groom and the clergyman and his wife. If a high-ranking church official performed the ceremony, or a judge or mayor, he is always placed to the left of the hostess and his wife, if present, sits on the left of the host. Very distinguished guests are seated at this table, but essentially it is for the parents and a few of their close friends and, possibly, close relatives.

In cases where a divorce has taken place the divorced parents are not seated together at the parents' table unless they are friendly. Another solution is to have a second table with prominent guests for the non-host parent and his new spouse, should he have one.

The Bride's Table

At large formal receptions there is sometimes a bride's table, especially decorated with white flowers and with the tiered and iced wedding cake in front of the bride and groom—the groom with the bride on his right. There are place cards at every place. Only members of the wedding party—the maid or matron of honor to the left of the groom, the best man to the right of the bride—are expected to sit at the bride's table, but if some of the attendants are married, and if there is room, it is courteous of the bride to in-

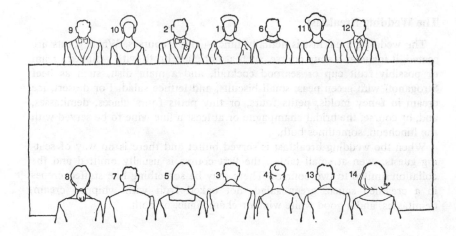

SEATING AT PARENTS' TABLE

(1) Bride's mother, (2) father of groom, (3) father of bride, (4) mother of groom, (5) officiating clergyman's wife, (6) clergyman, (7, 8, 9, 10, 11, 12, 13, 14) other family members and friends of parents.

clude their mates. Otherwise, they are supposed to enjoy themselves and take care of themselves independently of the bride's table.

Even when there is a buffet, the bridal table is waited upon. The bride is served first. If it can be arranged, the maid or matron of honor is served almost simultaneously. Then the groom is served, and the waitresses work their way out from the center to the ends of the bridal table. As soon as the champagne appears, the best man proposes the first toast to the bride, with other toasts following as the guests are inspired to offer them—not forgetting the groom. It might be awkward for your clergyman, seated at a parents' table, to bless the couple seated at another table, but discuss the matter with him. He can probably manage.

THE BRIDE'S TABLE

Reading from left to right: Usher, bridesmaid, best man, bride, groom, matron or maid of honor, usher, bridesmaid.

Food at the Reception

When food served at a reception is a simple hot, cold, or mixed buffet, guests can serve themselves from a buffet table, the major decoration of which may be the wedding cake itself. When there is room, guests should be seated at small tables set for eating (caterer's tables, or perhaps bridge tables for a home wedding).

While the guests eat and drink and enjoy themselves, the bridal party must remain in the receiving line without eating, and with only an occasional sip of champagne or a drink, until all the guests have supposedly arrived. When the line breaks up, they come into the area where guests are eating, drinking, and perhaps dancing and join the festivities. The wedding cake is not cut until the bridal party has finished eating, which is usually about three quarters of the way through the reception. Guests are supposed to stay at least until after the cake has been cut. If they have to leave early and the crowd is large, they should duck out inconspicuously, without saying anything to anyone.

Even at the most modest and informal wedding, it is not proper to use paper plates, napkins, and tablecloths. One can always borrow from one's friends, and this is one time when an effort should be made to "do it right."

The Wedding Toasts

If there is a bridal table at the reception, the first toast is offered to the bride by the best man. She remains seated during all the toasts to her, and she should not join in drinking from her glass when the others do, because she's not supposed to toast herself. She should smile and bow in the direction of each person who toasts her (and do her sipping in between toasts), and she should certainly return her new husband's toast. The toasts at the reception, particularly if there has been a rehearsal or pre-wedding dinner, are short. (The long ones are given at the dinner the night before.) The bride should also raise a toast to her mother and father, and perhaps even to the mother and father of the groom. She may want to raise one to her maid of honor. The wedding reception is a time for a few spontaneous warm words from anyone who wishes to give them. The best man can choose this time to read the cables, Mailgrams, and letters from very close friends who could not be present. He should read them over a microphone if there is one, so that others at the reception who are not close to the bridal table can enjoy the messages.

The Wedding Cake

Formerly, at large weddings, there would always be a white wedding cake for the bride and a dark fruitcake for the groom. There were also monogrammed white boxes with wax paper inside, one for each guest, into which one would put a small piece of the cake to eat, to save, or, for an unmarried, to put beneath one's pillow (in order to dream of the person one would marry). Today, probably because of the limitations of service and the high cost of doing everything, this charming custom is disappearing. The most popular cakes are the silver cake, which is made with egg whites alone and is light and airy; the gold cake, a yellow pound cake, which is richer; and the dark, rich fruitcake, which is the most expensive of all. It should have nothing "written" on it with icing, however. This sort of decoration is reserved for birthday cakes.

Cutting the Wedding Cake   At the end of the repast the bride rises—and with her all the gentlemen at the table—to cut the cake. Usually the guests are told that the propitious moment has arrived and gather around.

If the groom is in uniform the cake is cut with his dress sword, undecorated. At a civilian wedding a silver cake knife is used, and it may have its handle decorated with a streamer of white satin ribbons knotted with bridal flowers. The bride (standing at the groom's left) cuts only the first slice, with help, and she and the groom share it. Some member of the family, a knowledgeable friend, or a waiter then cuts and apportions the rest of the cake for service to guests, usually with ice cream.

The tiered, decorated cake is cut as follows, after the bride and groom's slice has first been taken: A long sharp knife is inserted vertically through the cake at the base of the bottom tier and that layer is cut into pieces. The top tiers are then removed and cut into pieces for the guests. The very top tier, which may or may not have the traditional bride and groom decoration —sometimes pastel icing flowers are used, for example—is gently lifted off, wrapped, and preserved. It can be stored in the freezer, of course (with the icing removed), for the first anniversary of the couple.

At second marriages, by the way, wedding cakes may be used but the decorative bride and groom or white bell should not be used at the top. The cake is traditionally a white cake, but it can also be a fruitcake, and some brides insist that it be chocolate. But whatever the interior, the outside is always white, although it may have pastel decorations.

Music at the Reception

It is not essential to have music at a wedding reception, particularly if there is a small space with numerous guests; however, a little music is a *great* addition to the festivities, whether or not there is room to dance. A trio is enough for most receptions. An accordionist who can move through the rooms or out onto the lawn, as the case may be, serenading guests, is a pleasant musical addition.

For very large weddings a dance band is appropriate. Today the band plays all through a large reception; it is no longer necessary to hold up the dancing until the receiving line breaks up.

The First Dance with the Bride Just as no one but the groom may kiss the bride first, so no one may dance with her before he does. When the receiving line at a large reception breaks up, the orchestra should stop playing the minute the group appears on the floor, perhaps rolling the drums to signal the groom's first dance with the bride. Everyone clears the floor and watches them in a circle-like formation. (If it's a small wedding, no one dances until the groom and the bride have their first dance.) The groom leads his bride onto the floor, she gathers up her train and veil, if they are long, and they glide into a waltz. (If they don't know how to waltz, no one will mind what they dance, as long as it's a dance where they are close to each other and not gyrating by themselves!) This can be a short dance; then the bride's father can step out on the floor with them, dancing with the groom's mother, while the groom's father dances with the bride's mother. Then attendants join in (while the candid photographer is shooting away), followed by the guests.

The bride must dance with her father and with the father of the groom, who should ask her just after she has danced with her own father (he may cut in), and the groom with his mother and with his bride's mother. The bride, after dancing with the fathers, dances next with the best man and then with each of the ushers. Guests may dance with the bride after all her "obligatory" dances are over.

If you want to encourage your guests to dance, it is best if you work out in advance an arrangement whereby ushers are paired with bridesmaids for at least one or two numbers. People will dance if they see others dancing.

After the bride has thrown her bouquet, dancing may continue, but usually the party begins to come to a close and guests are leaving. It is only the close friends and relatives who remain to see the bride and groom depart.

Throwing the Bride's Bouquet

The bride's bouquet is traditionally thrown to the assembled bridesmaids just before the bride goes to dress for going away. The bride often retains a flower or two for pressing. The girl who catches the bouquet is, of course, the one who is supposed to be the next to marry.

The bride's garter may be thrown to the assembled ushers. The catching of the garter by an usher means alternatively that he will have good luck and laughter for his whole life, or that he will be the next to marry, as with the bridesmaids and the bouquet. In either case, it is only the bridesmaids and ushers who participate in the attempt to catch the bouquet or garter, not the guests.

Problems of the Divided House

If the parents of the bride are separated but not divorced, they issue a joint invitation to their daughter's wedding and take their accustomed part in the ceremony as if there were no difference. For her sake, too, both officiate at the reception.

Sometimes when divorce has taken place the mother gives the wedding and the father the reception. If he has not married again, he stands first in line to receive the guests. If he has remarried, his wife acts as hostess. If the bride's mother should attend the reception under the latter circumstances, as might well happen in some instances, she comes as a guest, as she cannot stand at the side of her former husband in his new home and share the duties of hostess with his wife. If, however, her former husband has not remarried she could stand with him on the receiving line in his home, acting as hostess for the occasion, whether or not she has remarried. In this case, it is their choice who stands first.

If the mother, divorced, gives both wedding and reception, the father usually gives the bride away, calling for her at her mother's house in the bridal car. If relations are very strained some other male relative may give the bride away. Whether or not the father is remarried, he sits in the second or third pew on the left side of the church and, if remarried, may be accompanied by his new wife. She, in turn, may go with her husband to the reception if relations are friendly, but neither she nor the bride's father receives.

If the bride's mother has remarried, her husband sits with her in the first pew on the left and the bride's father sits behind them with *his* wife in the second or third pew. If the remarried mother gives the reception the bride's father, if present, attends only as an important guest.

It is far better to err on the side of too-friendly relations between divorced people on their child's wedding day than to keep reminding all present of their own failure in marriage. It must be the bride's great day, and even if her parents have been long divorced and long remarried they are probably to her forever a unit—the unit that produced her. She needs to feel, if possible, that on this day they are brought together, if only briefly, by this great common interest, the wedding of their child.

Guests at the Reception

A guest invited to attend the reception makes his own arrangements to get there from the church, either in his own car or by taxi, or he asks friends he may encounter at the wedding to let him ride with them. The bride's family is not responsible for guests' transportation to or from the reception. Guests leave the church unhurriedly by themselves only after the ribbons are removed, by either the center or side aisles.

As guests arrive at the reception they join the waiting line, staying together in family groups, if possible. They do not seek refreshments until
they have been officially received, unless it is clear that champagne or something similar is being served to them while they are waiting to go through
the line.

At large weddings there are always many people from out of town who do
not know each other. And as the parents of the couple are busy on the receiving line and introductions cannot be made in a general way by members
of the family in so large a group, it is up to strangers to make themselves
known to those in whose immediate neighborhood they find themselves
standing or sitting. The host's roof is sufficient introduction.

If a young person from out of town knows no one, all he has to do is go
up to another couple who obviously know many of the guests and introduce
himself, saying, "I don't know a soul here." The other couple will most
likely remedy that situation immediately and introduce the bachelor to
others, particularly members of the opposite sex.

At large weddings it may be impossible to say good-by to and thank the
parents of the bride. Every guest, however (or one of a couple), should
write a thank-you note to the mother of the bride, or whoever hosted the
wedding, commenting on how well everything was done, how handsome the
couple looked, what happiness the occasion brought, and so on. It is little
enough to do when one thinks of all the preparations, time, and expense that
went into the wedding.

Giving Your Own Wedding Reception

If a bride has an apartment of her own, and wants to give her own wedding reception, for one reason or another, she may—such as a simple breakfast or lunch or cocktail reception. She can act as her own hostess, and have
a friend or a caterer pouring champagne and passing hors d'oeuvres. If she
gives the reception in her own apartment, she might want to arrange to
change her clothes for her honeymoon at a friend's apartment where it is
less hectic.

Second or Delayed Wedding Receptions

A new custom, that of a second wedding reception following the one immediately after the ceremony, is being followed by many brides. The need
for this seems to arise sometimes when the bride, perhaps working in a distant city and perhaps marrying a man from that city, decides to be married
there, usually at a small ceremony attended by her immediate family and
that of the groom. Occasionally, the groom's family will lend their home for
such a wedding, following it perhaps with a small reception. The second reception then takes place in the bride's home city or town, so that all those
who were not invited to the wedding or who could not attend can meet the

bridegroom. The second reception, conversely, may take place in the groom's home town if the bride and groom plan a trip there shortly after the wedding and honeymoon and if many of the groom's family and his parents' friends could not travel to the first reception.

If engraved wedding invitations are sent out for the ceremony, invitations to the second reception may be enclosed or optionally they may be sent separately two weeks before the reception is to take place.

In today's world these second receptions are really informal cocktail parties, with informal invitations telephoned or put into the mail. If the party is informal there is no receiving line, but everyone should meet the honorees. Sometimes the groom's family gives this party, inviting, of course, the bride's family, which should certainly attend if possible.

The bride and groom wear clothes appropriate to the time of day, but such a reception is never formal.

Chapter 21

SECOND AND SUBSEQUENT MARRIAGES

With a rapidly increasing divorce rate, and with women frequently outliving their spouses, second marriages for one reason or another are increasingly common. And as second and subsequent marriages proliferate, so do the procedures and ethics concerning them grow and change. At one time few churches would sanction remarriage of divorced persons. Today, to meet the changing situation, churches and communities are revising their stand on second marriages. However, important distinctions still exist between first and second or subsequent marriages, and an enumeration of them makes things easier for all involved.

What Constitutes a Second Marriage

The single determining factor as to whether a marriage is to be considered a second marriage or not is the previous marital status of the bride, and only the bride. An oft-married groom will avoid such frivolities as a bachelor party, but if it is his bride's first marriage, she is entitled to all the trappings of a formal first-time wedding, should she desire them.

Any woman, however, who has been married before, no matter how briefly or unhappily or how long ago, and who is marrying again, is having, in society's eyes, a second marriage. It is not realistic or useful for a young woman who had an unfortunate marriage and who feels ready to marry again to pretend that her former marriage, even if it was a secret and short-lived one, never took place. In the case of an annulment, a person so involved may legally be considered as one who has never married, but socially it is another matter. Discretion and honesty are particularly advocated in this delicate situation. No person should ever try to hide the fact that he or she has been married, although one does not have to advertise it.

Engagements Before Second Marriages

Since most second marriages are small and informal, requiring much less planning than formal first-time weddings, engagements, if announced to friends at all, are usually brief and quite close to the date of the wedding.

No one in the midst of divorce proceedings should simultaneously announce remarriage. Such haste is tasteless and often risky. A decent interval should elapse, with perhaps therapy or other counseling seriously undertaken, before any remarriage.

No formal announcement of an engagement for a second marriage is required, although the bride may choose to write or call friends and relatives to inform them of her intention to remarry.

Invitations for Second Marriages

Invitations for second marriages, whether for widows or divorcées, are telephoned, sent by Mailgram, sometimes given by word of mouth if the ceremonies are small and simple, or handwritten. For example:

September 15

Dear Helen and Bob,

Richard and I have set the date. We'll be married, quietly at St. Andrews in the chapel, Friday, October sixth at five-thirty, with just the family and a friend or two. Please let me know if you can be with us and afterward at a small supper here.

Fondly,
Marion

Reception Invitations

Reception invitations, on the other hand, are engraved if the reception is to be sufficiently large to make this expense worthwhile. Such invitations may also be written, as may the wedding invitations, by a calligrapher. Separate reception invitations, say in the case of a young divorcée or a young widow, may be issued by her parents in this way:

Dr. and Mrs. Grant Kingsley
request the pleasure of your company
at the wedding reception of their daughter
Penelope Franklyn
and
Mr. George Frank Carpenter
on Saturday, May sixth
at five o'clock
Hotel Mark Hopkins, San Francisco

R.S.V.P.
15 Shady Road
Belvedere, California   zip code

An older couple issuing their own invitation jointly:

Mrs. Samuel Franklyn
and
Mr. George Frank Carpenter
request the pleasure of your company
at their wedding breakfast
on Friday, May fifth
at half after twelve
Hotel Del Coronado, San Diego

R.S.V.P.
Three Mark Lane
Santa Barbara, California   zip code

Wedding Announcements

Engraved wedding announcements of a second marriage may be sent, and, in fact, this is the best way to publicize the event, since engraved wedding invitations are not used. Announcements, which may be sent to a wide list even when the reception is small, should be mailed the day of the wedding, or as soon thereafter as possible. The bride may have her parents make the announcement, or, particularly if she is divorced, she may do it herself with her new husband. In the first instance, the announcement reads:

Mr. and Mrs. Francis Dorina Kipling
have the honour of announcing
the marriage of their daughter
Anita Kipling Benson
[maiden name, plus former married name]
to
Mr. Arthur Townley Bryant
Saturday, the fourth of March
One thousand nine hundred and seventy-eight
New York, New York

In the second case it reads:

Mrs. Anna Benson
and
Mr. Arthur Townley Bryant
announce their marriage
Saturday, the fourth of March
One thousand nine hundred and seventy-eight
New York, New York

The Divorcée's Announcement   If a divorcée is young, her parents issue the announcement of her wedding:

Mr. and Mrs. Leon Fuller
have the honour of announcing
the marriage of their daughter
Mary Louise Toure
to
Mr. Stephen Windham
on Sunday, the seventh of May
One thousand nine hundred and seventy-eight
Kansas City, Missouri

Or the divorcée may issue her own announcement, in conjunction with her husband:

Mrs. Mary Louise Toure
and
Mr. Stephen Windham
announce their marriage
on Sunday, the seventh of May
One thousand nine hundred and seventy-eight
Kansas City, Missouri

Or, more informally, and preferred:

Mary Louise Toure
and
Stephen Windham
announce their marriage
on Sunday, May seventh
in Kansas City, Missouri

The bride should submit a properly written (typed) announcement of the marriage to the society editor of the local newspaper a week in advance, with the phrase "Hold for Release." (Put the day after the wedding as the release date.) The announcement should naturally not appear in the paper until after the wedding has taken place. If for any reason, the marriage does not take place at the last minute, one must always notify the newspapers at once, so they can pull the item from the society announcements section. Mary Louise Toure might send in an announcement like this:

Hold for Release May 5

Mrs. Mary Louise Toure and Mr. Stephen Windham, both of Kansas City, were married here Sunday, May seventh, in the Sheraton Hotel by Judge Walter Smith of the Missouri State Supreme Court. Mrs. Windham is the daughter of Mr. and Mrs. Leon Fuller of St. Louis. She is a lawyer with the firm of Hayden & Hayden. Mr. Windham is the son of the late Mr. and Mrs. Philip Windham; he is the chairman of the mathematics department at the University of Missouri. Mr. and Mrs. Windham have two children each from their previous marriages, which were terminated by divorce. The couple will continue to reside in Kansas City.

Gifts for Second Marriages

The bride who has been married before, whether she is widowed or divorced, technically should not expect wedding gifts, although in actual practice many people do give them. Individual circumstances need to be taken into consideration. If the bride is a young divorcée who perhaps did not have a formal wedding with the usual wedding gifts, close friends at least and relatives will probably wish to give her gifts on her second marriage. If the bride has been married before and the groom has not, the groom's friends and relatives will very probably send wedding gifts to the couple. When the groom has been married previously and the bride has not, his friends are not expected to send gifts; some will anyway. (For gift suggestions, see page 782.)

Preparations for a Second Wedding

Because some clergymen are still reluctant to marry divorced persons, it is important that a divorced person visit a clergyman as soon as possible after deciding to remarry. Perhaps the clergyman will be unable to approve a church ceremony, but will be willing to perform the marriage in his study or elsewhere. All of these points should be brought up in the discussion. If he refuses to perform the marriage at all, and the couple wants very much to have a religious ceremony, they may approach a clergyman of another, more permissive, denomination, who would be willing to perform the ceremony whether or not either is a member of his congregation. Or they may approach a judge.

Since second weddings, even those held in a church, are small and simple, floral decorations and music are actually not necessary but, if used, should be minimal, as there is usually no processional or recessional in a second-marriage ceremony. A remarrying widow may be escorted in a simple processional by a son or family friend and accompanied by her matron of honor.

Attendants at Second Weddings

It is proper at a second marriage for the couple to have only one attendant each, who may be the sole witnesses of the ceremony.

As with attendants at any wedding, the bride and groom in a second wedding present their attendants with some remembrance of the occasion. The bride might give her attendant some small but attractive piece of jewelry, and the groom might give his attendant cuff links or any other personal gift of lasting value, as well as his tie, which should be either the same or a slightly different version of his own. If they have rented formal wear, the groom provides the boutonnieres for them both.

Children as Guests and as Attendants at Second Weddings

If a person's ex-spouse supports the idea, and if the children are mature enough to accept the new spouse, it is a good idea to have the children present at their mother or father's second wedding. When they are in their teens, the children are perfectly capable of deciding on their own whether they wish to attend. Whatever their age, they should be made to feel useful and given a job to do, such as opening the door, helping with the guest book, checking wraps, or passing hors d'oeuvres. Involving them in the occasion may make them feel important and less resentful of the new replacement for one of their parents.

We see many more marriages today where children serve as attendants. Whether a child serves a major role at the remarriage of a parent depends on his attitude toward the new spouse in particular and the remarriage in general. Parents who ask their children to serve in this capacity feel that the child's standing next to them is a symbol of a strong parent-child relationship that will remain intact in spite of the new spouse. This act should never be forced upon a child, who still may be in a state of shock over the breakup of his parents' marriage. Psychologists warn that young teen-agers are often not up to serving in this capacity because of their intense self-absorption at this time in their lives. In any case, it is a poor idea to involve the children if the other parent, who may resent the former partner's remarriage, is dead set against the child's major role in the remarriage.

Entertaining Before Second Weddings

Showers are not given before second marriages, since their purpose is to help the new bride furnish her household, and a widowed or divorced woman presumably has already established a household by the time of her second marriage. A rehearsal dinner is not needed, since the marriage ceremony this time is so short and simple, with only one attendant for each of the couple. Small parties, except for showers, are quite usual before second or even subsequent marriages. They may be given by close friends or relatives and may be buffets, cocktail parties, or luncheons with invitations sent either on fill-in engraved invitations or on ordinary fill-ins. A formal reception of any size may follow the ceremony and, if not given by the couple themselves, may be given by relatives or friends.

Dress for the Second Wedding

Whereas once it was absolutely taboo for a woman marrying a second time to wear a white dress, this is now acceptable, provided the dress is really off-white and does not attempt to resemble a formal white wedding gown. Depending upon the time of day and the degree of formality of the wedding, the bride may wear anything from a simple suit to a long gown in any color she finds becoming except true red or black. The second-time bride may carry a very simple bridal bouquet if she wants to, something like a spray of lilies of the valley or a Bible or prayer book, perhaps with a flower marker. The groom does wear a boutonniere.

Anything resembling a veil should not be worn by the second-time bride. It is not necessary in most cases for her to wear anything on her head if she doesn't wish to, but she may choose to wear a bow, flowers, or an attractive hat in keeping with her outfit.

The groom's clothes, whether or not he has been previously married, should be keyed to the degree of formality of his bride's dress. At an afternoon wedding taking place before six o'clock he wears a dark suit, white shirt, and conservative tie. His attendant dresses in the same manner as he does. The bride's attendant wears the same kind of costume as does the bride, and it should not be in any way a typical bridesmaid's gown.

Guests at a second marriage wear clothes suitable to the time of day, as they would at any other wedding.

Second-wedding Ceremony

The actual ceremony for a second wedding is greatly abbreviated from that of a first-time wedding. There is usually no processional or recessional. The bride in a church ceremony usually enters, following her attendant—but usually not escorted—from the vestry door to find the groom and best man already at the altar. In the case of a young girl, her father or another older male relative might still escort her and give her away, although this part of the ceremony is ordinarily dispensed with for a second wedding. The ceremony should be as brief and as dignified as possible with all procedures discussed in advance with the clergyman who will perform it. In a home, hotel, or club wedding, the procedure is equally simple, with the bride perhaps briefly escorted by a family friend, a mature son, or possibly her father. Music, if any, is never traditional bridal music—no usual *Lohengrin* or Mendelssohn, or solos.

Reception for the Second Wedding

Since this is a social event, it may be large and impressive if the bride wishes. If it is large, it necessitates a receiving line. The bride and groom greet people informally as they arrive, but neither sets of parents, nor even the attendants, stand in line.

It is permissible to have a wedding cake without the decorative bride and groom or white bell or lettering of any kind on top. You may want a pastel frosted cake this time. Naturally such traditions as throwing rice and tossing the bride's bouquet and garter are dispensed with the second time around.

Paying for the Second Wedding

The groom may assume all costs, or the bride and groom may split them. Rarely do the parents pay for this wedding, unless their daughter has been widowed or if neither she nor their new son-in-law is in a financial position to pay.

Remarriage of Divorced Persons to Each Other

When people who have been divorced decide to remarry each other, no formal announcements are sent out, but friends are informed of the good news by word of mouth, by letter, or by Mailgram. No formal announcements are released to the press. In such instances, children are often involved, so the reunion of the couple should be made almost as if the schism had never existed. In keeping with this, a couple who have been through such a parting should plan to celebrate their anniversary on the date of their first marriage. They should, however, subtract the years during which they were divorced from the total number for special anniversary celebrations. In other words, a couple married in 1960 but divorced for five years should wait until 1990 to celebrate their twenty-fifth anniversary.

Chapter 22

AFTER THE WEDDING

The Honeymoon

In most cases today the honeymoon is no longer a period for two people to adjust to living with each other, but it is a much needed period of rest and change after a hectic, overcharged pre-wedding schedule. The traditional wedding trip used to last from three to four weeks. In moneyed circles, a young couple would often take from four to six months while they made their way leisurely around the world on a series of ocean liners. In the early part of the twentieth century, scions of society spent a year on their wedding trips.

Today's average honeymoon lasts two weeks; sometimes it is simply a long weekend. Often it is delayed until several months later when both can synchronize their vacation schedules with their employers. We take the word honeymoon from the French term, *lune de miel*, which literally means "moon of honey." There is a historical significance to the term, because in some European countries the couple would drink every day for a month a special kind of mead drink called metheglin, or a honey wine—hence the term "honeymoon."

Where to Go   The place and duration of the honeymoon must depend on the amount of time available and the financial resources of the groom—for this is his expense, unless, of course, either his or her parents, or perhaps both together, are able to give the couple a honeymoon as a wedding gift, or unless the bride and groom agree to split the honeymoon expenses. Even if both bride and groom must go back to work immediately after the ceremony, some sort of quiet getting away together should be planned at the earliest possible moment before the two are caught up in the whirl of their new responsibilities. For the honeymoon a couple should choose to do something they both enjoy, whether it is traveling in a foreign country, skiing, camping, or soaking up sun at the beach. A lot of give-and-take should go into planning the wedding trip, and it is probably not the best time to introduce your mate to a new sport or interest. This trip is one that will always be remembered, as being very good or very bad. It is nice to have good memories of it to take through life.

Packed somewhere into the suitcase of every honeymooning couple should be a list of very special people's names and addresses, plus some note paper. A thank-you note for a wedding present written during a wedding trip is the nicest thank you of all.

Upon Arrival at One's Honeymoon Destination

Unless you are out of the country, it is nice to call both sets of parents from your honeymoon spot the first day you are there. Everyone at home will be exhausted and in a state of sentimental euphoria after your wedding; it will mean much to them to have you communicate—and say "Thank you for our wonderful wedding." A young woman who has left her only sister behind, perhaps feeling blue at losing her, should make a special call to her. In other words, the couple should make a list of special people whom they either talk to on the telephone or send a letter or a postcard.

The Newly Marrieds in a New Neighborhood

Moving to a new home is most difficult for the person who may have come from another city and who has no friends in the new one. It is up to the couple to take the initiative in making friends. The bride may meet a young woman from her apartment house while out walking their dogs. "Hello, we're new in this complex. My name is Margaret Stuart, and this is Pepper." The bridegroom may encounter his neighbor as he begins to clip his back-yard hedge. "Hello, I'm Jim Fordham. We just moved in." It takes very little courage to start the conversation, to give your names, and to set up an instant "Well, we must do something about this young couple" reaction among the inhabitants of that area.

People can make new friends in a community by taking an active role in their church or synagogue. They should introduce themselves to their clergyman, explain who they are and from where they have come, and ask about programs held at the church or synagogue. Everybody should fit some volunteer work into his schedule, so the couple should inquire about what needs doing in their community that lies within their talents and expertise. Usually it will be a different activity for husband and wife.

Behavior of the Newlyweds

Newlyweds should try not to overdo their togetherness, as it can be embarrassing to other people in social situations. When they are out dancing, the husband should ask his wife for the first dance, then his dinner partner, and certainly his hostess. They should not expect to be seated next to each other at dinner parties. As a married couple, they will find that they are supposed to spread their charm elsewhere at the dinner table, not solely to each other!

Chapter 23

WEDDING ANNIVERSARIES

Couples tend to celebrate their anniversaries in quiet ways as each comes along—perhaps by going to dinner in a restaurant, or having a bottle of champagne at home and exchanging small gifts with each other. A woman loves receiving flowers from her husband on this day, but a husband enjoys receiving them from his wife at his office, too. The tenth anniversary is often celebrated with a party, as are particularly the twenty-fifth and fiftieth, which are obviously very special ones.

When one of the spouses has died, it is thoughtful to remember the anniversary date by sending the survivor some flowers and a little note, which could say something like "This must be a sad day for you in many ways, but also one of lovely, tender memories. Anyway, we are thinking of you."

An Anniversary Celebration

Friends may give an anniversary party for a couple, or the couple may give one for themselves. According to the size and scope of the party, invitations may be engraved, printed, handwritten, or telephoned. The twenty-fifth anniversary ones may be engraved in silver lettering, the fiftieth in gold lettering. One would address the envelopes in black ink, not silver or gold! Couples usually adjust the actual anniversary date to a convenient one for a party, such as the Saturday after the actual date. If a couple wish their friends *not* to bring presents, they should send out dinner invitations that do not mention the anniversary. Then at dessert time, when champagne is poured, the host can rise and say, "This is a very special day in our lives, and we wanted the people we love best to be with us and share it. This is our fifteenth wedding anniversary, and I ask you all to join me in toasting my beautiful, wonderful bride."

A large cocktail reception or dinner dance is usually held only for the twenty-fifth and fiftieth anniversaries. It is a time when a receiving line should be held—with the couple only, if they are giving the party themselves, or the couple and their hosts. Champagne is served, and it is nice to have food that reminds one of a wedding—perhaps the same menu (except for the cake) that they had at their wedding reception, or at least something festive such as decorated petits fours. A great addition to a party like this is a group of blown-up posters for all the guests to see and enjoy—blowups of black and white wedding pictures and the newspaper announcement with the bride's picture. All of these things must be borrowed on the sly from the couple's wedding scrapbook, if the display is to be a well-kept surprise for them.

Formal Engraved or Printed Invitations to a Wedding Anniversary

1929   1979
Mr. and Mrs. Roland Purdy
request the pleasure of
the company of
Mr. and Mrs. Robjohn*
at a dinner to celebrate
the fiftieth anniversary of their marriage
on Saturday, the seventeenth of February
at eight o'clock
850 Park Avenue
New York, New York   zip code

R.S.V.P.   Black Tie

or:

In honour of
the fiftieth wedding anniversary of
Mr. and Mrs. Roland Purdy
their sons and daughters
request the pleasure of
the company of
Captain McMurray*
at dinner
on Saturday, the seventeenth of February
at eight o'clock
850 Park Avenue

R.S.V.P.   Black Tie
Mrs. Gibbs Purdy
88 Cricket Lane
Larchmont, New York   zip code

* Handwritten.

The above form is used where listing of all children would crowd the invitation.

or:

Mr. and Mrs. Gibbs Purdy
Mr. Allan Nye Purdy
request the pleasure of
the company of etc.

Replies to Formal Wedding Anniversary Invitations

One would write by hand on one's good note paper this kind of reply to a formal engraved or printed wedding anniversary invitation:

Mr. and Mrs. Robjohn
accept with pleasure
the kind invitation of
Mr. and Mrs. Roland Purdy
to dine [OPTIONAL]
on Saturday, the seventeenth of February
at eight o'clock

Captain McMurray
accepts with pleasure
the kind invitation
of Mrs. Gibbs Purdy
for Saturday, the seventeenth of February
at eight o'clock

For informal invitations, the usual informal handwritten acceptance is fine:

John and I wouldn't miss this celebration of your parents' anniversary for anything in the world. They are a model to every one of us, and I only hope we can live long enough and remain as happy together as they have for all these years! Thank you for including us.

Sincerely,

Anniversary Gifts

When invitations are sent out to a large number of guests for an anniversary celebration, it is not necessary for the recipients, whether or not they attend the party, to bring or send an anniversary present. Some hosts would really prefer that people not send gifts, and they may therefore add "Please omit gifts" on their invitations. For a formal invitation, however, I believe it looks better not to add extraneous text but rather to insert in the envelope a separate piece of thin paper upon which is printed "No gifts, please." If the party is an informal one, the task is easy. Simply explain "no gifts" over the telephone, or add a line to your invitational note.

If gifts are brought to a party, they should not be opened until after the guests have gone. When they are opened, someone should keep a careful record of who sent what so that thank-you notes may be sent efficiently by the recipients. If the couple are very elderly, one of the children can assume the thank-you note writing task.

Gifts are usually brought to a pair celebrating their anniversary if the celebration is a small dinner. One may bring something suitable for the numerical tradition of anniversaries or it may be the time to bring something frivolous and fun that the couple have not acquired over the years. (For specific suggestions, see Anniversary Presents, page 783.)

Anniversary Photographs

It is a good idea to record important anniversary celebrations when the family congregates from all around. A large, handsomely framed photograph of the entire family sent afterward makes a wonderful present to the honored couple. If the couple are elderly, with several generations of progeny, it is nice to give them a companion piece—a handsomely written and framed listing of the names, ages, and lineage of their spouses, the children, the daughters- and sons-in-law, the grandchildren, the great-grandchildren, and so on.

Reaffirmation of Marriage Vows

In some communities it is popular for couples to reaffirm their marriage vows after being married a number of years (at least twenty-five). This service may take place with only the couple and their family and the clergyman present, or with several other couples reaffirming their vows simultaneously. It can occur on any day during the regular service or at a special service; it does not have to coincide with an anniversary. The couple dress in their best daytime apparel. Their children should be present as guests, if possible; no one stands up for the pair. If the wedding rings are worn and battered, new ones may be placed on their fingers on this occasion. The ceremony may be followed by any celebration the couple wishes to have. There is no standard ceremony for this procedure; the clergyman fits it into the service where he feels it belongs. If there is no record of the exact exchange of vows that took place at the couple's wedding (such as that found in a Catholic wedding mass book), and if the liturgy or the customs have changed involving the marrying of two people, then the present ceremony of vows should be used.

If the renewal or reaffirmation is made with other couples at a regular service, no gift has to be made to the clergyman. If the service is a private one for a single couple, for which the church was specially opened, then a gift to the clergyman and one for the church should be offered.

The ceremony may be followed by any celebration the couple wish to have.

Chapter 24

FUNERALS

It is not strange that when people face the mystery of death they turn to religion for comfort and help. However unrooted we may be in our religious beliefs, in time of death we turn to the formalities and the solacing warmth of religion and the clergyman, the priest, or the rabbi. The final rites should be solemn, dignified, and supportive of those who feel the loss the most.

What to Do when Death Comes

Every individual should organize a file marked "To Be Opened upon My Death." The thought of death is a subject many people prefer to avoid, but such a file is of inestimable help to one's survivors at a time when they are emotionally upset. A family member should be told of the exact location of this file so it will be readily available when needed. Special needs to fit particular family circumstances should be included, but it is important that information such as the following be contained in the file:

Location of will
Name and address of attorney
List of bank accounts, savings accounts
List of all securities owned, and their whereabouts
Insurance policies
Location of safe deposit box and key
Name of preferred funeral home
Information regarding burial plot
Place where funeral should be held
Choice of funeral service
List of honorary pallbearers
Location of all silver
Location of all jewelry
List of items designated for special people
If cremation is preferred, a note to that effect
If vital organs are to be willed, a note to that effect

This information will enable the person making arrangements, whether it be with a doctor, lawyer, or funeral director, to do so in an efficient, orderly manner.

When death occurs, the attending physician fills out and signs the death certificate. If death occurs when a doctor is not present or when the person's religious beliefs preclude medical care, the county medical examiner (in some states, the coroner) must be called in to determine the cause of death and to issue and sign the death certificate. This must be done before even calling the mortician, for he may not act without the medical examiner's permission.

If the deceased has indicated a desire to donate his organs under the Uniform Anatomical Gift Act (whereby one makes such "an anatomical gift, if medically acceptable for the purpose of transplantation, therapy, medical research, or education"), it is most important that this request be honored immediately and the proper medical authority notified. The donor's wish should be given to authorities immediately. The reason for this urgency is that donor organs must be removed within hours of death.

Choosing Someone to Be in Charge

A mature member of the family or close friend should be chosen to be in charge of funeral arrangements. He or she will co-ordinate all events—dealing with the lawyer, the funeral home, and the cemetery, stationing someone by the telephone to answer calls and to dispense information, providing friends with a list of people to call to notify of the death, seeing to it that the family is fed, helping make decisions about flowers, meeting people at trains and airports and making sure they have accommodations, and, not least important, finding someone to stay in the house during the funeral service. Unhappily, there are people who read the death notices, note the time of the funeral, and take advantage of an empty house to rob it.

The one arrangement that should be attended to personally by a family member is the funeral service. The deceased may have made specific requests regarding the service or a family member may be familiar with certain prayers, psalms, or hymns that were favorites of the deceased. These should be discussed with the clergyman. It is best that the family member go to see the clergyman so that they can talk together in a quiet atmosphere, rather than at the home of the family, where there is bound to be a certain amount of confusion.

Attending to the funeral arrangements is an important executive job, and the person who assumes it efficiently and kindly makes all the difference to the comfort and emotional well-being of the bereaved family. No matter who makes decisions about funeral arrangements, the one important thing to keep in mind is that the wishes of the dead person should be respected, no matter what the personal feelings of those surviving might be.

The first step the funeral co-ordinator should take is to notify the deceased's attorney. He should then be in touch with the funeral home the family is accustomed to dealing with; if there is none, then a call to the family's church or synagogue will result in the recommendation of a suitable one. Someone from the funeral home will come as soon as he can to remove the body or discuss arrangements.

Dealing with the Mortician

For a long time the trend has been toward simple funerals, even among people who can afford elaborate ones. No one but the funeral director knows or cares about the fine details of caskets and their relative expensiveness or inexpensiveness. In fact, many people of sensibility shudder at the pretentious ugliness of expensive caskets, remembering that great heroes are often buried in simple, clean-lined pine boxes.

Whoever undertakes the responsibility of the funeral should realize that he or she is entering into a business contract—and under highly emotional circumstances—where those most involved may be of little help in making important decisions. Where expense must be regarded, he should discuss the necessity with the mortician and make as many decisions as possible himself. It is sometimes months before funds can be released for payment of bills incurred, and in complicated cases it is sometimes necessary to get the court's permission to have them paid. All these matters must therefore be handled with great care and conservatism.

If the deceased or his family has had some continuing religious affiliation, there is no problem concerning the choice of a clergyman to officiate. Otherwise a clergyman of any faith may, with the family's permission, be asked to read a burial service. When the funeral takes place in a city and the interment is in a family plot at considerable distance, one or more members of the family go with the body to the place of burial and a local funeral director is usually retained to handle the interment. A family member asks a local clergyman to conduct the brief service at the grave. A florist in the area may supply one or more fresh floral offerings.

Clothing for Burial

Among Orthodox and some Conservative and Reform Jews, the shroud is still used for burial. Otherwise, the person in charge of the funeral takes the clothing chosen by the family to the funeral director. The choice of clothing should be appropriate for burial and conservative in appearance. Children are often dressed for Sunday school or young girls in white. People are no longer buried with their jewels, although many are with their wedding rings. The funeral director should be given explicit instructions as to just what is to be buried with the deceased.

Hanging the Bell

The custom of hanging the bell goes back to the days when doorbells were bells with clappers. When someone died, the clapper was muffled in cloth. This later developed into ribbon streamers in white, purple, or black, with white or purple flowers. Like mourning, the bell hanging was for the protection of the bereaved, so that anyone approaching the house would do so with quiet dignity.

Today, few hang the bell. And it is never done except when the funeral is to take place in the home. When a family still wishes to adhere to the old custom, it so instructs the funeral director, who orders the flowers and has them hung just below the doorbell of either apartment or private house.

Where the Funeral Takes Place

Wakes are a long-standing custom and usually last a day and a half. A wake is basically a quiet social gathering of friends of the deceased and may take place at a funeral home or at one's own home. Funeral homes can be simple and functional or elaborate establishments with their own private chapels and organs. Today most wakes are held in a mortuary chapel even when home facilities are quite adequate to accommodate large numbers. The use of the funeral home is usually included in the over-all cost of the funeral, with the occasional exception of a charge for music. The religious service itself is held either in a chapel at the funeral home or in a church. In the latter case the casket is taken from the funeral home to the church on the day of the funeral. Immediately following the funeral service, the casket is taken to its final resting place.

If the funeral takes place at home, the largest room is usually selected, preferably one that can be shut off from the rest of the house. Folding chairs are provided by the mortician.

Death Notices

The person in charge of the funeral prepares the death notices, which are then inserted, often by the mortician, in one or more morning papers. In large cities, and if thought advisable, evening papers may also carry these notices. If the death takes place in a suburb the notices are carried by the nearest large dailies that are likely to be read by friends of the deceased. These notices are placed at regular space rates.

A paid death notice may be phoned to the papers selected, but it should always be *read* from carefully checked information. Where it is given over the telephone the newspaper's classified department usually calls back for recheck, to be certain the notice is legitimate. The form for either a man or a woman is:

Volkman—Lawrence Karl, on November 25 [year optional], husband [or beloved husband] of Helen Schroeder Volkman [his wife's maiden name is always given to aid identification] and father of Louise and Peter Schroeder Volkman [the daughters are listed first]. Funeral at [name of church and address, if necessary], at 11:00 A.M., Tuesday, November 28. Interment private [or give the name of the cemetery if the burial is not private].

Sometimes, especially when there was no generally known preliminary illness, the word "suddenly" may be added before the date of death.

The age is usually not given in the death notice, except in the case of a child. It is often mentioned in accompanying news stories, but need not be.

Obituaries for Prominent People

When the person who dies has been a prominent member of his community, it is probable that major papers in his city already have a prepared obituary on file, although it may need updating. But it can be helpful to the family of such a person to have their own obituary already composed, ready to type up and send when death occurs. The reasons for doing this are threefold: the family will not be bothered by having to do it in the midst of funeral preparations; the obituary will be included in the newspapers the day after the death so more friends will be aware of it; and the story will be accurate and contain the information the family wants it to contain. If an editor, upon hearing of the death of a prominent person, is unable to reach the deceased's immediate family on the telephone, he will write the story based on information in his newspaper files, thus missing perhaps more recent and important information about the person. Frequently the papers may also request a recent photograph of the deceased if they do not have one on file.

The obituary of a celebrity in the community that is meant for publication in the press or his or her college alumni bulletin, professional association or club newsletter, and so forth, should contain:

1. Name of deceased
2. Date and place of death (name of hospital or "at home")
3. Cause of death (this is optional; one can say "after a long illness" without disclosing its nature)
4. Age and home address
5. Important education details
6. What he or she contributed to society, to whom, and where
7. Military service record
8. Military decorations awards, books published, etc.
9. Membership in social clubs and professional associations
10. Names of survivors and their relationship

Attending a Funeral

Unless the words "Funeral private" appear in the death notice, any friend or acquaintance of the deceased or his family may attend the services. A divorced husband or wife of the deceased should most certainly attend the funeral, if he or she so chooses. It is not only appropriate but can be of comfort to any children of the marriage. The divorced husband or wife should not expect, however, to be seated with the family and would not do so unless asked. There is no specific age when a child should attend a first funeral; it is a personal matter that only a parent can decide. Some people feel, however, that if a child has never been to a funeral, it makes sense to take him to one for an older person who was a good family friend rather than wait until someone very close to the child dies. Close friends or relatives may ask the person in charge of arrangements for permission to attend the interment if they are able to provide their own transportation. They should be very certain that their presence at so difficult a time will be of real comfort to the immediate family, which usually prefers to be alone with the clergyman at the last brief rites. If it is known that the interment is private, no one should ask to attend.

The person in charge of funeral arrangements should see to it that relatives and friends from out of town are notified of the death and of the funeral arrangements. He also makes hotel arrangements for the people arriving from far away and sees that they are supplied with transportation. After the funeral, someone should give a luncheon for the out-of-town guests and the family. When the deceased lived in a large house, his or her house is usually the scene of this catered lunch, and it is hosted by the family itself. But if a prominent person's spouse lives in a small apartment, someone else should offer to host the buffet luncheon at his home. The out-of-town guests disperse after this event.

Sending Flowers

When flowers are sent for a funeral a plain white card is attached with the name of the sender, "Helen Murray" or "Mr. and Mrs. Hugh Wallace," and the message, "Deepest sympathy from Jean and Hugh," written in ink. The envelope is simply addressed:

> The funeral of Mr. Lawrence Karl Volkman
> Silvan Funeral Home
> 13 Morton Street
> Greenpoint, New York

When the funeral is to take place in a church but the body will first be at a funeral home, friends may choose to send flowers to the funeral home, provided calls are being received there. Or they may prefer instead to send them to the church in time for the funeral. In the latter case the flowers are addressed to:

> The funeral of Mr. Lawrence Karl Volkman
> Emmanuel Church
> 5 Hawthorne Avenue
> Rye, New York
> Funeral 2 P.M., Tuesday

Cards should include the name and address of the sender on the back if a plain florist's card is used. This is of assistance in the family's acknowledgments.

Sometimes the death notice reads "Please omit flowers," and this request should be respected. At some Protestant funerals the family prefers that the casket have only one floral offering, that of the family. One never sends flowers to an Orthodox Jewish funeral; often they are not desired at a Conservative or a Reform funeral. And it is preferable not to send them to a Catholic church, as they may not be taken into the church (only the family's one spray and occasionally an altar arrangement are permitted). Flowers are, however, often sent to the funeral home and later taken to the cemetery even though they may not enter the church. In Episcopalian funerals, flowers from the family and their friends are permitted in the church.

Mass Cards

Many Catholics prefer mass cards to flowers. When a Catholic dies, his friends and relatives, Catholic and non-Catholic, go to a priest and arrange for a mass to be said for the soul. The priest accepts an offering for the mass, fills in a card stating that a mass is to be said for the repose of the soul of the deceased, and presents it to the donor. Sometimes the exact time of the mass is indicated. The card is given or mailed by the donor to the family of the deceased, usually before the funeral. A tray is provided at the funeral home for callers who have brought mass cards. These masses may also be arranged on the anniversary of the death.

Funeral Calls

Now that the mortuary chapel is used in most cases rather than the home, people are often confused about where they are expected to make their funeral calls. If they are close friends or relatives they may call both at home and at the chapel if they wish, signing the register at the funeral chapel. The register is signed in formal fashion—Mr. and Mrs. John Brown, not Betty and John Brown—and the husband or wife signs for both. They don't each sign separately unless they visit the funeral parlor separately. The reason one should sign in this way is that, after the signatures have been seen by the family, some of these calls may be acknowledged with a brief note by a family member who would not necessarily know that Betty Brown is also Mrs. John Brown. The names should be signed very legibly, for some of the scrawls that confront families are impossible to decipher and many frustrations and inaccuracies can result.

Although funeral calls need not be acknowledged and customarily are not, sometimes the family wishes to make acknowledgment of such a call, especially if some have called when no immediate member of the family could be present to receive condolences. A family representative should be present during the afternoon and early evening when most calls are likely to be made.

If your children knew the deceased, it is nice to bring them to call at the mortuary chapel, to pay their respects. Be sure to impress upon the young ones to behave extremely well and quietly.

You do not need to worry about what you say to members of the family. Sometimes one is choked up and "I'm so sorry" is all one can get out. Everyone understands that this is not a time for great rhetoric. Just a few words from the heart, about how you will miss this person, how everyone will miss him, will mean a lot to his family. You do not have to stay longer than ten to fifteen minutes, and don't worry if you cry when talking to the deceased's family. Everyone understands if you can't control such an emotion.

The Funeral Service

It is a mattter of family choice whether the casket is left open or closed before the funeral, but the open casket is seen less and less today. At state funerals the open casket is optional, but it is always closed during an Episcopalian or Jewish service. At Catholic church services, the casket is open *only* for clergy and high-ranking laymen.

The Eulogy A eulogy may be given from the pulpit by the clergyman, or by a close friend or a relative of the deceased. It should be *short*. Essential details of the person's life, human-interest stories, and anecdotes—even with a bit of humor—are the most effective. The tribute in a eulogy should be a portrait painted of the person with warmth, love, and genuine affection. It should not be a grandiose sermon full of platitudes. The eulogy should certainly refer to "those left behind," too.

Pallbearers Among Christians, pallbearers are always men (although in our changing world this may very well change, too) and today merely honorary in that they seldom actually carry the casket. There are never fewer than four and rarely more than ten chosen for this honor from among those close to the deceased.

The pallbearers are usually notified by the person in charge of funeral arrangements, after he has received suggestions from various members of the family. Pallbearers do not volunteer their services; they wait to be asked. The family itself is often represented among the pallbearers, and the other men chosen must accept the honor unless there is some very valid reason for refusing, such as illness. When a funeral takes place at a funeral home, there is generally no extra charge for the professional pallbearers who actually carry the casket.

Sometimes the casket, which may be adorned with a blanket of flowers or surrounded by flowers, is already in place before the altar by the time the congregation gathers. In this case, just before the start of the service the family may file in from the vestry to the front pews: usually the pews to the right of the center aisle. The honorary pallbearers sit in the front pews to the family's left. At the end of the service, after the family has retired to the vestry, the pallbearers, walking two by two, leave the church, marching slowly in front of the casket if it is to be carried from the church at that time, or marching out slowly alone and into the waiting cars that transport them with the family to the cemetery.

If the casket is carried into the church, the pallbearers precede it, marching slowly, two by two, and stepping into the first left-hand pews as they reach the front of the church.

Pallbearers who have come from out of town and who may not be able to make their funeral calls to the family before leaving often call briefly at the vestry, before or after the service, to pay their respects.

Ushers and Procedures into and out of Church   While the mortician has men in attendance at every funeral who may act as ushers, and the sexton in a large church has a staff for the purpose, it is preferable that male relatives likely to know many of those attending the funeral act in this capacity. Like wedding ushers, they escort those attending the service to their seats but do not offer their arms, except to the old or infirm. Ushers are used for funerals of women as well as of men. A woman being escorted to her seat either by the usher or her husband walks on his right. Ushers do their best to place relatives and close friends toward the front of the church, keeping the front left-hand pews free for the honorary pallbearers or, if there are no pallbearers, for themselves. When there are no honorary pallbearers, the ushers selected by the family precede the casket in the same manner as the pallbearers, or march up the aisle, two by two, just before the service is to start. They march down the aisle at the end of the service ahead of the casket, if it is carrried out, before the rest of the congregation leaves the pews.

At Roman Catholic funerals the family does not enter from the vestry but follows up the aisle in the order of relationship to the dead when the casket is carried into the church. The family members are preceded by altar boys, priest, casket, and pallbearers. After the service they file out in the same order behind the casket. (On occasion this procedure is also followed in Protestant churches.) Outside the church the casket is put immediately into a hearse, while the members of the family take their places in the limousines or cars waiting behind. Some flowers from the church are put into a closed vehicle and driven out to the cemetery with the funeral cortege. The procession drives slowly to the cemetery; usually the cars have their headlights lit. Other drivers are not supposed to break into this cortege.

Jewish Services Funerals are not encouraged in Orthodox synagogues. Mourners of the Orthodox persuasion practice "Shivah"—they return to their home following the interment of the deceased, which usually occurs within twenty-four hours of death, and do not leave their homes for any business or social contacts for seven days following the death of their loved one. It is customary for neighbors either to bring food or to help prepare the meals. Friends in the community come to the home of the mourners at eventide and for seven days thereafter for the purpose of participating in a worship service.

Reform Jews return to the home of the mourners immediately following burial for a brief worship service. This religious service in the home is optional and is conducted by the rabbi or a layman at the suggestion of some member of the family. The men and women assemble side by side, the men with covered heads, the married women with some head covering. Reform Jews refrain from business and social contacts for a maximum of three days following the demise of a loved one.

Memorial Services Sometimes, for a variety of reasons, such as the expressed wish of the deceased or the difficulty of making public funeral arrangements, a memorial service takes place after the funeral. This usually occurs within a few days or weeks, but sometimes several months later. Memorial services usually take place in a church, but might be held elsewhere, for example at home, in a garden, or at a club or organization with which the deceased was identified. A few flowers are provided by the family or close friends for an altar arrangement. In large churches the mourners meet in a small chapel. There is often carefully selected classical background music—Bach is a favorite. Sometimes there is a choir or a solo rendering of the deceased's favorite hymns or other music. There is usually a brief eulogy either by a clergyman or by a friend, and the congregation joins in praying and singing hymns. The mourners are then received briefly by the family, say a few words of consolation, and depart. Those attending memorial services usually wear ordinary street clothes.

Cremation

Cremation is preceded by regular funeral services in the same manner as is burial. Usually just a few close relatives and friends go to the crematorium, where a further brief service is conducted. Subsequently, the family is notified concerning the availability of the cremated remains. Their care or disposal is regulated by various state laws. Sometimes, according to individual circumstances, they are interred in the family plot, placed in an individual niche in a public columbarium, or dispersed following a specific request in the will of the deceased. It is not considered good taste for a family to have the container of ashes of a deceased member on prominent display in the home. Any container of ashes should be kept in a very private place.

Interment and Grave Marking

The minister, rabbi, or priest goes along with the family and others to conduct the brief graveside service.

A grave is marked with the name of the deceased, the dates of his birth and death, and, frequently, his family relationship: "(beloved) father of," "(beloved) son of." In the case of a woman the inscription would read: "Sarah Morris [or Anne] Harrison [no 'Mrs.'], (beloved) wife of Francis Lee Harrison, 1910–1970." Women who have been married more than once are buried with, or in the plot provided by, the most recent husband or else in their own family's plot. Single women's names are engraved in full: "Sarah Anne Harrison" (no "Miss"). Sometimes a line or two of epitaph is added. The gravestone or monument bearing this information is ordered by the family from a monument maker. Cost of gravestones vary, but elaborate monuments can run into thousands of dollars. The monument maker installs the monument or marker at no additional fee. If no monument or gravestone is to be erected, the funeral director can at the time of interment place a simple bronze plaque on the grave costing considerably less than a gravestone and bearing the essential data. Some cemeteries require these for all new graves.

Most cemeteries provide perpetual care of graves as part of the purchase price, but families usually visit and tend their plots from time to time, especially on Memorial Day, religious holidays, and the anniversary of the person's death. Any fresh green plant, however simple, or even a single flower is preferable to plastic or other imitation flowers or plants. Everygreen shrubs around the grave, with either grass or ground cover, look well and require minimum maintenance.

Fees to the Clergyman, Sexton, Organist, Vocalist

It is usual for the minister to be given a fee for his services. Sometimes an appropriate amount is sent to him by the funeral director, who includes this expense on his bill. More often it is sent by a member of the family with a letter of appreciation for his comfort and help. The amount should be based on the family's ability to make a contribution. Simplicity of the funeral is today no indication of lack of funds. And certainly if the funeral has been large and expensive the officiating clergyman should not receive less than one hundred dollars. For the average funeral he usually receives twenty to thirty dollars. When checks are sent they are made out to the clergyman rather than to the church, as these fees are expected to contribute to his own expenses. In the Catholic Church, fees are set by the church according to the type of mass. The family is informed during the arrangements of the amount it is to pay.

The sexton, who opens the church, and the organist and vocalist should all receive a fee for their services. The amount will vary depending on the community, so it is best to consult with your clergyman about what is appropriate.

Acknowledgments for Flowers, Donations to Charity

If the funeral takes place at home, some member of the family should keep a careful record of the flower offerings as they arrive, removing the cards and noting a description of the flowers and the donor's name and address. The flowers from those closest to the family should be placed on or close to the casket, even if flowers arrive from associations or civic groups that are more impressive.

When the funeral takes place at a funeral home, the funeral director's staff will collect the cards and make a list of senders to give to the family. At a church funeral some member of the family, or a close friend, should go to the church ahead of the service to remove the cards and place the flowers around the coffin.

Whether flowers are sent or donations are made to a charity "in memoriam" or mass cards are sent from Catholic friends, everything should be acknowledged within a reasonable length of time, preferably within a month. Morticians usually suppply, as part of their service, engraved acknowledgment cards, which can be mailed by the family. I personally don't like them, as they are cold and impersonal. A handwritten note from some member of the family is far preferable—even if it is only two sentences: "You have no idea how much we appreciated your beautiful white carnations. Thank you for thinking of us at this sad time." When thanking for flowers or letters of sympathy there is no reason not to use your own stationery, provided it is conservative in style. It would be in poor taste to use fuchsia-colored note paper or "mod"-type cards for such an occasion.

When a public figure dies, there may be hundreds, even thousands, of letters, flowers, and gestures of sympathy to be acknowledged. In this case, the mailing of engraved cards in matching envelopes is the only answer to the logistical problem of acknowledgment.

The family of Mary Louis Montgomery
gratefully acknowledges your most kind expression
of sympathy

or, if one member of the family wishes to be the spokesperson, the card may read:

Mr. William Woodford
acknowledges with grateful appreciation
your kind expression of sympathy

Cards being sent to very close friends should be singled out, and someone in the family should pen a sentence or two on each of these cards:

> Dad loved you as a real friend, and we know how much
> you will miss him too.

> You'll never know how much we all appreciated your many
> kindnesses during the last months of Marie's life.

If there are a hundred or fewer gestures of sympathy to acknowledge, and one is writing a personal note, it can be short. One should mention the specific gesture—whether it is the Jewish gesture of having a tree planted in Israel, or sending a basket of chrysanthemums to the funeral, or making a generous donation to "Mother's favorite charity."

In the sad case of there being no living relatives of the deceased, the executors of the will often handle the funeral arrangements. I personally find it unrealistic to send flowers to a funeral of someone with no survivors. Instead, one should write a letter of condolence to a person one may have known who was very close to the deceased, and who will be affected by that death (a man's long-time personal secretary, for example, or his long-time housekeeper). If you know of no one who was close to the deceased, it is a nice gesture to donate some money in his name. The estate executors should send an acknowledgment card to everyone who did send messages, flowers, mass cards, or notice of a donation. Such a card might read:

> Your message of sympathy on the death of Mr. Jonathan Thomas MacArthur is greatly appreciated.

> Your most kind expression of sympathy is deeply appreciated.

> Your kind expression of sympathy is gratefully acknowledged and deeply appreciated.

Acknowledgments to Clergy, Pallbearers, Ushers

Shortly after the funeral a member of the family or a representative of the family should write a personal note to the officiating clergyman, thanking him for his spiritual assistance and enclosing a contribution made out to the clergyman. Honorary pallbearers and ushers should also receive prompt notes of appreciation of their services. Notes must also be written by a family member to close friends and neighbors who offered so much assistance before and during the funeral. Someone in the family should make a list of names and addresses, pointing out the reason for thanking, and then divide up the names among the family members before they go their separate ways after the funeral. In this way, the burden is shared.

Letters of Condolence

You should write a letter of condolence by hand and as quickly as you can after hearing the news of the death. If you do not hear about it until months have gone by—and this sometimes happens—you should still write that letter to the person you know best who was a member of the deceased's family. If you know well all the members of the family, write a good letter to one person only, mention the others' names. Your letter will be seen by them all. I feel that the age-old custom of merely sending your engraved visiting card, with "Deepest sympathy" written across it in black or dark blue ink, is wrong. You should be able to take pen to a piece of letter paper and write at least two or three sentences expressing your personal sadness at the news, and your love and admiration for the person who died. (See "Condolence Letters," page 519.)

If you send a Mailgram, you have the opportunity to express something more than just "Deepest sympathy," too. Come forth with something that the family will want to save, not just another name "signing in" as knowing about the death. Take some time to compose something meaningful. This is, after all, your last chance to honor the friendship.

To do nothing when a friend dies is heartless. It can mean a great deal on the anniversary of a friend's death to make a gesture to someone in his family—such as sending flowers, making a telephone call, or writing a letter that says, "I hope you're coming along all right." These are the truly meaningful acts of love and friendship.

Contributions to Charity

Sometimes the printed funeral notice states that "contributions may be made" to some specified charity or perhaps to a charity of their own choice. When someone chooses to send such a donation, he makes out a check to the charity and sends it with a note stating that this amount is contributed "in memory of" the deceased. The charity will then send the donor an acknowledgment, which may be used for tax purposes, and notifies the family of the deceased of the contribution. It is not usual to mention the amount, although there is no reason for the family not to ask the sum of the total amount of contributions the charity has received. A family member should, of course, write an acknowledgment to each donor.

Sometimes very close friends of the deceased choose to send flowers as well as make a contribution.

Food After the Funeral

In rural communities and small towns it is a kind custom for neighbors to prepare food for the family of the bereaved during the time of preparation for the funeral and immediately afterward. In cities the necessity for this kindness is lessened, in that there are many restaurants nearby or catering services to send in food. However, human kindness is still an effective ingredient in a big city, and apartment neighbors who bring the family a roast, a freshly baked cake, or containers of homemade soup are doing much more for the bereaved family than just giving them food. Among Jewish people, the custom of friends and neighbors supplying food is a tradition.

Distributing Family Possessions

You can help save your children a great deal of anguish by leaving instructions in your file "To be Opened upon My Death" about the disposition of certain personal possessions. By that I mean items that have particular sentimental or monetary value: a family portrait, a lace wedding veil, the family Bible, a diamond pin, or an automobile. Even in the closest of families disputes can arise, not so much from selfish reasons as from emotional ones. You should give considerable thought to your list, taking into consideration which child would most appreciate each object. While this list is not a binding one, in most cases it will be respected by the children.

The remainder of the furnishings and other possessions should be divided fairly and evenly among the children so that each receives an equal portion of the estate. There are a number of ways in which this can be accomplished, but I have yet to hear of a fairer one than the following. Write down the various categories on separate pieces of paper: e.g., rugs, lamps, tables, chairs, ornaments, pictures. Place all the slips of paper in a bowl and draw straws to see who pulls the first category and gets first choice. In rotating fashion, distribute all the items in the category. Next, the person who was second on the first draw becomes number one, pulls the second category from the bowl, and receives first choice. The system continues until the last category has been disposed of. This method virtually assures each child of an equal number of choices in a specific category and an equal share of the estate.

Mourning Dress

Visible signs of mourning are happily almost never seen these days. It is healthy to accept the loss as well as we can, and make an adjustment to daily living without the presence of the person we loved so much. Black used to be the badge of bereavement, but when it became a fashion color, too, it lost the meaning of mourning. One sees older women at a funeral wearing black for a member of their family, but it is rarely seen on younger people at family funerals. The family should wear conservative, somber-colored clothes; women should wear little jewelry. A woman may or may not wear a hat.

Men of the family at large, formal funerals in big cities may wear cutaways, but these are seldom seen today. Men wear dark suits (solid color or pinstripe), with conservative ties, white shirts, and black shoes and socks. A boy would wear his suit, with a conservative tie.

The Concept of Mourning

In times gone by, a family remained in mourning for a year, perhaps even two. Widows wore black until they died. Fortunately, today's world has discarded such a harsh attitude toward death. Instead, we try to develop positive attitudes toward our lives; it is the responsibility of each one of us to make the most of the gift of life while we have it, and to look ahead instead of behind. Today, a person returns to normal tasks shortly after the funeral. The abandonment of mourning is a mark of consideration to others.

People who have lost a close relative may not feel like engaging in a very active social life immediately after the funeral, but they should resume a normal life as soon as they are able to. A scheduled event, such as a wedding, should take place; summer vacation plans should not be changed; life should go on.

Christmas and Greeting Cards After Bereavement

People who have had a recent death in the family are frequently concerned about whether or not they should send Christmas cards. True friends are equally concerned about whether or not mourners should receive Christmas or other greeting cards. Probably at no other time do those who have lost a loved one more need the support and closeness of good friends than at Christmas time. The mourner should certainly send Christmas cards if he so chooses, although it might seem more appropriate under the circumstances to send a card of a religious nature rather than one suggesting merriment and Yuletide festivities. Friends should do all possible to help a bereaved person through the Christmas season, and instead of sending a Christmas card, it is nice to write a short note saying, "Dear Jane: I know this Christmas will be a sad one for you, but please know that you are in my thoughts and that I send you a great deal of love. Jennifer." Gifts should be exchanged, as they are expressions of love and affection and particularly appreciated by the bereaved at such a time.

Part Three

ENTERTAINING

Informal Entertaining 287

Menu Inspiration 310

Setting Your Table 327

Cocktail Parties 337

Informal Luncheons and Teas 347

Formal Entertaining 355

Entertaining Out of Doors 371

The Weekend Guest 381

Special Types of Entertaining 391

At Ease at Table 405

One of the most important facets in one's life is knowing how to entertain. Whether you live in a one-room apartment with an annual income of $6,500 or whether you live on an estate with an annual income of $300,000, the spirit of entertaining is the same. It is simply giving pleasure to others.

It is a gift to know how to entertain well. It is also one of the most creative actions we carry out in our lives. Possessing wealth does not automatically ensure being a good host, because affluence has nothing to do with a desire to please others, to be at ease with others, to be warm and welcoming.

If the host and hostess plan well in advance, even the most minute details; if they carefully compose their guest list; and if they look forward to an opportunity to please others, then the party will be a success. Whether trained staff pass platters of roast pheasant, or whether the guest helps himself to a casserole of stew, it is the attitude in the home that counts, the spirit, the atmosphere of real warmth.

Above all, remember one thing: entertaining is not easy. There is no such thing as the "Party-giving is a snap" hostess. Attention to detail, a continuing awareness of how the party is progressing and how the guests are feeling, requires constant alertness. This does not mean that one should be a nervous Nellie flitting about like a bird in frenetic, useless activity, but it does mean keeping a quiet eye on all details. It is no contradiction to say that you can work hard at your own party and still enjoy it tremendously.

Giving a good party is a creative achievement. It is also very satisfying to know that you have given your friends pleasure.

Chapter 25

INFORMAL ENTERTAINING

Although we may wear evening clothes to someone's house for dinner, the truly *formal dinner party* is fast becoming an anachronism. Today's life-style means informal dinner parties—of from four to twelve guests—or buffet suppers for ten to thirty people.

Invitations

Invitations to an informal dinner are usually telephoned, or are written on informals or on one's note paper. The wife usually does the inviting, but on occasion, for convenience' sake, her husband may do so. He might say, "Mary's at the convention, and she won't be home until Sunday. We would like you both to come to dinner two weeks from Friday at seven-thirty." It is also nice to explain briefly what type of evening you have planned.

Whoever telephones an invitation should remember that one can't press for an immediate answer, as both husband and wife will have to discuss their respective schedules together and agree on accepting the invitation. The wife usually has to say, "May I call you back tomorrow, after checking with Chuck?" If either the husband or the wife will be out of town on the night of the party, the wife should say that and regret for them both immediately. This gives the party hosts the option to come back a day or so later and say, "Please come by yourself to our dinner, Jane, *even if* Chuck is out of town. We need an attractive woman"; or "Make Chuck come by himself, even if we can't have the pleasure of your company, Jane." The couple inviting you will be grateful that you have given them this option, for guest lists are usually carefully thought out in advance, and having an odd number of either sex might throw the entire table off in its seating plan. (Buffets are a different matter; one does not have to try to maintain a balance of the sexes.)

If you know that one spouse of a couple you like is constantly out of town on business, it is very nice to invite the one always left at home to a dinner party, particularly if you are having the kind of social gathering where an extra man or an extra woman won't matter at all. There is no reason why today the spouse at home cannot accept such an invitation. Going to cocktail and dinner parties and attending sports and entertainment events in a group are certainly all acceptable, even recommended, activities for a spouse who is constantly left alone. One should, however, avoid invitations where one would be going out on a "date" alone with someone of the opposite sex.

If someone invites you to a dinner party for a night you are having out-of-town guests visiting, rather than hint for an invitation for your guests, too, always regret the invitation quickly and firmly. Otherwise your hostess is put on an embarrassing spot. "I'm terribly sorry we can't come, Anne, but we will have house guests visiting us that night. They're dear old friends and we will want to have a quiet reunion dinner." By saying that, you will have removed any feeling of guilt on Anne's part at not being able to absorb your guests at her dinner.

Invitations to dinners should not be treated lightly. The host and hostess are obviously going to considerable trouble and expense, especially if they have little help. Guests should not disappoint them at the last minute without a believable excuse such as illness.

A bachelor should not try to bring his own date, unless the hostess specifically requests it. Bachelors are usually needed as extra men for single women. It is also rude to ask a single woman to bring her own date to dinner, as this puts her on the spot. She may not know a suitable man to bring. The hosts should either provide a man for her or just not worry and have one extra woman on hand. In fact, most single women would prefer being an extra woman at a dinner to being matched with an unattractive man called in out of nowhere by a frantic host and hostess. If there is no suitable dinner partner for the widow, divorcée, or single girl, however, the hostess should tell her in advance.

The wise hostess sends out a reminder if she has issued her invitation by telephone. People should be invited to a dinner party at least two weeks in advance. Reminders may be as simple as the following, on the third side of an informal that bears your name: "Reminder—dinner Thursday, April 12, at 7:30 P.M." If your address is not on the informal, you should add it, complete with apartment number, if there is one. Such reminders may also be written on visiting cards in black ink at the top with the address lower right, if it isn't already on the card. Even a postcard will do. The wording can be quite telegraphic. Engraved fill-in reminders are also available for this purpose at good stationers. They read as example on page 289.

Reminder cards need no reply unless, of course, the person invited has mixed up her dates, has become ill, or has some emergency that makes it impossible to attend the function for which she has accepted the invitation.

The nicest addition to older people's dinner parties is an attractive, fresh young face. Sometimes, however, the older people may not know that the young person they wish to invite is secretly engaged or living with someone. When a young woman, for example, is invited by herself to a dinner party, she should tell her hostess on the telephone, "You're so nice to think of me.

This is to remind you that

René Dubois

expects you for *dinner*

on *May 5*

at *7:30* o'clock

May I ask for a rain check? I'd love to come another time with the man I'm seeing a lot of these days, Dale Kellon. I know you don't have room for the two of us this time, but I really want you both to meet Dale. Could *we* come another time?"

In this way, the young woman is telling her hostess something she did not previously know: that she has a serious relationship and prefers not to go out without her man. She is also letting her hostess off the hook, by turning down the invitation and referring to the fact that there is probably not enough room for both of them this time. If the hostess does indeed have a full table, she will welcome this way of handling it. The hostess can answer, "That's great news. We want to meet him. You can be positive that the next party we organize, the two of you will be the first ones we invite."

If the hostess does, however, have room at the table, she would answer, "That's great news. And we have room for Dale, too, at this dinner party. I insist you bring him along. We want to meet him right away."

The same goes for a bachelor who is almost engaged, or who is living with someone. He should tip off the hostess calling him as her favorite "extra man" that he is no longer free. He should say he hopes to have the pleasure of introducing his "friend" to them sometime soon. If a hostess is faced with a dinner party lacking three or four men, she would certainly not appreciate his suggesting he bring along his own woman friend.

Greeting the Arriving Guests

No guest should be allowed to arrive without being greeted. The maid takes the guests' wraps, or if she is busy doing too many things, she directs them to the bedroom or rooms where the wraps are to be left. Both host and hostess should station themselves near the front door in order to greet each guest with a warm handshake and a verbal greeting. If there is no maid and the wife is out in the kitchen when she hears a doorbell ring, she should get herself quickly to the front door, too, to say hello, however briefly. The smart hostess keeps a mirror in the kitchen, to make sure she is not frazzled-looking, with hair out of place and make-up messed up from bending over the steaming stove. She also keeps a turkish towel handy to wipe her hands clean of grease and other foods before dashing from the kitchen to shake hands with a newly arrived guest. A slip-on apron is an additional convenience, for there won't be time for endless tying and untying of sashes.

When an invitation is issued for seven o'clock, some guests may arrive promptly, others up to forty-five minutes to an hour late, pleading last-minute emergencies as their excuses. Once dinner is ready and it is time to proceed to the table, the hostess should not be expected to wait more than a few minutes for latecomers, unless one includes the guest of honor, who ideally should never be late but without whom it is uncomfortable to sit down. If the lateness is really very serious, guest of honor or no, the hostess proceeds with dinner. A latecomer enters the dining room as quietly as possible, goes briefly to the hostess (who remains seated so as not to disturb the table), makes an apology, and sits immediately in the indicated place. If the late one is a woman, the man to her left rises, or semi-rises, to seat her. Any long explanation of the reason for the lateness is uncalled for and should never draw in the others at the table. The hostess, no matter how she really feels about it, always minimizes the inconvenience to her as well as to the other guests. She says something such as, "It's really quite all right. I knew you would expect us to go right ahead."

Seating at Dinner

The hostess, when the meal is ready, should announce to her guests, "Let's go in to dinner now," and then lead her guests into the dining room or over to the dining area. The host usually brings up the rear. At a small, informal dinner, if some of the guests still have a goodly amount of their cocktails left, the hostess should say, "Bring along your glass to the dinner table." If it is a large, formal dinner, she would not welcome such an action, for there will be many glasses on the table, and additional non-matching bar glasses will detract from the table, both aesthetically and table-service-wise.

The hostess indicates where everyone is to sit, if there are no place cards. I find it easier to have place cards if the dinner is for eight or more. When the guests all know each other, the place cards carry first names only. Otherwise, the cards read "Mrs. Benton, Mr. Cunningham, Mrs. Smith." If two couples with the same surname happen to be at the table, then the cards must read "Mr. Robert Smith, Mr. Richard Smith." Titles are always simplified: "Justice Goldfrank," not "The Hon. Gerald Goldfrank, Justice of the Supreme

Court," and "Ambassador Bruce," not "The Hon. David Bruce, Ambassador of the United Kingdom to the United States." The title "The Hon." is not used on place cards; instead, Mr., Mrs., Miss, or Ms. is used with the last name. Even at a small party, place cards should be used if the hostess is likely to become flustered or forgetful of names.

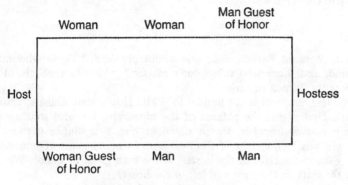

Seating Plan for Dinner for Eight

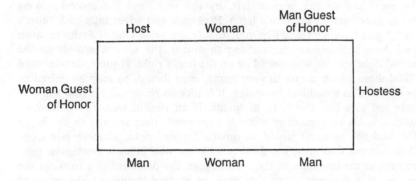

Seating Plan for Dinner for Eight, Alternative

In order to avoid having two men or two women sit next to each other, an alternative method of seating at a dinner for eight is to have the host sit on the side.

The woman guest of honor sits to the host's right and the male guest of honor is placed to the hostess' right. The second most important woman is seated at the host's left and the second most important man is on the hostess' left. A man seats the woman to his right, although this custom seems to be disappearing; in the mores of the younger generation, each woman simply seats herself.

Husbands and wives are never seated next to each other, unless it is a table for four and they have to. Even newlywed and engaged couples should be seated apart from each other on the basis that they already have enough time to talk to each other in private and should be pleased to have the opportunity to converse with others.

Protocol

The late Bernard Baruch once said about protocol, "Those who matter don't mind, and those who mind don't matter," which is a delightful and typically witty Baruch remark.

Nonetheless, protocol is not limited to White House state dinners, embassy diplomatic circles, and the palaces of the monarchs, but also touches each and every one of us when we sit down at our own dinner parties. The woman who sits to the right of the host is the woman guest of honor. The man who sits to the right of the hostess is the man guest of honor. Who deserves these seats on the right and left of the hosts?

If you have an official coming to dinner, that man and his wife or that woman and her husband deserve the seats of honor. (The second-ranking man guest sits on the hostess' left, by the way, and the second-ranking woman guest sits on the host's left.) Husbands and wives take each other's rank. If you have someone like your town's mayor, a United States senator, or an American ambassador coming to dinner, the man would sit on the hostess' right and his wife would sit on the host's right. If someone who used to hold these offices comes to your home, even though he may be retired or was defeated in a political campaign, it is nice to recognize his past achievements and give him the place of honor. If an elected woman politician or one who holds an appointive office is your guest, then she sits on the host's right, and her husband would sit on the hostess' right. If there is no one official coming to dinner, but there is someone who holds a prestigious position such as the president of the local college, the president of a bank, or the director of a museum, then that man or woman should be the guest of honor.

It is always correct protocol to give someone from another country the guest of honor's place at your table, because if you were in his home, you would be the guest of honor. Non-Americans are usually very careful about this. If you have neither an ambassador, congressman, judge, clergyman, nor a foreign guest in your home, you can get down to more basic matters. If you have a recently engaged or married couple, make them the honor guests. If your college roommate is visiting you, make her the guest of honor. Show respect for age by making an older person the guest of honor, and letting him or her know it. If there is a couple who have never been to your house before, they could be the honor guests. If you just have "old friends" to dinner, without any special occasion involved, the hostess puts one man on her right and his wife in the middle of the table; the host picks the wife from another couple and puts her on his right, and that woman's husband in the middle of the table. In other words, you are "sharing the honor." Do not put husbands next to wives, unless it cannot be helped.

Toasting

If wine is served, it is always a nice custom for the host to give a toast to both guests of honor (man and wife) at some point during the dinner. It is a great asset to know how to give good toasts. Toasting requires the ability to rise to one's feet and project with one's voice to the assembled audience a feeling of sentimentality, loyalty, praise, gratitude, or sheer humor in a very brief span of time.

You do not need to have a high official guest in your home in order to offer a toast at your own dinner party. Toasting becomes better with prac-tice, and I know some hosts who, over the years, have become experts in the art—hostesses also. It is immensely flattering to be toasted. The hostess' col-lege roommate passing through on her way across the country is pleasantly surprised—and delighted—when her old roommate's husband stands at his dinner party and reminisces in a light fashion to the gathering about seeing both girls in their college dormitory during his courtship period of his wife. He thanks the guest for "having pulled my wife through college by tutoring her"; he remarks how "the class of 1940 must have found the Fountain of Youth," because both the guest of honor and his wife look better today than they did almost forty years ago, and so on. Everyone laughs; it is all grossly exaggerated and mostly untrue. But the purpose of a toast, after all, is to make someone happy and feel proud. It is a charming, delightful thing to do.

People who want to give a toast should do so when everyone still has some wine left in his glass; the toaster should speak slowly and distinctly, so that all the guests can hear. Brevity is the key to success.

Traditionally, the host should to make the first toast. This is true at official dinner parties and in Scandinavian homes, where the host welcomes every-one with a warm word, ending with a *"Skål!"* which is the signal for everyone to begin drinking their wine or schnapps. Nowadays, if the host, for one reason or another, has not given a toast by the middle of the dessert course, an inspired guest may certainly rise and toast both his host and hostess (par-ticularly his hostess, if it was she who cooked the dinner). With this kind of informal toasting, the guests do not have to rise from their chairs except per-haps for the *first* toast. With each toast, everyone joins in raising their glasses of wine toward whoever is being toasted, repeats his name, and then drinks from their glasses. (It is most unwise to do what they did in ancient times and try to drink all of the contents of one's glass in one gulp.) When a person stands to give a toast, if the guests remain noisily unaware of his impending toast, people around him should help draw attention to his gesture by rapping a piece of flatware against the rim of a goblet, *carefully*. (It's pretty embarrassing to break a glass while you're doing this!)

People who do not drink alcohol should not necessarily raise a glass of water to join in the toast, as some people at the table may believe in the superstition that to toast in water is to invite bad luck. Instead, they might just make a token gesture with their hand and arm, as though they were holding a glass of wine. If they are drinking soda, they should toast with that.

If it is a big party and there are two separate adjoining rooms full of guests, the person who toasts should stand in the doorway and project his voice so all can hear. When I worked in the White House I discovered that the guests at a large dinner party who spilled over into the Red Room and the Blue Room were unable to hear any of the presidential or return toasts. I had the Signal Corps install a microphone for the heads of state to use, as well as hidden speakers in both rooms, so that everyone could hear all the toasts. These are still in use.

The person being toasted, of course, does not stand up or drink when the others are raising their glasses to him. It is nice if he responds to the toast, and either he can do this immediately following the first toast, or he can wait for another course of the dinner to be served before rising to his feet. At public banquet toasts are proposed toward the end of the meal. The first toast is proposed by the toastmaster, the honored person responds, and other toasts may be proposed, arranged beforehand, with the toastmaster's permission, by honored guests sitting on the dais. People sitting at tables "out in the audience" may not propose toasts.

In families with parents who drink wine regularly with meals, the art of toasting is usually learned by the children at at an early age. In many families the birthday child is toasted by everyone at the table, the younger ones using soda or mugs of milk. Children also toast their parents on their wedding anniversaries. Parents pass on this nicety of life to the younger generation, and it is an asset to be able to rise in a group and say something that gives pleasure to someone else.

I remember when I was a very young girl I was allowed to go to a "posh" black-tie dinner on a Long Island estate only because a young British girl my age had arrived that day to stay with our dinner hosts. She was one of the British war orphans, whose family had sent her to America to escape the Nazi bombs falling on London.

Our host and hostess kept eying the little English girl anxiously during dinner. She was tired from the long journey by troopship and was obviously feeling bewildered and homesick for her family and her country. When dessert time came, I will never forget what happened. Our host arose, turned toward the young girl, down the long table, and said, "We welcome you, Jennifer, but first, ladies and gentlemen, I propose a toast to His Majesty the King of England!" Her eyes large with tears, Jennifer arose with the rest of the group, turned toward her host with her glass of milk raised, acting as though she had done this all her life, and said in a solemn, clear voice, heard by everyone around the big table, "To His Majesty the King!"

Dinner Service with One Maid

If a family has a housekeeper or a maid, it is foolish to try to turn her into a cook-waitress who will handle a dinner party deftly all by herself. Entertaining causes a great deal of extra work, including marketing, getting the wines and liquor in order, polishing the silver, rewashing dusty glasses and plates, and a lot of other time-consuming chores, even before any cooking is done. Don't expect one person to do all this and take care of her other household or child-caring duties. A cook-waitress might be called in, if the host and hostess do not wish to (and don't *have to*) work on the party preparations themselves. Sometimes teen-aged children in the home are the answer to a well-served dinner.

A dinner that is to be both prepared and served by one maid should be kept simple—three courses. A freezer makes it easy to have some dishes prepared in advance. Canapés may be frozen, then thawed or put in the oven or under the broiler just before the guests arrive; so may the dinner rolls. Frozen vegetables cut down on preparation time; so do microwave ovens. The dessert may come from the freezer or refrigerator, too.

A simply prepared solid piece of meat, such as roast beef or lamb, carved in the kitchen and passed from a platter, cuts down work. Foods that require last-minute preparation and prompt consumption, such as soufflés and sauce Hollandaise, should be avoided. Some dishes just can't be held if guests are late. Roast meats and meat and fowl casseroles are the easiest to keep warm without overcooking.

The First Course If a first course is to be served at the table, a place plate is in place or the first course is actually on the place plate. In summer the first course may be something like jellied madrilène or vichyssoise, in winter a fish ramekin or hot soup in a bowl, a cup, or a flat plate.

A first course may be served by the maid once guests have been seated and have opened their napkins. All serving procedures described are intended to simplify work, save steps, and speed service. The maid comes in from the serving pantry or kitchen with the soup or other first course in her left hand, and at dinner of no more than eight, beginning with the lady at the host's right (never with the hostess), she serves counterclockwise, ending with the host. Everything is served from the *left*. Or, if there is no first course and place plates are on the table, she exchanges the place plates for heated dinner plates, taking off the place plates with her right hand to the guest's left *or* right and putting down the hot plate with her left on the guest's left side. Then she brings in the main dish and sets it before the host if it is to be carved. If the main dish is arranged on a large platter, she carries it on her left hand on a clean, folded napkin, steadied, if necessary, with her right.

Then she brings in the vegetables, one dish in each hand on the serving napkin. (A two- or three-compartment dish is excellent here, too.) She offers first the dish in her left hand, then that in her right. In each dish are a serving spoon and fork face down with handles toward the person to be served. Forks may be omitted if the vegetable is something like peas. However, with a vegetable like asparagus or a vegetable that actually needs to be lifted, both implements are provided. Asparagus, by the way, is often on a folded linen napkin in the dish if a sauce is to be served separately; otherwise it must be well drained before being placed on the platter. Sometimes toast, too, is used as a moisture-catcher for asparagus and, by the way, should be taken up by the guest when he serves himself, and may be eaten.

The dish or platter should be held at a level comfortable to the guest, never too high and never so far to the side as to cause him to twist around in his chair. Sauces or gravies should be served immediately after the dish they accompany. Hot dishes should be very hot, cold ones chilled. No lukewarm gravies, tepid chops, or cold biscuits.

If the Host Carves   Carving the meat at the table slows up the service. The custom of carving is, however, a nice one. When meat is to be carved at the table, the carving set with the sharpener is placed to the right of the carver above the place setting, so that when the roast is brought in the implements will be to the right of the platter. The maid stands at the host's left. Either she has removed his place plate and put before him a stack of hot dinner plates or he has before him one hot plate, which he fills and which the maid then takes with her left hand and places before the guest of honor, first removing the hot plate with her right hand, to the left or right. She then returns to the host, puts the new hot plate in front of him, serves it when he has filled it, and gives him another. Whoever carves should include on each plate a little of the garniture on the platter, whether it's parsley, watercress, thin lemon slices, or vegetables. A serving spoon should be placed with the carving implements so that the carver can serve a little of the sauce from the meat (like the "au jus" of the roast beef) onto each guest's serving of meat. The accompanying sauce or gravy is passed separately by the maid before the vegetables. Or she may place it on the table to be passed by the guests, which is faster and better.

If the host has before him a stack of hot plates the maid may stand at his left and take one filled one at a time, or two, if the table has been set with no place plates. Or she may let the host pass the plates right and left, as convenient, and she may bring the vegetables from the kitchen and serve them. With one maid, this is the best way to serve when the meat is carved at table. It ensures that the food will be served hot.

If the Hostess Serves   When the hostess is to serve, there are hot-plate mats, if necessary, in front of her place and to her right are arranged serving forks and spoons neeeded, the fork rested in the spoon. Silver (or china or glass) ladles for sauces are in the sauce when it is served, and the bowl or boat is on a serving plate. When jellies or condiments are in place on the table, to be passed, the spoon or fork for them is next to them on the table and is placed in them by the first person taking up the dish. A made dish or one to be portioned at the table, such as baked fish, may also be placed before the hostess. Or the host may serve meat or fish, and the hostess serve the vegetables. The maid first receives the plate from the host, takes it to the hostess' left for vegetables, sauces, or gravy, then serves it to the woman guest of honor (on the host's right) and so on around the table counterclockwise, serving the hostess in the regular order as she reaches her, unless she is serving (in this case the hostess is served last). If the dining room is so tiny as to make any service awkward or if the maid is inept at service, the best thing is to let her bring in the dishes for the host and hostess to serve, remove them at the right time, crumb the table, pour the wine when glasses are empty, and serve the dessert and after-dinner coffee, letting it go at that. Better no service than the bumbling kind. A tea table or serving cart may certainly be used. If it is placed at the hostess' right, it can greatly simplify the matter of service and prevent the overcrowding of the table with serving dishes. (The usual signal to summon the maid from the kitchen is either a buzzer pressed by the foot on the floor or a table bell that is rung.)

In America, to speed service with limited help, one serves from the left and removes from the *right*. However, the maid never reaches in front of a guest to remove from the right anything such as a butter plate on the guest's extreme left. These things are removed from the left, always. Conversely, she never reaches from the guest's left across to the right to take off water and wine glasses, but removes these always from the right.

Serving and Removing Two Plates at a Time In the most formal way of serving, a maid or waiter brings in one plate at a time, always serving a person from his left, and always removing one plate at a time from a person's right at the end of that course. To speed up service, however, this procedure is frequently changed as follows: a maid enters with a plate in either hand. She goes between two guests, lays down the plate in her left hand on the place in front of the guest on her left, and lays down the plate in her right hand on the place in front of the guest on her right. She removes them in exactly the same manner when the course is finished.

Clearing the Main Course Before the Service of Dessert The maid removes first the serving dishes and platters, then the soiled dishes, and finally the condiments. At an informal meal a wine decanter, if any, remains on the table. Unused silver is quietly removed to the same small serving tray that will accommodate the condiments. Glasses are never removed during the meal.

Crumbing the Table The maid crumbs the table just before the service of dessert. A folded napkin is used to the left of each guest to brush crumbs onto either a small tray or a clean plate or a "silent butler."

Demitasse Time When dessert is finished, some hostesses prefer to serve coffee at the table. Perhaps the conversation around the table is so spirited the hostess does not want to break it up and dispel the mood by moving. In this case, she serves the coffee cups right at the table and hands them down to the guests, one by one, after asking them what they want in their coffee.

If she feels it is more comfortable for the guests to relax in the living room, or on the patio, in the solarium, or wherever she wants to move the party, she rises, catches the host's eye, and says, "Let's go have coffee." She sits down before a low table, and pours each guest's coffee according to his preference. Her tray is laden with demitasse cups with their little spoons, neatly arranged to the right of the cup, on the saucer. There are cream, sugar, and sweetener on her tray as well. There are also two coffeepots, one of which is for coffee, the other for decaffeinated coffee. (A very thoughtful hostess will have tea available for non-coffee drinkers but she will not have it on the tray.)

The host passes a box of cigars at this point, too. (At a formal dinner, cigarettes stacked on a silver tray alongside a stack of cigars and a light are passed by the butler.) If a hostess is a woman who lives alone, she might ask one of her male guests to do the honors with the cigars and liqueurs, although I have seen many such hostesses do it themselves very well. The days are past when a woman who lives alone feels she has to lean on a male guest while entertaining. Many women make excellent drinks when they are handling a party alone; they pour the wine and cope with the bar very well. Their philosophy is that the men they invite are there as guests, to relax and enjoy, and not to work during their parties.

And as for the separation of the sexes after dinner, I am not even discussing it other than to say that the custom of the men having coffee and cigars by themselves while the women dawdle in the bedroom, sipping coffee and discussing the PTA, are finished. Most women feel that even though they may hate the fumes of a cigar (a lot of men do, too), it is still more pleasant to be together after dinner—more pleasant for both sexes.

The Buffet Supper

Only the very young (and for our purposes here, the "very young" means people still in their twenties) can be truly comfortable balancing a plate of food while reclining on the floor or sitting on a low cushion that requires the agility of a gymnast to spring forth from gracefully.

At a certain moment in our lives we have earned the right to be comfortable at parties. We want to have some back support. We want to relax while eating and not have to worry about knocking over someone's glass of sangria with an ankle.

The basic ingredient of any successsful buffet for the post-college set, and particularly for anyone in evening clothes, is to have every guest assured of a proper seat and a nearby space to place his plate and drink. Card tables,

TV tables, coffee tables, end tables, consoles, handy shelves, even the top of the TV set can be pressed into service for a resting place for one's party paraphernalia. There should be plenty of clean ash trays around, and coasters to hold wet-bottomed glasses. Napkins should be oversized, and there should be more than one for each guest; some will want to put one napkin on their lap, another by their side to use for fingers. It is also better not to serve runny food that will tend to slip off the plate while one maneuvers one's way to a seat.

Even more basic than providing anyone with a seat is following the rule of inviting only the number of guests that can be easily managed in one's home. When a host and hostess have reached their limit on the number of buffet guests, they should resist all attempts to pressure them into inviting more. If one of the guests you have invited suddenly is confronted with house guests and you have room, it is very friendly and nice to invite the house guests, too. (At summer resorts, weekend entertaining is always planned around the house guests.) But if you have reached your limit, explain to your friend how sorry you are that you cannot absorb everyone. You will ask him again to another party soon.

If you are having a buffet party, it is best to make it informal in dress, unless the group is going afterward to a benefit, a dance, or some other black-tie event. Evening gowns in general are expensive and difficult to dry-clean, and eating buffet-style at a crowded party invites spills and spots.

The smart buffet giver suggests to the guests (as they are standing in line to obtain their food from the sideboard or serving area) where they ought to sit. "John, why don't you take Mary and Gertrude and start a new group in the library?" "Denise, why don't you, Joe, and the Jenkinses use the card table in the living room?" "George, you and Jane stay right here in the dining room. There are two places left at the big table."

The napkins, eating utensils, and glasses of wine may be waiting at the various places around the home where the guests will seat themselves, or they may be on the sideboard for the guests to pick up themselves, once they have served themselves with food on a plate. The hostess who plans food that does not require a knife to cut it is doing herself, her guests, and her home a big favor.

There are many ways of organizing a buffet, whether a small or large one, and it is only after practice and experimentation that the hostess knows which way works best in her own home. One accomplished party giver I know has twenty-four attractive, lightweight square trays. When a guest has filled his plate with the food he wants, he is handed one of the litle trays by the hostess, each with its own flatware, napkin, glass filled with wine, and small salt and pepper.

At a buffet the host and hostess help serve their guests; sometimes there's a maid to assist; sometimes one guest will go through the line and fill two plates—one for himself, one for his dinner partner or for an older person who is comfortably seated.

As soon as a guest has served himself from a buffet, he may begin eating. One need not wait for everyone to be served at a big party. The hosts want their food to be enjoyed to its maximum, and that means consuming the hot food when it is piping hot and the cold food deliciously cold.

It is always very helpful if a couple of "helpers" volunteer to pick up their neighbors' plates and bring them back to the dining room when the guests have finished. Those same people can bring back plates of dessert to the seated guests. On the other hand, if one has been "stuck" in an unwieldy or boring situation, dessert time is the perfect excuse to arise from one's seat, go into the dining room for dessert, and then sit somewhere else.

There should always be enough food for seconds on every course served in a buffet. The organized host has someone—a maid, his children, the baby-sitter earning extra money—to take the dirty plates into the kitchen and to organize the cleanup squad. Guests should *never* have to traipse into the kitchen themselves. It destroys the party mood; it breaks the spell.

The host and hostess, or the maid, if there is one, should see to it that the guests' wineglasses are filled at all times. (Bottles or carafes of wine can be left in strategic areas of the house where people are sitting.) Ash trays should be constantly emptied, too. And there should be no "wallflower" guests. The hosts should see to it that everyone has someone to talk to.

The Buffet Table The buffet table should look as pretty as possible. It may be covered in any kind of linens, or, if the table surface is particularly beautiful, it can be left bare, with precautions taken to place enough heat-protectors beneath the food containers. Even through it is an informal type of entertaining, the hosts should use their prettiest tableware, glasses, and flatware. They should also use their handsomest serving implements and platters; although, with the new decorative oven cookware, one can now serve food in the very pan in which it was cooked.

Nonetheless, I feel that if you get out from storage your good silver hollow ware, polish it with enthusiasm, and use it for your buffet, the party will look more beautiful and festive than if you use your oven-to-table cookware. Something that has obviously taken time and trouble always pleases and impresses more than the "easy way." Though we are living in a world where the easy way is perfectly correct, there is always an unspoken feeling that passes between the guest and the hostess: "You thought enough of *me* to stay home Sunday and polish your silver all day?"

Serving areas for a buffet range from all parts of a dining room to many areas in an apartment or house. The hot food might be in one area (with the warm dinner plates preceding it); the salad and rolls might be in another serving area; the glasses of wine and the napkins and flatware might be in yet another. If the menu is very informal and beer is to be served, there could be a large container filled with ice and beer. Nearby there should be a large tray with attractive beer glasses on it.

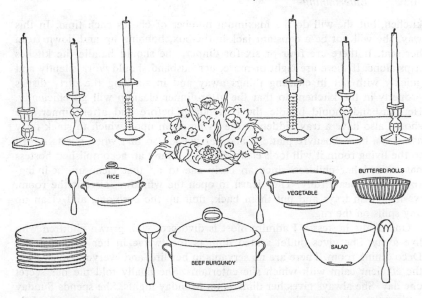

A typical one-plate, one-wine buffet service dinner. Since the plates are warm, they need a trivet beneath them, as do the beef Burgundy, the vegetable and the rice. Three pairs of candlesticks have been used on this sideboard. They don't match, but it doesn't matter. They are a handsome backdrop against the wall. The hot casseroles are covered until the guests line up to serve themselves, at which time the hostess removes the covers and places them in the kitchen. A free-standing buffet table should have one decorative element in the center, such as a three-armed candelabrum with the food and serving pieces attractively balanced around it.

A Sit-down Dinner Without a Maid

Certainly this is the type of dinner most often given today, usually for four to eight guests. It takes practice to get the whole dinner served and eaten while the hostess (or host) is acting as the cook, maid, and chief bottle washer. But it can be done. She must be well organized, and have everything prepared in advance and warming up in perfect synchronization during the cocktail hour, so that her guests will be aware of her existence. The hostess who says hello at the front door, hands her guest a cocktail, and then is not seen until she calls everyone in to dinner is not doing the job correctly.

With practice, she will learn what she can and cannot do in the number and kinds of courses. She will make the minimum number of trips to the kitchen, but she will do the maximum number of chores each time. In this way, she will not be a constant jack-in-the-box, bobbing up and down from her seat. If there are four or six for dinner, she should handle the kitches trips alone. If there are eight or more, her husband should work silently and quickly with her in clearing things away and in stacking the dirty dishes properly in the kitchen, so that the after-dinner cleanup will go efficiently. Her husband should handle the bartending, before and after dinner. He should also have a tray hidden in the living room upon which to stack dirty ash trays, hors d'oeuvre platters, and bar glasses, so that when guests return to the living room it will look clean and tidy. Many an accomplished hostess has trained her children since an early age to do that clean-up-the-living-room detail beautifully. They learn to open the windows, air out the room, wash the ash trays and put them back, fluff up the cushions, and clean up any spills on the rug.

One of the hostesses I admire most is divorced, with grown children who live away. She gives buffet seated dinners for twelve in her beautiful Art Deco dining room. There are no servants in her life, and everyone marvels at the efficient calm with which she entertains. She finally told me her secret one day. She always gives her dinners on Monday nights. She spends Sunday setting the table, cooking, polishing silver, arranging her flowers, and in other preparatory chores. She works all day Monday, comes home from the office, reheats her dinner food, and does some last-minute chores. By 8 P.M. she is bathed, freshly made up, and extremely glamorous. She serves pre-made martinis, scotch, champagne, and soft drinks so she can handle the bar easily herself. Once served, her guests go back to refill their drinks themselves, for everything is set up in the library. No need to go to the kitchen. When the guests go in to dinner, the twelve-year-old girl who lives across the hall enters the apartment, cleans up the entire living room and bar area, opens and closes the windows again, washes all the cocktail glasses and puts them back on the bar, refills the ice buckets with ice cubes, and steals away to her own apartment. She earns two dollars for those forty-five minutes of work.

Then, after dinner, two high school students who also live in her building come up to her kitchen through the service entrance and begin not only to wash all the dishes, but to clean the oven, and mop the kitchen floor as they go out the door. She pays each of them five dollars, plus a wonderful present at Christmas. They come faithfully, when she has lunch parties on Sunday, brunch parties before football games, or her famous "little dinners." She knows how to get things done.

Basically, there are three ways of efficiently giving a dinner party without the help of a maid:

1. Buffet-style—the Preferred Way

The food is served buffet-style from one or more serving surfaces in the dining area. An electric hot tray is a great help in keeping the food warm. There is usually no first course involved, and the dessert course is brought in

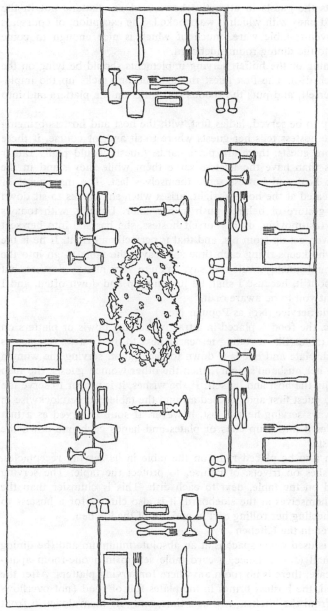

The sit-down buffet. This is the most comfortable way to dine buffet-style. The dinner table is set as usual, with the exception of place plates and serving dishes. On the table are all the silver needed, ash trays, salts, peppers, candlesticks, napkins, glasses for water and wine, possibly place cards and flowers. Guests serve themselves at the buffet, then take their seats at the table.

separately by the hostess after the main course is eaten. What is served, therefore, awaits the guests in attractive bowls and on platters, not in the original pots and pans with which it was cooked. The exception, of course, is the attractive oven-to-table ware, much of which is nice enough to come from the stove to the dining room sideboard.

At the beginning of the buffet, serving implements should be lying on the table beside each dish. The first guest through the line picks up the implements, serves herself, and puts the spoons and forks on the platters and into the bowls.

Guests line up to be served, ladies first, with the host and hostess bringing up the rear. The hostess tells her guests where to sit and, of course, if there are eight or more guests, there are place cards. Guests would really rather help themselves than have the hostess serve them while they stand in the buffet line. The host and hostess serve themselves last. The man guest of honor, who is seated at the hostess' right, arises when she comes to sit down and makes the gesture of helping push in her chair. Usually, with today's well-organized, fast-moving, do-it-yourself hostess, she has slid into her seat before he can even get up from his, and that is perfectly all right. If he is the kind of guest who keeps rising each time she leaves the table to go into the kitchen, she should quickly smile and say, "You're very nice to do that, but please forget about it, because I shall be jumping up and down often, and I really don't want you to be aware of it."

2. English-style Service (Not as Popular Now)

In this service, the food is placed in attractive serving bowls or platters on a small serving table (like a rolling tea cart) next to the hostess. She serves the food on each plate and hands it down to each guest, serving the woman honor guest (to her husband's right), then the other women guests, the men guests, and finally the host and herself. If she wishes, it is proper to serve the woman honored guest first and proceed around the table counterclockwise in progression, always serving herself last, however. If soup is served as a first course, she ladles it into soup cups or plates and hands each one down the table to the guests.

The food can also be placed right on the table in its serving receptacles, with the hot dishes on trivets, of course, to protect the table. The serving utensils are laid on the table, next to each dish. This is clumsier than the guests serving themselves at the sideboard; it is also clumsy for a hostess to have to keep wheeling her rolling cart in and out of the kitchen.

3. Plates Served in the Kitchen

This method is used when space is at an absolute minimum and the dining table is very small (for instance, a card table set up in a one-room apartment). In this case, there is no room anywhere for serving platters. After the guests are seated, the hostess brings in the plates full of food (not overflowing, however) from the kitchen, two at a time, and sets them down in front of the guests. The only dishes she brings in separately are a small receptacle with hot buttered rolls or breads (if she wants to serve them at all) or perhaps a small salad bowl. Such a small table seating four or five people should hold only the dinner plates, flatware, wineglasses (no water glasses), a salt and pepper mill, two small ash trays, a bottle or decanter of wine, and something small in the center. I have often seated six people at a round card table in an efficiency apartment I once had in New York. I used attractive little benches for people to sit on, and we actually all fitted in quite nicely. And one of the prettiest small tables I have ever seen was in a studio apartment only thirteen by eighteen feet. A white linen tablecloth covered the round card table to the floor; an occasional daisy had been embroidered on it by the hostess herself. The only centerpiece decoration was one large white porcelain candlestick, with a white candle. A fresh garland of long-stemmed daisies was wound around the candlestick. The china, ash trays, salt and pepper—everything but the goblets and flatware—were of white glazed porcelain. Simple, unpretentious, inexpensive, and perfectly lovely.

In the old days, it would have been unheard of to serve plates from the kitchen. In today's world of tiny spaces and relaxed entertaining, it often proves to be the easiest, the most efficient, the most graceful—and therefore the *best* way in which to do it.

Is the First Course Necessary?   The first course in the majority of informal dinner parties is disappearing. Some people like to serve it in the living room before dinner and have the soup cups, shrimp cocktail bowls, oyster plates, or whatever collected on a tray before everyone goes to the dining area for dinner. This is clumsy, however. The food often tends to spill; some people don't like mixing dinner food with sweet drinks like a gin and tonic or a daiquiri. If you are sitting on the edge of a sofa, balancing a Tom Collins and a cup of vichyssoise, it just doesn't seem to work, either from a physical-comfort or a gourmet point of view. The way to solve the logistics problem of the first course is simply to anandon it. The guests will feel more virtuous to have skipped those calories, and they will attack the dessert course with far less guilt and therefore greater enjoyment.

After-dinner Activities

What are we going to do after dinner? This can be an agonizing question for some women who are not sure about their hostessing abilities. The problem is solved easily if the entire group is going on to a dance or some other activity afterward. Or if everyone coming to dinner is an expert bridge player, there is no problem, either. But the key to what happens after most successful dinner parties is good conversation. There is nothing to replace it, and if you feel insecure about your own abilities to direct, monitor, and stimulate the conversation, then invite at least two people to your party who are gifted in this field. One person alone cannot keep the ball in the air without exhausting himself with his own efforts, which is why you should have two good conversationalists. Good listeners are important, too. The good listener goes about his business with intelligence, and with flattering concentration upon his subject. Even if you have a proper mix of conversationalists and listeners at your party, you still need to be relaxed, too. The jack-in-the box hostess, frenetically checking her guests' glasses, waving clean ash trays under their noses, and trying to move guests from one position to another ("Tom, you've been talking to that attractive Jane far too long; come over and spread that charm around Suzy"), makes everyone feel unsettled.

Good Conversation Why are some people so much better conversationalists than others? I think some are born good conversationalists, but after years of observation I have reached some other conclusions, too. It is an art that can be learned. For example, the good conversationalist is generally cheerful. He does not dwell on subjects that are sad; he refuses to let people continue discussions bathed in doom and gloom. He is blessed with a sense of humor and laughs a lot. There is nothing that fills the air more pleasantly than the ring of laughter. People turn toward the source of it, like the proverbial moth to the flame.

The good conversationalist does not have to be an intellectual genius, but he has to be informed. He reads; he listens; he is up to date on the latest news; his ear is tuned to the fads of the moment. Even if his knowledge about a topic at hand is sketchy, he knows how to bluff and is able to ask the right questions of someone in his vicinity who has something to contribute on that subject. It takes the right questions to turn on the quiet, shy guest.

Then there's the weapon of flattery. The good conversationalist knows how to wield it subtly and well. Flattery can bring the most reticent person out of his shell. Subtle flattery used on someone who merits it is kindness; it is also useful in any social situation. (Conversely, heavy flattery is artificial, phony, and crass; it makes everyone within earshot extremely uncomfortable.)

The good conversationalist does not talk about his children, except when there is something really important to say. To the polite question "How are the children?" he answers, "Just fine," "Just great," or however he usually expresses himself. However, when there is something important to say, he says it, as, for example, "Sally's in the hospital; she just had her appendix out," or "John has just been appointed class valedictorian," or "Jennie is off with a team to Nepal to climb Mount Everest." News is news; people enjoy partaking of it, but loving endearments concerning one's children, including the advent of a second tooth or a superb drawing of a robin, should be kept to conversations with one's closest friends and family.

The good conversationalist knows quite naturally from experience when to pull something out from his bag of tricks in order to wake up a dragging group of guests. He does it instinctively; he steps into the breach; it is an act of kindness. He may throw out a big piece of news, or a funny thing that happened on the street, or some inside information on a sports event. One of the greatest helps to the good conversationalist is, of course, the presence of another one. They act as foils for each other, and the combination of two plus a threesome of flattering listeners will pull an entire group of twelve people together in harmony.

It helps to set the scene for good conversation after dinner. Be sure that the room where everyone congregates is clean of all pre-dinner cocktail paraphernalia, including dirty ash trays. Turn on low, warm lights (which means, do not turn on the overhead ceiling lights). And be sure there is comfortable seating for everyone.

If you have records playing, turn the sound down low, too, and play music without singing, if possible, so that it will not compete with the conversation. Give everyone the drink he prefers, which may very well be a tall glass of water with ice cubes, and sit down yourself to enjoy your guests and your party in the moments that should be the most enjoyable ones of the entire evening.

Hiring Musicians Whether you hire a pianist for a small, intimate dinner or the leading society band to play at a large, formal occasion, you should make detailed arrangements beforehand with a representative of the group. You will have to sign a contract, complete with a cancellation penalty clause, guaranteeing to pay the union scale wage to each performer. You should discuss acoustics, space and electrical requirements, musicians' dress, the renting of a piano if you don't have one, and all other details well in advance of the date, so that on the actual day, when so many details will require your attention, there will be no crises concerning the music. Be sure to have extra extension cords on hand for the hooking up of their equipment.

The musicians, upon arrival, should be ushered in the front door. They should be shown to a room where there is a rack or a closet upon which to hang their coats and their clothes (if they will be changing). They should be shown to a bathroom they may use. Arrange to have them given refreshments during their "breaks" in the course of the party.

The host or hostess should talk to them soon after their arrival, to discuss last-minute arrangements about the type of musical selections to be played, any special song to be played at a particular moment, any rolls of the drums for toasts or special announcements, and so forth.

One usually pays musicians for a three-hour minimum; if you wish them to play past the minimum number of hours, warn them ahead of time. You can also request them to play longer when the time comes for the end of the music. If you have arranged with a band to play until 1 A.M., and there is a possibility you may wish them to continue until 2 A.M., tell the band leader this. He will come up to you fifteen minutes before one, to give you the option of paying for another hour beyond. If everything is talked out ahead of time, the party will go smoothly.

You do not have to tip the musicians. If they really did a superior job, write to the leader if the band and tell him so, and promise to recommend him to others.

Hiring an Artist If you invite a musical soloist or an actor to perform after dinner for your guests, you should provide a room for him or her in which to dress and stay until it is time to "go on" before the audience. Offer the artist something to eat or drink in the "dressing room," and make sure he is comfortable before you return to your party. If the artist is a personal friend, you should pay him regardless. Artists make their livelihoods performing, and asking one to perform free at your party is like asking a doctor friend to take care of your sick child for free. The only time it is proper to allow a friend to perform without payment is if the artist offers to sing at the wedding or the funeral of a member of your family—or something equally as important and personal.

When it is time for him to perform, the artist is introduced informally to the guests by the host or hostess. A few well-chosen words about the artist's past accomplishments will suffice.

If the artist is a personal friend, you might ask him to dine with you and your guests beforehand, but he will probably refuse. (It is difficult to perform well on a full stomach.) Whether or not he is a social friend, it is polite to ask him to join your friends *after* his performance, for conversation and refreshments. (Be sure you have discussed beforehand with him if there will by any encores, and if so, how many.)

After-dinner "Don'ts"

1. *Watching TV*

There are certain moments in history (very few) where there is a prearranged agreement among the guests to watch television at a certain hour. The President of the United States might be making a national announcement of great importance; the home-town team might be playing in the Rose Bowl; someone's godchild might be competing in the finals of the "Miss America Pageant." And, of course, there's always Election Night. On these unusual occasions, there is a reason for having the household sets turned on, but otherwise it is an unwanted intrusion at a party. Guests who wander off after dinner or during a cocktail party to watch their favorite weekly situation comedy or basketball game should be gently censured by the host or hostess, for the TV Addict Guest is in fact telling them that he finds them and their guests too boring a substitute for his favorite program.

2. *Making Everyone Dance*

The hyperthyroid hostess who rushes her guests into dancing the minute they leave the dinner table should take lessons in self-control. Not everyone is an aspiring Fred Astaire or Ginger Rogers.* The stereo music should be turned on softly. If some people start to dance after a while, then the mood

---

* However, one of the best parties I ever attended had two professional ballroom dancers come in after dinner. They wore Fred Astaire and Ginger Rogers masks and were dressed appropriately. They were such a surprise and handled themselves so well that before the evening was over they had the stuffiest group of non-dancers in America out on the "dance floor" doing the latest dances.

is right. It's probably going to be a "dancing evening." But a hostess should never force her guests into any actions against their will.

3. *Forcing People into Games*

Hosts who insist that everyone go swimming after dinner, or play in a Ping-Pong tournament, play poker, or whatever, are usually unable to attract desired guests to their home again. Have the Ping-Pong table ready for play, or the pool table, if you have one; suggest that anyone who wants to swim is welcome to. People will do what they really want to do. Many of them will just want to sit in your comfortable living room and talk. Let them do it.

Chapter 26

MENU INSPIRATION

There are so many great menus available to the public through cookbooks, magazines, newspapers, and TV shows that no hostess has the right to complain, "I don't know what to serve." Whether it's *Family Circle Magazine* talking about a budget dinner party or *Vogue* discussing the food served by a *principessa* in her Roman *palazzo,* there is a wealth of good menu ideas available to experiment with, to adapt, and to substitute, until we arrive at party menus that are both manageable and distinguished.

Dinner Menus

The White House releases the menus of its state dinners, and occasionally the chef's recipes, too. The most famous dinner given during the John F. Kennedy administration was in honor of the President of Pakistan in July of 1961 at George Washington's home, Mount Vernon. It was the first time that a historic shrine was used for a dinner. The food, provisions, everything, was brought from the White House to Mount Vernon; the guests were transported by boat down the Potomac; even electricity had to be imported for the event. A tent was put up on the lawn next to the house; mint juleps were served as President Washington did on the veranda of the house; strolling violinists entertained during dinner. The National Symphony Orchestra performed after dinner in a specially built acoustical shell on another part of the lawn. Yet, with all the pomp and splendor of that evening, there were only three courses served at dinner: avocado stuffed with crab meat; a chicken dish with white rice, accompanied by a salad; and fresh raspberries with Chantilly cream and crisp little cookies. A white wine was served with the first two courses, champagne with dessert, and liqueurs with demitasses after dinner.

The main factors to remember when organizing a menu for any party are:

1. Buy within your budget (you may have to forget the Mount Vernon dinner menu).

2. Serve only tried and true recipes—never experiment or try out new recipes at party time.
3. Serve fruits and vegetables that are in season; they are cheaper and taste much better.
4. Make *enough*. The worst thing that can happen, in many guests' opinion, is for the food and drinks to run out.
5. Keep it simple. Guests don't like to choose from too many dishes. They will overeat and regret it rather quickly. Also, for the host and hostess who are managing the logistics, it is far better to handle the timing and proper serving of their hot and cold dishes by keeping the number to a minimum.
6. Be imaginative in the presentation of the food. Sprinkle fresh herbs on dishes; serve your salad in an unusual bowl; try new things like serving hot soup in heat-resistant, long-stemmed crystal goblets; learn how to decorate your platters with radish flowers.

When I was Social Secretary at the embassy in Rome, I once managed to order an all-white dinner with a creamed soup, a main course of fish and boiled potatoes, and a fluffy white meringue and vanilla ice cream dessert. It was bland, boring, and very wrong.

When I read over some of my favorite White House menus served in the Kennedy days, I am struck by the balance of light and heavy dishes and by the fact that the dinners were not top-heavy at either end. The recipes can be found in any number of cookbooks, under their French names (French is the international language of cuisine). One can use the public library to research these dishes—there may be four recipes for any one dish, very similar, but some easier than others.

A few of my favorite menus, using part French and part English, from White House days are:

A White House state dinner menu of great elegance:

Chaud-froid de Truite Doria

Guinea Hen Santa Clara
Wild Rice
Asperges Sauce Mousseline

Mousse de Foie Gras en Gelée
Rubis au Porto

Bombe Glacée Rustique
Mignardises Assorties
Demitasses

A fish dinner served as a light Sunday night meal:

Cream of Tomato Carmen

Truite aux Amandes
Petits Pois à la Française
Pommes de Terre Persillées

Chiffon Rum Pie
Demitasses

Another light dinner:

Eggs Belle Hélène

Gigot d'Agneau aux Flageolets
Épinards aux Croutons

Salade Mimosa

Gâteau St.-Honoré
Demitasses

Cocktail Buffet Menu

Cocktail buffets are informal affairs and the menus are as varied as the hostesses. But one substantial hot dish should be served, which is kept warm on an electric hot tray or in a chafing dish with a burner beneath it. The hot dish could consist of anything from chicken Tetrazzini to Welsh rarebit, or from beef Stroganoff to crab meat au gratin. There is usually a platter of assorted cold meats offered (turkey, ham, roast beef, and so on) and a platter of different cheeses—cut into little pieces or served in chunks with cheese knives (an Edam, a wheel of Camembert or Brie, or a round of Fontina). There can be platters of hors d'oeuvres, like pieces of Bel Paese cheese speared on toothpicks with pieces of ripe pear. There is always a heaping platter or basketful of buttered rye or pumpernickel breads, as well as crackers, so that guests can make their own sandwiches.

A decorated platter of crudités (cold raw vegetables, cut into small pieces) is a good idea, with a dip in the center. A chafing dish of hot sausages wrapped in bacon, or of meat balls on toothpicks, is a perennial favorite.

Some hostesses can deftly use a cocktail buffet to give an ethnic food party—such as an all-Mexican or Greek or Chinese buffet. The cookbooks of those countries' specialties will tell you how to do it; so will a friendly chef from a good ethnic restaurant in your city. One should offer the guests the cocktails of that country, too, such as serving Margaritas with Mexican food.

Lunch Menus

I believe in serving the same food at lunchtime to mixed groups as to an all-women group. No one wants to eat too much at the noon meal. The following suggestions include summer and winter menus that are easy to prepare.

HOT-WEATHER MENUS FOR LUNCH

Melon and prosciutto (white wine preferred)

Cold salmon on lettuce with green mayonnaise
Buttered brown bread and cucumber sandwiches

Lemon sherbet with white crème de menthe
Demitasses

Platter of cold roast beef, tongue, and
corned beef, served with tray of
different mustards, horseradish,
etc. (red wine)

Cold rice salad; hot buttered popovers

Crème caramel (served with cookies)
Demitasses

Jellied Madrilène soup with lemon wedges
Hot buttered melba toast (red, white,
or rosé wine)

Chef's salad

Seedless white grapes in sour cream and brown sugar
Demitasses

Asparagus vinaigrette with buttered
rye toast (white wine)

Crab meat on bed of shredded lettuce
Waffle potatoes

Fresh fruit compote served in melon halves
Miniature cupcakes
Demitasses

Entertaining

COLD-WEATHER MENUS FOR LUNCH

Hot cheese soufflé (red or rosé wine preferred)

Spinach salad with bacon bits
Oil and vinegar dressing

Hot apple brown betty with cream
Demitasses

Seafood Newburg with toasted
buttered English muffins
(white wine)

Mixed greeen salad

Profiteroles au chocolat (puff
pastries filled with cream or
ice cream) and chocolate sauce
Demitasses

Creamed artichokes (red, white, or rosé wine)

Risotto alla Milanese

Hot butterscotch ice-cream cake
Demitasses

Consommé with sherry, with warm wheat
crackers (red wine)

Endive salad (with arugula and bibb)
Cannelloni

Apricot tart
Demitasses

Menu for an Easy Sunday Brunch

The menu for this most pleasant and informal buffet party should be light
and simple, one that makes it easy for the hostess-cook to entertain. When
the guests arrive, they find a large pitcher of bloody marys[1] awaiting them,
another larger pitcher of bullshots,[2] and, of course, a pitcher of spicy tomato

[1] Tomato juice with vodka, well spiced with seasoning, lemon juice, and
Worcestershire sauce, and served on the rocks.
[2] Bouillon with vodka, wedge of lemon, served on the rocks.

juice without vodka for the non-drinkers. The only food needed for this kind of party is:

Piping-hot quiche Lorraine (and plenty of it)

(Chilled dry white wine served)   A huge bowl of salad (such as spinach greens, fresh mushrooms, and chopped scallions)

Fresh fruit compote with chocolate lace cookies

Large coffees

The Least-expensive Menu Possible

You do not have to serve a lot of courses to impress people with your entertaining abilities. If you are on a tight budget, you can cut corners and still keep your dinner guests well fed, impressed, and happy.

For hors d'oeuvres, you can get by with one bowl of peanuts and one small platter of cut-up cheese. People who absolutely have to nibble with their before-dinner cocktail will find the nuts and cheese. As for the dinner menu, you can prepare a hearty casserole, a noodle or rice dish, and a large salad. You do not need rolls, bread, or even dessert. You can also dispense with candy and the serving of liqueurs after the meal. Buy your wine by the gallon, to economize, but be sure you know what the brand tastes like before you do.

When Disaster Strikes in Cooking

There isn't a seasoned party hostess alive who has not faced disasters in her entertaining. They can and do happen to everyone. The soufflé falls . . . the mold doesn't gel . . . the rolls are left in the oven too long and burn. When these things happen you should act fast, shift gears, substitute or omit, and then tell the guests what happened. Make it a part of a wonderful drama; your guests will laugh with you, not at you, and will love you for your emergency-coping.

I remember a busy working woman who took the afternoon off from work to put a very large roast beef into her oven for slow cooking while she went about all her party chores. Her guests were expected for an early dinner at 6:30. At 5:45 she hauled the roast from the oven to check on its final minutes. There had been a malfunction of the gas, and the oven had not turned on. The roast beef was raw.

After momentary panic, she made a quick call to her butcher's just as they were closing. Her child ran to the store with the uncooked roast beef, and returned with eight steaks. The guests were happy with the grilled steaks, amused by her story of the roast beef, and sympathetic with her over the fact that there would be no leftovers the next day. They also ate and enjoyed her special horseradish sauce for roast beef on their steaks!

How Many Courses Do You Serve?

An informal dinner usually consists of from three to five courses. The first can be a seafood dish or a cold or a hot soup. (Some people like to serve a seafood dish, then a light soup, and then the main course, although this is not necessary.) The main course may be meat, fish, or fowl. Salad may be served with the main course or it may be served afterward as a separate course with or without a variety of cheeses and crackers. Dessert is the last course, followed by demitasses served at the table or in another room, such as the den, the library, the porch, or the living room.

Special Needs of Guests

Guests on Diets   One of the great problems for a hostess is the guest who is on a diet; one of the great problems for a person on a diet is being a guest at dinner. People on diets should remember that no one else is truly interested in their heroic struggle. Dieting is not a topic for conversation at a party. It is probably the most boring subject there is.

If you are invited to a very small dinner party and you are on a severe medical or weight-loss diet, you should mention it to the hostess of your forthcoming dinner party at the same time that you accept her invitation. Be offhanded about it, but prepare her so that she will not be offended by your seeming lack of interest in her food. When you tell your hostess, she will immediately ask if she shouldn't have some special food prepared for you, which is your cue to say absolutely, positively not. Do not bring up the subject again, and certainly do not mention it to others the night of the party. If the dinner is large, you do not need to bring up the subject of your diet in advance with your hostess, because she will never notice. Diplomats, government officials, and business people who watch their weight and digestive systems are sometimes compelled to attend large luncheons and dinners almost every day. They learn how to take very small helpings, and to push the food around on their plates while talking. Everyone thinks they are eating, and no one has to listen to a conversation about "my agonizing diet."

Guests Who Have Allergies   If, for example, you are going to the expense and trouble of having Maine lobsters flown in for your dinner party, and your guest knows about it, it is up to the guest to tell you that he has an allergy problem and cannot eat shellfish. At the time the invitation is extended, he should say, "Why not give me a rain check? I would be unable to share in your great delicacy, and it would embarrass me greatly to have any substitute food planned for me." This gives the hostess the option of agreeing with him: "Yes, John, let's plan for dinner another night," or, "I'll heat up a frozen chicken pie for you. How would that be?" But if a guest does not know the menu in advance and one course turns out to be something he cannot eat, he should use the same technique as the dieter—take a small helping and discretely push it around.

Guests who must have kosher food or follow other religious laws governing their diets, or who have health problems, should inform the hostess well in advance. She may already be aware of it and not know quite how to cope with it. The guest should discuss it with her openly when she extends the invitation. Then the guest can either bring along something that can be heated quickly in its own container, or eat before coming, and still enjoy the party. He can also take a very small amount of food on his plate, and "push it around" so successfully the people around him will be unaware that he is not eating it.

Someone with a real dietary problem does not like to be deprived of the opportunity to attend a dinner party because of it. The compassionate hostess will see to it that he is taken care of, one way or another.

The Kinds of Wine to Serve

The subject of wines is fascinating, and one could very well turn the hobby of studying wines into a lifetime career.

In Victorian days no gentleman of fashion could possibly be ignorant of all the fine points of vintage and temperature, vintner and *endroit* of the wines at his table. He kept a proper wine cellar and tended each precious bottle on schedule. He knew enough not to permit his butler to wipe off a fine old dusty bottle, of, say, Château Mouton Rothschild of a superlative year and wrap it in a napkin to hide the details of its lineage from interested diners. His fine sedimented wines were kept on their sides at proper temperature and never put upright even before service. They could be decanted into beautiful clear glass decanters, slowly, after the cork had been eased—not yanked—out until the sediment was reached. Or they could be poured from a cradle or wine basket that held the bottle almost horizontal so that wine and sediment would not mix.

In those days, only families of great wealth could indulge in such pleasures. In our era, even couples of modest means are learning how to choose wines for special occasions, and how to enhance their food with the right kind of wine. The large American producers are primarily responsible for the wide selection of good wines now available at moderate prices.

There are five basic categories of wines, with variations within each category.

1. Appetizer Wines: Dry or sweet sherry, red or white Dubonnet, Lillet, Campari, and dry or sweet vermouth are examples of these. They are served chilled or "on the rocks" according to preference.

2. White Table Wines: These include chablis, Soave, Verdicchio, Pouilly-Fuissé. The best and most expensive chablis are from that area of France. California's "chablis" is usually a generic term applied to the mass-produced whites, which can be very pleasant. The better white wines from

America are now usually labeled by the grape variety—such as Chenin Blanc, Pinot Chardonnay, and Johannisberg Riesling.

These dry white table wines should be served chilled, but not so cold as to kill the aroma and flavor. Dry white wines are very popular as before- and after-dinner cocktails. They also complement and enhance the flavors of the lighter foods served during the meal—fruit, fish, chicken, veal, and the like.

3. Red Table Wines: Burgundy, bordeaux, and chianti are in this group of red wines. So are the "premium varietal" wines of America—such as Cabernet Sauvignon and Zinfandel.

These are served at cool room temperature (preferably not higher than 70° F), and are delicious with meat, game, or full-flavored cheese.

Rosé wines are served chilled, like white wine; they go well with most lightly flavored foods and are especially refreshing in the hot summer. They are not in the category of "great wines." The finest bordeaux, the best reds from the Burgundy area of France, and some red wines from the small, premium wineries of California are superior wines—usually expensive and served for special meals.

4. Dessert Wines: Port, sweet sauternes, and sweet sherry are typical of this classification of wine. Port is usually served at room temperature, but sauternes and sherry are served chilled. These wines are not as popular today as they were at dinner parties of twenty years ago.

5. Sparkling Wines: Champagne, of course, is the queen of this category, but sparkling burgundy, Italy's Asti spumante, and sparkling rosé are others. (The latter, like the dessert wines, are not as popular as they once were.) Champagne, if the budget will allow, is delightful when served through the entire meal. A wine like the Asti spumante is too sweeet for the main course and should be reserved for dessert or consumed by itself as an after-dinner drink.

Just as there are many kinds of wines, so there are many countries and regions producing them. American wines have come into their own in recent years, and we no longer need be apologetic about them. California wines are served proudly at state dinners at the White House, and cases of the very best are transported abroad with the President for use at his return dinner for the host head of state.

Excellent wines are of course still imported from France, Italy, and Germany, but now there are good ones also coming in from Yugoslavia, Hungary, Portugal, Spain, North Africa, Greece, and several South American countries. Russia is exporting a good champagne to us.

The Wine Cellar

Ideally, one should have a cool, dry place, such as a cellar where the temperature is 55 to 65° F, and where it is quiet (no throbbing washing machines and furnaces to disturb the rest of the wine). However, with apartment living and cellarless houses, such luxuries are often impossible. One can make do with what one has, even a closet shelf (but choose one near an inside wall and away from hot pipes). In a one-room apartment I had many years ago, I successfully turned the space beneath my sofa into my "wine cellar." Since the radiators were hardly ever turned on, even in the dead of winter, the wine was kept cool.

Wines that are corked should be laid on their sides, so that their corks don't dry out; the most efficient and safest way to store them is, of course, in a wine rack. There are many good ones on the market, made of wire, straw, plastic or wood, and holding twelve to sixteen bottles. Bottles with screw caps can be stored standing upright on a pantry shelf where it is dark and cool.

If you enjoy wine you may find it convenient to keep a little book in your wine cellar, in which you can record the following information under each of the five wine categories:

1. The name of the wine and the winery that made and bottled it.
2. The date each bottle was purchased.
3. The price of the wine and how many bottles were purchased.
4. The date each one is removed and consumed.
5. Your own and your guests' opinion of it.

Wineglasses

A thin, clear, sparkling glass is the major stipulation for a good wineglass. The rim should be smaller than the base of the bowl, so that the bouquet of the wine will waft upward toward one's appreciative nose. Today it is not necessary to buy a different type of glass for each wine. The all-purpose ten-ounce tulip-shaped wineglass or bowl-shaped glass is appropriate for red or white wines, sherry, or even champagne. The wineglass should be filled about halfway, unless you are serving an apéritif such as sherry, Dubonnet,

An all-purpose wine-
glass.

Another style of all-
purpose wineglass.

The correct placement of wineglasses at a formal dinner at which will be served (right to left): consommé (sherry); fish (white wine); meat entree (red wine); and dessert (champagne). The largest glass, of course, is for water.

or vermouth, in which case you would fill it one-third full only. You enjoy the aroma best if you can swirl a good wine around the inside of the glass. If the glass is more than half full, you're liable to spill it.

As for the champagne glass, the hollow-stemmed ones so familiar in the forties and fifties are no longer so popular today, for several reasons. First of all, you automatically warm the champagne with your fingers while holding the stem of the glass, which is undesirable, since champagne is better *very cold*. Additionally, these glasses are difficult to clean properly. If you like to have a special champagne glass, the best kind is a slim, tulip-shaped one, holding seven ounces. You should pour about four ounces of champagne into it each time.

The placement of wineglasses for a less formal dinner: the white-wine glass will be used only for the first course (soup). The middle, red-wine, glass will be used during the remaining courses. Glasses may also be placed on a diagonal, starting with water glass, leading to lower right.

A tulip-shaped champagne glass—the perfect champagne glass.

If you are fortunate enough to have a matching set of goblets, you probably have a service containing water, red wine, white wine, cordial (used for serving sherry), and saucer champagne glasses. Do use these whenever you have the occasion, for the full service adds a special elegance to any table. At a formal dinner where you use all these glasses, place them in a cluster at each table setting, above the knife. For less formal dinners, three glasses are sufficient. I prefer to line them up, more or less straight, beginning with the water glass to the left, the red wine in the middle, and the white wine to the right. This is primarily to help service. A maid or a hired butler will know to pour the white wine, the first wine, into the outside glass.

The Wine Service

The Temperature to Serve Wines   Most red wines are best served at "cool room temperature." It is usually helpful to uncork the bottle and allow the wine to "breathe" for at least half an hour before dinner. This tends to "mellow" the taste of the wine quickly and allows any unpleasant aromas to dissipate. If the bottle of red wine that comes to the table is too cool, the wine connoisseur guest can warm its contents by holding the wineglass by its bowl. The "room temperature" for wines is assumed to be about 65 degrees, but remember that most American homes in winter are much warmer than that.

Most white table wines and the rosés should be chilled in the coldest part of the refrigerator two hours or more before they are served. The finer the white table wine, the less it needs chilling. Champagne should be stored on the lower shelves of the refrigerator. Even the best champagnes should be served very cold. Never freeze wines (but how many of us can deny we have forgotten to chill a wine for guests and have put the bottle in the freezer for thirty minutes to cool its temperature effectively?). Today the ice bucket for wines and champagne is seen mostly in restaurants, but the new "wine cooler coasters" are practical for home use as they keep a bottle at a cooler temperature than it could be otherwise.

The appetizer wines are served chilled, according to preference; dessert wines may or may not be chilled also. After-dinner drinks such as brandy, grand marnier, and armagnac should be served at regular room temperature, and are often further warmed by cupping the bowl of the glass in the palm of the hand. Some people like a sweet liqueur, such as white or green crème de menthe, served over cracked ice, to make it even more refreshing.

Partly used bottles of red wine should be recorked and kept in a cool place, rather than in the refrigerator. They will probably start to turn sour within three days. A partly used bottle of well-made white wine, well stoppered with a cork, might be pleasantly drinkable even after two or three days in the refrigerator.

Opening a Bottle of Wine Some wines come with screw caps, but the best wines do not. Every household needs a good corkscrew, which does not necessarily mean an expensive one. The kind I like best has lever arms that project outward from both sides of the bottle when the long spike of the cork extractor (called the "worm") is firmly engaged in the center area of the cork. One presses the two arms down, and out comes the cork, gently and easily.

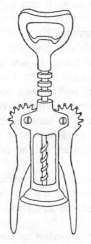

An easy-to-use corkscrew.

The red wine bottle should be opened at least a half hour before dinner. It's also easier to open the white wine bottle at this time, then recork and put it back in the refrigerator to wait for dinner. When the cork is removed, pour a very little of the wine out of the bottle into the kitchen sink, to remove any cork bits. Also wipe off the grime and dust around the neck of the bottle with a clean cloth, or a slightly damp paper towel. The host or hostess should now sip the wine to make sure it has not turned to vinegar. Some corks are very tough to deal with, and it is far better to do battle with bad corks *before* the guests arrive. (How many of us have had to strain the wine into a decanter to remove bits of cork when the cork popped *into* the bottle instead of out of it?)

Opening a Bottle of Champagne It is best to practice opening a few bottles of champagne in the kitchen before you try it in front of your guests; and when you do perform the operation in front of your happy, anticipating guests, aim carefully away from all those faces, as well as from the paintings on the wall, mirrors, chandelier, wall sconces, and any objet d'art or other fragile items.

First untwist the little loop of wire on the side of the cork and slip it off. Then remove the metal disk over the cork. Now, holding the bottom of the bottle against you, and pointing the mouth of the bottle into safe territory, *slowly turn* the cork and ease it up with your thumbs, or else give it a quick twist of your fingers. After you become adept at it, you will not even need to hold a napkin around the neck to catch spillage.

One bottle of champagne serves about four people for the dessert course.

Serving the Wine Butlers, waitresses, and waiters supplied by professional catering services are trained in the serving of wine. When there is a maid in the home, she should be trained to serve it and to keep the guests' glasses half filled. Until the maid is trained, it is best to leave the wine pouring to the host (or to the hostess, if she is a woman living alone).

When guests arrive at the table, they should find the wine bottles on coasters or the decanters of wine already in place. If you are having a fish course followed by a meat course, and if you are serving both a white and a red wine to accompany them, the white wine only should be in place on the table at the beginning of the meal. The opened bottles of red wine are on a serving table or sideboard nearby for the host to serve later. When the first course is finished, the host takes the white wine bottles or decanters out to the kitchen, and then places the red wine bottles on the table, one at each end for six or more guests.

If you are serving two wines you must have two separate wineglasses for each guest. It is not proper to pour red wine into a glass that was used for white wine, even if the guest has consumed the last drop of the previous wine.

Never bring a half-gallon or gallon bottle of wine to the table. (Decant them into smaller containers.) If you have an excellent wine, don't brag about it; let your guests discover it. It's a nice gesture for a guest to say, "What a great wine! May I see the label?" This is a great compliment to the host, and he immediately passes the bottle down to the guest for scrutiny of the label. However, the guest had better know what he is doing, for it would be embarrassing for both should the guest ask to see the label only to discover it's the least expensive wine available at the liquor store! (If wine is in a decanter, of course, one never asks to see the label, for the bottle is probably in the trash by then.)

If you are uncertain how much wine to buy for a dinner party, prepare to serve two bottles for four or six guests, but have a third standing by, ready to be opened, if necessary. Open three bottles for eight or ten guests; have a fourth in reserve. For four or six guests, if you are serving two wines, open one white and one red. Open two whites and two reds for eight or ten guests; have one of each in reserve.

Wine is cheaper to buy by the case, and it is best to have plenty on hand. More people, particularly women, are drinking wine these days as a before- and after-dinner drink, and I recently witnessed a group of guests go through their host's entire supply of dry white wine at the cocktail hour, leaving him embarrassed, with nothing to serve for his fish course.

When the guests are seated at dinner, the host should rise and walk around the table, serving the woman honored guest on his right first, and serving everyone else around the table, counterclockwise. He should have extra opened bottles in reserve on the sideboard to replenish his supply when necessary. Once he has passed around the table serving each guest once, he does not have to worry about refilling the wineglass at the other end of the table. He refills only those glasses at his end, and his wife or the male guest of honor sitting at her right will do the honors at their end. The host must keep an eye on both ends of the table, however, to substitute a new bottle when needed, or to slip out to the kitchen if the decanter needs refilling.

A woman who lives alone should pour the wine for her guests exactly as a male host would do, including serving each and every guest the first time around. She should serve her most important woman guest first, and then go around the table, counterclockwise. If she is recently widowed or divorced and is accustomed to having a man take charge of this part of the service, she should learn to handle it gracefully herself, rather than asking a different male guest to take over each time. I remember talking to a very well known, elegant older woman, now a widow with no help, but still giving dinner parties in her indefatigable way. "My dear," she said in a relieved tone, "you have no idea how nice it is to do it myself, *right*." Her voice was almost triumphant. "George was a good husband and we had a wonderful life, but as for the butler and maid I used to have in the kitchen, I spent my entire time telling them what they did wrong after a dinner party. Now I do it all myself, perfectly, you understand, and I go into the kitchen telling myself that 'I did it again. The dinner was perfect, and I'm wonderful.'"

The wineglasses are left on the table throughout the meal. They are not removed at any point in the service, a custom for which we should all be grateful, because carrying the glasses out to the kitchen between courses could be very risky.

Wine Spillage In order to avoid spilling drops, learn to turn the neck of the bottle gently before lifting the mouth away from the glass—in a circular motion. The mouth of the bottle should also be wiped clean after serving each glass of wine, if you are dripping as you pour. If, however, you have a lovely set of linens and someone knocks over a glass or spills wine accidentally, here is what you should do at once. (Your guests will understand your taking quick action and interrupting the dinner party for a quick moment in order to save your pretty cloth or the wood finish on your table.)

If there is no protective pad underneath the cloth, you must act quickly to save the finish of the table top. Slide a dish towel beneath the part of the cloth covered by wine, mop the moisture from the table top, then slide another dry towel (or paper towels) under the cloth, beneath the stained part only, to prevent further moisture from seeping through onto the table. Dab at the top of the cloth, too, with a clean wet cloth, to remove some of the red wine stain. Finally, take a salt shaker and pour salt heavily over the entire affected area. Rub the salt into the wine stain with your fingers and then either forget it, or cover it with a clean white napkin so it will not further embarrass the wine-spilling guest. (If white wine has been spilled, you do not have to go through the salt routine.) If you act swiftly, it will all be over in two minutes. The stain will come out of your linens (most fabrics, that is) when they are washed, and your table top will be saved. When the person who spilled the wine realizes everything will be all right, with no permanent damage, he will feel better. (When the guests leave for the evening, immediately soak the wine-stained linens in cold water overnight.) Some people prefer to pour soda water on red wine spots the minute they occur, but this can be messy when the linens are on the table and a party is in progress.

Chapter 27

SETTING YOUR TABLE

The Design Revolution

One of the biggest changes in table design is the linen revolution. Now anything goes, from patterned tablecloths to place mats printed in delicate florals or bizarre geometrics. Big, bold striped napkins in peach, lime, and yellow look perfectly at home on a cloth of delicate peach, lime, and yellow flowers. Hostesses are using fashion-designer printed sheets as tablecloths, combining them with co-ordinating solid-color napkins. Our grandmothers would have fainted at all this boldness in a field that has always been conservative, restricted, and bound by fast rules, but the setting of the table for guests is more than a perfunctory logistical detail. A pretty setting helps make the food look better and taste better. It makes the guests feel that an effort has been made on their behalf. It provides the host and hostess with an unlimited opportunity to express themselves creatively.

This does not mean that one must buy new decorative elements for the table each time there's a party. But it does require a fresh survey each time of the decorative elements already existing in your home. The creation of a new table setting means a shifting, a mixing, a matching of one's possessions. The marvelous mauve oblong low bowl in which you serve spaghetti alle vongole for big parties can act as a table centerpiece for another party—after you have filled it with little African violet plants. There may be some Victorian monstrosity you received twenty years ago as a wedding present that would make a sensational center focus for your dinner table. Some nights you may want to gather up all the plants blooming on your window sills and turn your table into a garden of greenery.

Table-setting design should never lose sight of its functional purpose. Using beautifully decorated fresh salad in a huge bowl as a centerpiece is a marvelous idea. But at a certain moment you are going to remove it in order to add dressing and serve it. So be prepared to substitute a bowl of fresh fruit, or a platter of cheeses and crackers attractively arranged, or a decorated cake, or a platter of chocolates in the table center during the salad course. One smart hostess whose major problem is a shortage of space in her one-room apartment always uses a decorative salad bowl as her centerpiece, which is whisked away after serving salad and cheese. Then she puts a steaming covered tureen in the center. The porcelain tureen contains espresso coffee, which she ladles into small mugs as though it were soup. She serves no dessert—only a plateful of delicious homemade cookies with the espresso coffee—and she passes a plate of lemon peel and cinnamon sticks for those who wish to use them in their coffee.

The taboos of table settings are relatively few, for informal entertaining. Candlesticks on the luncheon table do not belong, however. Candlesticks are for nighttime, when they serve a purpose. Paper napkins are an effrontery to a dinner served indoors; there are many attractive and inexpensive drip-dry napkins on the market to match table mats of stunning designs. Plastic flowers are out. Silk or beaded flowers or flowers made of porcelain are expensive, but they last forever, so they are a good investment. One can always buy a few fresh ones from the florist and then mix them into the arrangement of silk flowers, or buy fresh green leaves to mix in with porcelain flowers.

If there is one thing that is certain, it is that a bunch of florist-arranged flowers plunked down in the center of the table, flanked by four candlesticks, has become a boring and passé idea. Table decorations are now very personal statements of the host or hostess. One of the prettiest tables I ever saw was a springtime Sunday lunch one, when we all still felt chilled from winter. There was a bright yellow cloth, and in the center the hostess had placed a galaxy of silver mugs (her five children's christening mugs). Each had been polished to a beautiful high gloss, and each contained a saucy bouquet of dandelions the children had just picked. (The hostess had left the "table setting design" to her eldest daughter, then twelve.)

Hostesses are not only daring to mix different china patterns for each course on the menu, but are also mixing different patterns of plates within one course. If you collect beautiful plates, why not? And if you collect pewter, antique banks, old glass, porcelain birds, or early American wooden decoys, why not use them to decorate your table? Such a personalized table delights everyone fortunate enough to behold it, and that includes the host and hostess.

Hostesses are successfully using mother-of-pearl mats, or mats made of cork, wood, porcelain tiles, or sea shells. Polka-dot napkins are being used with plaid tablecloths. And why not, as long as the colors of the pattern-on-pattern theme are compatible. Some people are so proud of their table tops they like a bare table look. They place protectors under the plates, but the only linens visible are giant napkins. And why not? For others, the exact opposite—cloth-upon-cloth is their favorite way of entertaining. One well-known hostess at Christmas uses circular red velvet cloths to the floor for five little round tables in her dining room. Each is topped by a square crisp white embroidered tea cloth. Another hostess gives every spring a "pink and yellow" luncheon for her women friends, to thank them for working so hard on her charity benefit. She puts a yellow dotted-swiss-like cloth on her table, and over it places a smaller one of pale pink organdy. The napkins are yellow dotted-swiss. There are masses of pink iris and daffodils everywhere, in every type of white porcelain container. The candy mints in the little crystal-footed dishes are pink and yellow, too.

Praising Your Hosts

A hostess who has gone to a lot of trouble to make her table look beautiful, and to serve her guests great food, deserves some accolades. It is not rude, for example, to exclaim over a beautiful plate, to pick it up and turn it over to see the markings. This compliments the hostess. (Don't do it with a plate that is plastic, however!) If the guests know who did the cooking, who did the table setting, or even who grew the vegetables being served, it is a nice gesture for a guest to raise his wineglass in a toast to host and hostess, enumerating the delightful elements of the table, the food, and the whole party. Entertaining is a lot of work. One should always send a thank-you note after having lunch or dinner in someone's home, but it's nice to turn everyone's attention to it during the meal, too.

And whether your host and hostess have twelve guests to dinner, or just you, it's still a special meal.

The Logistics of Table Settings

Every table, no matter how informal, should be laid with care and attention to detail. The flatware is placed one inch or so from the edge of the table at place settings that are equidistant from one another on a table. The napkin may be placed on the place plate, unless the first course is in place, in which case it is to the left of the forks—but it should not obscure them, nor should the silver be obscured by the plate.

The table is set with whatever silver will be needed for the meal. Traditionally, that needed first is placed farthest right and left of the plate. The forks are usually two, for meat and salad; occasionally one more for the appetizer, but never more than three beside the plate at once. The dessert fork, when part of the setting, is placed above the plate. The salad fork is placed inside the meat fork, unless the salad is served as a first course, in which case it is the first fork in the setting. The knives are usually limited to two—one for the appetizer, if any, and one for the meat. If salad is to be served with cheese, a salad knife is needed. Spoons for soup are on the table, to the right of the knives.

Butter plates and knives are used with the butter knife placed in a variety of ways—across the top of the plate, blade toward the user; across the top of the plate, tip toward the center of the plate; or occasionally parallel to the knives, blade to the left. Butter plates are disappearing from the scene today,

FIRST COURSE: APPETIZER. *The appetizer is usually in place when the guest is seated. If not, the dinner napkin is on the place plate instead of to the left of the forks as shown. The seafood fork is shown in one of the three accepted ways of placing it. Ash trays are optional, since many hostesses do not offer cigarettes now. The butter plate is used less and less, and is optional. The salt and pepper are to the side so the set may be shared by the neighbor on the right.*

ANOTHER KIND OF FIRST COURSE: SOUP. *The soup may be served in either the traditional flat soup plate or in a creamed soup cup. If another appetizer is served, soup may be omitted. There are usually three or four courses served at an informal dinner.*

SECOND COURSE: ENTREE. *The table at the beginning of the entree course.*

THIRD COURSE: SALAD. *The knife is optional, depending on whether or not cheese will be served with the salad. (Some people like a knife, however, to use in cutting overly large lettuce leaves.)*

FOURTH COURSE: DESSERT. *If you have a sufficient number of waiters, you may prefer not to have the dessert silver in place during the meal as we have shown at left, but instead have the waiter bring in each dessert plate with the silver balanced on it, as shown at right. The guest then places the silver to the left and right of the plate.*

however. If you wish to have butter or margarine on the table, to pass around family-style, you should still make an effort to make it look pretty. Place the butter in a quarter slice on a pretty plate with a butter knife. As for the round tubs of soft margarine, there are pretty earthenware and porcelain, even silver, containers for sale that cover the whole plastic margarine container, and they're very decorative on the table.

If you want to be formal, you should use a salad plate. If you do not have a maid, and are trying to keep things smooth and easy, then dispense with the salad plate—provided you have not served as a main course something very runny or gooey. For example, if you serve a chicken-in-white-wine casserole and its sauce is very liquid, you should serve rice to soak up the runny sauce. Then the guests will be able to add salad to their dinner plates without having it become soggy.

The majority of food-spilling mishaps occur because the hostess has not provided dinner plates large enough. If everything is to go on one plate—meat, vegetable, salad, and roll—the plate should be twelve inches in diameter. Otherwise, give your guests a separate smaller plate for their salad and bread or roll.

Salts and peppers on an informal table may be in a wide variety of materials from the wooden salt and pepper grinders of the gourmets to cut crystal or smooth glass, porcelain, earthenware, stainless-steel, or vermeil sets. At a large table a salt and pepper for every two guests is appropriate. Little open dishes may be used with spoons. It is also well to remember that any salt cel-

FINGER BOWL AND DEMITASSE: *If there are finger bowls (a vanishing custom) the dessert service is placed before the guest this way: finger bowl on doily and/or small plate, flanked by dessert fork and spoon on dessert plate. Below: Guest rearranges dessert service like this: doily and finger bowl (including small plate, if any) upper left, fork left and spoon right of dessert plate, awaiting service of dessert. If demitasse coffee is to be served at the table, the cup and saucer are placed to the right of the dessert plate. The coffee may be poured in the kitchen or by the hostess at the table and passed, but only after the meal is finished.*

lar with a silver top must have the top removed and the threading washed completely free of salt after each use or the threading will corrode and the diner will get much more salt than he bargains for.

No one should smoke until the dessert course is finished. Individual ash trays are best, but one larger one for every two people is acceptable also. Hostesses do not often provide cigarettes for their guests these days, not only because no one encourages smoking any more, but also because smokers usually have their own brands and bring them with them at all times, including to the table. For people who do smoke there should be ash trays and matches; or if the hostess wishes to, there can be two cigarettes on the ash tray in front of each smoker's place, or a group of cigarettes in a nearby urn.

On an informal table the other appointments are geared to the size of the table, the amount of service available (which may be none at all), and the number to be seated. At a small round table, for example, a centerpiece may prove impractical if meat and vegetables are to be served at table. Perhaps all the table can conveniently hold at the center, in addition to the food, is the candlesticks or a single candelabrum. Candles may be in any color, but *white is always right.* Candles should be above eye level to avoid glare in guests' eyes. Candles are never placed on a lunch table, and if they are placed on a dinner table, they must be lit. (Candles on sideboards do not have to be lit, but it is prettier if they are at nighttime.)

Menu Cards

Menu cards in the past were used only by hostesses who gave sumptuous dinners, complete with liveried footmen and caviar in unlimited amounts. Now that most of us cook our own food we should be even prouder of what we serve, and menu cards are a lovely way of recording the event.

If you make menu cards for your special dinner parties, make one for each guest, or for every other guest. You can order menu cards at any stationer; if you have an engraved die of your stationery monogram, you can have it stamped at the top of the card, as well as on matching place cards. The menu card is placed on the table between two place settings or in a special holder at the top center of the place setting.

You can also make your own menu cards by cutting them out of any heavy white or cream paper. Approximately 4½″×6½″ is a good size.

Place the date at the upper right; put "Dinner" or "Lunch" in the upper center.

You can put your menu entirely in English, but certain things sound better in French. Many accomplished hostesses write their menu half in English, half in French, or in Italian if an Italian dish like pasta is being featured— such as spaghetti alle vongole (spaghetti with a sauce of small white clams). I have put the menus in this book in both French and English, as I did in my embassy and White House years. Hostesses may do as they prefer. Many good gourmet cooks who use the classic French cookbooks quite logically give the French names to their dishes. Leave a bit of space between courses, so that your guest will know how the meal is being served. Write or print the menus, in black ink, or type them. If your party celebrates an anniversary or birthday or some special occasion, indicate that on the top of the menu card.

LyB

Dinner

May 21, 1978

Inglenook
Pinot
Chardonnay

Salmon Mousse

———

Poulet Chasseur
Asparagus au Beurre
Potatoes Rissolé

Château
Margaux
1968

———

Gâteau Robert

———

Demitasses

A menu card shows what will be served at the dinner, including wines, and gives the date of the party, which sometimes has significance.

A friend who has an immense family kitchen, decorated in the French provincial style, became a first-class cook during the years she worked in France. She often entertains with a Sunday night supper in her kitchen. She covers the big table with a red gingham cloth, and next to the table is a student's blackboard, with the menu always written in French with chalk. It is an added touch that draws attention to her good food and wines, as well as giving the atmosphere of a French bistro to her kitchen. Dining in her home is always a special occasion.

Gourmet cooking has become big business in America. If you have labored long and hard on your own dinner or lunch party, you still have to remember the presentation of that food, the look of your table. The "little touches" are really very important.

Chapter 28

COCKTAIL PARTIES

Cocktail parties are on the wane in many large cities. First, people who have invited you to dinner do not consider your invitation to a cocktail party a realistic "pay-back." Second, most people do not have the inclination or the energy to go somewhere after a hard day's work and stand up. Many people who hate large cocktail parties enjoy an invitation "to come by for a drink," with just a handful of guests, and everyone seated and relaxed.

If you want to have a large group at your cocktail party, perhaps a hundred guests, invite one hundred and fifty. At large gatherings, usually only two thirds of those invited actually show up. Have your invitations printed or purchase the attractive ones available in the stores and fill in name, address, and date and time information. If you are giving the party in honor of someone, put that person's name on the invitation. Most people today use "Regrets Only" with a telephone number beside the phrase, signifying that if someone *is* coming, he does not have to respond. Nonetheless, most people ignore R.S.V.P.s on cocktail invitations in any case.

Send out your invitations two to three weeks in advance. It is also a good idea for a party this large to notify your local police precinct so they will be able to help with the traffic. When you make up your guest list, put people's telephone numbers after their names. It takes little extra effort on your part then, but it means that if you have to cancel the party for any reason, friends can easily help in notifying the guests of the cancellations.

Cocktail parties are usually held between the hours of 5 and 8 P.M.; guests are invited for a period of either an hour and a half or two full hours. Usually no one arrives during the first twenty minutes or so, unless a schedule must be adhered to because the party is held before a special benefit dinner or theater party.

Party Logistics

A large cocktail party at home inevitably means some damage to your furnishings. If you have a prized object, put it away. Clear all the surfaces of small bric-a-brac. Open up as much space as you can in the rooms that will be used by pushing back the furniture against the walls and removing small tripper-uppers like footstools and cigarette tables. If you have a table with an unattached large glass top, remove the entire table, for someone will hit it and knock it off its base (I have seen this happen three times, twice resulting in broken objects only, once resulting in a badly cut leg of a guest).

You no longer have to furnish cigarettes for your guests (they are supposed to bring their own), but you should put pocket matches around and large cheap ash trays in quantity, especially on table tops and large areas like the top of a piano. Someone—a waitress or one of your children—should be given "the ash tray detail," with the responsibility for regularly emptying those ash trays of their unattractive mixtures of cigarette butts, discarded paper cocktail napkins, toothpicks, and half-eaten hors d'oeuvres.

Children (unless they are big enough to help) and pets should be sent elsewhere for the duration of your cocktail party.

The strategic placement of the bar (or bars) is very important to the success of any cocktail party. People hate to fight to get a drink, and they detest having to stand in a long line trying to approach the source of liquor. Organize your traffic carefully. If the party is large, plan a bar in the dining room, one in the den, perhaps one in the living room. If the physical presence of these bars would overcrowd a tight space, don't have bars. Have all drinks mixed in the kitchen and have them passed—an assortment—on trays. Cocktails are always served on bare trays. Be sure every tray has several nonalcoholic drinks included in the assortment. Passing drinks frees up the space; it also means more dirty glasses, because every time a guest takes another drink, he puts his old one on the tray, and it must be washed. At a large party, it is almost impossible for a waiter to refill a guest's same glass; at a small party, it is not only feasible but advisable.

If your party is big and you live in an apartment, you should rent an adequate number of coat racks and leave them in the hall outside your door. If the elevator lobby on your floor is too small for coat racks, put them up in the main-floor lobby (with the superintendent's permission, of course) and have someone equipped with a guest list checking everyone's possessions and watching over them carefully during every second of the party. This is not a job for a child, particularly when fur coats are involved.

If the party is in your own house, you can, of course, assign two bedrooms, one for the men's and one for the women's coats. If it is raining, be sure to have large umbrella stands in the apartment hallway or in a protected part of your house (such as on the front porch or in the garage). If it is storming hard, put hangers on the shower curtain railings in the bathrooms, so the coats can drip happily away into the bathtubs.

Many people use plastic glasses for cocktail parties in their own home. I do not. I think it is tacky. Rent glasses for the occasion (the rental is inexpensive). If you frequently give this kind of party, buy a large quantity of glasses at a sale, as it will save you money in the long run. (Plastic glasses are for parties out of doors—poolside, picnics, on boats, at football games, and so on.)

The two kinds of bar glasses useful to have are the highball (right) and old-fashioned. The highball glass is used for scotch or Bourbon and water, vodka and tonic, beer, soft drinks, etc. The old-fashioned is used for apéritifs, with or without ice, martinis or manhattans on the rocks, wine served as a cocktail, and scotch or Bourbon on the rocks. The all-purpose wineglass (page 319) may also appropriately be used for apéritifs or wine at cocktail parties.

The host and hostess should stay near the front door in order to greet each guest. Let the first guest arrive before you take your own drink. Also instruct your help (and this particularly applies to eager children acting as waiters) not to pass hors d'oeuvres to a guest before he even has a drink in his hand.

When a drink is handed to a guest, be sure a paper cocktail napkin is given at the same time. (Alas, the days of the lovely embroidered linen cocktail napkins are gone, except for very small parties.) Also, be sure that whoever passes an hors d'oeuvre tray containing something even slightly messy gives a separate cocktail napkin to the guest who partakes from his tray. Guests who help themselves to hors d'oeuvres on toothpicks should *not* put back the toothpick on the platter. It is unappetizing to the other guests being served the hors d'oeuvres. Used toothpicks should be deposited in an ash tray or a wastebasket. (If you can find neither, put them in your pocket or handbag.)

The Bartender

If a couple are having a cocktail party with no more than twenty-five guests, they can handle it themselves, working in tandem to make the drinks, to pass the hors d'oeuvres, and to show the guests where to put their coats. However, neither will really enjoy the party or have time to talk to their guests; hiring a bartender can ease this situation. One bartender can handle the drinks for a party attended by fewer than thirty guests; more guests than that require two. A hundred guests at the party at any one time require three bartenders and two waitresses.

Bartenders should wear black jackets, trousers, and tie in winter, and white jackets in summer. (The waitress wears black in winter, a pastel uniform in summer, always with a little white apron.) In many summer resorts college men earn extra money by bartending. They are properly dressed if they wear a black tie with a white shirt (the sleeves are usually rolled up) and clean pants that are not in the jeans family. (Don't expect anything formal on their feet; you should feel lucky they are wearing shoes at all.)

The professional bartender will want to discuss the menu of drinks, the hors d'oeuvres, and the extra help needed well in advance of the event. He can usually supply all the extra help needed, for serving and making hors d'oeuvres, from his own coterie of colleagues, or he will work with the ones you wish to retain and whom you like from past experience. Of course, if you are fortunate enough to live in a college town, you are able to obtain excellent bartenders, male or female, who are college students, usually at very reasonable prices. In fact, resourceful hosts in large cities like New York can locate good university bartenders, too.

The bartender will be responsible for bringing extra glasses and for the ice, if you tell him in advance. When he arrives at your home, you should show him the location of all your glasses, serving trays, water pitchers, towels, paper cocktail napkins (order at least three of the latter per guest), lemons and limes, jars of olives, onions, cherries, and of course, the liquor. Let him set up the bar where you want it to go. Be sure you have several towels for him, bottle openers, a corkscrew, a bar knife, and a large receptacle, such as a garbage can, for him to stow his bags of ice. (Otherwise, the ice cubes will melt through the paper onto your floors.)

The Cocktail Menu

In determining how much to purchase, figure on about three drinks per guest. Most liquor stores will take back unopened bottles, so the safe thing is to order more liquor than you think you could possibly use.

There are so many new cocktails continuously being invented by America's bartenders that one would have to become a barfly to be truly au courant on the subject, and no one should aspire to that. There are many glamorous-sounding concoctions, too—cocktails like pink lady, Jamaica swizzle, brandy smash, silver fizz, and the like—but they are not often made in people's homes.

It can be confusing when organizing a cocktail party to know just what one has to serve. If you are going to give a large cocktail party (over fifty guests), it is far better to limit the types of drinks so that you and your bartenders can handle the logistics smoothly.

One should have on hand for the party:

1. Lemons and limes, and lemon peel should be precut.
2. A supply of soft drinks and low-calorie soft drinks; a pitcher of either tomato juice or orange juice.
3. Plenty of chilled white wine in the refrigerator to serve people who are watching their weight and their alcoholic consumption—but also for the

younger generation, who prefer wine. If there are many of this age group coming, have beer on hand, also.

4. Soda water (and tonic water in warm weather) and, of course, a large pitcher of plain water for those who do not want carbonated water in their drinks.
5. Vodka or gin and dry vermouth for martinis. Martinis can be mixed a day or two ahead of the party, and stored in a covered jar in the refrigerator, without ice cubes, of course. Some people put their mixed martinis right back into the vodka or gin bottle, being sure to mark on the label "Already mixed." This advance preparation means one less thing to do on party night.
6. According to the preference in your region, Bourbon or scotch, to serve either "on the rocks" or with ice and water.

For festive occasions, such as Christmastime, it's nice to have a bowl of eggnog for your guests, or if you're having a special party, such as a "Kentucky Derby on TV" party, you can serve mint juleps. They will taste good to your guests even if you don't have the sterling stirrup cups that were the tradition in the South. But whether you have made mint juleps, planter's punch, bloody marys, eggnog, or a batch of daiquiris as a special treat, be sure to have something else on hand for those who do not like your special concoction.

National statistics show that vodka is drunk by more Americans than anything else. Scotch is the number one drink for Easterners, Bourbon for Southerners. You should serve at your party what is popular locally. If you are new to a region and giving your first party, consult the catering services or your hired bartender.

Food for Cocktail Parties Every host and hostess must find their own way to make the service of the cocktail party work best. Hors d'oeuvres may be passed on trays, or guests may go when they feel like it to cocktail food concentrated in one area, like the dining room table. Little bowls or plates of food might also be placed in each room of the home used for the party, within easy reach of guests who like to nibble. Nibbling food includes popcorn, salted nuts, roasted soybeans, cheese straws, and pretzel sticks (but not your children's "junk food"). A large platter containing a variety of cheeses, several cheese knives, and an assortment of crackers or small breads is welcome in each room used for the party. A platter of crudités, with a dip in the center and also a little bowl of seasoned salt to dip into, is very welcome in each room used by party guests. Crudités (raw, fresh vegetables cut into bite-sized pieces) are very important in today's entertaining, particularly for dieters and nutrition-conscious people. Among the various raw vegetables that are adaptable for this (and they can be arranged in stunning patterns on a large platter) are carrots, asparagus stalks, mushrooms, cauliflower florets, broccoli, cherry tomatoes, string beans (slightly parboiled), zucchini, scallions, cucumber, and green pepper strips, with the seeds removed, of course.

Hot hors d'oeuvres can be left on heated trays in the dining room, and I have seen many wise hostesses passing around the hors d'oeuvres right on the hot tray (they have, of course, removed the electric cord before passing the tray). Some of the most popular ones are bits of rare steak on toothpicks, mushrooms stuffed with sausage, water chestnuts or pineapple pieces wrapped in crisp bacon and put under the broiler, cheese puffs, tiny pizzas, small squares of quiche, and fried shrimps.

A harried hostess without help (including children, who can be very useful in the kitchen, tending hot hors d'oeuvres) can make do at her party with all-cold hors d'oeuvres. But if she can handle the logistics of just one hot one, her party food will seem better.

Perennial favorite cold hors d'oeuvres include stuffed deviled eggs (these are beloved but messy and hard to handle—they need a cocktail napkin passed with them); egg salad sandwiches; small cucumber or watercress and cream cheese sandwiches; toasted rounds spread with peanut butter and chopped bacon; small open sandwiches spread with a combination of mayonnaise and mustard, topped with pieces of smoked turkey, rare roast beef, or baked ham; crab meat on toast, with a dash of Worcestershire sauce; squares of cheese and fresh fruit speared on a toothpick; and on ad infinitum.

If a cocktail hostess serves crudités with a curry dip, a platter of cheese and crackers, two hot hors d'oeuvres, and three cold ones, she has provided a more than presentable menu for her party.

If you hold your party in a special place other than your home—as, for example, in an art gallery to honor an artist friend who is having a show there—you can plan a much simpler party. You can serve only champagne or even white wine (and something nonalcoholic, too), and you can use plastic glasses. You can also serve a minimum of food (nuts, pretzels, cheese and crackers), which is passed by the waiters.

The Party's Over

Perhaps the most important element of giving a cocktail party is to know when to end it. Forty-five minutes after the party's ending time, as set on the invitations, the bar should be closed (in other words, if guests were invited from 6:30 to 8:00, the bar should close down at 8:45). Guests will still be finishing their drinks for another half hour beyond that. By 9:15, if it looks as though people are going to stay on forever, just tell them, "We are expected at some friends' house for dinner. They have gone ahead without us, but we really feel we must join them now." If your guests don't leave at that, it means that they are either rude or inebriated. Take steps to get the latter group home safely, and leave the former off your guest lists of the future.

The Problem Drinkers

If this book seems to furnish endless information on the drinking of wines and cocktails, I am also fully aware of the fact there are 10 million alcoholics in the United States, representing a very serious public health problem, but, far worse, a focus of personal tragedy in the lives of millions of families. A heartbreaking number of teen-agers and women who are mothers of small children are now included in this statistic. Our life-styles are contributing to the affliction. A victim can slip from heavy social drinking into the early stages of alcoholism without even noticing it. That is why it is the duty of hosts and hostesses to have short cocktail hours before their dinner parties, and to "shut off the bar" at a reasonable hour, whether they are giving the most formal of black-tie dances or the most informal of Sunday brunches.

If you are aware of friends who are having drinking problems that they won't recognize themselves, don't invite them to cocktail parties. Invite them instead to a weekend lunch or a small dinner where you can keep tabs on what everyone is drinking. As a host, you can control the amount of alcohol put into each glass and the number of times that glass is filled. Hide the bar paraphernalia in a closet, if necessary, to keep the guest from making drinks on the sly. When a friend with a drinking problem comes for dinner, try to serve the meal fifteen or twenty minutes after he arrives, so that the cocktail hour is short. In some communities the custom is to invite people for dinner at seven o'clock, and then feed them at ten o'clock, when the imbibers are all feeling the effects of alcohol and the nondrinkers are simply exhausted and hungry. This method of entertaining can only be described as barbaric.

Parents are at fault, too, when they think it's "cute" to supply their offspring at cocktail parties and at restaurants with their own cocktails in bar glasses "just like the grownups." Children are not little adults. There are many adult behavior patterns that children should not learn to imitate, because *they are not ready* for such activities. Nor should young teen-agers be urged to drink wine during the meal before they really want to. One hears parents actually bragging about how much wine their children drink at dinner, as though it were a meritorious performance, when in actuality some of them are starting their children on the road to alcoholism. Children should learn to drink in front of their parents when they become mature young adults, but it is quite another thing to force drinks on them.

We will have truly attained a golden age in our society when social drinking is not done to excess, when everyone knows the time to close the bar, and when the education of children on the subject of alcoholism is handled in the home—by parents who also handle their own drinking intelligently.

Handling the Out-of-control Alcoholic   Some alcoholics can go through an evening at a party with perfectly acceptable social behavior, but some of them cannot. If a guest becomes abusive in his or her language and gestures, the host or hostess must ask the guest to leave. If there is no spouse or date to get the guest home, then the host should either drive him home or ask one of the other guests to do so. Under no circumstances should he be allowed to drive, and, if necessary, his car keys should be taken from him. If the party is in the city, where guests come by taxi, the host should order a taxi and send him home with the fare paid. If he is in very bad shape, one or two people should accompany him home, because it is not the responsibility of the taxi driver to have to leave his vehicle unattended and cope with helping him to his door.

If all these attempts fail, the host and hostess should provide him with a bed in which to sleep it off.

The host and hostess should feel only sorrow when this kind of thing happens at their party, not anger. I remember the very compassionate act of a hostess in Paris who had to send a drunken guest home early to the Crillon Hotel in her own car. When he awoke the next day, there was a bouquet of flowers by his bedside, put there by the concierge after instructions from the hostess. The card on the flowers read, "We're sorry, and we missed you." The man in question called up the Paris representative of Alcoholics Anonymous that afternoon. . . .

Help for Alcoholics   A person in trouble deserves to be helped. When a person is an alcoholic, the entire family is in trouble, not just one member. Friends are meant to rally around at a time like this, not just witness the devastation. Help can be found. The person in trouble can be referred for psychological counseling; he can be urged to report his problem to the director of personnel of his company, in order to participate in various programs many corporations offer. A family member or a friend should make an appointment for the alcoholic to be taken to the local affiliate of the National Council on Alcoholism (which exists in all major cities), as well as to the local chapter of Alcoholics Anonymous. Both can be of great assistance, particularly when the alcoholic is ready for their help. So when you see a good friend becoming the life of the party too often, too much, and with loss of self-control, it is not a time to laugh. It is a time to act. And help.

Entertaining the Recovered Alcoholic   Sometimes a host is uneasy over what to do when a recovering or recovered alcoholic comes to dinner. You need not be. You treat him like all your guests. You ask him what he'll have when he arrives at your party; you do not force a soft drink or fruit juice on him. He wants to be asked what he would prefer, like every other guest. There is a dignity in being offered a choice. You also do not refer to the subject of his victorious fight against the disease. Let him bring it up if he wishes.

A very nice gesture to make before the dinner party is to ask a recovered alcoholic if there is some drink he or she particularly likes, such as iced tea or a special kind of juice. Some like to drink tea or coffee during the cocktail hour. A recovered alcoholic who doesn't want to be "different" might ask for ginger ale because it "looks like scotch and soda." I recently saw a host remove a cold soda from the refrigerator, put it in one of his children's cheap plastic glasses, and serve it to his recovered alcoholic guest without even a piece of ice in it. Soft drinks may be served to the children in Mickey Mouse glasses in that household, but adults deserve the finest bar glasses in the house for their soft drinks, and lots of ice, too. It's nice to ask a guest if he would like a piece of lemon or lime in his drink, too.

Fortunately, with the increase in dieting, there are many people now who abstain from alcohol for caloric reasons. The recovered alcoholic need no longer feel out of it by not drinking.

For a dinner party, the table should be set the same for all guests. You do not set the recovered alcoholic's place at the dinner table with the wineglasses conspicuously missing. When wine is served, this guest will simply make a "no, thank you" gesture when the wine is offered to him. He might also accept wine in his glass in order not to distract, but will, of course, leave it untouched. You are not putting temptation in his way by offering him wine, because a recovered alcoholic has to train himself with a fine-edged will power to refuse liquor of all kinds in all circumstances.

As for cooking, a hostess should be careful to use only liquor that burns off in the cooking process on these occasions. She should not, for example, pour a liqueur over ice cream or fruit. A newly recovered alcoholic who may be a little shaky and who does not know there is alcohol in the dessert may innocently take a portion of a dessert such as crème brulée full of cognac and go right back over the brink of alcoholism, based on that one experience.

Alcoholism is a serious disease, and those who have gone through programs and fought their way back deserve our sincere respect.

Special Kinds of Cocktail Parties

The Cocktail Buffet A cocktail buffet means a cocktail party with enough food on hand to serve as a buffet supper for the guests. It means a buffet table, but not necessarily an elaborate one. It means there will not be tables to sit at, and usually there is no dessert course, although some hostesses do offer one dessert and coffee on a side table.

A guest can take a plate of food at any point during the evening—early if he has to go somewhere else, such as the theater, and late if he arrives tardily from some other appointment. Guests eat standing up, while talking to people, or they sit down next to people who may be only drinking and not eating, or they find others who are eating somewhere in the house. (Many people, like me, are embarrassed to be eating in front of others who are not.)

The keynote here is informality. The invitations are telephoned or handwritten on informals or on invitations that have blanks in which to put the information giving date, time, and type of party. Many guests eat their "dinner" at this party; others attend who stay only for a short time before going on to something else they had previously accepted. Guests are usually invited for six or seven o'clock, and people come during the ensuing two hours.

Housewarmings A housewarming (a cocktail party with a purpose) is usually given by the person or the couple in honor of their new home, but sometimes a housewarming is given *for* a recently moved-in family to welcome them. For someone who is already known in the community, but who has simply changed houses, this party is to show off the new house and greet old friends. For newcomers to the community, the housewarming has a different purpose: one invites all one's neighbors on the street, the few people the family has already met, and the pastor or rabbi, the children's teachers, and the pediatrician, lawyer, and doctor, and their families.

Invitations to housewarmings are extended by telephone, by an informal note, or by printed invitations upon which one fills in the necessary information. During the week a housewarming is usually held at the cocktail hour, from 5:30 to 7:30 P.M. A housewarming can be given from 12 noon to 2 P.M. on weekends, or from 5 to 7 P.M. Usually entire families are invited (I remember one housewarming we were invited to on Long Island when, much to the delight of the children, even the new family's pooch "received" the dogs of the families invited). There should be a special table for children, perhaps with party plates and cups, and an assortment of soft drinks and huge bowls of potato chips or popcorn.

For the adults, a punch or mixed drinks may be served. A menu of cocktail hors d'oeuvres will suffice, although, if you so desire, you can shift the hours of your party to a later hour (6 to 8:30 P.M.) and give your guests a hot casserole, a salad, and rolls, as well as the regular assortment of cocktail food.

It is the custom for each guest (or each family, rather) to bring a small present to a housewarming (see "Gift Ideas for All Occasions," page 786). These should be left (with your name on the card) in the front hall as you enter. The hosts are not going to have time to open them during the party, but they will open them with great pleasure afterward, leisurely. When the housewarming is for people new to a community, there should be a "guest book" at the front entrance, too, with a place for names and addresses. It is very likely the newcomers may not know the addresses of some of the guests. This makes a nice record of their first party in their new home.

When an interior designer has been retained to give a town house or apartment an expensive face-lift throughout, the owners often have a cocktail party to "show it off." This is a type of housewarming, but no gifts have to be brought. The only thing really expected of the guests is a multitude of compliments on the new decor. (If you don't like it, praise it anyway, for taste is relative.)

Open House An "open house" is a term not used as often as it used to be. When people hold a housewarming, they are also holding an open house. The term is usually applied to family parties during the holiday season, or receptions held after football games. "Open house" is simply another term for a large cocktail party or cocktail buffet.

Chapter 29

INFORMAL LUNCHEONS AND TEAS

The Informal Luncheon

The term "luncheon" is not often used in conversation any more. We ask people "to come to lunch" at our home. We talk about "having lunched yesterday with so-and-so." Yet we still refer to "the luncheon cloth."

Invitations to lunch are extended by telephone or by written note. The hour is usually twelve noon, twelve-thirty, or one o'clock. When guests come to lunch, an attractive table is every bit as important as it is for a dinner party. Your prettiest linens should be used—whether you use place mats, a tablecloth, or large napkins combined with the "bare table look." By the way, if you are serving something with a rich sauce on your menu, give your guests dinner napkins instead of the little luncheon napkins. You do not put candles on your table, of course, even if they are unlit. One of the prettiest luncheon tables I ever saw was a white and pink crystal one. The shell-shaped candy dishes were made of Philippine mother-of-pearl, as were the place mats. The flatware was mother-of-pearl-handled. The pink porcelain plates were shell-shaped, while in the center of the table a lovely water lily floated in the thinnest of pink crystal bowls (a match to the tall-stemmed pink glasses for the white wine.)

If you are setting up several card tables for a buffet lunch, the cloths do not have to be identical, but they should be co-ordinated. Cotton or synthetic cloths made identically but of different colors (perhaps picking up the cloor scheme of the fabrics in the room) are nice; so are cloths of the same floral prints done in different colors. Women who sew, of course, have every advantage in being able to make marvelous tablecloths and matching napkins from inexpensive fabric, or even by cutting up the high-fashion sheets available in stores to fit their tables.

If a hostess wishes to serve only sherry, Dubonnet, some other apéritif or white wine as a pre-lunch cocktail, it is perfectly correct at her ladies' lunch. Salted almonds or something like small cheese biscuits are enough of an hors d'oeuvre. If the lunch is given on the weekend with men present, it is nice to serve something like bloody marys before lunch, in addition to the regular cocktails you serve. A platter of crudités and nuts is sufficient for hors d'oeuvres, even in mixed company, at lunchtime.

The flatware is set for lunch as it is for dinner. If there is no first course, only a fork and a knife in the usual positions and a dessert fork and spoon placed at the top of the place setting are required. (In former days, every bride had to have "luncheon"-sized flatware, but today she can use her dinner-sized flatware for all entertaining.) If there is going to be a hot or cold first course, the appropriate flatware is to be found at the outside left and right, just as at dinner.

For an informal lunch, one wine suffices, so as the guests approach the table, it would be set with a water glass filled with cold water and an empty wineglass at each place. The wine bottle would be on the table in a coaster, or the wine might be in a decanter.

At a warm-weather informal lunch, iced tea or iced coffee may be served. It is nice to offer both coffee and tea—a pitcher of each can be placed at either end of the table. The pitchers and their contents should be nicely cold from having been in the refrigerator for a few hours. A small tray with sliced lemon, cream, a bowl of sugar, and a sweetener is then passed around the table.

A tall glass filled with ice cubes on a porcelain saucer should be set at each place. The long iced-tea spoon is placed on the outer right of the flatware; it is balanced on the saucer when it is not in use. If your hostess does not provide a saucer, keep the long spoon in your iced-tea glass (a wet spoon may harm the linens or the table), and grasp it between the second and third fingers of the hand holding the glass, every time you take a sip.

Some of my favorite lunch menus are listed on pages 313–14. Lunch menus should be fairly light in composition, with a minimum of courses; I make no distinction between menus served at a ladies' lunch and those for a lunch attended by men, too. No one wants to be overstuffed at noontime. If it's a Sunday lunch, however, you should serve a dinner menu, unless everyone is planning on athletic activities later, in which case a light lunch is by far the best.

A lunch served buffet-style is the perfect answer for a household without help. Guests serve themselves from the serving area and sit down at the table, which is set with everything needed for service. Often the salad will already be on the table, served with small plates that sit to the left of each guest's place setting.

At dessert time the hostess can serve (seated at her place) from the bowl in front of her, with a stack of dessert plates next to it. Some women like hot coffee with their dessert; if that is the custom, then the hostess brings in a tray with coffee pot and large-sized coffee cups as soon as she has served dessert to her guests. She hands the filled coffee cup down to each person at the table (or, if there are card tables, she passes the coffee cups from a big tray to each guest). Or she can wait until everyone has finished eating dessert and then serve coffee in demitasse cups, as is done at dinners. The creamer and sugar bowl and a bowl of sweetener are passed from person to person on a little tray.

When There Is a Maid Serving   The guests come to the table to find the first course, hot or cold, already in place. When the first course has been consumed, the maid removes the soup cup and place plate (or fruit cup or shrimp cup, or whatever, and its place plate), moving from left or right. If the main course is hot, the maid should bring in warm plates. If the main course is something like a fruit salad or a shrimp salad, then she can bring in each plate already served with the salad from the kitchen. (I think it is nice to put the empty plates for anything being served cold in the refrigerator first for a few minutes, if there is room; it is just a nice added touch.)

When she brings in the main dish, she holds it on the flat of her left hand on a folded napkin, serving to the left of each guest, or she places it in front of the hostess for her to serve. She stands to the hostess' left to receive each filled plate, and then places it in front of a guest, moving always to the hostess' right first (to serve the guest of honor) and then on around the table, counterclockwise.

At the end of the main course, serving dishes are removed first, then the plates, left or right, then the butter plates (if there are any), bread tray, and condiments. The water and wine or iced tea or coffee glasses remain. The maid crumbs the table before bringing in the dessert course.

It is simple to serve dessert on the plates out in the kitchen, in which case the maid enters the dining room with a dessert plate in each hand, placing each one before a guest from the left. As an alternative, the hostess may serve the dessert from a bowl or platter set in front of her, alongside a stack of dessert plates. In this case the maid takes a filled plate in each hand and places one before a guest.

If there has been iced coffee or tea served, then hot tea never follows. If the hostess does wish to serve hot tea, she serves it at the table (it is never brought in already poured into cups in the kitchen). The teapot is brought in on a bare tray, with the necessary cups and saucers, spoons, sugar, milk, hot water, basin, strainer, and lemon slices. Tea bags should really not be used for a lunch party.

The Informal Tea

"Why don't you join me for a cup of tea?" Nice words, warm and kind, relating to one of the oldest customs in existence. A cup of tea signals a break in the afternoon's activities, a time for true relaxation, an inducement to gentle conversation. It is the perfect antidote for the visitor who arrives in your home tired from a long journey, or for anyone who comes in chilled from the weekend outdoor activities.

Invitations to "come by for a cup of tea" are extended, of course, informally by the hostess face-to-face or over the telephone. For elaborate teas that are held on special occasions, such as one honoring a debutante, the invitations are engraved or written by hand.

Tea bags should not be used when friends are invited in advance to your home for tea, and certainly never at a large tea. If you meet someone during the day and bring her home for a cup of tea, the tea bag is all right. (One of the reasons tea bags are not used at a proper tea is that handling the bag is inevitably a messy act.) When your tea is strong enough, lift up the bag by its string, and press a spoon gently against it on the inside part of the cup (to release as much liquid as possible from the bag), and then lay it on your saucer. If you really want to be thoughtful, have a small bowl nearby on the tray for discarded tea bags. (They are about as attractive as cigar butts!)

If you have invited a group of friends for tea, the first thing you need is a large tray, without a cloth on it. If you are using your silver hollow ware, be sure everything is polished beautifully. Tea plates should be stacked on the tray. Napkins may be folded beside them, or each napkin can be folded on top of each plate within the stack.

The following are needed for the tray: a teapot of any kind of heat-holding material; a pitcher of very hot water (for those who like to dilute their tea); a strainer; a bowl of waste leaves; a pitcher of milk (never cream); a bowl of sugar lumps with sugar tongs or a bowl of sugar with a spoon; a small saucer with lemon slices and a small fork; and cups and saucers and teaspoons. If you are having a large group to tea, set up some trays of empty cups and saucers in the kitchen, to bring in as needed.

SETTING UP THE TEA TRAY. The tea tray is always set up without a cloth and with all the things on it arranged in pleasing symmetry. Shown lower left to right: *Dessert forks (if pastry is being served), basin for leaves, teapot on alcohol lamp, milk, sugar, sugar tongs.* Upper left to right: *Tea plates and tea napkins, teacups with spoons shown on saucers to right of handles, hot water, lemon slices.*

Women dress for afternoon tea according to the regional custom, but usually a daytime dress is best. It is unsuitable to come in sports attire or in evening glitter. If you are having a warm-weather iced-tea party on the patio, then, of course, informal attire is correct.

Tea cools very quickly, so it is usually taken by the guest directly from the hands of the hostess. A hostess does not pour many cups at a time without being able to hand them quickly to her guests. She pours instead "as needed."

The Making of Good Tea The Far Easterners and the English make a proper ceremony out of serving tea, but we Americans still have a long way to go in this custom.

The first rule in making tea is to have the water actually boiling. It must bubble-boil three to four minutes and then be poured immediately over the tea leaves. Tea made with water under the boiling point does not have its flavor liberated and is flat and insipid. The tea made in most restaurants is tasteless, because the water for it is drawn from the coffee urn or from kettles kept hot for some time and is not fresh water, *freshly* boiled.

When the water is actually boiling, scald out the teapot so that the metal, china, or pottery is heated through. Then *dry* the pot and set it near the heat to keep hot. Now measure one teaspoon of tea for each cup to be served. Pour in the boiling water, cover the pot, and, if you have one, use a tea cosy, although there are excellent sturdy pots of various kinds that keep the tea piping hot. Let it steep three to five minutes. Stir before serving the first cup. Keep a pitcher of boiling hot water available (preferably on an alcohol burner) for those who like weak tea. If more tea is needed, it is best to start the entire procedure again instead of trying to add the somewhat cooled pitcher of water to the tea leaves in the pot. The result is usually poor. However, if you have made the tea at the tea table and are keeping the water at a boil over a spirit lamp or small electric stove, you may add the actively boiling water to the leaves in the pot when half the tea has been poured. The result is usually satisfactory. Good tea is easy to make properly if you follow these directions.

Kinds of Tea The dark teas—sometimes with a little green blended in—are good for every day. But there are delicious, and sometimes very expensive, mixtures one should try in tea-taster amounts to find the ones really preferred. People who know tea never put milk in a green tea (for it looks unappetizing), although they sometimes use lemon. The flower teas, such as jasmine, do not have a good taste with milk. They are so special that it is better not to offer them at large teas or to conservative tea drinkers. The herb teas, tisanes, are liked by some people before they go to bed, and are usually best with honey as the sweetener. Do not use milk with them, however, for they are green teas. Peppermint tea, camomile tea, and anise tea are among the easiest to find. Invalids and people coming down with colds often particularly enjoy these tisanes.

It is hard for people in many parts of the world to realize that many

Americans go through life without being exposed to tea drinking. I remember when I was in college, a friend of mine who had never seen tea drunk in her home approached an invitation to have tea with the mother of one of our New York classmates with some trepidation. When the hostess poured her a cup of tea from a lovely Lowestoft pot and handed it to her, my friend carefully opened her handbag, took out a tea bag, and plopped it in. Our hostess never batted an eyelash. After about eight seconds, she extended an ash tray to our friend and said, "Here, your tea looks just lovely now, just perfectly. Why don't you take the bag by the string and put it in here?"

Everyone survived the afternoon.

Coffees

Coffee parties are still enjoying popularity as an easy way of socializing for women in the morning hours, usually between nine-thirty and eleven-thirty. The parties have a different emphasis regionally. In California, for example, women with preschool children congregate at someone's house for coffee and conversation and the chance for their toddlers to play together for a short while (usually very short). The hour-long session, held at a different person's home each time, offers the women a touch of the adult world and the chance to compare notes on their children and their getting-back-to-work problems. In the Middle West, the South, and Texas, coffees are held by the younger women, but in New Orleans it is predominantly the older women who give and who attend the coffees. They still wear gloves when they go out in the morning to their coffee parties.

With the exception of the New Orleans parties, the food at these gatherings is usually informal and not extensive. Hot buttered croissants, coffee cake, or sweet rolls are often on the menu, or occasionally small finger sandwiches. Some serve hot tea.

Invitations to coffee are telephoned or made in handwritten notes. Like invitations to teas, they do not usually require or request an R.S.V.P., but it is a kind act to your hostess to let her know if you are coming.

Playing Bridge

If you are going to have a dinner party with bridge afterward, remember to invite only those who are avid bridge players. It is rude to have an "odd man out" who is supposed to kibitz happily while everyone else plays. Also, invite only people who play at about the same level. A beginning "hacker," attractive though he or she may be, would only disrupt the evening if everyone else is an expert.

If you are going to play for money and you have a steady group of bridge friends, there should be no argument by now about stakes. But if you are asking new players to dinner and you do not know about how much they like to play for, ask them. Make sure everyone agrees beforehand on the stakes. It is best to make the stakes low, so that you will not be indirectly responsible for a possible financial problem for one of your guests. If someone in a new group of players hesitates about playing for money at all, change the procedure. Just say, "We'll play for the fun of it and some silly prizes." If you do promise prizes to the leading scorers, make them suitable gifts for either sex, and wrap them prettily.

While the guests are enjoying their after-dinner coffee, the host or hostess should set up the tables. Be sure that each table has an easy-to-play-on surface, such as leather or another laminated surface. If not, use a bridge table cover. Do not ask your guests to play on uncomfortable chairs, either, such as a low sofa seat (lightweight, inexpensive folding chairs are easily available and can be stored in a hall closet with ease). Be sure that there are two good clean packs of cards, plus four score pads and four well-sharpened pencils with erasers, on each table. Each player should keep score, to avoid any disagreement or excuses for "having forgotten the score." The hosts should also provide a *current* book of rules and scoring count to settle the arguments that inevitably arise.

The hostess should arrange for proper lighting that falls upon the entire surface of each bridge table. She should see to it that the smokers have ash trays and the drinkers coasters for their glasses. And it helps if there are two little cigarette tables off to the side of each bridge table to hold this paraphernalia, plus a dish of candy.

Bridge players follow stringent rules of etiquette. Women who wear clanking bracelets can make others nervous; chattering during the game is cause for murder, in many serious bridge players' minds. Reading while you are dummy is rude; it shows you are bored when you're not in the play. The dummy, if no one else has freshened drinks or emptied ash trays recently, can offer to "get anyone anything they wish." Otherwise, he should sit engrossed in the play.

Bridge incites strong emotions in people, because it brings out one's character faults in a most concise manner. I can never forget the old *New Yorker* cartoon showing three bridge players, a dead body on the floor, and a police officer. One of the players is holding a smoking pistol. The caption read, "Well, Officer, the bidding went like this: Open with two spades; Pass; Pass; Pass; Bang, Bang, Bang!"

Players who are bad sports, who blame their partners, or who claim someone distracted them are suddenly destructive forces during what was supposed to be a pleasant evening. A player who insists upon discussing the last hand, rehashing every play, telling each person what he did wrong; the player who drums his fingers on the table, who takes forever making up his mind on a bid or a play; the player who smacks down his card on the table resolutely and lets no one see the trick he is taking; the player who issues a war whoop when he makes a coup and who agonizes vehemently when he loses a trick he shouldn't have; husbands criticizing wives and vice versa:

these are all major or minor irritants, according to each individual's anger threshold.

Bridge is really no different from any competitive game in that the rules of sportsmanship are the same. One should play quietly, quickly, modestly, and with concentration. One should win or lose without upsetting everyone else with a strong emotional outburst. If you are playing for money and lose, pay up quickly and cheerfully. There should be no arguments or recriminations. Bridge is a game. If you couldn't afford to lose, then you couldn't afford to play for money in the first place.

Serving Dessert   If you have invited friends to come after dinner for an evening of bridge, it is nice to serve dessert before beginning to play. You should set up a "dessert buffet" that is apart from the bridge-playing area. (Serving gooey cake on the bridge table is guaranteed to be regretted later.) Have a choice of two desserts and coffee, too. Nearby, set up a bar with the makings of a highball, liqueurs, and a tray with glasses of water and ice. Make beer available for your guests if they want it. After the guests have had their dessert, they may want to take their coffee and after-dinner drink to the bridge table. (Again, those little side tables to hold everything needed for smoking, drinking, and munching are very important.)

Afternoon Bridge   If it is your turn to "have the girls over for an afternoon of bridge," you can serve either the traditional snack of coffee and tea with sandwiches or cookies, or you can serve something different. A low-calorie treat would be welcome: for example, a plate of cottage cheese with fresh fruit, or a vegetable-juice or fruit-juice cocktail to ease late-afternoon hunger pangs. I have heard of bridge hostesses serving everything from miniature hot dogs (with rolls baked by the hostess) to mugs of ice-cold gazpacho soup and bowls of frozen yoghurt.

The smart hostess who serves food during these bridge afternoons also passes around moist towelettes, to ease the problem of sticky fingers ruining the cards.

Chapter 30

FORMAL ENTERTAINING

The Formal Dinner

The "truly formal dinner" is pretty much a rarity today. Few homes can accommodate a large group of guests at a seated dinner, with all the sterling flatware, stemware, and china required, plus a trained waiter to serve every six guests. Even the royal families who used to have a liveried footman for every two guests manage with a minimum of staff these days, and rely on hiring "extras" for their state parties (as does the White House).

The easiest way to give a formal dinner is, of course, to have it in a good club that handles food and service with distinction. But the nicest way to give a formal dinner is in one's home, and we are talking quite naturally about a large home or apartment.

Invitations Engraved invitation cards with blanks should be purchased from the stationer's for this kind of formal dinner. "R.S.V.P." will be on the lower left of the invitation, and you write your telephone number beneath, to accommodate guests who take the easy way of answering an invitation instead of writing and will not write a formal acceptance or regret.

The words "Black Tie" should be written on the lower right. In the upper left-hand corner one writes "In Honor of So-and-so" if desired. Invitations to such an event should be mailed from three to four weeks before the dinner.

Seating Even some of the strictest rules for the "truly formal dinner" have changed. The term used to imply that all guests had to sit at one long table, which made conversation difficult and required a very lengthy dining room. The John F. Kennedys helped change that rule in the White House. They began using round tables for eight or ten, instead of the large U-shaped one traditionally present for white-tie dinners in honor of visiting heads of state. Mrs. Kennedy used pale yellow and blue long circular cloths on these tables, too, breaking another rule that the formal dinner required a white damask cloth. Today's hostesses who give formal dinners either rent round tables from the caterer, or, if they have sufficient storage space, they own round plywood or plastic tops that fold in two and fit over their bridge

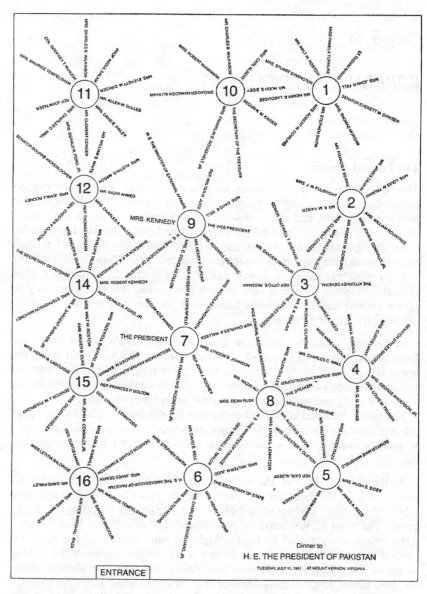

The nontraditional seating plan used by Mrs. Kennedy for the state dinner given at Mount Vernon in 1961 in honor of the President of Pakistan.

tables. Small gold ballroom chairs can be rented from the caterer, but, again, some hostesses prefer to buy their own pretty lightweight collapsible or stackable chairs, sometimes with upholstered seats to match the draperies or some predominant color theme in their dining room.

Another change in the very formal dinner is that the centerpiece decoration no longer *has to be* candelabra of silver with bowls of flowers lined up down the center. The hostess' own imagination should come into play in designing the table setting for her formal dinner, just as it would for any other party. If her formal dinner party will be seated at one large table, and the table surface is particularly beautiful, she can also set the table with the bare-table look of no linens except for large napkins.

The Service   There are two elements of the formal dinner that have not changed over the years: the use of a butler and waiters for serving and the necessity for a chef or cuisinière who can produce a fabulous meal of five courses—usually a soup, fish, meat or fowl, salad and cheese, and dessert. The formal dinner usually implies a white wine, red wine, and champagne served with the meal (sometimes sherry first, too). The way the food is served—its presentation—is extremely important at a formal dinner. The platters must all be garnished beautifully, so that the guests will admire each one as a work of art, not just the serving of a dish. The butter might be rolled into balls or carved into flowers; the vegetables and desserts served in imaginative ways (mushrooms served in tomato baskets; small peas in potato baskets; ice-cream balls served in large baskets of spun sugar, and so on).

The importance of the butler cannot be exaggerated. It is he who orchestrates the entire service of the evening. His aides can include the regular staff of the house plus hired "extras" from a local catering service or free-lance butlers and waiters of his choice (the chef or cook hires the additional kitchen service he or she may need). The hostess must discuss with the butler well in advance how the footmen will be attired, so that the proper uniforms will be rented for them, if they do not have the right thing.

Just before the arrival of her guests, usually a few minutes before eight, though sometimes formal dinners start at eight-thirty, the hostess checks the dining room and gives any last-minute instructions to the butler. He, in turn, makes his tour of the footmen and inspects their apparel, shoes, hair, and fingernails. In earlier times such serving men wore white cotton gloves because of the danger, as one writer put it, of a dirty thumb in the soup. The butler sees to it that there are no dirty thumbs or anything else that can't pass muster.

Arrival and Introduction of Guests   There are two ways of handling the seating logistics at a formal dinner. In one, after each man has given his coat to the butler or maid, he receives a small envelope with his name on it. Inside is a card bearing the name of his dinner partner. These envelopes with cards are kept on a tray in the front hall, alphabetized for easy finding. If the man does not already know the woman whom he is to escort into dinner, he finds her during the cocktail hour, introduces himself, and comes back when dinner is announced to walk into the dining room with her.

The more popular way, now that round tables are used more often than one large one, is for there to be an envelope for each guest, placed on the hall table in alphabetical order. As each guest arrives, he or she takes the envelope and finds inside a card with the proper table number written on it. There is no need to find one's dinner partner. Everyone will walk in informally to the dining room when dinner is announced and one will find one's dinner partners at the table.

At a large formal dinner there should be a *plan de table* (table chart) shown to each guest as he arrives. The butler either holds the chart in his hand, or, if there several round tables, the guests look at all the table charts on the hall table. The *plan de table* is a rectangular or round seating chart made of handsome leather, or perhaps of cardboard covered in silk. It has an easel back, like a picture frame, so it can stand on the table. Each guest's name is written on a little white card (or typed) and inserted in the proper place on the table chart.

When the party begins, the host and hostess should be near the entrance to the living room, so that they will be able to greet each arriving guest. They should see to it that newcomers are introduced to everyone through the cocktail hour.

When the butler comes to the hostess and announces dinner, she informs the host and they collect the guests of honor and proceed into the dining room (host and honored woman guest first, hostess last). Each man seats the woman on his left or right, whoever arrives at her place first at the round table. If a woman arrives at one of the tables before anyone else, she just seats herself, although, if there is a waiter nearby, he will rush to seat her.

The minute everyone is seated, the waiters remove the stanchions on the tables that hold the white cards with the table numbers. Since these are not attractive objects, they should not be left on the tables during dinner.

Place cards and matching menus, of course, are used for formal dinner parties. One menu is needed for every two guests. The menus may be printed but are usually handwritten in a handsome script in black ink. The same hand should write the place cards. The different courses on the menus are usually given their French names, since French is the language of international gourmet cuisine. The menu card can be placed flat on the table between two place settings, or it can be stood up in a holder specially made for menu cards (see "Menu Cards," page 334).

The protocol for seating guests is exactly the same as it is for informal dinners (see page 290). Husbands and wives do not sit next to each other; in fact, hostesses try to seat them at different tables. It is not necessary, either, for engaged couples to sit next to each other either at these dinners.

The Formal Dinner Table

The silver at a formal dinner must be sterling or vermeil (silver gilt). The large dinner napkin, folded, is on the place plate, no matter how decorative the latter may be. But the place plate, if it is pictorial, is carefully arranged so that the design is toward the diner.

It was traditional that no butter plates or butter knives appeared on a really formal table, as breads that were passed were placed directly on the tablecloth. The hard dinner roll, unbuttered, was in or on the napkin or to the left of the place plate as the guests were seated. Today, one may or may not see butter plates.

Silver and settings must be exactly arranged, as a crowded formal table is impossible to serve. There must be a foot or more between each guest, the space accurately measured. But there should never be so much space between guests that conversation becomes difficult. At a long, narrow table with few guests the seating is arranged so that host and hostess sit opposite each other at the center of the table with guests grouped right and left of each and with the ends of the table unset.

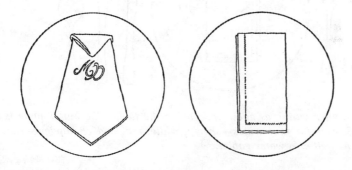

FOLDING OF NAPKINS, LEFT: There are many imaginative ways to fold napkins today, but for a more formal setting, simplicity is most appropriate. To dramatize initialed dinner napkins, first arrange napkins with loose edges upward on the plate. The fold of the napkin will then form the point of a triangle. Now fold over the loose edges to form a small triangle above the monogram, then fold under the other two points of the napkin to make the arrangement shown. Lay flat on service plate with the point of the napkin toward the diner. Monograms on napkins are, of course, meant to be seen. A napkin is folded to display them. (Incidentally, an embroidered initial looks best when the embroidery is ironed on a spongy surface such as turkish toweling, which permits the initial to be raised.) RIGHT: the simple fold of a large dinner napkin. The square is folded over left into a rectangle and placed flat on the plate with the edge either on the left (more conventional) or right. In picking it up, the diner takes it by the upper left-hand corner if the fold is to the right and by the right-hand corner if the fold is at the left. A large dinner napkin should not be completely unfolded but merely spread across the lap.

Formal dinner setting as guest approaches the table. The butter plate is op-tional. Glasses for four wines—sherry, white, red, and champagne—are in-cluded, as well as a water goblet.

At each place, in addition to the place plate, the butter plate, and the nap-kin, is the following silver: knives, to the right, never more than three—for appetizer, if necessary, fish, and meat, or for fish, meat, and salad. If more than three knives are necessary the additional one is put in place at the time the course is served. To the left are the forks, also never more than three at a time, one for the appetizer, if any, one for the fish, if needed, one for the meat, or the first for the fish, the second for the meat, and the third for the salad. If a fourth fork is needed for salad it is placed when the salad is served. If there is an oyster fork it is optionally placed, not with the forks, but on the side with the knives with the tines of the the fork placed, upward, across the soup spoon or parallel with the knives. With the exception of the spoons for soup or melon, there are no spoons to the right of the knives. The dessert fork and spoon lie at the head of the plate. Optionally, dessert spoons with their forks are in place, spoon right, fork left, on the dessert plates when they are brought in. Sometimes the finger bowl, on a doily or on a finger bowl plate or on both, is on the dessert plate, too. Sometimes the finger bowl is presented with fruit silver after the dessert.

On the formal table individual silver or silver-and-crystal salts and peppers may be placed, pepper first, a little below the line of glasses, one set for each guest or for each two guests. At a large table larger sets may be used rayed out, pepper above, salt below, from the corners of an imaginary rectangle around the centerpiece. Open salts and peppers require little sterling, ivory, or mother-of-pearl spoons. Mustard pots or other condiments are not set on a formal table but are passed, if needed, on the butler's tray. But I have even seen beautiful silver pepper grinders—two or more—on formal tables, where the hostess is one who makes a fetish of freshly ground pepper.

Formal glassware need not be in matching sets, but all glasses for a particular wine should match each other and all glasses chosen should look good together. A host might have a set of antique or modern light-green-bowled hock glasses for Rhine wine and like to see them used on a formal table with the, otherwise preferred, clear glass.

Glasses are placed in order of their use above the knives (see illustration) in a variety of ways. At a formal dinner, champagne may be the only wine served after the service of sherry with the soup.

On the really formal table there may be no ash trays and cigarettes at all during the meal. Or in front of each guest is a small silver or porcelain ash tray, with two cigarettes laid horizontally across the top and a small box or book of matches below. The match box may be silver, containing tiny dinner matches, or a plain gold or silver or sometimes black packet of book matches may be used, the smaller the better. Otherwise, cigarettes and cigars are passed with the coffee. Sometimes the butler brings cigarettes in silver cigarette boxes and individual ash trays on a serving tray, with a lighted taper or sometimes a large silver lighter, and passes them to guests after dessert, lighting each cigarette and placing the ash trays to each smoker's right.

The Service Begins The butler takes his stand behind the hostess. He moves from this vantage point only when a footman needs direction or when he himself pours the wine. He actually serves food only if there is not sufficient additional staff to do the serving, and then serves the main dishes only.

In a smaller household a butler and a footman can efficiently serve a formal dinner for eight to twelve guests. If he is quite adept, with adequate kitchen support a butler alone can handle a formal dinner for eight. At dinners larger than twelve it is necessary to have duplicate serving dishes presented simultaneously to each six or seven guests. In this way all food will be served so that the guests may eat more or less at the same time and hot food will be properly hot. The service begins with the lady at the host's right, and at a large dinner dishes are presented simultaneously to the ladies nearest, right and left, of the hostess. Butler, if he serves, and footmen present dishes with the left hand, right hands behind back.

At a very large dinner it is, naturally, not possible to wait until each guest has finished eating before the clearing of plates begins. In lavish service where a man was behind each chair, for instance at royal banquets, each plate was removed the minute the diner indicated by placement of silver that he had finished with it. Today, the butler directs the removal of plates, or begins the removal himself, when the majority has finished, bypassing the slower diners, but there must be no sense of hurry and certainly no clatter or audible staff directions.

At only one period is there ever a moment when there is not a plate before a guest. That is just before the service of dessert. Until then, beginning with the place plate with its folded napkin upon it, there is always a plate. Sometimes there is still another on top of it, as in the case of, say, a crabmeat cocktail, which would be in a stemmed double container, the "suprême" glass (sometimes silver) surrounding the "liner," on a small service plate. This complete unit is placed on the place plate. It is replaced, on the place plate, with the soup course—always in a flat dish. At the end of the soup course, plate and soup dish are removed, and, at a formal meal, removal is *only* from the left, except for those parts of the setting that are on the guest's right. As the place and soup plate are removed together, the warm plate for the fish course is immediately substituted. After the fish course has been removed the *rôti* appears, always hot, though not necessarily "roasted" at all. It is always completely arranged on a beautifully garnished platter or platters, often with its accompanying vegetables. Only the main course platters (the meat or fowl) are passed twice.

Leaving the Dining Room At the end of the fruit course, the hostess catches the eye of the lady of honor or some other lady at the other end of the table, bows, and slowly rises. The gentlemen rise and assist the ladies in pushing back their chairs. The hostess then indicates where coffee is to be served. In the English style, the men are served at the dining table with cigars, port, liqueurs, and demitasses. Or the men may escort their dinner partners to the living room, then leave them for the library or wherever else the men are congregating for coffee. The women then have coffee and liqueurs alone and, before the men return, supposedly "repair their make-up." In the continental fashion, men and women leave the dining room together, proceeding to the living room, where they enjoy coffee and liqueurs together. The "English style" very fortunately is going out of fashion.

Departing After the Formal Dinner Except for some very good reason discussed previously with the hostess, no guest should leave after a formal dinner in a private home until the guest or guests of honor have departed. At formal public dinners guests who must leave early go quietly either before the speeches begin or between them, never while a guest of honor is speaking or while a national anthem is being played. Those who must leave, leave by the nearest exit without stopping to talk or bid farewell to guests encountered en route, except to bow briefly.

Tipping members of the staff to get one's coat and hat in a private home is never done in the United States.

The Formal Luncheon

Today, although the formal lunch at home is rare, it does occasionally take place, at country places, resorts like Palm Beach, and in diplomatic circles.

Invitations to a formal luncheon are usually telephoned, but those to official luncheons are engraved. At official luncheons men and women guests are usually equal in number.

Greeting Guests The guests are met at the door by a domestic staff member who indicates where coats may be left. He or she then usually precedes the guest to the living room (unless all guests know the house well), walks to within speaking distance of the seated hostess, and announces the guest's name. The hostess rises in greeting, but there is no formal receiving line.

Sherry, white wine, and apértifs are often served. Occasionally cocktails are served, too, before luncheon.

After all the guests have assembled, the butler or waitress announces luncheon. The hostess leads the way with the guest of honor, if any, and the others follow along in any convenient manner, with any gentlemen present *not* offering their arms as at a formal dinner.

Place Cards and Menus At official luncheons both place cards and menus may be used, and place cards at other formal luncheons are necessary when more than eight are to be seated. The place cards (those for host and hostess are omitted) are placed upon the folded napkin, which is, in turn, *on* the service plate. A menu card, engraved or handwritten, is placed in its holder or flat on the table, either one for each place or one for each two or three guests. There should be one before the hostess and another before the host if he is present.

Arranging the Table Place mats are usually preferred for the formal luncheon. The silver must be sterling or vermeil, the china and glass of the best quality.

There are no candles on a luncheon table, but there are flowers or some other centerpiece. Butter plates are sometimes used.

If the table is large, the hostess' creative abilities (or her gardener's) come into play for the centerpiece decor. Decorative dishes of fruit, candies, or nuts may be spaced down the length of the table. A large epergne may contain both fruits and flowers, and on a long table the flower motif could be repeated in flower arrangements strategically placed.

The luncheon napkin is smaller than that used for a formal dinner, but dinner napkins are often used here, too. The napkin is folded as it is for a dinner.

At the formal luncheon no food is portioned or carved at the table but is brought in and passed.

If soup is served the soup spoon is at the right of the knife or knives (not more than two). If it is to be the less usual four-course luncheon, with the soup followed by an egg dish or fish, there is a small knife to the left of the spoon and next to it the larger knife for the main course. If it is a three-course meal beginning with an appetizer, the soup spoon is, of course, omitted. On the left of the plate go the necessary forks, not more than three, appetizer fork, meat fork, salad fork, with the one to be used last on the inside. Forks and spoons for dessert can either be included on a formal table at the top of the place setting or brought in with the dessert.

There are rarely more than two wines, and glasses for each wine may either match or just go well together.

If the hostess wishes, individual crystal, porcelain, or silver ash trays with their complement of cigarettes and matches are at each place, or cigarettes may be passed at the end of the dessert course or later in the living room after the service of demitasse.

The Food   As people prefer lighter luncheons today, even a formal luncheon is limited to a maximum of four courses, more often three. The food should be chosen for its seeming simplicity and deliciousness. Each course should balance well against the one to follow. There is expected to be a certain distinction about the food for any formal meal, and that for a formal luncheon is no exception. Menus are frequently written in French, and the service must be as faultless as the linen and silver.

Usually not more than two wines are served at a formal luncheon. Sherry, at room temperature, may be served with the soup (but not with fish). It may be poured from a decanter by the waiter, who, however, must not lift the glass from its place. Champagne, for some very special occasion, could be the only wine, served from soup to dessert or introduced with the entrée.

The Formal Tea

Occasionally there is an official tea or perhaps a large tea for a visiting celebrity where the guests are mainly feminine. In these cases, formal tea follows a traditional pattern. (See also "Debutante Teas," page 118.)

The Table and Lighting   The tea table must be large enough to accommodate two services on trays, at opposite ends of the table, one for tea, the other for coffee. On the table, too, are placed, buffet-style, the necessary cups, small plates, and silverware, as well as the special tea foods. The tea table, opened to its ultimate length, may be set in any convenient room to and from which passage is easy and where groups may stand about, or occasionally sit, and have their tea with access to the food, which they serve to themselves.

On the table itself is a white tea cloth, but the trays, usually silver, are bare. Each beverage service—a large urn is usual for coffee, a samovar good for the tea—is presided over by a hostess. The tea is set up farthest from the entrance, the coffee closest to it. At a large tea the hostess herself often reserves her energies for seeing that her guests enjoy themselves, and she delegates the actual "pouring" to two friends well acquainted with the ritual, or, at very large teas, teams of two that relieve one another. These ladies seat themselves at opposite ends of the table before the trays and serve each guest as she appears. It is permissible to return as many times as one wishes for more tea or coffee, but one waits until any who have not yet been served have received theirs before asking for more.

Very occasionally at a large tea, the tea or coffee is poured at the table but passed by maids on trays.

Of course, if gentlemen are present they may offer to get tea for the various ladies, but a tea is, essentially, a self-service repast and, aside from the receiving of the cup from the hands of the teamaker, guests are expected to help themselves to the various things upon the table.

The room in which formal tea is served is always artifically lighted, with the curtains drawn as if for an evening entertainment. Tall, white candles are the prettiest ones to use.

The Guest at Formal Meals

When a guest receives a formal invitation to lunch or dine, he should know the procedures; if he knows exactly what to expect he can be at ease. It is only the unknown that tends to shake our poise. Let us examine the guest's part in formal entertaining.

When a butler or waitress is serving at table, the persons served pay sufficient attention to the service to be ready to take their portions when dishes are presented to them (from the left) and, at a crowded table, to move aside, left or right, slightly, to aid the service or removal of dishes—the latter virtually always to the right, except for butter plates.

Second Portions At formal luncheons or dinners second portions are not properly offered (or asked for) because of the usual multiplicity of courses. But at meals where they are offered, any guest who wishes more may serve himself from the proffered dish or platter even if other guests have abstained. The hostess then takes at least a token amount to keep him company, or she has eaten so slowly as to have a little left on her plate from which to eat while any guest consumes a second helping.

Guests Do Not Assist A guest does not assist in the service of anything at the table while there is staff attendance. He never stacks dishes or hands an empty plate or glass to a waiter but permits these to be removed

or replenished for him. At a formal meal there should be no need for those
at the table to pass anything. There should be salt and pepper, ash trays,
matches, and cigarettes (if the hostess wishes) at every place, or at every
other place. Bread or rolls are passed at luncheon, or rolls are in place on or
in the napkin at a formal dinner or to the left of the plate, if they are served
at all.

Greeting Domestic Staff   A guest at table does not converse with the person serving him at a dinner party, even if it is an old family retainer he
knows well, or a member of the catering staff he may have had at his house
the week before. Instead, when the person he knows approaches him with a
platter, he smiles and calls him by name, saying something like "Good evening, Johannes," or "Hello, Mary." A personal conversation can wait until
after the meal.

Crumbs   When there is full service, crumbs and bits of bread are left on
the tablecloth by the guest and are removed by the waiter when he crumbs
the table. But if any semiliquid, such as a bit of jelly or sauce, has been
dropped on the cloth, the guest, at the time, if he sees it, quietly retrieves it
with some convenient utensil—butter knife, fork, or dinner knife—and
places it on the side of his plate. If anything is spilled while a guest is being
served, then the waiter or waitress attends to it. The guest should make no
more than a murmured apology, if any, and the hostess should take no notice of it except, if necessary, to instruct the waiter in the proper procedure.

Presentation of the Finger Bowl   Finger bowls are rarely seen in unstaffed
households these days, but of course do make their appearance in homes
where full service is still possible. (It is interesting that as early as the thirteenth century silver finger bowls were presented with flowered linen
towels.) They are filled three-quarters full with cold water when served after
dessert, and flower petals or tiny blown-glass fish, and so on, are often used.
Finger bowls are placed on the table in either of two ways, one of which
requires the slight co-operation of the guest.

If the finger bowl is on the dessert plate and a decorative doily (never
paper) is placed before a guest with dessert silver on each side, the guest is
expected to lift bowl and doily and small glass plate adroitly with the right
hand and place it in front and slightly to the left of his place setting. He
then removes the silver and places it, fork left and spoon right of the plate. If
the finger bowl is presented with no silver flanking it, this indicates that
there is no further course and the guest does not remove it from the plate.
Very occasionally, a small underplate on the dessert plate, topped by doily
and finger bowl, is intended for use. For example, strawberries Romanoff is
a difficult dessert for a flat plate. The menu or the hostess gives the cue.

In using a finger bowl, the guest dips in the fingers of one hand, then of
the other, lightly, then dries them on the napkin on his lap, but all so briefly
as to avoid the impression that this is a serious ablution. He may, too, of

course, touch his lips with his moistened fingers, then pat his lips lightly with his napkin, which he then places, unfolded and unarranged, to the left of his place. He never leaves it on his chair or tosses it onto a plate.

Finger bowls, even without service, are almost necessary after the serving of boiled or broiled lobster or steamed clams. In this case, they are filled three-quarters full with warm water that may be soapy. As a different and rather novel idea, to replace the use of finger bowls after lobster and such, the hostess might borrow the oriental custom of passing a flat dish or basket containing small napkins or terry towels wrung out in hot, scented water.

The custom before an oriental-style meal is to pass refrigerated scented towels on a tray so that guests may refresh themselves before eating.

Caterers

The busy host and hostess without household help and without the time to cook and prepare for a party themselves must depend on outside help of some kind. Usually there are several options open to them. They can use a caterer who prepares the food only but has nothing to do with the serving of it, or they can use a free-lance butler to "do" their party. Some people are fortunate in having a well-trained built-in serving and cleanup crew in their children. But if you are planning a large party and want the services of a smooth working crew, a knowledgeable crew, you must turn to a full-fledged caterer. The latter and his employees will cook, prepare, and serve, properly attired, the entire party for you, as well as clean up afterward (at times a feature almost as important as the party itself to the tired host and hostess!).

An experienced caterer should know the niceties of serving properly and not need direction from you. His waiters and waitresses are trained; indeed, they are often very skilled in their trade. For a staff of waiters and waitresses to move into a house they have never seen before, and to work for six hours handling under pressure a large group of guests in unfamiliar surroundings, requires patience, concentration, and the true ability to keep one's cool. I have seen caterers running parties smoothly on lurching trains, on tropical storm-swept terraces, under rain-sodden tents, and in offices where the service area for 300 guests seemed the size of a small coat closet.

Where to Find One   You find your caterer through word of mouth and the caterer's established reputation. You either attend a party that is beautifully done, or you hear about a successful one, or you read about one in your local newspaper. In the latter case, you might call the women's editor who wrote the story on the party and ask her who catered it. In a large city, when you know there are several reputable caterers, ask two or three by telephone to give you an estimate for catering a party for a given number of people with a certain menu. That way you can compare prices—but frankly, if they are good, the differences are usually minimal. Be sure that any "low price" quoted by a caterer does not depend upon his using a greatly reduced staff of people. This can only spell disaster for your party.

I know one woman who had just moved to the Middle West and knew no one. She read in the papers two days after her arrival about a catered party given on a coal barge and retained that caterer for her first large cocktail buffet, given for her husband's fellow executives and local business associates and their wives. "I figured that any caterer who could do a good job on a coal barge ought to be able to handle one in my totally disorganized house," she said, laughing. She turned out to be correct, for, from all reports, her party was an unqualified success.

Making Arrangements   One should book a caterer as far in advance of one's party as possible. For parties during the heavy entertaining seasons, like November and December or June, the caterer should be engaged five or six months ahead. Caterers are often walking information bureaus on who else might be giving a party on the same night you choose; their information enables you to change your date before it is too late. After setting the party date, the caterer will want to discuss the size of the party and the menu in detail with you. If you have no ideas on what to serve, he or she will make suggestions. Donald Bruce-White of New York reports he is delighted when hostesses offer new imaginative ideas for food and also provide the recipes for anything from an hors d'oeuvre to a dessert. But every caterer knows the limitations of his crew and the time, budget, and space allotted for the party, so miracles must not be attempted. The experienced caterer can also guard an untrained hostess from committing social faux pas.

The hostess should tell the caterer what she wants the waiters to wear—black or white jackets. The waitresses in hot weather may wear white, but some hostesses prefer them to wear black uniforms with white aprons winter or summer. Donald Bruce-White will, if the hostess prefers, put his waitresses in pretty pastels in summertime.

Some caterers will check over the hostess' china, silver, and stemware, as well as serving platters and trays, to see if anything else must be provided from his stock, or rented. However, most caterers prefer to bring everything, from bar equipment to demitasse cups and candy compotes. That way their staff will not be responsible for "breaking something precious" in someone's house. I might add that in my life and that of my mother's before me, no caterer ever broke anything in our home; all damage has been perpetrated by our own family.

They will also bring folding tables and chairs and pretty linens and, if asked to, will do all the flowers for the tables and the house. Sometimes the host and hostess supply their own liquor and wines rather than have the caterer supply them, which cuts down on his bill. The caterer can also arrange for a car parking service (which often consists of a group of students who welcome the extra money).

The caterer prepares the food in his own establishment, then transports it to your home, where it is reheated or refrigerated. If the party is held in a place other than your home—such as in a barn, on a dock, in a field, in the large lobby of a public building—the caterer will bring serving tables, screens to hide the working area, sit-down tables and chairs, warming ovens, and containers to keep things cold. Dinner will taste as though it had been freshly made in a nonexistent kitchen.

Gaper's, a famous Chicago caterer, reports that for its people everything works most smoothly if the hostess just greets them when they arrive a few hours before the event and then leaves them alone. They are professionals; they work fast; and the hostess interfering or "trying to help" can ruin their efficient schedule and routine. In other words, they hope that the hostess will say hello and then relax and be a guest at her own party.

The Cost Once the budget is set, it should be adhered to. The hostess should not continually call the caterer adding this and that, and expect her bill to remain the same. Gratuities are usually not included in the bill of a caterer like Donald Bruce-White or Gaper's, although it may be requested. When you are doing the tipping yourself, fifteen or twenty dollars to the "party supervisor," ten dollars each to the head waitress and head cook; and five dollars for everyone else on the staff is considered very nice. Some caterers use free-lance help. In this situation, the hostess pays each one a flat fee at the end of the party for the allotted hours worked; five dollars more per hour is paid to each for overtime; and a five- or ten-dollar tip over that is a very generous and appreciated way of saying that you thought they did a good job on your party.

The cost of a catered dinner party varies from city to city, but in New York, for example, it will cost a lot more per person than in Cleveland or Kansas City. Generally the price for everything for a beautiful dinner—service, food, and drink—ranges from thirty to seventy-five dollars per person in the more expensive cities.

Caterers around the country work in different ways. Some charge by the hour, with a four-hour minimum for parties; others charge a set fee for the entire job for a cocktail or dinner party, stipulating six or seven hours of work. The staff arrives from one and a half hours before the event, according to the amount of setup work involved. It usually takes the staff one hour to clean up afterward (and they clean up—everything). When the set number of hours are up and the remaining guests look as if they're going to "continue sitting around drinking awhile," the hostess would do well to tell the catering staff to set up a bar nearby, then dismiss them for the evening to avoid overtime charges.

Cancellation There is a legal cancellation clause in most New York caterers' contracts with their clients governing payment for a party called off at the last minute. Caterers in other cities are generally not as explicit and may handle this situation in a more personal way. But usually the client is responsible at least for the food if a party is canceled on short notice.

A Word of Caution Caterers have a justifiable complaint when the hosts let their small children run wild and unsupervised during a party. "We are not supposed to be baby-sitters, too," one commented. When I asked Donald Bruce-White, caterer to many of the New York area's "beautiful people," what upset him most about hostesses, the answer was simple: "When they're rude to us." Conversely, what pleases him most is "when the host and hostess take the time and trouble to come up to us at the end of the party to thank us." He also treasures a collection of nice thank-you letters sent to him after parties.

Chapter 31

ENTERTAINING OUT OF DOORS

Entertaining out of doors has so many pluses that they far outweigh the ominous threats of downpours or mosquitoes or too much sunburn. The major asset of entertaining out of doors is, of course, the beauty of the dining room—Mother Nature's own design.

Dinner on a City Apartment Balcony

Usually lunch or dinner for two or four is about as ambitious a project as one can undertake on the average city apartment balcony. If your balcony has a good drain, wash off the floor with buckets of water before setting up your dinner table. Be sure to wash off the grime from the furniture, too. Landscape the small area with flowering plants or greenery. One or two hurricane lamps make a delightful centerpiece when combined with flowers. No paper napkins or plastic plates for this kind of entertaining. Use your good china, silver, crystal, and linens. Making an effort for one's guests, even in a small space, brings large rewards.

An Outdoor Buffet

If you are having a large buffet lunch or dinner out of doors, place the serving table against a pretty backdrop in your yard or garden—an alley of trees, a vine-covered wall, an ivy-covered trellis, a rough stone wall, or a panorama of sea or lake or mountains. One woman I know, who lives in a small house in a crowded suburb, puts her buffet table against the painted side wall of her garage. She is a weaver of talent, and for each party she hangs a different large piece of her art on the garage wall as the center backdrop for her buffet table. Each time she manages to pick up the colors of the weaving in her napkins and tablecloth. When I asked her how she does it, she answered matter-of-factly, "I dyed them myself, to match my hand-dyed yarns."

In a place like Florida or Hawaii, the hostess usually does not need to tell the guests they will be eating out of doors. In more northern climes, she should tell her guests so that everyone will dress suitably. However, the efficient hostess keeps a supply of shawls and sweaters for chilly guests who forget to bring wraps.

Out-of-door entertaining presents the perfect background for stoneware, earthenware, and rustic pottery. The buffet table should look handsome, with the hot food served in decorative oven cookware. If you are having a big party that is informal in nature—such as an after-swim party, a Fourth of July lunch party, or a barbecue—then paper plates, napkins, and cups are suitable. But no plastic forks, spoons, or knives, please. The hostess should tell her guests when she is inviting them, "It will be a very informal party; come in comfortable clothes." Or, if she is going to wear a long dress and is using her good china and linens, she should tell her guests that she is wearing a long dress and her husband is wearing a jacket and tie. (In certain parts of the country, where informality is a way of life, the men might balk at being told to wear a jacket and a tie, but their attire will perk up the party, and it's good for everyone to get dressed up every once in a while.)

Patio Entertaining

Patio entertaining can also be as formal or as informal as you wish. Paper and plastic are suitable for lunch or a big daytime tea, wedding shower, or something of that type, but in the evening one should use one's good things —which can include the most informal of stoneware. Anything well designed is right for outdoor dining. If one is surrounded by the strong textures of nature, it is very pleasing to the eye to see strong-textured china, large bold-shaped glasses, heavy woven napkins. Yet candlelight dinners with delicate crystal plates and crystal candelabra look beautiful and right, too, on the patio. It's the hostess who decides; she can play it any way she wishes, but in my opinion, if she forgoes paper plates for her parties, she's doing the proper thing.

The food served out-of-doors can be the same as that served indoors (see Chapter 26, "Menu Inspiration.")

The smart hostess landscapes her patio and perhaps even repeats some of the same decor on her party tables: for example, large pots of pink and red geraniums against her patio wall, small clay pots of pink and red geraniums in the center of each table. Some hostesses cue their lunch party linens and centerpiece to match the gaily colored umbrellas over the tables on their terrace. (At night the umbrellas fold up, so that people can see each other more easily from table to table.)

There are many ways to fight bugs and mosquitoes on the terrace, and you should experiment to find the best solution for your home. It is always a good idea, too, to have on hand several containers of insect repellent for guests who are especially prone to insect bites. (The electric fly grid machines also seem to work well in ridding the area of biting insects.)

There is nothing more delightful and relaxing than enjoying an excellent dinner on someone's terrace, at a table that is set with taste, and surveying a patio and garden that are beautifully landscaped. I remember complimenting my hostess in Cleveland one summer night on the beauty of the scene she had set for her guests. "Thank you," she said, "for the wonderful compliment, but frankly I do it for myself, too. I like to look at all of this just as much as you do, every night. I cannot grow tired of it."

Picnics

There are two kinds of confirmed picnickers. There are those who own and use efficient, modern eating equipment, ready to go at a minute's notice in sleek, well-designed luxury; then there are those who have no regular picnic equipment but use any available container found in the house. The former look like a well-drilled Marine division; the latter like a group of nomad peasants crossing the mountains. (My family and I are in the latter group.) Either group can organize a sensational picnic, for it's the food that counts, and the spirit of the group, and the gracious caring of the host and hostess that everyone has a good time. Beer and soda taste refreshingly good whether the bottles are kept cold in the latest and greatest ice bag or in a tin wastebasket filled with ice cubes and topped by a makeshift lid. It looks a lot easier on the eye to do it in the professional picnickers' manner, with the handsome wicker baskets (instead of shopping bags), and hampers fitted with plates, cups, flatware, vacuum bottles, condiment containers, and, of course, special cold and hot maintenance features.

Wine bottles are carried efficiently in partitioned wicker baskets (whose primary use is to carry wine bottles safely from the wine cellar to their table destination). These wine-bottle carriers can also be used to pack the various thermos jugs of hot or cold soup and cold cocktails. (If you carry your wine bottles in a tote of some kind, wrap them well in newspaper or dish towels so they don't clank against each other.) If you have a cake carrier at home (the base and cover lock together, so the contents are unspillable) it is a wonderful way to carry a cake safely, but it can also be used to transport cold pieces of roast chicken or a whole roast beef you may wish to slice on the spot. (Those days of the simple picnic of peanut-butter sandwiches, deviled eggs, and soda seem to have disappeared, as people take their eating-away-from-home very seriously.) If you have made a Caesar salad, a shrimp salad, a Waldorf salad, or any kind for that matter, transport it in a plastic bag, firmly fastened, *with* the ice you are bringing for your drinks. You can bring your handsome salad serving bowl separately (and to save space, pack it with your table linens or some other bulky item).

Table Linens, Plates, et Cetera   Here again, the attitudes of the host and hostess come into play in the strongest possible way. Some people would not dream of going on a picnic without using paper plates, plastic glasses, and paper napkins. The one concession to style they make is that this paper wardrobe is all matching. Then there is the school of the perfectionist pic-nickers, who insist upon using fragile porcelain plates, linen tablecloth and napkins, and long-stemmed wineglasses (which they carry safely packed in wicker hampers). They carry a folding table and folding chairs with them, too. They are still living, attitude-wise, in the days when the family butler engineered the picnic and the domestic staff worked throughout the event (even though there may never have been a family butler in their ancestry). I must confess I love to go on these picnics!

Preparing the Area Bugs can ruin picnics even faster than a thunder-storm. (The rainstorm, after all, might blow away.) If you know you are going to have to picnic in a buggy area, and if you are the host of a large group, try to arrive there two hours before your guests, in order to spray the area with a yard spray purchased at the hardware store. Be sure to read all the directions carefully on the can, of course. There might be an unpleasant odor, which will disappear within a half hour. Keep children and pets away from the area while it is freshly sprayed, and keep your food well covered and away from this action. Some people prefer to light mosquito coils and place them around the picnic area.

If you are going to be eating on the grass (and be sure to pick a shady spot, as free as possible of anthills, on grass that has not grown too high), you can spread a tablecloth, an old bedspread, some beach towels spread out contiguously, or a blanket (if the weather is not too hot). Keep wind gusts in mind, and secure all four corners of your "tablecloth" carefully. If you're going to use park-provided picnic tables and benches, you can cover the table with a cloth or use mats. If you plan on using a paper tablecloth, remember the wind factor and secure it with four pretty rocks in the corners.

Check List Make a check list *the night before* of everything you are going to need. Assemble all the items in a central spot, and be sure all the equipment is clean and shined up. Thermos jugs often need airing. Make a note to yourself to bring twice as much ice as you think you'll need. Put out extra plates, cups, and utensils. There never seem to be enough, particularly when children are present. They somehow start to eat from the moment they arrive at the picnic destination, even though the meal is not supposed to be served for an hour or two. One efficient hostess I know gives each child his own junk food packet (a small ration) when he arrives at the picnic site, with stern instructions to stay away from the food and to refrain from ask-ing, "When do we eat?" She manages to assuage their hunger, earn their un-dying devotion, and save her food all at one time. Among the items on your check list, to be laid out the night before:

1. A first-aid kit, including insect repellent and sunburn lotion (and a snake-bite kit for rattlesnake country!).

2. Two bottle openers and two wine bottle openers (what if you are miles from any civilization and your bottle opener doesn't work?).
3. Salt and pepper; catsup and mustard; salad dressing—anything you need to spice up the food.
4. Sugar and sweetener for the hot or iced coffee and tea.
5. Count the soda in the icebox; add another six to what you think you'll need!
6. Linens (including paper napkins); plates, cups, glasses, utensils.
7. A booklet showing photographs in color of poison ivy and poison oak, to use in briefing the children before they go off to play.
8. Several large plastic bags and ties, to use for your garbage (and to bring back and dispose of at home). Also a roll of paper towels.
9. Several packets of matches.
10. If it's a beach picnic, supply extra beach towels, back rests, a big umbrella, some big straw hats, and several pairs of sunglasses.
11. If you are going to charcoal-grill your meat or fish, assemble the briquettes, and the lighter fluid with your equipment. If you are taking a portable grill with you, place it by the front door, so you will fall over it, or, even better, get it packed in the car.
12. Classical music for your picnic? Don't forget your portable radio or cassette player in your "take-along" pile.
13. Camera and film.
14. Last but not least, the sports equipment—the volleyball, the baseball bat and ball, whatever you are planning to do athletically—should be assembled in the staging area, too.

The importance of the list, which includes food that will be brought, cannot be overstated. The hostess should have that list in her hand when the time comes to return home, because it is her only way to know if everything goes back that should.

Preparing Food Ahead Since leaving for the picnic is so hectic, as much of the food as possible should be prepared the evening before. Make your fancy cocktails, if that is what you are going to serve, put them cold in thermos jugs, and place them in the refrigerator. Wash all the salad ingredients, prepare them, and place them in separate plastic bags before re-refrigerating. If you are having hamburgers, make the patties, put each one in a plastic sandwich bag, and wrap them into a single parcel before refrigerating again. Prepare the dessert, if you are having one; wash the fruit and wrap it; roast your chicken or beef, if that is what you are going to serve. Make your casseroles, cool them, and place them, well covered, in the refrigerator. In other words, do everything you can the night before. Again, listing all the food items is important, so you won't forget any the morning of the departure. Even count the numbers of soda and beer you are bringing. (The first large picnic I engineered, I left behind a complicated dessert I had spent hours making; but my niece outdid me—she left the entire main course behind.)

Epilogue Clean up the camp site or beach so fastidiously no one will know you have been there. Bring home your trash, if there are no proper trash receptacles on the spot. Never throw anything in the woods (not even a soda can top) or in the lake or sea. Gather it all and bring it home, to dispose of in your usual manner. Put out the fire, if you have made one. Pour water on the logs until there is no sign of steam, including on the beach. Never camouflage burning embers or coals with sand on the beach; someone could walk on it and be badly burned. Make sure, by consulting your equipment list, that each and every thing has been packed in people's cars to go back, including Junior's favorite football and Grandma's favorite fly swatter.

Tailgate Picnics The tailgate picnic is named for the custom of letting the tailgate down on the back of the station wagon and using it as a serving table for a picnic before a sports event. It is a phenomenon that grows more and more popular as Americans grow more and more spectator-sports-minded. All over the country, particularly during the football season but also in the racing season, the stadium parking lot or the field near the races becomes the scene of pre-game and pre-race gastronomic feasts. The hosts delight in the competitive spirit of preparing food and drinks that outdo the neighbors' tailgate offerings. When the tradition began, the menu used to consist of food like ham and cheese sandwiches with thermoses of coffee. Now out from large thermos bags and elegant picnic hampers, some with silvered fittings, emerge bottles of fine wine, well-made bloody marys or daiquiries, homemade pâté with imported pickles and French bread, hot turtle soup, cold artichokes, chicken tandoori, sliced London broil with special mustard sauces, lobster salad, and strawberries with whipped cream. One Yale football stadium hostess I know fed us royally from her station wagon and sent us off to the game, each with our own hot thermos of strong coffee to sip during the cold afternoon.

Poolside Entertaining

There is nothing more fun than a well-run poolside party. An invitation to a family swimming party usually means a "come for a swim and lunch" kind of event, where everyone will stay until quite late in the afternoon.

The lunch menu at such a party means simple food that children will like. There should be a bar for adults, but soft drinks for the young; barbecuing facilities for hamburgers and hot dogs; a big bowl of potato chips; a large salad bowl, and a freezerful of ice-cream bars and lots of fresh fruit. This is sufficient to keep everyone happy.

You should be explicit about details in extending your invitation. Don't just say over the telephone, "Come for a swim before lunch—come anytime." Your guests might easily spend an hour at home arguing about how your words should be interpreted, with their children pressing to arrive poolside by 10:00 A.M. (when you might still be enjoying your breakfast and the Sunday papers). You should also tell them to bring their own towels, if that is what you want—and you probably do.

State at what time they should arrive and at what hour lunch will be served (if the children know ahead of time they have to wait, they won't be so impatient for food). You should also indicate at what time you wish them to depart. "And we hope you'll stay around awhile after lunch—until about three" (otherwise, they might stay until six). You should also tell them if they can expect to stay in their swimsuits. If you are going to serve lunch in the house, tell them to bring along slacks, shorts, or something to change into, so they will not be in their wet suits while in your house.

As for the paraphernalia you should have ready and prepared by the pool: the barbecue equipment, of course; a big cooler full of ice for soft drinks and beer; a portable bar (with real glasses, not paper cups) and another cooler of ice for cocktails; a buffet table all set up for lunch service (this table can be a collapsible lightweight one and may be covered with any kind of attractive cloth, including one made of paper); paper plates, cups, and napkins, if desired; flatware from the house; some extra towels for the guests who inevitably forget theirs; balls and toys to float in the pool for the children's games and amusement; rafts for the adults to recline upon (or the children, when the adults are not using them); and perhaps a pair of those wonderfully decadent floating trays in which to place cocktails and soft drinks.

If you want to be a "super-host" in the eyes of your children guests, you'll organize a short and simple swim competition and diving exhibition—including letting the little ones dive off the side of the pool. At the end there should be an official prize-awarding ceremony, with each child given a prize.

The well-organized host has the Sunday newspapers for the adults to peruse, and a portable magazine rack full of the latest periodicals for the guests' enjoyment when desired. It is also very hospitable to keep a portable plastic "caddy" of some kind by the pool, containing paper tissue for the inevitable runny noses of the young ones, extra pairs of sunglasses, suntan preparation, some Band-Aids, and insect repellent (this avoids constant running up to the house).

The considerate host does not invite childless couples or single people to these family swimming parties. The noise, splashing, and mass confusion would be enough to keep a bachelor single or an unmarried woman from ever wanting to produce children.

The "Rules of the Pool" (discussed in detail in "The Considerate Sportsperson," page 717) should be posted for all to read and obey.

If there are plenty of food and sodas; if the rules are spelled out loud and clear; if there is a wonderful mixture of parents and children of all ages plus at least one hour of planned, supervised activity for the children (including the swimming and diving competitions, but also perhaps Ping-Pong or a cro-quiet tournament, pitching horseshoes, or whatever), then your party will be a great success.

Evening Pool Parties   Once again, the host and hostess should be explicit about the hours of the party, the dress suggested, and the activities planned. If there's going to be dancing to the stereo after swimming and dinner by the pool, the guests will want to bring dressier clothes to change into after swimming. If you don't have a pool house with dressing rooms, put a sign on the door of two bedrooms, one for men and one for women, so they can change in your house.

Tell your guests to bring their own towels, and let them know the timetable, as, for example,

5–8 P.M.   Swimming and cocktails
8 P.M.   Dinner served
           Dancing follows

One of the greatest swimming parties I ever attended was on the hottest night of the year in Washington, D.C. We stayed in our suits for dinner by the pool, and some guests stayed on the rafts in the pool for a nine-thirty performance of a movie (which had been rented for the occasion, with the hostess' son pressed into service as our projectionist). The only bad moment of the evening was when the family Labrador knocked down the portable screen at the most exciting moment in the film. It barely missed falling into the water, but it was soon righted and the show went on.

It is almost imperative that the pool be well lit if there are going to be parties at night; otherwise there could be some nasty accidents. Also, if you can afford to have a swimming pool, you can afford to have some pretty lighting around it for dinner parties. I have seen some ingenious pool-area lighting done with battery-operated lanterns and spots, all very homemade but nonetheless effective and attractive.

The use of hurricane lanterns and iron pots with oil or with wax candles—there are many beautiful ways to spotlight the out-of-doors and your dinner tables at night.

Barbecues

Barbecues have always been popular, particularly in the Southwest, but the advent of the Lyndon Johnson presidency made them a national institution. Barbecues can be organized in your back yard, if you and your guests absorb some western flavor and enter into the spirit of things. I remember once not being able to get through a blocked-off street in a medium-sized Ohio town. I parked my car, went to investigate, and was soon involved in a Ohio-style barbecue. (I missed my plane as a result, but it was well worth it.) It was a block party, a church fund-raiser. Everyone was in western dress. There were three separate square dancing groups in the street, each with its own fiddler and caller, and behind the houses succulent meats were being barbecued and long tables full of food were being prepared—and, I might add, were being continuously depleted and filled again. The food kept on coming. The entire city block was involved, with all of the houses' back yards full of activity, people coming and going, walking from the back to the street. As one of the townspeople said, "We're dancin' out front, barbecuin' out back."

Set your own barbecue feast on tables covered with gay checkered cloths, or do something creative with cotton. If you have a garage, you can use it for square dancing. If you do want to have square dancing at your own back-yard barbecue, you can probably locate a caller by inquiring around, and if you can't locate a fiddler, try using square dance records on your stereo. It works! (Be sure to put a rain date on your invitations, too.) At President Johnson's ranch in Stonewall, Texas, this was a typical barbecue menu:

Barbecued Beef and Ribs	Texas Cole Slaw
Chicken	Dill Pickles
Hot Link Sausage	Sliced Onions
Ranch-style Beans	Fried Apple Pies
German Potato Salad	Iced Tea and/or Coffee
Dough Biscuits	Fresh, Homemade Peach Ice Cream

The Johnsons would pass around mixed drinks, white wine, and beer before the barbecue; iced tea and beer were served during the meal—which was often served on tin plates, with tin mugs for the beverages.

Although you will be doing your barbecuing most likely on a charcoal grill, basting with a good barbecue sauce, here are Mrs. Johnson's instructions for constructing an authentic barbecue:

Dig a pit three feet deep, four feet wide, and forty feet long. Place a layer of wood across the bottom of the pit and start the fire. Keep the fire at the same height for about five hours and then let die down to coals. Any type of hard wood is suitable—pecan, oak or a similar wood.

Place iron pipe across the pit every three feet and cover with heavy wire mesh. Make sure that mesh is tied securely so that the meat will not be dumped into the fire. Make a one-foot opening under the wire at intervals through which additional coals may be added. Start another fire to one side so that additional coals will be available to add to the trench as needed. Start the fire at least six hours before the meat is to be put on. *Do not have any blaze after the meat is put on*—only coals.

Cut the meat into heavy pieces of six to eight pounds each. Salt and pepper the meat generously before putting it on to cook. Do not let pieces overlap—allow room for smoke to come up around each piece.

Pieces with adequate fat will be self-basting. For leaner portions, baste with cooking oil or melted margarine to which a small quantity of vinegar has been added. Turn the meat frequently so that it will cook evenly and allow at least eight hours of cooking time.

The barbecue sauce is, of course, the key to this festivity. The Johnson recipe is as follows and can be multiplied to suit the crowd:

¼ cup butter	¼ cup lemon juice
¼ cup vinegar	¼ cup Worcestershire
¼ cup catsup	Salt, pepper, red pepper,
(Sometimes add garlic or	tabasco
onion for variety)	

Melt butter in saucepan, add other ingredients and bring to a boil. Pour over meat to be barbecued.

The mode of dress at those Johnson barbecues was informal. The women wore pants or long cotton dresses (or long skirts); and the men wore "western gear" or slacks with an open shirt—no ties or jackets at this kind of party. It is great fun for your own guests to dress this way.

Chapter 32

THE WEEKEND GUEST

Invitations

If you haven't already had particular guests for the weekend, you're in for some very great surprises, and so are they. Friends do not really know each other until they spend a couple of nights under the same roof—particularly if the house is in a resort area dependent upon good weather and it happens to storm the entire time.

The major thing for people to remember when inviting house guests is:

1. Invite people for the weekend a full month or two ahead, so you will have a good chance of getting the people you want before they're booked up.
2. Do the different couples fit in with each other? Are they enemies or friends? If they don't know each other, will they get along?
3. Be very specific about:
   a. When to arrive and *when to leave.*
   b. The means by which your guests can arrive and the schedules for the best buses, trains, or planes, or a map for the best routes by car.
   c. What clothes to bring (which only you can know, since you're aware of the special sports or social events and the predicted weather). If you'll all be in jeans the whole weekend, tell them. Be frank if you are going to wear a short evening dress, evening pajamas or a long tailored skirt and blazer on Saturday night. Tell the men exactly what to bring—a black tie and dinner jacket, or sports jacket only with gray flannels, or "the loudest pair of pants you own." It is just as important for the men guests to be appropriately dressed for the weekend as for the women guests.

The Guest Room

Every hostess should sleep in her own guest room at least once before "inflicting" the experience on someone else. The mattresses may be lumpy and bumpy on those beds you inherited from your mother; the light in the bathroom may be so inadequate that it is impossible to shave properly or to put on make-up in front of it. I have listed below the items that should be on every caring hostess' check list under two main categories: Necessities and Niceties.

The Necessities

1. *The condition of the beds and the linens.* Will the guests be warm enough? Is there a good mattress pad on each bed? Are the pillows in clean condition; do they smell fresh? Are the electric blankets working?
2. *The heat or ventilation or lack of it in the room.* Do the windows go up and down with ease (or are they still painted shut from the painter's last visit?)? Are there giant cracks around the window frames through which the wind whistles? If so, place calking on your list of things to do. Does the air conditioner work, or does it just make a lot of noise? Would a good electric fan help cool the bedroom?
3. Are the window screens in good condition, or is there a symphony of mosquitoes playing every night in the room?
4. Are there large wastebaskets in both the guest room and guest bathroom?
5. Is there a good reading lamp with a strong bulb beside each bed?
6. If the arriving guests are smokers, alas, are there ash trays and matchbooks around for their convenience?
7. Are there plenty of coat hangers and pants and skirt hangers in the closet? Has room been cleared in the closet for the guests' clothes? Has the closet been aired of musty or mothproof odors?
8. Is there a notepad-pencil set on the table beside the bed?
9. Has bureau space been cleared in the chests of drawers? (There should be one *large* drawer cleared for each guest for a weekend visit, two drawers each for a longer stay.)
10. Are there a clock and a radio, so the guests will be able to set an alarm and know what goes on in the world?
11. Is there stationery in the desk (or the table that serves as one)? A work pad and a mug full of pens and pencils are certainly helpful for your guests, regardless of their ages.

The Niceties

1. A bouquet of fresh flowers, or a pretty plant (no plastic flowers, please).
2. A small TV set.
3. Some good books left in the room—and the latest magazines.
4. A tray of good perfume on the bureau.
5. A sewing kit tucked away in the top drawer.
6. An airtight tin box of goodies, such as brownies or special candy for the midnight snackers with an overly active sweet tooth.

7. A pretty scarf (for the woman who forgets something to protect her hair).
8. A thermos full of ice water.
9. A coffee maker with coffee and water in it; all the guest does early in the morning is plug it in and, presto, there's a cup of fresh hot coffee in the room.

The Guest Bathroom

The Necessities

1. Fresh bar of nonallergenic soap on washbasin; fresh bar of nicely scented bath soap in the bathtub or shower.
2. Shower cap.
3. Separate rack of towels for each guest, consisting of bath towel, face towel, and two washcloths.
4. Beach towel for each guest (stowed in bathroom or closet).
5. If several people will be using the bathroom, it's nice to have an extra dry bath mat for the latecomers to use.
6. There should be two hooks on the back of the bathroom door, to hang bathrobes, pajamas, and nightgowns.
7. *In the medicine cabinet:*
   a. Razor blades and a clean razor.
   b. Two new toothbrushes and a fresh tube of toothpaste.
   c. Aspirin.
   d. Package of adhesive bandages.
   e. Deodorant.
   f. Shampoo.
   g. Mouthwash.
   h. Styptic pencil.
   i. Hair spray.
   j. In hot climates: insect repellent and sun protection lotion.
8. *On or near the tub:*
   a. Bath powder.
   b. Sponge and small container of detergent.
9. *On a chest,* window sill, or small table:
   a. Box of facial tissue.
   b. Covered jar of cotton balls.
   c. Extra roll of toilet tissue.
   d. Container of mild soap for personal laundry.
   e. Container of air freshener.

The Niceties

1. An electric hair dryer.
2. Setting lotion and rollers for the hair.
3. An emergency make-up kit.

4. After-bath lotion.
5. Hand cream.
6. Toilet water for both men and women.
7. Hangers for drying personal laundry.

Good-looking bathroom accessories to match the room's color scheme can be easily purchased in stores and through catalogues, but those with artistic talent can do a masterful job on their own—as, for example, hand-painting ordinary food jars with pretty designs and using them to hide detergent containers or to hold cotton balls. (One of the prettiest bathroom accessories I've seen was made by a friend who covered a cigar box with decoupage and used it for storing flat items in her bathroom.) And if you want a tip on keeping the guest bathroom soap dish from becoming slimy and dirty; put a group of colorful marbles in the soap dish. The soap bar rests on top of them, and drains down, and the marbles need only an occasional rinsing.

Breakfast for Guests

Breakfast during the work week has to be, by necessity, a rather regimented meal. Everyone arises at the same time, eats breakfast more or less at the same time while jockeying for position to use the bathroom—if there aren't enough bathrooms to go around the family. The weekend guest should not have to follow such a regimented schedule. The "Let's all have breakfast at nine o'clock sharp" school is neither very popular nor very feasible.

Morning people want to have breakfast early in order to face the day. Night people usually do not even wish to discuss the subject. On Friday night the nicest thing a hostess can say to both her morning people and her night people guests is, "You're on your own for breakfast in this house. Get up when you please; eat what and when you please, and wear what you please." The hostess should then add, "But be on deck by twelve-thirty, when we're all leaving for the beach" (or going to the club for lunch and paddle tennis, or whatever the program is, winter or summer).

Someone, of course—either the host or hostess, whoever is the morning person in the family—has to rise and get the breakfast meal organized. One can prepare a large amount of scrambled eggs and leave them in a double boiler kept warm on the stove; one can make a pound of bacon, and leave it warm in the oven, well drained and wrapped in tin foil; and one can even make English muffins or buttered rolls and leave them well wrapped in foil in a warm oven. A large pot of coffee should be made; the plates, coffee mugs, orange juice glasses, utensils, and paper napkins left out; and various dry cereals and bowls available on the counters.

In a house without help, of course, each guest upon finishing breakfast, scrapes and rinses his own plates and puts everything into the dishwasher. If the machine is full, the last person to finish breakfast also starts the machine.

Organizing the Day

In most households it is really preferable to leave the morning schedule loose, in order to enable the serious sports people to pursue their interests and the need-to-relax people to do nothing. However, it is always wise to announce what time various activities will occur later in the day.

One of the best hostesses I know, with a house on Martha's Vineyard, is a paragon of efficiency, but, rather than remind us of a well-oiled machine, she just makes things wonderfully easy for her guests. It is a superorganized household; she has planned every single meal by the Wednesday before our arrival. Every year when we arrive we find in her kitchen the huge familiar blackboard, with all the information we need written in chalk. She puts on the board:

1. What time people are expected to be and where, wearing what, for each lunch and dinner. If we are going out for a cocktail party, she lists the time and the hosts and their address (for she has found out from experience that trying to get an athletic group back from different parts of the island to a cocktail party "on time, in a group, and smelling nice," as she puts it, is "impossible").
2. The greens fees at the local golf course and the best time to get there.
3. The hours of reserved tennis courts for the entire weekend.
4. The locations of the various beaches suitable for gentle swimming or rough surf.
5. The available transportation (most of it borrowed from her children, who are always off-island when these house parties occur, by mutual consent). It usually includes her car, a jeep, and four bicycles.
6. All the "in" shops on the island this season, and the "gotta see" art galleries.
7. The hours of mass on Sunday for those of us who are Catholics. (Usually no one ever thinks of that.)
8. Her last item on the huge board: the time the two island taxis will be coming to fetch all the house guests and their varied luggage for the Sunday night planes home. She always concludes her messages with: "And if you're fogged in at the airport, I don't even want to hear about it!"

For the Guest to Remember

Preliminary Organization

1. Arrange your transportation early, particularly on summer and holiday weekends. Airplane reservations may not be all that easy to get; rented cars are often gone by Friday morning on popular weekends.
2. Organize your luggage well ahead. You may need a new piece. Don't arrive in a car looking like gypsies, carrying everything in tote bags and

shopping bags. If you can't afford the proper luggage, borrow it from friends for the weekend.

3. Organize your wardrobe and your sports equipment, and this means everything from bathing caps and extra rolls of film to golf shoes and tennis balls. Don't arrive having to borrow all manner of things from your hosts. That is the best insurance for a non-repeat invitation that exists. Lay out on the bed all the clothes and equipment you'll need, and then list them. The list helps ensure that you'll return home again with everything you took with you. When you lay out your wardrobe three or four nights ahead, it enables you to sew things that need mending or get things back from the cleaners you thought were already back.

4. Plan your hostess' presents. A last-minute organization of this activity inevitably means you can't find the right thing. If there are children in the house you are visiting, remember to bring them something, too, whether it's a box of cookies or a new kite to fly on the beach. (See "House Guest Presents," page 787.)

5. Take certain steps in regard to the safety of your house, such as having a neighbor take in your newspapers and mail for you. Never leave proof that you are away from your house.

What Makes a Welcome Guest?

1. Don't under any circumstances bring your pet with you. It will only cause trouble and resentment, no matter how enthusiastically your hosts tell you to bring it.

2. Unless they are specifically invited, don't try to have your children included in the invitation, even if the house you will be staying in is tremendous. Many people feel more strongly about other people's children than they do about their pets.

3. On the subject of children, don't criticize or try to discipline your host's children, even if they desperately need it.

4. If you're not feeling well, cancel your visit.

5. Don't try to get your hosts to cancel their projected and probably much worked-over schedule in order to accommodate your special desires. Always accept your hosts' plans with enthusiasm.

6. Don't leave your room looking as though a tornado had passed through it—or a dirty washbasin, soap-splattered bathroom mirror, ring around the tub, or flooded bathroom floor. If you don't find available tools with which to clean up the mess, ask your hostess where you can find them.

7. Don't ignore something you break. It's easy to break something when you're a house guest. Whether it's the saucer under the window plant or the toothbrush glass in the bathroom, tell your hostess. If you broke something valuable, try to make amends by having it repaired or replacing it. If it's something minor, apologize profusely and then forget it.

8. Don't be late for anything, much less everything. When the host and

hostess are trying to organize a group (and they're always unwieldly on vacation weekends), moving guests from place to place and from activity to activity is logistically difficult. The prompt guest helps; the compulsively late guest penalizes the entire group.

9. Don't become so relaxed in the household you begin to put your shod feet on all the furniture; even informal summer furniture has to be treated nicely. In other words, treat your hosts' property with respect.

10. Don't rush out to the kitchen to help with anything and everything. Ask your hostess what helping hand you can extend, and when. If she's experienced in having house guests and has no help, she will tell you. Let her inform you of exactly what you may do to ease the load of organizing the weekend. Offer to do anything, and you will receive certain assignments—if, I repeat, the hostess is experienced and secure.

11. Don't ignore the hosts' family. There may be an aged parent in the house, or young children who need some supervision and attention while their parents are so busy. Devoting some time and attention to these other members of the family is "giving" to your hosts in the real sense. Engaging the children in a game of softball out of doors when your hostess is busy making hors d'oeuvres, or taking their grandmother on a shopping expedition, are ways in which a house guest goes to the top of the preferred list of house guests.

12. Never stay beyond your projected visit. Even "one more day" is too much. Your hosts in a flush of enthusiasm may have asked you to stay on, but it is much better to leave them sincerely sorry you are not staying longer. Don't worry, you will be asked back again if you were a "giving" guest.

If There's a Maid If you should be visiting someone still fortunate enough to have a maid, she might ask if she can unpack for you, which you may let her do, or you may say, "No, thank you very much. I'd rather unpack myself." A maid will ask if there is anything she might press for you; she will bring you breakfast on a tray if you wish to have it in bed. But don't overburden her with your personal demands. (In the old days, when there were plenty of maids in some households, a guest used to be able to ask the maid to do her personal laundry, too; her stockings might even be ironed!) If there are a butler, a cook, and a maid, you should tip them at the end of your stay. Tell your hostess you are "leaving something for the staff," and if you are in an absolute quandary about how much to give, ask her outright. Hostesses with a staff are used to the question; you won't be the first to ask it. If you and your family have been guests for a long weekend, you might give ten dollars to the cook, and five dollars to the maid. If you and your husband have stayed in the house with one maid for the weekend, you might give her ten dollars. Hostesses often discourage young people from tipping the staff, since the financial state of most young guests' wallets is limited: "No, forget about it. I always take care of it when we have young friends visiting." That doesn't mean, however, that those "young friends" don't go to thank each member of the staff who took care of them that weekend, before leaving the house.

Misusing the Telephone One of the worst transgressions house guests commit is overusing the telephone. Tying up the line is bad enough. Making long-distance calls without reimbursing one's host (or using one's own credit card or reversing the charges) is reprehensible.

If you come into a town and have a lot of local calls to make, don't make them from your host's home. Take an envelope of coins to a pay station and make all of your calls from there. You can use your host's home for a call-back number, provided you do it for only one night and you apologize profusely.

The Overnight Guest in Cramped Quarters

If there is a "guest room" in an apartment, then it usually means that the children have grown up and departed. With everyone home, however, a guest room in today's apartment is usually a family joke. The couch in the library-den or the convertible sofa in the living room usually translates to the "guest room." It is very difficult for both hosts and guest to live through these "overnights." The guest should make every effort to be so thoughtful that he will be asked to "stop over with us any time"—a tremendous compliment to someone who has just stopped over!

What the Host Does
1. Provides a bath towel, hand towel, and facecloths on a rack in the bathroom; also, a drinking glass and a glass to hold the guest's toothbrush and toothpaste.
2. Provides hangers in the hall coat closet for the guest's clothes or space there to hang his clothes bag.
3. Makes up the sofa bed with linens and sufficient blankets.
4. Gives the guest a clock.
5. Gives the guest a hint as to when to use the bathroom in the morning, according to everyone's departure schedules.

What the Guest Does
1. Observes the "to-bed" hour and bathroom and breakfast schedules and fits himself into the scheme in an unobtrusive manner.
2. Uses his suitcase as a bureau and does not unpack anything he does not immediately need.
3. Folds the bed linens, but makes up the bed with clean linens, then reconverts it to a sofa.
4. Makes his own breakfast and does his own breakfast dishes.
5. Writes a warm letter of thanks when he leaves and sends a little gift.

Saying Thank You After Being Entertained

When you attend a cocktail party, you don't have to write a thank-you note, but *if you do,* your hosts will really appreciate it. I strongly feel that if you are entertained at a meal in someone's home, or visit them for the weekend or even an overnight, you should write your thanks. The best time to do it is immediately after the event, but certainly within a time span of five or six days.

If you telephone your thanks, you're taking the easy way out. You are probably seated in your favorite comfy chair, with a drink or a cup of coffee. When you dial your host or hostess in their home you may be interrupting a warm bath into which the hostess has finally relaxed; an important conversation between husband and wife, just returned from work; an important helping hand being extended to a child with his homework; or a very strategic moment in cooking the family dinner. Who needs *that* kind of thanks from a guest?

The nicest thing to do is to take a piece of your best stationery and to write by hand how much you and your spouse enjoyed the party. The letter will be read by your hosts when they want to read the day's mail, when they are relaxed and receptive to it. Both husband and wife can share its contents, while a telephone call is received by only one person. If it is a particularly well written and delightful letter, the recipients may very well keep it, to savor again in the future.

This means, of course, that your thank-you letter is not a trite one. You can't write and expect great appreciation for a note that reads: "Dear Sally, Bob and I enjoyed the dinner party very much. Thanks for having us." You really should add some "yes, we were really there" comments. You might, for example, compliment the hostess on her cooking, or perhaps the host on his great choice of wine. You might mention a guest who was particularly fun to talk to, or the fact that you were fascinated by the naturalist who was holding forth on the disappearing species. Whatever it was (good) that really stood out at that dinner party, mention it. If you are thanking someone for a whole weekend visit, it should be easy to fill two or three pages with reminiscences and observations on the meals, activities, the people you met, the nice house, and so on.

In my White House social secretary days, I found it fascinating to observe the flow of beautiful, personal handwritten notes sent by Mrs. John F. Kennedy to her hostesses the day after a party she and the President attended, as well as the letters sent to Mrs. Kennedy by Mrs. Lyndon Johnson, Mrs. Harry Truman, and Mrs. Dwight Eisenhower, each after having been individually received at the White House. If the First Ladies of the land, past and present, have the manners and discipline to make time to put pen to paper, in order to say thank you, then the rest of us should be able to do it, too.

Sending a Gift to Say Thank You The fact that you wish to send a gift to your hostess does not mean that you no longer have the obligation to write a note to accompany it. Sending a visiting card with the present is not enough. The written message must still be added. You cannot "buy" thanks with a present.

If you have been the guest of honor at a party, or if you have been a weekend guest, you really should send or bring your hosts a joint gift, anythink from several bottles of wine to an art book, or from a basket of imported cheese to an impressive plant (see "Gift Ideas for All Occasions," page 787).

As for flowers, it is far nicer to send them the day before the party, so that they can help embellish the home of your hosts (and also save them expense on having to order flowers themselves). But if someone has given a dinner party for you, and you have sent flowers the day before with your card, you still have to write that thank-you note the day after the party. There is simply no way of getting around it.

Chapter 33

SPECIAL TYPES OF
ENTERTAINING

Children's Birthday Parties

For the very small child of one or two, it is best to limit "birthday parties" to the family, for the child is too young to understand or cope with so many things happening at once. By the child's third birthday, he becomes a more social being and can participate in the birthday fun to a certain degree. But it is still a period in which very few guests should be invited and not much activity should be planned. The ice-cream and cake celebration is still the most effective when it is part of a family meal—when it is dessert, and the family presents are presented to the "guest of honor."

For the school child, birthday parties are not only fun but are often the pivot of his social life. Types of party seem to have waves of popularity. One year every one has to have a bowling party, but it's a swimming party the next. The year after, it may be a feast at a fast-food restaurant chain that has special favors for children. It's always a challenge to be innovative—and successful, too. The parties that are the most trouble to give but usually the best are those given at home.

Certainly people who live in houses with big yards or nearby playing fields have a distinct advantage. On the weekend you can work off the excess energy of your children's guests—both boys and girls—before lunch, or, after school, before an afternoon snack by having them play kick the can, street hockey, or softball, or by organizing activities such as a kite-flying contest. A big family kitchen offers advantages, too, because children from the age of six can be sat down at the big table with different shapes of cookies, plus dishes of edible goodies like colored sprinkles, crushed nuts, candies, and shredded coconut. A cookie-decorating contest is great fun for all, and is usually successful, because any activity where everyone is involved simultaneously avoids boredom.

The problem of entertaining children is much more severe in small city apartments. A lot of children confined in an apartment are very likely to create havoc with the furnishings. There's a simple solution to this: don't invite that many children. If your child complains that he has to invite everyone in his class "because he's been to all their parties," explain that he may have only so many to his party, but that he may invite all the others separately on weekends to come for a "special Saturday lunch," or however you wish to arrange his paying back his social obligations. It is important for a child to learn at an early age the importance of repaying hospitality, even if it is offered in a totally different form from the original invitation.

I constantly admire the way parents who live in small apartments in Manhattan cope with their children's parties. They cannot let their children and their guests go to Central Park to play alone, but they manage to arrange for responsible teen-agers to accompany the children and to referee their games. The guests return to the apartment physically exhausted, at least temporarily, ready to sit down and enjoy the birthday food peacefully and with good behavior.

Party decorations in the home are fun, but they can be extremely expensive and are basically a frivolous purchase. I am envious of the parents who are artists and can make wonderful posters and create their own amusing decorations. One of the best child's party decorating schemes I ever saw was a dining room glittering from mobiles (made of shiny metal cans minus their labels), strung in silvery patterns across the ceiling.

I learned early in our children's lives to dispense with expensive table decorations, because we simply stopped using the dining room table. We put sheets all over the floors of the living room and dining room ("interesting" sheets, printed with cartoon characters, athletic league motifs, and so on). The children would remove their shoes, leave them in the hall, and then go sit in groups on the sheets of their choice. In this way we have always been able to invite a larger number of each child's friends home for lunch. We served them food on paper plates, not requiring forks and spoons, with the usual hamburgers or hot dogs and potato chips as the main course, and with ice-cream bars and pieces of birthday cake wrapped in napkins. The floors always stayed well protected by the sheets. At the end of the party, we would simply scoop up the sheets, including crumbs, food remnants, and spilled condiments and milk. Cleanup was easy.

When guests arrived with presents for our children, we put the gifts in a room separate from the guests' coats and paraphernalia. When present-opening time would arrive, usually just before lunch was served, a brother or sister would keep a careful list for his sibling of each present and donor, so that the birthday child would be able to write his thank-you notes the next day without a confusion in everyone's mind as to who gave what.

I find the whole atmosphere of materialism at birthday parties appalling. I remember a poignant telephone call from the mother of one of my daughter's friends who had just accepted our fifth birthday party invitation. The mother called to regret; I could hear the child crying in the background, so I kept insisting on knowing just why she couldn't come to the party. I felt money was the reason behind it, and it was. Her mother spurted out, "She doesn't have a birthday present to bring. She won't go without one, because everyone else will have one." My arguing that of course she did not need to bring a present had no effect. Finally I said, "Look, I have an extra present, because I purchased one game prize too many. It's already wrapped; I have no use for it. I'll leave it downstairs at the door, so when your daughter comes, she can pick it up and bring it to the party as her present." The problem was solved, and the little girl came. When children are little, these things mean much too much. I would like to start a movement where children who come to birthday parties may not bring presents. The waste of money all around is ridiculous, not to mention the harm done to all the children involved, who quite naturally compare lavishness and price of what they bring and what they receive.

Party Games When your children are young, you really have to plan every minute of their birthday parties. Everyone becomes bored or restless or aggressive very easily, unless things are planned to fill the entire time. The creativity of the parents comes into play here. Here are a few of the games that were successful with our children; you can always reinterpret them or make up your own. Half the fun is in the planning.

1. Drop the Clothespins in the Glass Jar
Each child sits on the edge of a bench or a chair, with his arm resting straight and motionless on his thigh, holding one of twelve clothespins in his hand. He takes aim and drops each clothespin, without moving, trying to get it inside the bottle or glass jar on the floor beneath him. The highest scorer (those with the most number of pins successfully dropped into the receptacle) play off against each other for the first, second, and third prizes. Experiment with your own child; see what size of jar opening he can successfully handle, and use that size for his party (naturally, the narrower the neck, the tougher the game). If the group is large, it is better to have four or five identical containers going at the same time, to speed up the game (one set of clothespins for each container for every five children).

2. Pin the Tail on Something or Someone
Instead of using the proverbial donkey and the tail, why not use any favorite cartoon character, athletic star, or rock or TV hero as your "pinning" object? Use a poster or photo blowup of the celebrity's head, and attach it to a wall. Make a funny-looking paper nose (one for each child), stick a pin through it, and put it in the guest's hand. Blindfold him well with a scarf, turn him around three times, and march him off toward the wall with the mission of pinning the nose as closely as possible on the poster character's nose. Once he has made contact with the wall, pin his nose securely to the poster, and mark his initials on that nose, so there won't be any arguing later as to whose is the winning nose.

3. Draw the Best Animal
Give the children a large piece of drawing paper each, make them put their name on the sheet, and set them to drawing a rendition of an animal—

real or fantasy. Have several boxes or cups of different colored crayons and pens and pencils, so that each child has a choice of colors and tools. Have an impartial jury (one year our jury consisted of two teen-agers who live in our building, our doorman, and a dog walker who happened to be passing by!). Give several prizes for this game, so that originality and a sense of humor, if not artistic talent, can be recognized.

4. Memory Game

This concerns memorizing objects on a card table and is for upper-grade children who know how to write words easily. The card table is filled with household objects of all kinds—a kitchen strainer, an emery board, a roll of stamps, a cutting board, a small clock, a tube of toothpaste, a cheese knife, a table bell, and so on. Assemble fifty or sixty things on the table. Give the children a specific amount of time to concentrate on the table (three to five minutes), and then cover the table with a sheet, or take it out of the room. Each child has a piece of paper and a pencil, and you give them ten minutes to write down as many objects as they can remember were on that table.

5. "What's in the Bag?" Game

Each child needs a pad and pencil for this game. Seat the group in a circle on the floor and begin passing around numbered bags, the contents of which each child is supposed to guess and write down on his pad, opposite the appropriate number, without telling anyone else. The bags, consisting of seven-inch-square pieces of fabric (such as old sheets) sewn together on the outer edges, contain common household objects. By not seeing what the object is, and by feeling it only through the bag, the child will have a difficult time identifying it. A bunch of loose rubber bands, a large safety pin with other pins hanging from it, a pair of book matches, a tea bag, a shower cap, some bandages, a scouring pad, a tape dispenser, a dog biscuit—these are only some of the suggested items.

6. Balance-on-the-Spoon Game

A game that has been played for centuries is one where a child walks and runs and turns around while balancing an object precariously on an object like a tablespoon. Make the children race in lanes to a goal and back again without dropping their orange; even the little ones can handle a hard-boiled egg balanced on a spoon. If you run each child individually, time him with a stop watch; otherwise, you can run five children at once in lanes, down a given distance and back again. (This game is better to do out of doors, although we've always managed in our living room without too much damage.)

Hiring a Professional to Entertain Children have a great time with movies—if you hire a projectionist, rent a good film, and do it right. (However, in my generation, before the advent of television, we appreciated the excitement of a movie far more than today's rather blasé generation of children.) If you are hiring a magician or a clown to entertain the small children before or after afternoon snacks, be sure you know what age group responds to that entertainer. I have seen entertainers labor under impossible circumstances—children who were too young and frightened to understand what was going on, or children too old, bored, and therefore almost rude in their reactions. One of the best children's parties I ever witnessed was one for ages four through seven. The only entertainment was a young college girl who played the guitar and sang simple folk songs. She knew how to hold her young audience's attention; the fact that she herself was young and pretty was important, too. But one of the secrets of any entertainer's success with children is the brevity of his program.

Prizes for Games   Organizing the prizes for games at birthday parties is no small feat. First of all, you must have on hand at least three more than you think you'll need. There may be ties in game winners; then, too, there is always the tearful, protesting child who says, "I won that game, not Henry!" —and he may be right. So you have to be able to mediate, judicate, and reward accordingly.

All prizes should be colorfully wrapped, but none should be expensive. It's the joy of winning a competition that matters, not the value of the prize. If you are having a party with boys and girls, it is wiser to make all the game prizes items that would suit either a boy or a girl.

The Loot Bag   The institution of the loot bag up through third grade is a nice one. (Even the older children like it, provided the contents are not "babyish.") A well-executed loot bag has all the makings of a successful Christmas stocking. One can buy them in stationery and department stores, but one can also take a small brown grocery bag, paint the child's name on it in bright colors, and let your family's "resident artist" paint a face on each bag. One can use the loot bag as the place card at the table, but the best thing to do with loot bags is to give each child his when he leaves your party. (Sad experience teaches mothers that children open their loot bags, begin to eat the candy, smear sticky fingers on the furniture, lose their favors, accuse others of taking them. . . .) The loot bag should have a balance between goodies (wrapped candies, gingerbread man, macaroons) and favors adapted to the age (small spinning tops and small soft animals for young ones, and objects like colored felt-tip pens, baseball or hockey or football cards, marbles, and miniature playing cards for older children). For years, every time I made a business trip to a foreign country, I would bring back two dozen small objects purchased very inexpensively in that country— tiny Dutch wooden shoes from The Hague, cowboy scarves from Australia, small Tower of London Beefeater figures from England, bright-colored embroidered tree ornaments from India, and mother-of-pearl shells from the Philippines. The children's guests always thought these favors were great.

Children's Manners at Parties   Children learn their manners gradually, not all at once. So a child who is host at his own birthday party should not be continually goaded and corrected by an overanxious parent. If he is old enough, he should be told just before the party that he must greet his guests when they come, thank them for the gifts they bring, and not ask "Where's my present?" if someone comes without one. The birthday child should be taught to act as enthusiastic about a duplicate present as he did about the first one. He should learn not to say, "Oh, I have that one already," which might hurt his guest's feelings. He should learn to thank each child with equal warmth and sincerity, regardless of the success of the gift. These are attitudes not easily taught—or learned—but in time they become automatic.

By the time the young host is nine, he should learn to see to it that all of his guests are enjoying themselves—that someone is not off by himself, shy and miserable because he knows none of the guests. He should say good-by to each guest, and thank him once again for bringing a present, and he should send a thank-you note to each guest within a week's time. (If he is too young to write, his mother should write for him, just as the mothers of his guests should write thank-you notes for the party on behalf of their guest children, if they are unable to write themselves.) Even a third grader who writes only the following words, "Dear Joe, Thank you for the party," is still learning a very important part of manners in life.

As for the child who is overtired and who acts up on his birthday, which one of us can say we never did that, too? The tension and excitement that build up to one's birthday party are almost too much, particularly in the earlier years, and can lead to tantrums and less than exemplary behavior. Rather than becoming upset, the parents should simply forget it, remembering that "next year will be better."

A Teen-age Party

Not too long ago, the major worry of parents helping their children plan a party at home was whether there would be enough sandwiches, soda, and potato chips for the crowd. Now, in many communities, the worry is whether marijuana will be smoked through the night and how many kinds of other drugs and liquor will be smuggled into the party. (The ways of doing this are legion.) Party etiquette doesn't seem very important when parents are faced with potential lawbreaking in their home involving their minor children and their friends.

Perhaps the first step in preparing for a party today is an open dialogue with one's children, a careful laying down of rules, and an agreement that there will be no "grass" or alcohol brought into the party by anyone (even if it's the most popular girl in the school or the football hero).

The second step is to ensure that a parent will be home during the entire party, preferably unseen after greeting the guests when they arrive.

The third step is to plan the best party of the year, with a schedule so full the young people will not have time to be bored or want to break rules.

A good dancing space should be cleared for the group. It may involve the inconvenience of moving furniture, but it's worth it. If you don't have a stereo system and the latest popular records, borrow them. If you can make a financial sacrifice in another direction in order to pay a small fee to hire the local high school band for dancing, do it. (It would be a good idea to write letters of apology beforehand to your neighbors, however, promising to cut off the noise of the music at a decent hour.)

If your teen-ager "would rather die than see Mom or Dad butting into things," get a college girl or boy whom your teen-ager looks up to, and have that college student bring a date. They can both chaperon the party for a fee. Then if someone tries to spike the soda or light up a joint, the college students can say, "Cut it out!" and the younger ones will usually listen and obey.

Ask around about successful games young people have played at other parties in your city. (A friend in Cleveland can also pass on to a friend in San Francisco some good ideas tried out in Cleveland.) Have chess and checkers set up in your home; some of the guests might begin to play; others can kibitz from time to time. Borrow a Ping-Pong tabletop and put it over a protective pad on your dining room table for the evening. Hang a dart board and leave some darts by it (but make sure your college student chaperons explain the ground rules to those who play a potentially dangerous game).

Have a superabundant supply of food and soft drinks on hand, and arrange everything attractively, just as you would for your adult friends. Put out your best bar glasses for their soft drinks. Give them a plate of fresh cut-up lemons and limes and maraschino cherries, even fresh mint, to put in their drinks. Have lots of sandwiches on platters (twice as many as you think you could possibly need). Platters of glazed doughnuts, cupcakes, and cookies will all go quickly. A friend of mine takes all the bright-colored plastic wastebaskets in her house, washes them thoroughly, and then fills them to the brim with freshly made popcorn. She puts one in each room used by the younger generation for the party, and reports that each basket is usually empty by 11 P.M. after an 8 P.M. starting time. (She patiently fills them again!) If you want to serve a hot dish, make a huge caldron of something like chili or spaghetti, and keep the contents warm by putting the servers on an electric hot tray. If you're serving pizza, make sure the guests eat it when it's hot, and that pizza is not simply left somewhere to be eaten as desired. (Cold, soggy pizza is no favor to a guest.) When you have only four to eight guests for a teen-aged party, you can involve them in the cooking—making pancakes, for instance, and letting them put on their own toppings; but with a large group, this is logistically impossible. A sure-fire hit is to have your college chaperons announce "dessert," to the guests and leave out on the buffet table four kinds of ice cream in gallon cartons, plus several ice-cream scoops (borrow some from friends, so that the guests can be served quickly), and a basket full of ice-cream cones, or a series of spoons and dishes and a mixture of sundae toppings, including whipped cream and crushed nuts.

College Entertaining

College students have their own imaginative ways of entertaining, but consideration of others, compassion for others—in other words, good manners —are sometimes forgotten in the priorities of campus life. For many young people, college represents their first adult social experiences, away from family guidance, and away from the security of their friendships at home. Many students attend college parties without knowing how to act, how to meet their peers, what to say. This is where the secure, poised, and compassionate student should step in—to help fellow students. He sees to it that the shy ones who don't have many friends are invited to college parties; he helps them meet new people. He "gives them a shove," so to speak, in mixing with their peers. One college senior, a very popular man on campus, told me he always seeks out the shy ones, in any case, because "they're usually the most interesting people at the party." Good manners require a little extra work, but they result in a good party, at which everyone has a good time. And a party always reflects the sum of its parts.

Many of the university and college entertaining ideas can be adapted for our more adult world, too, which is why I am always attentive to what is happening on college campuses today. My main source of information currently is one of my nieces, Megan Baldrige, who graduated from Yale University. She communicated with contemporaries on campuses all over America by telephone and by letter, so this section on college entertaining is really hers.

The First Step in Organizing a College Party Put all the requirements and plans down on paper, and make a detailed "battle plan" for yourself. Then there won't be too many unpleasant surprises of things forgotten or economic disasters or projects that become unglued because there was no glue.

Parties on campus today can range from a picnic after a group bike ride to a formal dinner dance. When a friend visits, it's time for a party; when you've been away for a while (on a work project or during a term abroad), it's time for a party to announce that you're back. One girl in a northwestern sorority threw a successful "Come Commiserate with Me" party when her roommates left to get married. University students have been going back to the customs of the college parties of their parents in the forties and fifties, and have resurrected everything from drinking too much to roller-skating parties and hay rides. One Ivy League coed decided the Kentucky Derby Saturday on campus was boring, with everyone just lounging around the television set, doing nothing, while they waited for the race. So she organized her own version of what a Kentucky Derby Party would be. She sent special invitations and made an event out of a TV party; the girls came in long garden-party dresses, and the men wore white suits. She served them mint juleps and tiny sandwiches, and they watched the race "on the tube" in great style. It was not just another Saturday afternoon on campus.

The Date Check out the date of your party well in advance with your good friends' schedules. You don't want to make an all-out effort when no one will be on campus, or when everyone will be in the library studying for exams.

The Place The place where your party is held is as important as the people whom you invite. "Even the most flamingly gregarious person cannot bedazzle in a closet," one student reports. In choosing a place for your party, consider space in terms of circulation and ambience. If you want to dance to stereo music or a band, you will need two or more rooms emptied of furniture for your party. It is a strain to talk in the same room where "the music is throbbing, the lights are dimmed, and everyone is pounding away to the beat," so have one room with the bar and food set up, and places to talk quietly, and reserve at least one room for the music and dancing. Even bric-a-brac should be removed from the dancing room; there will be spilled drinks and cigarette burns to ruin furniture, so anything good should be moved out of the space.

Lighting in the "dancing room" should be dim, but people should still be able to see each other. The other rooms devoted to the party should be brightly lit and cheerful, perhaps with some peppy posters to embellish the wall space. (One inventive student at Pitzer College in Claremont, California, took candid photographs of different students—all guests—before the party, blew them up to poster size, and then interposed different heads on different bodies, with amazing results.)

The bar and food table should be set up in the most convenient place in the area, to permit a good flow of traffic in and around it. You can use card tables or collapsible aluminum tables; cover them with quilts, bedspreads, or decorative sheets. If you don't have any comfortable sofas or armchairs or hassocks to use for sitting, borrow them. You can always use a mattress, too, for sitting, provided you cover it with something attractive. If you move the furniture out of your suite and borrow other pieces, organize your friends to do it with you; you might even give them a "post party" when everything is moved back again the day after the party.

If you plan far enough in advance and are on good terms with the head of the dorm, you may be able to use one of the college common rooms or your dorm dining rooms. However, in choosing a public place, you run the risk of gate-crashers. Students have been known to give successful parties in their college's art gallery, gym, locker rooms, art studios, squash courts, swimming pool (with a lifeguard present, of course), and theater. Innovative planning is the key, but just as important is proper respect for college property during the party.

If you hold your party away from the campus, you must remember the problems of transportation. Not everyone has a bike or a car, or can even borrow one easily. You should organize the cars yourself, if you are going to be a thoughtful host.

The Invitation   In order to have memorable invitations, you should design them yourself. For example, if you are having a tailgate football lunch party, you might make the invitation in the shape of a double-fold football, or a card covered with newspaper photographs or drawings of your campus football stars; or you might draw the invitation in the form of a picnic basket; or you might make a cartoon of students enjoying a feast on the spread of the tailgate. If it is a post-exam party, you can paste a snapshot of yourself sunk in dejection, studying for your exams. If you give an ethnic food party, carry the theme through on the invitation.

Some students print party invitations on cheap T shirts and send them around to guests; others have painted invitations on balloons, which were deflated and mailed to the entire guest list. If you can't think of a way in which to make your invitation "memorable," ask a friend to help you or design it for you.

Be sure that the invitation contains the following information: date, time, place, names of hosts, what kind of party it will be, what guests should wear, and what guests should bring, if anything, in the way of food or drink. Be sure to put an R.S.V.P. with your telephone number and address. If the party location is difficult to find, include a mimeographed map or explicit instructions on how to get there. The more information you provide for your guests, the more enthusiastic they will be about the prospect of the party.

If you have guests coming from other universities and colleges for the weekend, you should put a note inside their invitations saying you can arrange to put them up for the night.

One of the biggest problems in college entertaining is knowing how many are coming to the party. Most students ignore the R.S.V.P. sign on invitations, which is the height of rudeness. It is also rude to bring along a guest with you if you haven't discussed it first with your hosts. It is also rude to accept an invitation and then not attend, without letting your hosts know. This lament about college manners is heard on every campus today. One graduating senior sent out invitations to a large dinner party for his class at his parents' home. In each one he included a stamped, self-addressed postcard that stated: "Yes, I am coming" or "'No, I cannot come." There was a little box for a check mark by each statement. No one in his class even bothered to make the minuscule effort of making a check mark and mailing the postcard to the host. It is a sad commentary on college manners.

The Guest List   College parties are most successful when they are made up of a mixture of people—with students from other classes, departments, and sections of campus life. One can invite people one would like to know better, including people of different ages and one's professors. The latter are not asked to too many student parties, and even if they cannot come, they are complimented by invitations. One Radcliffe girl gives a party every year on some obscure anniversary like Joan of Arc's birthday and invites an equal number of faculty and students. It is always a sure-fire success.

The intelligent party-giver, of course, invites his or her immediate neighbors to the fete. There is no way to measure the hurt feelings of neighbors who are excluded from the fun but included in the noise of an all-night party.

If your school is coed, you would probably invite roughly an equal number of males and females (although it doesn't really matter). If you are at a single-sex school, you should consider what source you can utilize to even out the sexes. Maybe someone from a neighboring institution with a majority of students of the opposite sex should co-host the party with you. If you have friends who never seem to have any social life, the kind thing to do is to arrange blind dates for them to your party. Remember new students on campus are usually eager to meet people and attend parties, too.

However, while the chemistry of a party thrives on new blood, the presence of too many strangers in one room can have an alienating effect. One must be sure to have enough outgoing people present to get the group going.

Food and Drink   If finances are a problem, you can ask friends to bring their own liquor. You are still obliged to provide something yourself, however. This could be the old American college favorite of a keg of beer, or sangria, or a rum punch.

Some of your friends may offer to make food for your party, but you should provide the main course, whether it's hamburgers or beef stew or spaghetti. Keep a careful list of who is assigned to bring what, so there won't be fifteen desserts and one salad. Also keep a careful list of who brought what container, so they can be returned to the rightful owners the day after the party—beautifully washed, of course.

With a punch or beer, food like potato chips and pretzels are fine for munching upon, but there should also be something more substantial. The quickest and simplest college feast is a spread of cold cuts, fruit, cheeses, pickles, cheese spreads, and French bread. For an afternoon get-together, several kinds of ice creams with several kinds of nuts and seeds, plus a variety of sundae sauces, make a special treat. The art of gourmet cooking flourishes in off-campus apartments, as well as in co-operative dorms where students do their own cooking. Some really great cooks begin this interest in their college years. Students warn that the overcomplicated meal is a mistake, however. My Yale niece and a friend had to pitch in one night to save her younger sister from "social destruction" at Yale by having to cook and serve that sister's entire Mexican dinner of enchiladas, tostadas, tamales, and guacamole (all of which had to be prepared at the last minute and to be served at one time). Not all of us have generous sisters or friends, however.

Be careful not to put out too much food at once and have it all disappear too early in the party. Space it, and keep a little extra in reserve, just in case. Save some extra food and coffee for those who stay behind to help you clean up, too. It is wise to have a pot of coffee always hot and waiting for any guest who may have had too much to drink, and as one student hostess warned, "It's wise to have a large and compassionate friend alerted to assist anyone who needs help back to his room, quietly and unobtrusively."

Students report that it is all right to use plastic glasses, but not paper plates for parties indoors. If possible, you should borrow plates and eating utensils from your college dining hall.

Ask a few of your friends to serve as bartenders for forty-five minutes each. If you have several bartenders for a really large crowd, the lines will not be too long. If you can ask these helpers to dress the part, with black bow tie, et al., "it will add some class to the party." (A lot of students earn extra money in their communities as bartenders for cocktail parties, and they have the proper uniforms hanging in their closets anyway.)

One cannot discuss campus drinking without observing that there is a tragic excess of alcohol being consumed on campus today. Some think it's "smart and with it" to get drunk, but it's not smart and with it to become an alcoholic and ruin one's own life and the lives of one's family. Just as it is important for campus hosts to have enough to drink at their parties, so it is just as important for them to know when to turn off the bar, and to help their classmates who cannot hold their liquor. This is a time for real compassion and understanding, for never again in their adult lives will their friends be as close as they are in the campus environment.

Entertainment and Party Activity   Can you afford one of the college musical groups? (I know one girl who earns a free performance at her big annual party each year, because she designs, makes, and posts the musical group's advertising posters around campus.) Can you afford the special setup requirements the group may have, such as transportation of their instruments, musical stands, and extra sound and amplifying equipment? Make sure you have the arrangements understood about overtime charges, too. Do you have to borrow stereo equipment for your dancing? Remember to check out the availability of electrical outlets, extension cords, double sockets, and so on, particularly if you are holding your party in unfamiliar territory. If you borrow someone's delicate stereo equipment, will it be damaged when a small room is vibrating with many bodies doing the latest dances?

Maybe you can find a friend who plays great piano or guitar; ask her or him to play for your party. One student at Oberlin College invited her friends to a "Performing Genius Party." The guests soon found out that the geniuses were supposed to be themselves. Each one had to come prepared with five minutes' worth of proof of what "he was into." The hostess timed each student's presentation; no one was allowed to drone on, once the bell was rung. Drama majors enacted parts of scenes; a dance major played her own record and performed a short modern dance; a science student explained his latest experiment; and a French student translated parts of the campus newspaper into French and read them with hilarious results.

Ideally, the energy of the party should be combined equally in active participation (sports or dancing) and in passive participation (relaxing, eating, drinking, and conversing). The old-time "mixer" idea, where too many people stand in too small a space with no air and no place to sit down is happily occurring less often. Students want to be able to sit down and to converse without having their eardrums accosted.

Campus life-styles fluctuate in moods and customs every three or four years. Each new class seems to leave its imprint on how students entertain and what they like. But certain things do not change during the years, and one is the fun of college life—and the need for kindness, consideration, and thinking of others. It is a place where good habits are instilled, so that the next step into adulthood will not be such a difficult one. It is a good time—for most.

Post-college Entertaining

Young college graduates, beginning their careers and faced with the high costs of urban living, find that city entertaining can be a real financial strain. They solve the problem by continuing many of their college traditions in party-giving—sharing the hosting responsibilities as well as the provision of food and drink. They band together to co-host everything from Sunday brunches to formal dances.

Everything begins, of course, with a clever invitation, which they create. They often have a theme and ask people to dress accordingly. Spoofing past decades of American life is perennially popular—like the twenties of the F. Scott Fitzgerald generation, the days of the Capone gangsters of the thirties, or the "patriotic forties." They think nothing of inviting large groups to come at eight or nine (which to the older generation means the dinner hour, but to them means "eat your own dinner first").

They put on their invitations the kind of alcoholic drink they will be serving (beer or wine or a rum punch), which translated means, "If you don't like what we're serving, bring your own." I have seen on New York invitations, particularly those sent by girls, the phrase "No smoke please." I originally thought this was some kind of hidden reference to the fire laws, but was soon informed that the phrase means "There will be no drugs, but absolutely NO drugs, brought to my party."

When I think back on the parties we gave in Washington and New York when we were in our twenties and had our first jobs, I realize that today's generation has a tougher row to hoe than we did, but they also have a lot more imagination, too. Perhaps their creative imagination is a compensation for all those problems.

Special-event Parties

Any event is just cause for a party—Valentine's Day, St. Patrick's Day, Columbus Day, May Day (or as with the Radcliffe student, Joan of Arc's birthday!). If you are looking for an excuse to give a party, you will always find one without looking too hard. It is fun to select a theme and to be creative in the co-ordination of one's invitations, the food, and the party decorations. (Nothing is worse, however, than the overdecorated party, awash in crepe-paper streamers and confetti, in which the guests are forced to wear absurd hats and blow children's bugles.) Sometimes the special event will dictate what kind of a party it will be—such as an Election Night party, which means a late party and several television sets.

What really makes a successful party, anyway? A host and hostess may live in the biggest house in town, with a large staff and a larder stocked with the finest food and the most exceptional wines. Yet their parties can be cold and lifeless. Money is not the basic ingredient of entertaining. It helps, yes, but the first real secret of any party is the *attitude* of the host and hostess. Are they giving this party to give pleasure to their friends, to show their love for their friends—or are they giving this party to climb the social scale, to impress people with their financial success, and to further their business aspirations?

The atmosphere and the electricity in the air always give the answer to this question. If caring about one's guests and having an attitude of wanting to do everything to please them are the first secret of a good party, then proper planning is the second.

And I haven't mentioned money at all.

Chapter 34

AT EASE AT TABLE

A nineteenth-century editor in Boston wrote: "One knows the very nature of both man and woman by their actions at table. One suddenly sees their innermost characters, their attitudes, their breeding, but above all, one knows whether one cares to spend another evening at table with them."

Poor table manners can be a serious deterrent to a student's social life at school and college, to anyone's career, and to a happy marriage. Table manners are learned, but what cannot be learned and what is inherent in a person's character is the *desire* to have good table manners. We have all seen a woman marry a "diamond in the rough" and put the polish on that diamond, but very rarely have we seen the opposite occur. Women are supposed to lead in manners, to subtly instruct their husbands. When they do not, it is usually disastrous. We have seen men of medium ability rise to the top of their professions because of their polished manners and knowledge of what to do when and why; conversely, we have seen men of extraordinary talent consistently fail to reach the "big time" because others consider them gauche. Table manners are one of the most visible signals of the state of our manners. That is why good table manners are an absolute necessity for social success—and therefore business success.

Today's advertising does nothing to help us teach our children good manners. Take food commercials, for example. A food is touted because everyone is licking their fingers afterward, or because a child successfully grabs a treasured food off his father's plate when the father isn't looking. Yum, yum!

We have discussed previously the good behavior of a guest at dinner parties, but there are many more aspects of table manners to cover.

Who Is Served First?

When the hostess is serving at least part of the meal from in front of her place, with or without the aid of a maid, she serves the guest of honor (fe-

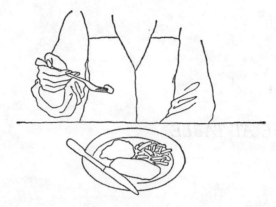

The American style of eating, fork in right hand, knife on plate.

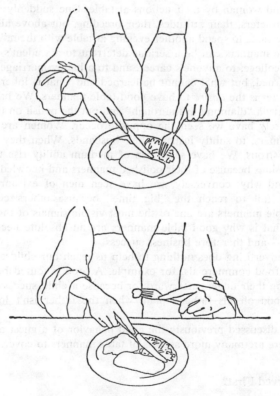

The European or continental style of eating; fork remains throughout in left hand, knife in right.

male) first and then proceeds counterclockwise around the table. She serves her husband next to last and herself last. Not only is this the gracious thing to do, but it means her own plate of food won't be obstructing traffic in front of her, with the food growing cold during her serving activities.

When to Begin Eating

Guests at a small dinner party (up to six guests) wait until the hostess has been served and she picks up her fork as the signal to begin. At a larger dinner party, the hostess urges everyone to begin eating as soon as they are served, in deference to the cook, who knows the food tastes better hot.

Children eating alone with their parents should wait until their parents begin eating before picking up their soup spoon or fork. Except for breakfast, the polite husband waits until his wife is served before beginning to eat himself is she has cooked the meal. If *he* has cooked it, she waits for him!

The Use of the Knife and Fork

Knives and forks may be used American or continental fashion, but the latter is much more sensible. American tourists abroad and American students living in European countries have noticed how easy the continental style is, have copied it, and usually succeed in never going back to the American system. It is logical and easier to eat the food one has just cut with the fork in the left hand, instead of having to change the fork to the right hand each time. In the continental style, the fork remains in the left hand, fork tines down, and the knife in the right, at all times. This style of eating entails pushing food onto the back of the fork (or impaling it, so to speak, on the tines), perhaps aided by a nudge with the side of the knife held in the right hand. Once firmly on the fork, the food is conveyed to the mouth.

Dessert eaten continental-style implies the same system, with the fork in the left hand and the spoon (or knife, as the case may be) in the right. If one is eating something with only a spoon or a fork (ice cream or cake, for instance) one holds it in the right hand.

In the American zigzag method, one cuts the food with the fork in the left hand, but before eating lays the knife down and changes the fork from the left to the right hand. In this case one eats with the fork tines up. For either style of eating, "lefties" naturally reverse which hands are used.

Placement of Used Silver   When a plate of food has been finished or the diner has had all he wishes, he places the fork and knife (but only if he has used one or both) on the plate, sharp side of the blade facing in, the fork tines down, to the left of the knife. In American style the tines would be up. They should be placed so that they do not slide off as the plate is being removed. Used silver is never placed on the table or left in a cup. A soup spoon is left in a large soup plate. Unused silver is left on the table.

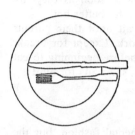

*When one has finished eating, the place-
ment of used silver is optional: either of
these two ways best ensures that the plate,
when removed, will have the utensils
firmly upon it.*

The Dessert Silver

The spoon and fork, or fork and knife, or fork or spoon alone that may be needed for the dessert course may be placed, along with dessert, on the plate. I prefer, however, to have the table set with the dessert implements placed above the dinner plate—with the fork, tines up, facing right, and the spoon or knife above it, facing left. There is occasionally some puzzlement as to where to place the dessert spoon after one has finished—in the dessert dish itself or on the service plate. Much depends on the size of the dessert dish in relation to the service plate and on the general shape and height of the dessert dish itself. For example, when you are served a dessert in a stemmed glass on a service plate, obviously the dessert spoon should not be left in the glass but should be placed on the service plate at the right. On the other hand, if you had a pudding-type dessert served in a plate that resembles a soup plate or sauce dish, there would be no reason why you cannot leave the spoon in the dish when you have finished.

Drinking Beverages at the Table

One should never take a sip of any beverage at the table until the mouth is empty and has been wiped with the napkin. This keeps the rim of your cup or glass free from food marks. Hot liquids such as soup or coffee are best tested with a careful sip from a spoon. One replaces the spoon when it is not in use on the saucer beneath the handle of the cup or on the plate beneath the soup plate.

The Napkin

Napkins are placed on the lap, entirely open if they are lunch-size or in half, folded the long way, if they are dinner napkins. Guests wait until the hostess has taken up hers before placing their own on their laps unless the service has been buffet and guests are urged to eat while their food is hot. Napkins are tucked in at the neck only for children or by anyone eating on an airplane who wishes to protect his clothes. For a lobster dinner, everyone should tuck his napkin under his chin, too.

The napkin should not be thrown in a heap on the table after the meal is over. Fold it casually. If the family uses napkin rings, each child should be taught how to fold the napkin when finished and insert it into the ring.

If at a dinner party you are having after-dinner coffee at the table, leave your napkin in your lap. Putting it on the table does nothing for the looks of the table.

If Silverware Is Lacking

If for some reason an eating utensil has been forgotten at your place, pause for a moment, and then if the hostess does not notice you haven't begun to eat, ask for what you need. Even if you know the house well and could find the missing implement in the kitchen, do not go yourself to the kitchen to get it. Never use your dessert spoon, for example, if the serving spoon has been forgotten on something being passed. Ask for the proper implement.

Tipping of Dishes

The tipping of soup or dessert dishes is acceptable, in order to enjoy every last sip of liquid, provided you tip the plate away from you, not toward you.

The Handled Soup or Bouillon Cup

Soup or bouillon served in a handled cup or even a small bowl (oriental fashion), may be drunk instead of being spooned. If there are dumplings or shredded mushrooms, vegetables, or other garnish floating on top, these should be eaten first by using the spoon, before the liquid part of the soup is drunk. Anything such as noodles that may be on the bottom of the cup or bowl is spooned up before the liquid may be consumed.

Care has to be taken not to slurp the soup. The only way to teach a child not to is to catch him each time he does it; eventually he will think before he drinks the soup—and the slurping noise will disappear.

Testing Liquids

If you take a large spoonful of soup that is far too hot, don't spit it out, but take a quick drink of water or wine to cool off the soup in your mouth. If you have burned your mouth, an exception may be made to the rule against drinking with food already in your mouth.

Coffee or tea may be tested for heat or sweetening by one sip from a spoon. If it is too hot, let it stand until it cools by itself. You must not blow it, spoonful by spoonful, until it is drinkable.

How to Hold Cups

A handled cup is held with the index finger through the handle, the thumb just above it to support the grip, and the second finger below the handle for added security. The little finger should follow the curve of the other fingers and not be elevated in an affected manner. It is incorrect to cradle the cup in one's fingers if it has a handle. This is done only when the cup is of oriental design, without handles.

How to Hold Glasses

Large stemmed glasses (water or wine goblets) are held with the thumb and first two fingers at the base of the bowl. If they contain chilled white wine or vin rosé, however, they are held by the stem, so as not to heat the wine with one's fingers.

Small stemmed glasses are held by the stems. Tumblers are held near the base, but, except by a child, never with both hands. A brandy snifter, of course, is held in the palms of both hands to warm the liquor. The delicate fragrance is thus inhaled, and finally the contents are slowly drunk.

Token Portions

If you are serving yourself from a buffet, you need not take anything you don't like if there is a wide enough choice of food. If the hostess notices you have left something off your plate and says, "Oh, please try the stuffed grape leaves—they're my greatest specialty," then of course you must put some on your plate. That does not mean you must eat it. If the main course is something you dislike intensely, take a small portion anyway and move it around on your plate. Don't mention it to your hostess. (If you're starving, you can always eat something at home afterward.)

The Use of Chopsticks

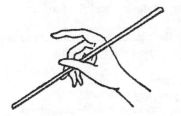

Pick up the chopstick almost as if you were going to hold a pen, but place it at the base of your thumb with the third and fourth fingers supporting it about one third up the chopstick, leaving your index finger free to use as a lever.

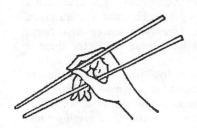

Now place the top chopstick in a parallel position, held firmly with the thumb and index finger. Practice picking up an imaginary grain of rice. (You should be able to pick up a real grain when you're adept.)

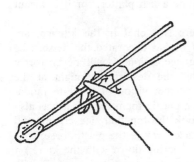

The first chopstick always remains firmly in position in the crook of your thumb, held there by your third and fourth finger. The top chopstick is used as a lever and should move freely. You use the pair as pincers to pick up any food you wish. Don't be embarrassed to ask your oriental waiter to help you get started. Eating oriental food with a fork is no crime, but it is not as much fun. The Chinese invented the fork but returned to the chopstick as a more practical way of eating.

The enormous popularity of Chinese and Japanese restaurants and of cooking with a wok has resulted in great interest in the proper serving of oriental foods at home. This, of course, includes being able to use chopsticks correctly. Just as pizza seems to taste better eaten with the fingers, oriental food seems to taste better when eaten with chopsticks.

Taking Portions from a Serving Dish

When a serving dish is passed with toast beneath some food immersed in a sauce, you take the toast (or English muffin, or whatever) and the food and some surrounding sauce.

When there are a serving fork and spoon on the platter being passed, you are supposed to utilize both utensils. Use one to support the food being taken with the other.

If there are little birds on the platter, you take one, never two.

If there are small lamb chops on the platter, you may take two.

If there is an enormous fish on the platter and you have trouble cutting off the portion of fish you wish, ask the waiter to assist you. If you are doing it yourself, look around the table and mentally count the number of guests, and serve yourself accordingly. It would be very embarrassing to take such a large piece that the people served last will be penalized. Take a small piece, and if you hear the hostess remonstrating, "Oh, that's not enough! Serve yourself well," she is giving you the cue to have some more, for there is more in the kitchen and plenty to go around.

If the platter contains various little sections of food items, take a little one of everything. There may be a stuffed mushroom or a square of aspic or a potato basket filled with peas, or some small new potatoes or a portion of spinach soufflé or a broiled tomato meant for each guest. After serving yourself with the main course, you help yourself to the other things arranged decoratively around the rim of the platter. If the meat platter is garnished only with watercress or parsley, you may help yourself to that, too; and take a piece of lemon if it is used to decorate a fish platter, for it is meant for your use on the fish.

If you are dining in a home where there is a chef in the kitchen, approach his very fancy dessert with care. If he has decorated the dessert, be sure you take the food part and not the decoration. I will never forget watching a well-known senator "attacking" the dessert one night at the White House. Chef René Verdon had created a vision of a white mountain of delicious fluff and spun sugar, atop a plastic foam base that was also decorated with spun sugar. The senator took the top fluff, ice cream, and sugary decoration, and then he began to hack away at the plastic base, convinced it was part of the dessert. He kept bearing down with the knife on the base on the platter, almost breaking the protesting waiter's arm. Finally the dessert in toto flew off the platter and landed in the lap of one of the women guests.

Adding Gravies and Sauces

If there is gravy for the meat, do not pour it over everything on your plate, but only over the meat. If there is rice or noodles with a main dish rich in sauce, like blanquette de veau or coq au vin, it is a good idea to ladle some of this sauce onto the starch dish. If you are in a restaurant, pouring that American institution, catsup, all over food is an insult to the chef and is exceedingly gauche. Catsup is for hamburgers and non-gourmet dishes.

Seasoning

It is an insult to the cook, professional or not, to shake salt and pepper indiscriminately over food you haven't first tasted. This is improper at home or in a restaurant or in someone else's home. This heavy pouring of salt is also very bad for your health anyway. If your hostess has not seasoned the food to your taste, use your salt and pepper in a way that she will not notice.

Additional Butter

If there is butter on your butter plate, and if there is no serving plate of butter on the table, do not ask for more. You are not supposed to butter your vegetables (with the exception of baked or mashed potatoes). If you were to slather the vegetables with more butter, you would be telling your hostess she does not know how to prepare her vegetables properly.

Jellies and Sauces

When jellies and conserves are served with the meat or fowl, you should spoon a small amount onto the side of your plate. (Additionally, there may be jelly or jam passed to place on your butter plate, and meant only for the hot rolls or biscuits.) The horse-radish, mint jelly, cranberry sauce, currant jelly, or apple butter that you spoon onto your plate should be incorporated onto your fork as the meat or fowl is taken into the mouth. Liquid sauces such as mint or cherry duck sauce are meant to be poured right on the meat or fowl. Be careful to take only a small amount of this liquid, for it may quickly flood your plate and overcome the flavor of the other food.

My mother tells me that when I was young and traveling with my parents, we were house guests in Pittsburgh, and I was allowed to attend the grown-up dinner party. I refused the ice-cream balls that were passed in a bowl for dessert by the maid, but then I saw the platter in her left hand, which contained two silver bowls full of sauce, one hot chocolate, the other hot butterscotch. Neither of my parents was watching me, but evidently the other guests nearby watched in fascination as I ladled out with great care spoonfuls of each sauce onto my plate and proceeded to spoon it up with exquisite delight. When my mother told me I could never pull that one again, I felt sorry, but it was one time when the learning process was very enjoyable.

If the sauce ladle falls into the sauce, by the way, you should retrieve it and not make the next guest correct your error. Fish it out and quickly wipe the handle and your fingers carefully on your napkin; then reinsert the ladle into the sauce.

Bread as a Food-pusher and Sauce-sopper

The exposure of many Americans to European travel since the war has brought European customs to our shores, including the use of bread, rolls, muffins, or bread sticks as "pushers" for food. One should adopt this rule only when handling difficult food, such as errant peas, or when one is anxious to have the last taste of an excellent sauce. As for the latter, make the piece of bread very small, spear it with your fork, squish it around in the sauce, and then deftly convey the soaked bread to your mouth.

You can use a bit of bread to push food onto your fork inconspicuously, but when you use bread as a sauce-sopper, you are conspicuous, no matter how well you execute the action. The French were the first to make it acceptable, for how else would one catch the last remnants of the fabulous garlic butter in which the snails were cooked?

The Left-handed Person

The left-handed person has sadly to learn to adapt to a right-handed world; the right-handed world won't adjust to him. If you as the hostess know someone is left-handed, it is considerate to seat the person on the left end of the table or at the table end, so he will be comfortable and will not have to worry about colliding elbows with his neighbor.

Rearranging the Seating

No diner, even a left-handed one, may change the hostess' seating plan. One often sees this in diplomatic life—a pushy social climber will sneak over to the table to change his place, in order to be seated in between people who will help him with that climbing. Such people are always caught in the act, and it inevitably means the end of their social reputations.

Getting Something Out of the Mouth

Nothing should ever be spat, however surreptitiously, into a napkin—not even a bad clam, and certainly not a piece of unchewable meat gristle or chicken bone. Roll the offending morsel of food with your tongue onto your fork or spoon, and then place it on the plate. Since a piece of partly chewed food is anything but attractive-looking to yourself or your neighbors, camouflage this morsel with another piece of food. When you are eating stewed or canned fruit with pits, push those pits onto your spoon, held to the mouth, and then place them on your plate. If you are eating a fresh cherry, hold it by the stem, and place the pit from your mouth into your cupped hand, and then onto the plate. If you are eating an olive, you remove the pit from your mouth with your thumb and index finger, then put it on your plate.

Accidents at the Table

Even the most careful eater occasionally has an accident at the table. If you spill food, even a bit of jelly or sauce, you may quietly retrieve it with any convenient utensil—butter knife, fork, or dinner knife—and place it on the side of your plate. Occasionally a little food or liquid will spill or drip onto a dress or tie. In such a case the best thing to do is to use a clean knife or spoon to lift off the offending substance if it hasn't soaked immediately into the fabric. You might also dip a small corner of your napkin into your water glass and then lightly rub the spot. Try to be as inconspicuous as possible, and don't be upset about it. It happens to every one of us. I think the Italians are the most intelligent about spots, even in the most luxurious of restaurants. When an accident occurs, the head waiter immediately sends to the kitchen for the can of talcum powder. Then, with great ceremony, the waiter or the *maggiordomo* pours talcum powder on the spot, and the diner finishes his meal or waits at least half an hour before he touches his tie. Usually, later right at the table, the powder is ceremoniously brushed off with a napkin by the head waiter and *ecco*—the spot has gone, the grease having been gradually absorbed by the powder. (It is almost an honor to be so covered in talc in a good Italian restaurant.) In someone's home, if you drop a piece of chicken or meat on the floor while trying to serve yourself from a platter, pick it up quickly with your napkin and put it on your plate. You should go ahead and eat this piece, as there may not be enough to go around otherwise. The waiter, holding a large platter, is in no condition to pick it up himself.

Swallowing the Wrong Way and Choking

All of us swallow the wrong way at times and suffer a minor choking fit. When someone chokes, it is the time for the other people at the table not to look at the person but to talk among themselves, so that he will be able to regain his composure in peace. But sometimes the choking is serious. A piece of food can become stuck in such a way as to cause death. The person who is actually choking to death can say *nothing*. Since this could happen in your own family as well as to a guest in your home, it is your responsibility to know what to do at once. Every kitchen should have posted on the wall the "Heimlich Maneuver," published by the Life Extension Institute at 1185 Avenue of the Americas in New York. Food choking is the sixth leading cause of accidental death. It takes only four minutes to die from it, unless immediate action is taken. If someone at your dinner table cannot breathe, becomes pale or cyanotic (blue), or becomes panicky, you must go to him at once. Don't let someone leave the room in this condition alone. The Heimlich Maneuver works as follows:

1. Stand behind the victim and wrap your arms around his waist.
2. Grasp your fist with the other hand and place the thumb side of your fist against the victim's abdomen, slightly above the navel and below the rib cage.
3. Press your fist into the victim's abdomen with a QUICK UPWARD THRUST. Repeat as often as necessary.
4. If the victim is sitting, stand behind the victim's chair and perform the maneuver in the same manner.
5. After the food is dislodged, have the victim seen by a doctor.

When the victim has collapsed and cannot be lifted, the following steps should be taken:

1. Lay the victim on his back.
2. Face the victim and kneel astride his hips.
3. With one hand on top of the other, place the heel of your bottom hand on the abdomen slightly above the navel and below the rib cage.
4. Press into the victim's abdomen with a QUICK UPWARD THRUST. Repeat as often as necessary.
5. Should the victim vomit, quickly place him on his side and wipe out his mouth to prevent aspiration (drawing of vomit into the throat).
6. After the food is dislodged, have the victim seen by a doctor.

If you yourself are choking, give the sign of choking by grasping your neck between the thumb and index finger of one hand. The victim of food choking is often mistakenly thought to be having a heart attack. If you are alone, try to self-administer the Heimlich Maneuver.

Sneezing

If you feel a sneeze coming on at the table, and you have no time to reach for your handkerchief, cover your nose and mouth area with your napkin, but never blow into it. If you are going to be in dire need of a handkerchief or some tissue, excuse yourself quickly from the table with an "Excuse me one second," directed at your hostess, and find your handbag or coat with the handkerchief—or find some tissue in your host's bathroom. When you return to your place, murmur a quick apology again to your hostess, and forget about it. When you have to blow your nose at the table, do it very gently, as it is hardly an appetizing sound.

If you are in an elevator or on a bus or in any close quarters with other people, and a sneeze suddenly overtakes you, cover your face with your hands and turn away from people as much as possible.

If you begin to sneeze during a concert or a play, remove yourself from the hall. One sneeze usually follows another. You can't hold back a sneeze, but you can do the best you can to keep it from being overly loud and disturbing to others. In other words, be a "polite sneezer," not a rude one.

Speaking with Food in the Mouth

We are constantly telling our children, "Don't speak with your mouth full." Our mouths should certainly not be full when we do talk, but if we waited to speak until every bit of food was out of our mouths, any conversation would be interminably delayed. It is possible to speak with a bit of food in the mouth and still not be offensive. If anyone directs a question at you and your mouth is full, naturally you must wait until much of it is chewed and eaten before replying. The person who asked you the question should realize your dilemma and quickly begin speaking about something to give you time to answer—perhaps more information concerning the question he asked you, or perhaps how he thinks you will answer it. It's embarrassing to be caught with your mouth full, and the person who puts you in this situation should be considerate.

Food in the Teeth

If food gets wedged in your teeth and can't be dislodged with your tongue, you may *not* sit there in front of people and get it out with a toothpick or with your fingernail. Leave the table and retire to the rest-room or bathroom mirror to get at the offending bit of food. If you have nothing sharp like a toothpick with you, often the rinsing of your mouth vigorously with water will correct the situation. People who have a constant problem with food sticking in their teeth should carry toothpicks with them.

Burping

The old saying " 'Tis better to burp the burp and bear the shame than to squelch the belch and bear the pain" is absolutely true. Burping is nature's way of getting rid of excess gas, and suppressing it may be physically harmful. When someone feels a burp coming on, he should cover his nose and mouth with a napkin at the table, or with a handkerchief when he is not at the table, in order to muffle the sound. When he burps, he should say, to no one in particular, "Excuse me!" If he continues to burp, he should remove himself from the dining room or theater or whatever public place he may be in, until the attack subsides.

When someone burps in your midst, you should pretend you did not hear it (unless you are in a smalll group of old friends, in which case a certain amount of teasing is inevitable). If someone burps at the dinner table, often all conversation will stop because the other guests are feeling such intense embarrassment for the sufferer. This is the time for a good guest immediately to introduce an interesting topic, to get everyone talking again. Those total silences at a party can be miserable for everyone involved.

Foreign Matter in Food

A foreign body taken into the mouth accidentally with food—gravel or bird shot, for example—should be removed from the mouth by rolling it forward with the tongue onto your spoon or fork held to your lips, and then it should be placed on the plate, hidden under a bit of food. If a gnat lands in your iced-tea glass, fish it out, but if a bug crawls out of your salad, you should ignore its presence and simply leave your salad unfinished. Calling attention to it will embarrass your hostess, even if her dinner party takes place in a fancy restaurant. (If *you* are paying the bill, call over the waiter and have him bring a fresh plate of whatever food it was.)

Leaving the Table

If you suddenly feel ill, or have an urgent need to go to the bathroom, no apologies are necessary. Just say to your hostess, "Please excuse me for a moment," and depart. You need make no explanations when you return, but after dinner you should explain to your hostess that you didn't feel well.

The guests do not arise from the table until the host and hostess do. The hostess should catch the host's eye and say something like "Shall we go into the other room?" to the guest on her right. Everyone then follows her. People who are engrossed in an exciting conversation should not linger at the table, but should carry that conversation with them into the area of the house where their hosts lead them.

Reaching Across the Table

There are various degrees of reaching for something across a table that are perfectly permissible, but one should not make an enormous stretch or rise from one's seat to reach across for something one needs at table. If you have easy access to the salt and pepper and your neighbor on either side does not, it is polite to offer it first to both of them before using it yourself. When passing the salt and pepper, pass them as a pair. If something is really too far from your grasp, address the person closest to it at the table and ask politely, "After you have used it yourself, would you please pass me the Hollandaise?"

Smoking at Table

If you must smoke at the table, please do it when everyone has finished dessert. Smoking in between courses is rude to the hostess, because it cuts down on the enjoyment of everyone's food. If the hostess herself smokes between courses, she is the rude one, and there is no reason for you to follow suit. Light up a cigarette or a cigar only when the dessert course has been finished and people are lingering over coffee or conversation at the table. And bring your own cigarettes. Hostesses are no longer supposed to furnish cigarettes for their guests at any time; only the ash trays and the matches should be in place on the table for those who smoke. If you are the lone smoker at the table, ask your hostess and your host first, "Do you mind?" They will most likely say yes, go ahead and smoke, because otherwise they would not have provided you with an ash tray. If there are no ash trays, and you notice a grim-lipped "yes" from your hostess, you would be far better off reconsidering lighting that cigarette. Your hostess may be making a mental check to remove you from her future guest lists.

Conversational Flow at Table

It is your hosts' duty to see that the conversational flow shifts smoothly at the table, and that no one is left out. Each guest has his own responsibility to change conversational partners, and to turn to the other side, when the entire traffic at the table seems to do so. In embassies and in the homes of the heads of state, there is a rigorous change of conversational partners after each course. One does not have to be that formal; but nevertheless, by the middle of the meal, the guests should have switched partners. A guest can help out, perhaps by engaging in conversation with two others, and then gradually weaning the closer of the other two toward his direction to converse with him alone. If you are having an absolutely fascinating conversation with one partner and don't want to leave, you should flatter him or her with the truth, but switch anyway, after saying something like "You know, I absolutely hate to leave you, but I'm getting signals from the other side that I'm being rude. May we finish this discussion later? Please?" Your dinner partner will not forget you, I promise!

What is deemed proper table conversation today is anything that is handled in a nonoffensive, tasteful way, which means without swear words and without the "dirty talk" that so many people feel they have to use in order to feel socially secure. I remember Winston Churchill once discussing how to decide what joke to tell at a dinner party. "Make a list of all of your best stories," he said with a twinkle in his eye, "and then throw out every one but the one you are certain is superb. Then try to control yourself and don't tell it unless some disaster occurs and everyone is exceedingly depressed. In this way, you won't make a mistake in thinking you're a good storyteller!"

One can discuss controversial topics, from politics to religion, remembering not to be pompous and overbearing. Almost anything except gore and violence may be discussed with taste at the dinner table. One should not dwell on depressing subjects. A dinner party is a festive gathering, a time to lift people's spirits and make them feel happy and good. To be able to contribute to that spirit of well-being is an art. It is the secret to the successful, sought-after guest.

Posture at the Table

Elbows on the table are permissible between courses but not while one is eating. Chairs should not be tipped back ever during the course of a meal. (Not only does it look terrible, but, more important, the chair has a good chance of being broken.) Sit up straight at the table as you were taught, we hope, as a child: with the base of your spine against the back of your chair and your feet flat on the ground.

We used to be taught to sit with our hands folded gracefully in our laps, a posture that today seems rather stiff and priggish. There is no reason in today's life why the hands may not stay on the table (with wrists leaning on the table's edge)—another custom we have absorbed from our European friends.

The main thing to remember with one's hands is not to let them drum nervously on the table or to play with the silverware, stemware, or other table accessories.

Saying Grace

The saying of grace is unfortunately not the daily custom it once was. In many homes throughout America, however, grace is still said. Among religious Jews, prayers are said after the meal—especially on Friday night. In many Christian homes the saying of grace is limited to special feast days, such as Thanksgiving, Christmas, and Easter; however, if a priest or a minister is present, the hosts should remember to ask him to say grace before the meal. Everyone remains standing with bowed head until he has finished.

The father or mother usually says grace in the home, although occasionally a child is asked to say it. Family grace is said either with everyone standing or with everyone seated with bowed heads. Nothing should be touched on the table beforehand—not even the water glasses or the napkins. If a hostess has invited guests, she should tell them as they sit down that it is the custom in that house to say grace, so that the guests will know not to unfurl their napkins.

In Reform Jewish homes the father or someone designated by him says the prayer with the "Amen" intoned by everyone. Christian graces, like prayers, may be extemporaneous, but there are many old familiar ones.

Here are two for children, the first an old Scottish one suitable for all religions:

> Thank you for the world so sweet,
> Thank you for the food we eat,
> Thank you for the birds that sing,
> Thank you, God, for everything.

A blessing for a Christian home:

> Bless this food
> And make us good
> For Jesus' sake.
> Amen.

In religious Jewish homes, after the father leads the general prayers before food, a child may say this:

> May the All Merciful bless my
> father, my leader, the master
> of this house, and my mother,
> my teacher, the mistress of
> this house.

Here is the most familiar grace of all, acceptable to all religions:

> For what we are about to receive,
> Lord, make us truly thankful. Amen.

An eighteenth-century grace from Charles County, Maryland, is for Christian homes:

> O Lord, forgive us our sins and
> bless these refreshments in
> Christ's name. Amen.

A simple one for a guest is Ophelia's blessing from *Hamlet:*

> God be at your table.

Various denominated prayer books, too, give graces.

Catholics are instructed in the saying of grace both before and after meals. A Catholic grace before meals is:

> Bless us, O Lord, and these Thy
> gifts, which we are about to receive
> from Thy bounty, through Christ
> Our Lord. Amen.

A clergyman who is a guest at a public function is also usually asked to say the grace if he is not already giving a formal invocation.

How to Eat Various Foods

Artichokes   A finger food. The leaves are pulled off, one at a time, the fleshy base dipped in the accompanying sauce, then dexterously pulled through the teeth to extract the tender part. The inedible part of the leaf is then placed at the side of the plate so that by the time the choke (the fuzzy center) is reached there is a neat pile of leaves which, if the artichoke is very big, may be transferred, in part at least, to the butter plate, for greater convenience. When the choke appears, it is held with the fork or the fingers while the tip of one's knife neatly cuts out the inedible gray feathery portion. Then the heart is cut into small pieces, each of which is dipped into the butter or sauce by the forkful.

Asparagus If it is full of sauce, asparagus is easier to eat cut into manageable portions, with a fork. However, asparagus stalks may also be eaten, one by one, with the fingers. Hold the stalk in your right hand, dip it in the sauce, and eat it up to the tough part. Then lay the latter part down neatly on the plate before you.

Bacon Very crisp bacon may be eaten in the fingers if breaking it with a fork would scatter bits everywhere. Bacon with any vestige of fat must be cut with a knife and fork and eaten with the fork, otherwise the fingers would be very greasy.

Birds, Frogs' Legs Small birds, such as squab and quail, and frogs' legs, too, may be picked up in the fingers after you have cut off as much meat as possible from the tiny bones. These small birds are slippery on the plate, difficult to cut, and almost everyone who eats them has had one fly off his plate at some point in his life.

Cake Cake is eaten with a fork, or with a fork and spoon, continental-style. A small fruit tart or petit four is taken by the dinner guest from the platter paper frill and all. If a round cake is served to you for dessert, cut yourself a wedge-shaped piece with the knife offered you. You may use the fingers of one hand to steady the piece of cake, to keep it from falling, as it goes from the platter to your dessert plate. If you are served a piece of fruit cake or pound cake with your ice cream, this kind of dry cake may be picked up and eaten with your fingers.

Caviar The eating of this luxury is becoming such a rarity today that few of us have the pleasure of this delicacy. Caviar is usually served in a small crystal bowl over ice, with a spoon tucked in among the salty sturgeon roe. It is accompanied by a plate of small round or square pieces of crustless toast. If someone passes you a platter of caviar, take some (not too much, never more than a teaspoonful, or you will have everyone glaring at you, thinking there won't be any left for them), plus one or two pieces of toast. Then serve yourself a bit of whichever garnish you want (crumbled hard-boiled egg yolk, chopped onions, or a piece of lemon), with the separate spoon you will find in each small accessory bowl on the platter. As the platter passes to someone else, use your knife to assemble your "caviar toasts" as you wish. If, however, the platter is left on the table next to you, you may assemble the caviar on toast as you wish, without putting it first on your plate. Some people like to put caviar on their toast with nothing else, but more people like to add a little lemon juice.

Champagne is the usual wine served with this hors d'oeuvre (or it may be a first course—certainly the most luxurious in existence!).

Celery and Olives Celery, radishes, and olives are often already on the table as you sit down to dinner; or they may be passed by the waiter. If you have a butter plate, put them there, and you may shake a little salt adjacent to them on the butter plate, into which you dip the celery before eating it. Usually these are not served now with the soup course; instead they are often served as an hors d'oeuvre before dinner during the cocktail hour. Olives, if stuffed, are popped into the mouth, one at a time. Olives used as a garnish on a salad or on a sandwich are eaten with the fingers. If they are part of the salad, then they should be pitless and are eaten with one's fork.

Chicken America's great tradition of fried chicken (but this goes for baked and broiled, too) should be eaten with the fingers only on such occasions as picnics, barbecues, boat rides, and other informal outdoor gatherings. Children should be taught from an early age to handle a chicken with a knife and fork. It is an important part of their table-manners training. Even at home, where life is often very informal, it is better if a child cuts the meat off the bones, eating it as he goes, so that these "chicken manners" will be automatic as he grows older. After all, at parties and in restaurants, too, he will have to eat chicken with his knife and fork.

If one is right-handed, one spears the chicken part with the fork in the left hand; then, with the knife, one strips the meat from the bones. The legs and wings are the toughest part for children to tackle, particularly since that drumstick is so enticing to eat with the fingers, without the bother of a fork and a knife! With practice, children become very proficient in handling chicken this way, as in anything, but if their parents never show them how, it will be a detriment to their manners later.

The best way to attack half of a broiler is to separate the leg at the joint, with the fork holding it in place and the knife cutting into the connective tissue. Then, with the fork, hold the leg in such a way that the meat may be sliced with the grain and cut into manageable amounts. Do not cut more than two or three pieces at one time. Whatever chicken is left that cannot be removed from the bones is simply left on the plate, and one does not pick up the bones to gnaw away at them—unless one is in an informal situation.

Rock Cornish hens, duck, pheasant—all birds are eaten with knife and fork. The joints are cut to dissect the legs from the carcass, in order to get at the meat easily; the wings are treated in the same way. With the fork in the left hand, impale the breast and slice the meat from the breastbone. On a small bird, just one slice will usually accomplish this. If the birds are extremely small, the tiny leg bones may be taken in the fingers, if the hostess so indicates by eating in that manner.

One should be very aware of grease on the mouth after eating fowl in this manner and blot the mouth with the napkin whenever necessary.

Chops   One should eat pork, lamb, or veal chops with a fork and knife, never with the fingers, even if there's a frilled paper "panty" on the bone end. That's for decoration only. This custom goes back many centuries to when there were no carving implements and the paper was meant to protect a lady's hand from grease when she picked up the bone, and then had to cut off some meat for her own plate. When eating a chop, spear the plump end with the tines of your fork (upside down) and with your knife proceed to cut out the center eye. Cut this, one or two pieces at a time, into bite-sized pieces. Then with the knife and fork clean as much meat as possible from the remaining bone. The frill end may be held with the fingers (but kept firmly on the plate), to facilitate cutting from the small bone. If you have been served very small, delicate lamb chops and your hostess picks up the bones to finish them off, you may certainly follow suit.

Corn on the Cob   This should only be served in informal entertaining for, delicious though it may be, it is messy and difficult to eat and creates problems of bits stuck in the teeth, lipstick smears, and stains on clothes. The cob should be held firmly by the fingers of both hands, at each end. You should butter and season a few rows only at a time, then eat them; then begin the process all over again until the corn on the cob is consumed. Some hosts serve corn on the cob held by silver skewers at either end—a fancy touch, but rather unnecessary. (A friend of mine used her grandmother's sterling silver cob holders for a summer dinner party and lost twenty-two out of the twenty-four pairs. The guests had all thought they were souvenirs, much like the book matches on the table!)

If someone is served corn on the cob and must cut off the corn for reasons of his teeth, the gracious hostess sends his cob out to the kitchen or does it herself. It is very difficult to sit at a dinner table and cut the corn off the cob. It is a slippery maneuver. One thoughtful hostess who throws large barbecues all summer keeps pretty little jars of toothpicks in all the bathrooms, for use by her guest after their corn feasts.

Crepes   The dessert crepes (like crepes suzette) are eaten with a dessert fork and spoon. There are other kinds, such as the very light Chinese ones filled with lettuce and other mixtures, that may be taken up and eaten in the fingers. If you are in doubt about what to do with a crepe that is passed to you, watch your hostess. She may have served you a delicious ethnic-recipe crepe that is meant to be picked up and eaten in the fingers.

Eggs, Soft-boiled   You may be presented with a soft-boiled egg, small end up, in an eggcup that resides on a service plate. The proper way to eat an egg like this is to crack the shell with the blade of a knife in a sharp horizontal stroke. You behead the egg, so to speak, and then you may season it in the shell and spoon out the contents from inside the shell. If you wish to order two eggs, they will come in a dish, of course, but there is something fun and flavorful about using an eggcup. I remember my utter delight in my student days in Switzerland when I would be confronted at breakfast with my soft-boiled egg in a beautiful china eggcup, topped with a minute flowered quilted "cozy" to keep it warm.

Fish Small fish, cleaned and then fried, are usually served whole, complete with head and tail. You cut off the head first, then hold the fish firmly with your fork, slit it with the tip of the knife from head to tail, and open it out flat. Then you insert the tip of the knife under one end of the backbone, which, with the help of your fork in a serving motion, is gently lifted out, bringing with it most of the tiny bones in the fish. This skeletal material is laid out on the edge of the plate. You cut the rest of the fish with your knife and fork into manageable portions. If some of the tiny bones are still in the fish and you discover them in your mouth, remove them with your thumb and forefinger and place them on the side of your plate. There is no objection to eating the head of the smaller fish; indeed, it is considered a great delicacy by true fish aficionados.

If you wish to serve your fish headless, that's all right, too. If you wish to serve the fish with its head reclining on a bed of lettuce or watercress, and with a slice of lemon in its gaping maw, that's all right, too. The fish eye, after all, in many countries of the Far East, is a great delicacy, and is offered first to honored guests, as is the sheep's eye in Arab countries.

If you take a piece of lemon, squirt it while holding it in your right hand over the fish. Use your left hand as a shield to keep lemon juice from hitting you or others nearby.

Fruit A bowl of fresh fruit is offered as the final course in many European and Mediterranean countries; it is also offered at the conclusion of a large formal dinner in this country. The first thing a child who is a fruit lover has to learn is to refrain from diving into artistic centerpieces of fruit. These are often for decoration only—or at least are meant to be the table decoration until the very end of the meal.

An *apple* or a *pear* is often eaten informally in the hand, but at a dinner party the fruit should be placed on your plate, halved, cored, then broken into smaller sections to eat with your fork and fruit knife. If you have to peel the apple or pear, you naturally do it before cutting it. If you know how to peel fruit in a deft spiral motion, so much the better. (If you're like me and are not a neat peeler, you learn to eat fruit with its skin intact.)

Apricots, cherries, plums, and *kumquats* are eaten in one or two bites. The stones, cleaned in your mouth, are dropped onto your fruit fork and then deposited on your plate. Kumquats are bitten into or eaten whole, depending on their size.

Avocado halves are eaten right in their shells with a spoon. Usually there is some kind of a fruit juice or salad dressing in the center cavity (where the pit was). Avocados that are peeled and halved or cut into small pieces are popular in salads; in this case they should be eaten, of course, with a fork.

Bananas may be eaten informally at picnics or on the beach just the way children eat them—by peeling down the skin and eating the fruit held in the fingers. At the table they should be peeled, broken into small bite-sized pieces with a fruit knife, and eaten with a fruit fork.

Berries are always eaten with a spoon. Large strawberries, however, may be served whole, complete with their stems. You grasp the stem and dip the berry into powdered sugar or something similar on the plate. You eat the strawberry in one or two bites, and deposit the stem on your plate.

A grapefruit half is best eaten with a pointed fruit spoon. If you are serving grapefruit to your guests, first loosen all the sections in each grapefruit with a fruit knife, so it will be easy to eat. Squeeze out the grapefruit juice into a teaspoon very unobtrusively, and without squirting in your neighbor's eye.

Grapes are cut with grape shears or with scissors in a cluster from the large bunches passed in a bowl. You eat one grape at a time, and the tiny pits are deposited in your cupped hand and then placed on the plate. It's pretentious to peel your grapes—leave that for gourmet recipes!

Some say that the only place to eat *mangoes* is in the bathtub. They are messy, so the best way to serve them is peeled, quartered, pitted, and chilled. A whole ripe (spotted) mango should be cut in half with a sharp fruit knife, then quartered. Then, with the quarter turned skin up and held in place with a fork, the skin should be carefully pulled away rather than peeled from the fruit. The juicy sections are then cut in one-bite morsels. Finger bowls or extra paper napkins are helpful at this point, as the mango is a fruit that stains badly.

Melons such as honeydew, cantaloupe, or Persians are usually cut in half or in quarter slices. This fruit is served chilled and well cleaned of any seeds in the hollow, and is eaten with a fork or spoon. Melon balls in syrup or wine are often served as a dessert and are eaten with a spoon.

The best way to peel *oranges* is with a sharp knife in one continuous spiral (this requires practice); then they are pulled apart into segments; if the segments are small, they are eaten whole separately. If the segments are large, they should be cut in half crosswise with a fruit knife, and consumed with a fruit fork or with the fingers. If you are serving oranges as dessert to guests, or even as a first course, you should peel and slice the fruit, perhaps adding a little sweetener. They may be served on a plate or in a compote dish.

Papaya is one fruit that is occasionally served with its black seeds. It is halved, chilled, and eaten with a spoon like melon.

Peaches should be halved, then quartered with a fruit knife. Lift the skin of each quarter at an edge, and pull it off. The sections should be cut into small pieces and eaten with a fork and fruit knife. Peach juice stains table linens, so care should be taken in eating them.

Whole pears or peaches in wine or syrup—a continental dessert—should be served with a fork and dessert spoon. The fork in the left hand, tines down, may be used to keep the whole fruit in place as the spoon cuts off manageable bites. If it is served with a dessert spoon alone, the spoon must be used with great care to prevent the entire fruit from skidding off the dish or splattering the syrup around. The soft flesh of the fruit is eaten with the fork rotating the fruit by the core to make the uneaten part available. When only a dessert spoon is served, then the dish itself is rotated with the left hand to make the fruit more manageable in its standing position. The core is left in the dish, but the wine or syrup may be spooned up.

Persimmons are often served as a first course with the top cut off well below the stem and the base cut flat so the fruit stands firmly on the plate. Grasping the persimmon with the left thumb and index finger, scoop out and eat a spoonful at a time, keeping the shell intact. Avoid the skin, which, unless really ripe, is puckery. The large pits are cleaned in the mouth, dropped into the spoon, and then deposited on the side of the plate. Persimmons in salad should be peeled and quartered.

Fresh *pineapple* is served peeled and cut in thin strips. One should use a fruit knife and fork to cut and eat it.

If *pomegranates* are served halved, you hold the half with your index finger and thumb, extract the seeds carefully with a spoon, and eat one or two of the seeds as you go along. (The seeds are used as a garnish, but some people enjoy eating them.)

Stewed fruit is served in a compote or dish and eaten with a dessert spoon and fork. The pits or bits of core of cherries, prunes, plums, apples, and so on, are dropped from the mouth into the spoon and then deposited on the side of the plate.

Tangerines are easy to peel, but the white pulpy covering is sometimes difficult to remove from the fruit. Pick it off with your fingers, and eat the tangerine segment by segment, pulling them apart with your finger.

Large pieces of *watermelon* are served on separate plates and eaten with a fork and knife (to help cut away the sections to be eaten). The fruit and its seeds are taken into the mouth; the seeds are cleaned in the mouth and dropped into the cupped hand for disposal on the plate. If watermelon is to be served cut into small pieces in a compote (sometimes in wine), all seeds must be removed beforehand.

Ice Cream Depending on how it is served, ice cream is eaten with a small spoon or with a dessert spoon and fork. When ice cream or sherbet is served in a sherbet dish, it is eaten with a small spoon. When it is served as part of the baked Alaska dessert, or in conjunction with cake or pie, it is eaten with a dessert fork and spoon. Ice-cream cones are not served at a lunch or dinner party, except for children, for the simple reason that they are messy.

Meat When a platter of meat is passed to you, whether it's a humble meat loaf or an expensive sliced tenderloin, take only one large slice at a time (or two small ones). The platter is usually passed again.

Meat served in large slices, such as steak or ham, is of course cut with a knife and fork.

Parsley and Other Garnishes Parsley, dill, watercress, mint, and other greens used as garnish may be eaten with the fork as part of the dish. Decorated lemon slices, or wedges of lemon, are meant to be squeezed over the food they accompany. This may be done through a gentle pressure of the fork, or the fruit may be picked up in the fingers if it is not covered with sauce or melted butter. In good restaurants, lemon halves or quarters are often served masked with cheesecloth to prevent squirting of the juice when the lemon is squeezed. You can prevent squirting, however, by piercing the slice of lemon with the fork tines, thus rupturing the juice cells. An even more basic way of preventing a squirt of lemon juice in your own or someone else's face is to shield the lemon with one hand while squeezing it in the other.

Pickles, Radishes, and Celery Whole pickles are taken up with the fingers, as are radishes; sliced or very small pickles are eaten with a fork. When a relish tray is passed to you, never take anything from the tray directly into your mouth. Always put it first on your butter plate, or on the side of the plate under your appetizer server, and then into your mouth.

Pizza Pizza is usually served to you in a pie-shaped wedge. You may eat it in your fingers (the sides gently held together so as not to lose the filling). More formally, it is eaten with a fork and knife, but then again, it is not a formal food. Some actually swear that a pizza tastes better when held in the fingers.

Potatoes One food that may be eaten with or without utensils is the french fried potato. If these are very small, it is better to use the fingers, provided they are not too greasy. If the shoestring potatoes have come into contact with any gravy or sauce on your plate, you should eat them with a fork. If the french fries are large, it is more correct to use your fork. As for a baked potato, you should hold it in one hand and make a large incision across the top, lengthwise, and then crosswise, in order to put butter, salt, and pepper (or sour cream with chives) inside the potato jacket. Use your fork to pick up the pat of butter from your butter plate or from the serving platter of butter, and put it right inside the potato. If you wish, eat the skin, too, cutting it first into small pieces as you go along. Only a child may have his potato contents scooped out of the jacket and then buttered, seasoned, and mashed on his plate. Some cooks, particularly in restaurants, bake potatoes in foil, to make them cook faster and stay warm longer, but the potatoes never seem to taste as good cooked this way.

Potato chips and sticks are, of course, eaten in the fingers.

Salad Hostesses who tear their salad lettuce into very small pieces (always at the last minute, in order to preserve the vitamin content), are doing their guests a favor. It is difficult to serve and eat (without cutting) enormous pieces of lettuce. A quarter of iceberg lettuce may be eaten with knife and fork. In fact, any salad may be eaten with a knife and fork, continental-style, if it is in front of you (not to the side), and if you are more comfortable using your knife. Many people use a bit of bread or roll as a pusher in eating their salad, and this is correct, too.

Salt and Pepper Pepper and salt sets that are not individual are always kept together in the passing, but pepper grinders may be passed without the salt. If the table is to be properly set, there should be a salt and pepper set for every two guests. However, if there is a large pepper grinder (a conversation piece), then there need be only a salt shaker or cellar of some kind (the latter with a small spoon) at every two places, and the pepper grinder may be ceremoniously passed around. If you want salt to dip your radishes or celery into, place it on your butter plate or on the edge of your luncheon or dinner plate—never on the table cloth.

Sandwiches Small tea sandwiches and canapés are taken in the fingers and bitten into or, if bite-size, placed whole in the mouth. Double- and tri-ple-decker club sandwiches are best eaten by cutting them into fourths before eating. You may have to use a knife and fork if the triple-decker sections are too messy.

Seafood The steaming process of *clams* is supposed to open the shell completely, but sometimes doesn't. If a shell is not fully open, pick it up and bend it back with the fingers. If it doesn't easily open, forget it; it is probably a bad one. With the shell fully open, take the shell in the left hand just over the dish and with the right hand lift out the clam by the neck. Holding the neck with the right hand, pull the body of the clam from it and discard the neck sheath. Holding the clam by the neck with the right hand, place the whole clam first in melted butter or broth or both alternately, then into the mouth in one bite. As empty shells collect, remove them to a large bowl the hostess has, we hope, provided her guests at each end of the table. The hostess should also provide plenty of extra napkins, and perhaps some finger bowls with warm water, too, to rinse the fingers after this messy but delicious job of clam-eating. The clam broth may be drunk separately from the soup cup. If the clams are fried, one should eat them with a fork after breaking them into two pieces, if necessary. These are greasy, so they should not be eaten with the fingers.

Lobster and hard-shelled crabs (broiled or boiled): The claws of both of these require dexterous handling. They should be cracked well in the kitchen, so that further cracking at the table will hardly be necessary (some hosts provide nutcrackers for each guest, regardless). The shells are pulled apart by the fingers and the tender meat extracted carefully, so that it comes out whole, if possible. An oyster fork or a nut pick can do this extracting efficiently; one dips the delicacy on the end of the fork into the melted butter or mayonnaise sauce and then pops it into the mouth. If the piece is too large, one cuts it into smaller pieces with a fork first. The green material in the stomach cavity, called the tamale, and the "coral" or roe in the female are delicacies and may be eaten with the fork, but some people don't like them. The small claws are pulled from the body with the fingers, then the body ends are placed between the teeth so that the sweet meat and its juice may be extracted by chewing and sucking (but without a loud sucking noise, please!). The major portion of the meat is found in the stomach cavity and the tail and is first speared, one side at a time, with the fork, then with the help of a knife, if necessary, lifted out and cut as needed into mouthfuls, then dipped into the sauce with the fork.

Crab "fingers" are often served as hors d'oeuvres; they are picked up by the small end of the shell with the meaty end dipped in the sauce and sucked out.

Mussels are served, pickled or smoked, on toothpicks as cocktail tidbits, and are taken via the toothpicks directly into the mouth. One of the most popular mussel dishes is moules marinières, which is served in a soup dish with a thin souplike sauce redolent with garlic. The mussels may be picked out of their shells with the small oyster fork provided, but it is also correct to eat the mussel right from the shell. Pick it up, place the tip of the shell in the mouth, and quietly suck out the mussel and its juice; then discard the shell onto the butter plate or an empty plate that may be waiting for just this purpose. You may spoon the soup sauce from the plate when you have finished eating the mussels; bread as a "sauce sopper" is again appropriate here. Since this is another messy dish, the gracious hostess serves her guest with hot moist towels or finger bowls before the next course.

For *oysters and clams* (half shell), you should hold the shell steady with your left hand and, using an oyster fork, lift the oyster or clam whole from the shell, detaching it, where necessary, with the fork. Then you dip it into the cocktail sauce container on the plate. (Others squirt lemon juice on the oyster or clam but not in the sauce.) You eat one of these in one mouthful, even the big Chincoteagues; don't ever try to cut them. Oyster crackers may be dropped whole into the sauce, then eaten by extracting them from the sauce with the oyster fork. Also, when eating oysters on the half shell, it is quite acceptable to pick up the shell after eating the oyster and to drain the juice into your mouth. This is not a particularly pretty sight; it should be done as gracefully as possible while holding the shell between your thumb and forefinger. If a chip of shell stays in your mouth, remove it unobtrusively with your thumb and forefinger.

When the *shrimps* in a *shrimp cocktail* are too large to be eaten in one mouthful, impale them on the seafood fork and bite off a manageable bite. Redip the portion remaining on your fork in the sauce, and eat it. Do not try to cut the shrimp on the plate beneath the seafood cup.

Sherbet When sherbet is served with the fruit cup or meat course, you may eat it with your fork or a spoon. The serving of sherbet is seen less and

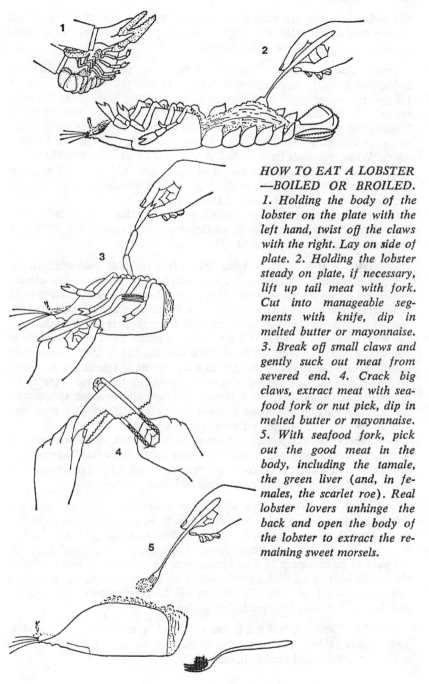

HOW TO EAT A LOBSTER —BOILED OR BROILED.

1. Holding the body of the lobster on the plate with the left hand, twist off the claws with the right. Lay on side of plate. 2. Holding the lobster steady on plate, if necessary, lift up tail meat with fork. Cut into manageable segments with knife, dip in melted butter or mayonnaise. 3. Break off small claws and gently suck out meat from severed end. 4. Crack big claws, extract meat with seafood fork or nut pick, dip in melted butter or mayonnaise. 5. With seafood fork, pick out the good meat in the body, including the tamale, the green liver (and, in females, the scarlet roe). Real lobster lovers unhinge the back and open the body of the lobster to extract the remaining sweet morsels.

less today in our more simplified, calorie-conscious way of living. When sherbet tops a fruit salad, you may eat it with your salad fork. When sherbet is a dessert, you eat it with a spoon.

Snails Snails are usually served on a hot metal plate. A special hinged holder that grips the piping-hot snail shells is usually provided in restaurants. (If you are served snails in someone's home and they have no such instruments, grip the snail shell with your fingers, protected by your napkin.) Holding the snail with your other hand, dig the body out by means of a pick or oyster fork with your other hand. Like raw oysters, snails should be eaten whole. When the shells have cooled, it is proper to tilt them into the mouth to get all of the garlic butter and snail juice. This will give you a greasy mouth, however. Some people prefer to get at that wonderful sauce by using the piece-of-bread-speared-on-the-fork method.

(If a couple plan to spend a romantic evening together, they should either both have snails or both abstain, as the smell of the garlic on the breath remains strong for a very long time!)

Spaghetti A true spaghetti lover knows that the only authentic, satisfying, and graceful way to eat real Italian spaghetti is to twine a few strands round and round a fork, until the long strands have all been wound around. A novice needs to use a large spoon as a buttressing operation against the fork as it twirls (to keep its spaghetti load from slipping off the fork), but the expert eschews a spoon. (Some "cheat a little" by holding a piece of bread in readiness in their left hand while they twirl their fork in their right —just in case assistance is needed in keeping the spaghetti on its fork.) When each forkful is ready, it is then conveyed into the mouth (the spoon remains on the plate, of course). If your spaghetti platter comes to you with the sauce and grated cheese on top, you may mix it all up with your fork and spoon, much as though you were tossing a salad.

It is heresy to cut spaghetti. A pasta such as thick macaroni may, of course, be cut as one goes along. With any pasta, fettucini, lasagna, cannelloni, or whatever, it is perfectly all right to go after the last remnants of the sauce on the plate with a small piece of bread.

Toast and Hot Breads You may butter your whole piece of toast and then cut it into halves with your butter knife or any knife before eating. Rolls, English muffins, brioches, scones, and muffins may be cut in half or slit into with a knife, with butter inserted into them. Long bread sticks do not have to be broken. You may butter them on one side, or you may stick the end of your bread stick into the pat of butter on your plate, and take a bite of it. Hot sticky buns (Danish) should be cut into halves or quarters and then each section buttered before eating.

Tortillas These are laid flat in the left hand or on a plate, filled slightly with frijoles (kidney beans) or some other appropriate mixture, rolled up and eaten like a rolled sandwich, endwise.

Part Four

MANNERS IN BUSINESS

Getting a Job   437

Men and Women as Colleagues in the Office   447

Business Entertaining   455

Telephone Manners   465

General Office Manners   474

Opening Your Own Business   485

BUSINESS

A revolution in the social mores of business has occurred. There is a new world, with women attempting to gain an equal footing with the traditional keepers of the corporate and professional keys—men. Yet many women who have succeeded in reaching the top echelon of the working world are unsure of how they should act while wending their ways through the intricate maze of corporate relationships. These women tend to leave the men around them confused, too, unsure of how they should treat the women and of how the women should treat them.

Something had to emerge from this state of flux—and something has. A type of double standard of behavior is developing, in which a man and a woman treat each other one way in the office, another way in their social lives. This dual standard has nothing to do with kindness or unkindness, but rather with external forms of behavior. In their business lives more men and women are treating each other as "people," a healthy development, while in their personal and social lives both tend to follow more traditional attitudes. For example, thirty-year-old Mary Jones, a lawyer, may want her fiancé to help her on with her coat, to push in her chair at the table, to hold open doors for her, and to treat her protectively; but she would most likely feel embarrassed if the men at her law firm were to treat her in the same way during working hours. It is not a question of Mary Jones' wanting to be "one of the boys" at the office; but rather of wanting to be "one of the people" in her firm.

I feel it is a good development that both women and men are coming to grips with the side effects of equal treatment in our society. There is indeed a lessening of deferential treatment of women in the business world, not by all men but by many. It is logical. Career women must help the men make this transition, particularly those who were trained from childhood to treat women as their fathers and grandfathers before them did.

This revolution of social behavior in the business world does not imply any lessening whatsoever of real manners. It does not imply that equality of treatment equals rudeness. On the contrary, manners are more important than ever. Real manners are the keystone of person-to-person relationships in the office, as elsewhere. Real manners mean consideration for everyone else. They require self-discipline, kindness, and foresight. They help make anyone's life easier and more pleasant. Therefore, if we see the male Sir Lancelot kind of gallantry disappearing in the business world, we should not lament it. In future years, business manners will have no reference to sex whatsoever, but real manners will, I hope, be even more strongly reinforced. In the "equal world" whoever happens to be in the lead opens the door and holds it for the other. Whoever first sees the taxi hails it. People emerge from an elevator in a logical procession, the front people off first, the people in the back off last. Each of us puts on his or her own coat; however, anyone who sees someone else struggling to get into a coat lends a helping hand. Each person lights his or her own cigarettes, but carries packages for someone who is overburdened. A person picks up a check in the coffee shop or a restaurant when it's his or her turn. A man or a woman stands up in the office to greet a male or a female visitor.

These newly emerging relationships do not imply the loss of a woman's femininity, either. Equality of good manners in business does not mean that a woman is less of a woman or a man less of a man. Instead each person treats the other colleague as an intellectual equal. There will always be some people who are better-mannered and more considerate than others, but that is a question of character and not of sex.

The tradition of parents teaching children will not change. Good parents will still teach their children to be thoughtful of others. Children will still be taught how to greet people, say thank you, apologize, and write a proper letter. Well-mannered people will still seek out the shy in a group to make them feel better, be kind to someone who is depressed, and congratulate someone who has good news. People will still be expected to develop good table manners, to train their voices into well-modulated tones, to act properly in public, to speak and write good grammar, to learn how to be a good host and a good guest.

In other words, real manners are not going out of style in this new "equal" business world. Both men and women feel better about themselves and live more efficiently when they are well-mannered. We are still in a state of flux in our handling of ourselves in the business world, but we are headed, I truly believe, in the right direction.

Chapter 35

GETTING A JOB

Looking for a job is a tough period in your life, whether you have just lost the one you had, or are a college graduate going on your first interviews, or a mother going back into the work force, or a bored forty-year-old looking for a new challenge and opportunity.

The most important weapon you can have is self-knowledge: to know well a complete inventory of your skills and what you like to do best. Then you should head in the direction of the companies that can use your areas of interest. You should research the companies themselves well, too, before you approach them. A good way to prepare is to read the company's annual report for the last several years. Know what goods and services they provide, how their profits are doing, and the name of the chief executive officer. Check the Reader's Index at the public library for news on the company that has appeared in major publications during the past year.

If self-knowledge is a necessary component of success in job hunting, so is self-confidence.

Writing a Résumé

The first task in job hunting for a man or a woman is the preparation of a good, selling résumé.

Men and women entering the job market for the first time, or women re-entering after a long time out for child-raising, often have a major problem: a lack of self-esteem. In order to succeed in writing an effective résumé, one must first convince oneself that one has value. A woman who has never before worked has to develop a good self-image and prove to herself that she would be an asset to whoever would employ her. I have seen résumés where the phrase "Have done only volunteer work" was scrawled under the heading "Professional Experience." Just a dismissed apology—"volunteer work." Some of the volunteer women I have known have had to exercise great executive judgment, seize responsibility, and carry out complicated tasks that would challenge a corporation officer of high rank and salary.

A woman should therefore take an objective look at her past work for charity, her children's schools or her alma maters, church or synagogue, and various community organizations. She should describe in professional business terms what were her responsibilities and what was accomplished with these groups. How much money was raised at the benefit she ran or during the year-long fund appeal she launched? How many Girl Scouts benefited from the course revision she accomplished? How many people did she supervise as chairman of the annual school fair? What constructive changes were brought about in her country club during her term as governor? Even if she never earned a cent for such jobs, she should describe her responsibilities and achievements with pride, without once mentioning the word "volunteer."

A person's résumé should possess as much "sales appeal" as possible. If you are just out of college, you should not be shy about a job well done, starting with your honors at college. If you were captain of the football team, state it. If you were on the dean's list, state how many times. Were you an officer of your class or of student government? Did you hold any paid jobs (self-help) while you were going through college?

If you have been working and are looking for a new position, be specific about what your duties and accomplishments were in your past employment. If you sold insurance, mention such things as the total value of the policies sold, the percentage of sales increase each year, and such important honors as "Chosen Salesperson of the Year in 1978." If you were in real estate development, mention the properties on which you worked, their location, and the success quotient involved. Always explain briefly but with a good summation what your role was on any project.

If you worked in personnel, describe how many applicants you screened or processed or trained weekly, or detail any new techniques you might have introduced to your section. In other words, look back on your past jobs as affirmative experiences. Even if you were unhappy in your last position, you learned or benefited from parts of it. Use those to your advantage now.

If you are a housewife returning to the job market, list the years you stayed home to raise a family, but mention certain skills you might have acquired during that period. For example, did you become a handicraft expert, an accomplished photographer, an expert gardener, a Shakespeare buff? Did you absorb a foreign language, help tutor children with learning disabilities, or write movie reviews for the suburban weekly newspaper? Whatever you did, describe it with pride.

A résumé should begin with a short paragraph that summarizes the major accomplishments in your life. If your credentials warrant it, this paragraph should portray an achiever with a strong and persistent record of specific, measurable accomplishment. It should make interesting reading for someone who has never met you. This paragraph might make or break your opportunities, so work hard at it. Many employers don't have the time to plough through a long résumé, but if you catch their interest right at the start, they will finish reading yours.

Your name, address, and telephone number should be at the top of your résumé, then the short summary paragraph of your achievements. Then you should list your work experience, starting with the most current or the most recent position and continuing in reverse chronological order. Give your job title, the name and address of the company for which you worked, and the dates. Follow this with a concise description of your duties and accomplishments. Then, in a separate category, list your education, special courses, and any free-lance writing credits, paintings sold, lecturing, or other outside talents that earn you income.

You should end your résumé with a description of your marital status and number of children. (By law you don't have to give this information, but I personally feel you should; you do not have to list your age, either.) If you know well-placed people who will give you enthusiastic references (and be sure to ask their permission before you furnish their names and telephone numbers to anyone), you may put on your résumé, at the very end, "References furnished upon request."

Almost as important as the contents of the résumé is the way it looks. It should be letter-perfect, well-centered, without even one typo. If you cannot type it perfectly yourself, have it done professionally, and have it offset or duplicated on good paper stock. Your résumé should say you are proud of yourself, that you're "quality material." There are excellent agencies in major cities that specialize in the preparation of résumés, so if you are uneasy, you should consult with one of them. Ask your friends who are well placed in business to criticize your résumé, too.

One should re-tailor one's résumé to fit each new type of occupation; a career counseling service or a knowledgeable friend can also help you with this.

Once the résumé is completed, send it to prospective employers with a neat, brief covering letter (on good stationery) asking for an interview "because I want so much to work for your firm and feel I could make a good contribution." That should be a tip-off to the person reading your letter that you feel enthusiastic—and competent.

Job Application Forms

You will probably be asked to fill out a standard job application form. Even though it may duplicate information, staple or clip your résumé to the completed form when you hand it in. If you do not have attractive, neat handwriting, take the application home and have someone (maybe yourself) type it.

Remember, in answering the questions on these forms, to project the same strong, positive self-image with which you imbued your résumé. If you are asked your reasons for leaving past jobs, stress positive reasons such as "To broaden my experience," or "To add to my skills." Never write a negative like "Became bored" or "Knew I could never get a promotion."

Find out the average salaries of people at your performance level before you go in to apply for the job. That way, you can mention a realistic amount when asked the "minimum salary requested." If you don't want the personnel department to contact your present employer, write that on the form. If you are taking or planning on taking any self-improvement or further-education courses, be sure to include that information under the "comments" part of the form. Make yourself sound like someone very worth while.

Going on a Job Interview

The easiest job interview to handle is when there is a definite opening in a company and you are being considered for that job. You can talk in terms of specifics—why *you* consider yourself a good bet for that particular job, and why you fulfill the requirements and have the needed skills.

The next easiest job interview is one where you know someone at a high level in the company and you have been called in for an interview as an accommodation to that person "with connections." You are at a disadvantage because there is no specific job opening for which you are applying; but you have the advantage of being "properly introduced," so at a minimum the chances are no one will be rude to you.

The toughest way of all is to obtain a job interview when there is no specific position available and you have not been "introduced" by anyone. If you do get in to see someone in personnel, you will have to act quickly to impress that person sufficiently for him to mark your application "Call back the next time there's an opening."

No matter what the circumstances surrounding your interview, it is difficult, nerve-racking, and sometimes demeaning. You have to prepare for all of this. You need to be clear-headed and clear-eyed (no late-night parties the evening before). You should be perfectly groomed: What about your shoes? Hole in your stocking? Is your handbag scuffed up? Is your dress long enough so that when you sit down it won't ride up above your knees? If you are a man, is your shirt clean, the collar unworn, your shoes shined, your tie spotless, your suit pressed and clean? Check your hair, your fingernails. A woman should take off any costume jewelry, except for one simple necklace or a pair of earrings. She should tone down her make-up and forget about heavy perfume. And she should not wear pants. Any of those items might "turn off" her interviewer.

If you have an early morning appointment, eat a good breakfast. Get up an hour earlier than usual, to be unhurried and to have time to psych yourself into feeling you would be good for that company or for that particular job. Make yourself feel self-confident. But remember, too, when you face your interviewer, there is a fine line between the braggart and the person who is sincerely self-confident.

Bring your résumé with you in a briefcase (your interviewer might have lost his copy). Bring samples of your work, commendations, and letters of reference in case he asks for them.

If you're kept waiting for your appointment, don't complain to the receptionist. Although you have presumably already researched this company thoroughly, use this time to read an annual report or other publications of that company that may be available. Make a casual reference to them as you shake your interviewer's hand. "I was just reading the company's latest quarterly report in the reception room. You must be very proud of the earnings increase."

Try to answer the interviewer with the right mixture of humility and certainty that you are the one to fill the job properly.

Be sure to mention any special skills you have that could relate to the position you are seeking. For example, if you sold 200 per cent more advertising space in the annual school benefit program than had ever been sold before, say so, and add, "Mr. Jenkins, I think that proves I know how to sell. And I could sell your products just as well—here or on the road."

Also be flexible, indicating you could fit into other jobs in the company that might be available. You might lose out on the one you are applying for, but if you make a good impression, you could be called back immediately for another job. If you have an opportunity, mention that you view a position with this company as a "career," not just a job.

Don't throw influential names around; any "pull" you have now should remain in your reference letters. Let your own record speak for itself, and if you are too young to have had a record, emphasize your enthusiasm about the idea of joining that firm. If you can get across to the interviewer there is *nothing* you want more than to work for his company, you have probably already earned an *A* on your file. It is a serious mistake for anyone inexperienced to say during an interview, "I'm trying to find out what I should be doing, where I should be heading. I need guidance on where I should go." (That guidance should be sought before he goes on the interview.) The job applicant should fire up his enthusiasm and say, "I'll go anywhere in this company I am placed. I know I could do any job you need to have done."

When the interviewer brings the meeting to a close, he usually asks, "Are there any final questions?" This is your cue to ask anything more you need to know about salary, employee benefits, and vacation time. Don't ask too many self-seeking ones, if you really need and want that job. Some young people are too intent on what they'll get out of the company rather than on what they can give to it. If possible, they should find out that information from other employees after being interviewed. There are pamphlets in the personnel departments of large companies that detail employee benefits, vacations, sick leave rules, maternity benefits, and so on.

After it is over, whether you thought it was a qualified success or an unmitigated disaster, always write a thank-you note to the interviewer.

Thank you so much for seeing me today. I know how busy you are, and I appreciate your taking the time to see me and patiently explain how the company works. I feel qualified for the job and hope to have an affirmative answer from you about it. Again, my thanks.

Sincerely,

[signature]

If you didn't get the job, ask *why.* Call the interviewer and say in earnest, "I know you're terribly busy. If you have any constructive comments for me —on my résumé or on how I handled myself on the interview—I would really appreciate them. I need to know how to handle things better for the future." If you're lucky and your interviewer is a person of any compassion, he will tell you, and those might be the most valuable tips you'll *ever* receive.

Also, when you finally land the job, you should call or write all of the people who gave you advice and helped you along the way to inform them of your good fortune. A little show of good manners never hurt any job applicant.

Employer's Responsibility Toward Job Applicants

There is also a corporate responsibility to show good manners toward job applicants—in the interest of the company's own public relations, as well as in the interest of being humane.

All job applications, solicited and unsolicited, should be acknowledged by the recipient company (whether large or small), even if by printed postcard.

If a person has been told he or she is "in the running" for a job, and then loses out, the company should send out a letter or postcard stating, "We're sorry, but we have filled the position in which you were interested." Otherwise, a person could continue to maintain false hopes, to the detriment of finding another job. Communications are very important in this world of job hunting, and no company is so big or so important that it has the right to ignore *human* responsibility.

Writing a Letter of Reference

A person who has worked satisfactorily for you—even for a short time, as for a summer job—deserves a letter of recommendation upon request. If you write a good, informative letter of recommendation for someone who leaves your employ, you will probably be saved bothersome telephone calls in the future from firms seeking references. A letter of recommendation may be written politely on three levels of enthusiasm, which are easily decipherable by the person's potential employer. This first example is a lukewarm letter—one that you may not want to write in the first place but do because you don't want to jeopardize the future of this person:

To Whom It May Concern,

Jane Doe was in my employ for a period of six months as a junior account executive. She dispatched her duties satisfactorily enough; she was always punctual and wrote neat reports. I wish her success in her future employment and in her quest to locate a job with more responsibility and with a higher salary than we were able to offer her.

Sincerely yours,

The second is more enthusiastic:

To Whom It May Concern,

Jane Doe was in my employ as a junior account executive for a period of six months this past year. She performed her work with great pride and care, and she maintained good working relationships in our crowded office environment. I feel she has good potential and will advance in her career with distinction.

Sincerely,

The third example is a one hundred percent recommendation:

To Whom It May Concern,

I have been privileged to have Jane Doe in my employ these past six months. During this short period of time she performed complicated assignments quickly and efficiently; she worked hard and enthusiastically at every task she was given. She managed to please both her clients and her fellow workers (no small task in our highly pressured, small office environment). Jane is an attractive, talented young woman with beautiful manners. She would make a great addition to any company, and I am only sorry that the size of our operation precludes us from giving her the kind of top-level position she deserves.

Sincerely,

If you have damaging statements to make about a former employee, whether domestic or office, never hint of these in a letter. Simply refuse to grant the letter of recommendation, and suggest to the person that he or she have "any prospective employer call me on the telephone." When the prospective employer does call, tell him the nature of your reservations about the former employee, in a calm, unvitriolic way, but don't ever make unproven accusations.

If you yourself have a position of importance and a friend or colleague seeks a change of executive position, either because he wants to better himself, or because he has been fired or retired, it is your responsibility to do the best you can to help. A thoughtful thing to do is to offer to write a letter of recommendation, rather than wait until the person, with inevitable embarrassment and hesitation, asks you. Then you should let the subject read over what you have written about him, and discuss how the letter could perhaps be made more helpful for the job in question. After all, the applicant's job, and perhaps even his life, is on the line, so to speak.

When you have finalized the letter and dispatched it to your friend's potential employer, be sure to send a blind carbon copy to the person involved. This is not a one-way street in good manners, for it is the responsibility of the subject of the letter to write you a very sincere and articulate "thank you" for the act.

The following is a sample of one type of letter of reference, written to an executive "head hunter" (executive search specialist), that could be helpful for an applicant:

Dear Mr. Jones:

I understand my former colleague, James Bearham, is being considered for the position of vice-president in charge of advertising and public relations of a well-known company. I have known Jim Bearham for twenty years. He has been not only an office colleague, but a great personal friend as well. He is a fellow Cub Scout leader in our community of Hinsdale. We have been fishing companions and, with our wives, tennis and bridge opponents. We served together on the management committee of our firm, and I have always found Jim Bearham the most responsive member of that committee.

Jim Bearham is a first-rate corporate team member. He is a man who likes responsibility, and he follows through. His creative approach for our corporation has always been out front, ahead of the competition, but always with the bottom line in view. He has an eye for important detail, and yet an amazing grasp of the far-ranging aspects of any problem. He knows how and where to tap outside expertise when it is needed. His departure from this firm left a vacuum in our creative planning that is a serious one.

I cannot recommend him more enthusiastically. Jim Bearham is a winner at any task he undertakes.

Sincerely,

[signed with executive's name]

Letters of Resignation

When an individual resigns from his job, he should address a letter of resignation to the president of his company, if it's a small organization, or to the director of personnel (with a copy to his supervisor), if it's a large one. This letter will become part of a permanent file and might be looked at years later by anyone from an executive search specialist to an FBI agent doing a check for a government security clearance. It is therefore important that the letter be neat, well written, and without mistakes. A reason must be stated for resigning, and an effective date for the resignation to take place must be given.

It is a mistake to make accusations in your letter. Even if you were driven to resigning by a scheming, unscrupulous co-worker, you must not make recriminations against that person in your letter. Think of someone going into your personnel file a year later, and reading your letter full of justifiable anger, a letter that cries for "the truth" to be known. The person reading that letter may very well say, "Here's a bad-mouther; we wouldn't want *him* in our company."

Always leave your post expressing a good feeling for it in your letter of resignation. An example of a letter that might be written to a company president by one of his top executives is:

> Home address
> Date

Name of president
Address of company

Dear Hal:

It is with great reluctance that I offer my resignation, effective June 1, 1979. As you know, personal family considerations which need attention, and which I have delayed too long, have reached the point where they urgently need my complete concentration of effort. I will look back on my long [or short, as the case may be] association with this company as an affirmative experience in every way. I admire the firm's philosophy; I have benefited from the learning and growing process here; and I have enjoyed the many close personal associations with my colleagues.

I leave the I. W. Platt Corporation with regret. I hope you realize that I have the highest admiration for your accomplishments as president of this firm. It is my earnest hope that you and the company will continue to enjoy great success.

> Sincerely,
>
> [signature]

A secretary who has found a better-paying job elsewhere might write her letter in the following manner:

> Home address
> Date

Name of head of personnel
Address of company

Dear Ms. Hathaway:

This is to confirm our conversation of this week in which I informed you of my intent to resign, effective at the close of the next pay period, March 30, 1979. If you need me to train my replacement, I can arrange to stay with you for two more weeks.

I am leaving Branwine's Department Store because of an opportunity for advancement and specialized training with another company. They made an offer I could not refuse, in the light of my earnest desire to progress in my career.

I leave Branwine's with regret because of the good friends I have made on the staff here. My contacts with management have always been affirmative experiences, and I shall always be grateful to them for their patience in training me and in teaching me the business.

Sincerely,

[signature]

Chapter 36

MEN AND WOMEN AS COLLEAGUES IN THE OFFICE

Women's Raised Consciousness

If you, as head of your company, have made the decision that everyone on the staff calls everyone else by their first names, that is your decision, and you should communicate it to all newcomers on the staff. If you insist that last names be used, communicate that, too, and hold firmly to it. If you are a man and you call your secretary Alice, meanwhile insisting that she call you Mr. Jones, be prepared for her to balk. The raising of women's consciousnesses has caused a sensitivity on this matter. If you want your secretary to call you Mr. Jones, and she asks you to call her Miss Williams instead of Alice, you should do so. If she is sensitive to the women's movement, she might consider your calling her Alice a put-down.

The owner of a business should be aware of all the nuances of the new roles of women in business, from the pique of the secretary at *always* having to make the coffee to the impatience of the women executives to be asked to serve on corporate boards of directors. A woman's employer should never use "honey" in addressing her. Older businessmen should drop their habit, if they have it, of referring to women as "the girls" or "the gals." Female office workers in both junior and senior positions want to be referred to as "women," and they certainly would never call their male associates "the boys."

The Use of "Ms."

Some women do not wish to be addressed as "Ms." and should inform friends and associates of that fact. A working woman will find, however, that it is easier to follow her firm's stated policy on addressing other women as "Ms." in correspondence. I personally favor using Ms. before a woman's first and last names (Ms. Anne Hutchins) for a very logical reason: the usage is a great timesaver. One does not have to research whether the woman one is addressing is married or not. Mr. has no reference to marital status.

Neither does Ms., which is why feminists have embraced it so wholeheartedly. The use of Ms. in addressing women in professional and business situations (except for women with titles such as Dr.) has made life easier.

In conversation, however, it is difficult to say "Ms." when making introductions; one sounds like a buzzing bee. In conversation, therefore, I prefer to use "Miss" unless I happen to know the woman is Mrs. and goes by that title. (See Chapter 58, "The Importance of Introductions.")

One must never use Ms., of course, before a woman's married name, e.g., Ms. Herbert Smith. One has to say Ms. Jane Smith, and if you know her only as Mrs. Herbert Smith, then she must be written to in that manner.

The inevitable outcome of dissent over whether to use Ms. or Miss or Mrs. is that some businesses are beginning to drop any title whatsoever and to write to women as, say, Jane Smith and to address them as "Dear Jane Smith." (The same holds true for men; many companies now address letters to John Herbert and use as a salutation "Dear John Herbert.")

I feel that such a procedure is wrong. Correspondence really should have a Mr., Mrs., or Ms. in front of names. However, the use of "Dear Jane Smith" or "Dear John Herbert" (as a salutation only) *is* permissible in the following circumstances: if you have met someone but do not feel you know the person well enough to say "Jane" or "John." Yet you do not wish to be so formal as to write "Dear Ms. Smith" or "Mr. Herbert." In this case you may address the person by given and last name, which is a way of indicating you know him or her but do not yet feel familiar enough to use a first name alone.

A Woman Picks Up the Tab

One of the things women who are reaching for the executive suite are going to have to accept is the financial responsibilities of their new status. They must learn how to do things gracefully that heretofore they may have regarded as a man's duty—such as paying the bill for meals, taxis, or rented limousines. When a woman lunches or dines with a man on business, they are not on a date. If he begins to act as though they were, she should quickly discourage such attempts. (It is up to her to set the mood of business for such meals.) It is perfectly proper for a man to pick up the check for the first business lunch they have together, but she should pick it up the second time, and they should continue alternating, as men properly do. Sometimes these lunch meetings occur twice a year only, so one should keep a record of who took whom to lunch the last time.

Some jobs necessitate the transaction of regular business over the lunch table. It makes the situation easier for a woman if that lunch table is situated in her company's executive dining room or at a club, where, as a member, she can sign the bill without a fuss. She should *not*, however, invite her male colleague to a women's club for a business lunch if that club is used almost exclusively by women at lunchtime. A woman does not mind being overpowered by the number of men in *his* club (in fact, she usually quite enjoys it), but a man minds being overpowered by the number of women in *her* club.

No one likes a man who is known never to pick up a check. In today's world, people are going to feel the same about a woman who is known never to pick up a tab. The woman executive is going to learn how to pay gracefully when it's her turn.

In order to save embarrassment all around, who will pay for the next business lunch should be decided without question in advance. If it's a woman's turn, she should make it very clear over the telephone or face to face when the appointment is made that she will be paying. She has only to say with a smile that it really *is* her turn. She should name the time and the place, call the restaurant, and make the reservation in her name.

At the end of lunch she should unobtrusively ask for the bill, add the waiter's tip to the total without an agonizing exercise in mathematics, and then use her credit card or sign her name and her company's address on the back of the check (if she has a charge account there). If she does this quietly, no one around them need be aware of her actions.

If the man she has invited to lunch is really uncomfortable about her paying (and a woman should sense this immediately when she is making arrangements with him beforehand), then it is better to settle the bill with the head waiter away from the table. She should excuse herself at dessert time on the pretext of going to the powder room and make the bill arrangements then.

If a head waiter has performed a lot of service at the table, a woman who is paying the bill at an expensive restaurant should tip him just as a man would (from one to three dollars, according to the restaurant and the service). She can include his tip along with the waiter's by writing it on the bill, if she wishes. (The subject of tipping is studied in another part of this book, page 685). The woman who is hosting the meal should also tip the hat check person for the coats of her guests, although any guest leaving separately should pay for his or her coat upon leaving.

A dilemma confronting men who are the guests of women at business meals is one that has worried women since men began taking them out to restaurants. Many women were taught by their families when they were young (and especially by older brothers) that a girl on a date must always order the least expensive thing on the menu, if she was to be invited out again. I think we should all be careful in our business lives, too, to watch the right-hand column where the prices are. A man who is a guest of a woman should follow his hostess' lead in respect to suggestions she makes from the menu. Particularly if you are the guest of a self-employed person, you should order carefully, because paying for the meal will affect that person financially much more than it would a large corporation. However, corporate expense account or not, it is always better to order moderate-priced items when you are another's guest, keeping a firm check on overly expensive preferences.

Lighting and Offering Cigarettes

Traditionally, if a man was seated or standing near a woman who took a cigarette from her bag or who reached for a cigarette from a nearby box, he was supposed to take a match or lighter and lean over to light her cigarette. Such an act is still a courteous one, but it is no longer considered ungentlemanly, particularly in a business situation, *not* to light her cigarette. A woman should equip herself with all the smoking materials she needs and light her own cigarettes quickly, so that there are no awkward pauses in the discussion at hand before they are lit.

Business Travel

Men and Women Traveling on Business When both sexes travel on business together, there are certain conventions of behavior that should be respected, if not for the individuals' reputations, then in consideration of the company they represent. Business colleagues of the opposite sex should not share a suite. They should have separate rooms, and when working in one of the bedrooms, both should be dressed. If a secretary who is accompanying her boss on a trip finds he is still in his pajamas when she arrives in his room to begin work, there is a quick solution to her dilemma. She should excuse herself and state she will return as soon as he is dressed.

An employer should assume all of his secretary's expenses on the road, even though she may actually be handling the finances when they are traveling together. A woman executive should pay her own expenses on a trip and put in for reimbursement from her office afterward; she can also travel on advance money. If a woman and her male colleague are dining in their motel, she should ask the waiter to put her drink and dinner on her bill. If they order a bottle of wine to share, the cost of the bottle should not be split but should be put on either bill. A woman executive should handle her own tipping, baggage handling, and airport limousine fee. Taxi fares should be paid for by either person, but should be split between the man and woman on the filing of the expense reports, and the woman should reimburse the man if he paid for all the taxis.

As for "what other people think" about a man and woman traveling together on business, if ordinary discretion is used, there is no need for concern. Most people realize by now that if two people want an illicit relationship, they do not have to travel to accomplish it!

A Woman Traveling on Business Alone Traveling alone is just as lonely for a woman as it is for a man, only more so, because a woman is more limited in what she can do by herself in the evening.

If you are "on the road," your briefcase can be your security blanket. If you go into the bar of your hotel or motel for a cocktail, or if you go into the restaurant for dinner, take along your briefcase or some file folders as a conspicuous sign of your business profession. Dress in business or travel attire rather than changing into anything that could be construed as a party dress. The people around you will know by the way you are dressed, by what you are carrying, and by your manner that you are obviously passing through town on business.

I have found people very friendly all over the country (except in large cities) when I am traveling alone. When someone starts to talk to me, I always smile pleasantly and answer, but if I am not in the mood for talking and have work to do, I simply go back to my papers.

If you are traveling and someone presentable begins to speak to you in a nice way and asks if he may join you (and you would like to talk to someone), say, "Yes, please join me." Make it clear you will put your own drink on your own bill, however. If he insists on paying for that cocktail and you decide to have one more with him, say firmly, but again with a smile, "I would like another one, but this time both drinks go on *my* bill." He will understand you are not letting him pick you up. It is better to stop with one drink when meeting a casual acquaintance like this, but you should most certainly stop after the second if you care anything about how people perceive your behavior in public.

If you decide to eat dinner together, once again you can avoid the possibility of complications later in the evening by stating before dinner that you will pay for your own meal, and by insisting that you are tired and have a lot of work to do—hence it will have to be "an early evening." If you continue drinking with him after dinner, and particularly if you leave the premises and go to other bars or to discos, you are asking for trouble, and not only in regard to your reputation, either.

In time we will all grow more accustomed to seeing women traveling on business. There are friendly and unfriendly women, just like men. Some people cherish their solitude when traveling on business, and others really enjoy the stimulation of meeting a new person and passing a couple of hours with him or her. There is nothing immoral or dangerous about this, and it is part of our changing mores. No longer is it true that a man automatically concludes that a woman traveling alone is a potential sexual conquest.

In addition, most of the men on the road are just as tired at the end of the working day as the women are: both are usually relieved to know that nothing more is expected of them than relaxed conversation during the cocktail or dinner hour.

Dress in the Office

Fashion fluctuates with such velocity that it is impossible for a book to be specific about what to wear in the business environment. One can, however, discuss appropriateness of dress and grooming. These are unchanging factors, not tied to the fickleness of fashion.

An executive in an undertaking establishment goes to his job in a somber dark suit, with black shoes and socks and a conservative tie. A fashion photographer goes to his job in faded jeans, a work shirt, and sneakers. The outfits are appropriate in their own situation, but they are not interchangeable.

A recent college graduate beginning a career in a conservative business establishment and owning a wardrobe of jeans, work shirts, and T shirts will have to invest in some new clothes. The best way to choose such purchases is first to take a good hard look at "what everyone else is wearing" in that office. In certain kinds of businesses the men wear only suits of a conservative nature with white shirts and dark ties; in others, men wear blazers and quiet-patterned sports jackets. In some staid institutions women know instinctively to wear skirts (there are no rules posted saying they should not wear pants). In other types of jobs women wear pants—well-cut, well-fitting ones—freely, and in certain other jobs that demand physical activity pants are almost a necessity.

In conservative business such as banks and financial institutions, insurance companies, foundations, and corporate headquarters, men and women should have one fashion dictate and one only: to dress in good taste. Good taste does not require a major investment in designer originals; good taste means dressing in an understated rather than overstated manner and without flamboyance and faddishness. A man who likes to wear his sports shirt open with a chain and pendant around his neck keeps this look for his weekend time; to the office he wears a pinstripe suit. A woman who chooses a sundress in summer with bare legs and open-toe high-heeled sandals keeps this look for her personal time; to the office she wears a fresh cotton dress that is elegant and modest; she also wears pantyhose and sandals with practical heels. Men and women who have their eyes on their careers dress carefully; they have edited wardrobes that are chosen wisely and well. How they dress on their own time is their own business. How they dress on company time is not, if they project an image that is contrary to the one desired by their company.

The importance of grooming cannot be overemphasized. Without it, there is no successful fashion. It would be helpful if everyone were to go over their grooming check list in front of a full-length mirror before leaving home each morning.

One of the problems career people have is dressing for the office in the morning when there will be an evening engagement immediately following, and no time to return home to change. The easiest solution is to keep a full set of toiletries and make-up stored somewhere at the office. A woman going to an evening party should dress in the morning in one of her "basic dresses" —the kind that can change into a different look with an added scarf or jewelry. In fifteen minutes, when her office day has ended, she can metamorphose herself into another person with freshly cleaned teeth, combed hair, a new face, a different and dressier pair of shoes, and some sparkly jewelry. If she must wear a long dress for the party, she should bring it into the office in a protective bag and store it safely until she has to put it on.

In addition to a razor and toothbrush, men should keep a change of shirt in their office so they can go off in the evening looking refreshed. If the occasion is formal they too must store their black tie paraphernalia and their dressy black shoes in their office.

There is no excuse for anyone's arrival at an evening function in office attire, looking disheveled and slightly dirty. A little advance planning, the carting of certain items to the office, and a good attitude toward oneself ("I look great tonight!") is all that is needed to turn around a hard-working executive or clerk a full 180 degrees!

Caring about how one looks is important to anyone's career. It is only logical to look as attractive as one can, for reasons of self-respect as well as for the image of the company.

Special Executive Facilities

The Executive Conference Room Even small companies have conference rooms. Large companies have several, culminating in the most royal of their kind—the board of directors' room. For important meetings and conferences, the secretary or administrative assistant in charge of the room should make sure that the following are present:

1. The agenda of the meeting and any pertinent material.
2. An adequately large notepad at each place.
3. A container every four places or so full of well-sharpened pencils and pens. (Some people do not like to use pencils.)
4. A jug of ice water on a tray with several clean glasses at each end of the table.
5. A set of quiet (non-distracting, non-gaudy) ash trays on the table (one for every two places).
6. A book of matches beside every ash tray (specially printed with the company logo, if possible).

The conference room should be well ventilated, with efficient air conditioning. The brain needs it as well as the room. Inside conference rooms with no ventilation become stagnant pools of heavy cigarette smoke, unbearably penalizing to anyone who is in the slightest way bothered by smoke. Anyone encased in such a "tomb" for a long time has the right to ask that the doors into the room be opened. One may also request a cigar or pipe smoker to cease. Ask them very graciously. (If it is the chairman of the board or the president smoking that pipe or cigar, forget it.)

It is important that a staff member enter the conference room to empty and wash ash trays every two hours or so during a long meeting, and that the water pitcher be attended to at this time, also.

A conference room should be equipped for an early morning meeting with a coffee urn on a side table, complete with napkins, insulated cups (paper ones are fine), sugar, carton of milk, and stirrers or spoons. Many companies serve "continental" breakfasts at important early morning conferences (coffee, danish, and orange juice). If it is not a breakfast meeting, the company would do well to dispense with the too frequently served sweet rolls. They do nothing but add to one's girth and create very sticky fingers.

The Executive Dining Room   Many companies have one or several executive dining rooms, in which they have inevitably invested a great deal of money on the interior design, the furnishings, and the table accouterments. Many have the company's logo design on the china, the crystal, even on the flatware and embroidered linens.

It is considered an honor to be asked to lunch in one of these executive dining rooms. Many executives like to entertain their clients and associates this way, so that there is no confusion over who pays the bill in a restaurant. According to company policy, usually laid down by the present chairman of the board, cocktails may be served before lunch, or there may be no alcohol whatsoever, or perhaps wine during the meal. If cocktails are served beforehand, it is considered unwise for a guest (or an employee) to ask for a second one. With the increased awareness of the problems of executive alcoholism, any excess of liquor at noon is open to criticism.

When there will be a large group of guests in the executive dining room, it is more efficient and easier to have the same meal ordered ahead for everyone. Such a lunch party should be treated as it is at home, with flowers or plants for a centerpiece, nice linens and table accessories, and place cards. It is permissible, indeed most helpful, if the group consists of people who do not know each other, to depart from the formal custom of putting only the last name on the place card. That is, one should write "Bill Holman" instead of "Mr. Holman," thus allowing guests the opportunity to learn the full names of the luncheon companions in their vicinity. (Many is the time I have wished my lunch or dinner companion's first name was written on his place card, for I am one of the many who never gets a name at the first introduction and thus suffer from a lack of name retention.)

The executive dining room is an area where the company should put its best foot forward with gracious hospitality. The menu need not contain caviar (in fact, it would probably be a bad idea if it did), but the operation should be well run and attractive, and serve good food. I remember asking an executive secretary who had been with her employer for thirty years and who was going through a series of retirement ceremonies in her honor what had been the most memorable part of her day. "Finally making it as a lunch guest to the executive dining room," she said, laughing, "and without having to bring my pad and pencil either!"

Chapter 37

BUSINESS ENTERTAINING

Invitations

Since business entertaining is an integral part of corporate life, it is important to follow certain basic forms in extending invitations. When you look at the layout and text of an invitation your company plans to issue, be sure it deals clearly with the following points:

1. *Exactly who is giving the party?*
The names of the executive or executives hosting the affair (their titles should be included if they are not well known to all the guests being invited) should be at the top of the invitation. Sometimes only a certain division of the company is host; sometimes the company itself is the host ("The Green Motor Company requests the pleasure of . . ."). I think an invitation is always more compelling if it has a human being doing the inviting, not just a company.

2. *What is the nature of the party?*
The invitation should state whether it will be a reception, a cocktail buffet, a breakfast, lunch, dinner, supper, a "lecture followed by cocktails," a "preview of the new models followed by dinner," or whatever. One should always be specific about what the guests will be offered. If you plan on serving them dinner, say so. Give them a time schedule:

Cocktails from 5:30 to 7:00 P.M.
Dinner promptly at 7:00 P.M.

If you are serving dinner and don't specify it, you might find your entire cocktail party evaporating at the dinner hour, since your guests would have made other plans.

3. *Is the party in honor of something?*
If your party is in honor of a person or in celebration of something, say so on your invitation:

In honor of the retirement of John Greene

To celebrate the fortieth anniversary of Mary Williams' service to this company

To a private preview of the *X* Company's sponsored exhibition of sculpture

To announce the Third Annual Golden Plum Awards

4. *When and at what time is the party?*

It is best to spell out the day of the week as well as the date on your invitations. When giving the hour, it is preferable to say "A.M." and "P.M." rather than just "o'clock." I remember once a colleague who gave a large party on behalf of her corporation and stated on the invitations "ten o'clock" as the hour. It was supposed to be a late evening reception after an affair all of the important people in her town would be attending. Half of her guest list arrived that day at ten in the morning, thinking it was a post-breakfast event.

5. *Where will the party be held?*

It is important to be specific about the place. If it will be in the executive dining room, give the corporate headquarters address and the floor of the building, too. If the party will be held in a hotel, give the name of the hotel, the address, and the name of the room. If it's going to be held in a country club, out of the city and unknown to some of the guests, include a map with your invitation.

6. *How does one dress?*

For an evening party, one always wonders what the prescribed dress will be. If the invitation does not say "Black Tie," it means "come in a business suit" for the men and an appropriate dress or suit for a woman. If you want your guests to dress in a formal manner, put "Black Tie" at the lower right of the invitation, to signal that the men should wear dinner suits and the women long dresses (or the fashion equivalent of the day).

7. *Spouses or dates*

This is one sticky issue in business invitations not found in social ones, and it should be clearly spelled out on the invitation, or with a printed insert in the invitation. One can say on a business dinner invitation: "We regret that, because of limited space, the dinner is for the recipient of the invitation only, and not for spouses and guests."

Most cocktail party invitations are considered an invitation for two by most recipients, and the hosts should take this into account when making a projected head count. If you prefer, you can say, "Each guest is welcome to bring a guest," which is another way of saying, "Bring your husband, wife, or friend."

8. *On the subject of R.S.V.P.s*

The R.S.V.P. belongs at the lower left of the invitation. List directly below it the name of the person in the office who will be handling acceptances and regrets. His or her company title, address, and telephone number should be listed on two or three lines below the name. Even if there is an enclosed R.S.V.P. card with a self-addressed, stamped envelope to make things easier for the recipient of the invitation, one should still include the R.S.V.P. information on the invitation, simply because enclosures have a habit of becoming lost.

Most people do not bother to respond to a cocktail party invitation. As a result, many business hosts today do not put R.S.V.P. on their cocktail invitations. They know from experience that a certain percentage of their guest list will show up, and they notify the caterers to prepare for that number. The percentage of "shows" versus "no-shows" varies according to the city. The larger the city, the smaller the number of "shows." The average number of "no-shows" is one third, but in New York, a 50 per cent appearance ratio is good, because many people who say they are coming do not come, and if it is raining, another 20 per cent do not come.

When an invitation says R.S.V.P. one should answer. There is no excuse for the bad manners of people in business in not replying to invitations. If the executive does not have good manners, then his or her secretary ought to handle the response quickly and efficiently.

How to Extend an Invitation

Invitations in the business world may be extended by any one of five methods:

1. *By a formal engraved invitation* on a traditional ecru or white heavy stock (or on any colored fine stock, for that matter) with a contrasting color used for the engraved text. Businesses may take license with their engraved invitations that brides and grooms should not in their wedding invitations. A corporation could send a gray invitation with a bright red border and bright red engraved lettering; or it could use a mint green stock with navy blue engraving; or fuchsia with brown—in fact, any combination desired if it wants to present a more creative image. If the company wishes to remain low-key and to reinforce its conservative image, it should use the ecru or white stock with black, navy, dark gray, or dark brown engraving. A company's embossed logo is always an attractive addition to the layout of an engraved invitation. The envelope for the invitation should have the company's address engraved or printed on the front upper-left corner of the envelope (so that the company's records may be corrected when incorrectly addressed invitations are returned).

The inclusion in either an engraved or a printed invitation of an R.S.V.P. card with a self-addressed, stamped envelope is an excellent idea. This means that a person may respond without any inconvenience. All he has to do is write his name, check the box that says either "Accepts" or "Regrets,"

LG

Fiftieth Anniversary
The Literary Guild
1927-1977

A corporation holding a social business event can effectively increase public recognition of its logo by using it attractively in its invitation graphics. The Literary Guild's LG logo, for example, is shown here on the outside of the ivory-colored dinner invitation, embossed in gold and with gold lettering; the text inside is engraved in black.

The Literary Guild
requests the pleasure of your company
at a dinner
commemorating its
Fiftieth Anniversary
on Wednesday, October twenty-sixth
at eight o'clock
Grand Ballroom
The Waldorf-Astoria
New York City

R.S.V.P.
Ms. Barbara Ann Bowden   *Cocktails at 6:30*
(212) 953-4747   *Black Tie*
Please present this invitation at the door

The logo appears again on the outside cover of what is a combination menu and program. The outside cover, in ivory chrome-coated stock, has centered on it a shiny gold embossed seal of the logo; an ivory silk cord and tassel at the fold make a decorative addition.

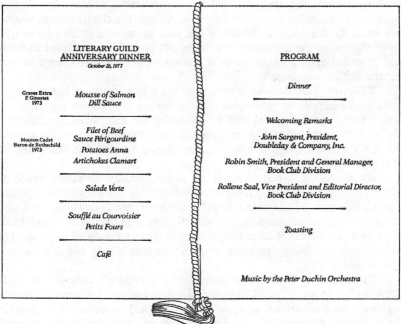

LITERARY GUILD
ANNIVERSARY DINNER
October 26, 1977

Graves Extra F. Ginestet 1973	*Mousse of Salmon Dill Sauce*
Mouton Cadet Baron de Rothschild 1973	*Filet of Beef Sauce Périgourdine Potatoes Anna Artichokes Clamart*
	Salade Verte
	Soufflé au Courvoisier Petits Fours
	Café

PROGRAM

Dinner

Welcoming Remarks

John Sargent, President, Doubleday & Company, Inc.

Robin Smith, President and General Manager, Book Club Division

Rollene Saal, Vice President and Editorial Director, Book Club Division

Toasting

Music by the Peter Duchin Orchestra

Inside, the menu and program are printed in black on a heavy cream-colored parchment.

and mail it off. These R.S.V.P. cards and self-addressed envelopes should be printed, not engraved (for to engrave them would be a waste of money).

There is no doubt about it: an engraved invitation is a signal of something very special. It means something out of the ordinary in the business main-stream, and engraved invitations should be used in business only when the event truly merits it.

2. *By a printed invitation* or through a process that results in an "engraved look." This is a much less expensive process than engraving. Printed invitations are appropriate in the business world for just about anything, short of an invitation to a ship launching or the hundredth anniversary of an august organization. In today's world, if a firm is on a tight budget, invitations printed on postcards are also permissible. A popular method, although I like it the least, no matter how clever the layout, is the double-postcard invitation. One postcard is used to invite the guest; the other half is torn off for the guest's response and is mailed back to the company hosting the party.

Printed invitations allow room for creative experimentation and amusing combinations and ideas. Through our office regularly pass invitations printed on velvet or on wallpaper, painted on gunny sacking, reproduced on Chinese parchment, or on news print, imitating a newspaper. One of the most ingenious and time-consuming invitations I ever received was from the president of a small company who sent out invitations to a dinner for fifty. An inveterate needlecraft exponent, she did her invitations in needlepoint! A company must remember its image, its products, and the clients or customers it has when sending out invitations. With that in mind, anything goes—provided the text of the invitation tells the guests everything they need to know, and provided good grammar is used. (Humor does not give license to murder the English language.)

3. *By letter.* This method is advantageous when an event is too complicated to describe in an invitation. A letter allows the host to explain in detail. A letter of invitation should be signed by the chief executive officer of the firm, or some other high-ranking official. His secretary would serve as the R.S.V.P. source, and this information should be placed in the lower left of the letter.

4. *By Mailgram.* When speed is of an essence, an invitation issued by Mailgram is very efficient. One gives Western Union a list of the recipients and a single copy of the message, and each Mailgram is delivered by a mail carrier to the recipient one day later. Although a Mailgram is not as handsome as a good-looking invitation, it carries with it a note of urgency. This technique is also fairly expensive to use if the text is long and if it must be sent to a long list.

5. *By telephone.* Telephoned invitations are perfectly appropriate, if the guest list is not too large. (Otherwise, the time element involved in contacting everyone is a serious deterrent.) A telephoned invitation is appropriate for a spur-of-the-moment business social event, and also to invite people who have been left off the invitation list by accident.

If there is time, it is always wise for the host to follow up an acceptance of a telephoned invitation with a reminder card, or with an informal letter that states "we are so glad you are coming," and that reiterates the information of time, place, and purpose of the gathering.

When There Is No R.S.V.P. Card Enclosed

It is proper to reply by telephone when there is no card provided. These telephoned responses are usually handled between the secretary of the invited guest and the secretary of the host. It is important for the executive's good public relations when he must regret an invitation that his secretary give a good reason for his refusal. She should explain carefully why he cannot attend, and she should add with sincerity, "He really is *most* sorry not to be able to come." The other secretary will report back to her employer the sincere regret and the nice message sent by the executive, and everyone feels happy.

Written acceptances or regrets are also appropriate (provided they are not last-minute). A secretary may type her employer's response on his office stationery in an abbreviated semiformal manner or in an informal letter style. An example of the former:

March 20, 19—

Mr. Thomas O'Neill
accepts with pleasure
the kind invitation of Ms. Anita Rubin
for lunch on Tuesday, April seventeenth.

An example of the letter, which gives one an opportunity to explain the circumstances:

March 20, 19—

Ms. Anita Rubin
President, Chemform Corporation
1314 Raleigh Street
Chicago, Illinois   zip code

Dear Ms. Rubin:

I am taking the liberty of regretting your kind invitation to Mr. O'Neill for lunch on April 17. Unfortunately, Mr. O'Neill will not be back from the Far East until April 19. I know how much he will appreciate having been invited, and how sorry he will be to have missed the presentation of your new products. I know he would enjoy seeing any follow-up material you will make available to your guests that day.

Sincerely,

[signed] Sarah Prendergast
Secretary to the Chairman of the Board

Thank-yous for a Business Social Event

One does not need to send a thank-you note for a business cocktail party, but it's nice to do so. One may even call the host's secretary and leave a simple message with her: "Please tell Mr. Reed that he gave a delightful party last night. I enjoyed myself very much." Very few people bother to thank the host after the cocktail party. It means a lot if someone does.

If one is invited to a lunch party, a dinner, a golf outing, a sports event, a theatrical performance—all in the line of business—one should send a short note afterward saying thank you. This may be handwritten or typed on office stationery. Brevity is permissible; it's the fact that *one does it* that matters.

Business Hosts and the Receiving Line

A receiving line is not only for debutantes and brides, and at formal affairs that are part of our personal lives. At many business functions a receiving line is called for. A receiving line can consist of one or two people, and those are the best, because they do not cause traffic jams at large parties. There is nothing colder than a party where guests have no idea of who is giving it. Since most business parties mix people who do not know each other, including the hosts, it is important at such an event for the host or hosts to stand by the door and to greet every single guest who arrives. The host should repeat the guest's name, and shake his hand, and wave him off in the direction of the bar or of associates who will help introduce him to other guests. Every person who comes to the party should feel he is wanted and that someone knows he has been there.

Badges

For many people, without a doubt the most unattractive aspect of a business gathering is having to wear a badge. On the other hand, badges are incredibly useful. (The kind that say "Hi!" and have smiling faces printed on them should not be inflicted on us.) It is worth feeling disdain for the ugly plastic thing that gets pinned on, inevitably at an awkward angle, in order to reap the benefit of wearing it: knowing the names of the people to whom one is talking. Badges are a wonderful assistance in the introduction of large groups of people. They help us remember to contact that person again; they help us find him or her, and to remember an important business conversation we shared. Badges are an affirmative tool in business—and in women's groups for large meetings.

They should be worn on the upper right shoulder, not on the left, where they are usually worn. People see someone's name more easily if one has the badge high on the right shoulder, close to the chin. In this way a person can check your name while he is talking to you, by dropping his eyes down so slightly you won't even be aware of it, whereas if you have your badge on the left shoulder, you will be aware of a strong movement of his eyes to his right.

In making up a badge, one should omit putting Mr., Ms., Miss, or Mrs. in front of names. Married women should go by their own names, and not their husbands'. In other words, the badge should read: ANNE WILLIAMS and not MRS. JOHN WILLIAMS, JR. If the gathering consists of a diverse group of people, it helps to put the company name under the individual's name; if the group is part of one national organization, then the individual's city or state should be placed beneath his name. This provides a conversation starting point. If a person has an important title, such as Congressman, Judge, Doctor, or Reverend, this should be placed on his badge; if he is a high-ranking officer of the organization, his title should be placed beneath his name. This helps people introduce others properly.

Like them or not, for large meetings, conventions, and gatherings where business is the purpose, badges help make all our lives easier.

Invitations from Business Associates

When a husband or wife, or both, work, there will probably be invitations forthcoming to the couple from their business associates. The best thing for each person receiving such an invitation, be it to dinner, Sunday lunch or a cocktail party, is to say, "That's very nice of you, but I'll have to check with my wife (or husband) tonight at home. I'll make sure our schedules are clear."

Since the spouses of the people who work together may not have had the chance to meet each other before the dinner, it is a gracious gesture on the part of the couple coming to dinner to bring a small present with them—a simple bouquet of flowers or a bottle of wine, a good book or a box of after-dinner mints. This act is merely a symbolic way of saying, "You know only one of us, but thank you for having both of us to dinner."

A spouse may not want to go to her husband's or his wife's associates' home for dinner. This presents a problem that is best worked out on a compromise basis between husband and wife. ("Okay, I'll go to their house this time, but then you have to go to that play with me next week!")

If both people work, and if the evening is something one of them "has to go through with" because of business relationships in the office, the spouse should be understanding and sympathetic, and bear with it. But no spouse should have to go to these dinners constantly; he or she should be able to say, "They're not *our* friends; they're your office friends." Then the person who keeps accepting these office invitations has the choice either of regretting them or of going without his or her spouse.

I never would have said that ten years ago. It would have been heresy for a man to go out without his wife or a wife without her husband to a work-related function. But now all our lives are so pressured, and family needs are so difficult to meet, that one person can and should go out without the other, if it's a business evening. I discussed this with a marriage counselor friend of mine. "Could such a system cause one partner in the marriage to begin 'cutting out' on the other?" "No," he replied, "if one of the partners wants to be unfaithful to the other, one doesn't need an office event to provide the opportunity. It will happen anyway."

Therefore, if one parent should be supervising the children's homework or attending a function at a child's school, it is better for the person concerned with the business event to attend it alone. No office socializing is more important than balancing the discharge of responsibilities, and one of the good things about our new world is the real sharing of those responsibilities that is going on today in many families.

When a husband or wife says to the other marriage partner, "This dinner means a lot to me and to my career," then there should be no question. Husband and wife go as a couple. That is what marriage is all about.

Chapter 38

TELEPHONE MANNERS

An efficient use of the telephone is woven into the fabric of good office manners. There are certain basics all should heed, whether one is chairman of the board of a large corporation or occupies the least important position in the office. Whoever answers the telephone for a business has tremendous power: to help further the company's objectives or to hurt them. When someone calls a company, the voice of the person who answers speaks for the spirit of the firm.

A good telephone voice contains a smile. It is a voice with variety in its expression and tone and one that pronounces words clearly and carefully. Even the choice of one's words is important. Technical jargon and slang are to be avoided. So is overfamiliarity.

We should listen to our voices, for we don't really know how we sound to others on the telephone. If a person possesses either a harsh, abrasive voice or one so soft and whispery that others cannot distinguish the words, it may cause a career stalemate, or even a job loss. Whether someone is selling his company and its products and services or himself, his voice represents him— the good or the bad, magnified many times.

Answering the Telephone

You must instruct your executives, as well as the secretaries, how the telephones are supposed to be answered. A lawyer who hangs out his shingle usually wants a conservative image, so that he will inspire the trust and confidence of the older clients (who in the begining will probably be more numerous!). He may instruct his secretary to answer the telephone, "Good morning, Robert Truman's office." A group of young documentary film makers might have their telephones answered by a cheery voice that says, "This is the Sunshine Group. Have a *great* day!"

Who Do You Say Is Calling? In former days, when calling a place of business, one was supposed to say, "This is Mr. Jack Smith calling." Now one hears in answer to "Who's calling, please?" "This is Jack Smith," or simply "Jane Teedman." It's abbreviated, but acceptable if one is pressured.

Putting People on Hold   If you are in the middle of a conversation and you are responsible for answering another call (even more than one) that lights up on your instrument (and this happens to executives as well as clerks), you should say in an apologetic tone, "Forgive me, I'll put you on hold one minute," and then answer the other call. Finish with the business of the second call immediately. If it cannot be done immediately, say you will call back and take the name and number of the person calling. It is your responsibility to finish with the business of the first caller. Do not forget him. There is nothing lonelier than being put on hold seemingly forever; people have been known to change their minds about making a sale of some kind simply because they were left neglected on hold too long. A cheery voice that returns to them every so often, saying, "Please forgive me; I promise I'll be back in one second," makes the annoyance, the interruption, and the delay much less irritating.

Transferring a Call   Another annoyance we all face is being transferred to someone else, having to start our story from the beginning, and losing time once again. Handle every call you receive, if you can. If you have to transfer the call, you should explain first why you have to do it, then be sure you make the transfer to the right number, without cutting the call off.

If someone starts a long-winded conversation you know you cannot handle, interrupt, but say apologetically, "Please excuse me, but I must transfer you to someone else who will know exactly how to handle this. Please hold on, and if the operator somehow cuts us off, please call back and ask for Mr. Culp on extension 307."

When Does the Executive Come on the Line?   The person who initiates a call should be waiting on the line when his secretary or assistant finally gets through to the person called. When an important executive is called by an unimportant one, and when the first voice he hears is that of the secretary of the man calling him, he is immediately put off. The most flattering way for an executive to handle telephone calls between peers is to make those calls himself, or to be ready and waiting on the line when his secretary makes them. It is the best kind of public relations.

When You Are Not There   One of the most important parts of telephone manners is the handling of a caller when the employer is not in the office. A secretary should be instructed to answer calls without saying where her employer is. The secretary should say, "Mr. Smith is out of the building on a business appointment" or something similar. It is better for Mr. Smith's clients not to know if he has taken the afternoon off for the opening game of the baseball season, or that he is having a doctor's appointment, or that Ms. Jenkins is having her hair done. In other words, it is the secretary's duty to protect her employer from any possible criticism or misinterpretation of his or her whereabouts.

If an employer wishes to remain at his desk working on something without taking any calls, the secretary should answer his telephone as follows: "No, Mr. Smith is not here. Who is calling, please?" If she were to ask who was calling and then announce that her employer was not in the office, it might leave the caller with the impression that Mr. Smith was talking to certain people but not to him.

Messages

How to Take a Message   There is a give-and-take responsibility on the part of both the giver and the taker of telephone messages. The giver's responsibility is to volunteer all the necessary information himself, without wasting the taker's time. The giver must enunciate his words, so that he is clearly understood. (Mumbling results in serious misinformation both in business and social life.) The message leaver should state:

His name (first *and* last)
His company (if pertinent)
His telephone number (area code if in another city, and extension, if he has one)
His message, briefly stated and to the point

If it is a personal matter the caller should so state.

The message taker (even if it's a busy executive who happens to wander by a sea of empty desks at lunchtime) has the responsibility for taking a full message. He should write it down on a proper piece of paper, not the edge of an envelope or the back of another piece of paper. The person taking down the message should add the time the message was received and his own initials.

I am reminded of an example of why the message taker should always identify himself. An executive on his way to the dining room in another building picked up a ringing telephone as he passed through the secretarial pool. He scrawled the following message and left it on the typewriter where it would be instantly seen:

Your son's morning nursery school called. He became ill right before closing time and they took him to the hospital's emergency ward. The baby-sitter is with him, and a teacher, too. Don't worry. Everything's going to be all right. Go right to the hospital.

There was just one thing wrong. The executive, who was obviously concerned about the message he had just taken, neglected to state which hospital it was, nor did he leave his initials or name on the message. The poor woman returned from lunch and spent a frantic time trying to find out in which hospital her son was waiting.

Always Leave a Message with the Secretary if You Can   Don't be afraid to discuss your business with an associate of the person you are calling. She is under orders to ask why you want to speak to her boss if she does not know you. A secretary or an assistant could turn out to be your best friend. If you get that person on your side with good manners and co-operation, then your calls will go through. An executive's staff assistant respects someone else's professionalism. The caller who refuses to discuss why he is calling, who masks his mission in mystery, gets nowhere. If your reason for calling is complicated, say so, but rough it out for the other person, nonetheless. If the secretary or assistant understands your reasons for speaking to her boss, she will present your request in an affirmative light. And, in returning your call, the boss will already have an idea of what the conversation will be about and will have the necessary information or materials at hand, thus saving time for everyone.

If You Can't Leave a Message with an Associate   If you feel you cannot leave a message for an executive with his secretary, tell the secretary as much as you can and explain why you cannot tell her more. "I have a personnel matter to discuss with him that is confidential and also extremely urgent." A good secretary will not press further and may even leave a message for her boss in the locker room of the country club, asking him to call his office, if she feels the situation warrants it. The gravity of the reason for the call must be communicated to the secretary by the caller. One must never play games with the secretary and overemphasize the importance of the call, for, if you do, you are hurting your cause with her and her employer.

The Secretary Who Will Not Take a Message   Equally annoying to a person calling on legitimate business is the secretary who refuses to take any message that is more complicated than a name and a telephone number. People working in hectic jobs do not, in many cases, have the time to call back when the person they are calling is not in his office. A secretary should always offer to take a message or help the caller in any way she can.

Executives Answering Their Own Telephones

When an executive answers his own telephone, either because he chooses to or because his secretary is out to lunch and he has to, he should "mind his manners" in the way with which he greets his caller. "Smith" is too abrupt a way to answer. "Smith here" is, too. One should be informative. "John Smith speaking" is informative and yet short.

Dispensing with a Pest   If you answer your own telephone by choice (and many executives do) you will inevitably receive a fair share each day of unnecessary calls or just plain pest calls——people wanting a job and refusing to go through the regular channels, people complaining because they know you are there to listen, or people calling you out of a lack of knowledge of who can solve their particular problem. The second an executive knows he is in the midst of such a call, he should suddenly interrupt his caller, and say in a very apologetic tone of voice: "My staff informs me an emergency call is waiting for me on the other line. Please forgive me, and put in writing the rest of your thoughts." (Or, "Call Sam Jones at this same central number—he will be able to take your call.") Sound breathless and apologetic. Don't give your caller a chance to say anything. Just cut him off with a final "Thank you for calling" and hang up.

Interrupted by the Telephone During an Appointment If you have someone in your office who made an appointment with you in advance and the person who normally answers the telephone for you is absent, you should pick it up each time and take the message quickly. Answer politely, but with a sense of urgency in your voice, "This is Mary Warden speaking. I am in an important meeting. May I call you back within the hour?"

The caller should give Mary Warden his name and telephone number without hesitation, and conversation should terminate right then and there. It would be rude of Mary Warden to continue to transact business on the phone when she had already set aside that time for her visitor.

If, however, staff members come into an executive's office without a prior appointment, that executive has the right to take any important incoming telephone calls and to interrupt the discussion. If certain matters to be discussed on the telephone should be handled confidentially, the executive should ask any staff member present to step out of the room for one minute.

Telephone Conversations

One Should React While Listening One of the more annoying telephone habits is to fail to react in any way to the person to whom you are speaking. For example, Mr. Judd is full of good cheer one morning as he calls to congratulate his friend on his television appearance and to discuss future vacation plans. But after talking to his friend's new secretary, who answers in monosyllables if at all, he feels as though he had been talking to a stone wall. It is a letdown, and he wonders why his friend would hire someone like that. (In fact, if his friend finds out that his new secretary is a non-reactor, he will probably find reasons to let her go.)

All a listener who is taking a message has to do is to utter an occasional comment. The secretary should interject an occasional "Fine," "Certainly," or "Yes, indeed" every once in a while. The caller should have the feeling he is talking to a human being.

Giving a Caller One's Undivided Attention When you are in the middle of a telephone conversation, you should not give orders to others in your office or make asides. It is very rude to be carrying on two conversations at once, one on the telephone and one with the people present.

If Disconnected   If you are disconnected during a telephone conversation, it is the responsibility of the caller to call again, even if the line was broken at the other end. If you are disconnected on a long-distance call, the person who made the call should call back the operator to report the interruption, and the operator will give him a credit on his bill and reconnect. If you are making an important business call from a pay telephone and you don't have any more change, tell the person you are calling that you are in a booth and give him your number, so that he will be able to reach you immediately if you are disconnected. This is also a good idea if you think you are going to talk a lengthy time.

Courtesy in Calling the Wrong Number   One of the rudest and most aggravating occurrences in our everyday life is to have someone hang up on us when they call us and find out it's a wrong number. It is a common courtesy if you dial a wrong number to say, "I'm sorry," or "Please forgive me," before hanging up.

Long-distance Telephoning

A person asking a favor should always pay for the long-distance call. What often occurs is this:

Mary Jones in New York calls Jane McGrew in her Los Angeles office to seek her help on getting her daughter into a certain college of which Mrs. McGrew is a trustee. The Californian is not in, so Mrs. Jones asks her secretary to please have her call back as soon as possible. Jane McGrew does call back; she is paying for the call now, and Mary Jones proceeds to outline in detail the reasons why she needs her help. She talks on and on, the clock ticks away, and Jane McGrew realizes Mary Jones has been bending her ear for a favor while she, Jane McGrew, is paying for the call. She naturally becomes resentful.

This is an error frequently committed by some people both in the office and at home. What Mary Jones should have done was either insist that Jane McGrew return her call collect, or place the call person-to-person and have the call returned on a "leave word" through the operator, so that she, Mary Jones, would pay for the call.

Business Calls at Home

No one should place a business call to another person at his home unless it is absolutely necessary. When a man or woman returns home, at night, that time is theirs, and it is poor manners to interrupt these private hours with a business call. Most calls made to someone's home can be just as well made the next day. If it is imperative to call someone at home, make your business short and to the point.

Dealing with an Answering Service

Small businesses, doctors, people who work out of their homes, or teachers who give private lessons are only a few of those who use—and need —an answering service in their home or office. Sometimes an annoying problem or a full-blooded crisis will occur simply because someone can't reach someone else by telephone. An answering service, either during the workday or on a twenty-four-hour basis, is an enormous help in avoiding such crises.

If the answering service slips up in properly relaying a message, the service is usually blamed. But more often it is the fault of the person who is the user of the service in not giving proper instructions, or the fault of the caller who leaves a muddled message.

The person who uses an answering service, to simplify his life, should leave explicit, clear instructions. If there is a complicated series of names, addresses, and telephone numbers involved in his general whereabouts, he should type up all these instructions and send them to his service, so they will have a clear record of how to reach him and what to do.

A person who calls someone with an answering service should be considerate when the operator answers. He should give that operator a lucid message, short and clear. If you are replying to a party invitation, for example, don't just say to Jane Johnson's service, "Tell Jane Johnson that Mary can't come to her party." First, Jane Johnson may be having a series of parties; second, Jane Johnson may have invited three Marys to her parties. You should ask the answering service to "tell Miss Johnson that Tom and Mary Duff cannot come to her dinner on the seventeenth."

Don't expect an answering service to cope with a long, rambling message. An answering service operator has many clients and calls to handle, and although she may be "fascinated" by the reasons why a caller can't make the dinner party, she has time only for a one-sentence message.

People who use an answering service for their livelihood as well as for their social calls are very dependent upon the quality of the people answering. And the quality of the people handling their calls very often depends upon how nice the subscriber is to the people employed by the answering service. An occasional "Thank you for doing such a great job for me" is appreciated very much. At Christmastime it is nice to send over to the people at the answering service a large box of candy, fruit, or something in the food or beverage line that can be divided among the hard-working staff. If they give you good personal attention, then they really care about your success in business or in social matters. If they give you bad service, your action is very easy: change answering services.

The Telephone Answering Machine

Many people are now using answering machines hooked up to their telephones. When you call, the voice of the person you are calling comes back to you in the form of a recorded message, usually sounding something like this: "This is Myrtle Masden speaking. I'm not home now, but if you'll please leave a message when you hear the beep [or signal], and leave me your name and telephone number, I will call you back as soon as I return."

This recorded-voice system infuriates some callers. Like many others, I am now used to such machines but am still put off when the recorded voice is not bright and cheerful. Many people record their messages sounding as though they were about to attend their best friend's funeral. The person with an answering machine should listen to his own message. He should go out and call himself, to hear how he sounds to the outside world. He should re-record it if it does not sound good. I remember hearing an executive comment, "I called his office, got one of those machines, and when he said his name and his company name, he sounded like such a 'down' type of man, I decided not to pursue our business conversations further."

Unnecessary humor is not appropriate if you are using your answering machine for business. You should have a businesslike relationship with your telephone messages recording device. You should sound businesslike, efficient, and cheerful; save the humor for the evenings and the weekends.

A word of caution, particularly to young women in large cities, who use such a machine: a criminal intruder might dial such a number, learn the occupant of that home is out, and then make an unlawful entry. Some women have learned to become crafty and they leave messages like the following: "I am working here with my staff and will not be answering my calls for the present. Leave your name and telephone number, and I will call you back as soon as I am able to."

Recorded Music

The chairman of the board of a major corporation remarked one day that the thing that irritated him the most was to be confronted by recorded music when he was put on hold in someone's office.

"There are only two places in the world where I don't feel like pulling the telephone out from the wall and throwing it away when I hear that music," he said, "and that's when I'm in the dentist's chair or when I'm trying to get through to an airline ticket agent. In the latter case, I can do my crossword puzzles while I wait."

Many businesses are using the recorded music idea when they have to put people on hold, feeling that soft music will perhaps soothe the caller's impatience. If an executive wants to know if such a custom will please or irritate his clients, he should *ask* them.

The most important thing to remember about telephone manners is always to return your calls promptly. Even if what you have to say is negative or unpleasant, make the call and get it over with. Remember, the telephone is the best tool any of us has in the business world.

Chapter 39

GENERAL OFFICE MANNERS

The Secretary

A good secretary is usually a firm's most important and perhaps least appreciated segment of the business. A good secretary bears a tremendous responsibility in the success of any operation with which he or she is associated. (A secretary may, of course, be male or female; the employer also. For the sake of brevity, we will refer to the secretary as "she" and the employer as "he.")

- She handles the telephone in such a way as to make the outside world impressed with her company, with her employer, and with her.
- She manages her employer's schedule and manipulates his time to allow him to best serve the company.
- She screens the telephone calls and visitors so graciously and adeptly that while she is saying no, and protecting her employer from a waste of his time or an annoyance, she is also making the person who wants to talk to him feel all right about the rejection.
- She knows how to redirect calls by finding out why the person is calling; she does this without antagonizing the person. She knows her organization so well that she can efficiently transfer all calls to the right person.
- She dresses appropriately, in order to reinforce the proper image for her company.
- She knows how to organize her employer's material so that he sees priority matters first, and so that he does not miss important information contained in the usual overly-large segment of "FYI" (for your information) material, as well as in the general reading material pertaining to the business.
- She corrects his writing and dictating errors; she suggests proper phrasing and points out factors her employer may have overlooked (if she is capable in these matters).
- She helps her employer do the gracious thing in his office relationships—including writing thank-you notes, sending gifts, and calling someone when the occasion warrants it—both inside the office and out of it.

- She reminds him of his appointments, keeps him on schedule, and acts as his listening ear in regard to company news and circulating rumors.
- She makes sure that his travel arrangements have been made satisfactorily; she organizes his briefcase before he goes and makes sure he has all the necessary tickets, stationery, pens, documents, schedules, and out-of-town telephone numbers and addresses he will need.
- She is always discreet about his business affairs, financial worth, and personal life.

Handling Personal Matters and Acting as a Gofer   Most good secretaries I know have never minded doing work that involves the personal side of their bosses' lives. In fact, most of them enjoy doing it. A woman easily becomes a member of his family in many ways, and takes vicarious enjoyment in the family's activities. However, in some firms a secretary is not supposed to perform any functions of a personal nature. If she feels her employer is loading her with too many personal things, she should speak to him about it in a very nice but frank way, so that he will not feel offended or guilty.

The symbol of a "gofer"—the secretarial responsibility of getting "coffee and danish for the boss"—has become a bone of contention in the feminists' movement. They look upon it as a symbol of servitude. During the years I myself was an executive secretary, I never looked upon it as such, but simply as a nice thing and also an efficient thing to do. If, however, an employer today senses a feeling of resentment in his secretary when she gets him his morning coffee, he should work out a system of taking that duty away from her. One woman executive I know brings into the office two or three times a week a giant thermos full of hot coffee for all her immediate staff. The other days her staff takes turns being gofers. An employer should ask how his new young secretary feels about this point; it is a sensitive one with many feminists, and all a person has to do is ask, *"Does* it bother you?" If it does, a lot of unpleasantness can be avoided simply by finding another system. A personnel manual cannot spell these things out; they are a question of one-to-one human relationships.

Upward Mobility for a Secretary   A talented, hard-working secretary can almost always "move up" today *if she wants to* and *if she has properly given her job enough time.* Many executive secretaries like their job immensely, have a lot of responsibilities, receive excellent perquisites, and are well paid. (They prefer to stay where they are, and with good reason.) A young woman who becomes someone's secretary and then asks for a promotion to a junior executive's job after six months is making an error. She does not deserve that promotion. It takes time to prove one's ability to act in an executive capacity. It takes knowledge and training. If she is ambitious and if she has proved herself, after serving in that job for well over a year, she should talk to her employer, communicate her feelings, and seek his approval and support of her move "up and onward." If he has any integrity, he will help her, even though it will be with regret at losing her. A good secretary is a rare jewel these days. She becomes an integral part of her employer's life at the office.

An intelligent, ambitious secretary makes use of all her time; she takes courses to broaden her horizons; she studies and reads. She becomes an expert on her own company, and when she's ready for that promotion to an executive position, everyone in that company will know she deserves it.

The Well-written Note: An Important Factor in Executive Relationships

The use of the personal letter in business is an important tool, not only from the point of view of manners, but also because it can influence one's career in a most affirmative way. Since no one orders us to sit down and write a personal letter in our adult life, the mere act of writing it is creative, and the motivation is usually unselfish. A well-written letter requires sympathy or empathy on the writer's part, so it does, in fact, denote a certain amount of good character.

The writing of personal letters in the business world should not engender self-consciousness about whether it is a man writing to a woman or a woman writing to a man. People write to people to console them, to make them feel better, to praise them, or to share in their sadness or happiness.

Personal letters to business acquaintances may be handwritten or typed. If the writer's penmanship is poor and hard to read, his letter should be typed. Office stationery is appropriate for all these letters. However, if one is writing a condolence letter, it is nicer to do it on personal stationery. (If the handwriting is bad, such a letter may still be typed.)

Typical situations that call for the writing of a letter to a business associate are:

To Say "Thank You"

1. For a lunch invitation, even if it was strictly business:

Dear Harry,

Thanks for yesterday's lunch. It was a very pleasant hour, even if we were both rushing against deadlines. I enjoyed the introduction to that corned beef you are always extolling. It even surpassed my inflated expectations.

Thanks again—
Jim

2. For showing one the ropes, for taking time to assist one on a project, for helping one learn the job:

Dear Jane,

I am such a raw recruit in this business, you have no idea what it meant to me for you to take an entire afternoon out of your tight schedule and show me the ropes. You are a real pro, and I benefited from every hour.

Thanks again—
Mike

3. For hearing another put in a good word for one with a superior, including hearing one's actions defended or especially praised:

Dear Joe,

I just heard what you did for me at the client meeting this morning. Since I wasn't there to defend myself, having the most respected and articulate member of this agency to do the job for me is something for which I shall be forever indebted to you. You are a real friend, and I promise I won't let you down for having faith in my capabilities.

Gratefully,
Alice

To Say "I'm Sorry"

1. Letter of apology for having seriously offended someone:

Dear Hank,

There is no way I can erase the tragic error of my bumbling tongue this morning. I never would consciously offend you in any way, because I respect you and treasure your friendship.

I hope that along with all the other good qualities you possess, forgiveness is among them. For I need your forgiveness now very much.

Sincerely,
Elizabeth

2. Letter of condolence to someone you do not know very well:

Dear Grace,

I write this note at a time when the entire staff is saddened by the tragedy that has hit you. Although I never had the pleasure of meeting your son, I have heard from everyone how close you were and what he meant to you. You were proud of him, and this is a terrible loss.

Come back to our office as soon as you can. Work is great therapy, and we need you. You are in all our thoughts.

In sympathy,
Helen

3. Letter to someone who has lost his job:

Dear Peter,

I was shocked when I heard the news. Your company must be in real trouble to let a man of your caliber and professionalism go. It will be their tough luck and someone else's great gain. I'm sure that after the usual painful period of job hunting you will end up with a much better position in a firm that will appreciate your talents. If there is anything I can do to be of help, let me know. I'll make any calls you wish.

And keep a "stiff upper." If I had stock in your old company, I'd sell it immediately. They don't know what they're doing to lose someone like you.

Sincerely,
Anne

To Say "Congratulations"
1. For a promotion:

Dear Emma,

Strike up the band! Hallelujah! You made it—the first woman senior vice-president of this august firm! The women executives of this company are all feeling a deep personal pride in your promotion. You have shown us the way, and it's wonderful news.

Sincerely,
Denise

2. To a colleague on a personal matter:

Dear Jerry,

I just heard your son won a scholarship to Yale for next fall. You and your wife must be bursting forth with unmitigated but understandable pride. What a great boy he is, and what satisfaction this must mean for the two people who did the job of raising him.

We are all elated for you. Please tell Jerry Jr. we are almost as proud of him as his old man!

Sincerely,
Allen

3. To someone who has been transferred:

Dear Al,

I read in the *Post* last night that you've been named to one of the top spots at Jefferson-Comford. It's a superior firm, and you are fortunate, but *they* are the lucky ones.

It will give me great pleasure to be your personal courier and inform any of your old pals who may have missed the news in the paper. Good luck in the new position, and let me know when you have finished your shake-down cruise. I'd like to hear all about it.

Congratulations again,
Gregg

Handling Executive Visitors and Appointments

The nicest way to greet someone from the outside world who enters your office is to rise with a smile and your hand extended. Both women and men should stand up for other men and women callers. The mere act of rising does honor to the caller. The warm smile, the stating of the visitor's name, and the firmly offered handshake are all important ways to help set a proper framework for the meeting.

I remember the story of one of my father's friends who always stood up to greet people in his office, even after he became president of his impressive corporation. Early in his career, a young typewriter salesman had come to call on him, and he stood up for him in his usual courteous manner.

Twenty-five years later he was quickly granted a very sizable loan by the president of a bank who told him, after the deal was closed, that he had been the young typewriter salesman for whom the older man had stood up. "You gave me an appointment," he explained, "even though you didn't need a typewriter; you stood up to greet me when no one else in the city would even talk to me, much less give me an appointment to practice my sales talk. I never forgot that."

If you are confused about whether or not to stand up when a visitor approaches your desk, the rule is: If in doubt, stand up. Standing up to greet an outsider is the nicest kind of welcome. It is not a mark of humble deference; it is a mark of simple manners.

Executives do not rise when members of their own company come into their office, with the exception of the chief executive officer or someone like the retired chairman of the board. A young executive should stand up as a sign of respect to greet a very senior officer who walks into his office. (One does not have to keep jumping to one's feet each time—one rises to greet a senior fellow member of the firm only once in the day.) Again, the rule applies to both sexes.

When an executive is interviewing someone for a job, he should rise to greet that person, even if he or she is very young, and shake his hand.

The rule holds that when you stand up to greet someone, you stand up to say good-by to that person.

When a man or a woman is late in coming into a meeting already in progress, he or she should quickly slip into an available chair and greet the other people in the meeting with a nod of recognition. When there is a break in the meeting, the person who was late should quietly apologize to the person chairing the meeting, and explain why he was late.

The Secretary's Responsibilities There is something very gracious, too, when a secretary arises to greet an executive from the outside who arrives for a meeting with her boss. If she rises smiling and greets the guest by name, she will make the best kind of impression on the guest and set the stage for a successful meeting with her employer. She should identify herself as she stands up: "Good afternoon, Mr. Fordson. I'm Mr. Smith's secretary, Miss Jenkins. Won't you be seated? Mr. Smith is on a long-distance call, but he won't be long." She shows him to a chair where he can wait comfortably. If the wait is long, she should give him access to magazines and the company's annual report. If her boss's conversation continues interminably, she should enter the office and remind him of his waiting appointment.

There are times, of course, when the secretary cannot rise. She may be typing something under pressure; she may also be juggling a telephone receiver in one hand and a notepad in the other. In this case, she should not rise, but she should still manage a smile of greeting. If the visitor should go right into her boss's office, she should motion him in with a wave of her hand. If he must wait, she indicates a nearby chair and finishes her telephone call; or she may put the telephone caller on hold while she handles a proper greeting for the new arrival.

If a visitor with an appointment is left waiting for more than ten minutes, with no sign of life from the inner office, it is the secretary's responsibility to remind her boss of his waiting appointment. I watched one smart secretary handle an executive with great skill while he was kept waiting for an hour. She continued to inform him of the current situation, while emphasizing how upset her boss was.

The Receptionist's Responsibilities   A receptionist in a public area does not stand up every time an outside person approaches her desk. There is too much traffic. She sometimes has to handle ringing telephones, arriving visitors, and messengers with packages and slips to sign. In some corporate offices, the receptionist is expected to escort the caller to his destination. In this case, she would rise upon hearing the person identify himself and show him the way, or she would first call the inner office to notify them of the caller's arrival, and then rise from her desk to escort him into the inner office.

Office Gifts

Office gift-giving has become grossly exaggerated in many businesses. It is wrong for a company to permit the constant solicitation of its employees by other employees who wish to purchase gifts for specific reasons. One woman told me that she had been solicited for contributions fifteen times in one year by her fellow employees in a big bank, including contributions to a bon-voyage gift for someone going on a cruise and a hospital gift for another who had had her face lifted. Since the woman was raising five children alone on her modest salary, the fifteen-dollar outlay was a real hardship. Some firms have solved this problem by laying down a policy prohibiting collections for gifts inside the office. (The soliciting also wastes a great deal of employee time on the job.) Otherwise firms allow an occasional solicitation in the office for a baby, wedding, or retirement gift, but only if the maximum amount allowable is something in the neighborhood of a dollar. If staff members wish to send gifts and cards on their own, they can always make individual or group arrangements outside the office.

Some firms have a small fund, supplied by management, with which flowers or a plant are automatically sent to each employee on his or her birthday, with a card enclosed that is signed by whoever wishes to sign. When someone in the immediate family of an employee dies, it is also proper for company management to pay for a funeral floral offering, or to make a donation to charity "in the name of" that employee's deceased relative.

There are many policies in effect, but the point is that every company, large or small, *should have* a policy, firmly understood by its employees.

It is unneccessary for staff members to give their bosses Christmas or Hanukkah presents. It is a nice gesture, however, for the boss to give a small gift to members of his or her immediate staff in the holiday season. This gift should not be too personal—gourmet food or a gift certificate to a fine store are always appropriate. One well-known woman executive gives the men on her immediate staff box seats to local professional sports games (or wine, if they prefer). To the women she gives certificates for an all-day "pampering job" at a local well-known cosmetics establishment, famous for its hair salon and face and body treatments.

It is nice during the Christmas season for a small business owner to give a token gift to the people who contribute so much to his comfort and efficiency during the year—the messengers, the elevator starter in the office lobby, the head of his mailing house or photo lab, the person who runs the downstairs newsstand or the shoeshine person, or the head of library research. An inexpensive box of candy is all that is necessary—something that says, "Thank you for being nice to us during this year."

Often a store-purchased gift is not the best remembrance. If a fellow office worker is seriously ill or injured, a series of telephone calls made through the months of recuperation means far more to the person than any one-time expensive purchase. One of the nicest "joint office gifts" I've heard described was one made to a popular woman junior executive of a large corporation. She was confined to hospitals and her home for almost a year following a serious bone operation. During that time her male and female colleagues, knowing she was a voracious reader, organized a lending library of their own books. Someone came to call on her every two weeks, bringing a fresh supply of books and returning the old ones to their owners. Most important, those visits kept her well supplied with office news and gossip and helped her settle back into her old routine with ease when she was finally able to return.

This was a perfect example of thoughtfulness, imagination, and friendship —a far cry from merely sending a studio card to which one signs one's name.

Office Party Behavior

When you attend an office party, whether it's held at Christmas, New Year's, or in the middle of the summer, the situation is fraught with potential embarrassment. Some people seem determined to abandon their inhibitions at these annual affairs, while others think they have to "grin and bear it," no matter what occurs.

The best way to handle trouble when it occurs at an office party is to walk away from it. There is no successful way for a young woman to deal, for example, with the amorous advances of an inebriated man who is her superior. If she tries to "jolly him out of it," she won't be able to; if she criticizes him, he'll remember it the next day and may deeply resent the rejections as well as his own guilt feelings. If she just smiles and drifts away, with a fabricated excuse, "for a moment," she can get her coat, leave, and solve the problem.

The same advice goes for a young man who is being pursued by a woman executive who partakes too heavily of the office party cheer. The only way to handle such a situation gracefully is to extricate oneself and leave the other person wondering where one went. And if the other person is confused tomorrow about what happened last night, all the better; then there is no need to refer to it or remind her of it.

Smoking in the Office

Some offices will not permit their employees to smoke while on the business premises. Some permit smoking only in the rest rooms and the cafeteria. (Those areas become insufferable, as a result, for nonsmokers.) If you make a business call on another person in his office, notice whether others around you are smoking. If you see no one, do not ask if you may smoke. If you sit down by the desk of an executive in an office where smoking is allowed but you notice the executive has no ash trays on his desk, the chances are he does not want you to smoke. Always ask permission if you are sitting by someone's desk and that person is smoking. If that person is not smoking, think before you even ask.

Never light up a pipe or a cigar in anyone else's office. If you smoke a cigar or pipe in your own office, be sure it is an enclosed area, so it will not offend others. Open the window regularly to air out the premises. Or regulate the air conditioning to pull the smoke out of the room.

Many people today keep signs that say "Thank you for not smoking" on their desks—an effective, polite way of discouraging smoking.

Some Office Do's and Don'ts

DO:

Be solicitous and welcoming to new personnel. Show them around; invite them to lunch; explain who does what to whom in the organization. Help the newcomer learn the names of all necessary office personnel. One's attitude in a new office situation is shaped by how others treat or mistreat one.

Offer to do errands for others if you are going out, such as picking up stamps at the post office, or supplies at the office supply store, or bringing back coffee for everyone.

Be creative in helping others in the office. Maybe it's a special container needed for everyone's umbrella to drip into on a rainy day; or a suggestion that a new coat rack or a small refrigerator needs to be purchased for everyone's comfort. Some of the best ideas for the bettering of the office environment stem from senior executives who care about the welfare of everyone on the payroll.

Try to help associates who have been fired to relocate themselves. This assistance may require a great deal of personal effort on your part—time spent in telephoning, writing letters, researching and "talking around." If you were in the same situation, you would certainly want someone to do the same for you.

Send a handwritten note to the home address of an associate who has just received either good or bad news in his life. To share in someone's happiness or sorrow, as the case may be, is the most supportive kind of action there is.

Take good care of the plants or flowers on your own desk, and take turns watering the community office plants. They are there for everyone's enjoyment, and should be jointly tended. Secretaries should take care of their bosses' plants; executives without an assigned secretary should take care of their own.

Be a neat smoker. Keep your ash trays emptied and wiped clean. If the sight of your dirty ash tray doesn't depress your associates, then the smell of it certainly will.

Keep a neat desk surface. If you have an ink-stained blotter, change it. Clean off paper clips that have become dust-clogged. Keep pencils sharpened and unchewed. Keep your notes and files in neat piles (you might even find things more easily that way!). Remove unneeded clutter from the desk, so it can be dusted more easily and so that you have more working space.

Do think of the night cleaners. Be careful about throwing ashes, cigarette butts, and garbage into your wastebasket. Throw all such waste into a bag or a large used envelope—something that will not require the washing out of the interior of your wastebasket. A sea of spilled soda, coffee, and orange peels is not the way to leave this receptacle for the cleaners. And pick up the dropped notes around your desk, too.

Keep the rest room neat and tidy. All litter such as paper towels should be stowed away. Washbasins should be rinsed clean, ashes disposed of, soda cans emptied and thrown into a receptacle, and toilets flushed.

DON'T:

The worst error anyone can make while on a business appointment is *to stay too long.* One should arrive on time, state one's case, and be gone. Executives who are important, overly busy, and polite find that "time wasters" are the biggest problem they have. Fifteen minutes is a good rule of thumb to use in deciding when to end an appointment. The caller who has been granted the appointment and who is asking for a favor, or seeking something, or simply informing, should rise and state, "I shouldn't take any more of your time; I know how busy you are." The executive will remember this person favorably, and will probably do what he can, within the context of the favor asked.

Don't be a manicurist in the office. It looks inappropriate to see a woman fixing her nail polish or filing nails at her desk; it looks just as bad to see a man cleaning his nails at his desk.

A woman should not fix her make-up and no one should do a hair-styling job on himself or herself at the desk. People of both sexes who are serious about their careers do their primping in the rest rooms.

No one should chew gum in the office. It is impossible to chew without the face becoming distorted. Someone once described graphically what it was like to be in a room full of gum-chewers. "It was like being in a jungle of chattering baboons, their faces vigorously exercising in unison."

The constant muncher looks very jarring, too, in the office landscape. One should eat at one's desk only at lunchtime, and only if the office permits it. Receptionists should never eat at their desks while dealing with the public.

Don't relive personal experiences concerning a social occasion outside the office in front of others who were not invited. People who lead lonely lives do not wish to have those feelings reinforced by hearing associates chatter in their midst about their own active social lives.

Don't borrow colleagues' telephone books, newspapers, pens, tape, scissors, ruler, or any supplies without immediately returning them after use. Secretaries who borrow others' typewriters should replace the margins and tabs exactly as they were, so as not to inconvenience the machine's owner when she sits down to use it. Executives who borrow reports and reference materials from associates should not forget to return them. A person who uses up all the paper in the duplicating machine should replace it so that the next user will not be inconvenienced.

Don't sit back with your feet up on the desk or the drawers. This denotes an "I don't care about anybody's property, including my own" attitude. It reveals a strong fault of character.

Don't take off your shoes at your desk or leave them sitting around. If a secretary goes out to lunch with her snow boots on and leaves her shoes sitting on the floor by her desk, it ruins the look of the office.

Don't use up the community supply of soda, coffee, tea, or snacks without resupplying or contributing toward their replenishment.

Don't borrow small sums of money without repaying. People who are always borrowing bus tokens and newspaper money, and who then forget to repay, move quickly to the bottom of the office popularity poll.

Don't drop by another person's desk to chat just because you are not busy at the moment. That person may be too polite to tell you he is meeting a deadline and must be left alone. People often have to stay after work at night to finish because an "office talker" wouldn't leave them alone.

Don't read magazines at your desk if you are not busy. One can always pass free time learning more about company operations instead of finding out about the latest fashions. Either read more about the firm's business or ask to be assigned more responsibility.

Don't clutter your desk with inappropriate souvenirs and mementos. They are dust collectors and can ruin the office landscape.

Chapter 40

OPENING YOUR OWN BUSINESS

I remember economist Bernard Baruch's answer when asked, "What do you have to have to open your own business?" He thought a short while and then said, "It's very simple. You have to fill an existing need; you have to believe you can do it; and you have to be *damned* lucky."

Success in a new venture implies a combination of factors, including luck, but one of the necessary ingredients is always good manners—to build up a reputation in your community, to develop allies who can help you succeed, and to inspire people to "give you a break," whether it's the owner of the office supply store who gives you an extra month of free credit or the local newspaper editor who writes a sympathetic story about your new business.

Good relations with present and future customers and clients are essential, but relations with suppliers, shippers, sales representatives—any human being with whom you come in contact in the course of your business—are equally so. Good manners underlie all friendships, and you are going to need every friend you have when starting a new enterprise.

Whether you are going to open a beauty salon, a catering service, a car wash, an accounting firm, a real estate agency, a costume jewelry boutique, or a public relations firm, you need to believe in your own capabilities to succeed. And you have to convince a lot of other people of that same fact, too, in order to establish credit, secure loans, and obtain sound financing for your project. Seek advice everywhere before you take the final step—and then never stop seeking it. Graciously thank anyone who goes out of his way to do some research for you, find information, or open up new contacts for you to approach. Do not, however, bend the ears of professionals whom you know socially, trying to get free advice. A lawyer should be seen in his office and paid a fee for his advice, and not be buttonholed on the dance floor by his wife's good friend who is opening her own business.

Once you are sure you are filling a specific need in your community, and are sure of what you want to do and where you want to do it, sit down and make a detailed list of how much money you will need in the first year—and in the second—in order to have the proper "Survival Kit" of funds organized. Be sure to add a sizable contingency fund to the total, to cover those unforeseen but inevitable emergencies. Ask experts to help you weigh your estimate on every item for which you will be forced to budget. The following are just some of the kinds of needs you will probably have and should be aware of. You should thoroughly research and specially tailor his general list to your own business and needs.

Budget Check List

Rent and utilities
Decoration of the office or shop, store, or restaurant, including signs
Maintenance (cleaning, snow removal on sidewalk, etc.)
Staff salaries (including Social Security payments, unemployment insurance, payroll taxes)
Corportate business taxes
Office furnishings and equipment (fortunately, everything from your executive desk to your adding machine, your electric typewriters, and your duplicating machine may be rented)
Printing, stationery, and office supplies (this can be a large item in some businesses)
Advertising and public relations budgets—including sales promotion pieces, mailers, etc. (this can be a very large item in your budget)
Telephone installation costs, equipment, and answering service charges, too, as well as monthly call bills
Licenses required in your business
Legal fees (can be very costly, but are very necessary)
Business entertaining budget (only if necessary)
Accountant's and/or bookkeeper's fees
Insurance (liability, fire, and theft, auto, workmen's compensation, medical plans, etc.)
Car rental, truck rental, or other transportation costs for all personnel
Mailing and shipping charges
Display designer fees (if yours is a retail business)
Messenger service
Start-up costs of raw materials and machinery, if manufacturing is entailed

Announcing You Are Open for Business

1. By means of a tasteful, professionally made *sign* on your door or on the outside of the building where you have your business. Your logo (if you have one) should be part of the theme. The sign should be informative, not confusing. It should have a "First Class" look. (Be sure that you are listed in the lobby directory of your building.)

2. By means of an *announcement ad* in the local newspapers and magazines, as well as spot anouncements on radio and perhaps even TV (if you are an establishment that requires instant traffic from the public). Use a professional ad person or a small agency for this.
3. By means of an *announcement mailing piece*—sent to business associates, friends, and possible customers (club and professional organization lists, magazine subscription lists, etc.).
4. By means of a *press release* sent to all local media—which may result in some good free feature story publicity on your new enterprise.
5. By means of an *opening party*—to which you invite future clients and customers, friends, influential people in your community, the other people on your floor (or the neighbors in your block), your lawyer, the head of the construction crew who worked on your space, the engineer, the interior designer, your banker, accountant, insurance agent—in fact everyone involved in helping you get started. (This might include the local stationer who gave you supplies on credit!) Three of the most important people who came to the christening party of my office when I started in business were the building manager, the captain of the local police precinct, and our Catholic priest, who blessed the office and every one of us.

Your opening party can be a fancy catered champagne and cake kind of affair or just a punch, coffee, tea, and cookies party.

Gifts to Send for the Opening of a New Business

If you want to send a "Good Luck" remembrance to a friend or business associate opening a new business, the traditional gesture is the sending of a basket of flowers with your card for the opening party. An even better idea is to send a card from the florist notifying him of a credit with that florist—to have flowers sent when they are truly wanted or needed. Credit for "A Lunch for Four" at a good nearby restaurant is also a welcome gift for the new entrepreneur, as are things like subscriptions to trade magazines and papers he or she will have to read; or a good-looking magazine rack stuffed with current periodicals to leave in the waiting room of the new office; or a handsome leather agenda for the executive's desk.

Stationery

One of the most important communicators of who you are and what you are is your stationery. As soon as you have an addresss and a telephone number for your new business, you should order your business stationery and cards. First consult a free-lance artist or graphics firm to assist you in developing a logo for your company or your store or restaurant. An attractive logo can help you to be remembered by the public; "instant recognition" is a great asset. A logo can symbolize what your company does, even in an abstract way. Once you have a logo, ask the graphics artist to work it into all your printed materials, everything from inexpensive memo pads to your good engraved business cards. ("You," of course, are the president of your company.) If you are running a baby-sitter service, you do not need engraved cards; if you are the head of a social-secretary service for diplomats and large corporations, you do.

Shop around for the printer who will give you the best deal, but also check with some past customers before doing business with him to assure yourself of his reliability and good workmanship.

One-color process is the cheapest in printing; the paper goes through the printing press only once. For example, your office stationery could have brown printing on beige paper and thus be a handsome one-color process. If your logo is yellow and brown, then the beige paper would have to go through the printing presses twice, which is why the two-color process is more expensive.

If your logo is universally regarded by your friends as well designed, and you are sure you will stick with it, you might as well have a permanent plate made of it, which can be left at the printer's. Then you can easily reorder anything you need in the stationery line just by calling the printer on the telephone. (One soon learns, however, to send confirming purchasing orders by mail for everything ordered by telephone in the business world.)

The heavier the paper, the more expensive it is. For important correspondence you should use a nice heavy stock for letterhead stationery, with matching envelopes. There is something about a good-quality paper when you are trying to sell yourself or your services to someone else—suddenly you become good-quality, too. Naturally, the majority of all office correspondence goes out on inexpensive letterheads or forms, but special letters from you (the chairman of the board, the president, and the chief executive officer of your little company) should have a "touch of class."

When you order your stationery, don't forget to order matching-sized envelopes (about two-thirds the quantity of your letterhead order), plus a small number of plain matching second sheets. And remember, it is much more expensive to order printed stationery in dribs and drabs. Always order in large lots, to keep the price low.

The basic stationery needs of most small businesses consist of a combination of any of the following:

1. Order forms, purchase orders, billing forms, multicopy memo forms.
2. Sales checks.
3. Good executive letterheads and envelopes (perhaps engraved for the president of the company, but printed for the others).
4. Inexpensive printed letterheads and envelopes on lesser-quality paper.
5. Message pads, interoffice memo pads ("buck sheets") of cheap stock.
6. Business cards for every executive or salesman. (These are a wonderful communicating tool, as well as effective reminders.)

7. Note cards and matching envelopes for companies where executives carry on a great deal of informal correspondence.

It is surprising the number of companies that neglect to include the firm's telephone number on the letterhead, but print only the name and address. This annoys everyone quite justifiably. One must search for the telephone number in the book, or make a call to information (for which, in many places, one is now charged).

If you operate your business from home, you might want to utilize a Post Office number instead of your address, for the sake of privacy.

If you are going to have to use rapid communications in your business, you should print your international cable address and your telex number on your letterheads and on your business cards. (See also pages 500 and 502 on personal stationery for the executive.)

Deciding the Office Image

When you open your own business, one important decision you must make early on is the image you wish projected to the public.

You should communicate this desired image well to your own staff so that they will act as a team. Everyone—from the office messenger to the president of the firm—should conduct business in an honest, efficient way, proudly in keeping with the desired image.

A small ad agency may well have an office that is a true contemporary environment, all shiny with polished chrome, fiberglass, soft leather, and hot, clashing colors in the framed graphics on the walls. In this atmosphere, it is perfectly appropriate for the men to come to work in their jeans, custom-made boots, and high-fashion shirts, and the women to arrive in well-fitting pants, sweaters, shirts, or jackets.

In another set of offices on the same corridor, those of a young business consulting firm, the women may be "asked" (never *commanded*) to wear skirts, not pants, and the men may very well arrive for work in dark pin-stripe suits. That office might be furnished in dark carpeting, dark, wood-stained walls, with antique furniture and framed maps on the walls. The entrepreneurs of both firms on that hallway may be of the same age and dress the same in their off-hours life. But the diverse nature of their business molds them consciously or unconsciously into projecting different images. One thing, however, is the same for both: the necessity for good manners prevails in both companies, not only in staff relationships, but also in relations with the outside world.

Free Advice About Jobs and Business Opportunities

If a woman has some financial backing and wants to start a small business of her own, she should write to the Small Business Administration, 1441 L

Street N.W., Washington, D.C. 20416, for advice and for printed materials. Help may also be received from organizations like the Association of Women Business Owners, 525 West End Avenue, New York, New York 10024. The national organization CATALYST, 14 East Sixtieth Street, New York, New York 10022, will refer women who write to it to professionally qualified Job Resource Centers, which exist throughout the United States. These offer educational and career counseling, job referral, and placement services. CATALYST also has booklets that comprehensively list career opportunities. If a woman wants to go into the lucrative franchising business, she should write for information to the International Franchise Association, 7315 Wisconsin Avenue, Washington, D.C. 20014. Good job information can also be acquired by writing to the U. S. Equal Employment Opportunity Commission, 1800 G Street N.W., Washington, D.C. 20506, and the Women's Bureau, U. S. Department of Labor, Washington, D.C. 20210.

Part Five

STATIONERY: AN IMPORTANT
COMMUNICATION TOOL

A Stationery Wardrobe 495

Letter Writing: the Ultimate in Human Communication 513

Invitations, Acceptances, and Regrets 533

The Etiquette of Calling Cards 547

Heraldic Devices 553

Over the past decade stationery etiquette—the do's and don'ts of what kind of paper is used for a specific type of activity—has eased greatly. For example, until recently acceptances or regrets for formal invitations had to be written in black or dark blue ink on white, gray, or ivory notepaper. Now they may be written on any color of good stationery, although for very formal occasions, such as weddings, debutante balls, White House dinners, silver wedding anniversary parties, and similar events, the conservative notepaper is still the best.

More and more men are using single cards with matching envelopes for correspondence, which were formerly regarded as women's stationery. Women who have large handwriting have begun using the larger-sized single sheets for their paper, a style once regarded as men's stationery. People who lead very active business, social, and community lives have greatly expanded their "stationery wardrobes" far above and beyond what used to be the traditional papers needed. People are buying stationery in newer and bolder color combinations, unusual sizes and textures. They are finding new forms of stationery on which to print or engrave everything from new, graphically exciting monograms to their own signatures reproduced in engraving. Everything is being printed, from multicolored bordered postcards to customized memo pads to use in offices or homes.

The one rule to remember when ordering stationery today is the Post Office restrictions on size. The smallest envelope now handled is 3½" × 5". No longer can one scribble a note on a small informal or on a calling card with matching envelope and send it through the mail.

Chapter 41

A STATIONERY WARDROBE

The Proper Form of Stationery

Engraving Versus Printing Engraving is much costlier than printing. The largest single factor in the price is the making of the special die. Since you pay only once for the making of the die, reordering engraved stationery is not such a major expense. Engraved stationery is special; it has a luxurious feel when you pass your finger over it. There are other processes that simulate it and give an "almost engraved" look and feel, and these processes are much less expensive. However, engraving is engraving and a substitute is a substitute, and a stationery buff always knows the difference.

Printing, of course, is the process we use the most and the one that is the least expensive. No die need be cut; instead, type is set. Printed stationery is acceptable today for everything except for acknowledging *formal* invitations (when, if you do not have engraved paper, you should use good-quality plain notepaper).

One should not combine engraving with printing (as, for example, having engraved letterheads made with envelopes on which the return address is printed). The exception to this rule is for charity or business invitations that may be engraved, but that include certain information or R.S.V.P. cards and self-addressed envelopes that are printed.

The Engraved Monogram on Personal Stationery It's wise to use two or three initials for your monogram on a letterhead. A single initial looks forlorn. If you use one of your stationer's simple monograms it will, of course, cost less than if you choose an intricate one. Some women like to have their own monogram specially designed, for they will use it (barring a change in matrimonial status) the rest of their lives.

I have known girls (for whom budgets presented no problems) who found a piece of some ancestor's silver or linen and who have used that unusual monogram for everything, from their stationery die to their monogrammed sheets and sterling-silver flatware and hollow ware. Nice, very special, but very expensive!

A sampling of various styles of monogram from the very traditional to the sharply modern.

Return Addresses Traditionally, return addresses in social correspondence are engraved, printed, or written by hand (or printed on address labels) on the back flap of the envelopes. Because Post Office workers must handle an ever-increasing volume of mail, and it takes time to rewrite the sender's name and address on the front of the envelope (if that piece of mail is undeliverable), we should all discontinue the back-flap custom. Instead, *we should put our name and return address on the upper left portion of the face of the envelope* by hand, engraving, printing, or the small paper sticker method. A majority of businesses have been placing the return address on the front for years, for the sake of Post Office efficiency, and the non-business world must do so also.

In women's stationery, a woman puts her name on her return address in the form in which she likes to be called; it's the clue to the title she wants. If she wants to be Mrs. David Smith, she puts that; or Ms. Marian Smith if she wants that usage; or Miss Marian Smith if she does not wish to be addressed as "Ms." (In her office stationery, she would put only her given name and the last name under which she works, without a title, in her return address.)

In men's stationery the return address on the face of the envelope carries the man's name without "Mr." preceding it. However, if he is doctor, a general, or a minister, his proper title should precede his name (Dr., Lt. Gen., Reverend), so that people will address him correctly. The same applies to a woman with a title. Also, if a man has a name that might be confused with a girl's, such as Marion, Lee, Beverly, or Evelyn, he would do well to place "Mr." in front of his name on his return address, and thus avoid endless inaccuracies in addressing him.

Telephone Numbers If a family has a telephone number that is unlisted in the local directory, it is a very good idea (unless there is a celebrity in the family seeking total privacy) to indicate the area code and the telephone number on the personal stationery of each member of the family. A person who lives in a large apartment house would do well to include the apartment number in the address, too, and the zip code must always be part of every engraved or printed letterhead address.

Lined Envelopes Envelopes of even the finest quality engraved paper are often unlined. If a colored lining is used, it is usually a plain, darker shade of the same color as the paper, or perhaps it is an attractive contrast, such as a ruby red lining for white notepaper.

There are some interesting linings made for social stationery today, but the plaids and polka dots should really be left to the teen-agers and younger children. So should the "pop colors" of ink (pink, purple, yellow, and turquoise blue). If you have black, blue, or brown color accents on your paper, it looks well to use matching ink. Red ink, except during the Christmas season, when used to match the red engraving on one's stationery, is a bit too strong.

Women's Personal Stationery

A woman should buy stationery according to her needs, her life-style, and the size of her handwriting. Some women need one kind of paper only; others need several.

A housewife who is heavily involved in community affairs, and who must write a lot of letters concerning her nonprofit projects, is as busy as any career woman. She needs a basic conservative and inexpensive set of stationery, printed with her name, address, and telephone number at the top. (If she goes by her full married name in these activities, she should have "Mrs. Robert Jones" printed at the top; when she signs her letters "Elizabeth Jones" people will have all the information they need in writing back to her. If she goes primarily by her given name, she should put "Elizabeth Jones" at the top; then under her signature she might type or write "(Mrs. Robert)" in parentheses.

A widow continues using the name she used when married, e.g., Mrs. George Greenberg. If she used her given name professionally, preceded by "Ms." when her husband was alive, she would, of course, continue to use it after his death: Ms. Carol Greenberg. She would not, however, use the name Mrs. Carol Greenberg, unless she had been a widow for many years.

Like the woman heavily involved in community affairs, a woman in charge of household bills, insurance, and other family business chores needs inexpensive stationery with her name, address, and telephone number. It is much easier to be able to write "Please contact me at the above address" (or "at the above telephone number") than to keep writing out all the information.

If she has big handwriting and does not use a typewriter, she is better off purchasing large single sheets with matching envelopes rather than the smaller standard stationery size.

No two women are alike either in their stationery tastes or in their stationery needs. A business executive who is also a homemaker needs a wardrobe of stationery in her office and a separate one at home. The following suggestions may give you some ideas of how to make your correspondence easier and more efficient.

Basic Stationery Needs   The stationery wardrobe of a hypothetical Mrs. Robert Latham Brown (Olivia Bakely) might be the following:

1. *A box of monogrammed informals* (a fold-over card with matching envelope), approximately 4"×5". She uses the initials of her first name, maiden name, and married surname in a monogram that is engraved in emerald green on pale green stock. She writes her thank-you notes and acknowledges invitations on this paper. She also extends invitations to informal meals and cocktails with it.

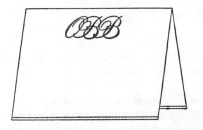

An engraved informal, monogrammed with a woman's initials—first name, maiden name, and married surname.

2. *A box of white or pale gray, absolutely plain informals,* which she uses for condolence notes or acknowledging the most formal of invitations (such as to a wedding or a dance or an anniversary dinner).

3. *A box of inexpensive printed stationery* with her married name, city address, and telephone number, which she uses for personal business matters such as writing to stores, her children's school, or the utility company.

> Mrs. Robert Latham Brown
> 1436 Hollow Lane
> Boston, Massachusetts Zip Code   Area Code
>   Telephone Number

A woman's personal stationery printed with her married name, home address, and telephone number.

4. *A box of colored-bordered postcards* printed with her married name only. These are for fast communications of a simple nature—nonconfidential items or quick personal messages. These are used at her Boston apartment and at the family summer home in Maine.

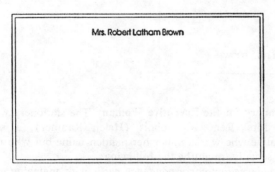

> Mrs. Robert Latham Brown

Informal postcards for quick notes, printed with name only.

5. *A box of engraved "Mr. and Mrs. Robert Latham Brown" visiting cards* with home address to use as gift or flower enclosures. (This is optional, not basic.)

6. *A box of engraved "Reminder" cards* for parties (fill-in kind).

7. *Printed memo pads* in a color on white, which Mrs. Brown uses in her work as chairwoman of the Women's Board of the Art Institute. These are used as in-house memo sheets and also clipped onto material mailed out to the public in the museum's regular envelopes. This kind of stationery must be ordered by Mrs. Brown at her own expense and with the charity's permission, but women involved in volunteer work find it very useful for their purposes.

Personally printed memo pads.

Basic Stationery for the Executive Woman   The stationery wardrobe of a hypothetical Mrs. René R. Dubois (Helen Rantner), a self-employed woman executive who works under her maiden name but who uses her husband's name socially, might be the following:

1. *Box of pale yellow correspondence cards* with matching envelopes (in lieu of informals) combining the initials of her maiden name and her husband's name in a very tailored royal blue monogram. She writes her thank-you notes and acknowledges invitations on these, and occasionally uses them for extending informal invitations.

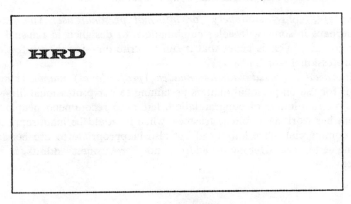

Correspondence cards printed with a combination of the initials of a woman's first name, maiden name, and married name.

2. *Box of absolutely plain informals* for condolence notes or acknowledgment of formal invitations.

3. *Box of inexpensive printed stationery* for personal business printed with "Mrs. René R. Dubois" and her home address and telephone number, similar to that shown for Mrs. Brown.

4. *Box of engraved "Reminder" cards* for parties.

This is to remind you that

René Dubois

expects you for   *dinner*

on   *May 5*

at   *7:30*   o'clock

An engraved "Reminder" card, used as a convenient follow-up to invitations.

5. *Box of "fantasy stationery for informal personal use.* This is fad paper, perhaps in some wild color combinations or designed in unusual textures or graphics. This is paper that is fun to write on—for the professional or nonprofessional woman.

6. *Letterhead engraved with her maiden (professional) name.* This stationery is for use on personal matters pertaining to her professional life—for example, writing letters of congratulation, letters to recommend people, letters about her work as a college trustee—when it would be inappropriate to use her commercial office letterhead but also inappropriate to use her married-name letterhead. Her home address, not her business address, is used on the envelope.

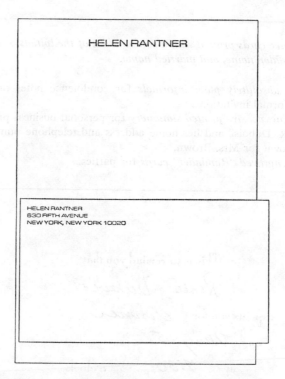

Engraved letterhead, with matching envelope, with professional name, only for use in personal matters pertaining to her professional life.

Men's Personal Stationery

Traditionally, a man's stationery has always been more subdued and conservative than a woman's. Until recently, a man would have only one kind of personal stationery to use both at home and in the office. This traditional style is engraved with his name and may or may not include his home or business address. (A company name is never included.) The paper is usually white, tan, or gray, with engraving in a darker color (maroon, brown, or dark green, gray, or blue; but the most popular is black). Today most men have this traditional stationery, but in addition use paper in a wide variety of sizes and color combinations: brown paper engraved in white; ecru stock finely bordered in brown and engraved in a lighter brown; light blue engraved in white letters, and so on. Many men use correspondence cards with matching envelopes. These may have amusing and innovative graphic designs engraved at the top center, at the bottom, or over on the left side. The design can consist of anything from a man's specially designed monogram to his own signature reproduced (at a high price) in colored engraving. The home or business address is optionally included.

Traditional engraved stationery for a man; for personal use, not business, it may or may not include the home address or the business street address.

Correspondence cards with matching envelopes are equally popular with men today.

A Married Couple's Personal Stationery

Traditionally a married couple have had their joint married names engraved on calling cards or on informals, such as "Mr. and Mrs. Harold Augustus Clayton."

If Harold's wife keeps her maiden name after marriage, and if she and her husband wish to have joint stationery (used for extending invitations, writing thank-you notes, sending condolence letters, and so on, when one writes on behalf of both), the following form may be used. The names and address are engraved or printed in the normal layout for a letterhead or a correspondence card.

Edith Barclay Woods   125 East 72nd Street
Harold Augustus Clayton   New York City   zip code

This stationery is not only convenient; it also helps communicate the fact that Edith Woods is married but has retained her maiden name.

Children's Stationery

It's important to let a child have his own stationery, even perhaps to let him pick it out, in order to encourage him to write thank-you notes and letters to his relatives. If a child begins to learn how to communicate on paper at an early age, he might very possibly sharpen that tool through the years and become an accomplished letter writer when he is older.

The best kind of paper to buy for a child who is still coping with the basics of penmanship is lined. Boxes of this paper are available with amusing and attractive illustrations at the top or down the side. When the child is more at ease with writing, it is nice to give him paper that has his first name at the top. When he is about ten, he may want paper such as his parents have, with his full name and address printed on top.

It is not necessary for a young person to have expensive engraved stationery until college age, and even then, only if affordable.

The House Stationery

The house stationery is a good-quality paper with matching envelopes, used by all members of the family (from ages thirteen up), as well as by house guests. (There should always be some of this stationery tucked into a desk drawer in the guest room for the convenience of house guests.) The paper is usually white, ivory, gray, pale blue, or pale green with a deeper hue or a contrasting color used for the printing or engraving. The street address, city, state, and zip code information is usually centered at the top. If you wish to include the telephone number, too, the address may be placed at the top left, and the area code and telephone number at the top right. (A telephone symbol may be used in conjunction with the telephone number on the right.) People with summer houses often have a house stationery for both their city and their country homes.

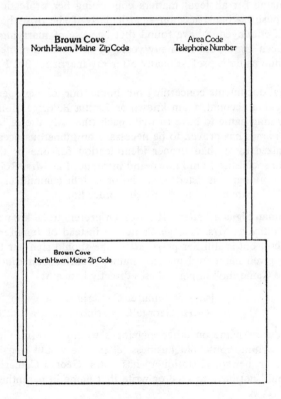

"House stationery" to be used by all members of the family and house guests.

Official Paper

When a couple occupy a government house, that house becomes their official address. The President, the First Lady, and their guests in the White House all use letter paper upon which is engraved simply "The White House." The American ambassador at his foreign post uses stationery engraved with "The American Embassy, Paris," or whatever the post. A governor's personal stationery reads either "The Governor's Mansion" or "The Executive Mansion," according to state preference.

Signatures

Signing Checks and Legal Papers In signing a check, a woman normally uses both her given name and her married last name for her personal checking account: for example, Mary Jane Broadhurst. Now, if Mary Jane Broadhurst works under her maiden name, Mary Jane Selden, she is advised to use that name for all legal matters concerning her professional life, including her business bank account—particularly if she owns her own business or is self-employed. I have found that because of marrying late in life and having been known for so many years by my maiden name, I logically had to continue using it professionally after my marriage. But I also *wanted* to.

For all legal documents concerning our home, our joint property, and my personal checking account, I am known as Letitia Baldrige Hollensteiner— an incredibly long name to have to write each time. My use of both maiden and married names has proven to be necessary on numerous occasions when I was recognized by or had proper identification for one or the other of two names. In social life I am known and introduced as Mrs. Robert Hollensteiner. When my name is listed on social or benefit committees, I use Letitia Baldrige Hollensteiner without any title preceding it.

How a Woman Signs a Letter If a woman prefers to be known and introduced in the office as Mrs. George Camerino instead of Jennifer Camerino, which is difficult but is still her prerogative, she should sign her business letters with her given name and married name, Jennifer Camerino, but place "Mrs. George Camerino" in parentheses directly beneath:

[signed] Jennifer Camerino
(Mrs. George Camerino)

Her return-address name on office envelopes would be Mrs. George Camerino. When writing household business letters she would sign in the same way. If, however, her social stationery has "Mrs. George Camerino" printed on it, she would not have to type or write that name in parentheses beneath her signature. Most women abandon the use of their husband's first name in business life because it is not the easy, efficient way to conduct business.

Listing Her Name in Clubs and Organizations Traditionally an officer of a women's club or organization always listed herself by her husband's name. Not so today. Women are using their given name with their married name more frequently. It looks better on the masthead of a letter or on a benefit program or in the paper if all names are listed in the same form. Otherwise one sees a benefit committee listing that looks like this:

Chairman:	Mrs. George Seebury
Committee Members:	Lorna Brennan
	Mrs. Richard Feidman
	Nancy Jones (Mrs. Seldon)
	Mrs. Jane Jordan
	Anne Panaggio Terhune

Here we had a hodgepodge of form. The Chairman and Mrs. Feidman use their husbands' names. Nancy Jones likes everyone to know her first name, so she uses it with her husband's in parentheses. Jane Jordan is divorced, and by putting a "Mrs." in front of her name she lets the world know it. Lorna Brennan is single, but she *could* be married or unmarried, or a widow or a divorced woman. By not putting a "Miss" or "Mrs." in front of her name, she is simply herself, without any marital status. Anne Panaggio Terhune is a professional woman known during the day by Panaggio. In deference to her husband on social listings, she includes his last name, which is what I do, too. If one is well known by one's maiden name, it is helpful to benefit groups and certain organizations to combine one's maiden and married names. What one can well conclude is that there should be a uniform system of listing names, and the easiest way to arrive at such a listing is to have women listed as Jane Smith, whether they are married, single, or divorced.

It also follows that when a husband and wife must be listed together, such as on a country club roster, they should use George and Jane Smith, rather than Mr. and Mrs. George Smith.

Divorcée's Listing The custom of a divorcée's using her own family name in conjunction with her former husband's last name is falling out of use. In other words, if Phyllis Goldfarb married Arnold Miller and they were subsequently divorced, she should not be listed as a club officer or committee member as Mrs. Goldfarb Miller but rather as Phyllis Miller.

Joint Signatures Even if a letter expresses the joint thanks of a couple, the letter should be signed only with one name (not "Denise and Larry"). The signer should refer to the other one in his or her comments: "Larry and I both agreed that you are one of the world's great chefs." Joint signatures are suitable for postcards, Mailgrams, greeting cards, or good wishes written on a card that accompanies a present.

A Common First Name   If you have a usual first name like John, Mary, Betty, or Robert, you should always sign your last name so that the recipient of the charity benefit invitation or the postcard from Marrakesh will know who sent it to him. Most of us know several people by each of those first names.

Illegible Signatures   If you have an illegible signature, you should use paper that is printed or engraved with your name as often as possible. Use name and address stickers on your envelopes, or type or print your name beneath your signature. And have your name and address printed (at a slight extra cost) across your bank checks. You will prevent costly delays and mistakes in this manner.

Changing "Jr." and Other Suffixes   A man who is a Jr., a II, a III, or possibly a IV, usually needs to take action when the preceding holder of the name dies. A Jr. usually drops the "Jr." unless both he and his late father were so well known that to drop it would cause public confusion. (For example, Franklin Roosevelt, Jr., kept it after his father's death.) A man with a "II" after his name is not named for his father but for someone else in the family, perhaps an uncle or grandfather of the same name. Upon the death of the original holder of that name, he would drop the suffix "II," unless, again, there would be public confusion because both names were well known. Someone carrying the suffix III or IV usually keeps it until he dies, or until his predecessors have died and he is tired of using it, in which case he just drops it.

When such a suffix is dropped, usually nothing is necessary other than notification of certain people: for example, the voter's registration office, the Internal Revenue Service, one's clubs and associations, charge card business office, and, of course, the personnel department of one's company. When one renews a driver's license or a passport, the deletion must be noted at that time, too.

Social Security concerns itself primarily with numbers. A man with "Jr." on his name, or any other suffix, does not change his Social Security number by changing the suffix. When a man receives a check made out the old way (with "Jr." or the suffix), he simply endorses the check on the back first with the old way and then with the correct way underneath.

The Use of "Sr."   When a man drops the "Jr." upon the death of his father, and lives in the same home or even in the same town as his mother, his mother adds "Sr." to her name. In other words, when John Wilson's father died, John Wilson dropped the "Jr." after his name, but his mother, who lived nearby, became Mrs. John Wilson, Sr., so that she and her daughter-in-law would not become confused. When a father and son work in the same organization, the father is called Herbert Costello, and the son is called Herbert Costello, Jr. A call coming into the office switchboard, however, might elicit as a response from the operator, "Which one, Junior or Senior?"

Addressing Social Envelopes

If letters are handwritten, the envelopes should be, too. (The handwriting should, of course, be legible and neat.) If letters are typewritten, then the envelopes should be, too. In former days, one either omitted people's initials entirely, or else wrote out the middle names in full. Today, this no longer holds. If a person is known as James A. Hancock, he is addressed that way in the most formal of social invitations. Street-address abbreviations, however (like "Ave." for avenue and "St." for street), should not be used in writing the envelopes for formal invitations. Names of states traditionally had to be spelled out on invitation envelopes, but in order to help the Post Office sort the mail more efficiently, it is now correct to use the official state abbreviations, as in San Francisco, CA 94109.

Keeping Her Maiden Name   It is no longer a rarity in today's world for a woman to retain her maiden name upon marrying. In addressing invitations to a married couple when this is the case, the envelope should read:

> Mr. George Nelson and Ms. Anne Roberts
> Street address and apartment number
> City, state, and zip code

Notice that husband's and wife's names are on one line. If Anne Roberts uses her maiden name only for her professional life, of course, social invitations to the couple would be addressed to Mr. and Mrs. George Nelson. In newspaper announcements of the birth of a baby to a couple where the woman retains her maiden name throughout, Anne Roberts and George Nelson's baby's birth would be announced in the newspaper in this manner:

> Son Born to Anne Roberts
> And George Nelson

A son was born to Anne Roberts and George Nelson of Lansing, Michigan, yesterday at the Such-and-such hospital, Lansing. The child's mother, who has retained her maiden name, is the daughter of, etc.

Couples Living Together Without Marriage   When you are addressing the envelope for an invitation or a joint letter to a couple who are living together without benefit of marriage, you do not put both their names on one line, as you do with a married couple when the wife retains her own name. When a couple is not married, you write each name on a separate line, in alphabetical order. In other words, if George Nelson and Anne Roberts were *not* married, one would address an envelope to them in the following manner:

Mr. George Nelson
Ms. Anne Roberts
Street address
City, state, and zip code

A Homosexual Couple An openly professed homosexual couple should be considered a social entity and be invited to social functions on one invitation. Their names would be listed alphabetically on separate lines.

Hyphenated Names Sometimes when a couple marries, they share each other's last names by using both names hyphenated, the woman's first and the man's second. Under this system Anne Roberts and George Nelson would be known after marriage as "Mr. and Mrs. George Roberts-Nelson." Their progeny would also carry the hyphenated name. If the child of one hyphenated-name family marries the child of another hyphenated-name family, they will have to decide between them which names they will drop, in order to avoid four hyphenated last names! If a couple with hyphenated names divorce, each drops the name of the other unless the woman has custody of minor children bearing that hyphenated name, in which case she may wish to keep it, at least until the children are grown.

Addressing Mail to Children A girl from infancy is addressed in writing as "Miss Susan Priddy." She may wish to be known as "Ms." from the time she is in high school. In addressing a letter to a young man in this country, one can use "Master" until he is about eight (when he might find it very sissified and embarrassing). Then he is simply "Malcolm Jenkins" until high school years, when he assumes the "Mr."

Change of Address If you change your address, promptly notify all your friends and correspondents. You should, ideally, change the subscription address for all publications two to three months before the move. Fill out the Post Office change-of-address card and give it to your mail carrier or send it to the Post Office.

Business executives and professionals often send engraved cards announcing their move to clients, customers, and colleagues. They also send out the same information in printed form for general distribution.

People sometimes send out formal engraved announcements to their friends, too, concerning a move from one home to another, but it is easier and more economical to use simple postcards that are printed with the information that:

The Thomas Durkees have moved to
Such and such an address
City, state, and zip code
Area code and telephone number

There are amusing "We've moved" greeting cards that may be purchased at a stationer's. One way to reinforce the fact that you have moved is to have new address stickers printed that say "New Address" on the top line. If you put these on all of your communications for a period of six months, people should finally record your move in their files.

You might find that the hardest thing to do is to change your address for your store charge accounts and your credit cards. Sometimes it requires several reminders on your part before the computer finally comprehends your new address.

Remember not to use crossed-out, corrected printed or engraved stationery for more than six months after you have moved. It looks bad enough whenever one uses it, but after a long period of time it looks downright tacky.

The Use of "Personal," "Please Forward," and "Opened by Mistake"

It is always assumed that a letter sent to a person's home will be opened only by the addressee. It is therefore rude to other members of the family to mark such a letter "Personal." If, however, you are addressing a purely social, and perhaps quite confidential, letter to a person in his or her office where there is likelihood that mail is first opened by a secretary, then the use of "Personal" in the lower left-hand corner of the envelope is permissible.

If you know only a former address, not the present one, of the person to whom you are writing, you may write in the lower left-hand corner of the envelope, "Please Forward."

In our urban areas, where many people live in large apartment buildings, there is often more than one resident having the same last name. This often creates the embarrassing situation of your receiving and opening another person's mail. In this case, you reseal the envelope, mark it "Opened by Mistake," sign your name, and mail it for the Post Office to redeliver. Do not attempt to deliver it in person. Legally, this will protect you in the event the mail is lost.

The Use of "Mesdames"

The French word "Mesdames" is used very seldom, only when addressing a group of women without any name as a reference, for example:
The Women's Christian Temperance Union
Address
Mesdames:

The title is not preceded by "Dear."

The Use of "Messrs."

"Messrs." is the abbreviated form of the French for "Misters." It should be used only for letters addressed to brothers, never as an address for father and son. It is always used instead of the English word. In sending a Christmas card or a wedding invitation to two young men in a family that includes several others to whom you do *not* wish to address the card or invitation, you write, "The Messrs. Guy and Donald Parsons." If there are merely the two brothers in the family you may address them as "The Messrs. Parsons" or simply "Messrs. Parsons." (See "Wedding Invitations and Announcements," page 136, for further information on this point.)

Chapter 42

LETTER WRITING: THE ULTIMATE
IN HUMAN COMMUNICATION

Long before telephones, Mailgrams, or television, people had to put pen to
paper if they wanted to express themselves to someone who lived elsewhere.
Today the easiest and the best way to communicate with one another is still
that written word. The letters left to us by the great figures of the seventeenth, eighteenth, and nineteenth centuries constitute a treasure trove of
history and sociology. (One may well shudder to contemplate the reactions
of our descendants in the year 2500 if they judge us by our TV tapes, records, telexes, and computer printouts!) We are not living in a culture of letter writers, but rather of fast communicators, with no motivation to pursue
the beauty of expression.

I often wonder when writing a letter to someone I haven't seen for a long
time and to whom I have much to relate, "Will he or she possibly save this
letter?" If I think the person might, I tear it up and start over again, paying
attention to the manner in which I express myself and the organization,
punctuation and style of the letter. (I also type it, so that no one in future
years will ever judge my bad handwriting!) I would hate anyone in the year
2050 to come across one of my usual hastily written, careless letters, and to
judge me on its merits.

There is nothing more pleasant than receiving a beautiful letter. It can inform, console, thank, express love, indignation. It can persuade, dissuade,
congratulate, chide, cajole, inspire, or say very effectively "I'm sorry." There
is nothing within the range of human emotions that cannot be expressed by
the reflective written word. It is sad that the world of instant communications has made us so lazy that we are losing the ability to communicate our real selves to each other on paper. It is easy to communicate
information via computers, but the computer cannot convey the emotions
of the heart.

It is often easier to write our deep feelings than to verbalize them face to
face or on the telephone. We should try all through our lives to develop
this gift of writing, to form good habits with our pen and paper, and never

to short-cut our friends and the people we love by ignoring the one most sensitive tool of communication we share.

The Form of Your Letters

The Correct Form for Social Letters If the writer's stationery bears no return address at the top, then she must fill in her own return address in the upper right-hand corner:

> 2450 Lakeview Avenue
> Chicago, Illinois   zip code
> The date

Dear Linda,
    The body of the letter begins here.

> Sincerely, [or affectionately, or
>   whatever you wish to use]
> [signed] Sandy

The writer should center the letter, leave good margins on both sides, and skip between paragraphs. A letter should not contain too many exclamation marks or dashes. If you misspell a word, try to correct it. If the word looks incredibly messy, start over again. If you don't have time, or if it's a very long letter, cross out the misspelled word and write it correctly directly overhead.

If you spill something on a letter that is just begun, start it over again. If you spill something on a completed letter, put a P.S. and explain at the end, "The baby just knocked my drink over on the letter. Sorry!" or "If you noticed a big grease spot, you are absolutely right. I put this letter down too close to the sizzling hamburgers. Apologies."

Dating Your Social Communications When you are writing a casual social note, it is all right to use just "Tuesday." But if your letter has any meaning, if it requires any answer or a follow-up, you should always date it in full. If you take the time and make the effort to write a good letter to someone, put the full date on it, because the chances are that letter will be saved, and it will have no value to anyone, sentimental or otherwise, if it is discovered much later and no one knows its date. I recently came across a letter that had been buried in an old school foot locker. It was dated August 14, 1945. I had saved it because it was beautiful and memorable, a letter charged with emotion, prayer, and retrospection. The word "war" was not mentioned once, but there were references to "it" being over. I checked the calendar, and the date was indeed V-J Day, when the Japanese surrendered in World War II. My friend had lost a brother in that war, but the letter expressed only joy and no sadness. Finding it again, more than thirty years later, it cut through time with incredible speed, and along with the bittersweet memories, it made me realize how few of us communicate anything of ourselves to anyone any more.

Sequence of Pages in a Letter   The envelope determines how a single sheet of paper is to be folded for insertion, in one or two folds. Either way, the writing goes from the top down, then again from top down on the other side, never crosswise, of a single sheet. When a double sheet is used for a short letter the sequence is to write on page one, finish on page three. If all four pages are used, they may be in the usual sequence, one, two, three, four; or the letter may go from page one to four, then the paper may be opened out flat, and the balance written down the full folded-out page, with the sequence of pages numbered. The sequence is not important, but remember that if your paper is at all transparent you should not write on both sides, for it is impossible to read.

Sequence of Pages in an Informal   If an informal has a monogram or the name printed or engraved in the center of the first side, nothing is written on that side and the note begins, if it is a short one, on the inside below the fold. If the note is to be long enough, it may begin at the top of the page when the informal is opened out flat with the fold in a horizontal position and may follow on to the last page. An informal is exactly that. It doesn't necessarily require a full salutation of formal close. It may be as brief as this: "Maria— We are delighted you both can come. We'll have supper waiting for you from seven on. Juanita."

Handwriting Versus Typing   Personal notes should be handwritten, condolence letters in particular. Acceptances or regrets to formal invitations should be handwritten, too. If, however, your handwriting is as illegible and as ugly as mine, and if you know how to type and have access to a typewriter, it is preferable to type as many communications as you can. A person with bad handwriting can force himself to write a short invitation acceptance legibly enough to be understood; however, if he wishes to regret an invitation when an explanation is in order, he should type his reply. An example of this would be a reply to an invitation to the wedding of the daughter of an old college friend who lives far away. He should not send a cold formal regret on note paper, written by hand. Rather, he should write a letter on good-quality paper (typed if the handwriting is bad, written by hand if the penmanship is good), explaining how sorry he is that he and his wife cannot make the wedding, and offering their joint best wishes to the future bride and groom and their families. He should include some personal news of his own family in the letter. How much warmer and nicer that kind of regret is than the handwritten one that says in black ink on white notepaper:

> Mr. and Mrs. Henry Hodkins regret
> that due to absence from the city
> they will be unable to accept the kind invitation of . . .

The Age to Begin Note Writing

Children should learn from an early age that everything they receive as presents will be thanked for on their behalf by their parents, and that it will eventually become their responsibility to write their own thank-you notes.

Once a child has learned the rudiments of writing, a parent should help the child write a simple thank-you message that the child can then copy in his own hand, such as:

Dear Jerry,
Your party was fun. I liked it. Thank you,

Joey

The parent usually has to write the envelope when a child begins letter writing (so that the Post Office will be able to read the address), but gradually, as the child develops, he should compose his own thank-you notes, write them, and address them, too. He should also learn to stamp and mail his letters, so that the entire process is completed. He will not always have a grownup around to do these things for him, so he might as well learn all these steps by the age of nine. Here's a typically delightful letter I found in one of my children's "saved" piles, written by an eight-year-old friend:

Dear Clare,
Thank you for my game. We played it the other nite and it was grate. I only hit Robby once when he cheeted. Thank you for coming to my party.

A child should send a thank-you note (or a young child's parent should write on his behalf) to thank for presents, parties attended, and having been asked to "spend the night." If a child forms this habit early, he will carry it through his life, and will find that his good manners will always be one of his greatest assets.

The Thank-you Letter

One should approach such a letter as if it were made up of several interrelated parts. It's almost like having a check list with the goal of making sure that everything on the check list is taken care of in one's letter.

In a thank-you letter the following elements should be present:

1. A statement to the people you are thanking. Is it one person? A couple? Mother and daughter? An entire family?
2. Who is doing the thanking? (You alone? On behalf of your husband and yourself? Your children, too?) Only one person writes, but that person should thank on behalf of everyone involved.
3. Mention something noteworthy about the event or gift. (Great food! Good music! Pretty flowers on the table. Usefulness of the gift.)

4. It's nice to remark about the warm hospitality of the hosts or thoughtfulness of the giver.
5. If you have spent time in someone's home, add a special word about "how nice it was to meet" some new member of the host's family.
6. Always end in an upbeat, pleasant key.

The following are some typical thank-you leters (not letters worthy of saving by any means, but good bread-and-butter examples):

For a Meal or Weekend

Dear Margaret,

We owe you enormous thanks for last Sunday's lunch in Lake Forest. It was the perfect antidote for the children and ourselves, suffering as we were from city exhaustion. Neither you nor Horace could imagine what it meant to us to spend the day at your lovely home in that good clean air!

We all voted your saddle of lamb the best we have ever tasted, and Kathleen, our thirteen-year-old resident expert in the decorative arts, was taken by your porcelain frog full of daffodils. She's been complaining ever since about our unimaginative table settings at home.

We enjoyed the quick glimpse of your mother, by the way, who is in such good form. She continues to inspire me with her energy.

There is no question but that you two are masters at the art of making your guests feel at home. We were delightfully spoiled, so thanks to you both from all four of us.

Affectionately,

For a Present You should always write a thank-you note for a present, regardless of the occasion. If someone shows up at your house for dinner bearing a bottle of wine, a brief note is sufficient:

Dear Mac,

You were wonderful to come bearing gifts last night, and we have decided we can wait no longer than tonight to christen that excellent bottle of wine. Many, many thanks. We will toast you on the first sip—and probably the last!

Sincerely,

If someone sends you a handmade present, you should be particularly thoughtful with your note:

Dear Sue,

Not only could I never learn to be as creative as you, but I would never know even how to select the perfect wool color, as you do. You are a marvel. You have knitted me the perfect shawl, and I shall wear it everywhere, whether it's to warm up a fireside dress or to lend a dash of bravado to my jeans and shirt. You are the best friend in the world, and I appreciate every knit one, purl two, or whatever you did to make this magnificent present.

Affectionately,

When Someone Sends Money   When a person sends you a gift of money, do not mention the sum in your thank-you note. Just express your gratitude for "your generous check" or "for being so wonderfully kind."

Refusing a Gift   If you feel you should not accept a present, don't. Let your instincts be your guide. If a young girl receives a piece of jewelry from a man she hardly knows; if a young person is paid a large sum by a much older person for performing a simple service; if one feels there is a hint of bribery involved—send the check or gift back and say, "Thank you anyway, for being so thoughtful and kind." Be sure to make a carbon copy of this letter for your files.

The Retirement Gift   A person should write a thoughtful letter to all those fellow employees or associates who contributed toward his joint retirement gift. After expressing his thanks, the retiree should wish them all continued luck and mention how much each one of them has contributed to his enjoyment of his years with the firm.

Printed Thank-you Cards   There are many classic and "cute" thank-you cards that may be purchased in the marketplace today, and some people buy them, sign them, and mail them, thinking they have fulfilled their social duty after attending a dinner party, a wedding, or any kind of celebration. I feel these cards cannot compare in graciousness to a handwritten note. Gratitude cannot be advertised with a printed sign that spells out "Thank you." Gratitude is transmitted through the written word or through the voice on the telephone. (It's still better to write it; it requires more effort, and it's a permanent record.)

The Congratulatory Letter

It's a gracious gesture to call someone to congratulate him on his good fortune, but it is even nicer to set pen to paper. The recipient can reread your letter and feel good each time—and that means rereading it years from now, too.

Dear Carolyn,
Congratulations, to our new congresswoman from the great state of New York! We are positive that all of our troubles in our state are simply going to disappear now that you will be representing us in Washington.

We sat up all night watching the returns, and are so proud of what you have done in this campaign. The job demands the ability to cope, plus administrative talent and political and financial expertise.

You have it all. Mike joins me in sending you our heartiest congratulations.

Affectionately,

When you are writing a congratulatory note to someone you do not know intimately, write in a more restrained manner:

Dear Mrs. Hansen,

Although I am just one of the high school volunteers in your campaign headquarters, I had to write to tell you how glad we all are that you won the election. We are proud that you are the first woman elected from this district and we know you will make a great United States representative. Good luck to you.

Sincerely,

Writing After Hearing Bad News

Sometimes the written word can bring more comfort than any other factor when misfortune befalls someone. Whether a person is in an accident, has a divorce, becomes ill, or loses a job, it is a mark of friendship and the best kind of support to write a good letter. Even a brief note, slipped under the door of a person who has been fired, can help in many ways.

Dear Alice,

We have just heard about Howard's having been let go at the plant. It is bad news, but anything can be turned around into something good, and this will have to be one of those. He'll get a better job, be appreciated for the fine person he is, and have more opportunities.

We'll be home all weekend. If you and Howard will share a meal with us, we'd be pleased. Jim has some ideas I know he wants to talk over with Howard about his future. We are right here, two strong pairs of shoulders, waiting to be used. We love you both and we are waiting for your call.

Love,

Condolence Letters

A good condolence letter accomplishes the following:

1. It proves to the bereaved that one understands what a terrible, crushing blow the death is.
2. It praises in a personal way the person who has just died.
3. It evinces a sincere desire to be of some help to the family.

This is a time when a carefully thought out letter is necessary, because that letter will probably be read by several members of the family and close friends. It might be saved and passed down through the family.

One should always refer to personal memories of the deceased, if possible, showing how that person influenced the writer. "I remember the first time I met her at college. I was a greenhorn freshman and she was a 'sophisticated' sophomore. She checked into my room in the dorm that night and found me in combat with a bad case of homesickness. In fifteen minutes she had chased the blues away. She gave me a tour, introduced me to twenty of her friends and gave me an album as a 'Welcome' present. She has remained that way all through her life, helping people, chasing their blues away. She always seemed ready, strong, creative, compassionate, always somehow replenishing that abundance of kindness. Her death is crushing to me, too. I will miss her for as long as I live on this earth."

Always end your letter by saying "always be around" to help when needed. (And don't forget to make good on your promise.)

If you are not a close personal friend of the family of the person who has died, it is still a gracious gesture to write a condolence letter to a member of the family, even if you have never met that person:

Dear Mrs. Cargill,
Although I have never had the pleasure of meeting you, I wanted to express to you the great sadness felt by all of the volunteers here at the hospital who worked under your late husband. His loss is our loss, too, for he was an extraordinary man, who typified excellence, devotion to service, and human kindness all at once.

I speak for all of us when I say we stand ready to help in any possible way in the forthcoming months. Perhaps you would come visit us in the hospital someday. We would like to invite you to lunch; we would like to show you how he organized the volunteer service in this hospital, and tell you, each and every one of us, how much he meant to us as a person. We will miss him very much.

Sincerely,

If you plan to use references to religious faith in your letter of condolence, it helps to understand the religion of the person to whom you are writing. Each major religion—the Protestant, Catholic, and Jewish faiths—has its own way of viewing the afterlife, so one should be on firm ground before launching into religion as a means of consolation. It is correct to say to anyone, however, even to an agnostic, "I will always remember him in my prayers," as that is a personal act of love. Discrepancies of religious belief do not really matter if the effort to console is a sincere one, such as this letter a young Jewish widow showed me that touched her greatly when her husband died. An eleven-year-old Catholic girl sent it to her. The religion of the writer and the recipient differ as to a belief in what happens at death, but their God is the same. The girl wrote:

Dear Mrs. Wise,
It's just terrible that God desided to take Rabbi Wise so yung. It's really very meen of Him, because He must have knon we wanted Rabbi Wise to stay longer. I dont know if you believ in Purgatory and saints and all that stuff, but I do, and I just happen to know that with all our prayers Rabbi Wise went thru Purgtory awful fast, sort of like a car racer. So he's already

in Heavn with God and His Saints. (my favrit Saint is Mother Seton). God will take care of Rabbi Wise and you, too, now that youre lone. I'll do your dishes or sit with the baby anytime. Tell Ralfie I have a new rattle for him anyway.

Love,

The Impulse Note

This is the nicest kind of note to write or receive. It is unexpected; it does not "have" to be written. It is not connected with any special event, but arrives out of the blue. Since it is motivated by a pleasant thought, it always brings happiness with it, as in this note from one man to another:

Dear Gerry,

I couldn't resist writing to tell you that quite by accident I happened to see Rebecca playing this afternoon in the interschool tennis tournament. Knowing you were at the office, I paused to cast a critical eye on her playing, so that I could report to you. The report is A plus. She is an excellent player, strong and fast, steady and accurate. She obviously can beat her old man to ribbons. You would have been very proud to see her win this afternoon. . . .

Or another example of one man writing another:

Dear Joe,

Although we haven't seen each other for years, last night I thought of you when I came across an old photo taken during our "Greek Classic" senior play. It certainly evoked a few memories, especially the sight of you with your hairy legs and white tunic, headband, et al., in the role of Apollo. I was a similar sight as Mercury, with my winged feet molting feathers all over the stage. No wonder we made college history that night!

How are you, anyway, and your family? Let's have some news of you.

It's nice to write a cheering note to someone who's been ill for a long time:

Dear Genevieve,

I passed you on Main Street today and called from the taxi, but you didn't hear me. For someone who has been in the hospital for so long and who has had such a hard time, you looked elegant, slim, rested, and just plain beautiful. The hospital must have agreed with you. But it's nice to see you around again. Stay well.

All the best,

The Recorded Message

There is another tool of communication in use today that is very effective for people who are close to each other but living far apart. Instead of writing long letters, some people make a recording or a taped cassette of their voices, which may then be played over the recipient's own equipment. For a student studying abroad who can't get home for Christmas, for example, a wonderful gesture is the sending of personal messages and holiday greetings from the entire family through a record or a cassette tape. If someone is in the hospital, friends who tape their own voices sending him wishes to get well quickly, telling him the newest joke or the latest office gossip, and saying that "we really miss you" are real friends. If the electronic world seems hopelessly materialistic, it has its human aspects, too.

Letters of Apology

A letter of apology should be sincere and rather humble, or it probably won't accomplish its mission. Of course, if you owe someone an apology, it's better to make it first face to face, and then reinforce it with a note.

If you absolutely cannot face someone to whom you have done an injustice, take pen to paper and humbly ask forgiveness.

For example, a woman who made an ethnic slur in front of a friend who she did not know was of that culture, might write the victim of her remark a letter along the following lines:

. . . In saying what I did, I realize I have offended you badly, but myself, too, because it was a cruel, stupid, and bigoted remark. I hope someday you will say you will forgive me. The episode has taught me a very valuable lesson. I am only sorry that, in learning it, I had to hurt a good friend at the same time.

If you forget an engagement you have accepted, such as a dinner party (and I have done this more than once in my life), you should telephone the hosts to apologize, but you should also write them a letter and accompany it with flowers.

Letters of Social Reference and Introduction

You should never send a letter of introduction for social purposes unless you know both parties extremely well. It is otherwise an imposition on the person to whom you write, for you are really commanding that person to entertain the people whom you are writing about.

If you have *really* good friends living in a city to which other very close friends of yours are moving, it is nice to introduce the newcomers to the established friends, but it is an imposition nevertheless. If there is any business connection between the two parties, the letter of introduction should emanate from one office to the other, rather than through personal channels, although the onus is still on the wife to entertain the new arrivals immediately:

Dear George,

Our corporate counsel, Keith Waddington, and his family are moving to your fair town. I told him that once he gets established in our offices there, he should call you, take you to lunch, and get some good tips on the business community. He also needs help on getting into the Athletic Club. He is a bright guy in his forties, and will make, along with his attractive family, a nice addition to Pittsburgh.

It is important that Keith make contacts outside of our corporation. That is why I am writing you to do me this favor. Thank you in advance, and I hope all goes well for you and your family.

Sincerely,

If a letter of introduction is a social one—for example, from one wife to another, introducing a new couple in town—the letter should be as informative as possible, without sounding like a recitation from a Personal History Statement. One should never ask for immediate action on the letter. Leave any action up to the person to whom one is writing, so she will not feel pressured and forced into doing something during an overly hectic time in her life:

Dear Madge,

Our very good friends Isabelle and Gerald Monahan are moving next week to Phoenix—he to be an executive vice-president of the Blank Corporation. Isabelle has run our hospital's women's board for the past five years, with a track record that has exceeded every other chairman's in the hospital's history.

The Monahans are our age; their two children (fifteen and seventeen) are away at boarding school. Both are passable bridge players, but are excellent tennis players. She is also a trap shooting expert (holds several titles) and he is an expert gardener and a conservation buff.

When you have some time, we would appreciate your giving them a call [insert the Monahans' new address and telephone number], but only when life is less hectic for you both.

We are well . . . [continue to give your family news and finish].

Sending Tourists to Friends Living Abroad

One often hears this reaction to someone's announcement that he is "leaving for Hong Kong next week": "That's great. You must look up my good friends the Johnny Peabodys."

Of course, the truth is that the Johnny Peabodys don't want friends looking them up. They are probably having a hard enough time trying to lead their own lives in Hong Kong without a continuous flow of American tourists and business people tramping to their door for free drinks or, worse, a free meal. Having myself suffered through eleven years abroad receiving "friends of friends of friends," I can only beg everyone not to send tourist friends, unless you make it very clear to the visitors that:

1. *They*, not your foreign-based friends, are to pick up the dinner check.
2. If they go to your friend's house for a drink, they should bring along a bottle of liquor or some other gift.
3. They should let your friends go home to bed at a decent hour, because the foreign-based friends, unlike your tourist friends, have to work the next day.

If you do send good friends to good friends in another country, be sure to write in advance. Explain who your friends are, where they'll be staying, and how long, and emphasize the fact that you understand perfectly if they are too busy to invite your tourist friends to anything.

Letters to Public Figures

One should never impose oneself or one's family on anyone who is in the public eye. People of prominence, politicians, and newsmakers have to devote a good deal of time fending off—or teaching their staff how to fend off—the public. And "the public" includes people who claim to be their good friends, too. Never presume too much. People who live in the limelight deserve their own moments of privacy. If you happen to be often in contact with a prominent person in your work or on some special project, don't overwhelm him with attention. Let the first invitation come from the prominent person. Don't pelt him with requests, invitations, and what you consider are ego-flattering moves. The celebrity might be antagonized by those moves.

If your child wants a special autograph or picture of someone you know, ask a member of that person's staff to cope with your request, whether by telephone or by letter.

If you have praise to send to an author after reading his book, or to an actor, singer, musician, or dancer, after seeing his performance, by all means write him. Even if the note is never answered, you will bring that person great pleasure. People who bring excellence to the world deserve to be praised.

As for the celebrity, he *should* acknowledge his fan mail, even if the acknowledgment is made by a staff member. I know many famous people who write little notes themselves to people who write them. Sometimes they carry little note cards or even postcards in their briefcase or handbag.

But do not expect a personal letter in return for your letter to anyone who is prominent in politics, the arts, sports, or the entertainment fields. This should not stop you from stating your views, however, or expressing your admiration or your criticism (constructively). If we place people in positions of power or adulation, we have a right to express our opinions to them.

Writing to the White House   Since a President and his family receive anywhere from two thousand to twenty thousand letters per week, there is probably no way in which your letter will be seen by any member of the presidential family, unless your letter is tagged as one of the "every thousandth" letters that are shown to the Chief Executive or the First Lady. Careful tabulations are made by the staff and sent to them, of course, on how popular opinion is running on each issue. Therefore, your voice is heard in those tabulations. But it is unrealistic to think your letter will make its way to the desk of a member of the First Family, except quite by accident.

Close friends and relatives of the First Family are often apprised of a code word that they are told to place on their envelopes in a certain place. These letters go directly to the First Family recipients. The rest of us simply have to recognize that an overburdened staff member is going to open our letters, comply with our requests (if they are possible ones, such as asking for a signed photograph), and acknowledge our letter with a short reply.

Persuading People in Power   You can exercise your rights in our free society and influence a governor, a legislator, the mayor, the school board or the chairman of the board of a company about to make a decision by writing a letter or sending an articulate Mailgram. But remember certain things:

1. Make your message short and concise. Never let a person reading your communication say to himself, "Whatever is this person talking about?"
2. No mater how furious or partisan you may feel, keep your emotions in check. Logic is effective; emotions are not, in discussing an issue. If your message is filled with emotional vitriol, the recipient's staff will probably throw it away, marking the sender as another crackpot.
3. Always be polite. Never criticize in a harsh, rude way. There is a great deal of difference between saying, "It might have been wiser to have considered an alternative to . . ." and "That was a dumb, stupid thing to do."
4. Define succinctly the group that you represent, whehter you are a party voter or speaking for a specific institution or organization, or just for yourself as a father, or a mother, a schoolteacher, an environmentalist, a teen-ager, or a pensioner.

Asking Permission to See a Private Collection   If you have an acquaintance who allows people to visit her private art collection or very special garden, you might write her a note like this:

Dear Mrs. Gardiner,

The next time you open your gardens to a visiting group, may I have the pleasure of seeing them, too? I have been so anxious to view them, but I also know how pressed for time your entire staff is, and I would never want to invade your privacy. If, however, you have arranged for a group to come at a certain hour, perhaps someone on your staff would call me at the number listed above, and I could tag along with them.

Now, Mrs. Gardiner might react by sending you a note telling you to come see her gardens any time. But then again, she might not. At least you will have tried to see the gardens "the polite way."

Writing for a Donation   One of the most effective ways of fund raising is the personal appeal, written by hand or typed, from one person to another. In writing a personal letter to raise funds, make your letter short and to the point, and instead of describing in detail what the charity does, send supporting materials—like a brochure, a pamphlet, or duplicated copies of good articles that appeared in the press. Don't send too much material: it will discourage the recipient and he or she might not read any of it.

Mr. Malcolm Cheevers
President, Cheevers, Inc.
Street address
City, state, and zip code

Dear Mr. Cheevers,
    The work of the Southwest Chapter of *Reading to Blind Graduate Students* has benefited from your company's generosity for five consecutive years. Because of your past contributions, Cheevers, Inc., has made it possible for many students to finish their studies, receive their degrees, and find jobs. I don't think I have to describe in detail what this means to those young people and their families.
    We have been so heartened by our past success that we have expanded our operations in this region and have doubled the number of students receiving assistance. (The attached brochure tells this story.) I am therefore asking you to double your contribution to our reading program and to sign the enclosed pledge card for $1,000 this year instead of $500. It is only thanks to you, Mr. Cheevers, and other concerned businessmen in our area, that we are able to carry out the ambitious task we are determined to accomplish. I will gladly visit your office any time to answer any questions you might have, or you may telephone me at any time.
    Thank you for your wonderful help and support during these important years of our efforts to help the blind.

Sincerely,

Writing Personal Business Letters

Ordering from a Store   If you order merchandise from a store or mail order catalogue, always be sure to list the name of the item, the page in the catalogue (or the page of the ad in the newspaper or magazine). State the size, quantity, pattern, and/or color of the item ordered (as applicable), as well as second color choice. If monogramming is to be done, draw the initials clearly. State whether you are enclosing your check (and give the check number and amount, if you are) and where the merchandise is to be sent. If you are charging it to your account number or a credit card, be sure to give all information. Make your letter so complete (be sure to keep a carbon copy of it) that the clerk handling your order can expedite it at once and will not have to write back to you for a missing piece of information. Our own inefficiency in ordering causes interminable delays in shipping, plus extra costs in postage and clerks' time in corresponding with us. Whenever there is an order blank available, as in a catalogue, one should use it, but catalogue executives tell a sad story of how many people fail to read the blanks entirely and consequently leave off important information time and time again. If you are writing a letter rather than sending in a mail order blank, end your letter with something polite: "Thank you so much for taking care of this order promptly for me." It will make the person handling your incoming letter feel he is dealing with an efficient, nice person. Even if you use a memorandum form to write to a company, the last sentence should be a polite one.

Making Reservations   I find that using a travel agent saves me an unknown quantity of time, money, and aggravation. If you like to arrange your own travel plans, here again you must carefully think through your communications with the place where you wish to reserve rooms, so that all necessary information will be given in one communication and so that time will not be wasted by the hotel or resort's having to write back before it can confirm the booking.

Remember, in writing for reservations:

1. Give the names of everyone in your party.
2. Give the number of rooms, the kind of beds, and the number of baths needed.
3. State the exact dates. If you will be arriving late in the evening, say so, to avoid having the hotel give away your rooms.
4. State how you will be paying (cash, personal check, or credit card).
5. If you are joining a special group but arriving separately from them, say so. (There may be a special rate involved.)
6. Ask the Reservation Department to call you immediately to inform you if there is any trouble in handling your reservations. And ask for a written confirmation on your reservation (which usually first requires a deposit).

Letters of Complaint   If you want to complain to a neighbor or a friend, whether it's about their dog, the way their children behave, or the fact they don't cut their grass and mow their hedges, it is better to talk to them face to face, keeping the voice pleasant and the mood light. The interreaction of human voices usually settles the problem more quickly than the exchange of letters. The written word, with emotional overtones, has too many interpretations.

However, all of us have problems, inquiries, and complaints to address to retailers, institutions, or government offices. Again, if you can handle a complaint or an inquiry by calling direct, do so. You will have less chance being the victim of an incompetent clerk or a stubborn computer.

When you do write a firm, be sure you have all pertinent information detailed and your case made clear in the letter or memorandum:

I would like to remind you of the following:

1. On January 13 I ordered by letter a man's bathrobe as pictured in your New York *Times* ad of that day, page 14. A copy of my letter is enclosed, as well as a copy of my canceled check made out to you for $48.50 to cover the cost of the robe and city tax.

2. On March 30, after telephoning your store three times to inquire what had happened to the robe, a package arrived from you containing a totally different robe in a different size. I notified your store immediately of the error and asked to have it picked up by your delivery truck.

3. On April 20 the package was picked up, three weeks after I had reported the error to you.

4. On April 25 I received my monthly statement from your store, on which is included a charge for $48.50 for a man's robe. Not only had you already cashed my check for the robe, but I was left without the robe and with an additional billing for it on my statement!

I hope you will straighten out this comedy of errors at once, because your store has always stood for good merchandise and superior service. I would hate to think I would have to discontinue my loyalty to you.

Since I had to purchase another man's robe elsewhere, I do not wish you to send me the one I ordered originally. Enough is enough. Thank you for attending to this matter.

Sincerely,

Sending a Memorandum The women's movement has made us very gender-conscious about the person to whom we are writing. There is no doubt that a man who handles requests for information at a women's college grows tired day after day of being addressed as "Dear Madam." And a woman who handles hundreds of letters a week in the store mail order department should logically become irritated by a constant stream of "Dear Sirs" passing through her hands. There is a very simple solution to this problem. When you have no information about the person to whom you are writing on a business matter, write your communication in a memo form, rather than a letter, because it makes no reference to gender. For example, if you want a college catalogue mailed to you, you would write a memo on your own stationery:

Marilyn Barnes
2450 Lakeview Avenue
Chicago, Illinois   zip code

July 24, 19—

MEMO FOR: Vassar College
Admissions Office
Poughkeepsie, New York   zip code

RE: Request for Catalogue

I would appreciate your sending me a Vassar catalogue to the above address. Thank you very much.

[signed] Marilyn Barnes

Or, if Ms. Barnes were writing about an order not received:

Marilyn Barnes
2450 Lakeview Avenue
Chicago, Illinois   zip code

September 30, 19—

MEMO FOR: The Penfarb Corporation
Street address
City, state, and zip code

RE: My order for pen-flashlights

I have not yet received the four pen-flashlights I ordered from a *New Yorker* ad of June 27. My check ⚡4301 dated 6/30/78 on the Northern Trust Bank for the sum of $32.85, which included shipping charges, was enclosed. Your ad stated delivery would be made within four weeks. I would appreciate an explanation for the delay as soon as possible, and thank you for your prompt reply.

[signed] Marilyn Barnes

By using a memo form rather than a "Dear Sirs" or "Dear Madam" or "Gentlemen," one does not make an error of sex in writing to an unknown person. Of course, if you have the name of the person in a company, it is always better to address him or her personally. Most of the time we do not have a name; we are writing into a void, so the memo form is the most efficient. It is important to remember to end the memo with some note of politeness, with the words "please" or "thank you for" somewhere in the text.

Using Postcards

Postcards are efficient, inexpensive ways of communicating. One may properly use a postcard for a thank-you for something like a cocktail party or an afternoon of bridge at someone's house; one would not write a thank-you note for a formal dinner party, a dance, or a weekend invitation on a postcard. Nor should a postcard be used to say thank you for a gift.

Postcards make good business communicators, when one is writing on personal business matters, whether it's to the dry cleaners about correcting a bill or to the head of the PTA about missing a forthcoming meeting.

Postcards are friendly communicators. When old friends congregate in a restaurant and send a postcard to a missing member, it means a great deal to the recipient.

One must remember, however, that many pairs of eyes see a postcard, so nothing of a serious nature or requiring confidential treatment should be written on them.

It does not matter whether the postcard you use is one of the Alamo, a Rubens painting, or a mountain in the Alps, or one that is printed with your name and address on it in letterhead form.

Greeting Cards

Just sending a greeting card with your signature below the printed text is not a proper form of communication. Greeting cards are fine in themselves, but they are not complete. They must be personalized. They must include a written message, however small, unless they are used merely as gift enclosures. (And that is an expensive habit!)

We Americans are the largest users of greeting cards in the world. Many are charming, amusing, and clever, and they fill many needs, like communicating on Valentine's Day or wishing the Irish good luck on St. Patrick's Day. They are, however, no substitute for written notes.

They should also be chosen with discretion. After attending a dinner party over which both host and hostess have labored long and hard, one would not send a card showing a house wrecked with the legend "Wow! What a party!" Nor would one send a young person a birthday card showing a drunk celebrating. (Come to think of it, that kind of card is suitable for *no one.*) One does not send the "dirty" studio cards available on the market to anyone. Poor taste is poor taste in any language for any age.

Generally a greeting card requires no acknowledgment other than a verbal one when you meet the person who sent it. If someone from another city, however, remembers your birthday or anniversary you should reply, even if it's a three-sentence note thanking that person for remembering.

Discretion must be used when sending a "get-well" card or a "Sorry you're in the hospital" kind. If someone is not going to get well and knows it, if someone is actually dying, it would be tactless to send a get-well card. There are cards to send that bring cheer without being ridiculous or ironic.

But it cannot be repeated too often: a greeting card sent without a handwritten personal touch—without even one written phrase—is sterile.

Christmas Cards

The spirit of Christmas is destroyed when someone sits down to address hundreds of engraved or printed Christmas cards without even signing a name to them by hand. It's an even more hollow gesture when the only reason motivating the person laboring away on the pile of Christmas cards is that he or his family will be deluged with incoming cards from the same people to whom he is addressing envelopes.

The only real card in the spirit of Christmas is one signed by hand or one with an engraved or printed name combined with a brief message such as "How are you? We miss hearing your news."

When the sending of Christmas cards begins to take on gargantuan and impersonal proportions, the time has come to reconsider the entire project. If others notice you have stopped sending cards, they will probably cross you off their over-swollen lists with relief (if they even bother to reconcile the names of those who sent them cards with their list of those to whom they sent cards).

The sending of Christmas cards makes sense when you are communicating with those whom you do not see for long periods of time—people who live in other cities or in other countries. Christmas cards sent to family and close friends (whom one seldom sees) that contain a family photo or the latest picture of the children are appreciated by most people. It is rewarding to watch the progress of the children through the years in their photographs contained in Christmas cards. However, a snapshot cover of the Christmas card portraying only the family pet can cause negative reactions. (I remember receiving one of a friend's family turtle in full color one year; we considered it a mockery of sorts of Christmas.) Christmas cards showing a drunken Santa Claus are also in poor taste, even for a business card.

The practice of buying one's holiday greeting cards from a museum or from a charity—when a large share of the proceeds from the sale of the card goes to that institution—is a laudable one.

Sending Cards to Jews   One should not send religious cards to Jews, and some are sensitive about receiving any "Christmas" cards whatsoever. Usually one knows how one's Jewish friends feel about it; the majority of them like to be remembered by a "holiday greetings" card. Some Jews send their Christian friends Hanukkah cards, too. This exchange of cards is done in a warm spirit of friendship and in celebration of each other's religious feasts.

Sending of Business Christmas Cards Business holiday cards have become a way of life for some companies. These cards are usually printed with the name of the firm (and not with the names of the owner or president of the company and spouse). In other words, most business holiday cards read: "With warmest wishes for a happy holiday season from The Jones Company" (and not from "Mildred and Roy Jones," particularly since Mildred Jones may not have ever met most of the recipients of her husband's firm's cards).

Addressing Personal Christmas Cards and Signing Them When sending a personal Christmas card, you should address it to both husband and wife, even if you know only one of the pair. If the wife has retained her maiden name, you address the envelope with the husband's name first and the wife's maiden name following on the same line. If you don't know the present marital status of your friend, send it to his office, not his home, addressed to him alone.

On signing the inside of the card, many follow the British tradition and put the man's name first on the card: e.g., "John and Marian Jones." However, it does not matter if it reads "Marian and John Jones." It is a question of individual preference. If a card is being sent from the entire family, one may take the family name and pluralize it: "From the Robert K. Reillys, Jr.," or "From the Robert K. Reilly, Jrs." (Notice how "Jr." can be made plural or the last name made plural, but not both at once, as in "the Robert K. Reillys, Jrs.")

Chapter 43

INVITATIONS, ACCEPTANCES, AND REGRETS

When to Invite

Invitations should be sent out three weeks before most events. They should be sent out four weeks before large formal parties; and during the Christmas holiday season, they may be sent out around the Thanksgiving holiday, in order to enable others to plan their own parties and still avoid a conflict with your date.

Formal Invitations

Formal invitations, engraved or handwritten on conservative paper, are used for occasions such as a large dinner party, a debut, a formal dance, an important lunch or cocktail reception, and a wedding. They are written in the third person. Today these invitations may also be engraved in color on contrasting stock; they may have a colored border, too.

"Miss" and "Ms." are now interchangeable in the wording of these invitations. It is a matter of preference, and if a young woman is sending out her own invitations, she may properly use "Ms." in referring to herself or her friends. (Ms. Janet Sorlen requests the pleasure of Ms. Blaine's company at dinner, etc.)

The Engraved Fill-in Invitation to a Formal Dinner   There are two kinds of engraved fill-in invitations suitable for a formal dinner party. In the first, the hosts' names are engraved:

Mr. and Mrs. Lawrence McKwaid
request the pleasure of

Ms. Tuckerman's*
company at   *dinner*
on   *Wednesday, the third of May*
at   *eight o'clock*

1000 Mason Street
San Francisco, California

R.S.V.P.   Black Tie

Another kind of engraved fill-in invitation, such as the sample below, which happens to be red engraving with a red border on white stock, has less engraving and more handwriting:

Mr. and Mrs. James Van Westering
request the pleasure of your company

at   *Dinner and Dancing*
on   *Saturday, January thirteenth*
at   *eight-thirty*   o'clock
The Onwentsia Club
Lake Forest

R.S.V.P.   *1500 Lake Shore Drive*
Chicago, Illinois   zip code   *Black Tie*

Invitation to a Formal Dance

Mrs. Richard William Horst
requests the pleasure of
Mr. and Mrs. Thompson's
company at a small dance
on Saturday the sixteenth of September
at half after ten o'clock
Lotus Beach Club

R.S.V.P.   Black Tie
One Silver Lane
Palm Beach, Florida   zip code

* *Italic* type indicates handwriting.

(The wording "small dance" in the above invitation is often used whether the dance is large or small.)

When a Guest May Bring Along an Escort

Mr. and Mrs. Gordon Smyth Cummings
request the company of
Miss Melissa McKee and escort
[OR IN THE CASE OF A MAN, MR. MARK MCKEE AND GUEST]
at a small dance
in honour of their daughter and son
on Saturday, June the tenth
at eight o'clock
Edgemere Country Club

R.S.V.P.   Black Tie
14 Apple Tree Road
Larchmont, New York   zip code

Invitation to a Formal Dance when the Reply Is Sent to the Social Secretary

Mr. F. Vernon Osborne
requests the pleasure of
Mr. Scott's
company at a small dance
in honour of his niece
Ms. Amanda Osborne
on Friday, the twenty-ninth of December
at eleven o'clock
Montclair Country Club

R.S.V.P.   Black Tie
Mrs. Van Broeck
8 East First Street
Montclair, New Jersey   zip code

Handwritten Invitation to a Formal Dinner   The formal written invitation may be written on any personal formal writing paper, usually white. If the stationery does not have the address at the top the address is written at the bottom underneath the time.

*Dr. and Mrs. Walter Mac Fee
request the pleasure of
Mr. and Mrs. Anderson's
company at dinner
on Wednesday, September the sixth
at eight o'clock*

*R.S.V.P.   Poppy Villa   Black Tie
Beverly Hills, California Zip Code*

For a Dinner in Honor of a Special Guest

Mr. and Mrs. Gerald Fox Healy
request the pleasure of
Mr. and Mrs. Buxton's
company at dinner
on Monday, September the eleventh
at eight o'clock to meet
Mr. Johnson Parker

R.S.V.P.   Black Tie
21A Sutton Place
New York, New York   zip code

Invitation to a Debutante Dance

Mr. and Mrs. Macy Linde Turner
request the pleasure of
the company of
Miss Lippincott
at a dance in honour of their granddaughter
Miss Charlotte Gilchrist
on Saturday, the third of February
at ten o'clock
River House

The favour of a reply is requested   Black Tie
998 Fifth Avenue
New York, New York   zip code

or, if the parents give the dance:

Mr. and Mrs. David Filmore Gilchrist
Miss Charlotte Sue Gilchrist
request the pleasure of
the company of
Mr. Butterly
on Saturday, the third of February
at ten o'clock
31 Sutton Place South
New York, New York   zip code

R.S.V.P.   Dancing
                                                                       Black Tie

Though on wedding invitations the "Miss" is virtually always omitted,
"Miss" or "Ms." appears on social formal ones. Note that the phrase "in
honour of" does not appear when the debutante's name is listed under the
parents'. (The reason for this is that a debutante can't "honour" herself.)
For an invitation to a small dance the guest's name is frequently not
handwritten and the phrase "request the pleasure of your company at a
small dance" is substituted.

Invitation to a Debutante Reception

Mr. and Mrs. David Filmore Gilchrist
Ms. Charlotte Sue Gilchrist
At Home
Saturday, February third
at five o'clock
31 Sutton Place South
New York, New York   zip code

R.S.V.P.

Invitation to an Official Luncheon

Mr. and Mrs. J. Peter Morton, Jr.

request the pleasure of your company

at a luncheon in honour of

His Excellency, the President of Chile

and

Señora de Martinez-Garcia

Sunday, the twenty-fourth of March

at one o'clock

R.S.V.P.   Aboard

17 Gracie Square   The "Mermaid"

New York, New York   zip code   Long Island Yacht Club

The abbreviation "J." above is permissible when the first name is never used. If necessary, engraved or printed directions with or without a map should be included when the party is held at a place not familiar to everyone.

More Than One Issuing the Invitation When friends are giving a party together, their invitations might be engraved as follows:

Ms. Alice Baldwin

Ms. Eileen O'Gara

Ms. Natasha Yatsevitch

request the pleasure of

Mr. Kahn's

company at dinner

before The Cotillion

on Saturday, December twenty-third

at eight o'clock

834 Fifth Avenue

R.S.V.P.   Black Tie

Mrs. Peter Yatsevitch

834 Fifth Avenue

New York, New York   zip code

If you are organizing a formal dance without the proper lead time (because, let us say, a good friend suddenly announces she will arrive from abroad), you would do better to invite everyone by Mailgram. Use the same terminology you would use on an engraved invitation in your Mailgram: even the same layout.

Accepting Formal Invitations

The manner of acknowledging formal invitations follows an exacting protocol with a handwritten note in the third person on very conservative stationery. Here is an example of such a formal written acceptance in the third person. It follows the same general form whether it is to a dance, dinner, reception, or any other formal entertainment. Incidentally, when replying to an invitation from people whose name is followed by Jr., M.D., or II, you omit these suffixes in your answer. Note, however, that the reply repeats the date and the time. The envelope is addressed, unlike answers to informal invitations, to *both* the host and hostess, as is the reply.

Mr. and Mrs. John Forrestal
accept with pleasure
the kind invitation of
Dr. and Mrs. Gudefin
to dinner
on Saturday, the fifteenth of June
at eight o'clock

Today it is also acceptable in replying to a formal invitation to use the telephone, send a Mailgram, or write a third-person acceptance on any good stationery, including letter paper in a color with a contrasting colored monogram or crest. In using the Mailgram acceptance be sure to write the hour and the day:

Mr. and Mrs. Clinton Dorchester accept with pleasure the kind invitation of Mr. and Mrs. Miller to lunch on December fourth at the St. Regis at two o'clock

The important thing to remember is that all R.S.V.P. invitations require an immediate answer.

If you should happen to run into your hosts on the street, and you mention, "We just received the invitation today, and we will be delighted to come," this does not constitute a reply. You must write one or telephone it. Otherwise, your hosts may forget to include you on the list of acceptances, in which case you would arrive at the St. Regis suite and find no places at the table.

R.S.V.P. Cards It is a matter of choice whether or not to include a printed or engraved R.S.V.P. card if you are giving a large dinner dance or a charity function or any event of importance. It may be a sad commentary on today's manners, but if you need to have an immediate response, such a card is useful. Even the laziest of recipients of an invitation, when confronted with a response card which he has only to put a check mark upon and then seal it in the attached stamped envelope, will tend to dispatch the envelope rather promptly.

It is too bad we have come to this; however, we are there, and therefore, one has to admit that a filled-in response card is socially acceptable for anything other than wedding invitations. Perhaps for the invitations of tomorrow we will only have to nod affirmatively or negatively at a computer screen when an invitation arrives in our mail! We seem to be headed in that direction.

When One of a Couple Accepts   If a husband and wife receive an invitation to a formal occasion, such as a wedding or a dance, and only one is able to accept, the acceptance is stated first and the regret follows:

Mrs. Henry Leary
accepts with pleasure
the kind invitation of
Mr. and Mrs. Greene
for Tuesday, November seventh
at ten o'clock
Mr. Henry Leary regrets
that he will be unable to accept
because of absence from the city

Regrets to a Formal Invitation

In regretting, as in accepting, a formal invitation there is an exacting protocol. A formal regret usually states briefly in a word or two the reason for the refusal—"because of their [her] absence from town," "because of a previous engagement," "because of illness"—but it is often better to omit the reason when illness is involved, except in refusing a most important summons such as one to the White House. If you refuse an invitation, you are not obligated to reciprocate.

Mr. Preston Moore
sincerely regrets
that because of a previous engagement
he will be unable to accept
Mr. and Mrs. Treadwell's
kind invitation for the third of August

When Not to Send a Formal Regret for a Formal Invitation   If you cannot attend a formal party, such as a wedding or debut, and you are very close to those extending the invitation, you should not just write the cold, formal reply dictated by strict etiquette. You should call or write a note, explaining the reasons why you will not be there. You should express your gratitude for being asked, and put your personal mark on the occasion through your good wishes sent to the bride and groom, the debutante, or the couple celebrating their anniversary.

How much we wish we could be there. If only Henry's medical seminar were not at the same time. What bad luck! We know Sue will make the prettiest deb of the year; we'll raise a toast to her that night wherever we are. Give her our love, save some photographs for us, and remember every single detail of the evening, so you can tell us everything when we get back from England.

Map Enclosure

If you live out in the country or even in a difficult-to-find urban center, you should have a good, clear map made, which you can have reduced to small sizes or enlarged to bigger sizes, according to need. You should always include this map in letters to people coming to visit, and in all invitations, even the most formal of invitations, if the majority of your guests have never been to your house or to the club before. Try out your map on people who are coming to your house for the first time; see if it really works and correct it if there is anything confusing. Be sure to put your street address and telephone number on it. An identifying landmark or two always helps. Print it in color, if you can, and have the artist (who may be yourself) make it attractive. As long as you live there you will make frequent use of the map, so it might as well be a professional job.

Extending Informal Invitations

Invitations to informal or semiformal dinner parties, lunches, teas, cocktails, buffet suppers, and children's parties may be extended by writing on informals or on correspondence cards, or they may be telephoned. (Remember when making telephoned invitations to send reminder cards or notes, except for children's parties.) Special invitations may also be printed, and these give someone with creative verve the chance to delight the guests with the imaginativeness of the invitations. You may also, of course, simply buy the attractive fill-in printed invitations available at stationers, in card shops, and at department stores.

Handwritten Note as an Invitation   When you are inviting a small group to lunch or dinner, it is nice to invite them with a note, because you can explain more things than you would be able to include in an invitation that is printed, engraved, or written on a *small* informal.

Accepting Informal Invitations

R.S.V.P.s   If you wish R.S.V.P.s to go to your office or your spouse's, you may so stipulate on the invitation. Give an office telephone number, or give a person's name, the address of the office, and the telephone number, if you wish. The latter is the kind of R.S.V.P. to use if you are having a big party, inviting people from other cities, or mixing both business and social friends. It is best to let your office handle these acceptance lists, unless

1220 PARK AVENUE
NEW YORK 10028

MRS. ROBERT PFORZHEIMER

Lunch

Sunday, June second

One o'clock

R.S.V.P. 832-5496

An engraved card the size of an informal may be used to extend an invitation to lunch or any other meal.

you're one of the few remaining people with access to a social secretary in your own home.

If you send out your invitations well in advance of a party and people do not reply promptly, you have every right to telephone them to find out why they have not responded. You use as your excuse, of course, that you "must know" for your food ordering, and your having to call to inquire should have a sobering effect on them. Parents should teach their children from early grade school years always to respond promptly to an invitation that has "R.S.V.P." on it.

Regrets Only It is helpful to know how many people are coming when you send out two hundred invitations to a cocktail party. Most people, unfortunately, do not even bother to respond. As a result, many hosts do not use an "R.S.V.P." but rather use the phrase "Regrets Only," followed by a telephone number, to make life simpler.

This helps only slightly; many people continue to ignore the duty of replying. Frequently one must resort to a system of calculated guesses as to how many are coming. My own rule of thumb is the following: in a medium-small community, I would expect three quarters of my guest list to come to a cocktail party; in a city like Chicago, two thirds. In New York, I would expect only one half; and if it's a stormy night, I would be surprised if even that number came.

The Nuances of Accepting Informal Dinner Invitations   If you're unsure whether, for example, your husband will be out of town on business the day of the party, call your hosts and ask "if it's all right to let you know in a few days' time." It may not be acceptable to the hostess, so you should add, "But if you must know immediately, I certainly understand. We'll regret and hope for a rain check." This gives your hosts the option of inviting another couple they know can both come, or waiting a few more days to see if you can both come. You should certainly not leave your hosts wondering about your plans any closer to the party date than one week.

If either spouse definitely cannot come, the one who *can* should say to the hosts, "Bob won't be back from Texas until the next day, so I'll regret for us both. We'd love to come another time." This gives your hosts an option. They can either ask you to come alone without Bob, in which case you should certainly accept, or they may say, "Yes, we do want the two of you together. We'll be having some friends to dinner very soon again, and you'll be the first ones we call."

If the wife is away, the husband is often a desirable dinner table addition, as there never seem to be enough men for all the single women around. It is unfair of a hostess, however, to "use" someone's husband this way and then never invite the man *with* his wife to dinner.

Postage Considerations

If you plan to include a single- or double-fold invitation, printed or engraved, plus a map, plus an R.S.V.P. card and envelope or any other informational cards, remember the postage costs of the total mailing. Ask your stationer or printer to weigh the stocks you would like for the different pieces that go in the envelope before making your final selection. You may want to use a much thinner paper for the mailing, or you may decide to make the whole thing smaller in size to save postage. If you are sending out, for example, a thousand social, charity, or business invitations, you could save a good bit of money by keeping the size and thickness of your invitation under the next-highest postal rate.

Reminders

If you telephone your guests to extend an invitation (which often happens when time is short, or when there are complications to explain), it is a good idea to send a "reminder" to all who accept. The most informal kind would be a note or a post card like this:

REMINDER
Lunch, Saturday, November 11th
at the Louis Bontemps' home
4713 Harvest Lane
12 o'clock
Come dressed for touch football!

The more formal reminder card is engraved, with spaces left to fill in the information.

A reminder that
you are expected for
Supper following the premiere of "Goldie"
on   *Wednesday, May third*
at   *eleven*   o'clock
Mr. and Mrs. Kenyon Bright
270 Eaton Road
Shaker Heights, Ohio   zip code

It is also proper to send an invitation already accepted by that particular guest, with "R.S.V.P." crossed out and with "Reminder" written in the upper left corner.

Telling Your Guests What to Wear

Traditionally one did not put "Black Tie" on formal invitations for events that begin at eight o'clock or later, because one was supposed to know that it was a black-tie affair. Today there is so much informality, and so many differing life-styles, no one is sure what to wear unless it is spelled out. Therefore, the rule to follow is that if you want your guests to come in evening dress, put "Black Tie" on the lower right of your invitations. If you do not, they might come in everything but appropriate evening attire.

If, of course, you are having an obviously informal barn dance or a beach barbecue, you should specify "Favorite jeans" or "Swimsuits and windy beach attire" or whatever you wish to put in the lower right-hand corner of the invitation. If you tell your guests on the invitation what to wear, you are helping them, and yourself as well, since your guests won't have to call inquiring about "what we're supposed to wear." If you stipulate "Informal" on your invitations for an evening party, your guests should know to come in cocktail dresses or dark suits.

Bringing a Friend

It is unpardonable to call up your host when you have accepted a meal invitation to say, "May I bring a friend?" It is quite another thing if he *asks* you to bring along someone of the opposite sex with whom you would enjoy spending the evening. Places at the table are very precious. The hosts usually have a long list of their own friends whom they would like to invite, but can't, because of space limitations. If the hostess has been slaving away over a gourmet feast for her friends, she would hardly appreciate one of her guests' trying to insert his or her own friend into the group.

A cocktail party is another matter. You may call your hosts in advance to request permission to bring along a date or an escort. Never ask to bring more than one person, however. You should not ask such a favor if you sense or if you've been told that the party is in honor of a woman—and you're one of the single men being invited to meet her; or if the honored guest is a new man in town, and you are being asked as "one of the girls he should meet."

If you are hosting a dinner party that includes a single woman and you do not know any unattached men, you may certainly call her and ask, "Is there any man you would like to bring along?" If she says "No," don't press further. Either get out your microscope to locate a suitable man or have an extra woman at the table. This is no disaster.

Bringing Along One's House Guests

Summertime brings the problem of people wanting their house guests included in any party to which they're invited. If John Smith and his family are invited to a Sunday back-yard barbecue, and if John's sister, brother-in-law, and their children are visiting it is *not* appropriate to try to wish off the house guests on the friends who are giving the barbecue. Space is limited even in a back yard; so are linen, silver, china, and glasses for a party; so is money to buy extra liquor and food. If the party is a bring-your-own-liquor-and-bring-a-casserole type, it is not rude to ask to bring your guests, provided there is space. One or two house guests are usually welcome at a cocktail party, but no one should automatically presume all his house guests are welcome.

Canceling a Party

If you are canceling a wedding or any large formal party in sufficient time, you may send out a printed or an engraved announcement, or you may communicate it through a Mailgram. If you are canceling one of your informal parties at home, you may do any of the following:

a. Ask your friends to help you make the calls by telephone, if you have a large cocktail party list. Give each friend a list of names and telephone numbers.

b. If it's a small lunch or dinner list, write a note by hand, but be sure to give an excuse for the cancellation: "for reasons of a death in the family"; "because of being called away on an emergency business trip"; "because we are all quarantined with chicken pox"; "because broken pipes in the walls have done extensive damage to our house"; "because Eve fell and has a broken leg in a cast."

c. If it's too difficult to telephone everyone and if time is of an essence, send the same Mailgram to the entire guest list:

Mr. and Mrs. Duncan Baldwin regret that because of illness it is necessary to cancel their invitations for the dance on Saturday, June tenth.

Formal Postponement In issuing a postponement, one has to call for R.S.V.P.s all over again: You do not have to give the reason for a postponement, as you should in a party cancellation.

> Mr. and Mrs. Charles Smith Danton
> regret that it is necessary to
> postpone their invitation to
> dinner from Tuesday, the second of May
> to Tuesday, the ninth of May
> at eight o'clock
> 3455 P Street N.W.
> Washington, D.C.   zip code

R.S.V.P.   Black Tie
247-6161

You do not engrave these postponement announcements and although you are issuing a formal invitation all over again, you would be safer to use a telephone number R.S.V.P. because of time limitations.

Breaking an Engagement

Just as it is important to explain carefully to your guests why your party must be canceled, so it is equally important for you to explain carefully the reasons why you break an engagement.

Don't just call the maid or leave a message with your hostess' child if you cannot make a dinner party very suddenly. Always give a complete explanation. And be sure to reciprocate your host's hospitality in some manner at the first available opportunity. I remember a couple who were invited to our house for a dinner party. The wife called that morning to say her aunt had died and they were catching the first available plane to Pittsburgh to be with her mother. At three o'clock that afternoon a basketful of beautiful red and yellow tulips arrived with a card written in her hand: "We hate not being with you tonight." She had arranged this on her way to La Guardia Airport. That's good manners!

Chapter 44

THE ETIQUETTE OF CALLING CARDS

Calling cards were one of the most important tools of social behavior in "polite society" through the first half of the twentieth century. However, as formal or informal "Calling" disappeared in most places (except for certain procedures in diplomatic or military circles), so did the calling card. This kind of card is too small to send in the mail in a matching-sized envelope any more; it is too small to write much of a message upon (people use informals or correspondence cards instead). Calling cards continue to be used with matching envelopes as gift enclosures, but almost any store or gift shop has a plain white card with matching envelope that serves the same purpose.

When you meet someone you would like to see again or should see again, you will need that person's name and address. A card containing this information is very useful, but in today's world the majority of cards exchanged in this manner are business ones. In other words, one no longer really needs calling cards (let's call them "social cards"), but if you wish to have them for gift enclosures, or if you want them with your address engraved upon them as information to give to friends, go to a top-quality stationer. They will help you choose the proper-sized white or cream-colored card and the appropriate typeface. The cards should be engraved, not printed, in black ink and should not be plate-marked.

How Names Are Used on Social and Business Cards

For a Man A man uses "Mr." followed by his full name on his *social card*. He does not use abbreviations or initials unless he dislikes those first names:

Mr. George Lee Meunier, junior

If he is a doctor, an officer in the military, a member of the clergy, or some such, he would of course use his title instead of "Mr." on his social card:

Doctor George Lee Meunier, junior

or

The Reverend George Lee Meunier, junior

If he wishes his address engraved on the card, too, which is only efficient, it would be placed in smaller letters at the lower right:

Mr. George Lee Meunier, junior

1120 Fifth Avenue
New York, New York   zip code

He does not use "Mr." on his *business cards,* although he uses his title if he has one (like "Dr."). Abbreviations are quite correct on business cards:

George L. Meunier, Jr.
Vice-president, The Jorkheim Company

909 Third Avenue
New York, New York   zip code   (212) 830-0000

If his company has a policy that the company name is the dominant factor, then his card might read:

THE JORKHEIM COMPANY
George L. Meunier, Jr.
Vice-president

909 Third Avenue   (212) 830-0000
New York, New York   zip code

The layout of a business card naturally depends upon graphic balance and the positioning of the corporate logo, if one is used, in the over-all design. The business card of someone of high rank must always show his or her title. For example, the governor of a state may simply state on a business card:

The Governor of Rhode Island

(One never uses "The Hon." on an American card.) The governor's card might also read in this manner:

Howard Hawkins
Governor of Rhode Island

A mayor's card follows the same form.

For a Woman A wife's card should match her husband's name on *social cards*. For example, Mrs. Meunier's social card would look like her husband's:

Mrs. George Lee Meunier, junior

If a man dislikes his first name and uses it only in initial form ("J. Jeremiah Frank") then she would put "Mrs. J. Jeremiah Frank" also on her social card (thus breaking the rule previously stated that initials should not be used on social cards).

A single woman would not put "Miss" or "Ms." on her social card, but just her name in full:

Alice Louise Hartwell

A widow retains her husband's name in all social matters, if she wishes, and the majority still wish to do so:

Mrs. Malcolm McFerguson

If she is a widowed businesswoman working under her own given name, however, she might use for her social card:

Jane McFerguson
(Mrs. Malcolm McFerguson)

If Jane Ferguson is a divorcée, she could choose any of the following forms for her card:

Mrs. Jane Ferguson
or
Jane Charter Ferguson
or she may take her maiden name again:
Jane Charter

The custom of putting on cards the woman's family name in conjunction with her divorced husband's last name ("Mrs. Charter Ferguson") is disappearing, I am happy to report.

It is no longer embarrassing for a divorced woman with children to be addressed by her maiden name and to be called "Miss" or "Ms." Many women are taking back their maiden names after divorce, particularly if there are no minor children. Our world is so full of different kinds of relationships, legal and illegal, with people marrying more times than ever before, that no one has the right to criticize a woman's desire to use her own name as part of her own identity.

For *business cards* a woman should never use her husband's first name, but rather should follow the same form as a man's business card:

Jane Ferguson

Brand Manager, Colgate-Bristol Company

Address   Telephone number

If she has a title she would be listed either as "Dr. Jane Ferguson" or "Jane Ferguson, M.D." If she is a married doctor, she might put "Mrs. Malcolm Ferguson" on her social card, but few women doctors do that today. Women have fought long and hard to become accepted in the medical profession, and most wish to keep the title in their social lives, too.

Joint Social Card

A joint social card used by a husband and wife usually carries their home address and is necessarily large enough to accommodate their names on one line. A convenient size is $3\frac{1}{2}'' \times 2\frac{1}{2}''$. Because of the necessity of combining many letters in a small space, titles may be abbreviated, as for example, "Dr. and Mrs. Grant Simpson," to avoid crowding the line.

When an officer has retired, his joint card with his wife would take this form:

Admiral John O'Hara, Retired

Mrs. O'Hara

When the wife is a doctor, the form preferred by most is:

Mr. Malcolm Ferguson and Dr. Jane Ferguson

Cards as Gift Enclosures

One may use either one's social or one's business card to accompany a gift or flowers. If you are sending a present to a good friend, you may run a fine line like a diagonal stroke with your pen through your name. When you do this, be sure then to sign the card at least with your first name in ink, or else write a message and sign it on the back of the card. This procedure, of course, personalizes an engraved or printed card, whether it is a social one or a business one. Always put your card in an envelope when you send it with a gift or flowers, and write the recipient's name and address on the envelope, even if it is recorded elsewhere.

Making and Receiving Calls

The etiquette and protocol books of the nineteenth and twentieth centuries have always devoted considerable space to the art of "calling" on people in their homes, an art practiced by people in social life, or in government, military, and diplomatic circles. Formerly even men would call in person on certain occasions, leaving their engraved calling cards in the sterling-silver card tray—the salver—that was in the front hall or the vestibule of every "proper" home. Since the endless rules concerning the hours during which you would make the calls and the reasons for them are now quite irrelevant, we will omit them here, even for nostalgia's sake.

What has not gone out of fashion, however, is one of the reasons behind this starchily programmed former mode of behavior: and that is the welcoming of a newcomer. It may be a newcomer to your neighborhood or to your apartment building. When a new family or a single person moves into your immediate environment, it is kind and thoughtful to welcome him/her/them in some generous way. It may be a note left at the door for the newly arrived occupants of the house:

> We welcome you! You will love this neighborhood, because we are all very civilized and nice, once you get to know us. And in order to help you get to know us, please call me [give the telephone number] and we will arrange for you to meet some of our friends in the area at our house for a drink the first night you are free. And bring your children, too. If there is anything I can do in the meantime to help you out—such as recommend a pediatrician, vet, playground, or greengrocer's, just let me know.

That kind of note is worth a dozen of the old-fashioned calls where people alighted from carriages and sat primly in the front parlor for thirty minutes of stilted conversation. The great thing about manners is that most changes are for the better.

Since in the former days of formal calls leisure time was inherent in every "lady's" daily schedule, people could call on her without notice. Or perhaps she had one day a week set aside during which everyone knew she would be "at home" to them any time between 10 A.M. and 6 P.M. In the world of today, no one has the time to receive callers unannounced. No one should attempt to see anyone on short notice, either. Everyone is too busy, too charged with responsibilities and appointments, to be "at home" for anyone who wishes to drop by for whatever reason.

When you wish to see someone, the best idea is to ask them over to see you. Then you can judge how busy they are by their response. Perhaps they don't want to do any "dropping by." Take a cue from the reception you receive when you telephone someone and say, "I'm free this morning. Would you like to drop over for a cup of coffee?" The person you call may very possibly have set aside that morning as the one time all month in which she can properly do her exercises, give herself a pedicure, and finish her gardening. Don't ever intrude on anyone's free time. It is one of the most precious commodities we possess. This is not to say we should not be friendly; it is to say we should be thoughtful of our friends and ask in advance when it would be convenient to see us.

Single people are often hesitant about inviting new arrivals who are also single and of the opposite sex to their homes, but it is perfectly appropriate to invite him or her to one's apartment or house, sight unseen, to meet the neighbors. If you stress the fact that you are inviting other "friends," then the new arrival will not suspect that he is being lured to a love-nest trap; he will probably gratefully accept your invitation. Your note to him might read something like this:

Dear Mr. Hellman,

Although I have not had the pleasure of meeting you yet, the building superintendent and Ms. Dawes told me you had just moved in. I am sure you are sick of unpacking, so I'd like to invite you up to my apartment for a real Kentucky mint julep and to meet some of my friends who live in this building. I think you'll like them, and I *know* they like my mint juleps. Just call me at this number, and tell me what evening would be convenient for you, at about six o'clock.

Sincerely,
[signed] May Newcombe
Apartment 12B

Chapter 45

HERALDIC DEVICES

The subject of heraldry, complicated but always fascinating, is enjoying a revival of interest along with the growing desire of many Americans to know more about their ancestors. Some people are even designing their own personal coats of arms just for fun, but the true right to use a historic one is limited to those who can claim direct descent from an "armigerous family" (one having a coat of arms in its history).

In the twelfth century the custom arose for warriors to emblazon their distinguishing devices on their shields so they could be recognized as friend or foe in battle. Armor was, of course, completely concealing when a man's visor was down as he prepared to engage. His device therefore became his trademark and was for further clarity also embroidered on the sleeveless jacket worn over the armor—hence "coat of arms." On his helmet a warrior wore a crest—say, a falcon or dragon—forged to the metal head-covering. The helmet itself might be of a distinctive shape and design. Today a coat of arms consists of these elements—the *shield* with its *coat of arms,* surmounted by the helmet, in turn surmounted by the *crest.* To these may be added "mantling," symbolic of the flowing cape or cloak that was attached to the warrior's shoulders, and "supporters," which are generally animals such as lions, unicorns, deer, or even human beings, and the motto on a "ribbon." Mantling is mere optional ornamentation but permission for the use of supporters must be granted by the Heralds' College in London, which is the best-known authority on heraldry. Some other countries have such governmental heraldic authorities—Holland, for one, with its *Koninklijk Nederlands Genootschat Voor Geslacht-en-Wapenkunde Bleijenburg* in The Hague.

By the sixteenth century many families other than the descendants of Crusaders and Knights bore coat-armor—hence the term "armigerous families"—and some merely assumed arms. It therefore became necessary for the Heralds' College, or College of Arms, established by law in 1483, to make an official "visitation" of all the families in each of the shires and counties, recording pedigrees and arms. These pedigrees form the basis of the mass of records collected in the College of Arms in London, England.

If you are of English, Scottish, or Welsh descent the College, for a fee (which may run to several hundred dollars), will examine your claim to the right to use a coat of arms. Or if that right cannot be established it will, for a fee, grant you a new coat of arms. If you are of Irish descent you may apply to The Genealogical Office, Dublin Castle, in Dublin, Ireland. If your family is of Scottish descent, the Lord Lyon King of Arms, Edinburgh, will verify your arms or make a new grant.

Although in the United States there is no legal, governmental authority that issues a coat of arms or rules upon your "right" to use a heraldic device, the New England Historic Genealogical Society, 101 Newbury Street, Boston, Massachusetts 02116, has had a Committee on Heraldry for many years. This committee will examine a claim to the right to "bear arms" and rule on its validity. If the claim is found to be authentic, the arms are included in the Committee's periodically published "Roll." As of 1972, 612 such arms were so registered in eight printed "Rolls of Arms." The Committee on Heraldry does not "grant" a coat of arms or do any genealogical search—it merely authenticates claims.

To determine your family's right to a coat of arms, you need to know not only the full name of your earliest paternal American ancestor, but his connection with an armigerous British (or continental) family and your own exact line of descent from him. If your name is Clark, Smith, Carpenter (all occupational names), or even such an unusual name as Blenkenship. Hungerford, or Cobleigh, you don't merely ascertain that there were coats of arms for these families and proceed to appropriate them for your own use. It may be happenstance that your name is the same. One Miller family, say, may have the right to use the coat as listed in Burke's *General Armoury;* another, quite unrelated, could not legally use that coat. Using a coat of arms not rightfully yours is like using another's trademark (as a matter of fact, some coats of arms actually are copyrighted in the United States).

The right to use a coat of arms was given in perpetuity to all direct male descendants *of the name.* In the early days of our country it was the younger sons who were more likely to emigrate from Europe than the oldest ones who inherited the title and lands. These younger sons sometimes came alone, sometimes with families, and with limited funds and even more limited experience in the kind of work they had to do in a new, rough country. In a generation or two, perhaps, former claims to gentility were forgotten, as all struggled together to build the new world. But the male heirs of the name, of direct descent from the original armigerous forebear, still had the right to the coat of arms, a right many a family here today doesn't realize it has.

The Lozenge

A woman who is an heiress or co-heiress (with sisters) of an armigerous family, and having no surviving brothers, has the right to use her father's coat of arms (as may her sisters) in a diamond-shaped "lozenge." If she marries she may "impale" her arms with those of her husband—the shield is divided in half vertically and his arms are blazoned on the left and hers on the right. Her children then "quarter" their parents' arms. Technically, if an "heiress" marries a non-armigerous husband she and her children lose their armigerous standing. An heiress may continue to use the lozenge herself even though she marries a non-armigerous husband. But if she is not an heiress she is not correct in using her family's arms on the lozenge after her marriage.

Full Coat   *Crest*   *Lozenge*

A complete coat of arms consists of the shield with the appropriate heraldic insignia, called the "charge," on it; in this example the chevron is the charge. A crest consists of simply the insignia (generally quite different from that on the shield) surmounting a "wreath" above the shield, which may be used separately on stationery or silver. The lozenge, the lady's equivalent of the shield, must be used with a crest.

Jones   *Brown*

If Mr. Jones marries Miss Brown (an heiress) their coats of arms are impaled thus:

Impaled coats of arms

and they may use this during their lifetime. Their son and heir quarters the
Jones and the Brown arms, and he and his descendants continue to use the
quartered arms.

Quartered arms

How Are Heraldic Devices Used?

The most common use of a coat of arms is on an *ex libris,* or bookplate;
or drawn or painted ("blazoned" is the technical term) and framed as a wall
decoration. It may also be used on stationery if the paper is of the best quality and the coat of arms engraved (in color, if you choose) or embossed.
This should appear only on the first sheet, and the envelopes should be
stamped in the same fashion as the paper. It is also proper to have the full
coat engraved on large pieces of silver, such as a tea tray. The crest only
may be engraved on smaller pieces such as flat silver or personal articles
such as a toilet set, cigarette case, or compact, or etched on glassware such
as goblets and cocktail glasses, or reproduced in wedding invitations, announcements, place cards and menus.

A Woman's Use The full coat of arms—shield, crest, and motto—or
what is known as a "gentleman's heraldic bearings," is never properly used
on personal belongings by a woman. Women in medieval days did not normally go forth in battle and therefore did not carry shields. It is proper form
in England, to which we look for precedent since we have nothing

resembling heraldic authority in our own governmental setup, for a woman to use a *crest* on her stationery, or personal linens, and so on, but never a coat of arms on a shield. The lozenge, however, is approved. If a British woman is titled she uses the coronet of her rank above it. But a woman of an armigerous family, especially if she is unmarried or a widow, may use just the crest or the coat of arms itself—but only if blazoned on a lozenge. No woman uses a heraldic motto, for these were often aggressively masculine and not suited to social use.

A Married Woman's Use of the Device A woman whose father has a coat of arms, but whose husband has not, shows better taste, actually, in saying good-by to it and its feminine modifications once her family has used it on her wedding invitations and announcements and, if she wishes, on silver her family has given her. A painted coat could be displayed on the walls, not too conspicuously, but the device may not be adopted by either her husband or her children.

Use on Wedding Invitations and Announcements When the names of a girl's mother and father appear jointly on wedding invitations and announcements it is correct, if the father has a coat of arms, to use it if desired either in its complete form—shield, helmet, crest, and motto or, more commonly, the crest only—embossed without any color at the top of the invitation. If the bride's mother alone—or some woman sponsor alone—has her name on the invitation or announcement she should not use her husband's or father's coat of arms. She may, however, use her crest or lozenge embossed without color.

Silver Marking and the Coat of Arms When the bride's family gives her silver they may mark it with her father's crest and motto without the shield and helmet. Very large plain pieces such as soup tureens, punch bowls, and tea trays may carry a full marshaling—shield, helmet, crest, supporters, and mantling, with the motto on a "ribbon" beneath. If silver is given later to match the original set, it *may* be marked the same way. Silver given at any time by the groom's family may bear his crest. Additional silver purchased by husband and wife during the course of their marriage may, if they wish, have their respective arms, "impaled," on it, but her family device should not be used, except possibly upon her personal silver—toilet articles, cigarette case, vanity. Even on strictly personal objects, however, it is better taste to use her husband's crest rather than her family's, or, if he has none, to omit it altogether. Today the younger generation tends to regard the entire subject as pretentious and stuffy, anyway, so no one should presume to engrave the family crest or coat of arms on any wedding silver unless the bride and groom are in agreement.

Part Six

YOUR OFFICIAL SELF

Correct Forms of Address 563

Parliamentary Procedure 630

Jury Duty 633

The White House 635

The Flag and Our National Anthem 640

Visiting a Naval Vessel 645

An Audience with the Pope 649

Social knowledge and expertise are learned throughout life. Often ways of behavior, learned years earlier, become useful only when one finds oneself for the first time at some official occasion strictly structured within a framework of protocol. Certainly each of us may at some time in our lives need to know how to correctly fly the flag, run a meeting, or serve on a jury. Few of us, perhaps, may be invited to a White House state dinner or have an audience with the Pope at St. Peter's, but I hope the brief descriptions here will provide an interesting glimpse into these protocol-conscious worlds.

Included in this section are charts that show how one properly writes to, addresses, introduces, and entertains people in official positions here and abroad. There is little agreement on the subject. Foreign etiquette books, the State Department in Washington, the White House Social Office, and the protocol division of the United Nations all have different variations and different rules. The entire subject needed standardization, particularly with the needs of American businesses in mind. I have looked at the variations and arrived at what I feel is a logical format that I hope will be useful to most Americans.

Chapter 46

CORRECT FORMS OF ADDRESS

When you introduce, speak to, or send a written communication of any kind to someone, it is natural to want to address that person correctly. If the person in question is an elected official, an officer in the military service, a clergyman, a professional person with a title, or person of nobility from another country, it is not only a question of politeness, but a question of embarrassment if you don't address him correctly. If you want to write to your governmental representatives; if you are invited to an embassy or a consulate for a party; if you dine on any army post or on a naval vessel; or if you have correspondence with a judge, you should know the correct forms of addressing them.

In the following charts I have included a simple formula for addressing officials and titled people of other countries with which we Americans have a great deal of commercial or social contact. Britain, the country with which we have the closest contact, shares a common language with us. Yet there are differences even with that country, particularly since it has a monarchy and titled nobility. Spain has a monarch on the throne. Neither France nor Italy does, but they have their own ranks of titled nobility left from the days when they, too, were monarchies.

It has been impossible to include forms of address for every country, and therefore many important countries have been left out. Although it is always preferable to learn the specific forms of address for each language, if one does not know the accepted form, following the more formal American usage would be appropriate. The exception to that is the use of "Madame."

In diplomatic language and in official life, any woman, married or unmarried, may be addressed as "Madame" instead of by her usual title (such as Mrs.) in her own language. The French word for "Madam" is always used in this situation. In other words, the wife of the German ambassador to Washington is accustomed to being introduced and written to (in any country in the world) as "Madame Hildebrandt" instead of "Frau Hildebrandt." Therefore, readers of the ensuing diplomatic charts will find "Madame" for the wife of an Italian diplomat (instead of "Signora," rightfully her title in

Italian), because "Madame" is always correct to use before the surname of a nontitled woman of another country.

By including the correct forms of addressing people in France, Spain, Italy, and Britain, I have, I hope, assisted the traveler and/or businessman in properly fulfilling his correspondence and entertainment responsibilities in the countries he visits.

I have combined the foreign-language forms of address with our English language forms so that, hopefully, a person or his or her secretary will be able to address a letter properly from this end, and the post office at the other end will understand to whom and where the letter is to go.

Having spent many years abroad in diplomatic service, I am intensely aware of the importance of knowing a country's customs before dealing with its people. No one has made worse gaffes than I, including when I was working for President and Mrs. Kennedy. I delivered some six dozen signed photographs of the Kennedys to the U. S. Embassy in New Delhi, all beautifully custom-framed in dark blue leather cowhide, stamped with the presidential seal in gold at the top. These were to be presented to officials all over India during Mrs. Kennedy's official visit to Prime Minister Nehru in 1962. The only trouble was, the gifts were totally unacceptable. The cow is sacred in India, and to present Hindu officials with something made of cowhide would be an affront. (The solution was a hair-raising one, with silver frames handmade and substituted within forty hours' time!)

UNITED STATES GOVERNMENT OFFICIALS AND INDIVIDUALS

Correct Forms of Address

In making *formal* presentations for banquets, and so on, the form is always that of the full title: "Ladies and Gentlemen—the President of the United States; the Vice President of the United States; the Honorable James J. Brown, Mayor of Trenton; the Honorable Eustis Coates, Associate Justice of the Supreme Court. . . ."

Unofficial Ranking of Government Officials

The ensuing list of United States government officials is called "unofficial" because each administration determines its own order of precedence for its members. In other words, each President has the right to create new commissions, or new positions of special assistants, meanwhile abolishing others; he also has the right to raise in rank certain White House and advisory positions, and to lower others from their rank in previous administrations. This list is carefully noted by the White House Social Office, but it is not officially published. Traditionally, the order of government positions of cabinet rank and above have remained the same over the years.

The President of the United States
The Vice President of the United States
The Speaker of the House of Representatives
The Chief Justice of the United States
Former Presidents of the United States
The Secretary of State
The Secretary General of the United Nations
Ambassadors of Foreign Powers
Widows of Former Presidents of the United States
Associate Justices of the Supreme Court of the United States
The Cabinet
    The Secretary of the Treasury
    The Secretary of Defense
    The Attorney General
    The Secretary of the Interior
    The Secretary of Agriculture
    The Secretary of Commerce
    The Secretary of Labor
    The Secretary of Health, Education, and Welfare
    The Secretary of Housing and Urban Development
    The Secretary of Transportation
    The Secretary of Energy
The United States Representative to the United Nations
Director, Office of Management and Budget
Chairman, Council of Economic Advisers
Special Representative for Trade Negotiations
The Senate
Governors of States
Former Vice Presidents of the United States
The House of Representatives
Assistants to the President
Chargés d'Affaires of Foreign Powers
The Under Secretaries of the Executive Departments and the Deputy Secretaries
Administrator, Agency for International Development
Director, United States Arms Control and Disarmament Agency
Secretaries of the Army, the Navy, and the Air Force
Chairman, Board of Governors of the Federal Reserve System
Chairman, Council on Environmental Quality
Chairman, Joint Chiefs of Staff
Chiefs of Staff of the Army, the Navy, and the Air Force (ranked according to date of appointment)

Commandant of the Marine Corps
(5 Star) Generals of the Army and Fleet Admirals
The Secretary General, Organization of American States
Representatives to the Organization of American States
Director of Central Intelligence
Administrator, General Services Administration
Director, United States Information Agency
Administrator, National Aeronautics and Space Administration
Chairman, Civil Service Commission
Director, Defense Research and Engineering
Director of ACTION
Administrator, Environmental Protection Agency
Deputy Under Secretary of State
Commandant of the Coast Guard
Assistant Secretaries of the Executive Departments
Chief of Protocol
Members of the Council of Economic Advisers
Active or Designate United States Ambassadors and Ministers (Career rank,
  when in the United States)
The Mayor of the District of Columbia
Under Secretaries of the Army, the Navy, and the Air Force
(4 Star) Generals and Admirals
Assistant Secretaries of the Army, the Navy, and the Air Force
(3 Star) Lieutenant Generals and Vice Admirals
Former United States Ambassadors and Ministers to Foreign Countries
Ministers of Foreign Powers (Serving in Embassies, not accredited)
Deputy Assistant Secretaries of the Executive Departments
Deputy Chief of Protocol
Counselors of Embassies or Legations of Foreign Powers
(2 Star) Major Generals and Rear Admirals
(1 Star) Brigadier Generals and Commodores
Assistant Chiefs of Protocol

The Use of "Esquire"

"Esquire" was originally used as a lesser English title. It indicated a knight's eldest son and the young male members of a noble house whose hereditary title was borne only by the eldest male heir. In addressing business or social correspondence to a British gentleman without title, use the abbreviation "Esq." (for Esquire) after the name, but do not precede it with "Mr." or "The Honourable" or, of course, use it with any title such as "Lord," "Sir," or "Dr." A British surgeon, however, is always addressed as "Henry Walters, Esq." and in conversation is "Mr. Walters," not "Dr. Walters." Professional men and those working in the so-called genteel callings—arts, letters, music—and members of the House of Commons and the landed gentry are addressed in writing with "Esq." following their names.

In our own country "Esq." is used by lawyers in written address to each other, a bit of old-school tradition the Correspondence Review Staff of our State Department is attempting to abolish in those few areas where it still persists. Some women lawyers like to use "Esq." If the "Esquire" is used, it follows the name and is abbreviated "Esq." or spelled out in full. The name is then not preceded by "Mr.," "Ms.," "Miss," or "Mrs." In the salutation of the letter, however, the lawyer is referred to as "Dear Mr. Jones," and in speaking he is called "Mr." When he and his wife are included in the form of address it is "Mr. and Mrs. Murray Price."

In diplomatic and extremely formal correspondence "Esquire" is written out.

If a lawyer has received the J.D. (Doctor of Jurisprudence) and uses it, he or she is addressed professionally as Robert Gray, J.D. ("Esq." is omitted.)

UNITED STATES GOVERNMENT OFFICIALS

PERSONAGE	OFFICIAL/ BUSINESS ADDRESS	SOCIAL ADDRESS	SALUTATION
The President of the United States	The President[1] The White House 1600 Pennsylvania Avenue Washington, D.C. 20500	The President and Mrs. Adams[2] The White House 1600 Pennsylvania Avenue Washington, D.C. 20500	Dear Mr. President,
Former President	The Honorable William R. Watkins Office Address	The Honorable William R. Watkins and Mrs. Watkins Home Address	Dear Mr. Watkins,[3]
The Vice President of the United States	The Vice President Executive Office Building Washington, D.C. 20501	The Vice President and Mrs. James The Vice President's House Washington, D.C. 20501	Dear Mr. Vice President,
The Chief Justice[5]	The Chief Justice The Supreme Court One First Street, N.E. Washington, D.C. 20543	The Chief Justice and Mrs. Meigs Home Address	Dear Mr. Justice,
Associate Justice	Mr. Justice Swenson The Supreme Court One First Street, N.E. Washington, D.C. 20543	Mr. Justice Swenson and Mrs. Swenson Home Address	Dear Mr. Justice,
Cabinet Member (man)	The Honorable[6] Joseph Suarez The Secretary of the Interior The Department of the Interior Washington, D.C. 20240	The Honorable The Secretary of the Interior and Mrs. Suarez Home Address	Dear Mr. Secretary,

[1] When writing or speaking to the President, his name is never used.

[2] When writing a letter to the President's wife, only her last name is used: e.g., Mrs. Adams, The White House, Washington, D.C. 20500.

[3] Out of respect and courtesy, it is correct for former staff members and close friends to continue using the title Mr. President, or President Watkins.

LETTER CLOSING	SPEAKING TO	INTRODUCING	PLACE CARDS
Most respectfully,	Mr. President or Sir	The President; The President of the United States	The President Mrs. Adams
Sincerely yours,[4]	Mr. Watkins;[6] Mr. President or Sir	The Honorable William Watkins, former President of the United States; Former President Watkins	Mr. Watkins Mrs. Watkins
Sincerely yours,	Mr. Vice President or Sir	The Vice President; The Vice President of the United States	The Vice President Mrs. James
Sincerely yours,	Mr. Justice; Mr. Justice Meigs or Sir	The Chief Justice	The Chief Justice Mrs. Meigs
Sincerely yours,	Mr. Justice; Mr. Justice Swenson or Sir	Mr. Justice Swenson	Mr. Justice Swenson Mrs. Swenson
Sincerely yours,	Mr. Secretary or Sir	The Secretary of the Interior; The Secretary of the Interior, Mr. Suarez	The Secretary of the Interior Mrs. Suarez

[4] An alternative and more formal closing of a letter is "very truly yours"; either closing is acceptable.

[5] A State Supreme Court justice would be addressed in the same manner, changing, of course, the address from Washington to the state capital.

[6] This may more informally be abbreviated as "The Hon." or "Hon." In this case the title and name would be on one line.

PERSONAGE	OFFICIAL/ BUSINESS ADDRESS	SOCIAL ADDRESS	SALUTATION
Cabinet Member (woman)	The Honorable Katherine S. Rheinhold The Secretary of Commerce The Department of Commerce Washington, D.C. 20230	The Honorable The Secretary of Commerce and Mr. David G. Rheinhold[7] Home Address	Dear Madam Secretary,
The Attorney General	The Honorable Arthur Gosling The Attorney General of the United States The Department of Justice Washington, D.C. 20530	The Honorable The Attorney General and Mrs. Gosling Home Address	Dear Mr. Attorney General,
Under Secretary of the Cabinet (man)	The Honorable Frederick Greenberg Under Secretary of State Department of State Washington, D.C. 20520	The Honorable[8] Under Secretary of State and Mrs. Greenberg Home Address	Dear Mr. Under Secretary,
Under Secretary of the Cabinet (woman)	The Honorable Sarah Thorne Under Secretary of Transportation Washington, D.C. 20590	The Honorable Under Secretary of Transportation and Mr. Wilson R. Thorne[7] Home Address	Dear Madam Under Secretary,
Assistant Secretary of the Cabinet (man)	The Honorable Robert G. Van Winkle Assistant Secretary of Defense The Pentagon Washington, D.C. 20301	The Honorable Robert G. Van Winkle and Mrs. Van Winkle Home Address	Dear Mr. Van Winkle,
Assistant Secretary of the Cabinet (woman)	The Honorable Alice J. Proctor Assistant Secretary of Housing and Urban Development Washington, D.C. 20410	The Honorable Alice J. Proctor and Mr. Douglas Proctor[7] Home Address	Dear Ms. Proctor,

[7] In the case of a woman, her husband's first name is included with his last name and two lines are used instead of the usual three.

[8] A less formal but acceptable form is "The Honorable and Mrs. Frederick Greenberg." This alternative form of social address may be used for all government officials except Cabinet officers.

ETTER CLOSING	SPEAKING TO	INTRODUCING	PLACE CARDS
iincerely yours,	Madam Secretary	The Secretary of Commerce; The Secretary of Commerce, Mrs. Rheinhold	The Secretary of Commerce Mr. Rheinhold
iincerely yours,	Mr. Attorney General or Sir	The Attorney General; The Attorney General, Mr. Gosling	The Attorney General Mrs. Gosling
iincerely yours,	Mr. Under Secretary or Sir	Under Secretary of State; Under Secretary of State, Mr. Greenberg	Under Secretary of State Mrs. Greenberg
iincerely yours,	Madam Under Secretary	Under Secretary of Transportation; Under Secretary of Transportation, Mrs. Thorne	Under Secretary of Transportation Mr. Thorne
iincerely yours,	Mr. Van Winkle or Sir	Assistant Secretary of Defense; Assistant Secretary of Defense, Mr. Van Winkle	Mr. Van Winkle Mrs. Van Winkle
iincerely yours,	Mrs. Proctor	Assistant Secretary of Housing and Urban Development; Assistant Secretary of Housing and Urban Development, Mrs. Proctor	Mrs. Proctor Mr. Proctor

PERSONAGE	OFFICIAL/ BUSINESS ADDRESS	SOCIAL ADDRESS	SALUTATION
Speaker of the House of Representatives	The Honorable Frank G. Conley The Speaker of the House of Representatives United States Capitol Washington, D.C. 20510	The Speaker of the House of Representatives and Mrs. Conley Home Address	Dear Mr. Speaker,
United States Senator (man)	The Honorable Prentice Gates United States Senate Senate Office Building Washington, D.C. 20510	The Honorable Prentice Gates and Mrs. Gates Home Address	Dear Senator Gates,
United States Senator (woman)	The Honorable Elizabeth Miller United States Senate Senate Office Building Washington, D.C. 20510	The Honorable Elizabeth Miller and Mr. George J. Miller[7] Home Address	Dear Senator Miller,
United States Representative (man)	The Honorable Richard Pellegrini House of Representatives Washington, D.C. 20515	The Honorable Richard Pellegrini and Mrs. Pellegrini Home Address	Dear Mr. Pellegrini,
United States Representative (woman)	The Honorable Barbara L. Wadsworth House of Representatives Washington, D.C. 20515	The Honorable Barbara L. Wadsworth and Mr. Gregory Wadsworth[7] Home Address	Dear Ms. Wadsworth,
U.S. Representative to the United Nations	The Honorable Roderick Horchow The U.S. Representative to the United Nations United Nations Plaza New York, N.Y. 10017	The Honorable The United States Representative to the United Nations and Mrs. Horchow Home Address	Dear Mr. Ambassador,

ETTER CLOSING	SPEAKING TO	INTRODUCING	PLACE CARDS
incerely yours,	Mr. Speaker or Sir	The Speaker; The Speaker, Mr. Conley	The Speaker Mrs. Conley
incerely yours,	Senator Gates or Sir	Senator Gates from Idaho	Senator Gates Mrs. Gates
incerely yours,	Senator Miller	Senator Miller from Colorado	Senator Miller Mr. Miller
incerely yours,	Mr. Pellegrini or Sir	Representative Pellegrini from New York	Mr. Pellegrini Mrs. Pellegrini
incerely yours,	Mrs. Wadsworth	Representative Wadsworth from Nevada	Mrs. Wadsworth Mr. Wadsworth
incerely yours,	Mr. Ambassador or Sir	The United States Representative to the United Nations, Mr. Horchow; Ambassador Horchow	The United States Representative to the United Nations Mrs. Horchow

PERSONAGE	OFFICIAL/ BUSINESS ADDRESS	SOCIAL ADDRESS	SALUTATION
American Ambassador[9] (man)	The Honorable Norman J. Fenton The American Ambassador American Embassy 2 avenue Gabriel 75382 Paris, France	The Honorable The Ambassador of the United States of America and Mrs. Fenton American Embassy 2 avenue Gabriel 75382 Paris, France	Dear Mr. Ambassador,
American Ambassador[9] (woman)	The Honorable Helen Povich The American Ambassador American Embassy Via Veneto 119 00187 Rome, Italy	The Honorable Helen Povich[7] and Mr. Albert G. Povich American Embassy Via Veneto 119 00187 Rome, Italy	Dear Madam Ambassador,
American Chargé d'Affaires, Consul General (man)	The Honorable Charles R. Edison American Chargé d'Affaires [or other of these titles] Office Address	The Honorable Charles R. Edison and Mrs. Edison Home Address	Dear Mr. Edison,
American Chargé d'Affaires, Consul General (woman)	The Honorable Lisa Vincent American Consul General [or other of these titles] Office Address	The Honorable Lisa Vincent Home Address	Dear Ms. Vincent,
Governor[10] (man)	The Honorable John J. O'Connell Governor of Connecticut State Capitol Hartford, Conn. 06115	The Governor and Mrs. O'Connell Home Address	Dear Governor O'Connell,
Governor[10] (woman)	The Honorable Louise Warburg Governor of California State Capitol Sacramento, Calif. 95814	The Governor and Mr. Richard Warburg[7] Home Address	Dear Governor Warburg,

[9] In presenting American ambassadors in any Latin American country, always include the phrase "of the United States of America" after Embassy. Avoid the term "American Embassy" or "American Ambassador." For the latter say, "Ambassador of the United States." The reason for this is that Latin Americans consider the South American continent and the Central American states "America," too.

LETTER CLOSING	SPEAKING TO	INTRODUCING	PLACE CARDS
Sincerely yours,	Mr. Ambassador or Sir	The American Ambassador, Mr. Fenton; Ambassador Fenton	Ambassador Fenton Mrs. Fenton
Sincerely yours,	Madam Ambassador	The American Ambassador, Mrs. Povich; Ambassador Povich	Ambassador Povich Mr. Povich
Sincerely yours,	Mr. Edison	Mr. Edison	Mr. Edison Mrs. Edison
Sincerely yours,	Miss Vincent	Miss Vincent	Miss Vincent
Sincerely yours,	Governor; Governor O'Connell or Sir	Governor O'Connell of Connecticut	Governor O'Connell Mrs. O'Connell
Sincerely yours,	Governor; Governor Warburg	Governor Warburg of California	Governor Warburg Mr. Warburg

---

[10] The term "Excellency" may be used as a courtesy in any state: e.g., His Excellency, the Governor, State Capitol, Hartford, Conn. 06115; or Her Excellency, the Governor, State Capitol, Sacramento, Calif. 95814.

PERSONAGE	OFFICIAL/ BUSINESS ADDRESS	SOCIAL ADDRESS	SALUTATION
State Senator, Representative, Assemblyman (man)	The Honorable Philip B. Hernandez Office Address	The Honorable Philip B. Hernandez and Mrs. Hernandez Home Address	Dear Mr. Hernandez,
State Senator, Representative, Assemblywoman (woman)	The Honorable Sylvia J. Wei Office Address	The Honorable Sylvia J. Wei and Mr. John Wei[7] Home Address	Dear Ms. Wei,
Mayor (man)	The Honorable Hugh O'Neill Mayor of Providence City Hall Providence, R.I. 02903	The Honorable Hugh O'Neill and Mrs. O'Neill Home Address	Dear Mayor O'Neill, or Dear Mr. Mayor,
Mayor (woman)	The Honorable Susan Bartlett Mayor of Chicago City Hall Chicago, Ill. 60602	The Honorable Susan Bartlett and Mr. Francis G. Bartlett[7] Home Address	Dear Mayor Bartlett, or Dear Madam Mayor,
Judge (man)	The Honorable Arnold Warner, Jr. Justice, Appellate Division Supreme Court of the State of New York Office Address	The Honorable Arnold Warner, Jr., and Mrs. Warner Home Address	Dear Mr. Justice,
Judge (woman)	The Honorable Barbara Cranston Family Court State of New York Office Address	The Honorable Barbara Cranston and Mr. Walter S. Cranston[7] Home Address	Dear Judge Cranston,

LETTER CLOSING	SPEAKING TO	INTRODUCING	PLACE CARDS
Sincerely yours,	Mr. Hernandez	Mr. Hernandez	Mr. Hernandez Mrs. Hernandez
Sincerely yours,	Mrs. Wei	Mrs. Wei	Mrs. Wei Mr. Wei
Sincerely yours,	Mayor O'Neill; Mr. Mayor or Your Honor	Mayor O'Neill of Providence; The Mayor	Mayor O'Neill Mrs. O'Neill
Sincerely yours,	Mayor Bartlett; Madam Mayor	Mayor Bartlett of Illinois; The Mayor	Mayor Bartlett Mr. Bartlett
Sincerely yours,	Mr. Justice; Judge or Judge Warner	Mr. Justice Warner; Judge Warner	Mr. Justice Warner Mrs. Warner
Sincerely yours,	Judge Cranston	Judge Cranston	Judge Cranston Mr. Cranston

PERSONAGE	OFFICIAL/ BUSINESS ADDRESS	SOCIAL ADDRESS	SALUTATION
Lawyer[11] (man)	Mr. Angus J. Gordon Office Address	Mr. and Mrs. Angus J. Gordon Home Address	Dear Mr. Gordon,
Lawyer[11] (woman)	Ms. Mary Leonard Office Address	Mr. and Mrs. Charles Leonard Home Address	Dear Ms. Leonard,
University President[12] (man)	Dr. Jonathan B. Horgan President Brown University Address	Dr. and Mrs. Jonathan B. Horgan Home Address	Dear Dr. Horgan,
University President[12] (woman)	Dr. Constance West President Carleton College Address	Dr. Constance West and Mr. Bernard West Home Address	Dear Dr. West,
Dean[13] (man)	Dr. Howard Williamson Dean of the School of Journalism Hamilton College Address	Dr. and Mrs. Howard Williamson Home Address	Dear Dr. Williamson,
Dean[13] (woman)	Dr. Joan Richter College of Business Administration Yale University Address	Dr. Joan Richter and Mr. David Richter Home Address	Dear Dr. Richter,
Professor[14] (man)	Professor George Bertolli Department of History Arizona State College Address	Professor and Mrs. George Bertolli Home Address	Dear Professor Bertolli,

[11] "Esquire" may be used after any lawyer's name: e.g., Angus J. Gordon, Esq. The practice is, however, not as widely used as formerly.

[12] Many prefer to use "President" instead of "Dr." in writing, speaking to, or introducing.

[13] If a dean does not hold a doctoral degree, "Dean" may replace "Dr." throughout.

[14] If a professor holds a doctoral degree, "Dr." may replace "Professor" throughout.

LETTER CLOSING	SPEAKING TO	INTRODUCING	PLACE CARDS
Sincerely yours,	Mr. Gordon	Mr. Gordon	Mr. Gordon Mrs. Gordon
Sincerely yours,	Mrs. Leonard	Mrs. Leonard	Mrs. Leonard Mr. Leonard
Sincerely yours,	Dr. Horgan	Dr. Horgan	Dr. Horgan Mrs. Horgan
Sincerely yours,	Dr. West	Dr. West	Dr. West Mr. West
Sincerely yours,	Dr. Williamson	Dr. Williamson	Dr. Williamson Mrs. Williamson
Sincerely yours,	Dr. Richter	Dr. Richter	Dr. Richter Mr. Richter
Sincerely yours,	Professor Bertolli	Professor Bertolli	Professor Bertolli Mrs. Bertolli

PERSONAGE	OFFICIAL/ BUSINESS ADDRESS	SOCIAL ADDRESS	SALUTATION
Professor[14] (woman)	Professor Josephine G. Butler Department of Mathematics University of Colorado Address	Mr. and Mrs. Roger Butler Home Address	Dear Professor Butler,
UNITED NATIONS Secretary General	His Excellency Pierre Meunier, The Secretary General of the United Nations United Nations Plaza New York, N.Y. 10017	His Excellency The Secretary General of the United Nations and Mrs. Meunier Home Address	Dear Mr. Secretary General,
FOREIGN AMBASSADOR	His Excellency[15] Ricardo Correia The Ambassador of Brazil Embassy of Brazil 3006 Massachusetts Avenue Washington, D.C. 20008	His Excellency The Ambassador of Brazil and Mrs. Correia Home Address	Excellency, or Dear Mr. Ambassador,

[15] Foreign ambassadors are referred to as "Ambassador," with the name of the country—e.g., Ambassador of Ireland; Ambassador of Peru—with the following exceptions: Ambassador of the Argentine Republic; British Ambassador; Chinese Ambassador; Ambassador of the Netherlands; Ambassador of the Union of South Africa; Ambassador of the Union of Soviet Socialist Republics; Ambassador of the Socialist Federal Republic of Yugoslavia; Ambassador of the Socialist Republic of Romania.

Ambassadors are addressed at the offices of their embassies: e.g., Ambassador of the Argentine Republic, Embassy of the Argentine Republic. Foreign Presidents, ambassadors, and cabinet ministers are referred to as His Excellency; if they have royal titles or military rank such as Baron, Lord, The Right Honorable, Sir, General, or Colonel, that title is included after "His Excellency."

The wives of all foreign ambassadors, with the exception of those from English-speaking countries, are given the French courtesy title of "Madame" and in speaking are referred to as Madame Correia, rather than Senhora, Signora, Vrouw, etc.

LETTER CLOSING	SPEAKING TO	*INTRODUCING	PLACE CARDS
Sincerely yours,	Professor Butler	Professor Butler	Professor Butler Mr. Butler
Sincerely yours,	Mr. Secretary General	His Excellency, Pierre Meunier, The Secretary General of the United Nations; The Secretary General	The Secretary General Mrs. Meunier
Sincerely yours,	Mr. Ambassador; Excellency or Sir	The Ambassador of Brazil; The Ambassador of Brazil, Mr. Correia	His Excellency, The Ambassador of Brazil Mrs. Correia

UNITED STATES MILITARY PERSONNEL

How to Tell Military Rank

Our armed forces, organized under the Department of Defense, consist of the Army, the Navy, and the Air Force. The Department of the Navy consists of two separate military services, the U. S. Navy and the U. S. Marine Corps. In time of war the Coast Guard is under the jurisdiction of the Navy but in time of peace operates under the Department of Transportation.

In all services staff officers, or noncombatant officers, are distinguished from line officers by a device signifying their staff corps. Line officers, generally speaking, are those entitled to command combat forces. There are certain specialists, however, who though technically line officers do not command combat forces.

In the Army, devices signifying the corps in which men serve—the caduceus of the doctor, the cross of the chaplain—are worn on the lapel. In the Navy these staff officer devices are worn on the sleeve above the stripes indicating rank.

The positions of General of the Army and Navy Fleet Admiral were created to give the highest ranking American military leaders acting on international joint staff during wartime a rank equivalent to the foreign position of Field Marshal. While the men holding this rank may not be actively engaged in military activities in peacetime, they are subject to call by the President if required.

The Army
Cap device—eagle clutching two arrows

In order of rank the officer personnel of the Army are:

GENERAL OF THE ARMY—Five silver stars
GENERAL—Four silver stars
LIEUTENANT GENERAL—Three silver stars
MAJOR GENERAL—Two silver stars
BRIGADIER GENERAL—One silver star
COLONEL—Silver eagle

LIEUTENANT COLONEL—Silver oak leaf

MAJOR—Gold oak leaf

CAPTAIN—Two silver bars

FIRST LIEUTENANT—One silver bar

SECOND LIEUTENANT—One gold bar

CHIEF WARRANT OFFICER—One gold bar, brown enamel top, gold longitudinal center

WARRANT OFFICER, JUNIOR GRADE—Same as above except gold center is latitudinal

The Navy

Cap device—crossed anchors, shield and eagle

On blue uniforms, rank is indicated by gold stripes on sleeves; on white or dress khaki uniforms, rank is indicated on detachable shoulder boards.

In order of rank the officer personnel of the Navy are:

FLEET ADMIRAL—Five silver stars, one 2″ stripe, and four ½″ sleeve stripes, with star of line officer

ADMIRAL—Four silver stars, one 2″ stripe, and three ½″ sleeve stripes, with star of line officer or corps device

VICE ADMIRAL—Three silver stars, one 2″ stripe, and two ½″ sleeve stripes, star of line officer or corps device

REAR ADMIRAL—Two silver stars, one 2″ stripe, and one ½″ sleeve stripe, star of line officer or corps device

COMMODORE—One silver star, one 2″ sleeve stripe, star of line officer or corps device

CAPTAIN—Silver spread eagle, four ½″ stripes, star of line officer or corps device

COMMANDER—Silver oak leaf, three ½″ stripes, star of line officer or corps device

LIEUTENANT COMMANDER—Gold oak leaf, two ½″ stripes with ¼″ one between, star of line officer or corps device

LIEUTENANT—Two silver bars, two ½″ stripes, star of line officer or corps device

LIEUTENANT, JUNIOR GRADE—One silver bar, one ½″ stripe with ¼″ one above, star of line officer or corps device

ENSIGN—One gold bar, one ½″ gold stripe, star of line officer or corps device

CHIEF WARRANT OFFICER—One ¼″ broken gold stripe and specialty device

WARRANT OFFICER—One ¼″ broken gold stripe and specialty device

The Marine Corps
Cap device—eagle, globe, and anchor

The top rank in the Marine Corps is general. He wears the four stars and shoulder rank of the Army. Other insignia in the Marine Corps are the same as those in the Army.

The Air Force
Cap device—wings flanking U.S. great seal

The top rank in the Air Force is general. All insignia in the Air Force are the same as those in the Army.

The Coast Guard
Cap distinguished by a single anchor, eagle, and shield

The top rank in the Coast Guard is admiral. All insignia are the same as those in the Navy.

Military Forms of Address

When two people in the service marry and the woman assumes her husband's last name, she naturally keeps her own rating or rank. If the wife outranks her husband, she comes first in formal address, in introductions, and in the way one addresses invitations to the couple: "Lt. Col. Marian Peabody, U. S. Air Force, and Captain John Peabody, U. S. Air Force, Andrews Air Force Base," etc.

Noncommissioned officers are addressed officially by title. ("Sergeant" is used for all grades of Sergeants, First Class, Master, and so on.) If you are writing a letter or sending an invitation to a noncommissioned officer, you may use Mr., Mrs., Ms., or Miss, followed by a first and last name.

A naval officer while in command of a ship is always called "Captain" during the period of command regardless of his actual rank.

A medical officer is called "Doctor" except if he or she is the head of a base hospital, in which case the actual rank is used; and if a doctor becomes a general or an admiral, he is always addressed by his rank, even socially, as long as he or she remains in service.

Chaplains in all branches of the Armed Forces are called by their military rank, officially and socially. Informally they may be addressed as Chaplain, Father, or Rabbi.

National Guard and Reserve officers not on active duty do not use their titles socially or in business affairs unless their activities have some bearing on military matters.

In any service branch a warrant officer, both officially and socially, is called Mr., Mrs., Ms., or Miss except for formal or very official occasions.

After retirement a person retains his military title except in any instance where it might look as though his activity had the official sponsorship of the Defense Department or any section of it. When a retired officer travels abroad, he or she should not use an official service title while making a public appearance, unless the appropriate overseas commander gives his approval.

Abbreviations of Military Rank

	Army	*Air Force*	*Marine Corps*
General	GEN	Gen	Gen
Lieutenant General	LTG	Lt Gen	LtGen
Major General	MG	Maj Gen	MajGen
Brigadier General	BG	Brig Gen	BGen
Colonel	COL	Col	Col
Lieutenant Colonel	LTC	Lt Col	LtCol
Major	MAJ	Maj	Maj
Captain	CPT	Capt	Capt
First Lieutenant	1LT	1st Lt	1stLt
Second Lieutenant	2LT	2d Lt	2dLt

Navy and Coast Guard

Admiral	ADM
Vice Admiral	VADM
Rear Admiral	RADM
Captain	CAPT
Commander	CDR
Lieutenant Commander	LCDR
Lieutenant	LT
Lieutenant, junior grade	LTJG
Ensign	ENS

UNITED STATES MILITARY PERSONNEL

PERSONAGE	OFFICIAL/ BUSINESS ADDRESS	SOCIAL ADDRESS

JOINT CHIEFS OF STAFF
Chairman
	General George S. Dudley
	or
	Admiral Franklin Gruen
	The Chairman of the Joint
	  Chiefs of Staff
	The Pentagon
	Washington, D.C. 20301
		General and Mrs. George S.
		  Dudley
		or
		Admiral and Mrs. Franklin
		  Gruen
		Home Address

Chief of Staff, U. S.
  Army
	General Arnold Gray
	The Chief of Staff of
	  the Army
	United States Army
	The Pentagon
	Washington, D.C. 20310
		General and Mrs. Arnold Gray
		Home Address

Chief of Naval
  Operations
	Admiral Philip G. Schwartz
	The Chief of Naval Operations
	United States Navy
	The Pentagon
	Washington, D.C. 20350
		Admiral and Mrs. Philip G.
		  Schwartz
		Home Address

Chief of Staff, U. S.
  Air Force
	General Malcolm Stoddard
	The Chief of Staff of the
	  Air Force
	United States Air Force
	The Pentagon
	Washington, D.C. 20330
		General and Mrs. Malcolm
		  Stoddard
		Home Address

Commandant of the
  Marine Corps
	General Frederick Heller
	The Commandant of the
	  Marine Corps
	United States Marine Corps
	Headquarters United States
	  Marine Corps
	Washington, D.C. 20380
		General and Mrs. Frederick
		  Heller
		Home Address

SALUTATION	LETTER CLOSING	SPEAKING TO	INTRODUCING	PLACE CARDS
Dear General Dudley, or Dear Admiral Gruen,	Sincerely yours, Sincerely yours,	General Dudley or Admiral Gruen	General Dudley or Admiral Gruen, Chairman of the Joint Chiefs of Staff	General Dudley Mrs. Dudley Admiral Gruen Mrs. Gruen
Dear General Gray,	Sincerely yours,	General Gray	General Gray, Chief of Staff of the Army	General Gray Mrs. Gray
Dear Admiral Schwartz,	Sincerely yours,	Admiral Schwartz	Admiral Schwartz, Chief of Naval Operations	Admiral Schwartz Mrs. Schwartz
Dear General Stoddard,	Sincerely yours,	General Stoddard	General Stoddard, Chief of Staff of the Air Force	General Stoddard Mrs. Stoddard
Dear General Heller,	Sincerely yours,	General Heller	General Heller, Commandant of the Marine Corps	General Heller Mrs. Heller

PERSONAGE	OFFICIAL/ BUSINESS ADDRESS	SOCIAL ADDRESS
THE ARMY, THE AIR FORCE, THE MARINE CORPS		
General	General Ann O'Hara, U. S. Marine Corps[1]	General Ann O'Hara and Mr. James G. O'Hara
Lieutenant General	Lieutenant General Ann O'Hara, U. S. Army	Lieutenant General Ann O'Hara and Mr. James G. O'Hara
Major General	Major General Ann O'Hara, U. S. Air Force	Major General Ann O'Hara and Mr. James G. O'Hara
Brigadier General	Brigadier General Ann O'Hara, U. S. Army Business or P.O. Address	Brigadier General Ann O'Hara and Mr. James G. O'Hara Home Address
Colonel	Colonel Joseph Schmidt, U. S. Air Force	Colonel and Mrs. Joseph Schmidt
Lieutenant Colonel	Lieutenant Colonel Joseph Schmidt, U. S. Army Business or P.O. Address	Lieutenant Colonel and Mrs. Joseph Schmidt[2] Home Address
Major	Major Albert S. Bowman, U. S. Marine Corps Business or P.O. Address	Major and Mrs. Albert S. Bowman Home Address
Captain	Captain Patricia Van Westering, U. S. Army Business or P.O. Address	Captain Patricia Van Westering and Mr. Edward Van Westering Home Address
First Lieutenant	First Lieutenant Gilbert Warren, U. S. Air Force	First Lieutenant and Mrs. Gilbert Warren
Second Lieutenant	Second Lieutenant Gilbert Warren, U. S. Marine Corps Business or P.O. Address	Second Lieutenant and Mrs. Gilbert Warren Home Address

[1] More informally, service designations may be abbreviated as follows: USA, USN, USAF, USMC, USCG. For Reserve personnel: USAR, USNR, USAFR, USMCR, USCGR.

SALUTATION	LETTER CLOSING	SPEAKING TO	INTRODUCING	PLACE CARDS
Dear General O'Hara,	Sincerely yours,	General O'Hara	General O'Hara	General O'Hara Mr. O'Hara
Dear General O'Hara,	Sincerely yours,	General O'Hara	Lieutenant General O'Hara	General O'Hara Mr. O'Hara
Dear General O'Hara,	Sincerely yours,	General O'Hara	Major General O'Hara	General O'Hara Mr. O'Hara
Dear General O'Hara,	Sincerely yours,	General O'Hara	Brigadier General O'Hara	General O'Hara Mr. O'Hara
Dear Colonel Schmidt,	Sincerely yours,	Colonel Schmidt	Colonel Schmidt	Colonel Schmidt Mrs. Schmidt
Dear Colonel Schmidt,	Sincerely yours,	Colonel Schmidt	Lieutenant Colonel Schmidt	Colonel Schmidt Mrs. Schmidt
Dear Major Bowman,	Sincerely yours,	Major Bowman	Major Bowman	Major Bowman Mrs. Bowman
Dear Captain Van Westering,	Sincerely yours,	Captain Van Westering	Captain Van Westering	Captain Van Westering Mr. Van Westering
Dear Lieutenant Warren,	Sincerely yours,	Lieutenant Warren	First Lieutenant Warren	Lieutenant Warren Mrs. Warren
Dear Lieutenant Warren,	Sincerely yours,	Lieutenant Warren	Second Lieutenant Warren	Lieutenant Warren Mrs. Warren

[a] In formal social correspondence, military titles are never abbreviated. When correspondence is more informal, lengthy titles may be abbreviated thus: Lt. Col., Lt. Cdr., 2nd Lt., etc.

PERSONAGE	OFFICIAL/ BUSINESS ADDRESS	SOCIAL ADDRESS
THE NAVY, THE COAST GUARD[3]		
Admiral	Admiral Russell B. Jordan, U. S. Navy[1]	Admiral and Mrs. Russell B. Jordan
Vice Admiral	Vice Admiral Russell B. Jordan, U. S. Navy	Vice Admiral and Mrs. Russell B. Jordan
Rear Admiral	Rear Admiral Russell B. Jordan, U. S. Navy Business or P.O. Address	Rear Admiral and Mrs. Russell B. Jordan Home Address
Captain	Captain Alice Engle, U. S. Coast Guard Business or P.O. Address	Captain Alice Engle and Mr. John Engle Home Address
Commander	Commander Rufus F. Williamson, U. S. Navy	Commander and Mrs. Rufus F. Williamson
Lieutenant Commander	Lieutenant Commander Rufus F. Williamson, U. S. Navy Business or P.O. Address	Lieutenant Commander and Mrs. Rufus F. Williamson Home Address
Lieutenant	Lieutenant Ann Schultz, U. S. Coast Guard	Lieutenant Ann Schultz and Mr. John J. Schultz
Lieutenant, junior grade	Lieutenant, junior grade Ann Schultz, U. S. Coast Guard Business or P.O. Address	Lieutenant, junior grade Ann Schultz and Mr. John J. Schultz Home Address
Ensign	Ensign Alfred Grimes, U. S. Coast Guard Business or P.O. Address	Ensign and Mrs. Alfred Grimes Home Address

[3] The rank of Commodore is omitted here since it is used only during wartime and there are no Commodores at present.

SALUTATION	LETTER CLOSING	SPEAKING TO	INTRODUCING	PLACE CARDS
Dear Admiral Jordan,	Sincerely yours,	Admiral Jordan	Admiral Jordan	Admiral Jordan Mrs. Jordan
Dear Admiral Jordan,	Sincerely yours,	Admiral Jordan	Vice Admiral Jordan	Admiral Jordan Mrs. Jordan
Dear Admiral Jordan,	Sincerely yours,	Admiral Jordan	Rear Admiral Jordan	Admiral Jordan Mrs. Jordan
Dear Captain Engle,	Sincerely yours,	Captain Engle	Captain Engle	Captain Engle Mr. Engle
Dear Commander Williamson,	Sincerely yours,	Commander Williamson	Commander Williamson	Commander Williamson Mrs. Williamson
Dear Mr. Williamson,	Sincerely yours,	Mr. Williamson[4]	Lieutenant Commander Williamson	Mr. Williamson Mrs. Williamson
Dear Mrs. Schultz,	Sincerely yours,	Mrs. Schultz	Lieutenant Schultz	Mrs. Schultz Mr. Schultz
Dear Mrs. Schultz,	Sincerely yours,	Mrs. Schultz	Lieutenant Schultz	Mrs. Schultz Mr. Schultz
Dear Mr. Grimes,	Sincerely yours,	Mr. Grimes	Ensign Grimes	Mr. Grimes Mrs. Grimes

[4] When speaking to a lieutenant commander, it is proper to say "Mr.," "Miss," or "Mrs." However, current social usage allows the courtesy title of "Commander." The actual rank is indicated by the two and a half stripes on the uniform.

PERSONAGE	OFFICIAL/ BUSINESS ADDRESS	SOCIAL ADDRESS

UNITED STATES
MILITARY
ACADEMIES

| Cadet of the United States Military Academy | Cadet Florence Kruger Company D-2, USCC West Point, N.Y. 10996 | |

| Cadet of the United States Air Force Academy | Cadet Frank Rudolph United States Air Force Academy Colorado 80840 | |

| Midshipman of the United States Merchant Marine Academy | Midshipman Alice Telson United States Merchant Marine Academy Kings Point, N.Y. 11024 | |

| Midshipman of the United States Naval Academy | Midshipman John Barker United States Naval Academy Annapolis, Md. 21402 | |

| Cadet of the United States Coast Guard Academy | Cadet 2/c Gregory Cowles United States Coast Guard Academy New London, Conn. 06320 | |

SALUTATION	LETTER CLOSING	SPEAKING TO	INTRODUCING	PLACE CARDS
Dear Cadet Kruger,	Sincerely yours,	Cadet Kruger; Miss Kruger	Cadet Kruger	Cadet Kruger
Dear Cadet Rudolph,	Sincerely yours,	Cadet Rudolph; Mr. Rudolph	Cadet Rudolph	Cadet Rudolph
Dear Midshipman Telson,	Sincerely yours,	Midshipman Telson; Miss Telson	Midshipman Telson	Midshipman Telson
Dear Midshipman Barker,	Sincerely yours,	Midshipman Barker; Mr. Barker	Midshipman Barker	Midshipman Barker
Dear Cadet Cowles,	Sincerely yours,	Cadet Cowles; Mr. Cowles	Cadet Cowles	Cadet Cowles

RELIGIOUS OFFICIALS

PERSONAGE	OFFICIAL/ BUSINESS ADDRESS	SOCIAL ADDRESS	SALUTATION
EASTERN ORTHODOX COMMUNION[1]			
Patriarch	His Holiness, the Ecumenical Patriarch of Constantinople Istanbul, Turkey		Your Holiness,
Archbishop[2]	The Most Reverend Michael Archbishop of Cincinnati Address		Your Eminence,
Bishop	The Right Reverend Basil Althos Bishop of Chicago Address		Right Reverend Sir, (business) My dear Bishop, (social)
Archimandrite	The Very Reverend James Papas Address		Reverend Sir, (business) Your Reverence, (social)
Priest[3]	The Very Reverend Nicholas Kontos Address		My dear Father Kontos,

[1] Greek Orthodox clergymen choose before ordination whether they are to be celibate or noncelibate priests. All highest clergymen—patriarchs, archbishops, and archimandrites—are usually celibates. There are three other patriarchs in ancient sees, those of Jerusalem, Alexandria, and Antioch.

[2] Metropolitans, who supersede suffragan bishops in rank, are found in large cities mainly among the Russian and Syrian Orthodox congregations, but in Greece they function, as well, for the Church of Greece. They are addressed as The Most Reverend Peter, Metropolitan of Boston, etc. and like archbishops are referred to as "Your Eminence."

LETTER CLOSING	SPEAKING TO	INTRODUCING	PLACE CARDS
Respectfully yours,	Your Holiness	His Holiness	
Respectfully yours,	Your Eminence	His Eminence	His Eminence
Respectfully yours,	Your Grace	His Grace	Bishop Althos
Respectfully yours,	Father James or Father Papas	Father James or Father Papas	Father Papas
Yours respectfully,	Father	Father Kontos	Father Kontos

* In the case of a noncelibate priest the form including his wife would be The Reverend Nicholas Kontos and Mrs. Kontos in the U.S.A., or, abroad, the Reverend Nicholas Kontos and Madame Kontos.

PERSONAGE	OFFICIAL/ BUSINESS ADDRESS	SOCIAL ADDRESS	SALUTATION
JEWISH			
Rabbi with Scholastic Degree[4] (man)	Rabbi Nathan Sachs, D.D., LL.D. Temple Emmanuel[5] Address	Rabbi (or Doctor) and Mrs. Nathan Sachs (some prefer Rabbi to Doctor) Home Address	Dear Rabbi (or Doctor) Sachs,
Rabbi with Scholastic Degree[6] (woman)	Rabbi Helen Kreisler, D.D., LL.D. Congregation Bnai Israel Address	Rabbi (or Doctor) Helen Kreisler Home Address	Dear Rabbi (or Doctor) Kreisler,
Rabbi without Scholastic Degree (man)	Rabbi Harold Schwartz Beth David Synagogue Address	Rabbi and Mrs. Harold Schwartz Home Address	Dear Rabbi Schwartz
Rabbi without Scholastic Degree (woman)	Rabbi Joan Friedman Central Synagogue Address	Rabbi Joan Friedman and Mr. Arnold Friedman Home Address	Dear Rabbi Friedman
Cantor (music minister of congregation; soloist at worship services) (man)	Cantor Chaim Levy Beth David Synagogue Address	Cantor and Mrs. Chaim Levy Home Address	Dear Cantor Levy,
Cantor (woman)	Cantor Marjorie Smith Central Synagogue Address	Cantor Marjorie Smith and Mr. Robert Smith Home Address	Dear Cantor Smith,

[4] All rabbis do not necessarily hold both degrees. In addressing a rabbi, give him whatever degree or degrees he possesses.

[5] The terms "temple" and "synagogue" are interchangeable, but Orthodox Congregations tend to prefer "temple" while Reform and Conservative Congregations tend to use "synagogue." The term "church" is not used.

[6] At the present time, women rabbis serve only in Reform and Reconstructionist congregations (the latter, a liberal interpretation of the Conservative tradition).

LETTER CLOSING	SPEAKING TO	INTRODUCING	PLACE CARDS
ncerely yours,	Rabbi Sachs; Doctor Sachs; Rabbi	Rabbi Nathan Sachs; Doctor Nathan Sachs	Rabbi Sachs Mrs. Sachs
incerely yours,	Rabbi Kreisler, Doctor Kreisler; Rabbi	Rabbi Helen Kreisler; Doctor Helen Kreisler	Rabbi Kreisler
incerely yours,	Rabbi Schwartz; Rabbi	Rabbi Harold Schwartz	Rabbi Schwartz Mrs. Schwartz
incerely yours,	Rabbi Friedman; Rabbi	Rabbi Joan Friedman	Rabbi Friedman Mr. Friedman
incerely yours,	Cantor Levy	Cantor Chaim Levy	Cantor Levy Mrs. Levy
incerely yours,	Cantor Smith	Cantor Marjorie Smith	Cantor Smith Mr. Smith

PERSONAGE	OFFICIAL/ BUSINESS ADDRESS	SOCIAL ADDRESS	SALUTATION
PROTESTANT CLERGY			
Clergyman with Doctor's Degree	The Reverend Joseph E. Long, D.D. Address	The Reverend Dr. and Mrs. Joseph E. Long Home Address	Dear Dr. Long,
Clergywoman with Doctor's Degree	The Reverend Agnes Godfried, D.D. Address	The Reverend Dr. Agnes Godfried and Mr. James Godfried Home Address	Dear Dr. Godfried,
Clergyman without Doctor's Degree[7]	The Reverend Frank K. Hanson Address	The Reverend and Mrs. Frank K. Hanson Home Address	Dear Mr. Hanson,
Clergywoman without Doctor's Degree	The Reverend Margaret Bruckman Address	The Reverend Margaret Bruckman Home Address	Dear Ms. Bruckman
Presiding Bishop of the Episcopal Church in the United States[8]	The Right Reverend Peter Flagg, D.D., LL.D. Presiding Bishop Address	The Right Reverend and Mrs. Peter Flagg Home Address	Dear Bishop Flagg,
Bishop of the Episcopal Church	The Right Reverend Gideon Carew, D.D. Bishop of Cincinnati Address	The Right Reverend and Mrs. Gideon Carew Home Address	Dear Bishop Carew,

[7] The use of "Father," designating an Episcopal clergyman or a priest who is not a member of a religious order, is a matter of the clergyman's own preference. When "Father" is used in writing it is usually coupled with the surname of the clergyman— The Reverend Father Huntington, O.H.C., without the Christian name. In direct reference, it is Father Huntington. However, in the Episcopal order of Franciscans, where there is a name conferred by the order (as among Roman Catholic religious orders) it would be The Reverend Father Joseph, O.S.F., in writing, and Father or Father Joseph in direct reference. Lay brothers are addressed in writing as Brother Charles, O.H.C., and in direct reference as Brother or Brother Charles.

LETTER CLOSING	SPEAKING TO	INTRODUCING	PLACE CARDS
Sincerely yours,	Dr. Long	The Reverend Dr. Joseph Long	Dr. Long Mrs. Long
Sincerely yours,	Dr. Godfried	The Reverend Dr. Agnes Godfried	Dr. Godfried Mr. Godfried
Sincerely yours,	Mr. Hanson	The Reverend Frank Hanson	Mr. Hanson Mrs. Hanson
Sincerely yours,	Ms. Bruckman	The Reverend Margaret Bruckman	Ms. Bruckman
Sincerely yours,	Bishop Flagg	The Right Reverend Peter Flagg, the Presiding Bishop	The Right Reverend Flagg Mrs. Flagg
Sincerely yours,	Bishop Carew	The Right Reverend Gideon Carew, the Bishop of Cincinnati	The Right Reverend Carew Mrs. Carew

[8] All church dignitaries in any formal presentation before audiences of any kind are given their full titles—for example, The Right Reverend Peter Flagg, Presiding Bishop of the Protestant Episcopal Church in America.

PERSONAGE	OFFICIAL/ BUSINESS ADDRESS	SOCIAL ADDRESS	SALUTATION
Dean	The Very Reverend the Dean of St. Matthew's or The Very Reverend John Brown, D.D., Dean of St. Matthew's Cathedral Address	The Very Reverend and Mrs. John Brown Home Address	Dear Dean Brown,
Archdeacons	The Venerable Charles G. Smith Archdeacon of Richmond Address	The Venerable and Mrs. Charles G. Smith Home Address	Dear Archdeacon Smith,
Canon	The Reverend Canon Charles Pritchard Thomas, D.D., LL.D. Canon of St. Mary's Cathedral Address	The Reverend Canon and Mrs. Charles Pritchard Thomas Home Address	Dear Canon Thomas,
Bishop (Mormon)	Mr. John Richards[9] Church of Jesus Christ of Latter-day Saints Address	Mr. and Mrs. John Richards Home Address	Dear Mr. Richards,
THE ROMAN CATHOLIC HIERARCHY The Pope	His Holiness, the Pope or His Holiness Pope Benedict I Vatican City 00187 Rome, Italy		Your Holiness or Most Holy Father,

[9] In the Church of Jesus Christ of Latter-day Saints (Mormon), the title of "Bishop" is used within the organization during the Bishop's term of office; otherwise "Mr." is used.

LETTER CLOSING	SPEAKING TO	INTRODUCING	PLACE CARDS
...ncerely yours,	Dean Brown	The Very Reverend John Brown, Dean of St. Matthew's Cathedral	Dean Brown Mrs. Brown
...incerely yours,	Archdeacon Smith	The Venerable Charles Smith, the Archdeacon of Richmond	Archdeacon Smith Mrs. Smith
...incerely yours,	Canon Thomas	The Reverend Canon Charles Pritchard Thomas, Canon of St. Mary's	Canon Thomas Mrs. Thomas
...incerely yours,	Mr. Richards	Mr. John Richards	Mr. Richards Mrs. Richards
...our Holiness' most humble servant,	Your Holiness or Most Holy Father	His Holiness; the Holy Father; the Pope; the Pontiff	

PERSONAGE	OFFICIAL/ BUSINESS ADDRESS	SOCIAL ADDRESS	SALUTATION
Cardinal	His Eminence, Patrick, Cardinal Terrance, Archbishop of San Francisco Address		Your Eminence; Dear Cardinal Terrance,
Bishop and Archbishop	The Most Reverend Peter Judson, D.D., Bishop (Archbishop) of Dallas Address		Your Excellency; Dear Bishop (Archbishop) Judson,
Abbot[10]	The Right Reverend Henry J. Loester or Abbot Loester Address		Right Reverend Abbot; Dear Father Abbot,
Prothonotary Apostolic, Domestic Prelate, Vicar General, Papal Chamberlain	The Right Reverend[11] Monsignor Robert McDonald Address		Right Reverend Monsignor; Dear Monsignor McDonald,
Priest	The Reverend Father James L. Cullen Address		Reverend Father; Dear Father Cullen,
Brother	Brother William O'Hara[12] Address		Dear Brother William; Dear Brother,
Sister	Sister Mary Annunciata Address		Dear Sister,

[10] After name add designated letters of the order; e.g., for members of the order of St. Benedict—The Right Reverend Dom Anselm McCarthy, O.S.B.

[11] If Prothonotary Apostolic, use initials *P.A.* after name; if Vicar General, use *V.G.*

[12] The use of the last name is a matter of choice; both Brother William and Brother William O'Hara are correct.

LETTER CLOSING	SPEAKING TO	INTRODUCING	PLACE CARDS
I have the honor to be etc.,	Your Eminence; Cardinal Terrance	His Eminence; Cardinal Terrance	Cardinal Terrance
I have the honor to be etc.,	Your Excellency; Bishop (Archbishop) Judson	His Excellency; Bishop (Archbishop) Judson	Bishop Judson
I have the honor to be, Right Reverend Abbot, etc.	Abbot Loester	The Right Reverend Henry Loester; Abbot Loester	The Right Reverend Loester
I am, Right Reverend Monsignor, etc.,	Monsignor McDonald; Monsignor	Monsignor McDonald	Monsignor McDonald
I am, Reverend Father, etc.,	Father Cullen	Father Cullen	Father Cullen
I am, respectfully yours,	Brother William; Brother	Brother William	Brother William
I am, respectfully yours,	Sister Annunciata; Sister	Sister Annunciata; Sister	Sister Annunciata

FOREIGN GOVERNMENT OFFICIALS AND NOBILITY

British Officials and Individuals

Where a man's name is combined with that of his wife, as in this country, the form is "Mr. and Mrs. Bertram Montgomery," but traditionally this form has been rare in Great Britain except on joint visiting cards. Although the practice is changing now, engraved invitations are customarily addressed to the wife alone. On the top of the invitation itself, or in the blank space provided, "Mr. and Mrs. Montgomery" is handwritten. Invitations written in longhand are also addressed to the wife only, with the exception of wedding invitations, which go to both. If a visiting card is used for an invitation, the envelope is addressed to the wife alone, while on the inside card "Mr. and Mrs. Montgomery" (no Christian name) is written.

There are some other differences between British and American forms of address. The American formal form—as "My dear Mr. Ambassador"—is never used in a letter to a British person with whom one is not on intimate terms; instead, one writes "Dear Mr. Ambassador."

French Officials and Individuals

For several centuries, French has been the diplomatic language the world over. As I indicated earlier, the title "Madame" is used before the name of the wife of any official of any country in any other country. One hears "Monsieur l'Ambassadeur" spoken at a polyglot gathering at any cocktail party around the world. This universal use is why the French language today is part of many schools' curricula.

France is a republic and, as such, no longer supports a monarchy. However, the legitimately titled people are still treated with great respect and a family often uses its royal crest on visiting cards and stationery.

Italian Officials and Individuals

Anyone who deals often on business or in government matters with the Italians learns to call them by their Italian titles (e.g., Conte instead of Count, Signorina instead of Miss). Since French is the diplomatic language, Madame is used throughout on this chart as the title to use before the name of women married to officials. However, if you are conversant with Italian, you would write to and introduce these women as Signora and not Madame. If a woman is titled, she is not addressed as Madame, but rather with her title before her last name. For example, an Italian ambassador who is also a baron would be addressed as Ambassador Piccione, but his wife would be addressed as Baroness Piccione. There are so many complicated factors regarding princely and ducal titles, including the ancient Vatican royal titles, that to do them proper justice would require a book on the subject alone.

Another custom the Italians have is that of using their professions in abbreviated titles before their names, such as Arch. Benedetto Empoli (Architect Benedetto Empoli), Avv. Maria Boncompagni (Lawyer Maria Boncompagni), and Ing. Luigi Carrara (Engineer Luigi Carrara). Anyone who graduates with the Italian equivalent of a B.A. college degree may thereafter be called Dottore or Dottoressa (feminine) for the rest of their lives. This title is abbreviated to Dott. in front of their names in writing.

The Italian military—Army, Navy, and Air Force—may be addressed and written to with the English names. Generale becomes General; Ammiraglio becomes Admiral, and so on through the entire military structure.

It is always best to write the street address in Italian, so as not to confuse the Italian postmen. For example, one would write Palazzo della Farnesina instead of Farnesina Palace.

In closing letters to Italians, it is fine to put "Sincerely," or "Sincerely yours," as you would in any social or business letter.

Spanish Officials and Individuals

Although there are differences in customs, idioms, and even protocol between one Spanish-speaking country and another, Spain is the symbolic matriarch of much of South and Central America. Most of the titles and protocol are a Spanish heritage to these newer countries, although today one is not allowed to use titles of nobility in some Latin-American countries.

In Spain, frequently one's family name and one's title are not the same. Titled people are therefore usually called by their titles rather than by their family names. Instead of saying, "His Excellency, Don Cristóbal Colón, Duke of Veragua," you would say, "His Excellency, The Duke of Veragua."

In Spain only one person in the family may bear a family title; usually the oldest son inherits it. If there is no son, the eldest daughter may bear the title. Brothers and sisters of the one who bears the family title either have another less important title of their own or use the family name with no title at all. Spanish titles are regulated by law and a tax is levied on the user. If the spouse of the person who bears the title survives him or her, that person can continue using the title, but must add the term "Widow" or "Widower" to it. In other words, if the Duke of Infantado dies, his wife would continue as La Duquesa Viuda del Infantado (The Widow Duchess of Infantado).

Another interesting thing about Spanish nobility is that one addresses a husband and wife not as say, The Duke and Duchess of So-and-so but rather as The Dukes of So-and-so.

When Spanish-speaking people write to the highest officials of the government, the Grandees of Spain (dukes and some marquesses and counts), ambassadors, or possessors of a "Grand Cross," a form of knighthood, they address their letter to "Excelentísimo Señor" (which would be "Most Honorable" in English, if we were to use this form). Lesser officials are addressed as "Ilustrísimo Señor," and those of no rank simply as "Señor Don" before the name.

PERSONAGE	OFFICIAL/ BUSINESS ADDRESS	SOCIAL ADDRESS	SALUTATION
BRITISH OFFICIALS AND INDIVIDUALS[1]			
The Queen	Her Majesty, Queen Elizabeth II Buckingham Palace London SW1A 1AA England	It is not usual to address letters to the Queen unless one is a head of state. Correspondence should be addressed to "The Private Secretary to Her Majesty the Queen," requesting that the communication be conveyed to the Queen.	
H.R.H. The Duke of Edinburgh	His Royal Highness, The Prince Philip, Duke of Edinburgh Buckingham Palace London SW1A 1AA England	Follow the same procedure used in communicating with the Queen.	
The Queen Mother	Her Majesty, Queen Elizabeth the Queen Mother Address	Follow the same procedure used in communicating with the Queen.	
Royal Prince	His Royal Highness, The Prince Charles, Prince of Wales Address		Your Royal Highness,
Royal Princess	Her Royal Highness, The Princess Anne, Mrs. Mark Phillips Address		Your Royal Highness,
Royal Countess	Her Royal Highness, The Princess Margaret, Countess of Snowdon Address		Your Royal Highness,

[1] Traditionally all invitations are sent to the wife alone.

LETTER CLOSING	SPEAKING TO	INTRODUCING	PLACE CARDS
	Your Majesty; subsequently, Ma'am		
	Your Royal Highness; subsequently, Sir		
	Your Majesty; subsequently, Ma'am		
ours respectfully,	Your Royal Highness; subsequently, Sir	His Royal Highness, The Prince Charles, Prince of Wales	H.R.H. The Prince of Wales
ours respectfully,	Your Royal Highness; subsequently, Ma'am	Her Royal Highness, The Princess Anne, Mrs. Mark Phillips	H.R.H. The Princess Anne, Mrs. Mark Phillips
ours respectfully,	Your Royal Highness; subsequently, Ma'am	Her Royal Highness, The Princess Margaret, Countess of Snowdon	H.R.H. The Princess Margaret, Countess of Snowdon

PERSONAGE	OFFICIAL/ BUSINESS ADDRESS	SOCIAL ADDRESS	SALUTATION
Royal Duke	His Royal Highness, The Duke of Trent, K.G. Address		Your Royal Highness
Royal Duchess	Her Royal Highness The Duchess of Trent Address		Your Royal Highness
THE PEERAGE A Duke, Nonroyal[2]	His Grace, the Duke of Norfolk, K.G. (formal) The Duke of Norfolk (less formal) Address		My Lord Duke (formal); Dear Duke of Norfolk (less formal)
A Duchess, Nonroyal	Her Grace, the Duchess of Norfolk (formal) The Duchess of Norfolk (less formal) Address		Madam (formal); Dear Duchess (less formal)
The Younger Son of a Duke[3]	Lord James Beaumont Address		My Lord (formal); Dear Lord James (less formal)
The Daughter of a Duke	Lady Bridget Beaumont Address		My Lady (formal); Dear Lady Bridget (less formal)
The Wife of a Younger Son of a Duke	Lady James Beaumont Address		My Lady (formal); Dear Lady James (less formal)

[2] The eldest son of a duke has the highest family title below his father's, such as Marquess. His wife has the corresponding title, such as Marchioness.

LETTER CLOSING	SPEAKING TO	INTRODUCING	PLACE CARDS
Yours respectfully,	Your Royal Highness; subsequently, Sir	His Royal Highness, the Duke of Trent	H.R.H. The Duke of Trent
Yours respectfully,	Your Royal Highness; subsequently, Ma'am	Her Royal Highness, the Duchess of Trent	H.R.H. The Duchess of Trent
Yours faithfully (formal); Yours sincerely (less formal)	Your Grace; Duke	His Grace, the Duke of Norfolk	The Duke of Norfolk
Yours faithfully (formal); Yours sincerely (less formal)	Your Grace; Duchess	Her Grace, the Duchess of Norfolk	The Duchess of Norfolk
Yours faithfully (formal); Yours sincerely (less formal)	Lord James	Lord James Beaumont	Lord James Beaumont
Yours faithfully (formal); Yours sincerely (less formal)	Lady Bridget	Lady Bridget Beaumont	Lady Bridget Beaumont
Yours faithfully (formal); Yours sincerely (less formal)	Lady James	Lady James Beaumont	Lady James Beaumont

[a] The terms "my lord" and "my lady" are forms of address used mainly by servants and tradesmen, although the usage is not necessarily menial.

PERSONAGE	OFFICIAL/ BUSINESS ADDRESS	SOCIAL ADDRESS	SALUTATION
A Marquess[4]	The Most Honourable the Marquess of Remington (formal); The Marquess of Remington (less formal) Address		My Lord (formal); Dear Lord Remington (less formal)
A Marchioness	The Most Honourable the Marchioness of Remington (formal); The Marchioness of Remington (less formal) Address		Madam (formal); Dear Lady Remington (less formal)
An Earl[5]	The Right Honourable the Earl of Leeds, G.C., V.O., C.M.G. (formal); The Earl of Leeds (less formal) Address		My Lord (formal); Dear Lord Leeds (less formal)
A Countess, Wife of an Earl	The Right Honourable the Countess of Leeds (formal); The Countess of Leeds (less formal) Address		Madam (formal); Dear Lady Leeds (less formal)
A Viscount[5]	The Right Honourable the Viscount Bemis (formal); The Viscount Bemis (less formal) Address		My Lord (formal); Dear Lord Bemis (less formal)

[4] The eldest son of a marquess has the highest family title below his father's, such as Earl—his wife has the corresponding title, such as Countess. The younger son and daughter of a marquess take the title Lord or Lady, respectively. The wife of a younger son of a marquess has the title Lady combined with her husband's full name.

[5] The eldest son of an earl has the highest family title below his father's, such as Viscount. His wife takes the corresponding title, such as Viscountess. The younger sons

LETTER CLOSING	SPEAKING TO	INTRODUCING	PLACE CARDS
Yours faithfully (formal); Yours sincerely (less formal)	Lord Remington	Lord Remington	The Marquess of Remington
Yours faithfully (formal); Yours sincerely (less formal)	Lady Remington	Lady Remington	The Marchioness of Remington
Yours faithfully (formal); Yours sincerely (less formal)	Lord Leeds	Lord Leeds	The Earl of Leeds
Yours faithfully (formal); Yours sincerely (less formal)	Lady Leeds	Lady Leeds	The Countess of Leeds
Yours faithfully (formal); Yours sincerely (less formal)	Lord Bemis	Lord Bemis	The Viscount Bemis

of an earl and their wives have the title The Honourable. The daughters of an earl have the title Lady combined with their Christian and family names.

The term "Dowager" is used as part of a title in England to indicate the earliest surviving widow of a preceding peer. She is known as the Dowager Duchess of Wickham. A later surviving widow who might be the widow of the first earl's son, nephew, etc., would be known as Mary, Duchess of Wickham, retaining this usage for life even if the dowager dies.

PERSONAGE	OFFICIAL/ BUSINESS ADDRESS	SOCIAL ADDRESS	SALUTATION
A Viscountess	The Right Honourable the Viscountess Bemis (formal); The Viscountess Bemis (less formal) Address		Madam (formal); Dear Lady Bemis (less formal)
The Family of a Viscount[6]	The Honourable Thomas Bemis Address The Honourable Mrs. Thomas Bemis Address The Honourable Gladys Bemis Address		Dear Mr. Bemis, Dear Mrs. Bemis, Dear Miss Bemis,
A Baron[7]	The Right Honourable Lord Lancer (formal); The Lord Lancer (less formal) Address		My Lord (formal); Dear Lord Lancer (less formal)
A Baroness	The Right Honourable Lady Lancer (formal); The Lady Lancer (less formal) Address		Madam (formal); Dear Lady Lancer (less formal)
A Baronet[8]	Sir Thomas Riddle, Bt. Address		Dear Sir (formal); Dear Sir Thomas (less formal)

[6] The eldest son of a viscount and also his wife have the title The Honourable. The younger sons of a viscount and their wives also have the title The Honourable. The daughters of a viscount take the title The Honourable with their Christian and family names.

[7] All the sons of a baron and their wives have the title The Honourable. The daughters of a baron also have the title The Honourable.

LETTER CLOSING	SPEAKING TO	INTRODUCING	PLACE CARDS
ours faithfully (formal); ours sincerely (less formal)	Lady Bemis	Lady Bemis	The Viscountess Bemis
ours faithfully (formal); ours sincerely (less formal)	Mr. Bemis	Mr. Bemis	The Honourable Thomas Bemis
	Mrs. Bemis	Mrs. Bemis	The Honourable Mrs. Thomas Bemis
	Miss Bemis	Miss Bemis	The Honourable Gladys Bemis
ours faithfully (formal); ours sincerely (less formal)	Lord Lancer (never Baron)	Lord Lancer (never Baron)	The Lord Lancer
ours faithfully (formal); ours sincerely (less formal)	Lady Lancer	Lady Lancer	The Lady Lancer
ours faithfully (formal); ours sincerely (less formal)	Sir Thomas	Sir Thomas Riddle	Sir Thomas Riddle

[8] A baronet has the title Sir and the abbreviation for Baronet (Bart. or Bt.) follows his name. The wife of a baronet has the title Lady with her husband's surname only. The sons and daughters of a baronet have no title.

PERSONAGE	OFFICIAL/ BUSINESS ADDRESS	SOCIAL ADDRESS	SALUTATION
The Wife of a Baronet	Lady Riddle Address		Dear Madam (formal); Dear Lady Riddle (less formal)
A Knight	Sir John Waugh, G.C.M.G. Address		Dear Sir (formal); Dear Sir John (less formal)
The Wife of a Knight	Lady Waugh Address		Dear Madam (formal); Dear Lady Waugh (less formal)
Member of the House of Commons with Title	Sir Henry Coakley- Smith, K.B.E., M.P. Address		Dear Sir (formal); Dear Sir Henry (less formal)
Member of the House of Commons Without Title	Roger Needham, Esq., M.P. Address		Dear Sir (formal); Dear Mr. Needham (less formal)
A Privy Counsellor with Title[9]	The Right Honourable Sir Percy Harron, Bt., D.S.O., P.C. (formal); Sir Percy Harron, Bt., D.S.O., P.C. (less formal) Address		Dear Sir (formal); Dear Sir Percy (less formal)

[9] A privy counsellor is addressed as The Right Honourable. However, a peer or peeress is more usually addressed according to rank, with, after the title, the letters P.C. and those of any Orders conferred. All members of the British Cabinet are members of the Privy Council and as such are entitled to the intials P.C. after their names. The wife of a privy counsellor has no title as such.

NOTE: British officials in Britain are not addressed as Excellency even when entitled to be so addressed in other countries.

NOTE: A member of Parliament has no special title except that the letters M.P. are written after his name.

LETTER CLOSING	SPEAKING TO	INTRODUCING	PLACE CARDS
Yours faithfully (formal); Yours sincerely (less formal)	Lady Riddle	Lady Riddle	Lady Riddle
Yours faithfully (formal); Yours sincerely (less formal)	Sir John	Sir John Waugh	Sir John Waugh
Yours faithfully (formal); Yours sincerely (less formal)	Lady Waugh	Lady Waugh	Lady Waugh
Yours faithfully (formal); Yours sincerely (less formal)	Sir Henry	Sir Henry Coakley-Smith	Sir Henry Coakley-Smith
Yours faithfully (formal); Yours sincerely (less formal)	Mr. Needham	Mr. Roger Needham	Mr. Needham
Yours faithfully (formal); Yours sincerely (less formal)	Sir Percy	Sir Percy Harron	Sir Percy Harron

PERSONAGE	OFFICIAL/ BUSINESS ADDRESS	SOCIAL ADDRESS	SALUTATION
Prime Minister (British)[10]	The Right Honourable Harley Asheden, M.P., P.C. The Prime Minister 10 Downing Street London SW1A 2AA England		Dear Mr. Prime Minister,
A British Ambassador[11]	His Excellency, The Right Honourable Sir Harold Pim, G.C.M.G. The British Ambassador British Embassy Zip code Rome, Italy		Excellency; Dear Mr. Ambassador

[10] A Prime Minister (being a Privy Counsellor) has the title The Right Honourable in addition to and preceding any other title.

[11] A British Ambassador is addressed according to his rank of nobility, if any, his title of rank being preceded by the diplomatic title His Excellency.

LETTER CLOSING	SPEAKING TO	INTRODUCING	PLACE CARDS
Yours faithfully (formal); Yours sincerely (less formal)	Mr. Prime Minister; Mr. Asheden	The Prime Minister; The Prime Minister, Mr. Asheden	His Excellency, The Prime Minister
Yours faithfully (formal); Yours sincerely (less formal)	Mr. Ambassador; Excellency; Sir Harold	The British Ambassador; The British Ambassador, Sir Harold Pim	His Excellency, The British Ambassador

PERSONAGE	OFFICIAL/ BUSINESS ADDRESS

FRENCH OFFICIALS AND NOBILITY

President of the French Republic (Président de la République Française)	His Excellency Jacques de la Roche The President of the French Republic Palais de l'Elysée zip code Paris, France
Prime Minister of the French Republic (Premier Ministre de la République Française)	His Excellency Jacques de la Roche The Prime Minister of the French Republic Hôtel Matignon zip code Paris, France
President of the Senate of the French Republic (Président du Sénat de la République Française)	His Excellency Jacques de la Roche The President of the Senate of the French Republic Palais du Luxembourg zip code Paris, France
President of the Chamber of Deputies of the French Republic (Président de la Chambre des Députés de la République Française)	His Excellency Jacques de la Roche The President of the Chamber of Deputies of the French Republic Assemblée Nationale Palais Bourbon zip code Paris, France
Minister of Foreign Affairs of the French Republic (Ministre des Affaires Etrangères de la République Française)	His Excellency Jacques de la Roche The Minister of Foreign Affairs of the French Republic 37, quai d'Orsay zip code Paris, France

SOCIAL ADDRESS	SALUTATION	LETTER CLOSING

His Excellency
The President of the French Republic
  and Madame de la Roche
Palais de l'Elysée
zip code Paris, France
	Dear Mr. President,
	Dear President and Madame de la
	  Roche,
		Respectfully yours,

His Excellency
The Prime Minister of the French
  Republic and Madame de la Roche
36, avenue Henri Martin
zip code Paris, France
	Dear Mr. Prime Minister,
	Dear Prime Minister and Madame
	  de la Roche,
		Respectfully yours,

His Excellency
The President of the Senate of the
  French Republic and Madame
  de la Roche
4, avenue Montaigne
zip code Paris, France
	Dear Mr. President of the Senate,
	Dear President of the Senate and
	  Madame de la Roche,
		Respectfully yours,

His Excellency
The President of the Chamber of
  Deputies of the French Republic
  and Madame de la Roche
34, avenue Foch
zip code Paris, France
	Dear Mr. President of the Chamber
	  of Deputies,
	Dear President of the Chamber of
	  Deputies and Madame de la Roche,
		Respectfully yours,

His Excellency
The Minister of Foreign Affairs of the
  French Republic and Madame de la
  Roche
21, avenue Georges V
zip code Paris, France
	Dear Mr. Minister,
	Dear Minister and Madame de la
	  Roche,
		Respectfully yours,

PERSONAGE	OFFICIAL/ BUSINESS ADDRESS
Ambassador of the French Republic (Ambassadeur de la République Française)	His Excellency Jacques de la Roche The Ambassador of the French Republic Embassy of the French Republic Washington, D.C. 20008
Consul General of the French Republic (Consul Général de la République Française)	The Honorable Jacques de la Roche The Consul General of the French Republic 934 Fifth Avenue New York, N.Y. 10021
PRINCELY TITLES Prince; Princess (Prince; Princesse)	Prince de la Roche[13] 7, rue de Balzac zip code Lyons, France
Duke; Duchess (Duc; Duchesse)	Duke de la Roche[13] 11, rue du Lac zip code Calais, France
Marquess; Marchioness (Marquis; Marquise)	Marquess Jacques de la Roche 24, rue Rivoli zip code Bordeaux, France
Count; Countess (Comte; Comtesse)	Count Jacques de la Roche 90, avenue de Champs-Elysées zip code Paris, France

[12] If the ambassadorial couple is titled, she is called by her title—Baroness de la Roche instead of Madame de la Roche.

[13] The titles of Prince and Duke are so important that one need not put the first name unless there is a father with the same first name or another brother with the same title and last name.

SOCIAL ADDRESS	SALUTATION	LETTER CLOSING

His Excellency[12]
The Ambassador of the French
  Republic and Madame
  de la Roche
Embassy of the French Republic
Washington, D.C. 20008
	Dear Mr. Ambassador,
	Dear Ambassador and Madame de la
	  Roche,
		Sincerely yours,

The Honorable
The Consul General of the French
  Republic and Madame
  de la Roche
934 Fifth Avenue
New York, N.Y. 10021
	Dear Mr. Consul General,
	Dear Consul General and Madame
	  de la Roche,
		Sincerely yours,

Prince and Princess de la Roche 11, rue de Savoie zip code Lyons, France	Dear Prince, Dear Prince and Princess,	Sincerely yours,
Duke and Duchess de la Roche 51, avenue des Châlets zip code Calais, France	Dear Duke, Dear Duke and Duchess,	Sincerely yours,
Marquess and Marchioness Jacques de la Roche 75, rue de la Faisanderie zip code Bordeaux, France	Dear Marquess, Dear Marquess and Marchioness,	Sincerely yours,
Count and Countess Jacques de la Roche 17, boulevard Raspail zip code Paris, France	Dear Count, Dear Count and Countess,	Sincerely yours,

<table>
<tr><th>PERSONAGE</th><th>OFFICIAL/
BUSINESS ADDRESS</th></tr>
</table>

PERSONAGE	OFFICIAL/ BUSINESS ADDRESS
Baron; Baroness (Baron; Baronne)	Baron Jacques de la Roche 83, rue de l'Université zip code Avignon, France

ITALIAN OFFICIALS AND INDIVIDUALS

President of the Italian Republic (Presidente della Repubblica Italiana)	His Excellency Pietro di Sangro The President of the Italian Republic Palazzo del Quirinale zip code Rome, Italy
Prime Minister of the Italian Republic (Presidente del Consiglio dei Ministri della Repubblica Italiana)	His Excellency[15] Pietro di Sangro The Prime Minister of the Italian Republic Palazzo Chigi zip code Rome, Italy
President of the Senate of the Italian Republic (Presidente del Senato della Repubblica Italiana)	His Excellency Pietro di Sangro The President of the Senate of the Italian Republic Palazzo Madama zip code Rome, Italy
President of the Chamber of Deputies of the Italian Republic (Presidente della Camera dei Deputati della Repubblica Italiana)	His Excellency[16] Pietro di Sangro The President of the Chamber of Deputies of the Italian Republic Palazzo di Montecitorio zip code Rome, Italy

[14] When members of high diplomatic circles write each other, the wife is not included in the address or salutation of the letter but is "referred to" in the body of the letter. Americans tend more often to include her in both the address and salutation if it is a personal matter, such as a thank-you note or a letter regarding, say, one's children.

[15] If he is a senator, he is written to as The Honorable Pietro di Sangro, Senator of the Republic of Italy, with a salutation of "Dear Senator di Sangro."

SOCIAL ADDRESS	SALUTATION	LETTER CLOSING
Baron and Baroness Jacques de la Roche 4, avenue Vendôme zip code Avignon, France	Dear Baron, Dear Baron and Baroness,	Sincerely yours,
His Excellency[14] The President of the Italian Republic and Donna Luciana di Sangro Palazzo del Quirinale zip code Rome, Italy	Dear Mr. President, Dear President and Donna Luciana di Sangro,	Respectfully yours,
His Excellency The Prime Minister of the Italian Republic and Madame di Sangro Via Condotti, 56 zip code Rome, Italy	Dear Mr. Prime Minister, Dear Prime Minister and Madame di Sangro,	Respectfully yours,
His Excellency The President of the Senate of the Italian Republic and Madame di Sangro Via Archimede, 19 zip code Rome, Italy	Dear Mr. President of the Senate, Dear President of the Senate and Madame di Sangro,	Respectfully yours,
His Excellency The President of the Chamber of Deputies of the Italian Republic and Madame di Sangro Via dei Tre Orologi, 1 zip code Rome, Italy	Dear Mr. President of the Chamber of Deputies, Dear President of the Chamber of Deputies and Madame di Sangro,	Respectfully yours,

[16] If he is a deputy, he is written to as The Honorable Pietro di Sangro, Member of the Chamber of Deputies, with a salutation of "Dear Deputy di Sangro."

PERSONAGE	OFFICIAL/ BUSINESS ADDRESS
Minister of Foreign Affairs of the Italian Republic (Ministro degli Affari Esteri della Repubblica Italiana)	His Excellency Pietro di Sangro The Minister of Foreign Affairs of the Italian Republic Palazzo della Farnesina zip code Rome, Italy
Ambassador of the Italian Republic (Ambasciatore della Repubblica Italiana)	His Excellency Pietro di Sangro The Ambassador of the Italian Republic Embassy of the Italian Republic zip code London, England
Consul General of the Italian Republic (Console Generale della Repubblica Italiana)	The Honorable Pietro di Sangro The Consul General of the Italian Republic 690 Park Avenue New York, N.Y. 10021
PRINCELY TITLES Prince; Princess (Principe; Principessa)	Prince di Sangro[18] Via Francesco Crispi, 12 zip code Bologna, Italy
Duke; Duchess (Duca; Duchessa)	Duke di Sangro[18] Via del Leone, 90 zip code Capri, Italy
Marquess; Marchioness (Marchese; Marchesa)	Marquess Pietro di Sangro Via del Marche, 70 zip code Naples, Italy
Count; Countess (Conte; Contessa)	Count Pietro di Sangro Piazza Victoria, 3 zip code Rome, Italy

[17] If the ambassadorial couple is titled, she is called by her title, Countess di Sangro, instead of Madame di Sangro.

SOCIAL ADDRESS	SALUTATION	LETTER CLOSING
His Excellency The Minister of Foreign Affairs of the Italian Republic and Madame di Sangro Via di Porta Pinciana, 16 zip code Rome, Italy	Dear Mr. Minister, Dear Minister and Madame di Sangro,	Respectfully yours,
His Excellency[17] The Ambassador of the Italian Republic and Madame di Sangro Embassy of the Italian Republic zip code London, England	Dear Mr. Ambassador, Dear Ambassador and Madame di Sangro,	Sincerely yours,
The Honorable The Consul General of the Italian Republic and Madame di Sangro 690 Park Avenue New York, N.Y. 10021	Dear Mr. Consul General, Dear Consul General and Madame di Sangro,	Sincerely yours,
Prince and Princess di Sangro Palazzo Sangro Via Ludovisi, 5 zip code Bologna, Italy	Dear Prince, Dear Prince and Princess,	Sincerely yours,
Duke and Duchess di Sangro Via della Stella, 3 zip code Capri, Italy	Dear Duke, Dear Duke and Duchess,	Sincerely yours,
Marquess and Marchioness Pietro di Sangro Via Monte Napoleone, 14 zip code Naples, Italy	Dear Marquess, Dear Marchquess and Marchioness,	Sincerely yours,
Count and Countess Pietro di Sangro Piazza Colonna, 24 zip code Rome, Italy	Dear Count, Dear Count and Countess,	Sincerely yours,

[18] The titles of Prince and Duke are so important that one need not use a person's given name. However, if there is another living male member of the family with the same title, the first name is used in order to avoid confusion. The children born to a prince bear the title Don (used before a male surname) and Donna (used before a female surname), as in Don Giulio di Sangro or Donna Elisabetta di Sangro.

PERSONAGE	OFFICIAL/ BUSINESS ADDRESS
Baron; Baroness (Barone; Baronessa)	Baron Pietro di Sangro Via Lazio, 72 zip code Livorno, Italy
SPANISH OFFICIALS AND NOBILITY His Majesty, the King of Spain (Su Majestad el Rey de España)	His Majesty Don Juan Carlos I The King of Spain Palacio Real Madrid zip code, Spain
President of the Spanish Government (Presidente del Gobierno de España)	His Excellency Señor Don José López The President of the Spanish Government Palacio de la Moncloa Madrid zip code, Spain
President of the Senate of the Spanish Government (Presidente del Senado Español)	His Excellency Señor Don José López The President of the Senate of the Spanish Government Plaza de la Marina Española 8 Madrid zip code, Spain
President of the Chamber of Deputies of the Spanish Government (Presidente de las Cortes Españolas)	His Excellency Señor Don José López The President of the Chamber of Deputies of the Spanish Government Palacio de las Cortes Carrera de San Jerónimo Madrid zip code, Spain
Minister of Foreign Affairs of the Spanish Government (Ministro de Asuntos Exteriores del Gobierno de España)	His Excellency Señor Don José López The Minister of Foreign Affairs of the Spanish Government Palacio de Santa Cruz Plaza de Santa Cruz Madrid zip code, Spain

SOCIAL ADDRESS	SALUTATION	LETTER CLOSING
Baron and Baroness Pietro di Sangro Via di Porta Liguria, 220 zip code Livorno, Italy	Dear Baron, Dear Baron and Baroness,	Sincerely yours,
It is not usual to address letters to the King unless one is a head of state. Correspondence should be addressed to the "Chief of His Majesty the King's Household" requesting that he convey a message to the King.		
His Excellency The President of the Spanish Government and Señora de López Calle Serrano 800 Madrid zip code, Spain	Dear Mr President, Dear President and Señora de López,	Respectfully yours,

His Excellency
The President of the Senate of the
  Spanish Government and Señora
  de López
Calle Velázquez 2000
Madrid zip code, Spain
	Dear Mr. President of the Senate,
	Dear President of the Senate and
	  Señora de López,
		Respectfully yours,

His Excellency
The President of the Chamber of
  Deputies of the Spanish
  Government and Señora de
  López
Calle Ortega y Gasset 2500
Madrid zip code, Spain
	Dear Mr. President of the Chamber
	  of Deputies,
	Dear President of the Chamber of
	  Deputies and Señora de López,
		Respectfully yours,

His Excellency
The Minister of Foreign Affairs of
  the Spanish Government and
  Señora de López
Palacio de Viana
Calle del Duque de Rivas 1
Madrid zip code, Spain
	Dear Mr. Minister,
	Dear Minister and Señora de López,
		Respectfully yours,

PERSONAGE	OFFICIAL/ BUSINESS ADDRESS
Ambassador of Spain (Embajador de España)	His Excellency Señor Don José López The Ambassador of Spain Embassy of Spain Belgrave Square London zip code, England
Consul General of Spain (Cónsul General de España)	The Honorable Señor Don José López The Consul General of Spain The Spanish Consulate 150 East Fifty-eighth Street New York, N.Y. 10022
PRINCELY TITLES Prince; Princess (Príncipe; Princesa)	In Spain there is only one Prince, and he is the heir to the throne. His title is Su Alteza Real el Príncipe de Asturias. He is addressed as Vuestra Alteza Real.
Duke, Duchess (Duque; Duquesa)	His Excellency The Duke of Hernández Calle de Serrano 42 Madrid zip code, Spain
Marquess; Marchioness (Marqués; Marquesa)	The Honorable[19] The Marqués of Vela Plaza de Salamanca 150 Madrid zip code, Spain
Count; Countess (Conde; Condesa)	The Honorable[19] The Count of Campo Rey Calle Ortega y Gasset 14 Madrid zip code, Spain

[19] In Spanish, a Marquess and a Count would be addressed as Ilustrísimo. Since this title has no direct translation in English, "The Honorable" may be used.

SOCIAL ADDRESS	SALUTATION	LETTER CLOSING

His Excellency
The Ambassador of Spain and
  Señora de López
Embassy of Spain
Belgrave Square
London zip code, England
	Dear Mr. Ambassador,
	Dear Ambassador and Señora de
	  López,
		Sincerely yours,

The Honorable
The Consul General of Spain and
  Señora de López
722 Park Avenue
New York, N.Y. 10021
	Dear Mr. Consul General,
	Dear Consul General and Señora de
	  López,
		Sincerely yours,

The Dukes of Hernández Calle de Serrano 42 Madrid zip code, Spain	Señor Duque, Señores Duques,	Sincerely yours,
The Marquesses of Vela Plaza de Salamanca 150 Madrid zip code, Spain	Señor Marqués, Señores Marqueses,	Sincerely yours,
The Counts of Campo Rey Calle Ortega y Gasset 14 Madrid zip code, Spain	Señor Conde, Señores Condes,	Sincerely yours,

Chapter 47

PARLIAMENTARY PROCEDURE

At one time or another, most of us witness or take part in some meeting that is conducted by the ancient and formal form of English parliamentary procedure. The American procedure is slightly different from the original English one. This highly stylized form is used for the conduct of various clubs, societies, and church bodies, as well as in ordinary business. Anyone who is asked to serve on a board of directors or elected to club or other office needs to know in greater detail than is here set forth the exact functioning of parliamentary procedure. The standard work on the subject is *Robert's Rules of Order,* obtainable in any library, but many meetings, particularly smaller ones, follow a simplified version of the procedure explained in this technical reference work.

The chairman of a meeting, in religious or debating assemblages sometimes called the moderator, must keep it in order and conduct its business. All members of the assembly are subject to the rulings of the chair. The chairman may not himself take part in debate unless he temporarily relinquishes the chair in order to do so.

Meetings conducted by means of parliamentary procedure may not transact any business unless a quorum is present: that is, a sufficient number of voting members to pass a resolution put to vote—normally a simple majority. The meeting is called to order by the chairman, who, if the secretary reports a quorum to be present, directs the secretary to read the minutes of the last meeting. The minutes are then approved as read, or corrected. Alternatively, the chairman may invite a motion to dispense with the reading of the minutes. The chairman then proceeds, according to the agenda for the meeting (usually prepared by the secretary), asking first for the officers' reports and thereafter for the various committee reports. These are followed by discussion, with each member who wishes to speak attracting the chairman's attention, usually by rising and saying "Mr. Chairman" or "Madam Chairman," sometimes "Mr. President" or "Madam President" (even in the case of an unmarried woman).

In small meetings the members often do not rise in order to be recognized especially if they are sitting around a table in a board room, but no matter how well the members are known to each other they are formally correct in reference to one another. "I am informed by Mr. Burns, etc.," instead of "Joe tells me, etc." The chairman, who may have known a member all her life, will still recognize her by saying, "The chair recognizes Mrs. Carlson," when she takes the floor, not "Yes, Mae." Since minutes of the meeting are recorded, it is important that the secretary have the correct names and, where appropriate, the identity of the speakers. In taking the floor, a person identifies himself and states that he "wishes to speak in behalf of—." It is better to err in the direction of overidentification than to assume that everyone in the room knows who you are and what you represent. You should identify yourself as "John Brown" or "Mary Smith," not "Mr. Brown" or "Mrs. Smith."

Sometimes acrimonious exchanges take place in board and other meetings, and keeping matters on a formal level in proper parliamentary style helps to foster the necessary objectivity, especially between chairman and assemblage.

In order to permit everyone who wishes to speak to be heard within the time available, it may be desirable for the chairman to limit in advance the amount of time to be permitted each speaker, and not to permit any speaker to speak more than twice on a given subject, except in clarification of remarks previously made, until all persons who wish to speak have been heard. No person may speak without being recognized by the chairman. The person who first rises to speak is entitled to recognition. The chairman should ask the person recognized to state his name for the record.

If disorder should occur, the chairman, at his discretion, can quit the chair and adjourn the meeting at any time. By common practice, the chairman is also entitled to recess the meeting at any time he feels it necessary or desirable to consult with his advisers in respect to any issue which may have been raised.

The main or principal question is the matter that is up for discussion. It is presented in the form of a motion or resolution. Except in the case of formal motions, such as to adjourn, motions and resolutions must be given to the chairman in writing if the chairman or secretary so requests. No motion may be proposed that is the same in substance as a motion which has previously been voted on. If a motion fails to be seconded, the chairman may refuse discussion or vote on it on the ground that the motion is not in order. After a motion has been made and seconded, the chairman customarily repeats the motion to the meeting and then asks, "Are you ready for the question?" This is an invitation for discussion. After discussion has been concluded, the chairman then puts the question to the meeting, i.e., states, "The question is on the adoption of the resolution [reading the resolution]" or "It has been moved and seconded, etc.," and conducts the vote. Except in the case of formal motions, such as to adjourn, the vote in large meetings should be by ballot. In smaller meetings, business is usually conducted by a voice vote, except for the election of officers or directors. After the voting, the chairman announces the results, saying, "The motion is carried," or "The resolution is adopted."

An amendment to a motion, like the motion itself, should be given to the chairman in writing, if requested, and should indicate clearly how the motion, as amended, will read. It should, of course, be seconded. An amendment to a motion must be relevant to the subject to be amended, and is not in order if it merely makes the affirmative of the amended question equivalent to the negative of the original question, or is identical with the question previously decided, or is a mere change in form. Discussion and vote on an amendment must be taken before discussion is resumed, and a vote taken, on the original motion.

A member of a board or committee should remain until the end of the meeting unless excused by the chair. If he has explained to the chairman before the start of the meeting that at some point he must leave, he may make his departure after catching the chair's eye at an opportune time and bowing. Sometimes in the case of an important member the chair makes some explanation, "Mr. Pryn has another meeting, ladies and gentlemen, and has asked to be excused at this time." The departing member then leaves without farewells, merely nodding to various members and the chair as he leaves. If in the middle of a meeting he is called to the phone, he may leave quietly without the chair's permission, unless a vote is about to be taken and his presence is necessary for a quorum.

When all items on the agenda have been covered, the chairman customarily asks, "Is there any further business to come before the meeting?" If he receives no reply, he may entertain a motion to adjourn or may say, after a suitable pause, "The meeting is adjourned." One then takes farewell of one's fellow board members or others in the meeting in a pleasant manner, even after heated and perhaps unpleasant discussion.

Chapter 48

JURY DUTY

Every voting citizen of the United States, except for a few like lawyers or newspapermen who are exempt, is eligible for and has the duty to serve as a juror when called. The way in which the names are chosen vary from state to state, even from county to county. But every jury panel is selected from a cross section of the community, and while certain temporary or permanent deferments are possible, most who are called must eventually serve.

One serves for a period of at least two weeks and receives a minor compensation for each day. If one loses a bit of money on one's business or is inconvenienced by serving, it is little enough to do on behalf of the justice system of this country. It is a responsibility and a privilege to serve.

When you receive your notice of jury duty, read it *carefully*. If it is absolutely necessary to request a deferment, the notice will state a date, time, and place to appear to request it. Many people do not read the notice carefully and wait to ask for the deferment until the day they are supposed to begin serving on jury duty. This upsets the entire system, as everyone who appears on that day is needed as a prospective juror.

Out of respect for the court, one should report for jury duty neatly dressed, as if for business. The period of selection of the jury can be a very tedious time, sometimes taking several days to complete, because each juror must satisfy the court, both parties, and their attorneys that he or she has no bias or prejudice in the case. The questions asked of each prospective juror must be answered carefully and honestly. During the long waiting time before being called for questioning by court or council, the juror should arm himself with ample reading material or office work (a lot of needlepoint and knitting can also be accomplished!).

No one can reach a juror during this time by telephone (except for a real emergency), but messages may be left at a special number, and there are pay telephones one can use to call out. A juror can talk to his home or office as much as he wants, but out of consideration to others wishing to make calls also, he should complete his own quickly. Once he is on a case, he can call out only during a break.

The jurors are together in close quarters for a long time, so their respect for cleaning up their own debris (emptying ash trays, coffee cups, and so on) and keeping their bathrooms neat is a community responsibility.

Once the entire jury has been selected, the judge instructs them on their duties and responsibilities. The judge must be treated with proper respect at all times. When he or she is talking, jurors should listen with close attention and not, as some have been known to do, leaf through magazines, write letters, or do handwork.

When a trial is under way, each juror should report promptly for each court session, since the trial cannot continue until all are present. It is inexcusable for a juror to be late. A juror should never falsely call in sick, for it wastes the time of the entire court and also wastes the taxpayers' money. A juror must concentrate hard on every question and answer during the trial. (It is better not to try to take notes, even when allowed, for one might miss subsequent testimony while writing.) The jurors are not supposed to discuss the case with each other or with anyone else until the case has been formally submitted to them and they begin joint deliberations in the jury room.

Serving as a juror can be a boring or an exciting experience, according to the case, but watching the process of justice in action is always impressive. Another affirmative note about serving on a jury is the friendships that are formed. The fact that a very heterogenous social, economic, and political group is thrown together in close circumstances, fulfilling an important civic duty that often entails dramatic and emotional circumstances, is bound to leave a lasting impression on its members.

Chapter 49

THE WHITE HOUSE

White House Invitations

It is an exciting event to receive a White House invitation. These invitations are always engraved with the presidential seal embossed in white or in gold; if it is a dinner or lunch, one's name is handwritten in the text in the most exquisite of calligraphy. If you are invited to a reception, which would usually be held from 5:30 to 8:00 P.M., you should make every effort to attend. The dress is almost always informal at this hour. You would not wear a long dress; a man would not wear a black tie. If you are invited to an after-dinner reception (9:30 or 10:00 P.M.) the invitation will probably read "Black Tie." Generally, you will be served champagne at this hour, and there will be either dancing or after-dinner entertainment of some kind in the gold and white ballroom that is known as the East Room.

If you are invited to a meal in the White House, it is, figuratively speaking, a command performance. The only reasons that make it acceptable to regret such an invitation are a death in the family, absence from the country, or illness. In all cases a White House invitation should be taken seriously.

You should handwrite a formal acceptance to a White House invitation no more than a day after receiving one and address it to "The Social Secretary, The White House, Washington, D.C. 20500." If you are invited by Mailgram, send a return Mailgram message. Do not ask the White House staff to make a hotel reservation or any travel arrangements for you.

At a luncheon naturally no formal dress is worn. A man wears a dark or light (according to the time of year) business suit; a woman, a suit or an appropriate nondécolleté daytime costume. If a woman has a smart-looking hat, she should wear it; she also looks more "complete" if she arrives wearing gloves, which are removed and put into her coat pocket or handbag. No one should shake hands with the President or First Lady while wearing gloves.

If you have received a dinner invitation to the White House, and "Black

Tie" is not indicated (informal dinners were started by President Carter), dark business suits for the men, and dressy late-afternoon dresses for women would be appropriate. Her choice may be velvet, lamé, silk, or some other formal fabric, but the skirt should not be evening-gown length. If a woman is unsure about her attire, all she has to do is dial (202) 456-1414 and ask for the Social Secretary's office to inquire about the appropriate attire for that particular presidential dinner.

If the invitation does say "Black Tie," the man wears a black tuxedo and the woman her prettiest long gown and jewels.

If, instead, the invitation says "White Tie," the man must dress in white tie and tails for the evening. There are several good men's-wear rental shops in Washington; and if he calls ahead and gives his proper size, his white tie and tails will be cleaned, pressed, and waiting for him on his arrival in the city. The woman wears her dressiest ball gown, jewels, and long white gloves if she so chooses. As mentioned before, gloves are always removed when shaking hands with the President or the First Lady, and of course when eating.

One must arrive at the gate stipulated on the invitation when attending any White House function. There will be a guard at the gate who will ask to see your "admit" card, which is sent with all White House invitations. After clearance, your taxi or car and driver will then be allowed to drive up to the entrance of the mansion. Do not bring your own car, as there are no parking facilities at the White House. Upon entering, there will be a guard at the door who will take your "admit" card and direct you to the area where coats are to be checked.

Almost immediately you will notice a number of handsome young men in military uniforms; they are the traditional "White House social aides" who have regular jobs in the military services, and who also attend White House social events. Their primary function is to circulate among the guests seeing that they are having a good time and answering any questions that may arise. The aides are enormously helpful in introducing guests to one another and in making people feel at ease. The social secretary will also be in evidence, as she has spent many hours organizing all aspects of the evening. She is in charge of co-ordinating the entire evening and will be watching out for guests who may have arrived alone and need introducing.

A State Dinner

Should the occasion be a state dinner, the guests first congregate in the East Room. There they are served a glass of wine or a cocktail, according to the custom of that particular administration. At an appointed time, the Marine Band, which has been playing in the large entrance hall of the house, strikes up a march, which is the signal that the President, the First Lady, and the honored guests are descending the grand staircase from the living quarters to join the party. There is a short photographic session at the foot of the staircase, after which the group proceeds to the East Room while the band plays "ruffles and flourishes." At the entrance to the East Room the President and those with him stand at attention while a social aide announces in a loud, resonant voice the arrival of the President of the United States, the First Lady, and whoever the dignitaries may be. Following the presentation announcement they enter the room with the band playing "Hail to the Chief." There is a military posting of the colors by the honor guard, after which the President, the First Lady, and the guests of honor take their place in the receiving line.

The social aides assemble the guests in an orderly fashion for the receiving line. Introductions are made by a State Department protocol official or by a military aide. The line should move swiftly, so the greeting must be brief. If an old friend of the President's is in the line, he should not hold everything up with a long conversation on "how things are back home." One shakes their hands and says something no more time-taking than, "You're doing a great job, Mr. President. We're so proud of you back home."

The guests are escorted from the receiving line into the State Dining Room and are shown to their tables according to the seating chairs and place cards. When the President, the First Lady, and the honored guests appear, they sit down first, and the guests then follow. If a leading clergyman is present, everyone remains standing until after the blessing.

No one should smoke until after the dessert has been served. No man should smoke a cigar, under any circumstances, until the footman passes him one. No one should light a pipe until the cigar smokers light up, and only if asking the others at the table, "Do you mind?"

Guests may take as souvenirs from the table the following items and nothing else: menu card, place card (both bearing the presidential seal in gold embossing, with one's name in calligraphy), and White House matches.

Coffee, always in small demitasse cups, may be served in the East Room or in the corridors outside the various reception rooms.

White House dinners follow regular social procedure. One talks to one's neighbor on the right for the first course, then one switches to one's neighbor on the left for the next course, then back to the right for the next course. At a White House affair you should not leave until the President and the First Lady return to the family quarters, except in the case of a real emergency. It is customary for the guests to depart soon after the President, although it is perfectly all right to linger for a *short* time.

After you have been to a White House reception, lunch, or dinner, always write a thank-you note. You do not write to the President's wife with anything other than "Mrs." and her last name. In other words, you address the letter to "Mrs. Adams," not "Mrs. John Adams."

Business Calls at the White House

In most cases, you will be instructed to come to the West Wing of the White House, where the President's offices are located. Follow carefully the instructions you receive, because once again security is strict. You will have to show identification at the specified gate, preferably a driver's license with your photograph. If you are carrying cases or tote bags they will be inspected and most likely stowed in lockers at the guard's station. These security measures unfortunately have become a necessary way of life for the White House in recent years. Arrive about ten minutes before your appointment with the President and be prepared to wait.

Do not bring the President a gift. It will only make things awkward and embarrass him. If you are a good friend and want to send him something inexpensive you feel he would like, call his secretary and tell her what it is. If she agrees he would appreciate the gift, she will explain how you should address the package so that it will reach his office. Otherwise he will probably not see it.

Gifts to the White House

If you are planning to send a gift to the White House, you should be aware that because of the great number of gifts received it is virtually impossible for the President and First Lady to see most of them. Every gift sent to the White House is X-rayed by the White House police, and all food is destroyed. While different administrations handle the disposition of gifts in different ways, it is not unusual for handworked gifts to be sent to the National Archives to emerge one day when that President has his museum and can display his gifts. On the other hand, one can labor long and lovingly over something by hand, whether it is a painting, a sculpture, or a crocheted afghan, only to have it returned with a thank-you note "on behalf of the President and Mrs. Adams." At this particular time, the White House policy is to return most gifts that are received regardless of monetary value.

An exception to the sending of gifts is flowers. If you have been received as a guest at a lunch or a dinner at the White House, it is a nice gesture to send flowers to the First Lady (if it was a stag dinner or lunch with the President, this would not apply) with your card, or with a note saying what a beautiful evening it was. Since there are so many places in which to put fresh flowers in the White House and it is so expensive to keep the house filled with flowers, guests can perform a valuable service by sending them.

Letters to the President and First Lady

Letters, on the other hand, are always welcome, as the President and the First Lady like to hear "what's on America's mind." Since many thousands of letters a week arrive at the White House, the First Family sees only a sampling of the mail, or a synopsis of public opinion expressed in them. It would be physically impossible for them personally to answer each letter, much less read each one. Letters are acknowledged by a White House staff member or the appropriate government agency.

Taking a White House Tour

The way most people see their President's home is on a free public tour, which takes about twenty-five minutes once one is in the main part of the house. The White House today is an exquisite museum of nineteenth-century Americana and of presidential memorabilia dating from George Washington's administration, thanks to the work of the original Fine Arts Committee for the White House, organized by Mrs. John F. Kennedy and carried on by subsequent administrations. Every American should try to see the White House at some point in his life.

Public tours through the main reception rooms on the ground floor and the first floor are held from 10:00 A.M. to 12 noon Tuesday through Saturday (except national holidays). People should go to the East Gate. Sunday is a day of rest for the household staff, and Monday is a thorough house-cleaning day, desperately needed after thousands of people have tramped through during any given week.

If visitors are lucky when they stand in line in the East Hall to go through the house, they may catch a glimpse of a member of the First Family or a top-ranking presidential visitor using the South Portico entrance. If they are very lucky, they will see the President's helicopter land on the South lawn to pick up the First Family. White House guidebooks (the proceeds of which go toward the restoration activities of the house) may be purchased inexpensively in the East Wing. It's a good idea to take the book along and read the history of each room as you pass through, since there is no tour conductor.

From 8 A.M. until the public tours start, there are special tours (with twenty to fifty people), which are escorted by a White House policeman-guide through the mansion. He gives the history of the room and its furnishings as you go along. It is not easy to be included in these tours, as they are arranged by your senator or congressman. Senators are allowed fifteen to twenty places per week for their constituents and representatives are allowed ten per week. Some of the legislators receive up to three hundred requests a week, particularly at holiday times, so don't expect instant success on your request to be put on a special tour. It is best to write several months in advance of your trip to Washington. You should always write your legislator a thank-you note for arranging it, and if you write a thank-you note to your White House guide, he, of course, appreciates it immensely.

Appropriate Dress In the summer in Washington the weather is usually incredibly hot and muggy, so tourists have the right to dress comfortably. However, there is no excuse for dressing as though one were sunbathing on the beach. One should dress with respect when one is in the house of a country head of state, whether it's the White House, Buckingham Palace, or the Elysées Palace.

Chapter 50

THE FLAG AND OUR NATIONAL ANTHEM

Regulations for Displaying the Flag

Many homes and most business houses, fraternal organizations, and all public buildings own and from time to time display the flag. Some in doing so do not realize that there are definite rules concerning the proper display of the flag that protect it from desecration. It can't be used, for example, as a trademark or part of a coat of arms, even in slightly altered form. There are state and federal statutes to enforce this ruling and others concerning the respectful use and display of the flag, although some are or will be relaxed.

Here are the major regulations concerning display of the flag:

1. Never fly it upside down except as a distress signal.
2. Don't let it trail on the ground—or even touch it—or in the water.
3. Display the flag only from sunrise to sunset out of doors and lower it promptly if it rains. Flags flown at night must be lighted.
4. Hoist the flag briskly but lower it slowly and reverently.
5. City and state flags or those of organizations flown from the same staff as the United States flag should be placed below the flag. No other flag is ever flown above it. On boats, signal and flag officers' flags are flown from the aft deck.
6. When organization or other flags are flown in conjunction with the U.S. flag on adjacent flagstaffs, the U.S. flag is always hoisted first and is last to come down (except in case of rain). Flags flown on adjacent flagpoles should always be placed on the left of the flag itself. No other flag is ever placed to the flag's right (observer's left).
7. When other nations' flags are flown with ours, they should be on separate standards, should be the same size as the U.S. flag, and should be flown at the same height. In times of peace, no nation's flag takes precedence in an arrangement of flags, but it is usual for the U.S. flag flown on U.S. soil, or on its ships or bases, to have the central position in such a groupings of flags. In wartime, no immediately adjacent flag

is ever flown at the U.S. flag's own right even in a grouping of allies' flags.

8. A flag flown from a staff fastened to a window sill or balcony or fixed to the front of a building must be flown with the union, or blue field, at the peak of the staff unless the flag is at half-mast. Flags are flown at half-mast only by official state, federal, or city order, never flown in such a manner to indicate personal loss to a family or to a business or other organization. In the last case, the deceased is so honored occasionally but then only by official decree if he has been of civic importance.

9. When a flag is suspended over a sidewalk on a cord from the building to a pole on the sidewalk, the flag is hoisted from the building to the pole, union first (so it may be taken in quickly in a storm).

10. When a flag is displayed without a staff, it should lie flat against an upright support, indoors or out, never draped or festooned. (Use bunting for this purpose.) When it is dislayed horizontally or vertically against a wall, the union or field is uppermost, to the flag's own right. When the flag is displayed from a window, it is always shown with the union to the left of the observer in the street.

11. A flag displayed over the middle of the street should hang vertically with the union to the north in an east and west street or the east in a north and south one.

12. In displaying the flag on a speaker's platform, place it above and behind the speaker, flat, union to the flag's right, observer's left. If it is flown from a staff on the platform, it should be flown to the speaker's right, in the place of honor. It must never be used to cover a table or desk. Never drape it over the platform.

13. Flags carried in a mourning parade or procession are never put at half-mast but may display a black crepe bow knot with or without two black crepe streamers at the fastening points by order of the President. It may not be used in this way for private funeral processions.

14. When the flag is to be flown at half-mast, it is first hoisted to the peak, then put at half-mast. Before lowering it for the night, hoist it again to the peak.

15. On Memorial Day the flag is flown at half-mast only from sunrise until noon, when it is hoisted to full staff.

16. Don't use the flag to unveil even a patriotic statue or monument, although it is properly used in the attendant ceremonies.

17. The only exception in the draping of the flag occurs when it is used to cover a casket, union at the head and over the deceased's left shoulder. The flag must not touch the ground or be lowered into the grave. The casket is carried foot first. The flag is used for this honor only for members of the armed services, for cabinet officers of the federal and state governments, and for others of national importance for whom the President decrees official mourning.

18. When a flag becomes torn, tattered, or otherwise unfit for display it is never heedlessly discarded. If it is beyond mending and cleaning it should be destroyed in one piece, privately, by burning. Its fabric may not be reused for some other purpose. An old flag, faded, worn, and torn beyond restitution, deserves and must receive respectful destruction so it will never fall into thoughtless hands.

19. The flag must never be dipped to any person or thing. Only personal, state, regimental or other flags may be used to render this honor.

20. Never place any object or emblem on or above the U.S. flag with the exception of the American eagle.

21. Never fasten the flag in a way that it can be easily torn.

22. The flag may not be draped on any vehicle. If it is to be displayed on a train, boat, or car it must be firmly fixed to a staff.

23. The flag must not be displayed from a parade float except from a staff.

24. The flag may not be used to cover the ceiling.

25. The flag may not be carried horizontally in procession, but must be aloft and waving.

26. Those who respect the flag are saddened by its commercial exploitation and lack of proper handling. If you have any questions, check The United States Flag Foundation, 39 West 53rd Street, New York, N.Y. 10019.

27. No lettering of any kind may be placed on the flag.

28. The pole from which the flag flies must never carry advertising signs or pennants. It may not be used in any form of display advertising, except that placed for the United States government.

29. A flag displayed in the body of the church is flown from a staff, to the congregation's right as it faces the pulpit. Service, state, or other special flags are flown to the left of the congregation. If the flag is to be displayed from the chancel or the platform it is placed on the clergyman's right, to the congregation's left. Other flags are flown from the clergyman's left.

30. Store the flag in such a way that it will be protected from moths and other damage. Never place it on the floor even for a moment, and never permit anyone to step on it or show it any disrespect, unwitting or not.

Invocation and Salute to the Flag

At a public dinner or luncheon meeting, or any other occasion where an invocation and a salute to the flag are given, the invocation precedes the salute—God, then country.

The Singing of Our National Anthem

When the anthem is played, you must rise promptly and stand at attention unless you are infirm or very old. Even young children should be taught to stand quietly and respectfully when they hear "The Star-Spangled Banner" and, like the rest of us, they should, as soon as possible, learn the words of at least the first and last stanzas.

The national anthem is not easy to sing, but most people can transpose the high notes an octave lower, as they go along, into something they can manage. Don't stand mute because you are afraid of those high notes. If you can't transpose, sing everything *but* the high notes and let the sopranos reach for them. It is sad that so few of us can sing the words accurately, although I can sympathize with anyone's difficulty with the range. The idea behind the mass singing of the anthem is to stir a feeling of patriotism and unity. Fine voices aren't essential. Enthusiastic, heart-warming, not half-hearted, singing by everybody does proper honor.

If you feel you can't sing, then you should stand quietly and respectfully without whispering, talking, or fidgeting until the anthem is finished. If a man is wearing a hat, he should remove it and hold it with his right hand over his heart. Others should stand at attention or place the right hand over the heart. It is usual if more than the first stanza is to be sung for the assemblage to go right into the last stanza, omitting the second and third unless the words appeared on printed programs. Memorization of the first and last stanzas should be sufficient.

"The Star-Spangled Banner"

O say, can you see, by the dawn's early light,
    What so proudly we hailed at the twilight's last gleaming?
Whose broad stripes and bright stars, through the perilous fight,
    O'er the ramparts we watched were so gallantly streaming?
And the rockets' red glare, the bombs bursting in air,
    Gave proof through the night that our flag was still there.
O say, does that star-spangled banner yet wave
O'er the land of the free and the home of the brave?

LAST STANZA

O thus be it ever, when freemen shall stand
    Between their loved homes and the war's desolation!
Blest with vict'ry and peace, may the heav'n-rescued land
    Praise the Power that hath made and preserved us a nation.
Then conquer we must, when our cause it is just,
    And this be our motto: "In God is our trust."
And the star-spangled banner in triumph shall wave
O'er the land of the free and the home of the brave.

—Francis Scott Key

As with many other such ceremonies, the singing of the anthem (which you may not like as music or for what are called, by some, its chauvinistic lyrics) is a mark of respect for one's country and flag. There are other patriotic songs—such as "America the Beautiful," "Columbia the Gem of the Ocean," "God Bless America," and "Yankee Doodle"—but they do not require the respectful response that must be given "The Star-Spangled Banner," designated as our official national anthem.

Traditionally, a public appearance of the President is preceded by the rendition of "ruffles and flourishes," a signal for all to stand at attention. The march "Hail to the Chief" is the signal that the President is arriving at once. Before the opening of ceremonies at which the President is to speak, "The Star-Spangled Banner" is played. It is played directly after a public toast to the President (on the rare occasions when one is proposed). Usually only the first stanza is played, and singing accompaniment is not expected, although it is not incorrect to sing. The singing or playing of the anthem is never applauded.

In an Orthodox synagogue it is not only proper but required that in any salute to the flag or singing of the national anthem the men's heads remain covered. It is forbidden in an Orthodox synagogue for men's heads to be uncovered at any time.

Anthems of Other Nations

In America public gatherings often open with the playing of our national anthem. If another country's representatives are present, as, for example, members of the cavalry teams from various countries in the National Horse Show, or a great pianist from another country at, say, a White House musicale, the visitors' national anthem is played first, ours second. For all national anthems, everyone stands at attention and all civilians place the right hand over the heart in salute. They may sing the anthem if they wish— many Americans seem to know the "Marseillaise" and "God Save the Queen" (whose music is the same as that of "America")—but they need not actually salute any but their own flag. Abroad they never pledge allegiance to another flag, just as no non-American ever repeats the words of our pledge.

Chapter 51

VISITING A NAVAL VESSEL

The Navy encourages people to visit ships in port and no special invitation is required, particularly on Sundays. On weekends and holidays every naval base has certain ships designated for "general visiting." These ships will be prepared with guides and welcome-aboard pamphlets. For the most part, crew members are proud of their ship and take a good deal of pride and enjoyment in showing it off to interested civilians.

If you are "in the Navy" as wife, mother, or fiancée, you will certainly be well schooled in the many visiting regulations. But the untutored civilian planning to visit one of our ships needs to know the accepted Navy way of doing things.

Aboard Ship

Embarking When you go aboard a naval vessel at anchor, you embark in a small boat that takes you out to the ship. The trip may be choppy and the seats uncomfortable. Even when the small boat is still fast to the dock it may heave and rock menacingly—from the standpoint of the less surefooted or queasy. A woman assumes her escort's position in the naval hierarchy and embarks and leaves the boat accordingly. Junior officers and guests sit forward, senior officers and distinguished visitors in the stern, for the good reason that even on the calmest day the front will get splashed and the ride is generally rougher.

When the small boat is alongside the ship the senior officers and their wives disembark first—wives first unless there is no one at the foot of the ladder to assist them and the sea is rough, when a younger officer or two may disembark first to help the ladies. Very young women hold back until older women or the wives of dignitaries disembark, then dignitaries and high-ranking officers leave before the younger men and women. It is an honor to be among the last into a boat, barge, gig, or any such ship's boat and among the first to leave. Children, therefore, should not be allowed in their enthusiasm to clamber up the ladder, perhaps past the captain himself, although in a rough sea a very old person or mother and small baby would probably be granted precedence.

Stepping from a small boat to a ship's gangway is sometimes quite an athletic undertaking even when the weather on shore looks perfectly calm. A visit to the engine room, when allowed, requires a perpendicular descent on steel ladders with blasts of air coming from beneath, so be forewarned. Descents on the ordinary ladders between weather decks are steep, too, and the wind seems to find them even when a ship is tied snugly up to the dock. Unless the occasion requires formal dress, in which case you will probably not be using the ladders, women should wear slacks or a pants suit and shoes with low, wide heels, as the ladders are made of metal gratings.

Making a Call Aboard a Naval Vessel   Some type of pass is issued to all visitors coming aboard the ship, usually on the quarter deck, by the officer on watch. There are no official calling hours, but the normal working day ends around 4 P.M. Visitors are frequently invited for dinner and the movie afterward, but must be off the ship promptly at 10 P.M.

If you are expected aboard by your host at a certain hour, he will probably be on deck to meet you, but even if you see him standing there as you come over the side, you first greet the officer of the deck (O.O.D.) stationed on the quarter-deck at the head of the ladder. He is, during his watch anyhow, in charge of the ship, the captain's surrogate on the quarter-deck. To you he is the official host, of whom you take cognizance the minute you arrive by saying, "How do you do," or "Good afternoon" (shaking hands after his salute, if you wish, if you are a civilian), and of whom you take polite official leave. If your naval host has come out with you in the boat, you precede him up the gangway, greet the O.O.D., and step aside to await your host before joining any groups already formed on deck, even when you know members of them.

Boarding   The quarter-deck is a small area of deck located at the section of the ship where it is convenient to rig a sea ladder or gangway. In ancient times it consisted of the small raised deck in the stern of the ship where sacred images of the altar were kept, and later the flags of kings. In deference to tradition, sacred in all the navies of the world, uniformed men, as they reach the upper gangway platform, face aft and salute the colors and, thereafter, the officer of the deck. Civilians show correct deference by stopping briefly and facing the colors, although with them the gesture is one of courtesy and not, as with the armed forces, obligatory.

Honors to Civilians   The President or some other official might receive special honors as he boards—a salute from the guns or the running up of his flag. If so, he remains on the gangway platform with his hand over his heart in the civilian flag salute until the honors have been completed. He then greets the O.O.D. by shaking hands before accepting the welcome of the captain and other officers.

Prohibitions Concerning Naval Vessels

The U. S. Navy is dry, so one should never bring liquor of any kind aboard a ship either for your own use or as a gift for your host. Traditionally the Navy did not permit cameras, but that rule has been relaxed and many ships will allow pictures to be taken, especially topside. The best procedure is to ask at the quarterdeck when you board if it is permissible to use cameras.

Meals aboard for the officers are in the wardroom, which is run like a men's club with meals billed to each officer on a monthly basis. Do not invite yourself to meals aboard under the mistaken assumption that they will always be on Uncle Sam. Your entertainment is provided by the members of the mess. If you do eat there, the senior officer of the wardroom and president of the mess is your official host. Excuse yourself to him if you must leave before the others. On most ships, enlisted men are allowed to invite guests for supper and other meals in the enlisted men's mess on the weekends.

Smoking is allowed in most areas of a ship, except for example, near ammunition. Because of the close quarters it is considerate to ask permission before lighting up, and do not smoke unless there is somewhere to dispose of ashes and butt. Do not litter butts on the deck, as some sailor has the duty of swabbing and polishing that deck every day and marks from cigarettes make his life harder.

Officers' Staterooms

With the exception of the captain and senior officers, other officers generally share their rooms with one or more other officers. While a woman making a tour of a ship may be asked to inspect these quarters, she must treat them as the communal rooms they are, even if it's her husband's room that interests her particularly. Doors must be left open—even when wives are inspecting the rooms—and congregating must take place on deck or in the wardroom, not in the individual rooms. Tender moments aboard a ship are best arranged by your host. He may be "off duty" officially, but he is under constant surveillance while he's on his ship. Don't try to break down his very necessary dignity and decorum.

Nautical Terms

Never refer to a ship or a boat as anything but "she." Only small craft, pulling boats, dories, and small power boats of various kinds are "boats." Anything from a patrol craft up is a ship.

Aboard a man-of-war there is no saloon, as on an ocean liner. Instead there is the wardroom for the officers' mess (dining) and recreation, the junior officers' mess, the warrant officers' mess, the chief petty officer's mess, and the enlisted men's mess. On large ships the captain's cabin is his mess hall, but on smaller ships he eats with the other officers in the wardroom. Enlisted men are quartered in compartments, and officers have staterooms, although they bear no resemblance to the luxurious staterooms of an ocean liner.

Floors are referred to as decks, walls are bulkheads. Topside is any exposed deck, and below deck is any covered deck.

Chapter 52

AN AUDIENCE WITH THE POPE

Visitors to Rome—Catholic and non-Catholic—often desire to see the Pope as well as visit historic Vatican City where he lives.

Every Sunday at noon, if the Pope is in residence at St. Peter's Basilica, he appears at the open window in his private apartments (a tradition centuries old) to speak to the masses of people in the square below. He gives a short message pertinent to the times in several languages, and when he imparts the final benediction Catholics generally make the sign of the cross and many kneel down in the square. No one *has* to do anything.

Tourists in Rome should always check for the weekly schedule of activities in the Vatican, because it is exciting to be in St. Peter's Square on the day when the Pope blesses all the cars driven in or the day he blesses people's pets brought to the square. The curving Bernini colonnade encompassing the church seems to expand miraculously outward in order to embrace hundreds of thousands of *il popolo,* and the people really love the Pope. At first it upsets Americans who haven't been briefed when they see people screaming, shouting, applauding, and laughing for joy when the Holy Father appears—as though everyone's favorite rock group or athletic hero were appearing. Although he is a figure that commands utmost respect, the Pope loves the "sound of the crowd" and is used to the applauding and shouting. More reserved tourists and pilgrims from other countries often get caught up in the noisy emotionalism and behave more Italian than the Italians.

Having a General Audience

If you want to participate in a "General Audience" with the Pope (held normally on Wednesday morning at 11 A.M.) you must write well in advance, particularly for the summer tourist season months, to the Office of the Papal Audience, Casa S. Maria dell'Umiltà, Via dell'Umiltà 30, Rome 00187. These offices are under the jurisdiction of the North American College, the official American liaison with the Vatican. It helps if you accompany your request with a letter of introduction from your parish priest. (If you are Protestant or Jewish, perhaps you know a priest or have a friend who would introduce you to one, so that a letter could be written on your behalf.) The letter is not absolutely necessary; it might speed things along, however. If there is sufficient time, you might receive back from the North American College a letter confirming you will be received in an audience. In any case, when you reach Rome, call the Via dell'Umiltà offices to ask if you are indeed scheduled, and arrange to pick up your entrance tickets there. They will instruct you when to arrive at the special Papal Audience Hall inside the Vatican grounds. Since thousands of people are involved in these General Audiences, it is best to arrive early. Do not drive your car; take a taxi or bus.

The seats down front in the Audience Hall are reserved for special VIPs. Most seating is first come first served, except that large groups traveling together (such as pilgrims from another country) sit together in blocks. The Holy Father usually refers to these special groups during his remarks in their native tongue, at which point loud, enthusiastic cheering breaks out from that section.

Everyone rises when the Pope appears, carried on a portable throne. The audience may sit after the Pope is seated on his permanent throne. The Holy Father speaks sometimes for fifteen minutes, sometimes much longer, and gives his remarks usually in Italian first, then French, English, German, and Spanish—according to the nationality of the people assembled in the hall. Everything is quite informal. People rise, clap, shout, and whistle when he arrives and then sits on his throne. They continue to express their love and admiration for him as he finishes speaking in each language. "Viva il Papa!" is a universal cry in Vatican City. Before he leaves the hall he raises his hand to give the papal blessing. Everyone should bow down at this moment; Catholics usually genuflect and make the sign of the cross.

Anyone who wishes to have anything blessed for relatives and friends back home should hold these articles in their hands, so that they will be blessed by the Pope during his final benediction. They can also be blessed if people hold them out in St. Peter's Square during the Pope's Sunday noon appearance.

During the summer months the Pope usually resides at his summer residence in Castel Gandolfo. General audiences are held there, too, once a week, usually at 10 A.M., but the crowd that can be accommodated is much smaller. Buses transport people from Rome to the Pope's palace. Ask your hotel *portiere* or any Roman travel bureau about the closest place to your hotel to board the bus.

Semiprivate Audiences

Semiprivate audiences are held for special groups of fifty to two hundred. These must be arranged months in advance and are difficult to achieve, because the Pope has so many demands for audiences from groups around the world. If you are going as a museum group on a special art tour of Italy, for example, or you are having special meetings of your profession in Italy, approach your city's bishop and ask his help in arranging a semiprivate audience through the offices of the North American College in Rome.

Private Audiences

A private audience is one where twelve or fewer people are received, usually very important people (such as heads of state or ambassadors) and their families. At these private audiences, which usually last only about fifteen or twenty minutes, the Holy Father presents each person with a personal gift, which might be a special rosary, a small bronze medallion, or a holy medal. When heads of state call on the Pope, there is always an official exchange of gifts. I remember that when President John F. Kennedy went to see Pope Paul VI in a private audience, he brought as his gift a handsome large letter box in sterling silver, for the official papers on the Pope's desk. The lid of the box was engraved with the date of the visit, the papal arms, and the Presidential Seal of the United States. (The Pope purportedly said to the President, "What a handsome gift, Mr. President, and I finally have something I can use!" A very human remark indeed.)

When the Holy Father enters the special room designated for private audiences, the small group is usually assembled in a kind of reverse receiving line. The Pope passes down this line as one of the assistants calls out the name of each person being presented. That person either goes down on one knee or bows low; if he is a Catholic he will take the Pope's hand in his right hand and kiss his ring. A non-Catholic will simply bow low in a sign of respect and shake his hand. The Pope pauses to say something to each individual, giving particular attention to children, and then he may sit down at a kind of table-desk to give a short talk to the group. There is no need to be concerned about what to do, as there are always friendly assistants and church officials who instruct you on where to stand and what to do.

How to Dress for an Audience

The formerly very rigid laws governing dress for anyone entering the presence of the Holy Father have changed drastically. No longer are women required to be completely covered up, including their arms, and heads. For a general audience you can wear your ordinary travel clothes, but they should be conservative in style and color. Women in pants are now admitted to the general audience, but women in shorts or sun dresses are not admitted. For a semiprivate or a private audience, men should wear dark business suits; women should wear their most conservative dress of any color, with a minimum of jewelry and no gloves. Children dress in their "Sunday best." Some women particularly from the Spanish-speaking countries, when received in private audience still wear the long black dress and lace mantilla, but that is not obligatory today.

The Pope in St. Peter's Basilica

When the Pope officiates at Mass in St. Peter's, which he does often during special religious feasts such as Christmas and Easter, special stands for guests are erected close to the altar. These are reserved seats for members of the Vatican diplomatic corps, high church officials from all over the world, and prominent Italians from social, business, and titled circles. Many thousands of *il popolo* crowd into St. Peter's, too, to witness the spectacle. The Pope is borne to the altar on a red damask sedan chair on the shoulders of the strong *Sediari*. The swelling shouts of the crowd and the sounds of the majestic organ music fill the basilica as he makes his way slowly through the roped-off crowds to the altar that Bernini designed under a swirling gold canopy. It glistens in the candlelight; the Swiss Guards in their costumes stand smartly at attention, and the clustering cardinals in their bright crimson robes make it all a most unforgettable sight.

Part Seven

YOU ON PUBLIC VIEW

You, Your Wardrobe, and Your Accessories   657

Men's Apparel   669

Dining in Restaurants   679

Private Clubs   694

The Considerate Sportsperson   699

The Important of Introductions   723

Public Speaking   729

Conversation: the Great Social Tool   742

Hospitals and Doctors   748

You are a combination of the sum of many elements: how you look, how you talk, how you move, how you act, how you meet people, how you handle yourself at parties, how you handle yourself at work, how you handle yourself with your family. Everyone is at his best when his behavior is spontaneous. If you learn the ways to behave and act so that your spontaneous behavior is also considerate of others, you are on your way to success on a human scale, the most important scale of all!

Chapter 53

YOU, YOUR WARDROBE, AND
YOUR ACCESSORIES

Your appearance tells everyone who sees you something very important: *what you really think about yourself.* You are a mirror of your own self-opinion. Whether you are in tennis clothes, or jeans and a sweater, or full evening regalia, you telegraph a message to those around you. They see you, hopefully, as a neat, clean, pulled-together person who cares about himself or herself.

Organizing a Woman's Wardrobe

A woman without budget problems can buy clothes indiscriminately, but she represents only one tenth of one per cent of the population. Apparel costs so much these days, a woman has to look hard at her life-style, her figure, and her budget before she assembles her wardrobe. The carefully dressed woman is relaxed about the planning of her wardrobe because she does it well in advance and allows time for necessary shopping. She never waits until she wants to wear an outfit to go shopping for it. At all times she has in her wardrobe something appropriate for the social occasions she is likely to encounter.

Budget Although every woman's fashion budget will differ, depending on her needs, income, life-style, social life, and the climate, there is one rule that applies to everyone: *it is better to buy fewer but better things.* Something that is not of good quality will not look right even at the beginning of the fashion season; something well made of good-quality fabric will look right season after season.

The demands on a woman to wear the "latest thing" differ according to her job or her social position. A woman involved in the world of design and retailing will try to wear the trends of the moment. A woman lawyer, on the other hand, must be well dressed, but she does not have to worry about current fads. A woman at home needs a more casual wardrobe than a woman who goes to an office. A woman whose husband entertains constantly as part of his business life needs yet another type of wardrobe. This variety in life-styles is why we must all read fashion magazines and fashion news reporting in the papers with intelligence, and edit out of our imaginations the items that look great on the page and might look great on us, but do not fit our way of life.

The well-dressed woman does not buy her wardrobe in a piecemeal fashion but at the beginning of each season gets out all of her clothes; discards those things that take up closet space without being worn, for one reason or another; decides what needs remodeling, shortening, lengthening, or other alterations; then, with a picture of what she needs firmly in mind, goes to her favorite stores or couturiers. She does not discard basic standbys of her wardrobe that have given good service and that are becoming. Instead, she integrates them into a wardrobe for the coming season, adding a new belt here, a scarf there, a blazer, a shirt, or costume jewelry to make something old and beloved look new and fresh.

Colors   The woman who has no basic color scheme in her wardrobe must have considerable money in order to be well dressed. She will need many more accessories than the woman who has accepted the idea that there are certain basic colors becoming to her and to which she should adhere if she wishes to dress well, within her budget.

Basic colors are black, blue, brown (with all its variations), and gray. On these four a good wardrobe can be built, allowing infinite fashion variety.

It is the interchangeability of accessories that makes one's wardrobe interesting. Even extravagantly well dressed women follow the basic plan of using colors that complement and contrast with each other in a logical way.

As a young girl's taste in clothes develops, she will find that she turns again and again to certain accent colors because they make her prettier or happier. Eventually she is guided almost unconsciously to these colors and variations of them. She will have decided early which of the basic colors go best with the accent colors she likes to wear, and she will buy her shoes, bags, belts, and coats in basic colors that will complement or match anything she is likely to buy.

Dressing Well and Following Fashion

The basis of knowing what to wear where and when is a question of proper guidance and self-education. Money spent lavishly on a wardrobe is not essential; what is essential is knowing how to select and assemble the elements together. Most important is putting your memory to work in order to recall the general type of apparel you've seen worn by most people on a certain kind of occasion. If you have an expensive suede pants suit and wear it to a wedding, you have missed the meaning of "the appropriateness of the occasion."

If you're at all unsure about what to wear to a party or what to take on a weekend visit, ask your hosts. A telephone call is the best insurance in the world. "I was just wondering what everyone will be wearing tomorrow night. . . ." I remember hearing one man deprecate another's well-known good taste in his clothes. "What does it matter, anyway," asked ths first man, rather sarcastically, "this being 'properly dressed' all the time? It makes no difference to a man's performance on his job."

The "properly dressed" one replied, "It makes only one difference. It makes me feel self-confident."

It should be the goal of every person seeking to have a successful career, social life, or position in the community to dress well. *"Dressing well" means being well groomed and having a good basic wardrobe that is appropriate for the occasion and that fits properly.* "Following fashion" carries dressing one step further. It means being properly dressed but also adhering to current trends, even following fads. "Being in fashion" can also mean economic suicide, since it is based on rapid obsolescence, unless one follows fads with a certain restraint and controls compulsive purchases.

The famous "naturally elegant" women who continually reappear in our press do not necessarily spend a lot of money on their clothes. Such a woman knows how to do the little things—how to tie a scarf, where to put a pin, when to wear a certain pair of gloves, how to angle a hat, what kind of bracelets to mix together. She buys good-quality clothes, well made and tailored. She spends a reasonable amount of money on each piece and keeps it in her closet for many seasons, always looking "just right" when she steps out of the door. This is the secret of good investment dressing and of dressing well. A woman who buys often but spends little on each thing and is continually dissatisfied with the fabric or the cut of what she brings home— she is the money waster.

It is wise to take along a good friend to shop with you—someone who is known for his or her taste—if you're not sure of your own. Or, if you go alone, go when there is little traffic in the store, and seek the guidance of the head salesperson or buyer. "I want something that is classic, well made, and right for my figure," is all you have to say; if you are in a reputable place, you will be shown the right thing.

The best teacher of good taste and learning to dress well is, of course, your own experience. If you have something that fits well, something on which you are always being complimented, it must be right. Choose something in the same cut and quality the next time. Your "taste buds" are forming.

Style

"Style" is something that is ethereal, elusive, and difficult to define. In fact, most people have their own personal interpretations of the word, but almost everyone wants to be thought of as "having style." To me, the term means far more than just dressing in an expensive, fashionable manner with good grooming and a proper balance of the classics and the fads of the moment. To me, style is a way of looking and a way of moving in one's clothes, and an elegant way of acting. It is a question of inside character as well as external characteristics, harmoniously combined. If you say, "She (or he) has great style," you are not just talking about the way the person looks, but the way she moves, lives, and interracts with others, her manners and general behavior toward everyone around her, from a bank president to a delivery boy.

I remember when I was a teen-ager, shopping with my mother in the designer salon of a department store. I recognized Mrs. Byron Foy because her photograph was in every magazine; she was constantly referred to for her chic and her style. I asked my mother, "What is style, anyway?" I was looking at Mrs. Foy's beautifully coiffed hair with its small veiled chapeau perfectly perched on the side of her head, the brown Balenciaga suit with its ruffled ivory silk blouse, the brown kid gloves, and the carefully polished calf bag.

My mother's answer seemed strange. "Ask the women in this department who wait on her what they think of her." I did and elicited the same response from all three women. "She's the nicest person . . . such a wonderful, kind woman . . . the loveliest, most thoughtful person."

When I reported these comments to my mother, she replied, "Well, now you know what real style is."

Grooming

The importance of grooming cannot be overemphasized. A man or a woman unable to purchase a new wardrobe because of financial problems can still look wonderful if he or she has impeccable grooming. On the other hand, someone clad in expensive new designer wardrobes can look like a "fashion minus" if his or her grooming is not impeccable.

Good grooming refers not only to one's clothes, but to oneself. The hair, for example, should be clean, even if it requires a daily shampoo. Problems like dandruff should be dealt with, not just "brushed off." A man should keep his face well shaven or his beard and mustache well trimmed; a woman should keep her make-up intact and check during the day to correct such common problems as smeared lipstick, powder caked around her nose, and smudged mascara. A good deodorant should be a basic fact of life in everyone's daily routine, and, along with a clean body, the nails need atttention each day, too.

One's clothes also need daily attention. A suit needs a brushing; clothes should be hung up carefully at night to avoid excess wrinkling. A steam iron should be part of everyone's household. A lot of men are learning how to use an iron today, as well they should! A daily exercise should be the laying out of the fresh clothes for the next morning: clean underwear, including socks for men and hosiery for women; shirt, dress, or suit; and freshly polished (or brushed, according to the kind of leather) shoes. Now, when you are not rushed, is the time to check carefully over the clothes. Is there a button missing on his clean shirt for tomorrow? Does a spot on a tie need removal? Is there an open seam on her skirt or a slip strap that needs sewing? Is there lint to remove from the fabric?

"To be in fashion" is really not enough. Spending lots of money on oneself is not enough. A good strong application of self-discipline is used by all those who look wonderfully put together; they have a "spit and polish" cleanliness and grooming. They have looked hard at themselves in the mirror and corrected the flaws seen there. It's not all that difficult or time-taking, but the difference it makes in the images they project is monumental.

How You Move in Your Clothes

An integral part of real style is the ease and grace with which the body moves and stands in its clothes. It is never too late for a man or woman to have his or her posture analyzed, and to go to work on it in a gym class or at home with exercises specifically designed by experts to straighten the spine and correct posture faults. A good trained instructor—either at the YM/YWCA, the YM/YWHA, health clubs, or spas—can give you supervised exercise. Even without losing a pound of weight (you may not have to), your posture will be greatly improved. You will learn to move properly, and your clothes will look a hundred per cent better on your body.

If you don't really know how you look when you move in your clothes, have someone borrow a family movie camera and make a short film of you in action—going, coming, rushing, and merely strolling along. Look carefully at your movements—several times. They will probably amaze you, for it's like listening to your voice recorded on tape for the first time—full of surprises.

How You Sit Posture governs how to sit properly, too. The best way to sit is the way least often seen these days (partly because we have so few good straight chairs). Your spine should be straight, hips flush with the back of the seat, feet parallel and flat on the floor. Today's furniture usually forces us into a lounging position when we sit down. The soft, cushy, modular units put us low on the ground and in need of a "hoist" to get us back up out of them!

If there is a straight chair in the room and you are neither young nor agile nor slim, head for it. Always glance back at the seat before bending your knees; the back of your leg should actually first come in contact with the chair. When you know where the chair is, bend your knees, lean forward slightly, and go down gently into it, body straight (not fanny markedly first), maintaining careful contact with the floor. In this way, if the chair is deep or unsteady, you won't be thrown backward or forward.

The deep, wide contemporary sofa is supposed to accommodate your entire thighs and all or part of your legs. The position of the cushions is an indication of where your spine is supposed to be, but if you are not supple, avoid sitting there. Don't flop down either and then squirm back into the proper position. Instead, sit down on the edge and then, placing your hands on the sofa, ease yourself back with a lifting motion. A woman can more easily handle sitting and getting up from this kind of furniture if she is wearing pants rather than a skirt. If there are some pillows against the back of the sofa, you can try rearranging them to make better back support for you, before you sit down.

Crossing one's legs while seated used to be a male prerogative, but now women *may* do it, too, without breaking etiquette rules, particularly when they're wearing pants. But women might bear in mind that medical science tells us this position interferes with circulation when done too often and for too long a time, helping cause varicose veins. A woman in pants does not look graceful if she sits the way men often do, one leg crossed at an angle, with the outside ankle resting on the other knee. A male business acquaintance of mine once said that when he sees a woman in pants sitting like that, "I feel like offering her a cigar."

The most attractive way for a woman to sit (even those in pants) is with knees and feet close together, or with the ankles gracefully crossed. If a woman wearing a short skirt crosses her legs, she has to be very careful that others do not see up under her skirt. Besides, the inevitable flab under the knee of a crossed-over leg is never a very aesthetic sight!

Pants

Pants for women are now an accepted way of life. Women who wear pants suits, or pants of any kind, should be careful that the pants are properly tailored to their figures, never too tight for easy movement, and always the proper length. If they are worn cuffless, they should be 1¼" longer in back than in front, clearing the ground and showing the heels of the shoes.

But some women were not meant to wear pants. Those with heavy figures and much older women should wear them in private as much as they want; in public, however, it is more appropriate for them to wear skirts. No one says, "You can't wear pants," but one can say, "You look much nicer in skirts."

Most churches have accepted pants suits, although pants are not really proper in church. Ministers would rather have their parishioners come dressed in pants than not have them come at all.

Evening pants and dressy pajamas come and go in popularity, but again, they look best on the slim and are most appropriate for at-home entertaining and not for formal dances.

Blue jeans, originally made for men working out of doors in the nineteenth century, are an accepted fact of life for everyone in the twentieth, for outdoor work, sports, and leisure wear. But jeans do not look well in a conservative place of business. There is a time and a place for everything.

Skirts

Women have options on their skirt lengths today; no fashion authority is in a position to "decree" that skirts this year shall be such and such a length. When the general fashion trend is to shorter skirt lengths, an older woman or someone with a figure problem will look better dressed if she keeps her skirt a bit longer. A very short woman, when skirt lengths grow longer, will wear hers a little shorter, in order to look in proportion. When a black-tie evening is called for, a woman may wear a short evening dress, one that is three-quarter length, or one to the floor. We are free to choose what is right for us and what we like. The only thing to guard against is a mistake such as wearing a floor-length dress before six o'clock—at least until the "Granny look" comes back in fashion again! As the French say, *plus ça change, plus c'est la même chose.*

Furs

You may wear a fur coat at any hour of the day. The old tradition of certain furs being "for evening only" has disappeared. The "fun fur" industry brought a great sense of informality to the coat world, and that relaxed attitude has rubbed off on the more classic furs, too. The main thing to remember when buying a fur is *not to buy one of the endangered species.* It does not matter whether you are buying a small scarf or a full-length coat.

Follow your furrier's suggestion about leaving the coat longer than you think it should be. The vagaries of the wandering hemline have outdated many fur coats long before their time. However, if you want to keep your coat long or short, it is your privilege, regardless of what fashion dictates.

A hat of wool or felt or any fabric is an attractive contrast to fur. Sometimes a fur hat of the same fur as the coat can be overwhelming. Also, one should not buy a fur hat of another fur that does not co-ordinate perfectly with one's coat.

Care for your furs. Store them in air-conditioned vaults at your store or cleaning establishment for the summer, and have them refurbished regularly (every two years). If you take care of your coat, have it restyled when necessary, and treat it with proper respect, it will look wonderful on you for several years. You can amortize the cost over those years and will find that your coat costs you very little to own each year.

Accessories

Accessories can make or break an outfit. A flower pinned on the belt of a dress you considered tired and dreary can change your entire way of feeling about it. A pair of white piqué gloves to match the white piqué collar on your navy blue spring dress may be just the look the dress needs. A bright-colored scarf, wound around your neck and attractively tied on the shoulder, may be just the thing to draw people's attention away from your nose, red and swollen from a head cold. A new leather belt can change the lines and entire look of the tent dress that has been hanging unworn in your closet. A great pair of shoes can give an entire fashion focus to your costume. The addition of two long chain necklaces may be just the shiny note needed to wake up a somber dress.

If you put on too many things at once, of course, the over-all look is like an overladen Christmas tree: off balance and fussy. But a deft touch here and there can add a strong dash of elegance to a costume you feel has the "blahs." We can learn how to add and subtract accessories wisely by watching what the fashion pages of the magazines show us, and by emulating the well-dressed women we see around us.

Hats   Hats sweep in and out of fashion. Most often today they are worn for warmth in cold climates. (Science tells us that a warm head helps keep the entire body warm in bitterly cold weather.) Some women, however, wear a hat as the perfect finish to their costume. There is nothing prettier than a handsome woman with the right hat on her head. It's up to you.

A woman should keep her hat on in a restaurant, but not if it's a rain hat or a wool helmet or a wind scarf. She can check any of these head coverings in the pocket of her coat.

Gloves   Gloves, like hats, used to be "the sign of a lady." Now they are worn for warmth. Many who work in hot cities also wear short cotton gloves in the summertime, to keep hands from getting too grimy and sticky. Buses or subways in the summer are good reasons for wearing gloves.

Long white gloves are still worn by some brides who wear sleeveless dresses, as well as by debutantes and by women who attend those rare "white-tie" functions. These long white gloves should be of kid or washable doeskin; in my opinion, long white cotton or synthetic gloves do not look right.

Short white gloves (kid, doeskin, or cotton) are still sometimes worn by young women with their summery dresses, or even graduation dresses, as part of their costume. At any time of the year wrist-length white gloves are attractive to wear en route to an evening party. They are also a co-ordinating and fashionable color accent for a special costume. Anyone looks more "finished" wearing gloves.

If a woman wearing long white gloves is part of a receiving line, it is proper for her to keep them on. However, any person going down the receiving line should have an ungloved hand to offer. A woman dining at a very formal dinner, such as a "white-tie" state dinner at the White House should remove her gloves before sitting down to the table. She can always put them back on again for dancing after dinner. Many people agree with me that a woman who rolls back her long white gloves to the wrist, in order to eat her dinner, looks off kilter. A woman can wear a formal bracelet over her long white gloves (not costume jewelry, however), but she should never wear rings over gloved fingers.

Gloves should be kept spotlessly clean, either by dry cleaning or by washing (the washable leathers) in very tepid water with a gentle soap. After rinsing well in cool water, stretch out the fingers, blow into them to puff them out, and then lay the gloves down flat on a towel to dry, away from any source of heat.

Removing Your Glove When Shaking Hands   As a point of etiquette, the American woman was always taught to leave on her gloves when she shook hands with a gentleman. The previous editions of this book, for example, state this as proper. The United States is probably the only place in which a woman keeps her glove on while the man is supposed to remove his.

After many years of living in Europe, I find our custom is an unfriendly, pretentious way to shake hands. It's as though the woman thinks the man's hand is not clean enough to touch hers. The real reason for a handshake is to say hello and to establish friendly contact between one person and another. Therefore for the man to remove his glove in greeting and the woman to retain hers is a contradiction. Regardless of sex, one should, I feel, remove one's glove on the right hand before shaking hands. The feel of one warm hand clasped in another's is the proper basis for a greeting—not the feel of one hand protectively sheathed in leather clasping a bare hand.

Handbags   One's handbag, if it does not match the leather of one's shoes, should at least co-ordinate. A woman wearing brown shoes and gloves should carry a bag in the beige to brown family. A woman wearing a black costume should not carry a navy-blue bag. The size of the bag should logically depend on the size of the woman carrying it, but this does not always hold. A small woman who is very busy and has to carry around a quantity of things in her purse needs to carry a large handbag. Some women who have to carry many items with them all day prefer to carry a small handbag and to put the rest in a co-ordinating tote bag or in a briefcase.

Glittery (satin, lamé, beaded) handbags are obviously for after-dark activities and should not be carried by day. Here again, co-ordinating the shoes and bag is important. If you leave for a trip with your large sporty daytime handbag, be sure to pack a small black satin clutch or a similar dressy bag to carry for your evening activities.

Organization inside one's handbag means an easier life. It's a good idea to put all make-up items in one separate, easy-to-open purse. One's keys should be on a light key chain. A pen clipped onto a checkbook or notebook is always easy to find; credit cards should be safely and efficiently stored in a little case or some kind of fold-out plastic cover. One's handbag should always be spotless—clean and polished outside, clean and neat inside. I will never forget reading part of a letter from a well-known English nobleman, a prize catch of a bachelor, written to his sister. He told her that his romance with a great London beauty was over.

"It's funny, how a little thing finally gave me the courage to tell her that our relationship wasn't working any more. Her handbag fell open when we were sitting at the races, and half the stuff inside fell out. The mess inside and outside was so disgusting, I swear only a vacuum cleaner could have properly cleaned it up. Anyway, that did it. I knew somehow she just wasn't —clean."

Shoes The primary things to remember when buying shoes are fit and comfort, and quality material. You can spend a fortune on your clothes, and if your feet hurt, the pain will show in every step you take. If you can't find the "latest thing" in your shoe size, then buy the non-latest thing and know you will be comfortable—and mobile.

Teetering heels are not for one's daily active life or for traveling or for any time at which you must be on your feet for a long period. In any case, always have an extra comfortable pair of shoes to change into. Keep a pair at work, and always pack an extra pair in your luggage that you're sure you won't need. They may save your life when your other comfortable shoes are drying out from the rainstorm or are being fixed at the shoemaker's.

Conspicuous, fun-fashion shoes are for women with slender legs and small feet. Women with the opposite kind of legs and feet should stick to classic, slenderizing pumps and sandals—the kind of shoes with an excellent, comfortable last. Keep patent, plastic, and calfskins well cleaned and shined; remove the spots from your suede shoes each night; keep your boots fastidiously polished and clean; brush off your silk evening shoes after each wearing. If you stick to basic design and buy good-quality shoes, you will find yourself spending much less money in the end.

If you are wearing boots, it is best to remove them at work; they might make your legs swell in an overheated interior, and they can also impede circulation. Take along an extra pair of shoes to change into at the office, or keep a pair tucked in a desk drawer. (You might also include a fresh pair of pantyhose or stockings to slip on when the runs occur—which they inevitably do on the days when you have to look your best.)

Jewelry When accessorizing with jewelry, the best rule to follow is "never too much, always too little." When you go out for the evening feeling you have left off one piece, you probably look just right. Always subtract one or two of the elements in a complete set of jewelry (necklace, pendant earrings, bracelet, ring). You can wear the rest on another occasion. Remember, too, that one can wear a jeweled necklace with jeweled button earrings, but that a jeweled necklace with matching long pendant earrings is too much.

A woman who wears several bangle bracelets on each wrist might conclude that she is wearing enough jewelry; a woman wearing a show-stopper of a necklace needs to add nothing else—in other words, an important piece of jewelry needs showcasing in a very simple setting. Jewelry should never have to compete with a loud print or pattern in one's outfit; a jeweler's work of art can be lost or even look tacky on a splashy print blouse.

A woman who wears a lot of rings should have lovely hands, with nails in good condition. If her hands are laden with rings, she will be drawing attention to them at all times.

Traditionally one did not wear sterling silver and gold jewelry at the same time, but women began doing it in the 1970s, particularly in the mixing of necklaces and bracelets.

All real jewelry should be cleaned regularly; usually soap flakes in warm water will do it, perhaps with an added touch of ammonia. A toothbrush can get dirt out from the crevices of intricately set jewelry, and there are also several excellent brands of liquid jewelry cleaner available on the market. A pearl necklace should be cleaned after each wearing with a soft cloth like chamois skin, to remove perspiration, make-up, or fragrance traces. A soft cloth can also be used to clean costume jewelry; the latter can be rinsed and dried with a soft cloth, but be careful not to unglue the stones from the setting while you are cleaning fake jewelry.

Fine Jewelry If you own real diamond jewelry set in gold, you can wear it all day long in today's world. Before the mid-fifties, women followed an unwritten law stating that diamonds should be worn only after five o'clock. Designers Jean Shlumberger, Fulco de Verdura, and David Webb led them away from this dictum by designing marvelous jewels set in gold that looked just as well at noon on the lapel of a gray flannel blazer as they did at night at the décolletage of a gleaming satin ball gown. (Elaborate diamond jewelry set in platinum, however, remains an evening rather than a daytime accessory.)

Another old custom that forbade one to mix different colored gemstones is archaic today. You can mix sapphires with emeralds or rubies as you please, particularly now that good jewel design often combines splashes of color by using pink tourmalines, aquamarines, amethysts, green peridots, turquoises, and other semiprecious stones together.

Remember when you're walking in public, whether you're wearing real or costume jewelry, to cover it up with a coat, cape, or shawl, so that you won't be an enticement to a mugger or a thief.

Wristwatches Again, old traditions have changed in the watch world. Women now wear men's wristwatches, if they want the big face and wide strap that goes with them. Watches that are fine for sportswear do not look well on the wrist of a woman in evening attire. However, pavé diamond-, lapis lazuli-, opal-, or malachite-faced watches, studded on their rims with small stones, may now be worn in the daytime as well as in the evening— not to a sporting event, but certainly to any city activity. If a woman wears one of these exquisite watches, she does not, of course, need other silver and gold jewelry. She wears the minimum: a necklace ring or chain, a pair of earrings perhaps, and her wedding and engagement rings. A wise woman keeps a wardrobe of straps on hand if she has a very special watch—leather to wear by day, correct even with a diamond-studded watch, and gold, silver, satin, or velvet by night.

A man can wear his watch with any kind of band day or night. If he is the kind who has to don a black tie for a formal evening event every so often, he would do well to choose a black leather instead of a brown leather band for his watch.

Chapter 54

MEN'S APPAREL

As with a woman, the major factors in a man's being "well dressed" are meticulous grooming and the proper fit of his clothes.

The majority of men are basically conservative in their dress, partly, I'm sure, because the business world requires it. Men in the fashion and advertising business may be avant-garde in their clothes; men who work in the financial community may not. A man should take a hard look at how the other men dress in his business situation, and act accordingly. It is a fact of life that dressing inappropriately can seriously hold back a career, not to mention the harm it can do to a man's social life. As the late Lucius Beebe, chronicler of society and fashion, said, "Whatever you do in fashion, do it *well*, not half-heartedly."

Business Suits

Business suits remain more or less the same through the decades. Sometimes trousers with cuffs are in, then they're out; the loose trouser leg is in, then it's out. The length of the jacket changes with time, up and down, and the lapels grow narrower and then wider, but the basic suit remains. The fabrics—flannels, gabardines, worsteds, blends—keep basically to conservative solid colors, plaids, checks, or pinstripes; the heavier wool tweeds have interesting textures and patterns, but the color explosions in men's fashions are left to the shirts and ties rather than the fabric of the suit. The two classics—the dark pinstripe and the gray flannel (with khaki-colored gabardine or poplin for summer)—remain popular, with brown suits increasingly seen. Suits are sold double- or single-breasted (the latter a slenderizing), with or without vests.

The most important factor to keep in mind when purchasing a suit is not the style or cost, but the proper fit. Unless the suit, either constructed or with soft shoulders, is well tailored to fit your particular body, it will never look quite right. Finding a good tailor can be difficult today, but every man should have access to one, whether he buys custom-made suits or carefully chooses a men's store with good tailors. The length of the coat is determined by the shape of the man. A suit coat should always be long enough to cover the seat of the trousers, but on a short man it should not ordinarily be longer than that, no matter what the current fashion. A man who is tall and very thin looks better dressed in a coat of medium length. A too-short one puts him on stilts, and one too long accentuates his thinness. Whatever the length decided upon, it should hang evenly all the way around, never hike up in the back. Even a ready-made jacket should conform to the figure.

A man's jacket must fit closely around the neck so that anywhere from one half to approximately one inch of shirt collar shows in back, depending on the style of the shirt. A man should know that sleeve lengths can be very deceptive, that it is the yoke of the shirt that seems to determine the actual sleeve length. In trying a new brand of shirts, not made to order, it is wise to try on the shirt, not go solely by the length of sleeve given. Even then some imported shirts, in particular, may shrink somewhat so that the sleeve length after the shirt is washed is even with the sleeve of the jacket instead of a good half-inch below. Too much cuff showing is better than too little. On the other hand, the shirt sleeve should not show above the cuff itself. The collar points, when not buttoned down, must appear perfectly even from a front view, never ride askew.

The trousers of the sack suit may have cuffs or be pressed straight down, depending on preference. If they are tailor-made and cuffless, the bottoms should be finished so they can be turned up in stormy weather. Length of trousers is again a matter of individual taste, but, fashionably, those with permanent cuffs should hang straight and not break over the instep. Plain uncuffed trousers should be slanted in back so that they are approximately one and a quarter inches longer there than in the front. The trouser width should be medium. A good tailor will proportion the trouser width to the size of the shoes a man is wearing, as well as to the size of his thighs and the current dictates of fashion, so the trousers will have the right "look."

The carefully groomed man limits his trouser pocket contents to his small change and his keys. The keys should be in a flat key case. A used handkerchief, folded as flat as possible, can be returned to his hip pocket, but his wallet there may make an unsightly rear bulge (and may be an invitation to pickpockets, who are not deterred by a button).

The main things to remember about the business suit are to keep it brushed and well pressed; to keep the buttons sewn on the jacket; and to wear it with a clean shirt and unspotted tie.

Shirts

The relaxation of the rule of strict conformity to a white shirt with a somber tie has meant a more cheerful and a far more creative and amusing environment in which men can dress for business. But, of course, as with all fashion, too much color for too long means a return to greater popularity for the white shirt!

Button-down-collar shirts are slightly more sporty and informal than plain-point-collar ones. Both are fine for either business or leisure wear. Town shirts are more formal; they require cuff links worn with their "French cuffs." A town shirt with contrasting collar and cuffs is the most formal of all (the shirt may be a solid color or striped, with all-white collar and cuffs). The addition of a collar pin (in gold or silver, fake or real), is a nice touch—more decorative than useful.

Many plain-point-collar and town shirts come with plastic "stays" to keep the points neat and uncurled; one removes them when laundering the shirt.

In hot weather, short-sleeved shirts are worn by some with business suits and ties. However, if the jacket is removed in the office, short sleeves do not look well. A short-sleeved business shirt is meant to be covered by a jacket in public.

When shirts are monogrammed, the monograms should be sewn unobtrusively on the left side, hidden beneath the suit coat unless one has one's jacket removed. A monogram should simply be "there," seen by others almost accidentally. I remember seeing a handsome red one on a friend's shirt when he unbuttoned his coat. I asked him why he didn't show it off to everyone. "Oh, no," he protested, "a monogram on your shirt is like a woman's wearing beautiful silk and lace underwear. Only the person wearing it is supposed to know it's there."

Ties

Bow ties for daytime wear wax and wane in size and in popularity. Bow ties come self-tied or pre-tied. Some men wear them always, making these ties a kind of trademark for them. The four-in-hand tie, however, changing in its width according to the dictates of the fashion at the time, is by far the more popular style. Four-in-hand ties are more slenderizing, too, and should be worn always by men who are not slim or who have round faces. On a very tall man, the four-in-hand tie often appears too short. Any man well over six feet should be careful to tie his tie in such a manner that it will appear long enough. Ties should be of good fabric with a well-designed pattern and color. A tie should be chosen to have a harmonious effect, rather than a strident one clashing with the rest of the man's costume.

Shoes

Well-dressed men are conservative about their shoes and very meticulous about keeping them shined. They buy relatively few pairs, but they buy the best quality. They do not follow fads—like the unfortunate one in the mid-seventies of high, chunky heels with squared-off toes.

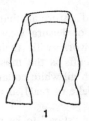

1   **2**

3   **4**

TYING A BOW TIE
(illustration shows the tie as seen in your mirror)

1. *Place tie well under the collar. Start with end in left hand extending 1½" below that in right hand.*
2. *Cross longer end over shorter and pass up through loop.*
3. *Form front loop of bow by doubling up shorter end (hanging) and place across collar points.*
4. *Hold this front loop with thumb and forefinger of left hand. Drop long end down over front.*
5. *Place right forefinger, pointing up, at bottom half of hanging part. Pass up behind front loop.*
6. *Push the resulting loop through knot behind front loop. Even ends, and tighten.*

5   **6**

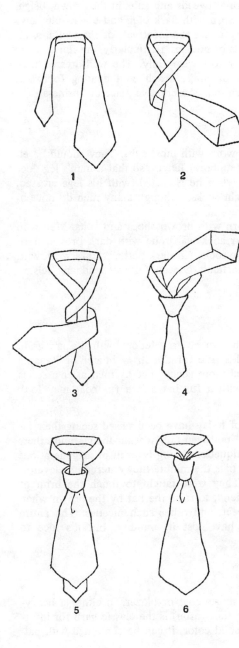

THE FOUR-IN-HAND KNOT (*illustration shows the tie as seen in your mirror*)

1. Start with the wide end of the tie on your right and extending a foot below the narrow end.
2. Cross wide end over narrow, and back underneath.
3. Continue around, passing wide end across front of narrow once more.
4. Pass wide end up through loop.
5. Holding front of knot loose with index finger, pass wide end down through loop in front.
6. Remove finger and tighten knot carefully. Draw up tight to collar by holding narrow end and sliding knot up snugly.

Brown shoes are worn with informal tweeds and suits in the brown, beige, and gray families. Black shoes are worn with dark blue and black suits, also with dark (Oxford) gray ones. Loafers are too informal for most offices, although the dressier ones, with tassels or buckles, particularly, are fine.

White shoes are for summer or resort wear only. The well-dressed man confines his "white" shoes mostly to tennis, beach, and boating footwear. The athletic shoe should not be worn to a conservative place of business.

Socks

Dark blue or black socks can be worn with most suits. They should be either garter length or over the calf (support) length, so that a man's leg does not show over the top of his sock when he is seated, with his legs crossed. There are winter- and summer-weight socks, although many men do not observe this change.

Dull black socks may also be worn with brown shoes and suits. Men who wear a lot of brown may vary their sock wardrobe with dark brown, dark maroon, or dark green socks. Argyle socks (in dark patterns) are worn with tweeds or gray flannel and look particularly well for weekend and leisure wear, with sports slacks and loafers.

Hats

After many decades of use, the brown or gray fedora with the grosgrain band still looks right; the same holds true for the straw boater or Panama hat in summer. Fur hats have gained more acceptance by men after a series of long, cold winters, but a man with a fur hat and a fur coat may look overdressed.

Hat Tipping   Since young men of today have been raised seeing their fathers more or less hatless, they have not been taught what their grandfathers taught their fathers: namely, hat etiquette. Young boys in prior generations were taught always to remove their hats the minute they entered an elevator, someone's home, or a restaurant. They were taught to touch the brim of their hats lightly when greeting a friend, to raise the hat by the crown when meeting a woman friend in the street, and other such niceties. The entire theory of hat etiquette seems to have lost its validity, but it's nice to remember what it was.

Leisure Wear

Sports Jackets and Blazers   The sports coat or blazer, in either a heavy- or a lightweight fabric (according to the season) is the classic garb for informal occasions. If the jacket is in a solid color, it can be combined with patterned trousers, and vice versa.

The navy blue blazer with its brass, sterling-silver, or eighteen-karat-gold monogrammed buttons is a staple item for every man's wardrobe. Today's blazer comes in many colors, but navy blue is still the most popular choice. In the summer, it looks well with anything from wild-colored patterned slacks to delicate pink-and-white-checked slacks. (Polished loafers and no socks are the accepted form with this extremely informal costume.) A blazer is a perfect "background coat" to set off any colored shirt and tie, as well as slacks. The blazer can be worn to the office, but a young man on his way up the corporate ladder had better wait a few years before emulating that look. A man can wear a navy blazer to a cocktail party in the city, as well as with white trousers to his summer wedding.

If a man dines in someone's house, a velvet blazer in black or a dark jewel color looks well with a black bow tie and the black trousers from his dinner suit. His black patent or velvet pumps are appropriate footwear. Alternatively, with this jacket he can loosen up on the color scheme with his choice of slacks and bow tie. It is a way of being comfortable and yet semiformal, just as with the long skirt his wife may wear to someone's home; even when it is not a "black tie" evening.

The tweed sports jacket looks well with or without a tie for off-hours leisure wear. It can combine with a turtleneck or crew-neck sweater, or with a sports shirt and an ascot. A man with a small wardrobe should remember that he and his friends will quickly tire of a pattern in his sports coat that is too loud or too memorable. This type of jacket should not be worn to business in a conservative office.

Ascots   An ascot is a scarf look only men who are very sure of their sportswear taste should affect. The name, of course, comes from the kind of neckwear men made popular at the races at Ascot, England.

The ascot is often of silk foulard or of a Madras-type cotton. It may be worn with any open-necked, long-sleeve sports shirt and topped by a blazer or sports jacket or sweater in cool weather. It is a leisure look and does not fit in with office life or an evening cocktail party in the city. I overheard a woman say once, "An ascot? Good Lord, only the art director of an advertising agency or Fred Astaire can get away with it."

Walking Shorts   Often called Bermudas, walking shorts are appropriate for resort wear, but not for city wear. The British colonial troops wore walking shorts with knee socks in the tropics, but a man walking down the streets of Syracuse, New York, in the summer does not have the same reason to wear them that the British had.

Without socks, walking shorts can be worn with loafers, sneakers, topsiders or espadrille-type leisure shoes. One can also wear white athletic socks with loafers or any other sports shoe except for espadrilles and sandals. If a man wears walking shorts with hiking boots, he of course wears knee socks or sports socks, whichever are the most comfortable.

If a man does not have good legs, he is better off wearing slacks. If he is very hirsute, he should give himself a good once-over in the mirror of the store, wearing the shorts, before he purchases them.

Polo Shirts   A man is always well dressed in summer with the classic polo shirt, short-sleeved, worn with any kind of solid-color or patterned slacks. A white polo shirt is always right on the tennis courts; a navy polo shirt goes with everything, and a man can wear a striking colored pair of slacks (chartreuse, shocking pink) with a white or contrasting-colored polo shirt. He can wear a sports jacket with it, too, for summer or leisure wear.

Jacket and Tie Code at Restaurants

Many of America's finer restaurants and hotel dining rooms, as well as clubs, will not admit men who are without jackets and ties. Often a headwaiter will have a few jackets and ties in storage in his checkroom, for just such an emergency. The reason for asking a man to wear a tie and coat is that when people choose to go to a fancier restaurant than usual (and pay more for doing so) they expect the others around them also to be suitably dressed for the occasion. No matter how clean or well tailored a man may be in his polished loafers, tailored slacks, and turtleneck sweater, he looks more formal in a coat and tie and therefore is less conspicuous in the overall scene of a fine dining place.

Formal Wear

Black Tie   When an invitation reads "Black Tie," it means both men and women are to come in formal dress. In a non-summer or non-resort situation, it means a man should wear a "tuxedo" jacket with matching pants, but an easier term for this outfit is a "dinner suit." Black is the best color for this suit, for it is appropriate winter and summer, spring and fall. Even if a man lives in a very warm climate, he should buy a black dinner jacket instead of a white one. There are lightweight fabrics for black dinner suits, perfectly suitable for the tropics.

A man should keep his "black-tie" bow tie in a fashionable width, according to what is being worn at the moment. It is a small enough investment, and a man who insists upon wearing his out-of-style bow tie calls attention to himself as a man who doesn't care. The well-dressed man at a formal event is the one who is clad in an impeccably cut black dinner suit, whose grooming is perfect, who wears good but quiet jewelry, and whose white dinner shirt and black tie are such that "one doesn't remember later what they looked like." That means he is perfectly dressed.

A man may wish to wear a cummerbund and matching bow tie of a dressy fabric like silk, satin, grosgrain, or velvet—or something made in needlepoint by a female fan. Many men prefer a waistcoat to a cummerbund; it may also be of velvet, a dressy printed fabric, or needlepointed. The preferred kind is the waistcoat made of a patterned black silky fabric. Some men are uncomfortable wearing either a waistcoat or cummerbund (the latter needs constant adjusting, as one sits down and gets up again). If a man wears a double-breasted jacket he doesn't have to wear either, for it hides his "middle."

Instead of a belt, one wears "braces" (suspenders) with a dinner jacket and trousers. Buttoned-down white shirts were once acceptable on young men wearing black tie, but no more. (As a man's daytime dress grows more relaxed and informal, his black-tie wear seems to grow more formal.) White, off-white, or pastel-colored shirts are the norm today, sometimes in a silk-like synthetic, and, for the lucky ones who have someone to launder them at home, in pure silk. Sometimes the shirt front is pleated; at other times it is plain, with a monogram embroidered on the left side. Ruffled, flouncy shirts are not in good taste, and never were, in the opinion of many. One of the perennially "best-dressed men" pronounced that the "ruffled shirt belongs on a stage."

For those in formal evening attire, a man should wear lisle, silk, or any lightweight black kind, garter-length or over the calf. Shoes should be black patent pumps with black bows or black patent laced oxfords. If a man does not have black patent shoes, he can wear black well-polished calf shoes, but the kind without any decoration such as wing-tips.

If a man is entertaining in his own home at a black-tie dinner, he may wear his black velvet or needlepoint slippers. It is his prerogative as host. His house guests may wear theirs, also, since they are temporarily "at home."

A dinner shirt calls for studs and matching cuff links. These can be of sculptured gold, gold with a diamond in the center, or a pearl. They may be of black onyx or mother-of-pearl. They may also be of semiprecious stone, such as jade, malachite, or lapis lazuli. A man may wear the wristwatch that he wears every day, but it looks better if it has a black strap on it (leather or suede) or perhaps one of a gold or silver or platinum. If he has no studs and cuff links, he can make out perfectly well by wearing a plain white shirt with a pointed collar.

If a man only very occasionally has to appear in a black tie, he would do well to rent this attire from a reputable place. If he will be wearing black tie several times a year (for association dinners, special meetings, or dances) he should invest in well-tailored jacket and pants, plus all the accouterments, except for the jewelry. (The jewelry can come later, as a present from someone who loves him—or from the one who loves him the most, himself!)

It is not correct, no matter what you occasionally see, for a man to wear a dinner jacket or tail coat in the daytime.

A white linen handkerchief (monogrammed or not monogrammed) might be put in his left breast pocket. If he uses a scarf or muffler, it should be white silk for a black-tie evening. His gloves can be dressy gray suede. If he has to go out often in black tie, he should invest in a coat for evening—of a black or almost black fabric. The most classic and beloved by many men of great taste is the dark wool chesterfield with a black velvet collar.

Since the black "Homburg" hat has all but disappeared for evening wear, if a man wants to wear a hat because he is cold, he may wear a fur hat or a gray fedora, with a black band.

Pastel-colored or Piped Dinner Suits   One is compelled to comment on colored dinner suits and those piped with black around the collar, lapels, and pockets. They are not elegant. Nor are the damask or patterned-fabric dinner jackets for winter, including the lamé type. If a man wants to know that he is going to look right, there is a very easy insurance: he simply buys a well-fitting black dinner suit!

Summertime Black-tie Variations   For resort wear and in the summer, men often throw off the all-black look for their black-tie evenings. If they are going to a dinner dance at the country club, they might still stay with all-black; but if they are going to a black-tie dance at the yacht club or in any informal resort place, they are perfectly at liberty to become "creative" in their black-tie assemblage. This means bright-colored linen pants and perhaps a dinner jacket of a patterned or solid-colored fabric, the color of which co-ordinates or at least does not swear at the color of the trousers. The white shirt and the black tie should remain as the steady note with all this color and pattern.

White Tie   If an invitation reads "White Tie" on the lower right (and your chances of receiving one today are very slim) it is a call for full evening regalia for the man and a ball gown and jewelry for the woman. There are still white-tie state dinners given at the White House for a visiting head of state; the fathers and the escorts of the debutante still wear white-tie outfits at many debutante balls; and there are formal banquets in hotels in major cities where the men seated on the dais have to wear white tie. If a man has received a decoration from a foreign government or military decorations, and if the woman has any decorations, these may be worn automatically at any public event with a white tie. At a private party they are not worn, unless the invitation reads "White Tie and Decorations."

Most men today rent a white-tie outfit, since they are so seldom used. The stiff wing collar and shirt, the evening studs, the white piqué waistcoat, the white tie, and long black tail coat worn with black patent shoes may not be the most comfortable outfit in the world. However, most men usually look so splendid in their white tie that the compliments they receive from all the women make up for the discomfort suffered!

Chapter 55

DINING IN RESTAURANTS

Americans are not only eating out more; they are entertaining outside their homes in increasing numbers. There are various reasons for this change, but the decrease in the number of people in domestic service has been a big factor in revolutionizing America's system of entertaining. Our homes tend to be smaller today and do not provide for large-party-giving. Another important reason, certainly, is that women have gone to work, so there is not enough time to organize entertaining at home. All of these factors have contributed to the continued growth and popularity of entertaining in a restaurant.

In a very expensive restaurant or hotel dining room, the hosts can put themselves in the hands of the headwaiter or a banquet manager, who will guide their clients as to menu, timing, and other important procedural matters. Even when you do not plan to entertain on such a lavish scale, restaurant entertaining can be easy and pleasant for both host and guests.

Good manners are as important in a restaurant or club as they are at a dinner party at home. One is dealing with a professional staff as well as one's guests. Both should be treated equally well.

The Fine Restaurant

The Staff: The Owner's and Manager's Pride

There is a hierarchy of jobs in any fine restaurant. The one in charge is the maître d' (headwaiter), who seats you at your table. The captain takes your order and supervises the service for your table. It is he who flames the soufflé, carves the duck or the smoked salmon, and filets your fish. The sommelier (wine steward—and a disappearing breed) is usually in uniform, with a large silver chain around his neck, from which are suspended either the keys to the wine cellar or an antique silver tasting cup. There is your waiter who serves you, and the bus boy who assists him and who keeps your water glass filled and your butter plate well supplied. When you receive your bill, you should figure on adding 20 per cent to the total for service (15 per cent to your waiter and 5 per cent perhaps to your captain). If there was a wine steward in attendance, and you consumed several bottles of wine, you might give him two dollars and another two to the headwaiter as you leave.

Making the Reservation The person in whose name the reservation is made should be either the host, the hostess, or the person who is organizing a "dutch treat" group. The table reservation is made in his name; he will get the bill and be responsible for settling it. Someone simply has to call the restaurant on the morning of the planned dinner: "I would like to make a reservation for Mr. James Morales for dinner tonight for six people at eight o'clock." If the restaurant in question is one of the currently popular "in" places, the reservation might have to be made from one to two weeks in advance.

Coat Checking Upon entering the restaurant, the host, hostess, and each guest should check their coats, briefcases, umbrellas, and/or packages. A man checks his hat. If a woman is wearing a fur coat, she should check it or keep it and throw it over the back of her chair, once she is seated. Many coat checkers will not take furs because of fear of theft. (When departing from the restaurant, one tips the person responsible for coats anywhere from a quarter to a dollar, depending upon the kind of restaurant it is and how much was checked.) A man usually handles this for the woman who has accompanied him, but if a woman has invited a man or a group to a meal, she pays for the coat checking of any guests who happen to be leaving the restaurant at the same time that she is. In other words, the host or hostess pays for the coat checking if present at the time the guests are picking up their coats; otherwise, each guest is responsible for paying for his own. If the hosts take over the entire restaurant for a private party, they should pay for the entire checking operation and post a sign that gratuities are being taken care of by the hosts. (The same holds true for private parties given in hotels.)

Greeting the Guests at a Restaurant The host and hostess should obviously be waiting at the restaurant for the guests. When the first guest arrives, they accompany him or her to the table and stay there (when the others arrive, they will be directed to the table by the maître d').

If the host knows the headwaiter, he should greet him by his first name. As the guests arrive, they wait at the entrance to the tables for the headwaiter to return, in order to learn where their host's table is. No one should barge into the restaurant without checking first with the headwaiter or owner. When you have given the name of your host to the headwaiter, he usually says, "Right this way," and then escorts you to the proper table. The host should rise to greet you and introduce you to any guests whom you may not know; then he or she seats you in your proper place. Either the host or the hostess should take a seat on the outside of the table while the guests are assembling, so that he or she may rise easily each time a new guest arrives.

If Guests Arrive First   If your host is late and you arrive first, you may either wait in the entry or go to his table. If the foyer is congested and uncomfortable, which it usually is, it is better for you to sit down at his table in an easily accessible seat. You may change seats later when your host arrives, so don't drink from the water glass, unfold the napkin, or use the butter plate at that place. It is not polite to order yourself a drink either, unless the waiting time drags on. After ten or fifteen minutes, you have the right to order a drink, since something must have happened (your host is stuck in a traffic jam or, worse, an elevator!). Any host would want you to order a drink and make yourself as comfortable as possible in such an embarrassing circumstance. However, it is not very polite for a waiting guest to sit guzzling a drink at the bar; he should drink at the reserved table instead.

Seating   The headwaiter usually pulls out the chair to seat the hostess or any woman guest as she arrives. A woman should therefore sit down in the chair the headwaiter or waiter is pointedly holding on to. If the guest has a legitimate reason for not wanting to sit in that chair ("I'm sorry, it's right under the air vent, and I have a bad sore throat"; "I'm sorry, I can't face the light from the window because of an eye problem"), it is appropriate for her to sit in another chair. (Not if it's a seated dinner party, however.)

There is usually one seat or one side of the table that is better than the others, for reasons of views of the out-of-doors, or of the decor, or perhaps of "the action" in the restaurant. The host or hostess should arrange to have guests occupying those seats, not themselves.

The banquette.   When a couple eats in a restaurant where there is one banquette wall seat and one seat opposite, the woman should take the banquette seat. When a young couple invites a much older couple to dinner, the older couple should be shown to the banquette seats, as should a couple visiting from out-of-town. The banquette seats have, of course, the best view of the restaurant. When two men sit opposite two women on the banquette, a husband should not sit opposite his wife. The strongest conversational lines emanate back and forth across the table in this kind of dining, not side by side.

Couples A and B, therefore, would sit like this:

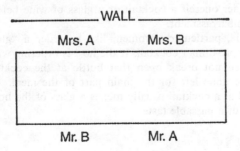

If several couples dine together in a restaurant, using a banquette wall, it is nice to separate couples and include the men on the banquettes, like this:

_____ WALL _____

Mrs. A	Mr. C	Hostess	Mr. B
Host	Mrs. B	Mr. A	Mrs. C

Booth seating. When two couples approach a booth, the two women slip first into the inside seats opposite each other, and the two men take the outside seats. If women are going on a dutch-treat lunch together, the younger, or the less important in the office hierarchy, stands back and motions the older or the more important woman into the inside seat. Or a woman hosting such a lunch ushers her guests into the inside seats first, and then sits down.

When you are sitting in a booth or on a banquette, don't put your handbag and parcels on the seat beside you. There often isn't enough room, and it is annoying to the person who has to sit on the other side of you. Put everything in the checkroom, or if that is not possible, stash it away quietly under your seat. Your handbag should be kept in your lap, however, because there are too many crawling bandits in good restaurants these days, collecting women's handbags from beneath their chairs!

Ordering

Cocktails As the guests "dribble in" for a dinner party at a restaurant, the host orders each a drink while they wait for the others. Cocktails are offered to every guest before the menu is studied. A nondrinker would, of course, order a soft drink (or a fruit juice, tea, or coffee) at a time like this without any embarrassment. Conversely, if one is dining with a nondrinker, one should order oneself a cocktail or a glass of wine before the meal with no sense of embarrassment.

Many people, particularly women, like to order a "glass of cold white wine" as their pre-dinner cocktail. If the host is ordering white wine with the dinner, he need not break open that bottle at the cocktail hour, because there might be none left for the main part of the meal. A "glass of white wine" ordered as a cocktail usually means a glass of the house wine, a community bottle of a passable taste.

If everyone has just come to the restaurant from a lengthy cocktail party, the host should tell the captain that the group will not be having cocktails and ask to see the menu right away.

The Meal In the "old days" a woman always relayed her order to her host, her husband, or her male escort. She was never supposed to speak directly to the captain or the waiter. Today most women have found their voices and handle their own ordering, although the "perfect host" is someone everyone admires—the person who memorizes the wishes of every single person at the table and who can relay this with total accuracy to the waiter. If the host knows the cuisine well, he should recommend to his guests the superior dishes of the house. If he doesn't, he might ask the headwaiter if he has anything special to recommend.

If you know your host has money to spare, you may order without paying too much attention to the price, but if you are not sure, it is best to order with restraint and compassion for the condition of his wallet.

If you order the "table d'hôte dinner" you are usually ordering in the least expensive manner. It is the opposite of ordering "à la carte," where each item you order is counted separately, including coffee and sometimes even rolls and butter. The price is set in a table d'hôte dinner, whether you eat all of the courses or not. People who eat very little food usually order à la carte, so that no food is wasted. They often order the main course and nothing else.

The restaurants that give a menu with prices *only* to the host are becoming rarer. Most guests would really like to know how much things cost so they do not overspend.

If you are in a food restaurant specializing in a foreign cuisine and do not understand the menu, have no hesitancy in asking the waiter to explain exactly what the main dishes are—of what are they made, and how are they prepared. If you are allergic to garlic or onions or peppers, say, ask if there is anything of that nature in the dish.

The Wine Wine is never ordered until all at the table have decided on their selections of food. Most people like to have the wine served as soon as they begin eating. If, however, you as the host prefer to serve one bottle of an excellent vintage, tell the waiter to save it until the main course is brought in.

If one is hosting a large party in a restaurant the wine should, of course, be ordered and opened beforehand.

Three couples are dining together and they all order different things, an easy solution is to order one bottle of red wine and one of white, so that the fish eaters can have their white and the meat eaters their red. A meat eater who prefers white to red should not be ashamed of it and should request the white wine.

Two people dining alone who are not great wine imbibers can order a glass of the house red wine or white wine, to suit their taste.

When you have ordered, the sommelier in residence, if there is one—but they are seen less and less—will automatically appear with the wine card. Since many domestic wines are superior to the lesser imported ones, the host should always ask the advice of the sommelier if he is not sure of his wines. ("A little learning is a dangerous thing" is a cliché that really applies in the subject of wines.) If a guest knows about wine, the host can ask him to make the selection. In this case the guest should order something appropriate for the dinner, but not too expensive.

It is very likely that the cork will be brought to whoever selected the wine to smell, or at least that the wine will be poured in a small quantity into that person's glass to sniff and sip and to grant his approval before it is poured to everyone.

If you do not wish to have any wine served to you, touch the rim of your glass with your fingertips as the waiter is about to pour wine into your glass. It is a signal he will understand immediately. And if you don't take any wine, do not order a cocktail as a substitute. Wine is a ritual for which there is no substitute.

Courses of a Meal   Many people omit the first course in a restaurant, and their host should not insist that "everybody have it." Others who are diet-conscious may order a green salad or a green vegetable or a melon or grapefruit while the others enjoy their seafood, rich creamed soups, or delicacies like quiche lorraine. The salad course should really be served after the main course, but in a restaurant it is now perfectly appropriate to order it as a first course (slender European women have been doing it for years on the Continent). If you are dining with someone on a tight budget and you are ordering your first course, be sure you check to see if it carries a special price with it. For example, pâté is usually on the regular table d'hôte menu, but fresh asparagus usually is not.

Vegetables and potatoes accompanying the main course are sometimes served in small dishes around your main plate. You may eat from them directly with your fork, or you may spoon them onto your main plate.

No one offends his host any more by refraining from ordering dessert in a restaurant. (In someone's home it is different; one should eat a little, if the hostess has spent all day making a great confection.)

After-dinner Coffee, Liqueurs, and Cigars   Demitasses or regular-sized cups of coffee are usually ordered to be served *after* dessert in expensive restaurants, although many Americans like their coffee with dessert. Remember that if you order an "espresso" or "café filtre" you are adding to your host's bill; American coffee is much less expensive. When coffee is served, the host may offer his guests a brandy or a liqueur, if the evening is not too late. And if circumstances permit (see page 689), the men may bring out their cigars, or the host may ask the waiter to pass the restaurant's offering of cigars.

Tipping and Paying the Check

Strolling Musicians You are under no obligation to tip the strolling musicians who stop at your table to play a few songs. One does not have to stay "enraptured" by their music the whole time, but it is polite to listen quietly to them for a few minutes, offer them a compliment, and then go back to one's conversation—keeping it low enough so that one gives the semblance of listening to them.

However, I feel it is nice to tip them something, whether they are a Mexican mariachi band, three Hungarian gypsy violinists, or an Italian accordionist singing Neapolitan love songs. A dollar or two is sufficient to give to a single musician who plays from three to five songs for you alone; five dollars is sufficient for a group of musicians. In many countries abroad, the strolling musicians do not receive any payment from the management and so they depend entirely upon the tips they receive from restaurant patrons. If you tip them abroad, it seems wrong to me not to tip them in this country.

Calling the Waiter In a good restaurant, where the service is really superb, one does not have to call the waiter. He is there, hovering nearby but totally inconspicuous in his actions. The minute he is needed, he is suddenly there, by your side, saying, "Yes, sir?" "Yes, madam?"

Since most restaurants do not fall into the above category, you can summon your waiter by calling out "Waiter" or "Waitress" in a pleasant voice—one that is not too loud, but one that is not too hesitant, either. If you are someone's guest, you should not call the waiter but tell your host why you need him. It is the host's job to call him. You may have spilled wine down at your end of the table; there may be a bug in your salad (don't tell your hosts about this one); you may be missing a fork; you may have lost your napkin. Of course, if it is an extremely large party, you may certainly call the waiter, if your host is far away. Don't make a big thing out of it, however, or be overdramatic about your reason for needing him.

In order to summon the waiter the host should try to establish eye contact with him, and then if that doesn't work, try subtle body language. If he sits upright and makes one vigorous wave, he will probably attract his attention. In Europe a smart flick of the fingers usually brings the waiter; on the Continent a kind of "St-st" hissing noise is made by the men (but if an American woman were to do this in a restaurant in Italy, for example, she would attract much more attention than the waiter's!).

Calling for the Check A host at a large dinner should arrange with the maître d' ahead of time to have the bill drawn up and ready to be signed with his credit card (or charged to his account or whatever the arrangement is) by the time the meal is drawing to an end. The host should slip away from the table, perhaps during the coffee hour, to accomplish this with the waiter or the captain.

When a person has invited a smaller group to dine in a restaurant and everyone has ordered individually, the host should catch the waiter's eye at the conclusion of the meal and say simply, "Check, please." If no one pays any attention, he should catch any waiter's eye and make a signal by motioning in the air as though he were writing with a pencil on a pad. An easy bit of pantomime, and a signal understood by any waiter or waitress.

When the check comes, it is presented on a small plate, face down, and often with a pencil. The host turns it over, without disclosing its figures to his guests, and checks it quickly for accuracy. If there is only one guest, that person should stare off into outer space, his eyes diverted away from the financial calculations. If the host has several guests, they should make a concerted effort not to watch him but to chat among themselves.

If there is something obviously wrong with the bill, the host should ask for the headwaiter, explain the problems, and then accept the explanation without unnecessary comment. If the waiter has undercharged the host, it is also the host's duty to correct this inaccuracy.

A host should never spoil what has been a good meal and an enjoyable time for his guests by making a scene over the bill. If he has a serious disagreement with the management, he should confer with them *afterward,* when the guests have departed.

If you pay by credit card, be sure to add the tip to the total amount of the voucher, as well as state for whom the party was given, and the names of your guests, if you have room to put them in (even with initials). One copy of this voucher goes to your credit card company so it can subsequently bill you back; the other copy goes to you so you will have accurate records for checking against the monthly statement. You will also need this for your records for the Internal Revenue Service, provided this was a business meeting and not just a social occasion.

Paying the Cashier If you are hosting friends in a more modest restaurant where the method of payment is to a cashier, you should send your guests out ahead of you with a "Wait outside for me" request while you settle the bill with the cashier. You should make sure that the tip has been left on the table for the server, of course, before you leave the restaurant.

Dutch Treat If it is a dutch-treat party, in which each couple (or individual) pays its own share of expenses, it is best to ask the waiter to make separate checks. Separate checks for more than two couples, however, make unnecessary work for the waiter. One person should assume the responsibility of handling the check (a decision that is made beforehand), and for telling the others how much each owes at the end of the evening. If one couple orders oysters and lobster with white wine, and if the other couple orders the soup of the day and salisbury steak, with no wine, then the bill should not be split in half. It should be settled as two thirds against one third. The couple who ordered the expensive food should take the initiative in insisting they pay the larger share when the bill arrives.

Women have been lunching and dining together for so long, there should be absolutely no truth to the old story that they can't split the bill without taking a half hour to apportion the cost of every piece of bread. This myth that they cannot handle the payment of the check smoothly and efficiently is demeaning to the image of women. The real secret is to trust completely the appointed treasurer of the group for that meal, to "ante up" one's share without question, and to do it all within two minutes' time.

Entertaining a Large Party at a Restaurant

It is always wise in this situation to arrange for an area in the restaurant where you can greet your guests, have a drink, and allow for some mingling and group conversations before going to sit down at the table. If that is physically impossible in your restaurant, you might try to arrange a short cocktail hour first in your own home, or the home of a friend. (Hors d'oeuvres are not necessary, just some nuts and minute crackers.)

With a large group, order the dinner for everyone beforehand. If one of your guests has a special diet problem or is a vegetarian, you usually know about it in advance and can ask the kitchen to prepare a special plate for that person. If what you have ordered is not to the liking of your guests, they would be rude to say so. They should pick at it anyway and get through it somehow, unless it is food to which they are allergic, food they think is bad, or food they should not consume for religious reasons.

It is always nice to have the florist send a pretty centerpiece for your table at a large party in a restaurant. (Some restaurants will do the flowers for you at an extra charge.) Make your table look pretty. If you have invited more than eight, use place cards to help your guests find their places easily. Bring some chocolate mints or something delicious to put on the table for after-dinner enjoyment. Some hostesses arrange the flowers at home in their own centerpiece bowls—it makes a very personal touch, as do beautiful linens brought from home. It is not advisable, however, to bring one's own china, crystal, and sterling flatware.

Restaurant Manners

One should always "give the other fellow a thought" when enjoying a party in a restaurant. *It's the host's responsibility to control the noise level* of his or her table, so that those around them are not upset. If it's a group of no-host friends who are ruining everyone else's enjoyment of their meal, someone in the group should take the responsibility of lowering the volume of hilarity, the uninhibited group singing, the angry arguing, or whatever is transpiring.

Everyone should be properly dressed in a restaurant. A woman in jeans may no longer be asked to leave, but she can destroy the glamour of an interior very quickly. When there is a house rule that men must wear a jacket and tie, they must abide by it. (Often the management keeps a supply of ties and coats just for the purpose of lending them.) A dress code is the restaurant owner's decision, not that of the guest.

Lovemaking at the table is conspicuous behavior that is better left in the boudoir. Passionate kissing, arm-stroking, and other signs of ardent attraction take away from others' enjoyment of their coq au vin.

Table-hopping is one of the most aggravating habits a person can assume. If you are someone's guest and you see friends at another table with whom you wish to chat, it is very rude for you to leave your table and to sit at theirs for a while. It is the mark of "a person on the make" either socially or in business. When you enter a restaurant and pass by tables of friends on your way to yours, you should greet those friends with a bow and a warm smile but continue on. The aisles are usually congested with people arriving and leaving and waiters carrying trays, and they have little room for people to stand chatting. One is supposed to go to one's table and sit down. If when you leave the restaurant it is empty enough to allow plenty of aisle room, it is appropriate for you to say hello to friends seated at another table and quickly to introduce the others with you.

It is perfectly all right to ask for a doggie bag if you have an excellent piece of meat that you cannot finish, provided there are enough waiters to ensure that making such a request is not too great an imposition on the staff. Whether the meat is for you to reheat tomorrow with a bit of homemade sauce Béarnaise, or whether it will go into your child's lunch box between two pieces of bread, the doggie bag is here to stay. Do not make a big thing out of your request of the waiter; do not try to draw attention to or laughs out of it. Do it quietly and discreetly.

If you wish to taste someone else's food, you should request it only of your spouse or your child, or a very close relative or friend. Pass a clean fork or spoon to the person upon which to receive back a morsel of that particular dish, or pass your plate over to have a bit of the food placed directly on your plate. It is rude to keep asking others if you may taste their food. "Why didn't you order it yourself?" is a logical retort. I have noticed that diet-conscious women will ask for one dessert that they then divide among themselves (with three or four forks). This, done quietly and inconspicuously, is perfectly all right.

Paper litter—packets of sugar or spices and paper containers of salad dressing or cream—is a distracting problem, whether we confront this litter on the breakfast tray of a jetliner or in the local coffee shop. One should first stuff the tops back into the containers when finished with them. The remnants should then be placed neatly on any empty, unused plate or the ash tray if it is not being used. As a last resort, they should be folded into the smallest possible pieces and tucked under the rim of one's plate. Empty packets of instant coffee should also be hidden under the nearest plate or saucer rim.

If you are smoking with your cocktail, you should put out your cigarette the minute the first course is brought to the table. You should not light another one until after dessert is served. If no one else at your table smokes, it is nice to ask before the first cigarette, "Do you mind if I smoke?" No one should smoke *during* a meal. The smell of cigarette smoke can ruin a gourmet meal, destroying the fruits of the chef's labors and the diner's enjoyment of them. Cigarette smoke and food are like oil and water.

Watch what the air conditioner does to your smoke, too. A draft can waft the smoke right into a neighbor's face. It's no fun to be downwind of someone's cigarette.

Ashes should be watched at all times. Be careful to hit the ash tray and not the table. If the waiter does not remove your dirty ash tray during the food service, it is up to you to do something about the offending object. Hand it to your waiter to empty and clean, or else put it on a nearby empty table, where someone will deal with it.

Your host should not offer his guests cigars, nor should you take out your own cigar or light your own pipe, until everyone around you in the restaurant has finished eating. Think how the person on the banquette next to you feels when he begins to enjoy his delicate smoked salmon, bedecked with olive oil, capers, and freshly ground black pepper, and suddenly a stream of thick cigar smoke hits his nostrils. He is paying a great deal of money for that smoked salmon and everything else in an excellent restaurant, and it is his right to enjoy it without the obliteration of the delicate flavors by thick smoke.

If you are the one enjoying the smoked salmon and someone nearby has lit up a cigar, you might try first pushing the smoke away with your hands and coughing a little. If the smoker refuses to take the hint, call the waiter and ask to be moved to another table. If there is no other table available and the headwaiter will not ask the person seated near you to put out his cigar, ask him yourself to extinguish it. If he refuses, then you have every right to walk out of the restaurant. (You should pay first, however, for what you have eaten so far, but you don't have to pay for the rest of the meal you ordered.)

There is an increase in the number of restaurants with smoking and no-smoking sections. It's the law in some states (for example, Minnesota). However it is difficult to take guests to dinner in this situation, since in a group of six or more there is rarely any homogeneity in smoking habits, and a smoker would feel hostile about having to spend an evening in a no-smoking section. Think, however, how a nonsmoker would feel having to spend his evening in the haze of clouds in the SMOKING section!

Table Implements The general rule to follow in using table implements is, of course, to work from the outside in, but some restaurants don't necessarily know how to set a table. When the traditional placement of the silverware has not been followed and you find you have used the wrong fork or spoon and are an implement short, ask for another if the waiter does not notice. If your salad plate has been incorrectly placed on the right, and you find it uncomfortable to use, move it over to the left, and if your coffee cup has been placed incorrectly on the left, move it over to the right. If one of your utensils doesn't seem clean, ask to have it replaced. (Never wipe off silver with your napkin.)

If you don't use all the implements placed on the table, don't worry about it; just leave them there. Don't put them on outgoing plates.

If you drop one of your eating utensils, leave it on the floor and ask the waiter to bring you a clean one. (The floor of a restaurant is never clean enough to allow you to put a dropped utensil back into your mouth.) If you spill something messy on the floor, something in which the waiter could slip, just drop a napkin over it, and then call the waiter to cope. Even a bus boy could handle this problem.

Functioning Properly at the Restaurant Table   If butter comes in a crock, take a portion from it with the small knife that usually accompanies the butter. Put it on your butter plate or your luncheon or dinner plate to use for the bread or rolls. Then replace the knife in the crock.

If a loaf of hot bread is brought in (usually on a wooden server), the host or hostess should slice it, or separate it, and pass it around the table.

If your salad dressing arrives in two crystal cruets, one for oil and one for vinegar, you must mix it yourself. Pour some from each cruet, rather sparingly, on your salad, add salt and pepper, and mix up the greens. Taste, and then add more oil or vinegar accordingly. If all of the guests at your table have to make their own, try to be quick about it.

If you order iced coffee or iced tea, the tall glass may be served on a saucer and will be brought to you with a long spoon. Use the spoon as a stirrer and then place it on the edge of the saucer. If there is no saucer, keep it in your glass. One is not supposed to put directly on the table (whether it's bare or covered with linens) an eating utensil that has been used.

Complaints and Compliments

The host should make any complaint in a firm but soft tone to the table's waiter or waitress, or to the section headwaiter, the dining room hostess, or whoever is in command (it may be the owner). These people are supposed to see that the service runs smoothly and that the guests are satisfied. Hot food should be really hot (particularly the soup, coffee, and tea); and cold food should be cold. It is better to send the food back to the kitchen without making a scene than to expect a guest to eat something not up to standard just because you're too embarrassed to complain.

A restaurant fusspot, of course, is just as bad as an I-could-care-less waiter. If you are in the proper mood, you will be able to find fault with anything and everything, which is unfortunate for you, either as a host or as a guest. Any good restaurant appreciates a customer who understands the niceties of dining and who exacts good service, but there are ways of complaining that are acceptable and others that are not. Making a loud scene and a public beratement of the service when the place is crowded are examples of the latter. The intelligent host writes a letter the day after, carefully detailing what went wrong and making suggestions for improving the situation in the future. A well-run restaurant appreciates this kind of constructive action, and any proprietor worthy of his or her profession will react favorably to such a letter.

Likewise, the management and your server both appreciate compliments if the service met your expectations. Thank both of them "for a very fine meal," and if you ask the waiter to "tell the chef that he did a great job tonight," you can rest assured the message will be immediately transmitted to the kitchen staff. Few people ever think of doing that.

Informal Restaurant Dining

Buffet Service A buffet service is becoming more and more popular in both hotel dining rooms and restaurants. One usually walks around the buffet clockwise. Most people make from one to three trips to the table. If you are making just one trip, you are probably combining the cold salad concoctions (everything from jello to chicken salad) with the main course (from roast beef to seafood Newburg), vegetables, and breads on your plate all at once. If you make two trips, you have probably eaten the first course all by itself. If you make three trips, you have probably eaten a plate of the cold salad items first, then a hot plate of meat and fish, and finally a plate of different desserts. (The antacid awaits at home.) It is all right to have one's plate well supplied with food, but constant trips from the buffet with overflowing plates might make onlookers suspect you of an advanced state of gluttony!

In the "old days" a gentleman was supposed to go to the restaurant buffet, fill up his lady's plate, and return it to her at her place at the table. In today's world, each one of us wishes to choose our own—ignoring certain items and taking a large portion of some very favored food. It is very nice of the men present at the table to order everyone's drinks from the bar, or to fetch a glass of wine for every person at the table. The philosophy of who goes to the buffet to put food on a plate for someone else is based upon kindness and need. An older person should be waited on, as should someone who is not feeling well, someone with a leg in a cast or some similar problem, or a child who might not pick healthful food. If the old custom of a woman sitting helplessly at the table while the man fetches her food is disappearing, the reason for someone helping someone else in need is *not* disappearing. We should welcome the shift in emphasis.

Cafeteria Service   If there are coat racks in the cafeteria, it is advisable to use them in order to make others' passage behind your table less congested. Be sure you are sitting where the coat rack is within your view, however, and never put a fur coat or a fur hat upon it. When you're going through the food line, don't hold up other people unnecessarily by taking too long to decide. And it is rude to push back into line to get something one has forgotten.

If you sit down at a table for four in a crowded period, the chances are strangers will have to join you. They should be polite and say, "May I sit here?" or "Do you mind if I join you?" and you should be polite and respond quickly, "Of course, please sit here." You are under no obligation to talk to strangers, but if you are sitting alone at a table with one other person, it can be a very frigid atmosphere unless one of you says something. It can be something as exciting as "It's really beautiful outside today, isn't it?" That is all you need to say, and the other person can respond with "It certainly is." Each has made a gesture, the tension barrier is broken, and you can both eat in peace.

Lunch Counters   If you and a friend finally find two seats at a popular lunch counter, but there is one person separating the two seats, it is proper for you to ask apologetically, "Excuse us, please, but would you mind moving over one seat, so that we may sit together?" If your sitting together with your friend involves three people getting up and playing musical chairs, in order to give you those two seats, do not ask it of them, for you are imposing too much. If you are alone at the lunch counter, never criticize to your neighbors the food or the service, for you are interrupting them with something depressing and negative. If you want to speak to your neighbor, do it very sparingly, and make it an affirmative comment (or at least show a sense of humor by making a funny comment—we all need that in our lives).

The importance of "real manners" manifests itself even at the lunch counter. The way in which you ask your neighbors for the catsup or mustard, and the way in which you thank those who pass it to you, show the kind of person you are. If you are just lingering over a cup of coffee and there are many people waiting behind you who are frantic to be served, real manners mean you quickly pay your check and free the seat.

Fast-food Service   Usually a child's first "eating-out" experiences occur in fast-food establishments. This is a perfect training area for parents to teach their young children manners. If they behave well in a hamburger, pancake, or fried chicken place, they will behave well in a hotel dining room or in any expensive restaurant.

The way in which a family acts together while eating out is one of the basic ways in which children learn to think of others, to be unselfish. The first thing they must learn is to keep the noise level down, to control their natural ebullience or a possible desire to "show off" by talking or laughing loudly. Teen-agers particularly have to watch themselves on this point. Many people who come to the fast-food places are tired, in a hurry, or preoccupied with their own problems, and the interruption of their peace and quiet with loud noises is very thoughtless.

Children watch the way their parents pick up litter and carry it to the big trash receptacles, so that the bus boys and girls will have an easier, quicker time of cleaning up their table for the next occupants. Children notice their parents doing little things like cleaning off the side of the catsup or mustard container. By wiping it off with a paper napkin, someone is making it pleasanter for the next family to use.

A child observes; a child learns; and a child will behave in the same way as he grows into adulthood. This is the way character is formed, even in a frozen custard drive-in.

Chapter 56

PRIVATE CLUBS

America is unique in the world with its intricate network of private clubs used for family, business, and social entertaining, for intellectual pursuits, and for sports activities.

Almost every large city has an in-town athletic club with a pool and squash, tennis, or handball courts. There are eating clubs for men or women where members can invite those of the opposite sex and where a great deal of entertaining is done. There are still a few men's clubs that will not admit women guests (except perhaps around the Christmas holidays). There are private bridge and chess clubs, and clubs for graduates of a specific university; there are those that sponsor lecture-luncheons featuring celebrities and experts who lecture on everything from gardening, wines, and art to philosophy, investing in the stock market, and foreign affairs. These in-town clubs, as well as country clubs, are much used for luncheons, dinner parties, club dances, private dances, debuts, and wedding receptions. In most clubs a non-member may use club facilities to hold a cocktail party or any large function, provided he or she is sponsored by a friend who is a member in good standing. Most clubs welcome this outside entertaining to help them pay their bills.

Clubs can perform many services for their members, but their over-all function is to provide a meeting place for people of similar interests. They fulfill a very important service for business people, for many a deal has been sealed at the eighteenth hole or at the end of the third set of doubles.

Country clubs and athletic, beach, golf, racquet, shooting, and yacht clubs have very strict rules regarding members' use of their facilities. Members—and their guests—must observe the rules of the club in regard to the dress codes for the various sports, and for the dining rooms. I asked the governor of a famous country club what was his definition of a "good club member," and he laughed but came up with a fast, no-nonsense answer.

A good member obeys all our rules, entertains a lot here so the club can remain solvent, pays his bills on time, and likes what he sees.

Private clubs usually require an initiation fee after the age of thirty or thirty-five, which may be anything from five hundred to several thousand dollars. The dues are usually billed on an annual or semiannual basis, or they are prorated monthly along with the house charges. When members do not pay their bills, they are often "posted," and it is embarrassing to see one's name up on the board in the main hall with those of others delinquent in paying. In most private clubs neither members nor guests tip the coatroom attendants or waiters; a service charge is usually tacked on to each bar or restaurant bill. One signs checks in a private club; cash is usually not handled. An exception to the no-tipping rule is often seen in the golfing part of a private club, relating to caddies, locker room attendants, and so on. (See "Golf," page 708.)

Members must adhere to regulations on bringing guests to the club. They must never bring so many that the existing athletic facilities are taxed. Bringing a gang to the swimming pool can antagonize the club membership when they find they can't get near the snack bar. Some clubs restrict the number of times any one person or family may be invited during the season by any one member.

Joining a Club

Joining a private club requires soul-searching from a financial viewpoint. Not only do you have to be able to pay the initiation fee, which may be steep, but you must also pay the annual dues and the monthly house charges, make a contribution to the Employees Christmas Fund, and be prepared to accept without complaining emergency assessments (the pool needs refinishing, the clubhouse needs a new roof, the greens must be redone, the dining room needs redecorating . . .).

Many clubs have long waiting lists, and being accepted for membership may take years. If someone wants to join such a private club, he should evince a casual interest to his friends who are members, without pressuring them. If one of them offers to help him join, he should give his sponsor the names of other members who might logically second his application, as well as send supporting letters. Some clubs require five such supporting letters in addition to the proposer's and seconder's letters. It is, of course, highly embarrassing to the sponsors if the proposed new member is rejected by the Membership Committee for any reason. The rejected member must accept the situation gracefully, and not probe or keep forcing himself on his club member friend, asking that he put him up again.

Letter of Proposal for Membership   If a club member wishes to put up a friend for membership in his private club, he might write a sponsor's letter, such as this:

Date

Mr. James Elliott
Head of Membership Committee
Racquet and Greens Club
St. Louis, Missouri   zip code

Dear Jim,

I would like to propose for a family membership in the Racquet and Greens Mr. and Mrs. Earl Whitman and their family of four children. Earl is a graduate of Tufts and the Wharton School of Finance and is a Senior Partner of Gordon, Milliken, Whitman & Co. His wife, Nancy, graduated from Vassar, did graduate work at New York University, and teaches at the Persons School. The four children, Earl, Jr., Randolph, Agnes, and Emily, range in age from twenty to fourteen. All attend boarding school and college away from St. Louis.

The Whitmans recently sold their farm and moved into the city. The senior Whitmans need a place like our club in which to do their extensive business and social entertaining. Both are excellent golfers and tennis players; three of the children are tournament-quality golfers. Mr. and Mrs. Whitman are civic leaders in this city and would make a great addition to the club. I most heartily endorse their candidacy for membership to the Racquet and Greens Club.

Sincerely,
William Garrett

The seconder writes a letter stating that he is seconding the membership application, knows the Whitmans well, and finds them attractive and likable. The writers of supporting letters say how long they have known the Whitmans, and that they wholeheartedly endorse William Garrett's sponsorship. It is up to William Garrett, as sponsor, to send a carbon of his proposing letter to all the others who are helping the Whitmans attain membership; he should keep track of who has not sent in his seconding or supporting letter, so that he can complete the required preparations.

Letter of Resignation   When one resigns from a club for whatever reason (not using it enough, too expensive, moving away), one should write a short letter of resignation for the record, to prove that one resigned in good standing.

Date

The Board of Governors
Racquet and Greens Club
St. Louis, Missouri   zip code

Dear sirs,

It is with great regret that I submit my resignation as a member of this club, effective July first of this year. The pressure of work is such that I am unable to utilize the club and feel I should withdraw so that someone who has more leisure time may enjoy the great facilities. I have enjoyed my associations with the members of this club and wish you continued success in your efforts to keep it the pleasant place that it is.

Sincerely,
Norris Lanson

Naturally, all club bills and dues for the year must be paid up at once upon resignation.

Staying Overnight

Some clubs offer a limited number of rooms for overnight guests of members who live a hundred miles away or more, or for out-of-town members. If you, for example, wish to stay at the River Club in New York and you know a club member well, you should call and ask him to "have you put up" for the weekend of such-and-such. These reservations usually have to be made far in advance. You can have the bill sent directly to you after your visit for your room and meals and any other club charges. Your sponsoring member has to call the River Club and make the reservation. Some clubs require a letter from the sponsoring member in order to make the reservation. Some clubs allow the visitor to sign his own name on all checks; others require that he sign with the sponsoring member's name or account number. A guest should act circumspectly while at the club, because otherwise he will reflect badly on the sponsoring member; he should pay his bill with dispatch.

Using Club Facilities for Entertaining when You Are Not a Member

Many clubs, in order to make ends meet, welcome the friends of members giving cocktail parties, wedding receptions, and dinner parties in their private rooms—even in the ballroom. If you wish to have your daughter's wedding reception, for example, at a good friend's club (and as I said before, you would not ask this favor of anyone but a *good* friend), you should plan it far in advance with the member. If permission is granted, you should talk to the banquet manager or maître d' or catering director of the club about the details concerning your party. Don't ask to break club rules. Be sure to invite the member who sponsored you, and to pay your bill the day it is delivered to you. You may tip anyone on the club staff who worked especially hard on your reception. This would be over and above the service charge that is added to your bill.

Christmas Fund for Employees

Club members receive a notice every year before Christmas, asking for contributions to the employees fund, which, when received from all members, is divided up and given to the employees as a Christmas bonus. It is the membership's way of saying "thank you and you did a great job in taking care of us this past year." A single member who rarely uses the club might send a check for ten or twenty dollars; a family that uses the club constantly might contribute one hundred dollars and more.

Other Clubs and Organizations

There are many organizations that revolve around special interests, volunteer work, community service, hobbies, politics, and foreign affairs. The National Federation of Business and Professional Women's Clubs, Inc., has a list of clubs in every city in America to which women who are interested may apply for membership. For gardening enthusiasts there are the Federated Garden Clubs, as well as the Garden Clubs of America. Women who can prove that an ancestor aided the revolutionary cause in the American Revolutionary War days may qualify for membership in the Daughters of the American Revolution National Society, or, if their ancestry was established here before the Revolution, in the Colonial Dames of America. There are similar organizations for men, such as the Society of Colonial Wars. There are clubs for stamp collectors, antique car owners, skiers, wine lovers, and scuba divers. Just as the big labor unions have committees that plan for members' special interests, so do the management or professional organizations (lawyers, bankers, designers, medical associations). Many powerful membership organizations address major national issues, such as preservation of our landmarks (the National Trust for Historic Preservation), foreign affairs (Foreign Policy Association), and ecology (the National Audubon Society, The Wilderness Club, The Sierra Club). Almost every cultural institution, including opera companies and major museums, has its own membership assoiation, with special benefits and social activities. It is easy for anyone "to belong" to something, whether it's strictly for pleasure, for self-enrichment, or for helping the common good.

Chapter 57

THE CONSIDERATE SPORTSPERSON

As Americans push into the few wilderness areas still remaining with their enthusiasm for cross-country skiing, snowmobiling, hiking, or camping, and as millions more each decade take up traditionally popular sports like hunting and fishing, it is apparent that *there is a desperate need for a set of good behavior priorities.* Simply put, these rules have to do with consideration of other people and consideration of our environment. If we do not live by these rules and teach them carefully to our children, we will lose what is left of our beautiful natural areas. Snowmobiles are already relentlessly ripping up precious timberland and disturbing the fish beneath the iced-over surfaces of streams and lakes. Selfish fishermen are bespoiling the waters with litter and overfishing; animals are killed by forest fires caused by careless campers. The movement of Americans to the outdoors is exciting, because physical activity provides the greatest relief there is from the tensions of our everyday life. But we must have manners in that great outdoors, or we will destroy the very thing that gives us so much happiness.

The American passion for physical fitness is also reflected in the tremendous growth of traditional sports like skiing and tennis. People are out jogging, bicycling, tossing the volleyball around on the beach, racing each other over frozen ponds. In this section on sports I do not attempt to teach you how to perform them, for such information is available elsewhere in much more detail than I could possibly provide here. I can only skim the surface of certain activities, to point out the continuing importance of good sportsmanship, as well as the importance of proper preparation and rigorous adherence to safety rules.

A child should be taught that he has a tremendous responsibility toward others as well as himself whenever he embarks on a sport—whether he's skateboarding in the neighborhood, skiing at a large resort, or fishing from the town bridge with his buddies. Adults should remember this responsibility as well.

Yachting and Sailing

Boating is one of those sports requiring advance planning, rigid adherence to safety rules, a constant alertness on the part of the person in charge, and a show of consideration for others at all times. The captain of a sail- or powerboat is responsible for his craft, the lives of his passengers, and the lives and property of other people in the water around him. Today, with waters congested with boats, swimmers, surfers, water skiers, and fishermen, the skipper has little chance to relax. His guests, too, have a definite responsibility in following the rules of water safety, in thinking of others, and in showing a concern for the environment.

There is certain basic required equipment, such as one Coast Guard-approved life preserver per passenger. A child or anyone who is not an excellent swimmer should wear one at all times. There are four approved PFD (personal flotation devices), and the Coast Guard recommends different kinds according to the size of the boat. One popular type is the buoyant cushion device, designed to be thrown from the boat or grabbed in the water. It is filled with plastic foam, kapok, or fibrous glass material. The buoyant vests come in three sizes (adult, child-medium, and child-small), as well as in many styles and colors. The store where you buy PFDs will help you select the suitable ones. If you are alone in a boat, always wear a life preserver of some kind, and be sure that everyone wears his own when you begin to encounter rough ocean or stormy lake waters, rushing streams, or rapids.

An excellent boating guide furnishing important information at a small cost is the Coast Guard Publication 340, entitled "United States Coast Guard Recreational Boating Guide."

For people who are around motorboats, it is an excellent idea to enroll in one of the free boating courses offered by volunteers in your area. Write to the United States Power Squadrons National Headquarters, 50 Craig Road, P.O. Box 345, Montvale, New Jersey 07645 for information. If you have a choice of instructors, ask around as to who is the best.

Any boat designed purely for pleasure is technically classified as a yacht. However, to refer to one's rowboat or little sailboat as a yacht, except in fun, is very pretentious. The Coast Guard classifies any boat under sixty feet in length in the "small boat" category. The main types of boats are runabouts, powerboats for cruising, fishing boats, and sailboats used for racing and cruising.

Before Boarding a Sailboat   If you have never before been on a sailboat, you might find it useful to familiarize yourself with some basic terminology of sailing (available in numerous books in the library), such as:

On the wind; off the wind; tacking; jibing—terms to describe the maneuverings of the boat in relation to the wind.

Mast, boom, stays, mainsheet, helm, cleats, halyards—parts of the sailboat with which you should be familiar. If the captain yells at you, "Watch out for the boom!" you had better know what the boom is before it hits you in the head.

Mainsail, jibs, spinnakers—the basic sails that drive the boat.

Port, starboard, forward, aft, cockpit, below—terms to differentiate the different physical locations on the boat.

Head, galley, dinghy—nautical terms for the toilet, the kitchen, and the small boat used to get people to and from the shore.

A smattering of these general terms should be memorized before you take such a trip. And remember to excuse the captain's language and tone of voice at all times. His job is to watch out for everyone's safety, and he usually feels the responsibility heavily.

Clothes to Take Wear a hat that will stay on your head in the wind; take two bathing suits, if it's swimmable weather, a windbreaker, jeans or slacks, shorts, a long-sleeved shirt (to protect you from sunburn), T shirts, and a sweater. Skirts are a nuisance except on shore. Even in hot weather, when it "blows" it may become very cold at sea. Foul-weather gear is a must, such as a slicker and matching hat or poncho. (Ask your host first, however, whether he already has these items stowed on board for his guests.) A woman, of course, needs a couple of scarves to protect her hair from the wind. Most important, you should have non-skid sneakers or similar soft-soled shoes. The deck of a boat when it's wet can be extremely slippery. And the worst offense is to wear hard-soled shoes aboard any craft. They not only damage the boat but are dangerous. Also be sure to include in your gear a strong sun-screen preparation, sunglasses, and any personal medicines (such as motion sickness pills and aspirin).

As far as the skipper is concerned, the container in which you bring your belongings is as important as what you bring in it. No hard suitcases should be brought on board (unless you are on a big yacht). They are too difficult to store below. Pack your things in squashable canvas or denim, like a sailor's duffel bag.

If you and your spouse are going to be someone's guests at a yacht club after a day of sailing, ask your host about wardrobe requirements for this event. At many of these clubs a woman might need a short or long dress (the packable jerseys are the easiest to take along) or a man might need a blazer, shirt, and tie, or even a dinner suit. Some people don't want to be bothered with taking their formal clothes on board. They send them ahead to a hotel, motel, or a friend's home in the town where they will be spending the night. They arrange to have their clothes pressed and waiting on their arrival.

Guests' Rules of Behavior on Board

1. Always defer to the skipper (captain), because he is responsible for everything on board, including human life. Always obey him swiftly.

He is aware of things you are not; never argue with him. Ask him if you can be of any help, perhaps with the galley—although this small area is usually the carefully organized province of one person. Inexperienced though willing help might turn careful organization into chaos.

2. Watch your smoking. Some skippers will not allow smoking at any time. Ask when you may, but remember never to light up when a boat is being refueled. Never stamp out a cigarette on deck or toss a lit cigarette overboard. The wind may throw the burning cigarette back on deck or into someone's face.

3. Stay out of passageways.

4. Never let out a playful scream when you're underway. The captain will probably react with the belief that there's a man overboard.

5. Never throw anything down a ship's toilet (the "head"). It is a delicate instrument, and you should ask the captain or mate exactly how it works before using it.

6. Use water sparingly. Never wash any personal laundry on board. Wait until you are on shore to wash your hair, and always take your own soap and shampoo with you on shore. Shower very lightly on board, since water is at a premium.

7. Never swim unless you have the skipper's permission, and dive off the boat only from the positions designated by him. Don't dive off a moving boat, either. The true speed of a boat is deceptive; you may find yourself frighteningly far from the boat when you surface.

8. When there's dirty work to do on board, be the first to offer to help—whether it's cleaning, shining, pumping, or bailing.

9. If you are prone to motion sickness, take a seasickness medication prescribed by your doctor before and during your sea voyage. If you still become seasick, don't be embarrassed by it. Even the most experienced sailors are subject to it from time to time. If you feel queasy on a boat, don't go below. The closed atmosphere of the cabin and the boat's motion may only aggravate the problem. Stay on deck and keep your face to the wind. Fresh air is the best cure, and if you become hungry again, salty crackers are surprisingly soothing to the stomach.

10. If you are a first-time guest, above all have a relaxed attitude. Even if sailing is an unpleasant surprise and you are seasick, overly sunburned, or just plain exhausted, don't complain. Keep smiling and remain good-natured. After all, if it rains the entire time and the trip is a grueling experience, you can always refuse to go on another boat. But if your experience is like most people's, you will become addicted to the sport.

Host's Rules of Behavior on Board

1. The person at the helm cannot afford to be a show-off. It is a time for self-control and proceeding with caution at all times.

2. Be efficient in briefing your first-time guests about what to expect—the limitations of space, the possibility of being seasick, the necessity for proper clothes.

3. Be patient and kind with your inexperienced sailor-guests. Teach them how to move fast and respond to your directions on board.
4. Don't overindulge in alcohol; the skipper must be alert at all times.
5. When under power, be considerate of smaller boats; try not to rock them.
6. Don't allow anyone to throw trash overboard. Collect it in a plastic bag and dispose of it properly at the marina or club in the specified place.
7. Faithfully observe all channel markings. Don't rev up your engine early in the morning upon departure, as it will wake up everyone else around you. Be careful of fishermen's trolling lines and water skiers' lines. Careful navigation and the strict observance of nautical rules avoid accidents.

Powerboats These pleasure craft are often larger, more formal, and better equipped for "gracious living" than the sailboat. The large powerboat often has all the comforts of home, including an ice-maker, microwave oven, TV sets, and even bathtubs. Usually you will need some dressier clothes on board, for cocktail parties on shore and on other boats docked nearby. Again, ask your hosts exactly what kind of clothes you should bring. Take along your needlework or reading material for hours of total relaxation; you will not be as busy as on a sailboat. A good guest leaves everyone else alone part of each day. Companionship is the essence of boating, but time apart enhances it.

The responsibility of the skipper to his passengers is identical to that of the captain of a sailboat; their lives are in his hands.

The social life revolving around powerboats, particularly at the larger marinas in season, is intense. If you and your passengers are invited to many parties and you accept those invitations, you should invite your hosts back to your own boat, whether informally or for a party. If you borrow food or drinks from a neighboring boat, be sure to replace what you took.

Gifts For sail- or powerboats, space is always at a premium, so do not buy something too large and therefore useless as a thank-you present for your host. Either bring a gift of food that can be consumed and enjoyed by the entire group on board, or send something you know from experience is lacking on board. It may be a weighted, non-sliding ash tray or an ice bucket, but be careful not to purchase a gimmicky "nautical" gift. Skippers are very careful about what they put on their craft; frequently they are more particular about their boats than about their own homes.

Yacht Clubs There is a great diversity in yacht clubs. Some of them are steeped in tradition and are very posh and snobbish. Others are creaky one-room wooden clubhouses that look like waterside shacks. Most of them, of course, are on the water, but then there's the renowned New York Yacht Club (the repositor of the America's Cup for the prestigious international sail race held near Newport, Rhode Island). This club is located on a busy midtown street in New York City.

A large yacht club usually offers sailing classes for children. It organizes and supervises races for all classes of boats and awards trophies to the winners. It has docks for securing boats for short lengths of time and a fueling service. It offers launch service (the boats that ply back and forth in the harbor, picking up sailors and bringing them to shore, or back out to their boats again). A yacht club usually also has varying degrees of restaurants and bar services.

The clubs are pivots for a great deal of social activity. Each year, for example, many large yachts from all over the world put in at Edgartown, Massachusetts, and often the entire New York Yacht Club fleet arrives at this island club during its cruise, giving the signal for a crowded weekend of dinner-dances and parties. Many such clubs grant reciprocal privileges to members of other clubs. However, in the busy summer months, one cannot assume that one can easily moor one's boat at another club's facilities without booking well in advance. One may be charged a nominal fee for obtaining one of these reserved moorings.

Each major yacht club has its own insignia, its own flag staff, and its own traditions of ceremonies relating to the flag. Sometimes a cannon is shot off at 8 A.M. and again at sunset each day to alert all those not under cover to stand quietly while the colors are raised in the morning or brought down and furled for the night.

Life Aboard the Big Yachts   Life aboard one of the great yachts, like the late Aristotle Onassis' *Cristina,* is about as glamorous as one can imagine it to be. The guest staterooms are larger than most people's bedrooms at home; the bathrooms are palatial. There is a swimming pool with automatically sliding covers that form a dance floor for evening festivities. A yacht like the *Cristina* has its own medical department, small powerboats for sightseeing and water-skiing pleasures; full skin-diving equipment; its own movie theater, and its own airplane. If you are invited to cruise on such a yacht, you would take the same wardrobe you would take to visit a friend at a very social summer resort—including formal clothes for "on board" parties, or the black-tie dinners at friends' homes on shore. You don't have to worry about bringing aboard easy-to-stow canvas duffel bags for luggage. You may bring as many hard suitcases as you wish.

You tip the crew as you would tip the staff of a private home or of a luxury hotel on the shore. If the owner is not on board, you should tip the captain—but a nice present might be a more diplomatic gesture. The stewards should receive anywhere from ten to twenty dollars each, according to how much service they rendered you.

Your hosts on a cruise would like nothing better than to have you an independent guest, resourceful at entertaining yourself, even when on shore, in between meals. No one likes the thought of having to entertain a guest and tell him what to do every second of the day. A cruise is the perfect time to catch up on intellectual pursuits, needlework, or just plain healthy sleep and exercise.

Tennis and Racket Sports

Tennis has enjoyed a greater surge of popularity in the past decade than any other sport in America. The major reasons for its tremendous growth are the increasing availability of courts and the game itself, which affords an easy way to get hard, fast exercise within a short period of time. This is an unbeatable combination for any sport in our exercise-conscious society.

Along with the year-round sport of tennis, other racket sports have also drawn more advocates. Squash, played only indoors, is an even faster, harder game, and until recently was played mainly by men. Women are now adopting this sport with great enthusiasm, although the availability of courts for them is a continuing problem, since many squash courts are in men's private clubs. Paddle or platform tennis, often referred to as the perfect cold-weather game, is enjoying greater popularity, too, although it is still available mainly through private clubs. This game is played outdoors in a fenced-in area on a platform made of wooden boards, with a special type of paddle and ball. Badminton is another good although less strenuous racket game. It has the advantage of being playable wherever there is a flat lawn. It requires a special net, rackets, and a feather "bird" instead of a ball.

Tennis is a great unmasker of people's character. The negative side of some people is brought out faster on a tennis court than almost anywhere else. A person of a perfectly nice social demeanor can suddenly flush scarlet, throw his racket, and make accusations of his partner, his opponents, or himself. Equally odious is the tennis "excuser" who is ready with a different excuse for each bad shot. "The sun is in my eyes. . . . The net is too high. . . . My tennis elbow is acting up again. . . . The blister on my heel hurts." Perhaps a definition of the kind of social tennis player one wants to have around is the following (the professionals have a different set of rules):

1. He plays steadily, not flashily. He is in control of his shots.
2. He never brags about his tennis abilities in order to be matched with people of superior playing ability.
3. He never complains about his partner's shots, no matter how bad they may be.
4. He watches his language and never throws a tantrum on the court.
5. He has a sense of humor, knowing when and how to laugh at his own playing or at something someone else just did on the court.
6. He knows when and how to compliment partners and opponents alike. He knows how to buck up a depressed or embarrassed partner.
7. He never "hogs the court." When it's rightfully his partner's shot, he lets him or her take it, even if he knows he could win the point by taking it.

8. He always thanks each player at the end of the match, as well as shaking their hands. He compliments the winners, consoles the losers.
9. He never makes excuses for his own playing.
10. When he has ten minutes to spare, he hits some balls with a child or a beginning player who's dying for the chance to play with "someone good."

There are more formal rules of tennis etiquette, many of which apply in particular to private tennis clubs or at public courts where serious tennis is played. For example, one should bring one's own balls (good, playable ones). Some people never bring balls and are as popular as those who never pick up a check at the restaurant. If you have to cross over courts where people are playing in order to reach your own, wait patiently to the side until the ball is no longer in play on each court. When there is a quick pause between points, ask politely, "May we go through?" Permission will of course be granted, but you and your fellow players should move quickly *across the back* of others' courts, so as to hold up their game as little as possible.

If your partner or opponent makes a bad call or insists upon a score you know for certain is inaccurate, don't dispute it. Agree with him or her, and be a good sport. To lose a point or two is insignificant; to lose your reputation for being a good sport is serious.

Don't be lazy and stand there while your partner picks up all the balls when your side is being served to. And when your partner is serving, you must always keep him well supplied with balls. Return any stray ball that bounces into your court to its rightful owners the moment there is a pause in your own game. If your ball goes over a fence, you should shout, "I'll get it at the end of this game." Then go and get it.

When you are ready to play, one player from each side tosses his racket to win serve and desired court. This is the time you decide, too, whether you will change sides every odd game (the most accepted procedure), every three games, or after each set. Both sides should keep score, but the server should announce the score right before he serves—so that any disagreements can be settled before proceeding. Loud talking and laughing is very upsetting to neighboring players, so one must keep jokes and ebullience under control. If there is any distraction that interferes with your opponent's shot, the nice thing to do is insist that he take the point over.

When you arrive at the given hour to claim the court, you should call out to those who have been playing on it, "Go ahead, finish your game." This does not mean that they should finish the set. If you arrive on time without your opponent, tell those playing, "Please, continue playing until my opponent arrives." If you will be playing doubles and three of you are ready to play at the beginning of the hour, you can claim the court in order to "warm up." Adult members of a club usually have the right to take away from junior members the court upon which they are playing—because the chilrden supposedly have many other hours during the working day when they can play.

Learning players should occupy the courts very early or late, in order to let proficient players use the courts at peak hours. Fast, able players must also be satisfied with shorter court time on busy holidays. If two people are playing singles on a busy weekend, they should graciously offer to play doubles with two other players, even if they do not wish to.

Spectators should have good manners, too. They should not make any comments, critical or laudatory, from the sidelines, unless it is to applaud the winner in the finals of a tournament. The most objectionable "spectator" is someone's small child, begging for attention or to be allowed to chase balls. As one pro put it, "Children should not be seen, heard, or even present during a tennis match."

If you play on grass (and you are indeed fortunate if you can, since there are so few grass courts left in this country), remember always to fix the grass if you have made holes in the turf with your shoes or racket. If you are fortunate enough to have the use of a friend's private court, you and your children should offer to help in the maintenance of the court—helping to water, roll it, sweep the lines. If you are the last one to leave, know the rules of what to do with the net.

Proper Attire In the "good old days" tennis dresses were designed and manufactured by people who followed utilitarian, functional principles in their designs. As a result, they were easy to wear and performed efficiently. Today high-fashion designers have suddenly turned their attention to the lowly tennis dress. Fashion tastes aside, the girl who looks best on the court is one who is clad in a dress or shorts in which she is obviously prepared to play a fast, rugged game. White used to be de rigueur, but the advent of colored piping and trimming has started a whole color revolution. Now anything seems to go, except blue jeans. Very few clubs still hold to the "all white" rules of former years. White shorts and polo shirts often in colors are still in the most popular attire for men. Women have the option of wearing socks or no socks, or the ankleless socks with pompoms at the heels to keep them from sinking down into the shoe. Men are still wearing long white stripe-trimmed or plain white socks, usually a blend of wool and synthetic, worn straight up or cuffed over. Sneakers or tennis shoes with bright-colored trim are acceptable today, but what is *not* acceptable is filthy dirty ones.

Because of a dramatic increase in severe eye injuries suffered by players who rush to the net and receive a hard ball in the eye, one sees more eye protectors or impact-resistant sunglasses being worn today on the courts. Other players disdain them, because they feel they automatically protect their faces with their rackets when necessary.

Because people are wary about the danger of skin cancer today, players are wearing better sun-screen protection on their faces along with visored hats. The less conspicuous the hat, the better. As for jewelry, the only items that should be worn on the court are plain earrings for pierced ears, wedding rings, and shockproof watches.

Golf

Golf is a competitive game that can bring out the best and the worst in a player. Courtesy and patience are as much a part of a good golf game as a perfect swing. One should be friendly with one's group, but not talk too much. The noisy player or chatterer is unwelcome, as he disturbs everyone's concentration, including probably his own. Individual honesty is an integral part of golf, for each player has to call errors on himself and should take any penalties without discussion. He must keep his own score accurately and always play with the attitude that his opponent is equally honest. In other words, he never challenges his opponent's score.

Players are given handicaps in golf, which have been carefully checked out by the tournament committee in advance. One should never apologize for one's handicap. It is, after all, as true a reflection of one's sustained game as it is possible to have. When golfers hit the ball badly, they should not make excuses; when their opponents hit the ball well, they should compliment them. A pleasant, congenial attitude on the golf course is paramount to everyone's enjoyment of the game.

Golf courses fall into two categories: the private club to which one must be invited by a member, and the public course open to all upon payment of a fixed greens fee and caddie fee. Both of these fees vary greatly with the public or private course.

At a private club hosts usually pay for their guests' greens fee and caddie fee. At the "nineteenth hole" men sometimes throw dice to see who is going to pay for a round of drinks. Sometimes each player pays for his own.

At the first tee players have different ways of deciding who shall play first. One popular way is to hold a ball in your hand and ask a member of the opposing team whether the number on it is odd or even. If the player guesses correctly, he or his team tees off first. If he guesses incorrectly, you (or your team) have the honors. Thereafter the winner of the previous hole always tees off first.

Each club has its own way of handling such matters as who takes precedence at the tees. Guests at clubs should always refer to their golf score cards to find out what the local rules are. Men have priority over women in teeing off at many clubs. Women are not allowed to play before noon at some, and they are sometimes barred from playing on weekends except in mixed foursomes in the afternoons. Let us hope these rules will begin to change to allow working women the same privileges as men.

Two players sometimes take precedence over a foursome, which must necessarily play much more slowly. It is good golf manners for a foursome to allow a twosome to play through. On the other hand, a twosome that is playing a leisurely game always permits a businesslike foursome to play through.

Any other combination of players, from the lone golfer to the "gang"—over four—must allow the twosome or the foursome precedence. On many courses, especially on public ones, only foursomes are permitted on crowded weekends.

Even non-golfers should know the rules concerning quiet as a player tees off. Players should stand still—not even make practice swings with their clubs or talk with their caddies as another player takes his turn. Spectators, too, should be sure to keep absolutely quiet so as not to disturb the golfer's concentration when making his shot.

Great care must be taken not to tee off when others are in line with what a player hopes will be the flight of his ball, and certainly never until the players ahead have each had their second strokes. The warning "fore" may not carry sufficiently against even a light wind, so it is not used much any more. Instead a player should wait until golfers immediately ahead are out of range. On blind holes the caddie or another golfer should go ahead to see if it is safe to hit, and then signal when it is safe.

When a ball is lost, other players in the group help look for it, but the search is never drawn out to the extent that it holds up the play. Players searching for a ball should allow other players coming up to pass them. They should signal to those following to pass and then should not continue their play until those players have passed out of range.

The greatest problem on golf courses today is the slow player. Golfers should be aware of their own actions and not contribute to the traffic jam on the course. The polite, efficient golfer knows all the local rules and the handicap allowances before he starts. He knows when it's his turn to play and he's ready. He has sized up his next shot and decided which club he will use while another of his group is hitting. When he hits off the fairway, he judges where his ball went so he can find it easily, but has a second ball handy in case of need. He does not practice-swing or waggle unnecessarily. If he shares a caddie and goes in a different direction from the other player and the caddie, he takes two or three clubs with him to speed his selection of them for the next hit. He does not indulge in idle chatter, distracting the others and delaying the game.

Handling a Golf Cart A guest of a member should read the posted rules governing the use of golf carts at that club before taking one. There are certain universal rules, however, that are essential to the maintenance of the course and personal safety.

Before starting out, you should check to see if your cart is set to go forward or backward, and act accordingly. Be sure you don't start until everyone has driven from the tee, and never drive out ahead of someone playing a shot. You should not put the cart too near the putting greens, for it ruins other players' approaches to the green. You should park the cart, instead, on the side of the green nearest to the next hole and then move away from that green quickly as soon as you have finished putting. If you have a gasoline cart, you should turn off the motor while the rest of the group is playing their balls. When hunting for a lost ball, don't leave your cart on the fairway where it will be in somebody's way coming from behind; instead, leave it in the rough.

Fashion on the Golf Course   Golf apparel is quite varied today, although there are fashion fads that come and go—certain types of hats for men and women, or a special kind of short skirt for women. Above all, one should wear clothing that allows free movement of the upper body, but not clothing that is garish or in bad taste. Many clubs set definite standards of dress for tournaments, and some clubs will not allow women to play in slacks or shorts. Short-shorts and bra tops for women are taboo. A member reflects, after all, the club's image.

The one required item for golfers is, of course, a pair of regulation cleated golf shoes. A golfer also wears a thin leather glove—on the left hand if he is right-handed; on the right, if he is left-handed.

Riding and Fox Hunting

Although big private stables are much less in evidence today than they were on the big estates of the first half of the twentieth century, there are many more one- and two-horse owners.

Riding is a sport for people of all ages. Many young and not so young new riders are coming into the sport with no background whatsoever as to its conventions and rules of safety. A horse is an individual. Some are skittish, some passive, some reliable, some so unpredictable they require a highly experienced rider. Never mount a strange horse without first inquiring about its disposition and experience.

When riding in a group be very careful if you are on a kicking or biting horse. Do not ride too close to the others. If he is a kicker, see that he sports a red ribbon on his tail as a warning. Keep a horse-length behind the person in front of you and avoid crowding other animals on the path. Never be diffident about refusing to mount a horse you feel incapable of handling. If you wish to gallop when the others are walking, trotting, or cantering, explain this to the other riders and ride your horse at their pace far enough in advance of the group so that a sudden gallop will not disturb them.

When coming upon another group, slow down until you are past. Don't pass other riders at a gallop, which could cause their horses to break into a gallop as well. On a narrow path, slow down in passing until you are well ahead of other riders. Slow your horse to a walk when you approach roads.

Accidents can happen if someone dismounts momentarily and others don't rein in until he has remounted. In fast riding on woodland paths watch for low limbs on trees, holes, or logs in the path and warn those behind you.

Always walk your horse back to the barn, hence avoiding any chance of a runaway, as well as helping to cool and relax the horse.

Hacking Hacking is informal riding in the country, the kind of riding many young people have taken to. The dress is very casual—blue jeans, sweater, open-neck flannel shirt, typical country clothes, worn preferably, of course, with boots. Boots are proper protection and are relatively safe. Sneakers, loafers, or bare feet are not. It's a good idea to wear a riding hat or helmet.

There are, however, correct and traditional hacking clothes for men and women, which consist of a single-breasted tweed coat with back vent; breeches in buff, canary, tan or rust; a waistcoat (in cold weather), either checked or plain, single-breasted; shirts tailored in wool or cotton, possibly button-down, worn either open or with a tie (which in turn should be well secured). A turtleneck sweater may also be worn, in hunting yellow or any of the leafy muted colors. For this kind of riding the boots should be brown and as long and as narrow as the leg can accommodate. They may be laced field boots. For safety's sake, particularly when one is riding alone, one is well advised to wear a hunting cap. For hacking, either breeches or jodhpurs are worn. They fit the leg tightly, Indian fashion, and are worn with jodhpur boots under them. These boots are also worn with slacks or trousers for informal wear by both men and women. With jodhpurs, knitted shirts, turtleneck sweaters, and tailored sports shirts are worn, with the formality of a tie usual in city park riding, but not obligatory there. Stocks are not worn for informal riding, but ascots, properly secured, are often worn with collarless shirts. Suitable gloves are required in leather, cotton, or string, lined or unlined, the latter advisable in wet weather particularly. In warm weather just a shirt may be worn, with short or rolled sleeves and open collar. A waistcoat alone is not worn.

The traditions governing riding garb have been greatly relaxed, and today more attention is paid to such things as providing protection during the deer hunting season by wearing something bright red or blaze-orange while riding.

Western Riding In western riding the stock, or working saddle, is used with a horn in front to which the lariat may be attached. To someone used to an English saddle, to ride in a stock saddle often seems like riding in a secure rocking chair. The stirrups are covered (tapadero) to protect the legs in brush country. The reins are held in one hand, leaving the other hand free for work with the rope.

Western boots have a high heel, with a pointed toe. Western gear for riding can be very elegant and is often terribly expensive (especially the hand-tooled, custom-made leather boots). However, jeans (riding pants aren't necessary in this activity), a work shirt in wool, flannel or cotton, a bandana, and a broad-brimmed hat (which may be an expensive felt or straw with a brim to shade the eyes), are all that are needed to complete the costume. Chaps are often worn to guard against chafing, briars, and inclement weather. For warmth in the mountains and protection against the elements, a full-length slicker or jacket is added.

The men who handle the horses are called wranglers, never cowboys. In riding with a wrangler who is the leader, never pass him.

As in all safe riding, keep one horse-length between your horse and the one in front of you. Careful respect for gates is very important. The fences not only mark boundaries, but often restrain valuable herds. When a gate is opened by the wrangler, the following riders ride through slowly until all are through with adequate space between the animals. All then wait until the wrangler has closed the gate and resumed his position at the head of the line. It is not only incorrect riding manners to ride ahead of the wrangler, but unsafe. Even if you are a good rider, the rest may not be able to control their horses as well.

Only when there is room on the trail for horses to come abreast should you allow yours to do so, and then only at a walk. Horses may kick if a rider comes too close to their heels, dangerous to both you and your horse.

Keep your horse up with the others. If you feel unable to keep up with a fast ride, say so in the beginning and ask to be placed with a slower group.

Your hat and your scarf should be well secured. If you must put on a jacket or slicker, don't do so while in the saddle. Dismount for this purpose, preferably telling the rider ahead so that he'll slow down if necessary and not let you get too far behind. Or wait until the whole group stops for this purpose or some other.

Don't try to carry anything in your hands or strapped to you, or around your shoulders. If you take a camera, picnic lunch, blanket, or sweater, have the wrangler secure them to the saddle or place them in saddle bags.

Do not smoke except at cigarette breaks. Break used matches and finished cigarettes. Be sure that they are cold before you throw them down.

Safety in Riding   If you are an inexperienced rider, do not go out on the trail for the first time without instruction. If possible, get to know your horse and his idiosyncrasies. Don't feed him sugar or apples until instructed on how to do it safely. Don't make sudden, quick movements around a horse, and keep away from his hoofs. They are highly dangerous.

Always wear a hard hat when jumping. Many people also feel a hard hat should be worn whenever one is riding.

Never ride your horse or pony into a stall with a low ceiling or under anything low.

Fox Hunting

This is the most formal of all the sports, even for children, who must be neat and efficient in their attire. Any infringement of the rules of fox hunting etiquette is intolerable to those who take this very special sport seriously.

Like other sports etiquette, that of fox hunting is based on a concept of sport combined with safety. But in addition, there are certain traditional customs that are not always explicable but should be followed nonetheless, out of deference to the conventions of the sport as well as to the Master and the staff of the hunt.

Those riding to hounds are referred to as "members of the field." The Master of Foxhounds (M.F.H.) can be compared to the captain of a ship, commanding total respect. His orders must be followed without question. Each member of the field rides up to greet the Master at the meet before it starts. At the end of the hunt, the riders say good night and thank the Master for having provided them with the day's sport. The hunt staff consists of the huntsman (sometimes the Master), who hunts the hounds, assisted by the "whippers-in." The Master, or someone appointed by him known as the field master, directs the staff and is in charge of the field.

The Spectators   Watching the hunt on foot is almost as exciting as riding to hounds, but foot-followers can cause havoc, especially if they follow the hunt by car. Anyone bringing a car should park well out of the way of the staff and field; avoid loud talking, laughing, or honking of horns; and keep the engine turned off. Followers must never in any way interfere with the hunt either at the meet or during the chase. Spectators should assiduously avoid littering or damaging the fields and fences in any way.

Joining the Hunt   If you have had no experience with cross-country riding and jumping, do not accept a hunting invitation. Various hunts have differing rules in the matter of guests. In some, one must be an overnight guest of a member in order to be allowed to hunt, but in most hunts all that is necessary is for the person wishing to be a guest to write to the M.F.H. or the secretary for permission. One does not need sponsors. The "capping" fee or "cap" is a fee paid by the guest or his host on his behalf, to hunt that particular day. The money should be sent or given to the hunt secretary *before* the meet.

Some hunts require that those seeking to be regular members of the hunt live in the area and be landowners. With urban spread and consequent limitation of areas for fox hunting, some hunts have to tightly limit the number in their field. Other hunts restrict a guest to three "caps," and if he is not asked to join the hunt as a regular member at this point, he should not cap again until next year.

Hunt Colors   Every hunt has its distinctive colors. Not all members wear them, however. Those who have been regular members of the hunt and have proved to be knowledgeable fox hunters are invited by the M.F.H. to wear the hunt colors, which are then sewn on the collars of their hunting coats. The honor extends to buttons, which are usually made of dark bone, silver, or brass, depending on the color of the coat. The hunt insignia is usually engraved on these buttons.

Hunting Attire   If you are invited to join a hunt and plan to hunt more or less regularly, traditional hunting attire is called for. If either the rider or the horse turns out improperly, it is a great rudeness to the Master. "Ratcatcher" attire is permissible during one's "cubbing period." This would consist of a tweed jacket, well-fitting jodhpurs, shirt, stock with an appropriate plain gold safety pin (worn horizontally), brown gloves, plus the black hunting derby. (Women should put their long hair neatly in a net.) The stock is said to have been designed to serve in an emergency as a sling or bandage, and is therefore truly functional. The plain safety pin is used when necessary to secure the sling or bandage. If the Master of Foxhounds is a stickler for form, he will not put up with anyone's being dressed too informally. If you are invited for the first time, you should ask your host to be specific about what you should wear.

Formal hunting attire, whether worn by members of the field or by professional hunt staff, is rigidly prescribed. For example, the "pink coat," cut as a frock coat, or cutaway (shadbelly) worn by men is really a vivid scarlet color. It may be worn only by those receiving a special invitation from the M.F.H. Although each hunt has its own colors and livery worn by the Master and staff, only those invited to wear the colors may do so. All others wear dark gray or dark blue coats, according to the tradition of that hunt, with breeches in white, canary, buff, or brick. Only black calf boots are correct. With scarlet, or the gray melton frock coat or shadbelly, black calf boots with tan tops are de rigueur.

A high silk hat is always worn with a scarlet coat, a frock coat, or a cutaway. A guest, if formal, should always wear a top hat and the gray melton frock coat. A black derby, never worn with a pink coat, is worn with every other outfit. The black velvet hunting cap is worn only by the M.F.H., by other masters or ex-masters, by the staff, or by juniors under the age of eighteen. (The Master will grant permission to others to wear the black velvet cap upon special request.) The waistcoat is usually a tattersall or canary wool flannel one, or it may be of any distinctive color that has been adopted by the hunt.

Swimming and Water Sports

Of all the sports, swimming is the best all-around for all ages and is the one most available to us. The sport usually involves many people enjoying it together, so manners are terribly important in helping us get along with each other—whether it's in the locker rooms or cabanas or on the beach or by the pool.

The Swimsuit This is a sport where one's attire (or lack of it) is important, because the body is shown off to its best advantage or disadvantage. Both men and women should take a good long look at themselves in a three-sided full-length mirror in the store before buying their bathing suits. They should also try sitting down in them, as they will be spending a lot of time in that position on the beach. Bikinis are meant for lithe young bodies. A woman with a figure problem should veer toward a one-piece suit, perhaps with a skirt, for there is nothing less appealing than billowing layers of flesh between the two parts of a bikini. For men a conservative pair of swimming trunks that fit well is always right—good figure or bad.

Children's Safety and Manners Children who are not excellent swimmers should always wear some form of life preserver, whether they are playing on the beach, on the edge of the lake, or at poolside. A child is apt to run compulsively into the water or fall in. A baby playing with a toy at water's edge may be knocked down by an unexpected wave and carried out by the undertow long enough to fill his lungs with water.

Children behave quite naturally in a boisterous manner when they are near water. It is clearly the parents' responsibility to teach their children appropriate manners, to remind them over and over of their duty to think of others, and to make them obey the rules. No running or screaming, for one thing. No playing with a ball near sun bathers. When they walk by people lying on the sand, they should do it with great care, so as not to kick up sand into people's faces. No splashing—this may be fun for the splasher, but it is always a bore for the splashee, and it may result in a water accident, too. A child should be taught never to dunk another: his victim, if caught unaware, may find his lungs filling with water, and may become frightened and panicky.

As for the parents, they must be responsible for their children. It is not the duty of their host at the pool or the lifeguard at the beach to keep their children from harm. Young children should be watched *every minute* around water for their physical safety, but also to ensure that they do not bother others.

Ocean Swimming and the Lifeguard One should not swim alone in the ocean without a lifeguard present, for the ocean is very deceptive. On what looks like a calm, sunny day there may be a serious undertow; there may be Portuguese men-of-war in the area; there may even have been a shark scare. If there is a problem the lifeguard posts warning signals or flags, or orders everybody out of the water if the situation is serious. Usually he orders people out of the water in a storm, for lightning is attracted by water. The lifeguard must always be obeyed, and quickly.

You should never wave at someone on shore when you're out swimming, because the lifeguards may think you are calling for help and spring into action. Neither should you hang around the lifeguard stand chatting, because it is distracting and keeps the lifeguards from being able to scan the water with full attention.

Beach Manners If you are floating on a rubber mattress riding the waves, keep a careful watch on the people in your path. Like a surfboard, if a mattress hits a swimmer in its path, injuries may result.

Littering of the beach or lakeside is absolutely lamentable; even leaving behind something as small as the cap of a tube of sun cream or a paper tissue is noticeable. If you've made a fire in the sand, remember to throw water on your coals or embers, not just cover them with sand. Someone with bare feet might come along later and step right on them. If you bring a portable radio to the beach, use an earphone instead of playing it out loud. People around you may be reading, sleeping, or concentrating on something, and not particularly interested in either your favorite rock group or your special ball game.

Check List for a Comfortable Day at the Beach   It is wise to make a list of things you will need for an all-day trek to an inaccessible beach:

1. First-aid kit (if there's broken glass anywhere, your barefooted children will probably find it!).
2. Food and drink, including water (very thirsty children need water, not just soda).
3. Sun protection devices, including a beach umbrella, sunglasses, a preparation for your skin, a nose guard (if you have a sensitive nose), and a sun hat. Each member of the family should have a cover-up, too, preferably long, to protect their skin when they've had too much sun.
4. A pair of sneakers for each person, if the beach area consists of rocks and pebbles instead of soft sand.
5. A bath towel and a beach towel for each person.
6. Collapsible beach chairs to ensure your reading comfort, and to allow you to keep a watchful eye on the young children.
7. An insect repellent (especially for sand flies and late afternoon insect visitors).

Beach or Swimming Clubs   You should never lay down your beach towel on the property of a private beach club when you are walking along the beach. You will run the risk of being asked to leave, which is embarrassing, to say the least.

When you are invited to a private beach club, you should check first with your hosts whether you should bring your own towels, and whether you are allowed to pay for your own food and drinks in cash. You should also know the tipping rules in advance. Beach clubs adjacent to each other sometimes have totally different rules. In one, guests may pay their own entrance fees and may use cash for their meals and snacks. In the other, everything must be signed for by the club member. In one, the tipping of the locker room attendant and the boys who put up the beach umbrellas may be encouraged; in another, it may be forbidden.

Always bring a modest cover-up to the beach club to wear over your suit. Some clubs will not allow people in beach garb in their dining room or even in their outdoor seated buffet area. Usually there is an outdoor snack bar where one may lunch on hamburgers, hot dogs, and ice cream cones. Here, too, there may be a requirement for some kind of top to wear with a bathing suit. By far the wisest thing to do is ask your hosts these questions in advance so that you won't inadvertently commit a faux pas.

Pool Swimming   A pool owner once said in an exasperated, weary tone, "I wish our friends would start thinking of our pool as if it were our home, instead of a public swimming hole!"

Guests innocently take advantage of their friends who have pools, but part of it is their hosts' fault, too, for not properly communicating their rules and regulations.

The wise host has the "rules of the pool" well posted, and the cleverest one I ever knew had two sets of rules made and posted on the front of his pool house. One was in printed text for the adults. The other was for children, consisting of little text but a lot of illustrations of what not to do at the pool. Here is what the rules for adults said:

1. Always call us first to see if it's all right to come. [Even if you have a standing invitation to use that pool, your hosts may be having a private party or be cleaning the pool or may wish to sleep late on a certain morning.]
2. No pets allowed.
3. Watch your own children.
4. No swimming in the area of the diving board.
5. No running in the pool deck area (it's slippery and may result in accidents).
6. If your hair is long, wear a cap.
7. Bring your own towels.
8. No radios, please.
9. Place all your trash in the receptacles by the pool. Use the ash trays provided.
10. Shower before entering the pool. If the shower is not working, use the garden hose.
11. Use the plastic bags we leave in the dressing room to carry away your wet suits.
12. Have a good time as our guests.

Your family, as guests, should never bring along extra children or even adult guests without first receiving permission. And don't ask to do this often, either. Teach your children not to enter the house in wet suits, for upholstery stains very easily from chlorinated water marks.

You should not turn anyone's pool area into a picnic ground. Do your eating at home. Bring your own sun protection items; they are costly, and you should not keep asking to borrow your hosts' preparations.

It's a nice gesture if you or your children ask if they may clean the water surface of any insects, grass, or leaves that might be floating on top. Someone in your family might sweep the terrace around the pool or pick up any trash other people might have carelessly left from the night before. One family I know is always welcome at their neighbors' beautiful pool because they never leave without watering the bushes and flowers around the pool; they even do some weeding, if it is needed. It is part of their "thank you" to their hosts for the use of the pool.

Pool users should always understay rather than overstay their welcome. Two hours is about enough time when you are not invited to a meal or a party at your hosts' pool. And if you are habitual pool users, you should send your hosts a nice gift at the end of the summer—something appropriate for their poolside entertaining—as well as a letter of thanks.

Water Skiing   Water skiing is another popular water sport. Provided you know someone with a boat to tow you, or can rent such a boat, the sport requires a minimum of equipment: skis, tow line with handle (or two handles, as the case may be), and a flotation belt. The latter safety measure is required by law in many states. It is very easy for a skier going close to thirty miles an hour to fall, hit his head on a ski, and be knocked unconscious. Even a strong swimmer, therefore, should not pooh-pooh that belt.

There should be two people in the boat—the driver and a spotter, who watches the water skier at all times and who informs the driver of other activity in the area. The driver should handle the boat according to the skill of the skier he is towing.

This is a sport that is relatively easy to learn; in one's enthusiasm for one's increasing skills, it is important to remember the others in the water. The skier who purposely or carelessly sprays other people in boats is exceedingly rude. Water skiers should stay out of crowded territory where there are swimmers, sail races or any kind of heavy traffic.

The water skier must be careful of cutting others' buoy lines, log lines, fishermen's lines, or others' tow ropes. Skiing close to shore jeopardizes swimmers' safety. One should also respect peoples' private beaches and not take them over to use for one's water skiing pleasure without first obtaining the owners' permission.

Winter Sports

Skiing

Skiing is at an all-time high in popularity. It's not only the exhilarating exercise and the camaraderie of skiing with one's family and friends, it's also the beauty and peace of the snow scene that is so magnetizing. Even the après-ski night life and the daytime social activities of non-skiers who remain at the foot of the mountain have become a way of life for people of all ages and economic strata.

Skiing is a sport that requires good equipment that fits you and is in excellent condition—whether you rent or buy it. It requires expert instruction, too, and the novice had better begin his career safely in a ski school where he will receive lessons from a qualified instructor.

Any skier should be in good physical condition, because it is an arduous sport. Getting in condition for skiing requires a regular program of exercise over a period of several weeks before the skiing season starts. There are certain basics to remember about skiing, but the first one is *never to ski alone.* Always patiently await your turn at the lift, and don't be afraid to ask questions about how to cope with the lift. A swinging T bar could seriously hurt another skier, so when you get off a lift, gently let go of the T bar or Pomalift. Don't swing or bounce on the lift. That's "kid stuff" and it's dangerous.

Always ski under control. The show-off usually goes out of control and accidents result. Experts should remember to ski more slowly and take extra precautions when they are on the lower, more crowded slopes. Likewise, novices should not venture onto expert trails that they cannot handle and where they will interfere with the enjoyment of more skilled skiers.

You should always wear skis when walking or climbing in a ski area; and keep to the side of the trail or slope as you do it. All skiers should follow the Golden Rule and help keep the slope free of hazards. If your body or equipment makes depressions in the snow when you fall, pack the snow and smooth it over. If you come across any debris on the trail, stop and move it off the trail. Holes, bumps, and litter are dangerous to the skiers coming behind you. When you feel tired, *stop* skiing. This is when most of the accidents occur, and that mountain will still be there on other days.

Equipment There is such a variety of skiing equipment available today and it is so expensive that one should seek expert advice before making any purchases. Most new skiers rent equipment at first until they are sure they enjoy the sport. When you are ready, buy your equipment from a reputable store where you will be given guidance on the best type of skiing equipment for your ability, and where all of your equipment, boots, skis, and poles, will be properly fitted.

Apparel Ski clothes should be warm and functional and should fit properly. Bright-colored attire is the safest, for it allows other skiers coming down behind you to see you sooner. Your outer clothes should be made of a fabric that will reduce sliding after a fall. They should be warm without bulk, and, of course, water-repellent. If you dress in layers of wool underneath, you will be toasty warm and can remove layer by layer as the sun becomes hotter. Many younger skiers prefer to wear blue jeans, with warm-up pants over them if it is extremely cold.

Be sure your clothes are tight at the cuffs and the ankles, so the snow doesn't seep through to ruin your insulation. Thermal long johns and warm socks are needed, too.

Mittens retain more heat, but they do not allow the hand the same control of equipment that gloves do. All of your head gear, whether cap, headband, scarf, or mask, should offer wind protection, absorption, and insulation. Don't wear a long, furling scarf, for it's dangerous around a tow or lift. As for your goggles or glasses, they should be shatterproof; they protect your eyes both from the sun's glare on the snow and the winds.

Après-ski Apparel Before you go skiing, it is best to check the customs of the resort you will be visiting and the life-style you will be following. The dress habits of the guests of the Palace Hotel in St. Moritz and those of the guests in a communal A-frame house in Vail are decidedly different. If you are in a quandary, remember that in the mountains it is better to underdress than to overdress at night. This does not mean that everyone has to wear jeans and dirty sweaters, for everyone should be freshly bathed and well groomed and make an effort in the evening. A wardrobe of warm casual separates for women, involving pants and long skirts with different tops and sweaters, is usually appropriate.

The Injured Skier If you come across an injured skier, don't move him. Place his ski poles upright in the snow above his head as a marker. Stay with him to comfort him if another skier is around who will report the accident at once to the Ski Patrol. If you have to leave the injured skier to report to the Ski Patrol yourself, be sure to remember the exact location and any details of the injury that you can. (Having broken a leg myself in Stowe, Vermont, one year, I am an ardent fan of the patrol's rescue work.)

If you want good information on the sport of down-hill skiing, and the good maintenance of your equipment, write to the National Ski Patrol, 2901 Sheridan Boulevard, Denver, Colorado 80214.

Cross-country Skiing In wintertime the Scandinavians have been getting to and fro on cross-country skis for hundreds of years, but Americans just "discovered" the sport with enthusiasm in the late 1960s. Special attention is increasingly being paid to cross-country or ski touring in this country because of its growing popularity. Now there are marked trails, inn-to-inn tours, and patrolled paths all over the country. Ski shops and ski tour organizations have excellent cross-country tours for their client enthusiasts.

This is a much slower sport than downhill skiing, but it is much more strenuous, for one often does it for hours on end, and there are no restful lulls while waiting in line for a ride on the ski lift. Cross-country skiing is good for any age, provided one is in good physical shape. It's not as expensive a sport as downhill skiing; the equipment is not as costly, and there are no high-priced ski lift tickets to be purchased.

Be sure to ski with a group and never set out without knowing the weather and trail conditions ahead. Stay on the trails so you will not become lost; if you plan to cross private property, always ask permission first.

Cross-country skiers are notably more relaxed about their attire than downhill skiers. Most important, you want to be warm and dry. A hat is a must, because without it almost 90 per cent of your body heat will be lost. Wear long johns and layered clothing, which you can shed and put in your pack as you go along. You will be warmer and drier performing this sport in the Rockies than in the East, which has more damp cold.

Most cross-country skis are made of fiberglass today (because the old wooden ski tips broke too easily). These skis are lighter, more flexible, slimmer, and less expensive than downhill skis. Cross-country boots may be almost any kind, as long as they are comfortable, sturdy, and warm. Just as this equipment is less expensive than that for downhill skiing, it is also easier to maintain. It is wise to rent it at first, and then you will have time to experiment enough to know what you wish to buy.

One should never venture too far when learning this sport, even if one is in good physical shape. The trip back, through deep snow, can be very tiring. Like anything else, this is a sport to be practiced in moderation until skill and good physical condition combine to allow you to press harder and farther.

Skating

Skating is a great exercise for everyone, no matter what their age. Strong ankles and a determination to learn are the only major requirements, along with a properly fitted pair of skates.

Manners are of great importance here, for everyone's enjoyment on the ice can be ruined by ill-mannered skaters. All too frequently one sees teenagers skating four and five abreast, and in the process knocking down everyone in their path. The sad thing is that no one ever taught those children "skating manners," so how can we expect them to behave? It is up to the parents to teach their children how to control their natural ebullience on the ice rink. Parents should teach children that the pair of skates they own carries with it a responsibility to be a "good citizen" on ice.

The following are some fundamentals to which every skater should pay attention:

1. Skate in the same direction as other skaters; don't get smart in a crowd and go counter to everyone else.
2. Skate in the part of the rink where others of your level of skating ability are to be found. The fast skaters usually frequent the area several feet away from the outer fence of the rink. The fence area is usually populated by beginners who lurch to the fence for protection from falling and who need the fence to rest upon when the effort becomes too much. Figure skaters use the center of the ice, as do the instructors and their pupils.
3. Watch out for little ones—children who skate between your legs, change direction without thinking, and bump into you simply because they don't know how to stop. (The same goes for quite big beginners, too, including, I remember so well, a six-foot-five football star who learned how to skate while knocking down everyone within a radius of ten feet on his travels around the rink.)

4. Do not skate several abreast, and don't play ice hockey when regular skaters are on the rink.
5. Never trip anyone. At times young people think it's a smart, funny thing to do. It's not. Serious injuries may result. If you do accidentally trip someone, help that person to his feet and apologize profusely.
6. No shouting or raucous laughter is appropriate at the rink. Others are concentrating on their steps or perhaps on listening to the rhythm of the music.
7. Don't take candy and gum onto the ice, because it is too easy to drop the wrappers. Litter on the ice is the biggest safety hazard of all. If you see someone else's litter—or Mother Nature's litter in the form of a leaf or a branch from a tree—always pick it up. It might save someone else from a serious accident, if not you yourself.
8. Reckless skating is absolutely prohibited. Some people think they're trying out for the Montreal Maple Leafs by the way they move relentlessly over the ice, disregarding everyone and everything in their path. Perhaps if they knew that, instead of impressing people, they were causing others to pity them for their pathetic need to show off, they would cease and desist from their aggressive behavior.

Dress Ice-skating garb should be warm and windproof and nothing much else matters. The neophyte who goes out in her ballerina skating costume for the first time, without benefit of warm tights, learns a costly lesson—a terrible cold—from the attempts to look like an Olympic star. When I was young, we all had to appear in those costumes. Today it's blue jeans over woolies, and how much more efficient it is! Warm slacks, wool skirts, wool sweaters, Viyella shirts, windbreakers, and down jackets are all great for the sport.

Remember wool underwear (or thermal); remember, too, to cover your head because of the cold emanating from the ice, and to wear gloves, for to fall without them on that hard, cold ice is an unhappy experience indeed.

Skating on a Pond or a Lake There is one prerequisite in this kind of skating that supersedes anything else: safety. Test the ice carefully on all parts of the pond before you skate there. The ice may be deceptive. Even if it appears solid, *never* skate there alone. Anyone who skates on a pond should have in his possession a very valuable booklet, published by the American Red Cross, entitled *The American National Red Cross Lifesaving Book,* where there's an entire section called "Ice Safety and Rescue." This book states that small bodies of water such as streams that flow slowly and small lakes usually make the best outdoor skating areas. They freeze more rapidly than larger bodies of water and the ice formed is usually longer-lasting and smoother.

Chapter 58

THE IMPORTANCE OF INTRODUCTIONS

Knowing how to introduce other people is an integral part of good manners. There is one very good rule to follow concerning the need to introduce someone you know to someone standing near you: *If in doubt, introduce them.* Ever since my days as an embassy social secretary where much of my job consisted of introducing people, I have been making introductions, often blundering my way through some pretty embarrassing situations, introducing men to their ex-wives, employees to their bosses, or married daughters to their mothers. But for each innocent mistake I made, there were many more groups of people who felt more comfortable in particular situations because they had been introduced and could now talk with ease to each other.

Who Is Introduced to Whom

A young person is always introduced *to* an older person. A person is introduced *to* someone of a higher position or, as in the case of the military, higher rank. The old rule that a man "is always introduced to a woman" is no longer invariable. An eighteen-year-old girl is introduced *to* a forty-year-old man. A young man in his teens or twenties, however, would be introduced *to* a young woman, because they are more or less equal in age and in station in life, so the traditional way would be in force.

In other words, put on your thinking cap if you are in a quandary about who gets introduced to whom. If one person is much older or more important than the other (more important for offices held or achievements in life), you introduce the younger or the less important to the older and the more important—regardless of sex. If your town has a young mayor, say thirty-five years of age, and you have a middle-aged woman in your group, you would introduce that woman *to* the young mayor. His high elective office deserves it. If, however, you have an eighty-year-old woman in your group, you and the young mayor would feel better if you introduce him *to* the eighty-year old. In other words, there are no hard and fast rules, except in the military and in diplomatic protocol. The rest of the world should be introduced one to another on the basis of good sense or of good feeling.

The New Informality of Introductions   When one is a child, one learns to say, "How do you do [or 'hello'], Mrs. Smith." When adults are introduced to each other in normal everyday situations, they do not have to be so formal. When you're introducing a woman to a group you can say, "This is Mary Smith." If she has a title, you of course would say, "This is Dr. Mary Smith." It is the same with a man. Similarly, when you meet people on the street you do not have to say, "Mr. Johnson, I'd like to have you meet Mrs. Jonathan Swift." Instead, you may say, "Bob, I'd like to have you meet Gwen Swift. Gwen, this is Bob Johnson."

Whether one refers to the people one is introducing as Mr., Mrs., Miss, or Ms. no longer has the same importance. It is much more intelligent for people to be introduced in a warm, smiling fashion than for the introducers to worry about formal protocol restrictions.

Of course, if you are introducing the people on the dais during a banquet dinner, you should do it properly, with everyone's title and full name properly announced. If you are at a diplomatic or high-level government dinner, you would be careful about proper titles. (See Chapter 46, "Correct Forms of Address.") There are times when formality and obeying strict rules of protocol are meaningful, because public introductions are made more efficiently as a result. When friends and acquaintances meet other friends and acquaintances, however, the warmth of the action can outweigh the placement of the words.

Standing Up to Be Introduced   Traditionally in this country the woman has remained seated when new people enter the room and are introduced. She would rise only to greet a much older or a very prominent person or a member of the clergy. But today everyone in a small group rises to greet the newcomers, extends a hand, and says hello to each person. There is no reason why a woman should remain seated and aloof when new people are being presented. If the group is very large, only those nearest the newcomers should rise and say hello.

The Importance of the Handshake

Every bit as significant as the smile and warm tone of voice people should use to greet each other is the warm handshake that should accompany them. Your grip should be a firm one, a handshake of substance—but not a bonecrusher or too long-lasting, either. Two or three seconds is long enough to hold someone's hand in greeting. Don't let your handshake be a dismal, lifeless one, for people tend to think that character matches a handshake. If you start to shake hands with someone who has lost an arm, shake his other hand. If he has lost both arms, shake the tip of his artificial hand (be quick and unembarrassed about it).

Whether you are a man or a woman, extend your hand. The old days are gone, thank heavens, of a man's having to wait until a woman extends her hand first before he can put out his own. Whoever gets there first puts out his or her hand.

Remove Your Glove   Always remove your glove when you shake someone's hand: one cannot feel human warmth and life through the fabric of a glove. The exceptions are when you are wearing white gloves at a white-tie ball; when your hands are full of things and you cannot physically remove the glove; when you are out of doors and it is sub-freezing temperature.

Husbands and Wives Introducing Each Other

A married person should let everyone know in social gatherings when he or she is introducing his or her partner. A wife could say to an older hostess, "Mrs. Johnson, I would like to introduce my husband to you—Ralph Weigert. Ralph, this is our hostess." Or a husband could say to his boss, "Mr. Talcott, this is my wife, Erica. Erica, I'd like you to meet our chairman of the board, Mr. Emerson Talcott." (The husband would use formality in his introduction if this is the first time his wife has met the head of the company.)

When a man is at a business function, he should take care to introduce his wife to everyone in the room, because in all likelihood she will know few of those present. When a woman has her husband present at *her* business function, she should likewise carefully introduce him to all her business associates and their spouses.

When a Woman Keeps Her Maiden Name After Marriage

A woman who keeps her maiden name professionally (or even if she retains it for everything) should be very sensitive to her husband's ego when they are in social situations where she is known and he is not. People who do not know them well will tend to assume the woman and her huband bear the same name. It is important for the wife to introduce her husband proudly and distinctly. If Mary Branton, for example, is accompanied by her husband to her firm's annual convention, she should always introduce him as John Kushell, saying his name slowly and carefully so the difference is clear. Then people will not introduce John Kushell around as John *Branton*.

Introducing Strangers at Parties

Hosts should take newly arrived guests around and introduce them to at least six or eight people before abandoning them to greet other arriving guests. If you are the only person in a group who knows the others' names, it is your responsibility to introduce people. A stranger can, however, go around the room and introduce himself or herself. One should try not to interrupt two people in earnest conversation, but come back to that pair later when they're not so engrossed. If you see a likely-looking group engaged in pleasant conversation, stand patiently until the person speaking stops. Then introduce yourself: "Hello, I'm Heidi Greene, and I don't know anyone here except my hostess. Will you forgive me for barging in on you like this?"

People are often shy and insecure about introducing themselves to others. If you are one of these, just tell yourself that it's far worse to stand around talking without any introductions than to have people wonder who you are and why you're there. Summon your courage and admit your insecurity. Everyone has compassion for a stranger who admits he or she knows no one; the others will see to it that that person is properly "introduced around."

Forgetting Names

It's embarrassing to forget names, but it happens to everyone. If you know a person well and suddenly can't recall his name when you have to introduce him, just bluff your way through. The easiest way is to make a very complimentary introduction, perhaps in an amusing way. What usually results is that the person being introduced is so flattered he is unaware you have not uttered his name!

For example, if a man and his boss run into the man's college classmate on the street and he has forgotten the classmate's name, he might introduce him: "Mr. Cantwell, I want to introduce to you one of my college classmates. He's the only one who ever got top honors in our senior class while making the football team, running the newspaper, and winning the popularity poll with the girls at Wellesley." Mr. Cantwell and the young man will in the meantime be smiling and shaking hands. After the threesome part, Mr. Cantwell may very well say to his employee, "What *was* that young man's name?" to which his employee would say, "I knew him well, but momentarily can't remember his name!" Mr. Cantwell should be impressed that his young associate knows how to get graciously through an embarrassing moment.

If, in the middle of introducing him, you have to admit someday to your "best friend" that you can't remember his name, laugh about it but don't make a big thing of it. The more embarrassed you feel about your own little mishaps, the more it upsets everyone else. Some politicians move successfully through an entire campaign without remembering most of the names of those around them. They smile so quickly, grasp people's hands so warmly, and appear to recognize all their "friends" so readily that no one every suspects them of not knowing names.

People Greeting Each Other

When two people meet, whether by prearrangement or accidentally, the first to spot the other should say with a smile, "Hello, how are you?" and extend his hand.

The other should answer, "Fine, thanks, and how are you?" (Variations are: "And how are things with you?" or "How are things going?" or "It's so nice to see you.")

No one should answer an informal greeting of "How are you?" with a listing of complaints and ailments. No one *wants* to hear anyone else's bad news. So even if you feel terrible and the whole world is crashing down around you, answer simply, "Fine, thank you," to a simple greeting. Don't pour out your troubles except to close friends and relatives, and only when the timing is suitable and *if* they really want to hear them.

Acknowledging Compliments

When a compliment comes one's way, always acknowledge it with a "Thank you" in a sincere manner. A compliment should never be greeted with "But . . ." The person who gives the compliment does so to give pleasure, and is rebuffed if the recipient of the compliment downgrades the praise: "What, *this* old thing? I've had this dress for five years!" "She wasn't in top form. Our daughter usually plays *much* better than she did today." The self-deprecating reaction of the recipient makes everyone feel uncomfortable.

Compliments should be made graciously and often, even from one stranger to another. We are all in need of praise in this life, and it is as important to know how to receive a compliment graciously as it is to be able to give one. A person who gives and takes compliments with ease is a secure person.

Receiving Lines

To go through a receiving line may be bothersome for people, particularly if they know hardly anyone standing in it. But it is a lot more tedious for the people who have to stand in the receiving line.

Brevity and a smile on the face are the two things to remember about receiving-line conversations. When you are going through the line, introduce yourself with perhaps an explanation of why you are there. For example: "I'm Jane Shaughnessy, and I'm your granddaughter's college roommate." Or "Hello, Mr. Greene, I'm your son's squash partner at the club. Richard Foster's my name. I sure hope the wedding doesn't mean our squash game will be affected!" Or "Mr. Gordon, I'm really honored to meet you. I'm the eighth-floor receptionist."

As for those standing in the line, they should try to alternate their trite replies to guests going through: "I'm so glad to meet you." "It's nice to have you here." "Thank you, too, for coming." "Yes, it is a happy occasion." "Thank you for saying so."

The Use of "Ma'am" and "Sir"

"Yes, ma'am" and "No, ma'am" were used in the Old South and in the days when Northerners had servants. They are still in use in some parts of the South, by children and young people in particular, as a mark of respect and deference to someone older. The fact that the young people show this respect is very laudable; however, I feel it would be better if they were to say "Yes, please," or "No, thank you." Even nicer for a young person is to use the name of the person being addressed: "Yes, Mrs. Jenkins"; "No thank you, Mr. Brown"; "Yes, please, Miss Smith."

The use of "Yes, sir" and "No, sir" has traditionally been taught in prep schools for addressing male teachers. The phrases have also been regularly used in conservative business circles by polite young men and women in addressing senior male officers of the company. They are still used by many, but we seem to be moving away from this form of address in the business world. One reason for the change is that there are many women moving up in the executive suite and to say to a woman company president "Yes, ma'am" would sound wrong, even though it is the equivalent of saying "Yes, sir" to a male president of the company. It is better to say "Yes, Ms. Smith" or "No, Miss Watkins" instead.

The Use of "Lady" and "Gentleman" Versus "Woman" and "Man"

In the first half of the twentieth century the terms "lady" and "gentleman" were used much more than they are today. They were terms of class distinction. Today even the humblest person can act like a "lady" or a "gentleman," but men and women seldom use the term.

If you don't know whether to refer to a female as a "lady" or as a "woman," try using the male equivalents of the words. For instance, "There's a lady in our district who is running for Congress" versus "There's a woman in our district who is running for Congress." You wouldn't say, "There's a gentleman in our district who is running for Congress," but rather, "There's a man in our district who is running for Congress." The same usage follows if it's a woman.

A businessman, in referring to female employees, should never say, "the ladies in our firm." (Even worse is "The girls" or "The gals.") But he should refer instead to "The women in our firm," just as he would say "The men in our firm."

"Lady" and "gentleman" today are often used to mean a well-mannered person. A parent will say to a child, "Now, behave like a lady" or "Behave like a gentleman," and the child usually knows what that means.

Chapter 59

PUBLIC SPEAKING

Most of us have to speak before a visible or an invisible audience at one time or another in our lives. Some people remain genuinely terrified of the experience; in fact, some of the best-known cinema and stage actors and actresses visibly suffer when they have to make a speech in public or have to be interviewed on television or radio.

Most people, however, become practiced with experience, begin to relax on their feet before an audience, and eventually start to enjoy this very human experience. As with anything in life, the more skilled and effective one becomes, the greater the enjoyment—for both audience and speaker. Many high schools and colleges today offer public-speaking courses on their curricula; it's a good way to begin. In most medium-sized and large cities there are voice coaches who teach us how to project our voices, properly enunciate our words, and learn how to convey emotions through the expert manipulation of one of a person's greatest tools and assets: the voice.

A child sits and watches his parents "perform in public" when they rise to give toasts at important family celebrations. Before long he is reading aloud an essay in class. In high school he may become a member of one of the civic societies and be called upon to stand up in front of the class. In college he may be on his feet, too, whether it's to read in drama class, to make a recommendation before the student council, to speak as a member of the debating team, or to "roast" a popular fraternity brother who has just received a special honor. At his own wedding or at the wedding of his good friends, he may find occasion to toast the bride, the parents, the bridesmaids, or even the groom's great-grandmother. As a member of a business organization or a club, he makes presentations, or gives a report as secretary or treasurer; as program chairman, he introduces the monthly speakers. Many organizational positions require "rising to the feet" upon occasion. As a person matures and takes an active role in his community, there is everything from the PTA to the local fund-raising drives that require him to be articulate; there are the demands of his job, which may require him to address a sales meeting, make a presentation, or give a report and defend it. Even an activity like being a member of the grounds committee for his country club might force him to his feet, pleading for a larger budget next year.

The woman's role in speaking equals the man's; she is required to speak in public as often as he. Becoming an assured, adept speaker takes practice for either sex—preparation, organization, and a firm resolve. When the results are successful, it is worth all the effort, for one projects oneself as someone of value, intelligence, and persuasive power.

Your Voice

The first thing anyone should do who has to speak in public—whether it is a short introduction of the main speaker or a major address—is check out his own voice. You can do this by listening to yourself on the tape recorder. Prerecord your address before your business lunch appearance, your anniversary dinner toast, your introduction of the guest speaker, or your advertising strategy presentation. Make corrections and re-record your voice on tape, enunciating more efficiently and weeding out any imperfections you possibly can without the aid of a speech therapist. Work on your breath if you are too breathy, or if you drop your voice at the end of words so no one can understand them. Work on a tone that is not too loud or too soft, a pitch that is neither too shrill and high, nor too husky and low. If you have a tendency to speak too fast, try consciously spending three days speaking with an exaggerated, irritating slowness. You'd be surprised how this exercise will ameliorate the rate of speed of your normal speech. Re-record your remarks until they sound wonderful to your own ear. You will have practically memorized your remarks in the process, and you will have a new confidence when you stand up to speak.

The Microphone

If you have to speak to more than thirty people, request a microphone. Otherwise, if you speak longer than ten minutes, you can strain your vocal cords. Listen to your own voice volume, so you'll know whether to pull back from the mike or move closer to it. Even though you may have checked out the mike before the audience came into the room, the acoustics may change drastically when the room is full of people. Consequently I find that having a friend signal one from the back of the auditorium or hall is very helpful. Work out a code signal whereby the person in back can tell you with the motion of his arms whether your voice is coming through "okay," or "move in closer," or "back off."

If several people are speaking on a program, the sound engineers set the volume for the average level; often the engineer does not stay to make constant adjustments, so if you have a soft voice, force yourself to speak up. If you're a tall person, the person preceding you inevitably is short, and vice versa. Learn to adjust the height of the mike to the level of your mouth before uttering a word.

Remember, when you turn your head to the right or left, your words will be lost to your audience. Unless you are equipped with a "necklace mike" (a small mike that hangs like a pendant from a necklace wire), you should keep your mouth aimed straight at the mike. You will find certain podia are equipped with one mike on the left, and another on the right, allowing you more mobility of head movement.

Some people like me cannot use necklace mikes (those of us with a long neck and prominently jutting chin). The sound vibrations of our words don't reach the mike nestled in under our chin. When I'm given one of these, I unhook it from around my neck and hold it in my fingers in front of my mouth, turning it as I turn my head. (Television necklace mikes work beautifully, however; they are far more sensitive.)

Stage Lighting

Stage lights should be checked out ahead of time by the speaker at the same time the microphone is checked. A combination of pink and amber lights makes a white skin look well; a combination of pale pink and "special lavender" looks well for a black skin. If you are in doubt, ask the stage electrician to experiment a bit with you as you stand on stage, and ask your friends to sit in the audience and tell you what looks best. I always enjoy watching actors and actresses prescribe the exact lighting they want before their speech. Experience has taught them what to do. I know only one thing about lighting: that it's easier to talk in a theater with the house lights turned up enough to allow one to see faces in the audience. If you're standing in a bright glaring spot and the audience is in a sea of velvety black, there is no humanity to reach out to.

Introducing a Speaker

Perhaps the most important thing to remember in introducing a speaker is to put pep and enthusiasm into your voice. Sound as though it is the greatest privilege in the world to introduce this person, because the way you introduce him is terribly important. How many times have you heard people leave an event muttering, "What was our speaker's name? Who was she anyway?" The introducer has a great responsibility: to present the speaker to his audience with deftness, to set the scene for him, and to put the audience at their ease, so that the speaker will find a sympathetic atmosphere.

No one should ever simply read aloud a dry biographic sheet usually furnished by speakers' bureaus or the public relations office of a company's executive. The introducer must keep in mind, too, that it is the speaker who is to make the speech, not he, the introducer. No speaker likes to sit while the introducer drones on, praising him, quoting endlessly from some newspaper publicity, or reading unimportant detailed trivia. The introducer should couch his remarks within a tight frame.

Whatever you do, open with a smile, a joke, after thanking everyone for coming. Flatter the audience with some general compliment, even if tongue-in-cheek. Give only the *salient* biographic facts on the speaker's life. If the speaker is unknown to the audience and has a difficult name, the introducer should pronounce it carefully two or three times in his remarks. But the important thing to include is something personal in the remarks, perhaps something gleaned when sitting next to the speaker at dinner.

After a fast-moving introduction, turn over the microphone to the speaker, sit down, and reclaim the microphone at the end of the speech to thank the person warmly and congratulate him. End by saying, "Thank you, John Wyatt, for being with us tonight, and thank you, our wonderful audience, for coming. Good night!"

Master of Ceremonies

If you are master of ceremonies for an entire evening's banquet program or a luncheon (if you're a woman, I prefer the term "master" of ceremonies instead of "mistress," because to be a "master" in the art of anything is not a gender word), you should open the program with a note of welcome and introduce yourself unpretentiously—with a touch of humor, if you can.

As master of ceremonies, it is imperative that you establish good communications with all participants before the event occurs. You should call or write each one of them, give them the sequence of events, provide transportation, if necessary, and define their duties; make sure you state the exact hour at which they should appear backstage or in such-and-such a hotel room prior to the march onto the dais or onto the stage. You should guide them on how to dress ("the women will wear long dresses, the men dark business suits"). You should ask the guest speaker if he or she has any special requests. You make arrangements with the guest speaker to check the microphone and acoustical arrangements and podium lighting before the audience comes into that room (and don't forget the glass of water!).

As master of ceremonies, you are the first to step up to the mike and gain the audience's attention. If there is to be an invocation, blessing, or special grace said by a minister, priest, or rabbi, ask the audience to rise, then state the name and the church affiliation of the person giving the blessing. When he or she is finished, step up to the mike again. "Please be seated, and enjoy your meal. You'll hear again from me later."

When it's time for the program to start, you should rap a gavel or make any pounding noise near the mike. If the hall does not quiet down when you rise to begin, signal some people at nearby tables to help you get everyone's attention. Keep repeating into the microphone, "Ladies and gentlemen, your attention, *please*." If you have a musical group for entertainment during the meal, a flourish executed with the drums can easily quiet a large, noisy hall. An efficient headwaiter and his men can assist in quieting the diners, too.

Make your introductory remarks brief, no longer than four or five minutes, then get on with the introductions. Introduce each person *flatteringly, amusingly,* and *quickly*. Keep those three adverbs in mind, and you'll be a good M.C. If the speaker steps up to the mike smiling or laughing at your introduction of him, half the battle is already won for everyone. The mood in the hall is right. If you are someone who makes quips quite naturally, and you think of something funny to say right after the previous speaker and before you introduce the next speaker, make the quip—but no long stories, no "Now that reminds me of . . ." Make a quip only if it directly pertains to what the previous speaker said or if it relates to the next speaker. If you're not a natural comedian, don't try to be funny. Play it straight, but keep your voice cheerful and peppy. A light touch is what counts. Have your notes on each speaker so thoroughly learned your eyes have to dart down to your notes or script only on occasion.

The M.C.'s face should always be relaxed and smiling, not tense with worry, no matter what happens during the events, such as a singer flatting badly, a mike not working, a waiter dropping an entire tray of food, a noisy drunk having to be evicted. As in every occasion in life, a sense of humor helps!

When a speaker finishes, you as M.C. should jump up fast, shake his hand warmly, point him toward his chair or the stage exit, and thank him enthusiastically in front of the microphone. Your actions will whip up the audience applause.

If it's the end of the program, finish it for everyone by saying, "That was an inspiring talk, Jim, and you left us with many wonderful considerations to remember and to think about," or, for an amusing talk, "That was great, Irene, and I hope you don't mind if I use all those good jokes of yours from now on, because yours are better than mine!" Then, "Good night, everyone. Thank you for coming." Walk away from the mike, for this will signal to the audience to rise and leave. If your musical group is still in evidence, they should play a peppy, happy march-out song. Everyone should leave smiling and more or less pleased with the entire program.

One of the responsibilities of a master of ceremonies is to keep the program running on time, and this may entail slipping a note to the speaker on his lectern. Don't be diplomatic with the note. Be blunt. "Please end. We're off schedule." If there are four or more people, each of whom is supposed to make remarks for five minutes, everyone in the audience will register anxiety, if not overt hostility, over the delays. Each one of them will be counting out the five minutes that you, the master of ceremonies, announced each speaker had at his disposition. Keep your group running on schedule. Warn those on the program ahead of time that you are going to be unmercifully strict on this point.

If You Are the Major Speaker

If you are to give the major address, be sure to ask those who invite you exactly how long you should speak. This is as important a detail as the subject on which you're to speak. A good length for a major after-dinner or after-lunch speech is thirty minutes. If your sponsor says, "Please speak for forty-five minutes to an hour," then you know that people are coming from far and wide to hear you, and that for them to "get their money's worth," you must give them that amount of time. Professional lecturers, for example, sometimes have audiences that come from farms and hill towns a hundred miles away. They make their trip into the nearest city on lecture day as an all-day excursion. They pay for their tickets. If you speak for forty-five minutes, you can always stretch it to an hour by having a fifteen-minute question-and-answer period. (With many interesting celebrities, this is often the best part of the entire speech.)

If you are asked to speak for fifteen minutes, make it fifteen minutes only. Practice and time your remarks. One of the WORST crimes a speaker can commit is to go over the allotted time. If you want to make a successful appearance, leave your audience with the feeling of "I wish she had talked longer."

When you begin your talk, always thank the person who just introduced you to the audience. Then proceed to say something complimentary about the city or the audience if you are a stranger in their midst. Then say something funny about yourself and jump into the substance of your talk. The nature of the subject does not forbid humor in your remarks. One of the best and funniest talks I ever heard was on the subject of nuclear energy.

Mannerisms to Avoid   Your hands will be a telltale sign of nervousness, so keep them in check. Don't rattle your notes or twist a brooch you are wearing. I sat through one hour-long talk by a professor who kept fingering his suit jacket lapel the entire time. By the time he ended, he had his audience practically jumping from nervousness and as a result none of us really heard what he had to say. At the same conference I watched fascinated while another speaker carefully shredded to tiny uniform bits each page of notes as she finished with it. I have also seen a speaker carefully defoliate a plant on the lectern, leaf by leaf, as he spoke.

Watch those hands. Place both at the very front of the podium, if you want to appear totally relaxed. If you have to clutch something for support, clutch the two sides of the podium or lectern. Also avoid the following annoying habits:

Fingering one fingernail with finger of another hand . . . clinking your bracelets, or touching the pendant that hangs from your necklace . . . clutching a button on the front of your blouse or suit jacket . . . sliding a ring up and down your finger . . . constantly touching your hair or brushing back a forelock . . . shaking a finger at the audience when making a point (although the entire Kennedy family has affected this mannerism for years with success).

You should be at ease with the mike, because, of course, you will have pretested it before the audience comes into the room.

Each of us needs his own paraphernalia at the podium. Be sure you have everything you need up there before you have to speak. Perhaps it is a watch with which to time yourself (make sure the dial is large enough for you to read). Maybe you need paper tissues for a runny nose, or a glass of water, or a throat lozenge if you're having coughing spasms, and, of course, your notes. Twice in my life I have had to speak extemporaneously without any cues, because I thought the notes waiting up on the lectern were mine. I had put them there, but they weren't mine; they were someone else's, and I have not yet learned how to give someone else's talk!

Delivering Your Speech Each of us arrives at a personal best formula for delivering an address. The most difficult way to give it successfully is to read it word for word from a printed text. However, this technique has been developed successfully by more than one American President (reading from a TelePrompTer), and some people are at home with it. If you must have your text written out in full, practice it over and over and then practice it again, until it is almost memorized. In this way you'll be able to look up often from your text and gain your audience's attention.

Many people write out their key sentences, underline them, or make notes in a wide margin. Some use different-colored pens and pencils to make certain points jump out from the page.

Some talk from a spare outline which gives certain key phrases, but which has none of the sentences written out.

Others talk from cue cards, or from a paper with key words written on it. I am always fascinated to see what comes out of great lecturers' pockets when it comes time for their address—one sees scribbles written on the back of laundry and grocery lists, or torn menus, and I watched one man give an incredibly stimulating talk using notes he had written on the back of a cereal box (the only thing he could find to write on that morning).

You should experiment to find out what system of notes suits you best, and practice and develop your skills—whether you're rehearsing in front of an overly critical family or before the puzzled family dog. Standing up in the bedroom and speaking into a full-length mirror is great practice, for one can see posture faults, the awkwardness of one's hands, and the possible hangdog look on one's face that must be changed before facing the public!

Slides Adding a note of excitement with good colored slides is very effective. The slides must be clear and strong, and pertinent to your talk, not just a "throw-in." There are certain things to remember if slides are on your program:

1. Insist that a professional be retained to set up and be present at your slide presentation. It something goes wrong (and it often does), such as a bulb blowing out, a slide sticking, or the fan breaking, the professional can cope with it. All you have to do is tell a few anecdotes and stall for time while he repairs the damage. A club member working the club machine may not be able to deal quickly with such an emergency.
2. Always open your program with the house lights up, so your audience gets used to you and knows what you look like. Then you can plunge them into darkness and become a voice accompanying the slides.
3. If you travel around with a slide set, be sure to check before each performance the sequence and position of the slides in your tray or drum. They are often rearranged by a projectionist or by an interested member of the committee. Clean your slides every so often with a soft cloth to remove dust specks and fingermarks.
4. Try out your slides with the projectionist before the audience comes into the room. Be sure the slides fit properly on the screen (or screens); your rehearsal may indicate that another type of lens is needed.
5. Be sure you and the projectionist have an understanding about your cues, when the lights are to be doused, when the house lights are to come up, and so on. This requires a mini-rehearsal in advance with the projectionist and perhaps the house electrician. Leave nothing to fate, for fate is rarely kind with audiovisuals.
6. Change your slides quickly during your talk. The impact of one slide on the audience diminishes quickly, particularly a statistical slide or a name slide. Make your last slide either visually smashing or amusing, so that when the house lights come up, the audience will have cause for sincere applause. Always end on an "up" note in your remarks as the house lights come up, so that your audience feels good.

How You Are Dressed   If the evening affair is formal, a woman speaker (or a woman sitting on the dais) wears a long or very dressy short evening dress. This is preferably not an occasion for party pajamas or evening pants. The days of a gala banquet with speeches that calls for white tie and tails for men and full ball-gown regalia for women have disappeared.

In the daytime a woman speaker should make an effort to be smartly dressed for her audience (not in a pants suit or even in too sporty a tailored suit, but rather in a dress or a softly tailored costume). She should try to be in fashion, in order to live up to a female audience's expectations of her. If the speaker is a "hat person," she should by all means wear one, if it is in fashion and if it does not cover her face in any way. If she has one beautiful jewel, she should wear it, but be careful not to wear competing jewelry with it. (Also, a big jeweled flower may look perfect on the lapel of a black moiré suit and out of place on a splashy flowered jersey dress.) The only rule that really applies to what one should wear on the stage or dais is the rule of good taste.

For an evening affair, if a man wears a dinner jacket with its lapel width sadly out of date, probably few will notice. If a woman wears an out-of-date dinner dress, almost everyone notices. Equality in dressing is not yet a fact of life!

A woman speaker should not be made to wear a corsage, for inevitably it either conflicts with the color of her costume or the design of the fabric, or makes her look fussy and top-heavy. Flowers are a wonderful present for a woman speaker—but the flowers should be sent to her home *after* the talk.

Men look best on the speaker's platform in quiet, conservative suits for daytime affairs (no sports jackets, open-necked shirts, or sweaters). In the North, a conservative suit means a dark one, unpatterned except perhaps for a pinstripe; in the South, a conservative suit may well mean a light tan one.

If a company meeting is held in a resort area and after the seminar everyone is going out on the golf links, the speaker may dress like the audience—in golf slacks and sports shirts.

For evening affairs, a man looks better in a black dinner jacket (not colored), with or without a black evening vest. Colored cummerbunds are distracting on the dais, and men usually fidget with them. White unruffled dinner shirts look best, in the opinion of many.

Coughing or Sneezing If you have to cough or sneeze while speaking, turn quickly away from the mike and do it with your handkerchief to your face and your back to the audience. (One should always have a handkerchief or a tissue ready for such emergencies.) Then turn around, apologize, and begin again. It helps if you can joke about it, and put your audience at ease: "Before I was so rudely interrupted by that ragweed . . ."; "I've just come from Sun Valley, Idaho, and that clean air there is finally getting to me." Anything you can say to make your audience relax again helps, because almost all of them will be suffering with you.

Taking Care of the Celebrity Speaker

The proper care and feeding of a celebrity speaker is a delicate matter, in that some of them are temperamental. (Most of them, fortunately, are not.) It is not easy for speakers on the road, often for months at a time, going from town hall to women's club, from campus to businessmen's luncheon. It is an exhausting experience; at each stop the speaker has to "give" with every bit of enthusiasm and charm he can muster, from the time he is met at the airport until he gratefully says good-by and moves on to the next appearance.

A little planning ahead will make everyone's life easier, and your association's task more enjoyable, too, because you will know that you are making life easier for the speaker. Once you have been notified by the lecture bureau or the speaker's agent when and how he or she will arrive, you should write a warm letter of welcome to the celebrity. Your letter might contain the following:

1. Warm words of welcome. "It means so much to have you come to our town. . . ."
2. The names of the people who will be welcoming the speaker at the airport (hopefully, not more than two).
3. If the press will be at the airport, say so, for the speaker will want to be properly groomed for the cameras.
4. Give the complete schedule, with a warning to the speaker to "call me at once if there is any detail that must be changed." Every movement should be detailed, particularly such possibilities as an early morning TV talk show or a radio interview. Give the scheduled time, the network, the interviewer's name, and the type of show it is. This will enable the celebrity to protest ("I NEVER get up at that hour of the morning"), which some will do, and give you time to cancel the shows. It is much better to cancel in advance than to have to call the people the morning of the show and say, "He won't go on."
5. If the speaker is an author, ask if he wishes to have an autographing session of his book right after his speech at the place where the talk is to be given. If the answer is yes, ask him if his publisher will arrange with a local bookstore to supply your organization with books, a table to put them on, and a salesperson to write up the orders, or if you, the sponsoring organization, should arrange all of this yourselves. Always carry a couple of extra copies of the speaker's book, because he may not have one, and it is needed for TV appearances.
6. Give a very short statement explaining your club, group, or organization, particularly in regard to any philanthropic work you do. This will enable the speaker to include in his opening remarks a salute to the organization that brought him here—"I have every admiration for the work of . . ."
7. For women only: ask if a hair appointment is needed.
8. If the speaker will arrive too late for his hotel to offer pressing service, ask if some emergency pressing service will be necessary.
9. Ask if the speaker would enjoy a tour of the city or local museums during any free time. If he says no, that means he wants to stay in his hotel to rest or work, or just be away from people. Sometimes, after he speaks, the lecturer likes to enjoy the city's cultural assets in the free time before the airplane leaves.

It is nice to leave some fresh fruit or even some candy for the speaker to nibble on in his hotel room. If he will have to get up early to make a seven o'clock TV show, a breakfast of sorts should be left in his room, because room service will not be operational at that hour. (One woman left a coffee percolator in my room the night before, filled with coffee and water, all ready to be turned on, and a basket of homemade bread, butter, and jam, as well as fruit. It was a breakfast banquet at 6 A.M., appreciated beyond belief, before leaving for that TV studio!)

But the greatest gift the sponsoring group can give to the speaker is to make sure he doesn't have to speak to too many people before his hour-long address. Having to shout in order to be heard in a reception room packed with people and smoke fumes is exhausting and damaging to the speaker's vocal cords. He should be spared this as much as possible. It will be difficult enough for him to make charming conversation on the dais, keeping the person on his right as happy as the person on his left. The time for private questioning, hand-shaking, and autograph-giving is after his speech. (Many women's clubs handle this situation beautifully by scheduling the speaker before lunch or by scheduling him in the afternoon before a tea-reception.)

What Not to Do for a Celebrity Speaker

1. Take him from the airport to your home, so he can "meet the family" when he's inevitably tired from his trip, anxious to unpack and have a moment's rest in his hotel room.
2. Keep him out late the night before his talk, subjecting him to a long cocktail hour, and then an even longer dinner hour. It will sap his good humor and vitality and affect his mood for the next day.
3. Ply him with hackneyed, gossipy, personal questions, the kind he gets everywhere, but the kind that irritate him beyond belief. I heard a famous actor supply the perfect "put-down" to a woman who relentlessly asked these pushy questions. "Mrs. Blank," he said coldly, "may I ask if you are in charge of my lecture arrangements or if you are being paid a great deal of money by a movie magazine to write an exposé article? Frankly, I'm amazed at your rudeness." (*He* was rude with her, too, but she learned a very valuable lesson in life.)
4. At the end of the speech, don't give the speaker a framed plaque, a figurine of your club logo, or anything that is hard to pack, heavy, and destined for the garbage on his return home. The best thing you can send him is a letter from the organization sponsoring him, telling him how great he was (with a carbon copy to his lecture bureau). Be sure to send him a copy of any newspaper publicity concerning his appearance.

Handling Press Relations

For Your Club or Volunteer Activities One of the most important public relations tools for any organization is the well-written press release. A press release should be sent to one's local newspapers, radio and TV stations, and magazines *only* when there is real news to communicate. A good press release is neatly typed, double spaced, fully informative, with accurate information and names properly spelled. A well-written press release is often

responsible for an important piece of publicity in the newspapers on your
activity or your charity.

If you are associated as a volunteer with a large group, like a major hospital or your local affiliate of the American Cancer Society, there is usually
a professional on staff who handles public relations and publicity. But if
you are part of a small local effort, helping your house of worship, your
garden club, your children's in-school or after-school activities, or a neighborhood project, you may need to learn how to work with the press.

First, as I said, one does not bother the local media unless there is major
news to report. If you have an upcoming event you think would be of interest to their readers and something they would want to cover, with good picture possibilities, include this information in your release. Send your release
a week before the event. Be sure it contains in the first paragraph the who,
what, where, when, and why. No editor wants to have to read through pages
of text trying to find the time or the date of the event. After you have stated
what it is that is newsworthy, and where and when it is, give a synopsis of
your organization.

Get everything on one page, if you can, and be sure to include a "contact"
at the top right of the page—the name, address, and telephone number of
the person the press should call if they have further questions. That person
should also be available during the event to handle any reporters or photographers who appear. The press contact is usually chosen by the officers of
the organization and is assigned the task either for the one important event
or for news all during the year.

A release should be sent to the city editor or to the women's news
(family/style) editor. The city desk can always tell you where to direct
your release if you call and state its nature.

Don't forget free radio "public service spots"; some local TV stations will
also run them. Take your release to the manager of your local stations and
ask if he or she would place the information on the air prior to the event
free of charge. You should write a short fact sheet and put it on top of your
release; the announcer may even use your exact text on the air. For example:

> The Mohegan Girls' Club, celebrating its twenty-fifth anniversary this
> year, will hold a major bake sale in the Fulton High School parking lot
> next Saturday, the twenty-ninth, from 10 A.M. to 3 P.M. Every kind of
> homemade delicacy will be sold, from brownies to pecan pie and upside-
> down cake. All proceeds go to the Mohegan Girls' Club scholarship fund."

When Your Family Makes News   Most families live out their lives having
little to do with the press, other than placing wedding announcements, birth
announcements, and obituaries. It is possible, however, that you or a
member of your family may at some time become involved in a news story,
good or bad. In that case, it is quite likely that reporters from the local
media will call and ask for details. Whether the news is something pleasant

(your daughter is going to marry a very famous person) or very unpleasant (your child has been arrested for manslaughter and drunken driving), you should handle reporters politely, giving as much information as is necessary, but no more. If your news event concerns anything legal, speak with your lawyer before talking to the press, so he can guide you in your answers. Give as many accurate answers as you can to a reporter's questions. Otherwise he will have to get his information from other sources, and he may print inaccuracies that result in a story far less favorable than if you had helped him originally.

If a news story breaks in your family, choose a mature person to stand by and handle all telephone queries in your home; direct everything to that person, so he or she can keep a careful record of all incoming calls, "needs to call back," and names and telephone numbers of reporters. If you don't want to answer a reporter's questions inside your home (and many people don't), talk to him outside. The same holds true for talking to a reporter from a TV station who arrives with his camera crew.

If you do not wish any member of the family to be interviewed, type a statement (and give a copy to each reporter) in which you say whatever you want to say, and then end with "There will be no further comment." At least the reporter will be able to write something for his story. He can repeat the statement.

The press has to do its job. If one is polite and co-operative, if one gives them as much accurate information as one is able to, then a good story will be made better and a bad story less harsh.

Chapter 60

CONVERSATION:
THE GREAT SOCIAL TOOL

One of the greatest attributes of social acceptance, even of popularity itself, is the ability to converse. There are two kinds of conversation: polite and real. A thoughtful person knows how to do both.

Polite conversation is reserved for people who start to talk to you—in airports, on buses, in doctors' waiting rooms, in the checkout line at the supermarket. It is polite to answer whenever someone speaks to you, and not just with a simple "yes" or "no." Some people talk to others for reassurance; others because they are lonely. You will find it is not difficult to engage in polite conversation with people if your motivation is to be kind to others. "Polite conversation" is not a long-drawn-out one. A few sentences are all that is necessary in order not to be rude.

A successful *real* conversation requires perceptiveness, mental agility, and education and cultivation or self-education. A good conversationalist is a self-confident person. He or she is always a desirable element at any social gathering. Some of the most sought-after dinner guests are not particularly attractive physically, but they have conversational prowess.

A group, even a large one, needs only two good conversationalists, exchanging ideas, attitudes, and information, in order to make the evening a memorable one. An intelligent host and hostess see to it that there are two good conversation-carrying guests at their dinner party, if they themselves are not easy leaders in this art.

A good conversationalist stimulates, inspires, and teaches us. He may also tease and flatter us. Underneath his wonderful "gift of the gab" inevitably lie two ingredients: an honest desire to please *and* a sense of humor.

The Way You Talk

No matter how intelligent you are, if you pepper your speech with grammatical errors, swear words, or too much slang, you will make a bad impression. People will not perceive the depth of your conversation or its intelligence; they will hear only its harshness and vulgarity.

Bad language can be weeded out of your speech through a conscious effort, but errors in grammar require more work—perhaps private lessons with an English teacher, or enrollment in an English class (through adult extension services or classes in high school or college). Going to night school, and doing the assigned homework faithfully while holding down a demanding job or running a busy household, is a tough task. However, it has always been possible for those who want it badly enough to reach their goal. People had successfully changed their speaking habits through the years long before George Bernard Shaw wrote *Pygmalion.*

Watch "cutesy" and cliché expressions, for they are out of date almost before they are in fashion. If you use slang in your speech, it must be fresh—and minimal—and in the natural flow. It is better to avoid slang completely unless one is sure the terms are completely current, and not just in one's home town.

A good vocabulary is one of the most impressive assets a person can have. A plain sentence is just like a plain dress; it is more attractive when properly accessorized. Add a rich-sounding word here, an amusing, delightful, and appropriate word there, and the sentence becomes more elegant and "finished" than it would be otherwise.

Foreign words, unless you pronounce them perfectly, should not be used. And if no one else will understand them, don't use them, for people will consider them affectations. When I lived in Italy, I constantly used the Italian expression *piano, piano,* which means "slower, go more slowly." When I came back to America the Italian expression stayed with me—until my senior executive chided me. "There's something you ought to know," he said; "people think you're slightly nuts when you go around saying 'Piano, piano.'" I have stopped using the Italian phrase—almost.

I remember having lunch on a business trip one day in a small midwestern town. A man arose and departed saying, *"Ciao, everyone." (Ciao* is the Italian expression for good-by.) Another guest remarked to me critically, "There he goes again, dropping Chinese words when he doesn't even know what they mean!"

The Basis of Good Conversation

In order to be a good conversationalist, one must be up-to-date and current on life in general—whether it's a question of the latest coup in the Middle East, the election of a home-town girl as the new Miss America, or the latest news in the puts and calls of the options market. You never know whom you'll be sitting next to.

You don't have to be a member of the rich, much-traveled "jet set" to keep current, but you do have to read and listen a lot. If a certain newspaper in another city is full of special political and social stories that people constantly refer to, take a subscription to it, or read it in the public library. If you hear everyone talking about a controversial magazine on current life-styles, buy it on the newsstand, or read it in the library. Read a financial publication regularly. Even if you don't like sports, it's a good idea to listen to the TV news segments on sports and at least have a rudimentary knowledge about events such as the Olympics, the World Series, the international soccer champions, the American winners at Wimbledon, and who is playing this year in the Rose Bowl. (To one wag, "Speaking knowledgeably about something on which one knows nothing and cares less means simply nodding in agreement and looking intense at the right moments.")

There is no excuse for not keeping current on the mainstreams of our lives —including local and national events, such as tax reform, legislation on welfare, political elections, and cultural events of great distinction. The daily newspaper should be read, for TV news does not give us all we need in order to speak intelligently and be truly informed. The mind is kept limber by mental exercises—like a ballet dancer's working out at the bar every day. But unlike the body, the mind can continue to be stretched and stretched as we grow older.

It also helps to become an expert in one field so that someone, in conversing with you, will receive some nice feedback in answer to the perfunctory question "Well, what are you up to these days?" Whether you are a stamp collector, a photographer, or a specialist on mushrooms, come out with it. Be able to describe your field intelligently, without embarrassment, but with a light touch. If you play the harp, have some interesting comments to make about its history, and be able to name some of the great harpists in the world. But if you have been talking with enthusiasm about your favorite subject and you note a dull glaze in the other person's eyes, change the subject. He is not receiving your message.

And whatever your interest is, learn to talk about the other person's. Don't make your own interests so refined and specialized you can talk about nothing else. Soon your language will become so technical, no one will understand you—or worse, even want to understand you.

A good listener is a necessary ingredient to any conversation, so never feel shy about being a person of few words. You can be an interesting quiet person. If what you say counts when you finally get it out, you will find people listening intently to you. So feel good about yourself—whether you are a talker or a listener. Just be sure to keep carefully sharpened whichever tool you use.

Appropriateness of Subject

Notice something about your dinner partner's attire—the color of a woman's dress or her earrings and bracelet, the pattern of a man's necktie or his cuff links. There's always something one can find that will stimulate a compliment. Look at the person before you make it; then come out with it, even if there has been an embarrassing silence between you. If you are on the receiving end of the compliment, say, "Why, thank you. Aren't you nice!" Never kill a compliment by saying "What? *This* old dress?" Always accept a compliment gracefully.

If you know for a fact that the other person has children, ask him about them. Whether your dinner partner is temporarily miffed at his children or enormously proud of them, the conversational box has been opened. It will be endlessly full of material and comments. You are not being too personal if you ask a stranger if his children are in school, how old they are, or where they are working. People with children inevitably find a large field of common experiences to exchange.

If you strongly disagree with the majority opinion on a subject at hand, like politics or abortion, you should speak up. Show you are not of the same opinion, but without an emotional discussion. "Look, I don't agree with what you just said, but a pleasant party like this is really no place to carry on this discussion. Why don't we change the subject for now?" Having suggested a change of subject, it's really up to you to do just that: change it to another topic, and quickly. Your adversary will be compelled to lay down his verbal sword and follow along.

There are unwritten rules of inappropriate topics of conversation, all based on common sense. Don't, for example, ask someone to confirm an unfortunate rumor—"Is it true, Mike, that Mary has left you?" Don't interject a sad subject at a party, like someone's family tragedy that has just occurred. However, if this is the first time you have seen that person since he suffered a great personal loss, you cannot just ignore it. Reach out early in the evening, pat his hand, and say, "I'm terribly sorry about what happened. We *all* are." Enough said. The other person will appreciate your acknowledgment of the sadness, and then he will be at liberty either to pursue the subject a little further with you, or drop it completely.

Don't get things off your chest that have been bothering you all day. There is nothing that turns off someone more quickly than to be confronted in a social situation by someone saying, "You just wouldn't *believe* what happened to me today. Just let me tell you!" Never overdramatize small incidents in your life—unless there is a lull in the conversation and unless you are a good comedian.

Don't criticize or initiate juicy gossip about someone in your circle of friends or acquaintances. If you know something scurrilous or just mildly scandalous, save it for a private talk with your spouse (or if you have no one at home, a talk with yourself).

Don't bring up an obtuse subject, such as the wheat crops in Afghanistan or the change of climate in the lowlands of Australia. Your dinner partner might feign interest in the subject, but he is probably more interested in the parsley on his plate than in the subject you just launched.

Don't discuss your health. In answer to the perfunctory question "How are you these days?" answer, "Fine, thank you," because that's the only answer the other person wants.

Don't tell dirty jokes. A person who gets attention by telling off-color stories is also telling the world he or she is a very insecure person, trying to gain attention. However, there is a difference between a "slightly naughty" story (which is all right in most groups) and a dirty story. And everyone knows the difference.

Don't tell a tasteless ethnic joke in any group, because there may very possibly be someone of that nationality present.

Don't begin by saying, "You're not going to like this, but . . ." Immediately the other person unleashes a security mechanism; an unpleasant alarm sounds.

When people pass the age of thirty-five, don't ask them their ages or their college year (which is the same as asking their ages). Always imply they are young; you can never use too often the phrase "Of course, you'd be too young to remember this, but . . ."

Never bring up a subject on which a bigoted person will rant and rave in his usual style. Some people do this to make fun of bigoted people. It is no fun for the people around the lecturer who have to listen to him.

Don't show someone up with your superior knowledge on a subject. If you come forth with facts, figures, and superior knowledge, you are putting down the other person, an unnecessary and a cruel act most of the time.

In other words, one should be sensitive to who is in the group, and help interweave the topics of conversation into subjects that are of general interest to the group, ones that won't depress or upset anyone, and ones that stay far afield from people's troubles and anxieties. The old wives' tale that one should never discuss politics and religion is not true; but in anything discussed, conversation should progress without rancor or overemotionalism.

Talking to a Celebrity

Celebrities like recognition; they also like privacy and hate trite questions. They spend their lives seeking the first two and escaping the third. If you wish to flatter a famous person whom you happen to be sitting next to at a party, say something nice about his latest movie, play, or TV appearance (or corporation). Don't give him a critic's appraisal of his work or of his product.

If you can say anything knowledgeable about the play he has appeared in or something about his firm, or his government department, come out with it. He will enjoy an intelligent comment about his work, and it will help him open up new lines of conversation with you.

Talk to him about outside interests, including his charitable activities. If he is an actor, suggest a great book, the hero of which he could play well. Never tell him he looks much younger and thinner in real life than he does on screen or on stage. (You will make him think he looks old and fat to the people who see him on camera and on the stage.)

Never criticize any of his colleagues or fellow performers. Even if he agrees with you, he will have to come out in their ardent defense, and no one likes to be on the defense.

Never pry into his personal life, even if rumors have been printed in the papers. Never question his marital status, or ask personal questions on subjects like how much income he earns. Wait until he brings up the subject of his family.

If he is a performing artist, don't ask him some intricate question on international foreign affairs (he will feel inadequate and unprepared to answer in most cases). Likewise, one does not ask a Cabinet officer what he thinks of the latest underground movie one may have seen.

The worse thing you can do to a celebrity is ask his help in getting a friend or relative of yours a job in his movie, play, or corporation. And one of the nicest things you can do to a celebrity dinner partner is say, "Would you mind signing your place card for my son, John Deems? He is a great fan of yours, and it would mean a lot to him and me."

Chapter 61

HOSPITALS AND DOCTORS

Visiting the Patient

A visit from a friend or relative is worth far more than an expensive present to the person who is confined in a hospital. Often those who get to the hospital to visit most frequently are the busiest people with the most responsibilities; somehow they manage to fit compassion into their well-organized schedules, too.

Visiting rules in a hospital are usually strict, although private patients may have callers at more flexible hours than the semiprivate or ward patients. Be sure to call the hospital to find out before you come. Unless you are a close friend or relative who is needed to help in the nursing of the patient, visit only a short time. If the patient has been very ill, don't stay more than five minutes; if the patient is recovering and doesn't tire too quickly, a visit of twenty minutes should be the maximum. If the patient is well enough to be leaving the hospital shortly, a longer visit may not tax him.

Gifts One should use common sense in bringing a gift of food. If your friend is in the hospital with a broken leg, you can bring him a freshly made batch of brownies without fear, but if he is recovering from an internal ailment, he is probably on a special diet and you should not bring any delicacies. When you ask a friend what she would most like as a present and she replies, "A good cold martini," don't smuggle one in to her. It could conflict with her medication and you would be innocently compounding her troubles.

A small plant that requires no care and that can be taken home from the hospital (or flowers sent home the day the patient gets out of the hospital) are far better than sending a huge bouquet that will only die quickly. (See page 789 for additional suggestions.)

Visitors' Manners One or two visitors at a time is easiest for a sick person or someone in pain to absorb. In many hospitals there is policy limiting the number of visitors at any one time, so don't come to see a friend with a

party of people. Aside from its violating hospital rules, the patient will become exhausted trying to carry on several conversations. Keep your voices
low, so that you do not disturb others nearby. Under no circumstances
smoke. Even if the person you are visiting is smoking, or the patient in the
next bed is smoking, there is not enough air in the small room to handle
your cigarette smoke, too.

Use your discretion in asking for information on the patient's health.
Most nurses will give you a general assessment of patient progress.
Remember that patients have rights to privacy and hospital staffs are expected to protect those right. Only a very close friend or relative should
take it upon himself to question the doctor about a patient's condition.

Don't belittle or make jokes of the patient's problem. He will probably
laugh with you, but he deserves sympathy, not ridicule. If you send a studio
card to your friend in the hospital, be sure to send an appropriate one.

The Terminally Ill Terminally ill patients often feel abandoned. So if you
have to choose between visiting someone who has just had an appendectomy
or someone who is very ill with cancer, choose the latter. Many people are
so uncomfortable with ill people, they cease to communicate with them. This
is an unforgivable rejection.

If you visit someone facing death, let him talk about how he feels if he
wants to. Let him voice his fears of the unknown and his frustrations about
"what has been left undone." But take your cue from the patient. Listen to
what *he* says. Let him guide the conversation. Don't smother him with sympathy when he is anxious for cheerful news of the outside world he used to
inhabit. He may be longing to hear an "upbeat" conversation again. Ask him
how he feels, of course, when you enter the room, and in a manner that
shows you recognize his suffering.

"Hello, Amy. How goes it today—any better? You've been having a tough
time, old friend." Don't be afraid to kiss her check. Squeeze her hand or pat
her arm gently; establish body contact in some way. Don't remain coldly removed from the body in the bed, as though she were an untouchable. Pull
your chair close to the bed, and when you talk, look her in the eyes. If she
starts to tell you how tough it is, listen carefully. She may need at that very
moment to "get it all out," and you may be the one person to whom she can
talk. If you start to cry when she tells you of her fears of death, don't worry
about that, either. No one is going to fault you for your own emotions.

But if she keeps asking you about what *you* are doing, what your family,
her old friends, and her associates are up to, don't discuss health and hospitals. Tell her the news, the gossipy, funny stories, exciting events. Keep your
conversation cheerful, or at least fascinating, but above all, don't sit there
and expect the patient to entertain you. And when you see that she is beginning to tire, wind down quickly and leave. One can absorb only so much
stimulation when one is very ill. Take her hand again, and tell her "you'll be
back." And go back.

Tips for the Patient

When you pack your bag for the hospital, include a couple of nightgowns or pajamas, clean bathrobe or dressing gown, and bedroom slippers. You'll want to be properly covered up when walking through the hospital halls. And as for the hospital gowns, which are unsightly and scratchy, patients seem to recover faster when they get out of the hospital gowns and into their own things.

A woman should bring her prettiest bedjacket, too, in which to receive visitors when she feels better. (If, as a visitor, you notice she does not have one, this is a perfect gift to send her.) Someone who is hospital-bound should bring a large supply of stationery, note paper, pens, stamps, a clock, a radio, and any good reading material at home. Anyone who does needlepoint or any kind of handwork can probably get a lot done in the hospital, too. But remember, your locker or closet is inevitably Lilliputian-sized, so don't overpack. One should, however, bring one's own good soap, talcum powder, hand lotion, and face creams or emollients of any kind. The hospital air is very drying to the skin, and anything that lubricates the skin and smells fresh feels extra good.

Don't pack any of your own medicines, even aspirin. There are strict rules in every hospital against a patient's having any of his own medicine. All drugs ingested in a hospital are prescribed by the physician and carefully controlled in the dispensing by the hospital staff, so don't try to sneak around them. I knew one woman who smuggled in her diet pills, took them, and had to stay in the hospital an additional three months as a result of complications from conflicting medication.

How a Woman Registers

For years, women have been known in hospitals by their first name and last name, and not by the husband's name. For example, a woman may register as Mrs. Roger Tuckman, but she will be listed officially by the hospital as Betty Tuckman. To avoid confusion, you must ask for her by "Betty" and not "Mrs. Roger" when you call, and mail or flowers should also be addressed in this manner.

Services in the Hospital

You should have a minimum of cash with you when you come to the hospital and leave all jewelry at home. Usually a newspaper/magazine cart from the gift shop passes by daily, and you can also send a friend down to purchase certain items for you in the gift shop. When you are better, you can go yourself. You can rent a television set by the day or by the week.

You may also have your own telephone line installed if you are going to be there for a while. These expenses are usually charged to your hospital bill. If you have a telephone or television, keep your calls to a minimum and never play your TV or radio so loudly or so late at night that the noise will disturb your roommate.

Your Hospital Roommates

Because of the astronomical cost of hospital care, many people who would like private rooms find themselves in a semiprivate room with a roommate—or even in a ward, with several. This can be a very good experience or a very bad one. If you have a roommate who insists on playing the television set all day with loud volume, who has a constant stream of visitors and telephone calls, and who smokes (with or without permission), your life can be miserable, and you should tell the head nurse or your doctor. You cannot get well as quickly under such conditions. On the other hand, having kind, considerate, and interesting roommates can forge lifelong friendships.

Your Nurse

Since a private nurse is a rarity these days, most patients are cared for by nurses on the regular staff. These nurses must necessarily be professionally businesslike toward each patient, because they have so many to help and so many duties to fulfill. Sometimes the nurses do not have much time for talking, although they like to when they can, for getting to know a patient helps them in planning appropriate care. Despite the pressures of their day, most remain consistently kind to people who ask questions. They are truly unsung heroines. Patients often make the mistake of asking a nurse too many detailed questions about their own condition. Ask your doctor such questions, not your nurse.

It is a nice gesture when you leave the hospital to put a large box of candy at the nurses' station for the enjoyment of all those who helped you. If you write one nice note to the administrator of the hospital expressing your gratitude to the doctors, nurses, aides, and housekeepers, chances are it will be distributed and read with equal gratitude by everyone. Never try to tip a nurse or a resident or intern, by the way, for it is the height of bad taste to do so.

If you have had a private nurse (and most people live their lives through without knowing that luxury), it is appropriate when she leaves you to give her a personal gift, like perfume, a book on a subject that interests her, or anything you happen to know she likes—whether it's recordings or seeds to plant in her garden. If you've had a baby, it is a nice gesture to leave something for the head nurse of the hospital nursery, if your baby stayed there.

Remember above all that your nurse is an educated, professional person worthy of your respect and consideration.

Your Doctor

Every doctor has office hours, and these should be respected. Don't drop in on him before or after these hours just because you are passing his office and think it might be a good time for him to look at Danny's tonsils. If an emergency arises, telephone his office, not his home. It is not fair to interrupt his family life if by telephoning his office, day or night, you can reach him through the service most doctors maintain. When you do go to your doctor's office, remember that he has little free time for unnecessary conversation, even if he is a personal friend. His time is precious; your relationship with him when he is "at work" should be dignified and serious. Don't try to solicit information about his other patients, whether they be friends of yours or celebrities. He would be unethical to answer you. Always go to your appointment dressed cleanly and neatly, inside and out.

If he makes a house call, don't expect him to give a once-over to all the members of the family without billing you for his additional attention. Offer him, if you wish, a soft drink, coffee, or tea. Think twice before you ask him to make a house call at night or in very bad weather. Often telephone advice will tide you through and save the doctor's energy. Many mothers of young babies pay a doctor a flat fee for one year's care of the child, and this service includes telephone consultation as often as necessary. But calls should, even then, be made during office hours, if possible. A list of questions, prepared beforehand, saves the doctor's time as well as your own.

Please remember not to seek professional advice when you see a doctor socially. Some doctors are inundated by subtle searches for free diagnostic information from friends and strangers alike at parties. I know doctors who won't go to large parties as a result of this annoying behavior.

Be chary of suggesting any social invitations to your doctor, unless he indicates a desire for them. A doctor should never be put in the position of either having to see his patients socially or losing them. Again, objectivity between patient and doctor makes for the best professional relations.

The Psychiatric Patient

Psychiatry, psychoanalysis, and their language have all become a familiar part of our society today. It is, however, therapeutically unwise and socially tasteless to proclaim this confidential material. It is usually the beginning patient, fascinated by the experience, who feels impelled to tell everyone about it. On the other hand, today no one undergoing such treatment should be embarrassed to mention the fact if there is reason to do so. The diabetic does not arrive at a cocktail party announcing his illness, but he may mention it if some unthinking guest forces alcohol upon him when it is forbidden. The analogy is not farfetched. Mental illness, whatever its degree, is a disability that may be cured, helped, or at least made tolerable through therapy. Stigmatization, which formerly concerned individuals suffering from psychiatric illness, has subsided markedly as the probability of successful treatment has become better known.

To be avoided in regard to the psychiatric patient: Never ask a patient what he has discussed with his doctor or how much his sessions cost. Avoid asking how long treatment will last—even his doctor probably can't give a definite answer to that. Imply neither that his trouble is minor nor that psychiatry is in his case a waste of time. Resist being a parlor analyst. It is easy to take your friends apart, but difficult to repair the damage you may do.

It should go without saying that you should never ask the doctor about one of his patients when you meet him socially.

You don't make a special point of your medical or dental appointments, nor should you with psychiatric or psychoanalytic ones. If you have a regular session at the same time each day or each week, explain this if necessary to your family and associates in a casual fashion, as is your right.

Part Eight

GIFT GIVING:
AN ACT OF HUMAN KINDNESS

The Philosophy of Giving   759

Gift Ideas for All Occasions   766

GIFTS

The giving of gifts is a ceremony as ancient as any in existence today. Gift giving began as a ritual to appease the gods. Today we may give a gift to help appease someone we have angered or disappointed, but there is a much broader philosophy to the "art" of gift giving today.

One gives a present to say, "I'm sorry" . . . "Congratulations" . . . "Thank you" . . . "Let me console you" . . . "Don't worry" . . . "Have a good time" . . . "I love you" . . . "Feel better" . . . "Let's celebrate" . . . "You're a real friend."

The best gifts are those that come from the heart or those that are given for no reason other than friendship. One cannot purchase affection with presents, but one can demonstrate thoughtfulness, imagination, and caring about someone in an important way. Whether the present is costly or inexpensive is immaterial. Giving comes from the heart, and the well-mannered, popular, successful person knows how to use his heart when sending someone a present. Imagination helps, too!

Chapter 62

THE PHILOSOPHY OF GIVING

Gift giving is one of the nicest and warmest of customs, followed throughout the world. The manner in which a gift is presented, unselfconsciously, in fact with enthusiasm, is really as important as the gift. The personal touch must be there too.

A store-ordered item, sent with the donor's name but without any attempt at personalization, lacks humanity. I remember one Christmas receiving an enormous box of candy from one of my firm's suppliers. It arrived with a printed card from the company without even a name of one of the people with whom we did business. The very same evening there was delivered to our door a small box of homemade fudge from a friend who was in difficult economic circumstances. Her candy was wrapped in a newspaper, tied with bright red ribbons. The newspaper happened to have been printed the day of our wedding, December 27, 1963, so we sat down and read every word of her Christmas wrapping. The message wishing us Merry Christmas and a Happy Anniversary was handwritten in rhyme. The difference in our feelings toward these two gifts of candy was, of course, very marked.

The handwritten word cannot be given too much importance. Some people buy an expensive greeting card and simply sign "Jane" at the bottom, to accompany the package. How much nicer to send a short, handwritten note of greeting that says, "I hope this will be the most wonderful birthday ever! Love, Jane."

Shopping by mail-order catalogue is very easy and efficient, but the thoughtful donor plans far enough ahead to write a card or a note that is then mailed to the catalogue headquarters along with one's order, so that it will accompany the gift to its recipient.

The two major elements to successful gift giving are timing and creativity. The former implies thinking ahead, buying or making a present ahead, and having it ready to arrive on the proper day. In fact, timing implies thinking of sending the gift in the first place! But the creativity factor is just as important. One should ask oneself these questions:

What does this person *need* or what could he or she use?

What does this person *want* that he or she doesn't have?

How can I surprise and delight this person with the unexpected? Being creative goes back to being organized, too, because it takes time to find or make the useful, the needed, or the unexpected. One should never be ashamed of spending very little on a present. The old cliché "It's the thought that counts" is really true. The ultimate goal of gift giving should be to give pleasure. It's a selfish act in one way, because a person who gives a delightful present with the right timing and in the right spirit usually receives more in return than he gave.

The Universally Accepted Gift: Money

Money is, of course, a great common denominator—it is always a popular and appropriate gift. However, an important part of its appropriateness is the manner in which it is given. The act of giving money must be carried out with proper timing and with discretion. To some people the giving of money is a controversial subject. There are those who claim it shows a lack of imagination and is a "last-resort" gesture. I do not agree. Money is appropriate in almost every case, if given in the right spirit. To make a contribution to a joint gift to enable a piece of engraved silver to be bought or someone to take a nice trip is a gracious gesture. If you are hosting a party where you would like the guests to contribute toward such a present, include a short, informal note with your invitation explaining what is being planned. Some party givers use the "Money Tree" device at the party, where the donors' checks or bills are suspended from a tree-like display item. Often guests are permitted to see who gave what, which to me is vulgar. I feel it is far more tasteful to have the lump sum presented to the recipient or recipients, accompanied by a card upon which every contributor has signed his name. There should also be a legible (preferably typed) list of all donors with their addresses, so that the recipients can write each a thank-you note. No one, except the organizer, need know how much each person gave. If Uncle Harry is rich and Cousin Louise is not, whose business is it that Uncle Harry gave a thousand dollars toward the project and Cousin Louise only fifty? The important thing is that the money was raised to send the couple celebrating their anniversary to Europe. The person who did the collecting might simply say to the anniversary couple, "I think you ought to know that Uncle Harry was particularly generous with his gift."

A gift of cash is an easy one to give, an easy one to accept. This is usually a privilege of adults; a young person does not give a gift of money. When a nephew or a goddaughter lives far away in a region with a climate, manner of dressing, and life-style different from yours, money might be a far wiser present than anything else. The best idea is to ask the child's parents for a clue. One's nephew might be saving money to buy a guitar; one's goddaughter, to go abroad next summer. In both cases, a gift of cash would be the most welcome surprise.

Money should be sent in the form of a check or a traveler's check, for cash is too easily stolen in the mails. Always stipulate in a note how much money is enclosed, in case something is stolen from the envelope.

A gift of stocks or bonds is always an appropriate gift even for someone in high school or college. Remember to have the certificates of ownership made out to the recipient's name. (If the recipient is a minor, have the certificates made out in the name of the child, care of a logical custodian such as a parent.) A young person can become interested in and knowledgeable about the stock market while following his few shares on a daily basis in the newspaper, watching them increase or decrease in value. Savings bonds are another excellent gift for someone of any age and for any occasion.

Gift Certificates

If you are at a complete loss about what to buy someone, a gift certificate is always a solution. (Its only drawback is that the recipient knows exactly how much you have paid for the gift.) Gift certificates to one's local stores, health clubs, beauty salons, flower shops, and bookstores are great presents. For people who live in rural communities, far from good shopping, the sending of a luxury mail-order catalogue with a gift certificate enclosed is a wonderful present.

Gifts Made to Charitable Organizations

There is nothing nicer than a gift made by one person to another in the form of a charitable contribution. It means the most, of course, when the charity involved is one in which the recipient has a personal interest. For example, as a gift to "someone who has everything," a donation made to the museum or college or library or health organization that person particularly espouses would mean a lot.

The Unexpected Gift

The nicest presents to give and the nicest to receive are the no-occasion, unexpected kind. These are truly gifts of love, whether from one woman to another, one man to another, a woman to a man, or an older person to a younger one. To make a gift without any specific reason is the nicest thing to do for someone. The gift should be personalized with a card that says, "Because I was just thinking of you" . . . "Because we miss you" . . . "Because we love you" . . . "Because I was wondering how you were coming along" . . . "Because I wanted to make you smile." These are gifts from the heart, and their monetary value is irrelevant. It could be a box of freshly baked cookies, an amusing tie for a man, a pot of growing herbs, two tickets to the opera, an art book, a porcelain box that says "Thou art so sweet" on

the lid, a box of unusual stationery bearing the recipient's printed monogram, a terrific-looking sweater, a tiny toy animal that evokes past memories
shared by giver and receiver, or a record that does the same, the newest garlic mincer for a gourmet cook, an irresistible watering can for an inveterate
gardener, or perhaps one beautiful rose accompanied by a card that says,
"Just because it's such a beautiful day." These are all impulse gestures, some
sentimental and romantic, some teasing and funny. But all are acts of the
heart, and because they are unexpected they are doubly appreciated.

Flowers

For Men Flowers and plants (always fresh, never plastic) are considered
a welcome and appreciated present for women and couples; yet many of us
never think to send them to bachelors who also entertain and take great
pride in their homes. As a result, single men hardly ever receive flowers.
Flowers are not a "sissy gift." If you know, for example, a divorced man
who has just moved out of the family home and into his own apartment,
why not send him an arrangement of flowers to cheer up what is probably a
depressing new environment for him? A man will always enjoy a birthday
gift of an attractive, easy-to-care-for terrarium for his office. If he is giving a
dinner party, ask if you can send him flowers of his choice for the center of
his table. If he is in the hospital, send him a flowering plant that will
brighten up his room but will require little or no care from the hospital staff.

For Anyone Flower traditions come and go, but it is still a gallant gesture for a man to send flowers to a woman to whom he is attracted; it is still
a very polite gesture for a young man to send flowers to the debutante and
her mother on the night of her debut party. It is important to send flowers
intelligently. For example, when you send flowers, you should know whether
the recipient prefers the cut kind that one can arrange oneself, or an arrangement of flowers that demands no more attention than the adding of
water to the bowl. It also helps to remember the color scheme of the recipient's living room or bedroom, and to match it with your floral gift. If you
want to send the table centerpiece for a dinner party, you should first talk it
over with your hostess and order the kind and color of flowers she wants.
(Most hosts or hostesses want complete control of their dining table decorations.)

Many people send flowers to their hostesses after the dinner party to say
thank you, but it's nicer to send them before. In fact, the best time to send
them is the night before or early in the morning of the dinner. This will
allow your hostess enough time to place them to their best advantage in her
home, and she won't be wasting unnecessary money in purchasing too many
flowers herself. She should be made aware in advance, if possible, of your
plans to send her flowers.

As a last-minute impulse, it is nice to bring cut flowers to your hosts when they are having a small, informal dinner. You should ask for a vase and arrange them yourself, however, and you should ask your hosts where they would like them placed. They will be too busy coping with the bar and the cooking logistics to have the time to stop to arrange flowers.

Don't ever be embarrassed about what kind of flowers to send to your friends, or how much you pay for them. Whether they are beautiful peonies picked from your own garden, a modest cluster of daisies and cornflowers bought at a corner street stall, or a lavish spray of tiny orchids flown in from Hawaii by your florist, all flowers bring beauty to any interior. They are a gift that says, "Congratulations," "Get well," "Thank you," "I'm sorry," or "I love you" most articulately. The written word should accompany the flowers, however—not just a business card. A human hand should write an appropriate line on the card. It can be short: "Our thanks for what will be a great party tonight," followed by your signature, will do it.

One of the nicest things about sending flowers is their convenience. You can pick up your telephone and have your local florist take an order for delivery in almost every major city in the world. Since you often will not be able to include your own card, you should have the florist arrange to have your flowers delivered in the other city with a short message dictated by you and written on a card by his associate florist.

If you want to send flowers to someone who is allergic to them, particularly in the hay fever season of August and September, you can always send a non-flower flower gift—flowers that are beaded or made of metal, silk, fabric, or porcelain (*not* plastic!).

When you commit a social error or have inadvertently offended someone, which I have done through my own life far more than I care to admit, flowers sent with a note of apology make a strong statement on one's behalf. Once, after telephoning my apology, I sent someone a bunch of white lilacs with a note. She forgave me, but she said later, "It was the white lilacs that did it!"

Gifts of Fine Jewelry

For Men   There are some controversies on the subject of men's jewelry of which a woman should be aware before making a "surprise" purchase for the man in her life. One of them is the buying of diamond rings for men. Some people consider them in bad taste (Tiffany, New York's biggest jeweler, has always refused to make or sell them for men). It would embarrass the recipient of her gift if a woman were to spend a lot of money on a man's jewelry gift he would never wear. The same can be said for the gold or silver identification bracelets and necklace chains. Many men refuse to wear these and consider them effeminate, so a woman should be sure of the tastes of the man for whom she is buying a gift.

A good watch is a fine present for a man. Even if he has an old one, he can enjoy a new one, perhaps with changeable straps (one for daytime in black leather, another for evening in gold or silver or platinum or suede). If he wears shirts with French cuffs, even occasionally, new gold (fourteen- or eighteen-karat) cuff links should please him. The most inexpensive kind are those with small round or oval discs, upon which his initials are engraved. If he wears a blazer, fourteen-karat-gold blazer buttons are a nice gift. If he wears a black tie upon occasion and owns "dress shirts," a set of evening jewelry—studs with matching cuff links—is in order. These may be the traditional black onyx or mother-of-pearl, or they may be small sculptured gold designs, or gold or platinum settings holding a tiny stone (gemstone or pearl), or they may be made of some semiprecious stone like jade, quartz, malachite, or lapis lazuli. Don't forget to give him on some occasion a handsome leather or silver "stud box" in which he can store this lovely jewelry.

For Women A young (pre-teen) girl's first real jewelry is usually tiny gold or silver earrings for pierced ears, a gold bangle bracelet, a chain with a small pendant like a gold heart, or a small gold ring. Her first brooch, most often of gold, can be a simple circle, a flower, or a small animal pin. When she is in high school, it is time to think of giving her a good watch. At graduation from college, a pearl necklace with a small jeweled clasp is an appropriate gift; so is a good wristwatch.

For a woman, any special occasion, like a wedding, an anniversary, an important birthday, or the arrival of a baby, is a cue for the husband to present his wife—to the extent he can afford it—with a piece of fine jewelry.

If a woman has "no man in her life," she should go out and buy beautiful jewelry as a gift to herself whenever she feels like it—if she loves it and can afford it. Along with everything else that has changed in the world, the old tradition that a woman's jewelry has to come from a man has gone by the boards.

The Don't-give Gifts

There are certain gifts that are simply not appropriate to give because of the timing or because of the price or because of the reasons for giving them. Pets should never be given to children or adults unless explicitly requested by them or at least agreed to. There are serious responsibilities involved in the proper care of living creatures, and one does not give them "as a joke." Cruelty is never a joke.

Vulgar, bad-taste gifts may be hilariously funny for one second, but then they leave a bad taste permanently in the mouth. The easiest solution is never to buy them. The same goes for silly joke presents. Everything costs so much these days, there is no reason to buy something that provides a short laugh and then is useless.

Be sensible with your gift ideas. An elaborate pair of silver candelabra for a newlywed couple living in a one-room apartment and struggling to earn their living is hardly an appropriate (or welcome) gift. One should think ahead and act with intelligence in selecting presents. One should never give anything ostentatious or patently expensive in a "show-off" manner. A child should not be sent to a birthday party with an enormous, expensive stuffed animal as a present, when everyone else will arrive with modest gifts. (Also, the child won't play with it—it is an adult's pleasure.) A man should not give a woman an expensive fur coat unless they plan to be married; a woman should not give a man expensive jeweled cuff links unless they plan to be married. A man does not give his secretary for Christmas expensive, lacy underwear; a secretary does not present her employer with a high-priced all-leather desk set, either.

For an occasion like a graduation, a birthday, an anniversary, or a wedding, the expensive gifts should be given only by close friends or relatives, and they should be presented quietly, without fanfare or publicity. A check should never be on view with the wedding presents. The bride can always say, "And Grandpa gave us such a nice check!" when showing her presents to her friends.

It is wrong to give a person an oversized gift when he will have to tote it home with him on a plane or train (unless there is a strong box in which to place it as checked baggage). If you wish to give someone a bulky or fragile gift before he returns home, the nice thing to do is to show it to him, then take it back and say, "I'll have it shipped to your home."

One of the things to remember about your own supply of gifts is that items which were once exciting or useful to you and which you no longer want or need make the greatest of gifts to the needy. Clear out your house every so often of "addenda" and be the nicest gift giver of all to those who are less fortunate than you.

Chapter 63

GIFT IDEAS FOR ALL OCCASIONS

The custom of exchanging gifts is as old as civilization itself. As man became more civilized, so did his gift-giving techniques. Today, in our materialistic society, the custom has grown to exaggerated absurdity, and if you peruse the following pages of suggestions, you might accuse me of aiding and abetting that exaggeration.

The attached lists are meant to be a frame of reference—something to make your own creative juices flow. The lists contain suggestions of things you might do as well as things other people have done. If you grow something in your garden, bake something in your kitchen, write a poem from your head, or make something with your hands as a present, you are giving to another in the purest, truest sense. If you contribute to charity in someone else's name, you are giving in the purest sense, too, for without those gifts our great philanthropic and educational institutions might not survive.

Let us say you buy something very humble, all you can afford, and you don't know how to wrap gifts very well. But you present it to someone with perfect timing and you accompany it with a note that is rich in expressions of friendship or love or joy or consolation; well, then, you are a very successful gift giver indeed.

Christening or Baby Presents

Many of the jewelry, gold, and silver gifts listed as baby presents are items to be saved for when they are older, even adults. The sterling silver mug, traditionally given by someone very close to the baby, such as a grandparent or godparent, goes right through the child's life from a milk container to a flower vase or a pencil mug or cigarette server when he is grown up. One can give a baby girl a tiny bracelet for her to wear until she is two for special occasions, but this seems a waste. If one gives her a bracelet sized instead for a young girl, she will be able to wear it until she reaches adolescence. A baby can't appreciate a piece of jewelry, anyway—but a four-year-old girl looks forward to every birthday party and special occasion when she will be allowed to wear "her very own gold jewelry."

Jewelry for a Girl

Silver mug with name and birth date engraved

Gold name-tag bracelet with name and birth date engraved

Gold bangle bracelet

Baby pin (gold circle or enamel or antique seed pearls)

Saint's medal in gold or silver (for Catholics)

Jewelry for a Boy

Silver mug

Silver frame with his hospital or christening picture inside

Antique cuff links or studs

Gold tie bar with birth date and initials

Saint's medal in gold or silver (for Catholics)

Sterling jewelry box lined in velvet and engraved

Sterling pusher, sterling fork, knife and spoon set

Good group presents are a piece of needed baby furniture (bureau, bed, etc.) or a good-quality carriage that can convert to a stroller. This kind of present should be sent the minute the baby is born, so the parents won't invest in it; tell the parents you are buying it for them.

Set of utilitarian bibs ("feeders")

Baby blanket

Baby dress for girl, suit for boy

Playsuit, nightshirts, etc.

Cardigan sweater (perhaps with matching cap and booties)

Baby pillow and two pretty cases for it

Crib comforter

Mobile for crib

Pretty box for diaper pins

Silver barbell rattle

Set of hangers for baby clothes

Electric bottle warmer

Electric two-sectioned feeding tray

Music box

Handsome leather photo album for pictures and record of the baby

Savings account opened in baby's name with twenty-five or fifty dollars deposited as a starter; the passbook is wrapped as a gift and presented to the parents.

Savings bond, purchased in the baby's name

Baby's first good book—a starter on his or her library with the birth date and donor's note in the front: a good edition of a child's classic.

Note: Clothes should be bought in size 1 or larger, as the baby usually has a wardrobe of sorts when he or she is born, and fast grows out of it. One should let parents choose important items, like the baby's coat and hat or snowsuit. Give the parents a gift certificate for something that utilitarian; they usually have set ideas.

Classic Presents for Children Ten and Under

Books of all kinds, including those on history, wildlife and flora life
Telescope
Bank or toy safe
Cash register (it's nice to put some change inside the drawer)
Disguise kit
Magician's set
Fancy kite (always bring extra balls of string)
Slide viewer with popular cartoon sets
Two-speed portable record phonograph and records
Ice-cream sundae making equipment
Popcorn popper
Games
Old clothes for dress-up
Portable blackboard, chalks, and erasers
Painting set
Sandbox toys and bath toys
Puppet theater, puppets, or hand puppets
Simple arts and crafts kits

First Communion Presents

It is no longer obligatory to give religious gifts to children making their First Communion, but relatives and godparents should see to it that the child has a rosary in a little case (mother-of-pearl, sterling silver, or any small rosary), and perhaps a saint's medal, engraved with the date of the First Communion on the back. A small Bible or a book for children on the lives of the saints is also appropriate.

For girls: a bracelet with a saint's medal in sterling silver or gold, engraved on the back, is attractive.

Also, a small silver or gold cross on a fine necklace chain.

And for either a boy or a girl, a photo for their bedroom in which they can put their class First Communion picture is a gift they will enjoy.

Otherwise, one can give a child a game or a toy—in celebration of a very exciting day.

Classic Gifts for Teen-agers

Dictionary
Set of encyclopedias
Set of the classics

Invitation to a play, concert, ballet, opera, or movie
Invitation to a fancy restaurant for lunch or dinner
Backpack or piece of luggage
Photo album
Game of skill
Money
Leather wallet
Stereo and recording equipment: speakers, turntable, records, cassettes, etc.
Shortwave radio
Private telephone line
Camera or camera equipment
Musical instrument and music lessons
Sports equipment desired
Ten-speed bicycle, or bicycle accessories, moped, etc.
Books pertaining to a special hobby or interest
Trip with historical interest (Washington, Williamsburg, the Alamo)
Trip with sporting interest (fishing, canoeing, backpacking, mountain climb-
    ing, skiing)
Typewriter and typewriter lessons
Sewing machine or carpentry equipment
Season ticket to football, baseball, basketball, soccer, or hockey games
Pet of one's own, provided the parents are in full agreement
Clothing of all kinds
Overnight suitcase or tote
Rock concert tickets
Magazine subscription, according to his or her interests
Pierced-ear earrings for girls

Christian Confirmation Presents

Cash
Savings bonds
Leather-bound Bible or lives of the saints
Holy medal of confirmation saint, engraved with date of confirmation, and
    hung on necklace chain for a girl, attached to key chain for a boy
Silver cross and chain or gold cross and chain
Sterling silver rosary in a pretty case
A family heirloom, such as a gold signet ring
(Check "Classic Gifts for Teen-agers" for additional ideas)

Gifts for Bar and Bat Mitzvah

Cash
Bonds

Initial ring
Engraved prayer book, Bible or other Judaica items
Jewelry of all kinds for the girls
A trip
(Check "Classic Gifts for Teen-agers" for additional ideas)

High School Graduation Gifts

(Many of these suggestions are particularly appropriate for students going on to college)
Bicycle
World atlas
Dictionary
Thesaurus
Desk/studio lamp
Luggage
Set of wineglasses
Corkscrew
Electric typewriter
Lighted mirror for make-up or shaving
Luggage tags (with name and address printed)
Stationery printed with student's name and college address
Clock-radio
Stereo equipment
Gift certificate for records and cassettes
Tape recorder-player
Coffee mugs
Coffee serving set
Framed art prints to embellish dorm walls
Bed and bath linens
Thermos for cold-weather sports events
Popcorn popper
Bridge lessons
Potted plants
Watering pitcher
Airtight container for storing food in one's room
Small refrigerator
CB radio
Subscription to home-town newspaper
Magazine subscriptions
Pair of canvas directors' chairs
Umbrella
Electric blanket
Basics for dormitory cooking, like mixing bowls, spoons, and saucepan

Hair dryer

Electric curlers

The nicest graduation gift I received was an old foot locker that a friend had conditioned and painted in bright colors with a Pennsylvania Dutch stenciled design. In my college dorm, it served as much-needed storage space and alternately as a seating area or our cocktail table or a bridge table.

Gifts for a Debutante

The only people who give gifts to the debutante are the adult members of her family, her godparents, and perhaps some old family friends. It is nice for the young men escorts to send her or her mother flowers at the height of festivities (and in some cases, if she wants to wear a corsage, to supply that), but a deb's escort does not have to give her a gift. (Instead, he is supposed to fulfill his duties extremely well as her escort, and give her a good time.)

Anything to do with the care of her hair is a good present—either a portable home dryer, electric curlers, or a gift certificate to the top local hairdresser.

It is the time when a debutante loves something luxurious—a fur hat (if she wears hats), a cashmere sweater, or a beautifully embroidered nightgown.

One of the nicest debutante presents I ever heard of was what the uncle of my college roommate gave her: her portrait painted by a talented artist. She was captured at the height of her young beauty; this was a present of meaning to her, to the man she eventually married, and now to her children.

A dressing table set (mirror, comb, and brush, in silver, tortoise, mother-of-pearl) is appropriate

Piece of luggage or a good traveling make-up kit

A sterling compact, monogrammed, perhaps with matching lipstick case

A series of gold or silver bangle bracelets

If she has her own apartment, some pretty china or stemware or something in silver

A sterling frame in which to put her debutante photograph, with her initials and the date of the debut

Necklace—a heart on a chain, or a tiny diamond or pearl suspended from a chain

Gold or silver earrings (find out whether she prefers silver or gold, and if her ears are pierced)

Gold finger ring

Evening bag (gold, silver or white is best, for patterned or colored bags might clash with her evening dresses)

Gold charm, perhaps with a small stone or two, to wear on a bracelet or necklace chain

Evening scarf for her hair

Buying an "extra" for her car she cannot afford, such as installing a tape deck

Cultured pearl necklace and/or bracelet

Box of quality note paper, perhaps with her first monogrammed die included in the gift

Good leather wallet

Notebook for her handbag (perhaps with agenda attached)

Leather handbag

Gold or silver pen

Season tickets to concert, ballet, or opera

Gifts for the College Graduate

A briefcase or attaché case or a desk set for the office, if the graduate is going into the business world.

A pocket calculator

A piece of luggage (ask the graduate what is most needed, don't guess)

Sterling silver pen and pencil set or gold pen

Handsome leather-bound dictionary

Stationery die with graduate's name or monogram, and a box of good stationery engraved with the new die

Set of beer mugs

Set of all-purpose wineglasses

Set of coffee mugs

Set of stainless-steel flatware

Ask the graduate which of these items he or she wishes most:

    Stereo equipment

    Portable radio

    Coffee maker

    Wall clock

    Kitchen equipment

Picture frame

Shares of stock

Telephone answering machine

Binoculars

Gift certificate to clothing store (to enable young person to be suitably dressed when applying for a job)

Cash—always suitable, always appropriate!

Gifts for Priests, Ministers, and Rabbis

Food (including baked goods, tins of delicacies, cooked turkey and roast beef)

Wines
Smoking accessories (if the person smokes)
Gift certificate to a good store to buy clothing of one's preference
Personal stationery of good quality and a good silver pen and pencil set
Cash—always a welcome gift

If you take the time to find out what special interest your minister or rabbi has, it is nice to send him a gift certificate from the store catering to that interest—whether it's sporting goods, books, art supplies, or music.

Subscriptions to good magazines are always welcome. So is membership in a book club.

A good color TV set is a great present; or perhaps he needs a portable recorder-cassette player or another piece of electronic equipment.

One of the nicest gifts I ever saw given anyone was from a man of means who had purchased many raffle tickets to a charity. He won the main prize —a new car—and since he had all the cards he needed and his parish priest needed a new car badly, he gave the priest the newly won car. But he also paid the income tax on the gift and the first two years' insurance on the car. That is a well-thought-out gift!

If he belongs to a club, such as a golf club, a *really* generous present is to pay his club dues for the year.

Gifts for a Nun

Cash—always the best
Food and wine
If she does not wear a habit, a gift certificate to a good clothing store is welcome; so is a gift certificate to a good mail-order catalogue and to local stores specializing in her particular interest—whether sports or music
A lunch or dinner invitation at an elegant restaurant
A play, concert, ballet, or opera invitation
A briefcase, if she needs one in her work
A suitcase
Subscriptions to good magazines
Membership in a book club
A good TV set
A portable cassette-recorder-player
House plants for her room, apartment, or office
Some good soap; nice-smelling potpourri in a pretty container for her room; hand lotion and bath oil
If she has an apartment, gifts of china, crystal, flatware, cooking equipment, pretty porcelain decorative objects
Good-quality stationery
The most welcome gift a group can give her: a trip to a place she has never been (provided her community allows such travel)

Teachers' Presents

It is not obligatory to give presents to your children's teachers. However, it is a nice gesture, either at Christmas or at the end of the spring term, before everyone goes on vacation. An elaborate present is not called for, and I like to give the women something frivolous, like a bottle of perfume or a pretty scarf that they would not ordinarily buy; to the men I give things like wallets, ties, diaries, and bar glasses.

Some of the most successful and least expensive presents for teachers are homemade foods. If you don't give the main teachers in your young child's life a present, at least you should write a note at the end of the year, saying, "Thank you for working so hard with Ruthie. We appreciate it." A letter of thanks is often the very best present of all.

Kitchen Shower (also good for gourmet cooks and for housewarmings)

The bride's friends attending the shower might decide in advance to give an expensive gift, like an electric blender or grill or food processor, instead of purchasing individual gifts.

Other group gifts might be: a set of fine-quality, graduated-size saucepans with covers, and one-quart and two-quart covered casseroles (from oven to table).

Set of kitchen towels
Set of hot pot holders
Whisk and egg beater
Rolling pin
Food storage jars
Set of canisters
Spice rack
Set of sharp kitchen knives
Cutting board
Cookie jar
Set of trivets
Fruit or vegetable peeler
Double boiler
Two sizes of frying pans (the larger one with a lid)
Crêpe pan
Two sizes of aluminum or Pyrex baking pans (one square, one rectangular)
Meat broiling pan
Colander

Small strainer
Juicer
Two aprons (one for him, one for her)
Dish cloths
Dispenser for paper towels, aluminum foil, and plastic wrap
Set of measuring spoons
Set of measuring cups
Spatula and scraper set
Recipe file and cards
Cookbooks
Kitchen shears
Cheese grater
Coffeepot or coffee maker
Large roasting pan with fitted lid
Rack to fit in roasting pan
Meat thermometer
Tea kettle
Tea strainer
Earthenware teapot

Cookie sheet
Cake baking pan
Salt and pepper set for the stove
Set of mixing bowls
Flour sifter
Toaster
Fire extinguisher for the kitchen
Crock pot (great for people who
  work)
Wok (for lovers of Eastern food)
Electric food processor
Electric can opener—or just a good
  plain can opener
"Cleanup caddy"—rubber or plas-
tic wash basin jammed with items
like liquid soap for dishes, scouring
pads, sponges, to keep beneath the
sink
Rubber draining pad for sink side-
  board
Rack to place on draining pad for
  drying dishes (useful even if one
  has a dishwasher)
Timer
Kitchen clock
Garlic press
Spaghetti pot

Linen Shower

These are expensive items, so the guests should form groups, choose the gift they wish to present the bride, and ask her her color preferences for her bedroom and bath. A linen shower that is a total surprise to the bride usually means she has not been consulted about what she likes, and this may spell disaster and permanent displeasure for her. She may have planned her bedroom and matching bath in blue and white, so why risk bringing her something in green? She may hate floral patterns, so why not find out in advance? What kind of bed will they have? The size of the bed is of paramount importance before ordering any bed linens.

Needed Bed and Bath Linens
(The bed linens are all "per bed")
2 bath mats
4 bath towels
4 hand towels
8 facecloths
1 set of guest towels
1 electric blanket
2 blanket covers
1 thermal blanket

1 bedspread
2 mattress pads
3 sets of sheets
3 pillow cases to match
Pillow cover for each pillow
Pillow for each person (but find out
  if they sleep with two each)
Dust ruffle

Lingerie Shower

To many brides, the lingerie shower is the least important of the three common kinds. To some, however, it is very important in that it is the most personal of the showers.

The first thing a lingerie shower hostess should do is get the bride-to-be's sizes and color preferences. Then she should make a list of the important lingerie items and allow guests to bring the item of their choice. Many of these things are so expensive that two or more will have to join forces in order to afford what they would like the bride to have. Some of the items on the list might be:

Matching gown and peignoir
Matching bedroom slippers
"Every-night" nighties
Set of matching bra, panties, half slip—or shifts, or whatever is in fashion
Long half slip (for evening length)
Lace-trimmed slip
Bedjacket
Pretty nightgown for winter (brushed nylon, cotton flannel)
Winter robe
Summer robe
Lingerie cases for bureau drawers
Sachets

Christmas Gift Giving

The main thing to remember about Christmas presents is that they should be given in the spirit of Christmas, *from the heart*. Christmas is not only a time to please someone one loves, but also to say thank you to someone who serves one well—whether it's the family doctor, the minister, or one's hairdresser. The spirit of Christmas is based on love and gratitude. If we often seem to forget that fact, it's probably the plethora of Christmas advertising and commercialism that encourages us to forget it.

Christmas giving is easier and more efficient if it is organized well in advance. We all of us have our own system of Christmas priorities, but not all of us stop to write our priorities down on a piece of paper, where we can analyze them.

How to Organize Your Gift List   Figure out your budget, the amount of money you wish to spend on gifts for the coming Christmas, and write it down. Let that figure guide you. Second, list the names of all the people to whom you gave gifts last year (to some, like your children, you gave more than one). Write down new names that should be on the list this year, and delete those that do not have to be on the list any more.

Assign each name an approximate maximum sum that may be spent on that person's gift, in order to fit within your budget. Remember, when buying, to keep that allocation in mind for each person. For example, it doesn't make sense to splurge on your goddaughter and buy her a sixty-dollar sweater because you happen to see it and know it would suit her well—and then find yourself with only five dollars for a gift for your younger sister.

I have found it helpful to list names under the following categories, to assist me in the rather gargantuan planning Christmas requires in our household:

1. Immediate family
2. Peripheral family (in-laws, cousins, nieces, and nephews, etc.)
3. Godchildren
4. If you live in an apartment building, the tip money for the superintendent, doormen, servicemen, elevator operators, etc.
5. Service presents: mail carriers, parcel post carriers, milkmen, newspaper delivery boys or girls, hairdresser, gym instructor, etc.
6. Important people in our lives (minister, pediatrician, secretary, housekeeper, children's teachers, baby-sitter)
7. Good friends
8. And if you're in business for yourself, the immediate staff in the office or your place of business

The reasons for organizing in advance are pretty obvious, but the most important is that everything is that much easier. You can also pick up items of excellent value during the summer sales. If your recently married child and spouse need, for example, more linens or another piece of furniture, what better time to buy it and lay it away for Christmas than during the traditional late summer sales?

Planning ahead also helps you to buy more appropriate gifts for the people on your list, since you have the time to look and find what you want. Such plans help you set aside money and budget yourself for Christmas, instead of facing economic disaster in January when all the bills pour in at once. Of course, if you are a participant in a bank's save-for-Christmas plan, you have already dealt with this problem. If you like to do handcrafts, organizing well in advance for Christmas means you can also have all your presents finished well ahead of the busy holiday season.

If you find yourself a willing or unwilling "Chief in Charge of Christmas," you may find the following suggestions helpful:

1. Use fresh large plastic trash bags to collect your gifts for each member of the immediate family. Label each bag with the person's name, and be sure to find a safe hiding place for the bags.
2. Buy decorative wrapping paper (if you bought it at half price last January, so much the better!) and Christmas-wrap as you buy during the summer and fall, being sure to tag each item with the recipient's name. Put each wrapped item in the proper bag. Also maintain a written list of each item you buy, so you'll know what you or your spouse bought for each person.
3. For young children, include in each large bag a smaller plastic bag, into which you put little items that will serve as stocking stuffers.
4. For your peripheral family, begin to assemble presents, wrap them, and put each family's in a large shopping bag, so they are ready to be

handed over, or sent at Thanksgiving time. If you have a lot of nieces and nephews and godchildren around the same age, it is practical to buy all of them the same thing.

5. As presents for your own family are dropped off at your home, you can put them in each person's big plastic bag and thus keep them separated efficiently.

Some famous very large families I know have simplified gift giving in the immediate family. They each draw a name from the hat at Thanksgiving time; that person is the one to whom they will give one important present at Christmas. In other words, each person has to buy only one present, and everyone in the family is taken care of handsomely.

Mail-order Catalogues   These are blessings in that you can send a present to friends and relatives who live far and wide, without stirring from your chair. If you give an order to a mail-order company for gifts, be sure to include your personal gift tag or note card, to personalize the operation. The better mail-order catalogues ask you to order monogrammed gifts in September or even August, so that they will arrive at their destination in plenty of time.

If you are faced with sending one gift for an entire family, the food gift box—cheese, cakes, candy—is always welcomed.

How Much You Spend and Making It Yourself   There is no need to spend a lot of money on Christmas presents. Any friend who judges your friendship by the amount of money you spend on him is one worth losing quickly. Imagination fills any void left by money. A fresh loaf of bread baked and tied up in pretty paper and left on someone's doorstep on Christmas morning; a small notepad with some of last summer's wildflowers pressed between the pages for someone who shared a vacation spot with you last year; a set of scented homemade candles; a drawing made of the front of someone's house; a poem, written carefully on a piece of good-quality paper; a needlepointed case for someone's glasses; a cutting from someone's garden, planted in a hand-painted clay pot; a silhouette cut out in black paper of someone's child, and framed; one bar of an unusually exotic soap "because I know what a soap lover you are"; an apron stitched together from pieces of leftover fabric in a bright patchwork design—these are gifts of the heart and of the hands that bring enormous pleasure.

It is wonderful to teach one's children to make their own presents from an early age; it is wonderful to teach them to give, of their own accord, something that would please a child in a hospital ward, a rehabilitation clinic, or an old person sitting sad and alone in an old people's home. That is the true meaning of Christmas; it transcends all the glitter and glamour surrounding the giving of gifts.

Wedding Gifts

Thank heavens few people still follow the rule that says when you receive a wedding reception invitation, you have to send a present, and if you don't receive such an invitation, you are "off the hook." Today relatives and good friends of the bridal couple, as well as close friends of their parents, send a gift to wish the couple well. The gift is sent whether or not there even was a wedding reception. If a couple elopes, or if they choose to have a wedding with immediate family only present, they deserve to receive wedding presents—from people who know and love them. Today, if you are invited to a reception or not; if you are sent an announcement or not—if you are close to the pair, or one of the pair, you should send a gift or at least a warm personal letter.

Suitable Gifts   Any gift that matches the interests or life-styles of the couple is appropriate, even if it costs very little money. The wedding gift is perhaps the most sentimental and important gift of friendship that one ever receives. The money spent is not what is important. If the bride's family is rich and the wedding will be large and much publicized, don't be afraid to send a modest present—even if you know the gifts will be on display—if a modest present is what your budget calls for. If you buy or make something in good taste, your present will look as good as anyone else's, and certainly in the eyes of the bride and groom.

One young friend of mine is constantly at work making needlepoint telephone book covers. As she says, "All my friends keep getting married on me," and for each she needlepoints a telephone book cover; she includes their monogram and puts the wedding date in the lower right of her design. (Subsequently, one of her married friends did a needlepoint telephone book cover for her, with her initials and a bridal bouquet included in a corner of the design, telling her "you're the next to be married!")

Choosing the Wedding Gift   The first decision one should make is the amount of money to be spent on the wedding gift. When young people begin to marry, there are often several weddings in their group in one year. Most people have to budget very carefully for these expenditures, which is why a group gift from several friends of the bride and groom is an intelligent choice. A person should also not be embarrassed to buy only one cup and saucer in the bride's patterns, or one dessert plate. No one should ever feel embarrassed by how little is spent on *any* present. Sometimes it is the note that is sent with a small gift of no monetary value that makes it a very large and important gift in the eyes of the bride and groom.

Most brides register with the bridal consultant at a local department or jewelry store, and shopping through them can be the easiest way to select a wedding gift. There is only one minus in buying a wedding present from a registered list; the recipients will know its exact monetary value. However, that minus is small in comparison to the vast advantages of buying something that was preselected by the bride and groom.

If you do not wish to buy something from the bridal registry, your next decision (after setting your budget) is selecting the type of present. To me, there are five major categories of gifts, some of which can be equally as well given as bridal shower presents:

Money. Cash or checks—bonds—stocks. Money in some form is by far today's most popular wedding gift.

Practical Items. Needed expensive items like a vacuum cleaner, dishwasher, electrical coffee maker, blender.

Art Objects. Paintings, framed graphics, etchings, lithographs—sculpture—antiques.

Entertaining Assists. Electric hot tray—trays—table stemware—bar glasses—pitcher—ice bucket—tureen for table centerpiece—candlesticks—flatware—plates and serving dishes—casseroles and decorative bowls—salts and peppers—table linens, mats—serving cart.

Furnishings. Card table—hall mirror—table lamps—small cigarette tables—wall sconces—folding buffet tables—coffee table.

As with most wedding presents, they are chosen better and appreciated more if one has spoken to the couple beforehand so that the giver knows what the couple particularly want and need. If you do not understand their life-style and tastes, do not try to get them a present in this category. (Or else give them a gift certificate to the local reputable home furnishings store.)

The One-of-a-kind Wedding Present Some people prefer to give a gift that would never be duplicated—an original work or an antique that was handed down in the family or found while browsing in antique shops. These are very special gifts, requiring a lot of thought, sometimes weeks of searching, sometimes years of saving the object for just such an occasion: a very special wedding. When one gives such a gift to a couple, the story or history of the object should be written on a card, so that they will know how very special it is.

Gifts of Money Gifts of money in cash, checks, or bonds are often presented the day of the wedding or even well before. Some engaged couples wisely open a joint savings account before their marriage to take care of gifts of money that come in after their engagement announcement. The account should contain both their names, as in this example: "Sarah Jane Parker and/or Richard Mooney." Checks sent before the wedding may read "Sarah Jane Parker and/or Richard Mooney" or they may be addressed to the bride alone. Checks presented to the couple at their wedding reception read "Mr. and Mrs. Richard Mooney." Bonds and securities sent to them jointly should read "Sarah Jane Mooney and Richard Mooney."

If the couple is going to move far away and would really prefer money instead of gifts that they will have to move at great expense, they should let the word get around through their mutual families.

Monogramming One has to be careful about having a wedding gift monogrammed. First of all, your gift might be a duplicate and if it has been monogrammed the couple may not return it. Also, today you may not be sure of how the couple will call themselves. It is better, if the couple lives in the city where you purchased the present, for you to pay the store for the engraving or monogramming but not have it done. Ask the store to furnish you with proof of this payment, and include it with the gift, together with your enclosure card. The bridal couple can then have the initials put on the present in exactly the style they want.

Double Wedding If you are invited to a double wedding and you know only one member of the party well, you do not need to send presents to both couples, even if there are brothers or sisters involved.

Timetable for Sending the Gift The best time to select a wedding gift is immediately upon receipt of the invitation. Engraved gifts and special orders, for example, take time. One's enthusiasm is much higher when the invitation has just arrived, and it is somehow easier to find the right thing than it is the day before the wedding.

Another reason for sending a wedding present as soon as possible after receipt of the invitation is that it is tremendously helpful for the bride to be able to write thank-you notes in a steady stream *before the wedding*. Since problems of time grow so much more acute after a wedding, the bride who "thanks as she goes" is a wise one.

Sometimes, because of absence from the country, ill health, financial reverses, or other reasons, one cannot send the wedding present before the ceremony. In such cases, wedding gifts have been sent as much as one or two years after the event. The couple should be touched and grateful to receive a delayed wedding present; there is no time limit to a kind and thoughtful gesture. However, people who delay in sending gifts through sloppiness and forgetfulness are displaying bad manners.

Where Gifts Are Sent Wedding gifts are addressed to the bride only before the wedding. After the wedding, they are sent to "Mr. and Mrs. John Grace."

Even if the bride has her own apartment, it may still be easier for everyone if you send your wedding presents before the ceremony to her parents' home, provided, of course, that is where the wedding arrangements will be handled. It is a good policy to ask her which address she prefers you to use. (If she is as busy as most brides-to-be who are also working, send her a self-addressed stamped postcard, which will come back to you with the proper address written on the postcard.) In some parts of America, it is customary for guests to take wedding gifts to the reception, but this can be very inconvenient for everyone.

If it is certain that the gift will arrive after the wedding or if it is sent in response to an announcement, and you do not know the couple's new address, the gift is sent to the home of the bride's parents. Of course, if one knows exactly where the couple's future home is to be, the gift may be sent there provided it is certain someone will be present to receive it should it arrive while the bride and groom are still on their wedding trip.

Enclosure Cards   Any wedding gift you send should have your calling card or your engraved informal or correspondence card inside. Write a little note of good wishes, and sign it "Jim and Janet" or just with your first name, if you are not married. If you are much older than the bride and groom and are not intimate, sign as a couple "Jim and Janet Goodwin," or "Alice Metcalfe." On a calling card, you'll have room to write only "Best wishes," or something similar, but it is cold to send a gift card that has nothing written by hand on it.

Be sure your card or the outside envelope of the card contains your address, as it will help the bride do her thank-you notes promptly and accurately.

Gifts for the Second and Third Weddings   No one should feel obligated to give a wedding gift to someone who is marrying for the second or third or fourth time. However, if the person is someone close to you, of whom you are really fond, it is nice to send a wedding present as a mark of affection and your good wishes for the couple's future. The present might cost a few dollars. It might cost a hundred dollars. That does not matter. Even if you have not yet met the new spouse of your friend or relative, it will mean a lot to both of them to have everyone's good wishes and support for their marriage. It's a time when good friends should really rally around. (If you can't send a present, write them a warm letter.)

Usually the woman in a second marriage already has her good silver, china, and crystal, or at least enough of it to get by. If she does not, and if the couple has to watch their pennies, you should ask the bride or groom (whichever is closest to you) what they really need most. It may be some dinner plates; it may be a lamp; it may be an electric can opener. If it is something you cannot afford to pay for yourself, find a friend or two to go in with you on a group present. If the couple seems to be one of the few who "have everything," present them with something sentimental. Once I bought a group of little porcelain boxes very inexpensively on one of my travels. They have little romantic sayings hand-painted on their lids. I use them as "second marriage presents," and they always accomplish their mission: to please the recipients greatly.

A fully equipped picnic basket is a great group present. A small radio is a useful gift, because one can always use a second one for traveling or, to leave in the bathroom or kitchen.

If the newly marrieds are avid games players, a present directed at their favorite game is a good idea. They may need a bridge table cover, or a set of cards, with matching score pads and pencils. Maybe they would like a good new leather cup with dice for their backgammon game. Or a subscription to a magazine that addresses itself to one of their favorite hobbies or interests (art, sports, gardening, cooking, investing).

One of the nicest thank-you notes I ever received came from a young couple who had both remarried and moved to another city. I was aware of the low condition of their finances, so our wedding present to them was a year's subscription to the local newspaper, delivered daily to their door.

Since the "second-time" bride usually has a new monogram, some monogrammed linens are in order, too. And if you have a photo or snapshot of the couple, present it to them in a frame. (It does not have to be an expensive one.)

I remember a lovely wedding when a widow in her sixties married a widower in his seventies. Their two families gave each of them an engraved fourteen-karat gold house key to their new apartment. The gift was presented at their reception, complete with a card signed by each member of both families, wishing them "all the love and joy these keys to happiness can provide." The couple framed the card and are still living happily ever after, complete with his and her gold door keys!

A lot of things may go out of style, but sentiment never will.

Anniversary Presents

People who have been married twenty-five years or more are usually fairly uninterested in adding more possessions—knickknacks and household items —to their lives. They are beginning to think about moving into smaller quarters, living more simply and ridding themselves of superfluous things. Therefore, for older people, anniversary gifts should be chosen carefully and from a sentimental point of view. Joint presents from the family or a group of friends are often the best solution—such as a trip to a vacation resort, or perhaps an expensive gift like a new color TV set, or even a refrigerator. One of the nicest anniversary presents I've heard of was the air-conditioning of an elderly couple's home, a joint present from the children, who decided their parents should spend the remainder of the long summers in comfort, removed from the usual symphony of electric fans.

Another group of children provided their parents on their fiftieth anniversary (and renewed it every year thereafter) with a free limousine pickup service. Neither of the parents could drive any more. They went out only once or twice a week, but they went out now in comfort and safety, thanks to their children's thoughtfulness.

Some nice anniversary presents for older people are:

A group family photograph, presented in a lovely frame

A tray with their original wedding invitation painted on the tole surface

A huge bouquet of flowers—perhaps the same flowers that were in the bride's original wedding bouquet

A gold bracelet for her with each grandchild or great-grandchild's name and birthday engraved on a gold disc; a necktie for him with the children's names painted on the silk surface

A small, nicely framed painting of their first home—made from an old photo

A rental service on films—where the projectionist will come once a month with his equipment to show a movie of their choice (this would also give them a chance to entertain friends easily)

A cassette player; the children and grandchildren and great-grandchildren can record messages on cassettes, which the couple could then play on their own player

Anniversary Gifts Pegged to the Year   It is nice to be able to give an anniversary gift to a parent or a close friend or relative that fits the traditional gift for that specific anniversary:

1st	Clocks	15th	Watches
2nd	China	16th	Silver hollowware
3rd	Crystal, glass	17th	Furniture
4th	Electrical appliances	18th	Porcelain
5th	Silverware	19th	Bronze
6th	Wood	20th	Platinum
7th	Desk sets	25th	Sterling Silver Jubilee
8th	Linen, lace	30th	Diamond
9th	Leather	35th	Jade
10th	Diamond jewelry	40th	Ruby
11th	Fashion jewelry and accessories	45th	Sapphire
12th	Pearls or colored gems	50th	Golden Jubilee
13th	Textiles, furs	55th	Emerald
14th	Gold jewelry	60th	Diamond Jubilee

One does not have to take literally the symbol of the anniversary in selecting a gift either for one's spouse or for friends celebrating their anniversary. If you are bringing presents to friends celebrating their diamond jewelry anniversary, for example, you can bring "joke" presents festooned with rhinestones. If you are attending a ruby anniversary party, you can bring the honorees a ruby red velvet tie and a ruby red chiffon scarf. For a bronze anniversary, you can always find a small piece of bronze, like a paperweight or letter opener, that is not too expensive. A wood anniversary can bring forth anything from a wooden salt and pepper set to what some friends did recently for the honorees: having a tree planted in their badly-in-need-of-landscaping front yard!

If a couple wishes to (and is financially able to) take their diamond jewelry anniversary seriously, it is the time for the wife to present her husband with something like evening cuff links of gold with a diamond in the center of each, and for the husband to give her anything from an expensive diamond wristwatch to a tiny gold leaf brooch with one diamond in the center.

One should not overspend on gimmicky or expensive gifts for close friends or relatives on their anniversaries. Buy something simple and useful, or something that is fun. Write an appropriate card with it—either funny or sentimental. The card should set the pace of the gift. And if the party invitation says "no gifts," follow those instructions.

Birthdays

One will find in other parts of this section lists of gifts suitable for people of special interests or people at certain age levels, which would be suitable for birthday presents.

Birthdays are for everyone; birthday *presents* are for children, for families, or for those who are very close to us. Birthday presents are also for those who may be going through a difficult period of their lives.

A host and hostess who are giving a birthday party, and who list it as such, should say to their adult guests, "Absolutely no presents are to be brought." The guests should follow the instruction; it is rude to try to be the exception. If the host and hostess proclaim it to be a birthday party, but do not mention gifts, then you would be better off if you brought something.

An adult birthday present does not have to be expensive. One perfect rose from the florist; a box of homemade fudge; some delightful scent; new playing cards—anything small and not too expensive will do. One of the best birthday gifts I ever received was from a friend who was "flat broke," in her own words, who knew I wanted to read a certain book. She got it from the library on her own card, and when I had finished it, she picked it up and returned it. She saved me time and money; her gift cost her nothing, but it meant a lot to me, and we laughed and had a good time over her "birthday present."

Suggestions for Birthday Jewelry   It is a gracious gesture to give someone a birthday present containing his or her own birthstone. Whether it is a pendant with a tiny stone or a pair of impressive cuff links, it's a gesture of extra thoughtfulness.

Month	Birthstone
January	Garnet
February	Amethyst
March	Bloodstone or aquamarine
April	Diamond
May	Emerald
June	Pearl, moonstone, or alexandrite
July	Ruby
August	Sardonyx or peridot
September	Sapphire
October	Opal or tourmaline
November	Topaz
December	Turquoise or zircon

Housewarming Gifts

A "Welcome" mat to go outside the door (a practical kind, for bad weather)

A beautifully illustrated art or travel book

Book ends

Gift certificate to the nearest bookstore

If you know the color scheme of the living room or library or family room, a pair of fresh decorator pillows

Large box of white candles

Gift certificate to local liquor store

Arrangement of silk flowers to brighten up a dark corner

Wine rack

Notepads with pens attached, one for each telephone extension

Decorative telephone book covers

Large supply of stationery printed with the new address and telephone number of the house or apartment—which can be used by every member of the family

Plastic organizers of all kinds: for kitchen or bureau drawers; knife holder for the knives; tool drawer organizer; umbrella stand; spice rack, bathroom shelves, etc.

String dispenser; Scotch tape dispenser; scissors in a big box

Stamp box full of stamps

Pen and pencil set for each member of the family

Lovely tall plant (that requires little care)

Knife sharpener

To send in advance: several rolls of shelf-paper (with co-ordinated-color thumb tacks if the paper is not adhesive)

House Guest Presents

Set of guest towels
Box of guest soaps
Porcelain soap dish with matching tumbler for guest bathroom
Pair of lap supper trays for the hosts to use for themselves or for their guests
Set of breakfast china—and, to be terribly luxurious about the gift, a matching plastic breakfast tray and linen set
Cachepots, jardinières, or any kind of attractive containers (porcelain, wood, straw, pewter) for any kind of household plant or indoor tree
Place mats (in straw, plastic, linen) with matching or co-ordinating napkins in linen or polyester
Set of canapé knives
Set of fruit knives
Saucy little bell, in porcelain, crystal, or silver—to use as a table bell, but useful also for anyone who is sick in bed
Ice-cream scoop
Place card holders (decorated with little shells, pineapples, figures, or whatever), including a set of handsome place cards
Coasters for cocktail glasses
Bar glasses—the newest fashion glasses (always useful, too, because they're constantly being broken)
Laminated plastic canapé trays
Paper dinner napkins, cocktail napkins, and coasters, with your hosts' monogram in color

For Hot-weather Entertaining
Hurricane lamps for patio dining
Votive candles set in all kinds of decorative holders, including hanging garden lamps
Oversized bucket and tongs
For the pool:
  Rubber mattresses and blow-up plastic animals and balls
  Floating candles for nighttime illumination
  Terry robes for the pool house or dressing room
  Large beach towels—amusing ones
  Bath towels with hosts' initials
Noncapsizable, nonrusting ash trays to leave out of doors
Plastic insulated bar glasses
Matching plastic tray, ice bucket, bar glasses

Earthenware and stoneware garden china sets

Summery linens (be sure you know the measurements of your hosts' table before buying linens; otherwise buy mats and napkins)

Wire-meshed food protectors (to keep insects off food)

Large, well-insulated metal cans full of popcorn or potato chips for patio or poolside entertaining

Barbecue chef's apron and gloves

Two-tiered rolling cart that becomes a portable bar or buffet

Iced-tea glasses and spoons

One inventive woman I know happened to notice her hostess' pool house had no proper dressing-room equipment for guests, so she made up two tortoiseshell trays of preparations—one for the men's side, one for the women's side, equipped with sunglasses, bathing caps, deodorants, tissues, sun protection, sunburn relief, talcum powder, etc. Her gift was a smash hit with both hosts and guests.

Food and Liquor as Host and Hostess Presents

A host and hostess are always glad to see someone arrive with any of the following in their baggage (even better if they know it in advance, to help them in their weekend grocery planning):

Cooked, large rare roast beef

Tins of imported pâté—with some special crackers

Freshly baked loaves of bread and other delicious things from a special bakery, or from one's own oven (croissants, brioches, cookies, cake)

Fruit cake in a tin

Several quarts of ice cream packed in dry ice—and jars of different toppings

Homemade casseroles (that the hostess has only to reheat during the weekend)

Prosciutto (Italian ham) or a baked or smoked ham of any kind

Gourmet cheeses—a large wheel of Brie of Camembert, or a giant hunk of Wisconsin cheddar or a crock of Vermont cheese

Basket full of homemade jams, jellies, and relishes

A jar of freshly made (and freezable) spaghetti sauce

Big box of candy

Frozen hors d'oeuvres and frozen quiches (all frozen or cold goods should be packed in thermo packs or in dry ice)

Fresh Beluga caviar, if your ship has come in

Case of fine imported beer

Selection of red and white wines

Gallon jug of homemade Sangría

Case of assorted liquor

Basket with assorted small bottles of liqueur

Large plastic container of raw vegetables, all washed and chopped for hors d'oeuvres, packed in a little water

Gifts to Send Someone in the Hospital

One should not send food unless the patient's doctor specifically grants permission. Hospital staffs are too overworked to take care of special foods for the patient, so one should ask the patient "Is there anything you're allowed to have that would taste good that I can bring you?"

An easy-care flowering plant, much better than flowers that require daily care

A marvelously scented soap—a good present for men or women (hospital soap usually leaves a lot to be desired)

Bottle of a good cologne (for men or women)

Talcum powder

Hand cream

Books—nothing depressing, but light reading, mysteries, cartoon books, or even a beautiful art book that will keep the patient opening its pages for visual pleasure

An attractive loose-leaf notebook, with your card that says, "It's time to write down all the things you have to do when you get out of there!" The patient can make notes of thank-you notes to send, people to call, etc.

Box of good notepaper for patient to use in writing thank-you notes; if you have stamped all the envelopes for him, even better

If the patient cannot afford to rent a TV during the hospital stay, your paying for the rental is the nicest present you could make

Pair of pajamas for a man, pretty nightgown or bedjacket for woman, or a dressing gown for either

You might have a private telephone installed at your expense for someone who has to be in the hospital for a long time

You might also want to send any of the following:

Crossword puzzle books

Book of bridge hands (when appropriate)

Games, like Scrabble

Book of stamps

Pretty postcards, prestamped

If *you* are in the hospital, when you leave you should have someone bring in a huge (ten-pound) box of candy to leave at the nurses' station for the nurses, the orderlies, the interns, resident physicians, and all. Leave a note with it thanking all of them for the wonderful care they gave you.

Gifts for the Traveler

Ask the recipient what is needed in the luggage line, and then buy it. Every traveler has specific wants and needs, and it is impossible for someone else to divine what they are without asking specific questions. However, no matter how much luggage a person has, he can always use another light-weight nylon tote, a crushable item that can be packed in one's baggage and used when needed.

A handsome new set of printed luggage tags, with the owner's name, address, and telephone number, is always useful

A "stationery kit" with airmail paper will be useful for anyone going overseas

A leather passport-money case is another item for an overseas traveler

Money exchange calculator

Portable radio (small and lightweight). I have kept myself from being homesick all over the world by tuning in on my radio.

Travel mirror (regular mirror on one side and magnified one on the other). This helps a woman with her make-up in badly lit hotels and a man with his shaving duties, too.

Small folding picture frame, to give to someone who is going on a long trip and would like to have family pictures with him

Small travel alarm clock (mine is the size of a small matchbox and goes into my handbag instead of my suitcase)

Hidden money belt

Plastic bag full of the right-sized film for the traveler's camera. Most travelers forget about taking this along, and it is difficult to buy film in many parts of the world.

Room scent (I've been in so many hotels and motels that have smelled badly, I learned this trick through necessity)

Set of lingerie cases for woman's underwear and hosiery

Lightweight washable robe that fits into a small pouch—a wonderful present for a man

Shoe covers (keep them from soiling your clothes and also help keep them shiny)

Trip diary with a good pen attached

Tiny pocket dictionary of the language of the country (or countries) the traveler will visit

Travel guides to the countries the traveler will visit

Make-up kit or toilet kit for a woman or a man

Small emergency sewing kit for woman or man

Good laundry soap in packets and collapsible hangers for personal laundry chores

A plastic "pill organizer" for someone who has to carry a lot of medication with him

Lightweight nylon raincoat that folds into a small packet

Folding umbrella

Shoeshine packets

Bon Voyage Gifts for Ship Travelers The era of multitudinous delivery boys struggling past the rich and the famous on the gangways of the great ocean liners is long gone. In the "good old days" the delivery boys would be laden under jeroboams of champagne festooned with orchids; a roast suckling pig with an apple in his mouth, reclining on a silver platter, could be seen making his way to a stateroom in a cabin boy's arms; a messenger from a famous furrier might be scurrying to deliver a present for "Madame" from "a certain someone" to "keep her warm against the ocean breezes."

Nowadays the lavish bon voyage gifts are a thing of the past. One can still get a basket of fruit delivered, but the easiest thing to do for a friend is to have champagne delivered to his or her table on a specific night during the cruise. (You arrange this with the cruise line office ahead of time.) The bottle will be presented as a surprise with your card.

If you're going on board to wish someone happy cruising, you might give him or her some good books to read, particularly about the countries to be visited.

The most generous bon voyage present of all is to pay for the cocktail party given in the cabin before sailing. The passenger must provide his own liquor for this party, since the ship cannot sell alcohol in port, so it's very nice of a passenger's friend to say, "Let me provide the liquor for your bon voyage party."

Gifts for Special Interests

The Gourmet Cook   Don't forget that a lot of the gourmet cooks in this world are men, and they love to receive presents for their kitchen interests. Here are some suggested items:

An apron that's functional but unusually attractive, too
Large fish platter
Fish poacher
For a lobster lover, claw-shaped shellfish crackers and plates decorated with bright red lobsters
For a bread baker, new items to try, like loaf pans made of glass or terra cotta
Kitchen scale
Aluminum or iron or copper rack to attach to the wall, from which large kitchen utensils hang
Dishwasher-safe polyethylene cutting board and chopping knife
Portable timer (for sixty minutes or less) to clip on a belt or slip in your pocket, so you will be reminded of whatever needs attending to in the kitchen
Lemon stripper (to make strips and twists for cooking and for the bar)
Spice jar set—a shelf that sits on the counter or hangs from the wall
Good kitchen shears that will cut even small poultry bones
Collection of different kinds of pepper
Collection of different kinds of mustard
Collection of different kinds of pâté in tins

Set of mixing and measuring spoons (one always needs "an extra set")
The perfect pepper mill
Tea towels to dress up the kitchen, perhaps with matching hot pads
Fancy new copper or aluminum mold
Electrical gadgets that help get the work done and are fun for children's par-
    ticipation, too, such as:
      Frozen yoghurt maker; ice cream maker; peanut butter maker; pop-
      corn popper; hamburger and french fry fryers
Anything new on the market to make whisking easier, beating faster, and
    blending more efficient
Fancy butter cutter and egg slicer for those who like to "present" their food
    well

Any gourmet cook likes to have handsome new things in which to present
the food—earthenwear platters or glass bowls, whatever the material, if it's
good to look at, it will help the food taste good, too.

One of the nicest gifts I know of for a gourmet cook is to take her out to
an excellent restaurant meal!

Someone Who Is Good with a Needle
A new sewing basket
Stand-up tote bag to allow the efficient carrying of one's needlework, includ-
    ing canvases, wool, embroidery frame, knitting needles
Package of good needles in a pretty slipcase
Decorative thimble—perhaps in porcelain or silver
Stitchery scissors
Acrylic yarn keeper
The perfect pincushion
Pretty white linen towel in which to wrap one's handiwork to keep it clean

The Gardener My sources, gifted gardeners all, were adamant on the
subject of books on gardening and flower arranging. They love to receive
books, but they maintain there are as many bad as good books on the
market, and that one should ask the gardener what new book he or she
would like to have.

Most gardeners have many of the following items, but since many tend to
wear out from use, fresh replacements are always very welcome:

An attractive watering can
Kneeling pads
Gardener's apron, with pockets for tools
Gardener's gloves
Baskets for transporting flowers, vegetables, fruits, and weeds (with handles,
    of course!)
Cachepots for indoor gardeners

The Cigar Smoker
A box of *good* cigars—or even four good cigars
An efficient, handsome humidor
A cigar cutter (to put in his pocket)
A cigar case for his pocket (perhaps of crush-proof leather, to enable him to
    carry three cigars)

The Pipe Smoker
A new pipe (talk to the tobacconist first)
Some fine pipe tobacco
A handsome tobacco carrying case (make him one in needlepoint)
A special lighter for pipes
And, for someone with a sense of humor, a Sherlock Holmes hat!

The Lover of Wine
Several bottles of a very good wine
Wine rack (a real enthusiast can always use more of these)
Sterling wine pourer (to keep the wine from dripping on the table)
Wine basket (to place on the table)
Pair of wine bottle coasters (to place on the table, one for white and one for
    red)
The latest cork remover (a wine connoisseur is always eager to find the
    perfect cork remover)
Half-dozen beautiful new wineglasses
The latest well-reviewed wine book

The Collector   When you make an addition to someone's collection, you
are giving the nicest present of all to that person, for you have shown foresight and thoughtfulness and obviously had to research your present. If you
have a good friend or a favorite relative who collects one particular thing, if
you see something that would make a nice addition to his or her collection
you should buy it and put it away until Christmas or the upcoming birthday.

When you wander through a flea market here or abroad, when you rum-
mage through an antique shop or attend a tag day sale, you may see something that would really please a friend. That is the time to buy it. Save it for
the right occasion, and give it. It's a gift of the heart.

And don't forget that collectors like tools to help them display their objects, too—such as easels made of wood or metal, or any kind of display
rack that is suitable.

The Sportsperson   Gifts pertaining to sports are always popular with
sport-loving individuals and families—whether the occasion is Christmas, a
birthday, Easter, graduation, or a weekend visit. If you are making a present
to a family and you know part of its regular sports equipment is old or mal-
functioning, to replace that particular item is especially nice: such as a
volleyball net or shuffleboard discs and cues, or the ping-pong table top or
the net and rackets.

A book on the subject of a person's favorite sport is always a good gift. So is a gift certificate to a sporting goods store or a sports catalogue. For the *golfer,* a dozen balls are always welcome, as is a new set of club covers. Other ideas: an electric practice putting cup to use in the living room or office, a ball retriever (to fish the ball out of the water); a golf utility brush; a golf umbrella; or even the epitome of luxury—an electric golf ball warmer.

For the *hiker* and *camper,* there is always some new gadget to make life easier in the woods or on the road, including a compact first-aid kit in a waterproof container, a new backpack, a foam pad to go inside the sleeping bag, a camper's cooking kit, a new flashlight, knife, or camping lantern. A logbook for recording catches and game bagged is a good present for a *hunter* or *fisherman.* For the hunter, a good cartridge-carrying bag for his ammunition, an efficient rain hat, a sitting stick that converts to an umbrella (that's for me!), or a lightweight chair that one carries by the top (foldable, of course, and again for people like me). For every person who takes the wilds as they are, without creature comforts, there's someone who goes along, and enjoys it, but likes to have as many creature comforts as possible.

For the *tennis player:* the latest tennis hat, cans of balls, a tennis towel, a towel-holder that is attached to one's belt, an amusing racket cover, a tennis tote, and, for the lucky owner of his own court, an extra "tennis ball picker-upper." (Of course, the best present of all for a tennis court owner is to do some work on his court.)

For the *young swimmer,* a gift of goggles or fins or a mask and snorkel set makes a hit. For people with their own pool a new kind of inflatable mattress or floating lounge chair is welcome. For a *scuba diver,* one can buy a good depth gauge, or a knife to attach to the belt, or a compass, but since this is such a specialized sport, a gift certificate to an established scuba diving equipment store is probably best.

Don't forget binoculars for any family who loves the out of doors, whether they are near the sea and race sailboats or go on early morning bird walks; or whether they cheer from the upper tiers of the football stadium or sit in duck blinds by the hour.

For someone on a *physical fitness kick,* a good exercise mat or slant board to use at home is welcome. If you know the size of the recipient, nothing will inspire him or her more to get out there and "go to it" than a new jogging or warmup suit.

If you feel your friends are past the age of violent exercise, when a basketball and basketball net would be extremely inappropriate, if they have access to a good, flat lawn, get them a croquet set. It's a good game and one gets exercise, too!

Part Nine

THE ETIQUETTE OF TRAVEL

Basic Travel: Public Transportation   799

Travel by Motor Vehicle   814

Planning Your Vacation Trip   822

Taking a Cruise   834

New transportation methods and economical tours have put travel within the reach and budget of many more people today, but the biggest change of all is that women are no longer hesitant to travel alone. More and more women are getting themselves to every kind of place—either in a charter group, with another woman friend, or by themselves.

The great crowds of travelers on planes, trains, and buses, particularly in the summer months, can make the "getting there" arduous and exhausting. Self-restraint and a sense of humor are often necessary: things go wrong; reservations are fouled up; accommodations are disappointing. The wise traveler in such situations controls his temper and restrains his language; and instead of using his energy to complain vociferously, he uses it to extricate himself from the situation. The frequent traveler becomes the wily one. He knows where and how to complain, and when to change reservations or revise plans completely. In other words, he doesn't let the inevitable frustrations undo the therapeutic rest of a vacation.

The following section does not deal with travel abroad per se, because, in order to do so properly, one would have to include a detailed section on the customs and ceremonies, country by country. This is not a travel book, and a traveler to a foreign country should consult a good guide book and devour the brochures available at the country's tourist information center or travel agencies before leaving.

Whether one travels in the United States or anywhere in the world, the mainstay of a successful traveler is always consideration of others. If one keeps this in mind and goes with an open attitude and a taste for new adventures, travel, wherever it may take you, will always be a truly exhilarating experience.

Chapter 64

BASIC TRAVEL:
PUBLIC TRANSPORTATION

By Airplane

There are many different air fares available today, and so many types of aircraft, you should check carefully with an experienced travel agent or airline to find out which one is most advantageous for your trip. Sometimes you will hear different information from each agent to whom you speak, because it is so difficult for the travel industry itself to keep up with all its special rates.

Points to Consider when Booking Your Flight

Differences Between Classes on Airplanes There are definite distinctions between first-class and economy-class travel (even more marked on overseas travel). Unfortunately, there is also a large difference in price. Among the advantages of first-class travel: the configuration of the first-class section allows for only two seats on each side of the aisle (instead of three), and thus a wider seat and considerably more leg room. The meals are much more elaborate in first class; free champagne, wine, and cocktails are served; when a movie is shown, there is no charge for it, as there is in economy. There are more flight attendants in first class per passenger, and there is a larger baggage allowance overseas. On night flights many airlines give first-class passengers complimentary slippers and eyeshades, if the trip is a long one. If you travel first-class overseas, you may also ask for an airlines flight bag (a shoulder-strap tote, advertising the line) free of charge. There are closets for coats and clothes bags in first class.

Speaking of clothes bags, you are not supposed to bring larger than a "three suiter" aboard. The closets do not have room for both coats and the huge broad clothes bags that look as though they contain an entire wardrobe. Such a bag jams the closet and should be checked rather than brought into the cabin.

Many companies that used to send employees first-class now have a general rule that everyone, the chief executive officer included, should travel economy-class on business trips. However, many of these same companies also permit employees traveling great distances, such as coast to coast, to go first-class.

There is no question but that the long-legged passenger is penalized in economy class with its crowded seating arrangements. The savvy economy passenger who happens to be tall learns to ask for a seat on the aisle, not the window, and learns the configurations of seating in the different types of aircraft, so he can request one of the few seats that have more leg room—sometimes the bulkhead seats, sometimes the emergency exit rows.

Questions to Ask Since the rules and regulations change continually, and airlines offer various services, it is always best to ask the following questions of your travel agent or airline agent when booking your reservations:

1. Will you have to reconfirm your return flight, and how far in advance? (On overseas travel, you must reconfirm every reservation, as soon as you arrive in any one city.)
2. If you are obtaining a special rate for early payment, when must payment be made, and by what means?
3. Find out if a meal will be served on board, because otherwise you may be left very hungry with a small packet of peanuts as the only food served. On certain lower-cost flights you may buy a simple meal or bring it.
4. If you are traveling with a baby, notify the airline in advance. An infant under two travels free but has no seat, so the airline will try to seat the adult in the bulkhead, with no one next to her, so the baby can be stretched out safely in a bassinet or in an infant seat, which some airlines provide.
5. If you plan to travel with your dog or cat, make your reservation in advance. You will pay a flat fee for its transportation. Small animals may be brought on board in small carrying cases that fit under the seat, like a suitcase. (Some airlines provide cardboard carriers free; some charge a few dollars for a plastic container that is reusable.) Only one or at the most two pets are allowed in the cabin on any one flight, usually one in economy and one in first class. Some airlines will allow no pets in the cabin, so it is best to check beforehand. Large dogs travel in the pressurized, temperature-controlled cargo sections. For dog transportation, some airlines provide three different sizes of "kennels" that you buy and keep. Because of security precautions, the days of checking on one's pet in the cargo during stops of the plane en route are over. The baggage handlers usually will see to it that your dog has water on a long flight. As for taking a dog overseas, the complications of long flights, quarantines, and so on, are so numerous that you should never put a dog through the experience unless you are moving overseas. Whether to tranquilize a pet before he makes the trip, is a decision that should be between you and your veterinarian.

6. If you need a "special meal," inform your agent when you book your flight; you will be served that meal automatically when the rest of the meals are served. The flight attendant may call out on the public address system, "Will the passenger who ordered the special meal please identify himself?" Special meals offered include: bland, diabetic, low-cholesterol, low-sodium, low-calorie/low-cholesterol, vegetarian, and Kosher.
7. If you need a wheel chair, order it when you make a reservation and the skycap should have it ready for you as you arrive at the airport.

No-shows, Overbooking, Stand-bys It is inconsiderate and unfair, both to the airline and to fellow travelers, not to cancel plane reservations you will not be able to use. Some secretaries will make several reservations for their boss for the various times he might wish to depart. Unless she cancels the ones he does not use, the secretary may deprive someone else of space on that flight. Those who do not cancel and don't appear at flight time are called no-shows. When there are epidemics of this malady, the airlines retaliate by overbooking their flights, which means passengers will show up with definite reservations (perhaps booked weeks in advance), and there will be no seats available for them. If you are "bumped" off a flight in this manner, and the airline cannot find you good alternate transportation within two hours, you are entitled to as much as $200 as a refund, depending on the value of your ticket. If you are bumped, you have every right to be angry and full of emotion, but try to control it. The poor passenger agents at the airport gate are blamed, but they have nothing whatsoever to do with these overbookings.

If the airline says, "The flight is full, sorry," you still have a good chance of obtaining a seat by reporting to the gate to "stand by" for the flight. You should arrive well in advance, at least an hour. Give your name to the agent as a stand-by, and when the plane is boarded, the stand-bys will get any seats left vacant by no-shows. The real inconvenience for stand-bys is not being able to check their baggage curbside. They must carry it to the gate.

Checking In for Your Flight On international flights, you should check in one hour before departure time; on domestic flights, you are supposed to check in one half hour before, although at large airports it is usually wise to give yourself more time. (The early birds get the choice seats.) In most cities (all the larger ones) you can check your bags curbside on domestic flights. The skycap will put tags on your bags marked for the airport destination, and give you the other half as your claim check. You should pay him a minimum of thirty-five cents per bag for this service (many give fifty cents per bag). If you wish to avoid tipping, carry your bags in to the airline counter inside the terminal, and check them there. Forget about being able to push your baggage to the gate yourself in one of those handy baggage carts. They are harder to find than winning lottery tickets. The best piece of advice anyone can give any traveler is: travel light. Take only baggage you can carry yourself, and if you can, take only a carry-on piece.

If you check in for your flight at the counter inside the airport, the agent will examine your ticket and check your baggage (giving you a receipt for each piece). This is the time to take out baggage insurance, if you are carrying valuables with you. If your bag is lost, the airlines will reimburse you only up to $500 as of this writing.

You are allowed three bags on domestic flights. You may carry one of these on board, provided it fits beneath your seat or the seat ahead of you (this is a strict government regulation). You may carry your briefcase on board, but this, too, has to be stored beneath a seat for take-off and landing of the aircraft. On the jumbo jets the closed overhead racks are fine receptacles for coats, hats, umbrellas, small packages, briefcases, and totes. According to government regulations, the first bag you check may not be more than 62" over-all (total of length, height, and depth), the second not more than 55" over-all, and the one you can carry on may not be over 45" over-all. The only weight restriction is that any one piece may not weigh more than seventy pounds. If you take more than three pieces, you are charged a flat fee per piece.

Security In order to protect passengers from hijackers and bombs, the government enforces strict security requirements. Each passenger must walk through a screening device like a gate. Also, separately, all carry-on bags, totes, briefcases, handbags, and shopping bags must be inspected by security agents or passed through an X-ray device called an ASE X-ray machine. (In certain foreign countries each passenger has to be frisked or body-searched in a small curtained booth by a security official of the same sex.) In busy airports, one often has to stand in a queue at the security checkpoints, another sometimes exasperating delay, so allow extra time for this. When you walk through the gate-like device, if there is something on your person that sets off the buzzing device, security personnel go over your person with their magnetometer instrument to try to find the metal source that sets off the buzz. Sometimes a woman's heavy metal jewelry or a man's belt buckle or the change in his pocket will set off the alarm. Camera film will not be affected by the ASE X-ray machine. Everyone should show consideration toward the security officials instead of the antagonism and sarcasm that one often witnesses at the checkpoint. They are, after all, doing their job, and the ultimate goal of their job is to protect us.

Seat Assignment At the gate you will be assigned a seat, if reservations are permitted on the flight. (On shuttle flights and short hauls, seats are not reserved.) You will be asked "Smoking or nonsmoking section?" This is the time you should also stipulate whether you wish a window or an aisle seat. If you arrive late and are an economy-class passenger on a full flight, your chances of getting one of the middle seats—the least desirable—are very good. This is your guarantee of an uncomfortable journey, as you will be wedged into a narrow seat with your fellow passengers' elbows and shoulders constantly reminding you that you are the piece of cheese in the sandwich.

Unless you are a small person, sitting in the middle seat in the economy section of a plane is only barely tolerable.

In Flight When the plane begins to taxi down the runway for its take-off, a flight attendant will give you instructions over the public address system on what to do in case of emergency. He or she will explain where the emergency exits are and how the oxygen mask system works; if you are going to fly over the sea, the inflatable life jacket is demonstrated.

If you are in a smoking section, you may begin smoking when the plane has reached its flying level, and when the "no smoking" and "fasten seat belts" signs are turned off. The captain of the aircraft will soon identify himself and the crew over the loudspeaker and may comment on your position as the trip proceeds.

You should bring your own reading material. There are only so many magazines available for passengers, never enough. Flight attendants wish the passengers would stop keeping the magazines, too, which are there supposedly for everyone. Also, it is extremely rude of a passenger, as often happens, to ask for some special magazine and then berate the flight attendant for not having it on board. (Passengers who tear pages out of the plane's magazines are also on everyone's "irritants list.")

Your Seat Mate It is unfortunate that airline personnel don't ask one more question of the passenger before assigning a seat: are you a talker or a nontalker? The constant chatterer is nothing short of an affliction to someone who is tired, who wants to be left alone, or who has a great deal of work to finish. One is a captive audience to the chatterer, and as someone who often has to work through every minute of airtime, I have had my share of suffering on this point. It may be that your seat mate is talking nonstop because of nerves—a genuine fear of flying. In this case one should show compassion and help the person get through what is a real and frightening experience. You should inquire of your talkative seat mate, if you can interrupt the person long enough to insert a question into the conversation, "Do you fly often?" Then it should all come out—the fear, that is, if it is indeed fear causing all the nervous conversation. If it develops that your seat mate flies often, then you may easily say, "You know, you are a very interesting person. I wish I had more time to chat with you, but I am working on something here that has to be finished by the time we land. Please excuse me if I concentrate on *this*."

When the meal is served, it is rude not to say anything to your seat mate. One should make a stab at a polite sentence or two. It doesn't take too much effort to say, "Dinner looks good tonight, doesn't it?" If your seat mate does not pick up the conversational ball, then it means he is more antisocial than you are. You can eat in peace and then turn to your briefcase, magazine, speech, needlepoint, crossword puzzle, or transcendental meditation with a clear conscience the minute the tray is removed. I usually enjoy the short conversations during a meal with my seat mate. In one month of flying I managed to sit next to a woman dog-breeder, a juvenile court judge, a TV games star, a Buddhist monk, and a night-club female inpersonator.

Food and Drink One is served free drinks in first class, and unfortunately there are no real restrictions on how many a passenger obtains. If he becomes unruly, of course, the flight attendant will not serve him any more; if he becomes obstreperous, the flight attendant will call a member of the crew from the cockpit for assistance. In economy class, you will be served free soft drinks, but you must pay for beer and hard liquor. Try to give the exact price of the drink to the flight attendant. She has a difficult enough time as it is trying to serve everyone on short trips without having to cope with changing large bills. Naturally, you do not say to the flight attendant, "Keep the change." They are not to be tipped under any circumstances. If you are going to want two drinks eventually, order and pay for both at the beginning to save the attendant extra time and trouble. On crowded economy-class flights, the attendants simply do not have the time to make repeated trips to satisfy the needs of any one passenger.

Remember your flight attendants are not waiters and waitresses. Their primary purpose is your safety, and then your comfort. They are skilled, trained people. When one sees a passenger flicking his fingers at one of them, as though he were in a restaurant arrogantly demanding service, one feels only embarrassment for the flight attendant and pity for the crude, ignorant passenger.

Smoking on Board Even when you are sitting far away from a passenger who lights up his cigar or pipe in the plane, you will know it. The air is quickly polluted in the small space of an aircraft. No one on American aircraft is allowed to smoke a pipe or cigar in the smoking section, because the heavy smoke immediately engulfs everyone. But on foreign lines the problem still exists. If you are the one complaining about the smoker, you should not try to handle it yourself. Tell the flight attendant quietly; he or she will ask the passenger to put out the smoking material. If the passenger refuses, the attendant will go to the crew in the cockpit for assistance in handling the passenger.

Landing Formalities When the plane begins its approach to the airport for landing, the captain and the flight attendants will announce that seat belts must be fastened, smoking materials put out, and trays and reclining seats put back in position. Some people try to get up from their seats almost immediately after the plane has hit the runway to collect things from the overhead racks and to don coats. One should not take lightly the captain's warning to "please remain in your seats until the plane has come to a complete stop." Sometimes a plane has to pause on the runway several times before the captain can turn off the engines. The plane lurches, stops suddenly, and makes sharp turns. This is why passengers must remain seated. Every

year some passengers are slightly injured because of disobeying this steadfast
rule.

Traveling with Children Babies and children can be a first-class problem
if the parents do not plan their trip properly. If a mother is carrying her infant, she must inform the airline well ahead, as I mentioned before, and
request an infant seat or bassinet. She should bring her own baby food, for
the airlines do not have it, but the flight attendants will heat the baby's
formula whenever asked to. If the mother is carrying tins of food requiring
a can opener, she must bring it herself, as the airlines do not carry can
openers. Most airlines provide disposable diapers. The mother should change
her baby's diaper in the lavatory, not in her seat. She should stow the soiled
paper diaper in one of the airtight "airsickness bags" she will find stashed
away in the seat pockets on the plane; this bag should then be thrown into
the paper towel disposal chute in the lavatory. Flight attendants report that
it is not uncommon for mothers to throw diapers beneath their airplane
seats—a terrible display of a lack of manners, thoughtfulness, and human
decency.

Mothers should bring extra food for their children up to the age of ten.
The young ones are inevitably excited, often eat very little on the tray of food
served to them, and then, an hour later, are ravenous again. There is no
food available on board to cope with those sudden hunger pangs, so parents
should bring along some sandwiches, cookies, or crackers for these mini-
crises.

Children of any age should not be allowed by their parents to wander up
and down the aisle. One often sees the proud parent beaming as a two- or
three-year-old goes "exploring," talking to all the passengers, being petted,
cooed at, and given favors by people on the aisle. Such children are creating
a hazard. They are interfering with the work of the flight attendants, and
they might be responsible for other passengers, if not themselves, being injured. If a child is told well before the trip that he is to stay in his seat with
the seat belt fastened through the entire time, except to go to the lavatory,
he will accept it better than if one surprises him during the flight with the
news that he must remain immobile. The secret to keeping the child from
crying or becoming unhappy on the trip is to bring along sufficient toys and
games to keep him occupied—perhaps a nice combination of some of his old
favorites with some exciting new little things. Stuff them in your carry-on
bag; you will be glad you did. The airlines have a few games and comic
books for children, but they are not really set up to run a nursery school on
board.

Clothes to Wear The main thing to remember for long air flights is to
dress comfortably, in something old that washes or dry-cleans easily. Spilled
food on trays, air sickness, or any number of things can ruin your clothes.
Sitting for long hours in a small seat will put nasty wrinkles in anything. If

you have a tendency to a swelling in ankles and legs in flight, don't wear anything tight, either. On overnight flights, bring a toilet kit in your carry-on bag, so you can refresh yourself and even brush your teeth before landing in the morning. Bring a pair of bedroom slippers or slipper socks to change into, also, if you know the airline will not provide you with slippers. You will be given pillows and a blanket, but you should have a sweater available, in case the cabin becomes chilly. I always put a scarf around my neck to ward off air vent drafts.

Portable radios must not be played in flight, because they can interfere with the cockpit's communications system. (One has to be grateful for some of these restrictions.) Bring your own stationery, writing pens, and playing cards. Gone are the days of there being a plentiful supply of these items. They are expensive, and people tend to steal the cards rather than leave them for the next passenger. Evidently theft is so prevalent people don't think they're doing something wrong when they take blankets, as well as the china, flatware, and stemware. It is not souvenir-collecting, however; it is *stealing*.

The Golden Rule Travel by air probably puts people closer in contact with each other for a longer period of time than almost any other activity. It is important to remember others, to be considerate, because everyone is in a group from which there is no escape. The first thing to remember is, of course, to leave the lavatory clean behind you. Attendants say this seems to be the main fault of the air traveler. He selfishly thinks, "Oh, someone will clean up after me." It's not the flight attendant's job, and it certainly isn't the next passenger's responsibility, either.

People who bring on board too many carry-on items are very rude to their seat mates. Every item that can be checked should be checked. When someone sits down surrounded by several items—totes, camera cases, shopping bags—he uses all of the room around him. The other occupants of the row hardly have room for their feet.

The person on the aisle should get out into the aisle to give free passage to the person sitting by the window or in the middle seat who wants to go to the rear of the plane. It is very difficult to jump across someone's body in order to reach the aisle when there is no room between the obstructing body and the seat in front of it.

People who recline their seats in economy class are very inconsiderate. These seats are so close together that they are not really meant to go back if there is someone behind. The knees of that person are probably close against your seat, and when you recline the seat, the eating or working tray of the person behind is suddenly jammed into his stomach by your action. Unless you have a small child sitting behind you, it is kind and thoughtful *not* to recline your seat.

It is the little things that can make air travel more pleasant for everyone. If a short passenger near you in the aisle has trouble reaching up to the overhead racks, why not accomplish the task for him? . . . Don't let your child disturb your seat mates. . . . Don't borrow someone's paper or magazine and not return it. . . . If you're a woman, don't hold up the line waiting to get into the lavatory while you put on a whole new make-up job. (Do it in the middle of the trip, when fewer people are trying to use the lavatories, or, better yet, do it on land.) . . . If you sit next to someone from another country who has a language problem, and he is going to have to change planes at the next stop, patiently explain to him what he will have to do and make sure he is helped at the gate. . . . Thank the flight attendants and smile at them when you depart. If you see the captain or co-captain as you disembark, compliment them on the trip and the great landing. They will really appreciate such a rare occurrence in their lives—a compliment from a passenger.

If, upon landing, you find your baggage missing, report it at once to the airline baggage office personnel. They will give you a form to fill out, describing the bag and its contents. If the missing bag arrives on a subsequent flight, they will have it delivered to you.

And if you are bumped from your flight the next time around, write five letters of complaint to the management of the airline, instead of just one. As a beautifully mannered passenger you deserve to be better taken care of!

By Train

Today's passenger on long train trips is a special breed. The experience can be an utter delight, or a saga of frustration. Until the end of World War II, intercity land travel in this country usually meant rail travel. Even during the war, 97 per cent of all troop movement was by train. Then came the freeway, motels, and the jet age. The result is that today a traveler, contemplating a long-distance rail journey, often is doing so for the first time—or else trying to evoke old memories.

Train travel is the most "social" form over land. It's easy to meet people and strike up conversations. If you savor the scenery part of the trip and like to sit at a window, watching the different landscapes and towns roll by, you will probably enjoy the long ride and hate to see it end. Automobile and air travel have their own advantages, but the train offers something different, and it is very special. Also, a train may run late through snow and rainstorms, but at least it runs. Trains are very rarely canceled.

Planning Your Trip   Amtrak (the National Railroad Passenger Corporation, the public-private corporation that runs the intercity passenger trains) has changed many things in train travel. Since it is virtually all one system now, you deal with one company instead of many; you can read one timetable, obtain information, and purchase tickets anywhere in the country by calling one toll-free number, listed in your local telephone book. Tickets may be purchased by check or credit card and will be mailed to you, if there is sufficient time. Tickets may be picked up at the station, or, in some large cities, at downtown ticket offices. Travel agents handling rail transportation usually say so in their advertisements, or in their windows. A knowledgeable travel agent can give you advice about routes and services, arrange stopover accommodations, and generally take the worry out of your planning.

Even if you are depending on someone else for advice and reservations, get a copy of the latest national timetable that Amtrak publishes. It is revised at least twice a year and is jammed with information on schedules, cities served, services offered, special discount prices, and much good advice on how to travel easily and comfortably by train.

Travel by Coach or Parlor Car   No matter in what part of the world you travel, there are two kinds of train accommodations: coach and first class, or their equivalents. In this country, first class usually means sleeping car space if you are traveling long distances or overnight.

The difference between the two classes is significant. Coach travel is intended to move large numbers of people inexpensively. Most coach passage, especially for short distances, is unreserved. This means that your ticket, which is not dated, is good for transportation—but does not guarantee you a seat. That's one reason why it is less expensive. Not having a reservation usually doesn't matter, but if you travel by unreserved coach on weekends and during the holidays, prepare for crowded trains and perhaps even standing for a stop or two. The railroad adds more cars at these times, but sometimes the number of riders simply exceeds the capacity. Guaranteed seating in the coach sections of most trains may be obtained by paying an additional fare and traveling first class.

In the first-class or club car section of regular daytime trains, there is more room to stretch out; also, personal service from an attendant assigned only to that car is available. Food and beverages are served at your seat, which is great if you wish to read or work quietly and are not interested in socializing in the diner or club car.

The coaches are informal, but there are some rules. One of the most important concerns smoking. Interstate Commerce Commission regulations require separate smoking and nonsmoking areas. In trains of more than one car there are designated smoking and nonsmoking cars. Smoking is usually permitted in lounge or snack cars (which is why some passengers avoid them), but it is not permitted in the food service area of dining cars. First-class parlor cars are usually divided, with nonsmokers at the front of the car and smokers to the rear. Smoking areas should be clearly designated. If they aren't, ask the conductor. Smoking is always permitted in private first-class compartments.

Everyone would prefer having a double seat to himself, but when coaches are crowded and people may have to stand or tramp through several cars, lugging baggage while they look for seats, it is selfish and wrong to leave packages or papers or a briefcase on the seat adjacent to you as though it were occupied by someone temporarily away from his seat. If conditions are crowded, the conductor will ask you to remove your belongings from the seat next to you; it is much better when you do it without being "required" to. If there is plenty of room in the car, you may curl up in two seats to take a nap. Remember to remove your shoes if you do. And if there is plenty of room and you are unhappy with your seat mate, you can always move, muttering some sort of apology or excuse, such as "I'm in a draft in this seat."

Don't play your radio on the train, unless you use earplugs. It is bound to upset passengers around, even if they're fans of baseball, or rock, or whatever it is you are listening to.

Children love trains for many reasons, and they have a certain mobility on trains, but don't let them become aisle-running pests, or bother passengers in their wanderings.

Don't take your dog on the train. He will be very uncomfortable in a crate in the unheated, uncooled baggage car. Travel with sensible amounts of luggage. If you have a trunk or oversized suitcase or packages, check them in the baggage car, and just take one or two small pieces of hand luggage into the coach. Don't block the space in front of your seat mate with your totes or briefcase, either.

Pick up your own litter. Just because the car attendant will eventually pick up your trash is no reason to drop every candy bar wrapper or sandwich bag underfoot. Watch your cigarettes and soda cans or bottles. If you or your children leave cracker or cookie crumbs all over your seat, remove them before you leave the train. Think of the next person who must sit in the mess you have made.

Eating on the Train   There are several kinds of dining or food service cars on trains today. On most short-distance daytime trains (and we are of course not talking about commuter trains) the diner has been replaced by a limited-menu, self-service food counter where food is purchased and consumed at the passenger's seat. You would tip here if you generally tip at coffee shop lunch counters (which I do). Drop-down trays fold out of the back of each seat, much like those on an airplane, and can be used for eating, working, or playing games.

The dining cars of fabled trains like the Southwest Limited, the San Francisco Zephyr, and the New York–Miami Silver Meteor still exist, with white cloths, fine porcelain, silverware, and fresh flowers on each table, but they mark an era that seems to be quickly passing us by. If you are in one of these long-distance overnight train dining cars, you will find it under the supervision of a steward or a headwaiter. He will seat you or ask you to wait in an adjoining lounge car, if the diner is full. He will provide you with a check and a pencil with which you are to write your order. Dining car waiters traditionally do not accept verbal orders, although spoken amendments usually may be made after the initial order has been taken. Major credit cards are accepted in dining cars.

You do not have to tip the steward, unless he goes to great pains to seat your large family together or does something special for you. You tip the waiter or waitress as you would in a restaurant—15 per cent of the bill if the service was good, and more if you felt it was outstanding.

The Sleeping Car   Your first trip overnight in a railroad sleeping car is a unique experience. There are the sounds of the train's signal and the clicking of the wheels over the tracks in the night; there is the gentle (and sometimes not so gentle) lurching of the train on the curve of the tracks. Amtrak put in service in 1978 the first of their new double-decker sleeping cars, but for a while yet we will still be using the old sleeping cars—the ones built by the private railroads in the 1940s through the early sixties. The fact that they are still in service is a tribute to their original design and construction, and to the money Amtrak invested in their refurbishment.

In the sleeping cars of the first-class section of the long-distance train, there are a few traditions that still deserve to be honored. The first is the relationship between the sleeping car attendant (the Pullman Company used to call them porters) and his passenger. If you are fortunate enough to be in a car administered by one of the great veteran sleeping car attendants, or one of the eager young ones, you will probably receive very special attention. The attendant will meet you on the platform at the entrance to your car. He will help you with your luggage and show you to your accommodation. He should volunteer to explain the workings of the switches, buttons, and levers that produce your wash basin, toilet, or bed.

If you are in a bedroom or double-bedroom suite, your problems are fairly simple when bedtime comes. You simply tell the attendant what time you wish to retire, and he will fold out your bed from the chair seat, and will pull down the upper berth from the wall, if there are two of you. He will set up a ladder and webbing safety harness for the upper berth. In the bedrooms and bedroom suites, the lavatory, including sink, mirror, and toilet are in a separate telephone-booth-size cubicle inside your compartment, called the annex.

The single traveler in a roomette is on his own, although the attendant will come at a pressing of the call button, to assist or to answer questions. The first thing to notice is that each roomette is closed by both a sliding door and a full-length zippered curtain of heavy material. Both have a purpose. During the daytime, the bed in a roomette folds up into one wall. However, when the bed is pulled down for sleeping purposes, even the toilet is covered and inaccessible. If you need to use it, the bed can be raised or lowered easily by the passenger himself. In order to have enough space to lower the bed, however, or to get in or out of it, one needs to leave the roomette door open and position oneself slightly out into the corridor. The curtain ensures that this may be done with privacy, except that anyone coming down the corridor might catch a fleeting glimpse of a pair of feet and ankles, plus a backside bulge of the curtain!

Normally, the sleeping car attendant is responsible only for the passengers within a single car; therefore he is able to pamper you. He will make up your bed when you are ready to sleep, wake you in the morning at the time you specify, direct you to the diner, and advise you as to the best times to eat. On some trains, if you request it, the attendant will bring you complimentary orange juice and coffee in the morning.

In every sleeping car compartment there is a small metal door in the outside wall. This is your access to the shoe locker. Another door in the locker opens to the corridor, and if you put your shoes in the locker overnight, the attendant is supposed to shine them. This is one of the unknown factors: will he or won't he? Don't ever put your money or valuables in this shoe locker, however, for petty thieves can easily steal it.

The sleeping car attendant, male or female, wears a uniform with a name plate. It is nice if you learn his name and call him by it. You should always tip him as you get off the train at the end of your journey. The minimum tip is one dollar, but most people give more.

In the Station   Stations in the larger cities are often confusing. Train platforms may be a long distance from the taxi stand, and sometimes it's difficult to find the right track and even the right car on your train. The tracks are posted only a short time before departure, but it is still best to get there twenty to thirty minutes before departure; allow much more lead time if you have to pick up reserved seats or buy your ticket at the station. If you have arrived by car or taxi with baggage, a redcap (baggage porter) will help you at the curb to reach the right car. In Amtrak stations, redcap service is free; it is part of your fare. However, many people tip $.35 to $.50 per bag.

Summary of Train Tipping
Redcap: Not necessary, but some people do anyway ($.35 to $.50 per bag;
Sleeping car attendant: $1 per person per night, but usually more
Dining car steward: Not necessary, except for special service
Dining car waiter: Usually 15 per cent of the total bill or more
Coach car attendant: Not necessary
Parlor or club car attendant: Usually $1 plus 15 per cent of the food or beverage bill
Conductor, brakeman, or other operating crew: Never

By Bus

If your experience with buses has been limited to crowded city vehicles, there is a treat in store for you on many of the cross-country bus systems in the United States or in Europe. For today long-distance buses are usually quite comfortable, with air conditioning and large windows through which to watch the world go by as you sit relaxed. It's a good idea to bring along a good pair of sunglasses, however. Your reclining seat allows you to nap or sleep through the night, but you might be wise to bring earplugs and an eye shade if you are really serious about that sleep! Bus travel is the least expensive mode of transport, and sometimes it is the only way to get to your destination, aside from driving yourself.

There are toilet facilities in the rear of the bus, but most passengers prefer to wait until the bus makes one of its regular rest stops. Meal stops last about thirty minutes, but you can always bring your own box meals or snacks. Travel-wise passengers use every rest stop or meal stop to get a little exercise and get their blood circulating. They also wear non-wrinkling, loose, comfortable clothing and don a pair of soft slippers for all those hours of bus sitting.

Students are avid bus users; business people generally are not. The former keep themselves updated on the various bus passes of different lengths, which enable them to travel anywhere in the United States on that bus line and many connecting lines during the specified time of the pass.

One is allotted 150 pounds of baggage on the intercity lines, and no more than three pieces of luggage or boxes. However, these rules change frequently, so passengers should call the bus line before departure to double-check. The overhead rack on the buses do not hold large, heavy bags or packages.

The driver or the supervisor has the final say on whether a passenger has had too much to drink to be allowed to board the bus. Children under the age of twelve must be accompanied by an adult, although this rule is sometimes waived if the child is mature and experienced enough to travel by himself. It is always possible to ask for special attention for any elderly person traveling alone, too. Pets may not be carried on a bus, with the exception of a guide dog for the visually handicapped.

If you want social life, you should sit in the back of the bus, because that's where the rest room and the smoking section are, and people tend to sit in the back and chat. If it's a smooth ride you care about, sit in the middle of the bus.

If you wish to sleep, read, or just not talk, and you sit next to a chatter-box, answer politely in monosyllables. If that does not deter the person, come right out with your desire to be left in peace. It's the tone of voice that counts. "I'm really sorry, but I have to finish this work," or "I'm sorry, but I'm awfully tired and would just like to close my eyes." If the person remains a pest, change your seat, or speak to the driver at the next stop, if there are no empty seats.

Some people play their transistor radios, which is extremely rude. They should play them using their earplugs, so that the other passengers are not a forced audience. If you are an avid picture-taker on a sight-seeing trip, don't hold your camera right against the window from inside the bus. The vibration of the bus, of which you may be totally unaware will blur the shot for certain.

When traveling with small children, keep them in their seats and provide them with lots of games, books, and amusements. If they become car-sick easily, give them medication in advance of departure; be sure to carry some plastic bags with which to handle the emergency. The bags are also useful for gathering all of your snack or reading material litter, for disposal at a rest stop.

Chapter 65

TRAVEL BY MOTOR VEHICLE

Taking Taxis

When you hail a taxi that carries a meter, be sure the driver pushes the flag up to start the meter again. Otherwise, the previous passenger's fare will be added to yours. The minute the cab pulls to a stop the meter should be stopped by the driver's pushing the flag down. The driver is not supposed to let the meter run while he makes change. It is against the law for a metered taxi to proceed while carrying a passenger without the meter running, unless it charges according to zone, as in our nation's capital, or unless the taxi has been engaged for a trip out of town at a flat rate. In some cities, there is a charge for each extra passenger. (Rates are always posted in a taxi.)

Protection When you enter a cab, look immediately at his or her posted license to be sure the driver's face corresponds with that in the picture on the license. If you entrust a woman or child to a taxi, make a notation of the driver's license and that of the car. For safety's sake, in the case of a child or sick person, have someone telephone you on his arrival. All taxi drivers must be licensed and fingerprinted. To ride in a cab not driven by its proper driver as indicated on the posted license is to risk accident, robbery, attack, or worse.

You and the Taxi Driver Many people behave in cabs as if the drivers were wooden Indians. It is quite possible for drivers to hear all conversation in the back of the cab and many cabs have strategically placed rearview mirrors that permit the driver a full view of the back of the cab. A taxi, therefore, is as public as the library, about as private as the back seat of a bus.

Taximen are a philosophical, often cynical crew. They must drive all day, relatively unprotected from the weather for eight hours—sometimes longer, if they have the stamina to work for overtime pay. To pass the time they often open conversations with passengers—if the passengers don't get the conversational drop on them first. Such conversations should be kept impersonal. Why take violent issue—say, on politics—with a taximan whom you will probably never see again. It is easy enough to be monosyllabic in your replies, if any, if you don't want to talk or if his remarks get out of hand. The law says, that, with or without conversation, he must deliver you where you want to go within the area in which his cab operates.

Taxi drivers have legitimate complaints against people who behave rudely in their cabs. Manners come into play at the first hailing of a cab. If someone else has obviously hailed the cab first, and the driver stops to wait for that person, you have no right, just because you now see the cab and are closer, to jump in and claim the cab. Or if you have hailed a cab stopped at a red light, and the driver acknowledges you with a wave or blink of his lights, you should not jump into another cab that just happens to turn the corner in front of him. You should wait for the one you hailed.

But the worst complaint cabbies have about their passengers is the littering of their cabs. They start off the day with everything nicely clean. Some cabs have large signs asking smokers to please use the ash trays, but many smokers can't read, it seems, for the back seat and floor are soon littered with ashes, butts, and crumpled cigarette packs, along with gum wrappers and dirty tissues. Some people leave newspapers in disarray on the seats or, worse, rumpled on the floor. All litter should be taken from the cab and deposited in a public trash receptacle on the street. If you start to enter a cab that is filthy, get out again and say nicely, "I'm sorry, but your cab is too dirty back here." The driver should clean it—and you shouldn't have to ruin your clothes and shoes, either.

When a driver has posted a "Please Don't Smoke" sign, one should respect the driver's wishes. If you are a cigarette freak, and cannot wait a few minutes for a smoke, get out, pay what's on the meter, and take another cab. That driver would rather lose the tip and the remainder of the fare than have you filling his cab with smoke. Likewise, if it is *you* who is the non-smoker and the cabbie is puffing on a big cigar, you have every right to ask him to put it out during your ride.

Losing Articles in Taxis In all big cities drivers must keep a log of each trip they make. You have seen them filling the log or trip sheet out as you enter and leave the cab or sometimes when they must stop for a light. These cards note where the passenger—or passengers—was picked up, the number of passengers, and where they alighted, together with the meter reading for the trip. The cards must be kept over quite a long period of time in case of police check-up. If you leave something in a cab and do not remember what company operated it, it is still possible to trace your property. Notify the Lost and Found Department of the police at once and tell them where and at what time you took the cab and how many passengers were in the car. If the article has not been turned in to police headquarters, a fairly quick check on your driver can be made. Most cab drivers are honest, and there are many regulations they have to observe. They must, for example, check the cab for forgotten articles as you leave, for they can be held responsible if a subsequent passenger appropriates lost property.

Where a taxi driver does turn in something of impressive value left in his cab, it is usual to give a reward of at least 10 per cent of the actual value of the article.

Tipping   Never give less than a quarter. Drivers work on a base salary plus tips. Every time you undertip or—as some parsimonious people do—fail to tip at all, you cut their salary. For longer rides 15 to 20 per cent of the total is fair.

The Sensible Driver

The masterful, safe driving of a car is inextricably tied in to good manners. In fact, the two are synonymous. A good driver is a courteous driver. He is thinking all the time about somebody other than himself. Sometimes this may be defensive thinking—he's wary of other people—but at least he is thinking about them!

A good driver is constantly alert, and knowledgeable about the local speed limits and the meaning of the signs. He does not drive too slowly, either, for this action creates as much of a safety hazard as speeding. The courteous driver does not sneak through at the beginning or end of red lights. He thinks ahead on his turns and consequently carefully works his way into the proper lane for turning. He always uses his signals—in plenty of time. Even if his anger is aroused, he dispenses with clenching his fist at another driver, because that could incite unreasonable behavior in another hostile person. He looks before he backs into or out of a parking space—and he parks carefully, within the prescribed lines, so that he is not hogging two parking spaces. He also doesn't fight over a parking space, because he's smart enough to know someone's car will probably be damaged, and it might very well be his.

A courteous driver thinks about pedestrians on rainy days. He goes slower than his normal speed, particularly when turning corners, if the streets and gutters are filled with rain or slush.

An honest driver, when he scrapes the fender or inflicts minor damage to a parked car without its owner present, leaves a note giving his name, his telephone number, and the name of his insurance company. If he has no insurance for damage inflicted on another car, he knows he should pay for it himself. In some states, any damage over a certain amount inflicted on another car must be reported to the police.

The courteous driver *never* double-parks his car and leaves it, thus blocking traffic and entrapping the legally parked driver at the curb.

The well-mannered driver lowers his headlights the minute another car approaches. If the other car fails to do likewise, he blinks his lights. As for the horn—he uses it for real emergencies, not to express displeasure at traffic conditions or to show disapproval of someone's inferior driving technique!

The good driver keeps his back window, rear mirror, and side mirrors clean, for good vision. He pulls over to the side of the road and naps if he is sleepy or groggy. He locks the doors of his car whenever he parks his vehicle or leaves it. He keeps a flashlight, a signal blinker, a small first-aid kit (and some change in the kit to use for making emergency telephone calls) in the glove compartment of his car. If he lives in a northern climate, he puts on snow tires every winter, checks his anti-freeze regularly, and keeps an ice-chipper on hand to use on the windshield. He also puts a plastic bag full of sand in the trunk of his car for emergencies.

When his car is disabled, he manages to get it *completely off the road* onto the shoulder, in order to avoid accidents. He puts the hood of his car up as a distress signal; some prefer to tie a white handkerchief to the radio aerial.

The person who drives a car constantly would do well to join the American Automobile Association (AAA). For modest dues, he will receive emergency road service, and a travel service that can route his trips, supply him with road-condition information, and provide him with bail bond protection.

The most important part of well-mannered driving is to know not to drive when one has had too much to drink. No matter how much you may not want to, if you've been drinking, give your keys to someone who has not. Your reactions will no longer be sharp, and your reflexes will no longer be fast. The courteous driver is an alive one.

Car Travel with Children

Long car trips are a difficult experience for everyone concerned. Make your trip as easy as humanly possible by starting it early in the morning and stopping in the afternoon. A parent should make it a hard and fast rule that *everyone,* and that means the adults too, must use a seat belt. If a child weighs less than forty pounds he should have a car seat. The proven safety value of seat belts is so strong that it should be a family rule that the car does not start, even for a trip to the supermarket, until everyone has buckled up.

Try to keep small children on their regular eating schedules by making regular "pit stops." Stopping frequently will make a long trip easier for you as well. Every time you stop, have the children run around a bit to let out their accumulating energy. To make the trip as pleasant as possible for everyone, including the adults, it is a good idea to bring along a quantity of inexpensive toys and games that can be brought out as boredom threatens. If the children are old enough, word games are a wonderful way to pass long hours in a car.

When my two older brothers and I were very young, we made what seemed like an endless car trip across the United States each summer (from Nebraska to Maine). One of my parents' friends packed a duffel bag for us each year full of small, gaily wrapped gifts. Each package had one of our names on it, plus the day it was to be opened, plus the hour it was to be opened. She had wrapped something for each of the three of us to open on the hour from nine in the morning until four in the afternoon. We could hardly wait for each hour to strike so we could open another surprise package. Inside we might find a little crossword puzzle, a cookie or two, a miniature book, or a small notepad and three crayons—with instructions for "drawing the best picture you can of a gas station sign." Sometimes the instructions inside the package would read: "Take bets from everyone in the car on how many cows you will see as you drive this next hour. You do the counting, and mark it on this piece of paper." None of us will ever forget that woman—the work we caused her, the joy her gifts gave us, and the labor of love she executed out of friendship.

It is essential, also, to take along a plastic jug of water with paper cups to use whenever thirst takes hold. Also a few light snacks—crackers, fruit, hard candy, chewing gum—can relieve boredom. A pillow and a favorite blanket will often induce a child to take a nap.

Motion Sickness Wise parents bring along small plastic bags to use in the car for problems with motion sickness. Often the knowledge that something of this kind is readily available, and that there need be no hurried stop by the road, will steady a child. When the parents are tense, in a hurry, and grumbling, their own feelings are often communicated to the children, who may react with a case of car sickness. Give your children small, leisurely meals with a minimum of liquids and act in as relaxed a manner as possible. But despite your efforts, there inevitably are some children who throw up even during the course of simple travel. Ask your doctor about a simple medication to give the child before he has to make a major car trip. Needless to say, warning a child not to be sick or scolding him afterward is useless and unkind.

Taking Along the Baby The baby is usually safe and snug in its carrying cot, which can be wedged lengthwise between the front and back seat for safety. When the child can sit up well, he will probably enjoy and be more content riding in an infant seat. Manufacturers are constantly coming up with new safety designs for these seats, so you should ask about the latest safety features before purchasing one.

The world of disposable diapers and disposable bottles has made traveling with an infant much easier, but no matter how many preparations you make, the baby is certain to show the same fatigue and stress over being in the car for a long time as the other passengers. Carry a washcloth that has been rinsed in cold water and placed in a plastic bag. Use it to wipe off the baby's face every few hours. It will greatly refresh him. Also bring along a bottle of water for him, because he will grow thirsty.

It is important to have telephoned ahead to the motel where you will spend the night to reserve a crib for your room. If something goes wrong and the crib is not available, put the child in a single bed pushed against the wall, and then protect him on the other side by pushing two chairs to form another protective wall. (Of course, if your baby is very small, he will be safe and happy in his little carrying cot.)

When your young children are in strange beds in strange rooms, the presence of their favorite toy is reassuring at night. Always remember to bring night lights when you are "on the road" with children; place one in the bedroom and one in the bathroom (and if you're in a suite, place night lights in the corridors or hallways, so that they can find their way to the parents' room).

Rental Cars

For big-city dwellers or the frequent business traveler, rental cars have become an institution and way of life. There are now many local car rental agencies in addition to the big national ones, and they have outlets conveniently located at airports, hotels, and in downtown areas of cities. If you plan to use a rental car for your vacation travel, particularly on summer weekends, it is necessary to make a reservation well in advance. This is especially true if you want a specific type of car, compact, or station wagon.

In order to take possession of the rental car, you must be at least eighteen years of age (in some states the minimum age is higher), have with you an up-to-date driver's license, and have either a charge card or a "cash qualified" status with the agency. Although your spouse may drive the rented car on your trip, too, only you (with your own driver's license) have the right to pick up the car and sign the contract, if the car was reserved in your name. It is a good idea, if your spouse will be driving the car, too, to put both your names on the contract before it is signed.

Before leaving, make sure the mileage shown on the car matches the "Out" mileage stated on your rental contract. Sometimes mistakes are made, and you certainly don't want to pay for any mileage that is not yours.

Keep all gasoline and oil receipts on your trip. In some rental contracts one is reimbursed for gas or oil purchased en route. One is also reimbursed for breakdown repairs made, but keep careful receipts and notes of telephone numbers and name of mechanic, and so on, in order to back up your reimbursements. If you have an accident while driving a rented car, make out your own complete accident report, with date, time, location, names of all vehicles' passengers, license numbers, and so forth. (You will need this information for the detailed accident report that you must file with the rental agency.) Be sure to wait for the police to arrive and make their report, if your accident is a major one, or if any injuries were sustained by anyone involved. Call your rental agency as soon as you are able, to report what happened; they will give you further instructions.

If you rent a car, it should: (1) be washed and freshly vacuumed after the last passenger's use; (2) have a full tank of gas; (3) have its oil, radiator, and battery water in order, its windshield wipers working, the air pressure correct in the tires, the spare tire inflated in the trunk, and so on. It should be in perfect driving condition. If it is not, return the car for another, either at your point of departure, or in the next city at your rental agency station.

When you eventually return your car on the day you said you would at the designated station, hand in your contract with the present car mileage marked. This figure, minus the mileage already on the car when you took it over, plus the number of days the car was rented, plus insurance, will constitute the charge you must pay. Your bill will be mailed to your charge address within a few days, although some companies are so computer-prepared, they present the total bill to you right then and there. You do not, by the way, tip any of the car rental agency personnel.

The rental agencies all report that young people in their twenties tend to be the worst offenders in mistreating the cars. These vehicles should be treated with respect, for if one drives them badly, races them, and handles them recklessly, they are ruined for the other, safer drivers who will come along afterward. One should treat any rented car as though it were one's own property. The ash trays should be used, not ignored. Many of these cars come equipped with litter bags, and one does not have to throw soda cans, waste paper, chewing gum wrappers, and empty cigarette packs on the floor. When your children eat in the car and leave a mess, clean it up before you return the car. I remember a rental agency in Paris I used to frequent that had a huge poster right inside the door, depicting a monstrous pig, with the words printed large and clear beneath: "NE SOYEZ PAS UN COCHON!" (Don't Be a Pig).

I doubt if Avis, Hertz, or National would dare post something like that for their customers, but I can well imagine they would like to!

Recreational Vehicles

There are between 5 and 6 million recreational vehicles (RVs) on the roads of America—a formidable thought—proving that American families are really on the move. Motor homes are a relatively new event on the travel scene. In essence, the *motor home* is a self-powered unit similar to a bus. The driver's section and the living space are all under one roof. Another kind of RV, the *travel trailer* (often called "hardtop"), is very like a small cottage on two wheels, towed behind a small truck or full-sized automobile. You can purchase a basic camping trailer for a few hundred dollars, or you can buy a customized motor home with added touches given by your own interior designer, resulting in a fifty-thousand-dollar price tag!

Since RVs are very limited in space, never invite a large group to travel with you. There certainly isn't enough closet space in an RV to take extra clothes or sports equipment for guests. One RV owner told me that packing for a trip is like a mountain climber filling his backpack. One takes only what is necessary.

An RV traveler has to like other people and be able to tolerate close quarters (a special gift), because the largest RV units are smaller than the average home living room. The RV must provide in that one small space for activities involved in sitting, cooking, washing up, sleeping, and bathing. As in boating, the smart traveler learns to organize the space around him to its maximum efficiency. He takes no extra paraphernalia. Even an unneeded pair of knitting needles can present a problem.

Leaving on a Trip The main things to observe and remember as you pull away from home in your RV are these:

> Drive Carefully
> Reserve Your Camp Site Ahead Each Night
> Have Good Manners at the Camp Site
> Observe Good Security Rules

Don't plan on parking for the night by the road in the country or on a large highway. There are too many muggers driving around in cars today. The safety and convenience of the public or private camp sites make it well worth putting up with possible crowded conditions or extra fees to be paid. The average parking area makes available a water supply, toilets, fireplaces, and picnic tables and benches, and some offer hot showers, laundry facilities, and playgrounds for the children.

City Ordinances Good parking manners are as important as good road manners for owners of RVs. Many communities have zoning ordinances forbidding the parking of recreational vehicles anywhere in certain residential districts. Therefore you may have to store yours in a commercial building or build an addition onto your existing garage to house the vehicle and hide it from the street.

RVs are here to stay. The way their owners handle them and the manner in which the owners arrange to park them are very important. Sometimes a visit from the driver of an RV to a merchant with a polite request to "park here for the night, if it's perfectly all right with you" is all that is needed. What is also needed is great respect for the property on which the RV owner parks.

Inquire about the rules and regulations of the town you visit by going directly to the police station. Knowing the law is half the battle, and showing consideration for others is the other half.

Chapter 66

PLANNING YOUR VACATION TRIP

So you're going to take a trip. Bravo! Half the fun is in the planning, so take your time and explore every possibility. The three basic factors that should govern your trip are:

How much can you afford?
How much time do you have?
What time of year are you going?

For the bargain hunter or the person seeking solitude, a resort in the off-season, when the rates are low and life is tranquil, might be just the answer. Many winter resorts such as the Caribbean Islands are pleasant and inexpensive off-season; many ski resorts in the summer are also just as much fun and certainly just as beautiful as they are in winter.

Travel Agents

There are numerous reasons why you should avail yourself of a qualified travel agent. The most important one is that you will save yourself money, as well as obtain valuable services. Since travel agents receive their commissions from the carrier, hotel, or tour operator, and not from you, it does not cost you a penny to use a travel agent.

Check out your travel agent's reputation before you deal with him. Call up people who have used that particular agency to see if they received good, accurate information and were well served. You particularly want to use a travel agent who is sympathetic and interested in the kind of travel you wish to do.

The agent should be familiar with the intricate maze of special packages, charters, family plans, and off-season rates to help you plan your trip at the lowest possible cost. He should be familiar with all phases of travel, and if he has not been to the place you are inquiring about, the chances are that someone else in that agency has been, and can answer all your questions.

Travel agents keep up to date on the many complicated systems of air fares, as well as on the different price structures of hotels and motels every-where. They therefore offer you a wide variety of choices. A good travel agent with experience can often obtain space that you, as an individual, might not be able to procure. He is apt to have "friends" to call upon in an emergency. Since hotels rely on travel agents for a good part of their business, they like to take care of these special requests.

Travel agents are usually walking encyclopedias on the subject of travel. They know about passports and visa requirements, what kind of inoculations are necessary in foreign travel, what the climatic conditions are all over the world at every season, where you can change your money into foreign currency, how and what kind of car to hire, how to charter boats, and how to obtain services, from a hairdresser to a guide, and from a baby-sitter to an emergency dentist. The travel agent thinks of things you haven't thought of —port taxes, national holidays abroad on which you cannot shop, difficulties with obtaining international driver's licenses, and so on. The agent saves you endless telephone calls, letter writing, and frustrations caused by a lack of communication with the places you intend to visit. A good travel agent likes and knows people; he is sympathetic to the reasons why you are taking a vacation. He makes very little money booking your short-distance trips; he earns his real livelihood from your long stays at hotels or long-distance air or cruise fares. So if your travel agent has been putting himself out for you for your short-distance travel, be sure to give him your business for the long-distance kind.

Other Sources of Information If you are planning a trip abroad, you should check with the nearest consulate and the government tourist bureau of each country you will visit—either in person, or by writing for information. You will find these in many major American cities. You can also obtain good, up-to-date information on the countries by asking for the latest pamphlets and brochures made available by the international air carriers, who also have offices in large cities.

Another invaluable source is the latest guidebooks, many of which are directed at specific interests or needs, such as visiting the wine countries of the world, or eating with distinction on an international culinary binge, or visiting all the great antique and auction rooms of the world. It is important to consult guidebooks that have been published within the past year, for, like everything else, travel conditions may change overnight.

Before You Go

You should make certain your home—whether a one-room apartment or a twenty-room house—is in a secure condition, before leaving on your trip. If you live in an apartment, it's fairly easy. You give your key to a neighbor friend or a trustworthy "super," instructing him to put all mail and package deliveries inside your door, and you give him your address and telephone number, so he can reach you in case of an emergency.

Closing a house is a more complicated procedure. A house-sitter is the best solution if you are to be away for an extended trip, but if that is not possible, give a key to your neighbor and tell him where you'll be, in case a fire occurs or your house is broken into. You should also ask if he will collect the mail and packages for you daily (and if he does all this, be sure to bring him a present to say thank you). You think it will never happen to you, but pipes burst, trees fall down on roofs in storms, and fires break out in the best of families. Leave a report at your local police station of where you will be and how long you will be gone. Some families also hire off-duty guards to check on their houses every night.

If you are prominent in your community and the society editors report the goings and comings of your family and guests, ask them please not to mention your "big trip" until your return. Burglars read the newspaper carefully.

Before you leave, you should, of course, cancel your newspaper and dairy deliveries; you should place your jewelry in the safety deposit box of your bank. As you go out the door, be sure to make a last-minute check that all water faucets are closed, gas jets turned off, and household appliances like the washing machine and television sets disconnected. If you are on an extended trip, defrost the refrigerator and leave it turned off and disconnected.

Many homes are now protected by one of several good alarm services, to guard against theft or fire. It may be an expensive investment, but it is worth every dollar in terms of peace of mind, especially when you are away. There are also simple timers that will turn the lights on automatically in the house at night and turn them off again in the morning—another wise expenditure to help with the security of your house—whether you are away for two months or just overnight. So are the special safety locks that can be attached to window frame sides and extra-strong, double-cylinder dead-bolt door locks. Cellar doors and dumb-waiter and service doors should be checked, but don't padlock anything, for this is tantamount to waving a red flag in a burglar's face. Smart homeowners also take snapshots of how every room looks on the interior before leaving on a long trip, including close-ups of tabletop objects and items in library shelves or on mantelpieces. These photos would be invaluable for insurance inventory purposes in the event one's home is robbed or burned in one's absence.

Travel Preparations

Be sure your passport is up to date, with visas for any countries requiring them. When families travel together, they sometimes go on one passport, but this often proves to be unwise, in case family members have to separate. Every member of the family, except for infants, should have his own passport. (It takes about two weeks to obtain one after submitting the photos and necessary forms, properly filled out, plus the fee; in the rush travel times it can take longer.) If you need special medication, be sure to consult your doctor and have a plentiful supply. Pack your pills and medications in plastic containers, by the way. (A great pill carrier is the transparent plastic cylindrical container sold in sporting goods stores for fishermen to carry their fly baits; each small compartment screws into the next one, like a continuous tube.) On a cruise ship a doctor is available for passengers if you have a stomach ache or the flu, but if you are off in the Canadian woods, you had better carry a basic medicine supply with you.

Travel Check List

1. Type several copies of your complete schedule, and leave it with whoever might need it, such as your building superintendent, your neighbor, your office, your lawyer, and your in-laws.
2. Assemble your camera equipment, and lay in a full supply of film, flash cubes or bulbs, or whatever you need. It is usually difficult to buy such items when one needs them on a trip.
3. Bring your own soap (hotel bars are either too small or too strong a soap for sensitive skin, or you may be in a place with no soap provided at all).
4. Bring your own shampoo, make-up, and toilet articles in a rubber-lined toilet kit. Whenever possible, transfer anything liquid into plastic bottles, and fill these only three-quarters full, giving a little squeeze to get the extra air out before closing the cap. (On planes, increased air pressure causes the air to expand, so if the bottle were full, it could burst.) It is also a good idea to choose the smallest bottles and discard them as they are used.
5. Many hotels and motels do not have washcloths, so bring a pair of your own (you can keep packing damp ones in plastic sandwich bags).
6. As for plastic bags (the food storage kind and the sandwich size), they are the traveler's best friend.
7. Save some of the plastic garment bags from the dry cleaner's, too. They can be used as a bottom cushion in your suitcase and are great liners for drawers of questionably clean bureaus in the hotel you have chosen. They are also useful for wrapping around shoes in suitcases to keep them from soiling your clothes.
8. If you wear glasses all the time, be sure to have an extra pair packed safely; also some sunglasses.
9. It is best to bring a lightweight poncho unless you are wearing or carrying a raincoat. Pack a rain hat, too, or some waterproof head scarves. A collapsible umbrella is fine, too, if you have the room; the same can be said for rubber boots.
10. Take along three or four good ballpoint pens (you will keep losing them), and stationery is essential. For travel in the United States, bring along a large quantity of stamps for postcards. Really organized people

type labels with a series of names and addresses, which they pack, too. Then all they have to do is buy postcards, jot a quick message on each, attach the label and stamp, and they've taken care of "all the friends back home."

11. Arranging for money is an absolute necessity. If you buy traveler's checks, be sure to make a note of the numbers of all unused checks, so you can replace them in case of loss or theft. If you are going to be in or near a large city, have your banker give you the name and address of someone who can help you cash your checks and establish credit locally. If you are forgetful—or overanxious—you should put your cash in a money belt and wear it underneath your regular clothing.

12. Take along a miniature alarm clock and a small transistor radio, if you are going to be staying in a place where there are no radios or TVs in the rooms. (But remember, play the radio quietly.)

13. Don't take good jewelry with you. As for your costume jewelry, it is fragile and should be packed in something like a jewelry roll, an easy item to tuck into a corner of your suitcase.

14. The way to avoid having to carry or ask for an iron is to pack only drip-drys and the "shake out the wrinkles" jerseys. If your suit, for example, is full of wrinkles, hang the garment in the bathroom while you take a hot shower; the hot steam should work out the wrinkles. For a stubborn wrinkle, put on a glove and unscrew a light bulb that has been lit for a while and is piping hot. You can then go after that wrinkle with your "substitute iron" light bulb!

15. If you are carrying a wig, pack it flat in tissue paper, but carry some balloons and thumb tacks. When you reach each destination, blow up the balloon, secure it to a surface with a thumb tack, then shake out the wig and place it on the balloon. You'll have an "instant wig stand."

16. It is helpful to take along a collapsible canvas suitcase or one of those stretchable hemp tote bags in which to stuff presents and souvenirs you collect en route. (It also makes things easier for the customs, too, when you return to the United States, to have your customs sheet and all your dutiable items in *one* place to show the customs official.)

Packing Your Suitcase

For a long trip, the best large suitcase is one in which you can layer the clothes in such a manner that they all cushion each other.

1. To start, you might line the bottom of your suitcase with a dry cleaner's plastic bag (which you can also use, as we mentioned before, as a bureau drawer lining).

2. Place heavy items on the bottom—opposite the handle, so that when you pick up the suitcase they won't all avalanche downward and crush your other things.

3. Pack shoes at the sides and bottom of the suitcase (or at the bottom of a hanging bag, if you have one of those). Instead of shoe trees, you can stuff socks, jewelry pouches, facial tissues, and even belts in the shoes to help hold their shape and utilize the storage space, too. Shoe mittens, old socks, or plastic bags pulled over the shoes will keep them from soiling the clothing and serve as yet another layer of cushioning. (Don't put plastic bags over handbags, by the way. The leather has to breathe.)

4. To save space and keep belts from cracking, stretch them around the perimeter of the suitcase.

5. Stuff underwear, washcloths, or other soft bundles in the crannies.

6. Make yourself a flat shelf by cutting a piece of cardboard to fit exactly inside your suitcase. It should be placed on top of all the bulky items, thus separating their hard edges from the clothes you will layer in on top. If you are carrying another suitcase, place all your bulky items and shoes in that one, and put nothing but clothes layered neatly in your large suitcase. This method is called the "fold and cushion" technique. When you have to fold something, you cushion each fold with a non-wrinkling item.

7. Many items can be rolled up, sailor-style. When rolling, line up the creases, then roll tightly, beginning with the cuff. Roll all knits, lingerie, and scarves. As for a pleated skirt—it's the only thing to do.

8. Put the rolled items aside for the moment, and begin with slacks, long skirts, and dresses. Lay one item at a time, putting the waistband at the edge and letting the other end hang out over the opposite edge of the suitcase. Alternate placement of waistbands on each items so that there is not a build-up of double fabrics at one end. When folding the sides of the skirts into the suitcase, take a rolled scarf, for example, and put it where the crease would be. The scarf will prevent that crease from forming. Dresses need more protection. Put tissue in the sleeves and shoulders to prevent extra wrinkles. Sometimes it helps to fold skirts, sweaters, and even dresses inside out, for any creases that do occur will be inverted and won't stick out as much. When folding a garment, do it at the hip and shoulder line. Your own hips and shoulders will then act as "a natural iron." Always try to fold things along the body lines.

9. Now add shirts and blouses, which should be laid in front-to-front, with collars in the opposite directions. You might roll up a necktie and place it in the open area of the collar, to help the neckline keep its shape.

10. After the flat folded items are safely in place, put in the rolled garments. When you have built up enough height with these items, bring the bottoms of the slacks, skirts, robes or whatever was left hanging over the sides of the suitcase up and over the rolled items. In this way they will not be creased in the packing.

11. Jackets are tricky to pack. You might fold the unbuttoned jacket inside out, with the collar turned up and the shoulders touching. (Jackets of

flimsy fabrics should not be folded this way, but should be stuffed with tissue paper.) Check to see that the sleeves lie straight inside, and then fold over the jacket double to fit inside the suitcase. (If your suitcase is small, fold it over triple.)

12. Put your nightgown or pajamas on the top. After a long trip, nothing feels better than slipping out of your travel clothes into something loose and comfortable.

13. Make a list of everything you have packed, and its approximate replacement value. The total will surprise you, but now you'll be ready to insure your baggage for the trip!

Hotels and Motels

Every year first-class motels are becoming more like first-class hotels. Some of the large luxury motels in big cities are frankly thought of as hotels, and they contain the same services, with bellmen, restaurants, a sauna, beauty salon, and a variety of shops.

Today it is absolutely necessary to reserve your room in either motel or hotel ahead of time by writing, telephoning, or having your travel agent book it. Many hotels and motels are part of nationwide chains, reservations for which can be made anywhere in the country by calling a toll-free number. Even if you have not been to a city, you can decide which hotel to stay at on the basis of its reputation, the strength of its advertising, what you hear about it from others, or what your travel agent advises. Regardless of the season, the place you choose may be full (a convention might be in town), so you cannot expect to arrive without a reservation—even in early afternoon—and be accommodated. Gone are the days when a family would get in their car on a cross-country trip and drive as long as they felt like it before stopping for the night, whenever the spirit moved them.

Checking In When you arrive with your car at a motel, you leave the car with your baggage in it in front of the office of the motel and go inside to check in. When you arrive with a car in front of a hotel, either a doorman will have someone take your car immediately to the hotel garage, or you proceed to the hotel garage yourself, following the doorman's instructions. In checking in at the front desk or the "reception," only one person in a family need handle these formalities. Next to this desk will be the cashier's desk, where you will pay your bill upon checking out. You also use the cashier for turning large bills into small, or for cashing traveler's checks or personal checks. (Attention on the latter: some establishments will not cash personal checks unless your credit has been established beforehand or unless they know you well. Your credit card might stand you in good stead, if the amount you are trying to cash is not too prohibitive.)

When you check in, write your name, address, and business address (if applicable) on the blank furnished you. In some motels, you are required to give the make and license number of your car accompanying you. Often the clerk will ask you for a credit card (for credit checking purposes), even if you say you are going to pay your bill in cash when you leave.

If you are a married professional woman who works under her maiden name or another name, you should sign the register with both names. In that way, family, friends, and business associates will all be able to reach you quickly in an emergency.

In a hotel, once you have checked in, a bellman takes your baggage to your room for you. You are not supposed to take up your bags yourself. If you have only one small bag, he still takes it up and ushers you into your room. (When you check out, you do not need to call a bellman, however, if you have just one small bag; you can carry it yourself.) When the bellman takes you to your room, he opens the door, turns on all the lights, hangs up your coat in the closet, puts your largest bag on the luggage stand, opens the window if the room needs air, or turns on the air conditioner. He will show you how to work the air control units, and how to work the television. Sometimes, during a busy check-in period, several hotel guests' luggage will have to be taken care of by one bellman, who will use a baggage truck. In this case he sends you up ahead with your room key, and he will arrive within minutes with your baggage. The average tip to a bellman for admitting you to your room and bringing up your bags is one dollar. If he handles your whole family's luggage, you naturally give him more.

As soon as you are safely in your room, stick your head out in the corridor to check the location of the illuminated EXIT signs. Memorize whether the nearest exit to your room is to the right or to the left; this would be invaluable information in case of fire and smoke-filled hallways.

There is often no bellman as such on the staff of a small motel. You must handle your own bags, no matter how many (unless you happen to be in a small southern town, where gallantry still persists—and the manager will even make the cook come out from the kitchen to carry a large suitcase for "a lady"). In the average-sized motel you check in, sign the register, obtain your key, and go back to your car parked outside to drive it around to an empty parking space in front of your room.

When checking out, you may pay your bill the night before you leave; then you just leave your key in your room the next morning, telephone the desk to say you're leaving, close the door, and leave the premises.

Tipping and Room Service Details In motels there is no doorman; in good hotels there is always one. The quality of the hotel, the amount of baggage coped with, and the service expected all have bearing on the size of tips the hotel doorman receives.

If he merely opens the door of the cab and sets bags on the curb before calling a bellman to take over, no tip is required. If he dispatches your car to the garage, or if he carries heavy bags inside the hotel lobby, he should be tipped about a dollar. For summoning taxis for you, he should receive a quarter each time, but if he must venture forth in the rain or snow or really work to find your taxi, you should give him fifty cents to a dollar.

Tip the waiter and the captain in the hotel dining room as you would in a good restaurant—a total of 14 to 20 per cent of the entire bill. If you are signing the check with your room number for a dinner costing $50.00, for example, you would write "$7.50 to waiter, $2.50 to captain." If the head-waiter made a very special effort for you, give him $5.00 to $10.00 on the way out.

Some motels have no room service whatsoever, but all of the larger ones do. Most motels have an ice machine on each floor; some have snack-dispensing machines and soft-drink ones, too; others even have a "necessities" machine with items like razor blades, combs, and toothpaste. If you bring your own liquor and soft drinks, the use of the motel ice machines will save you a lot of time and money that would otherwise be involved in room service. I usually have my dinner sent up via room service in a motel, and since time is not a problem in an evening of working in bed and listening to television, it works very well. Sometimes the food arrives lukewarm on an overladen tray, but that is all right, too. I could have chosen, after all, to go to the motel restaurant for a hot dinner, which is what most people do.

In contrast, if one orders dinner in a hotel room, it often comes on a large table, covered with a formal white cloth, ceremoniously wheeled in by the waiter. Hidden beneath the white cloth are the warming ovens for the hot food. It makes me feel pretty silly, when I've ordered something as simple as consommé and an omelet, to have it arrive grandiosely on a table (set with a rose in a bud vase) that seems to take up half my room. I usually specify. "Please send my dinner on a tray."

You either give the waiter who brings you a meal 15 to 20 per cent tip in cash or add it onto the check he gives you to sign. If the kitchen makes a mistake (they often do), and the waiter has to return again (classic omission: the wine bottle opener), you should not tip him further.

When you are finished with the table or tray, put them both outside your room in the hall, flat against the wall, so as to be as inconspicuous as possible. Call room service and tell them you have done this, so they will dispatch a waiter to pick it up. Often in motels the tray won't be picked up until the next day, and it looks pretty unattractive to the other guests who walk down the hall past it. (The alternative is worse for you, if your room is one of the sealed-in ones; you will have to smell food remnants all night if you keep the tray in your room.)

Room service in most hotels and motels begins at 7 A.M., and if you are in a hurry for breakfast, in order to be punctual for an early morning appointment, forget about room service. It never comes on time in the morning, even in the best of establishments. Get yourself to the coffee shop.

You are not morally obliged to tip the maid who cleans your room every day after you leave, but it is nice to do so anyway. Leave a dollar for her in some conspicuous spot. She will know it's her tip, whether or not you bother to slip a piece of paper under the bill that reads "For the Maid." It is nice to leave behind a dollar-a-day tip for each day of your stay.

There is no valet service in most motels, but, of course, there always is in first-class hotels. Consult the instructions on your telephone dial, and then dial the valet to arrange for the picking up of your clothes that need cleaning or pressing. (If there is no dial, ask the main operator to give you the valet.) Most modern hotels and motels have telephone systems where the guests dial automatically for local and long-distance calls. If you have a great many calls to make and your telephone is not equipped with this system, take your coins and go to the lobby pay phone. You will go stark raving mad going through the switchboard, and you won't be contributing to the mental health of the motel or hotel operator, either.

If you find the bed in your room has not been made, or if you find there are not enough towels on hangers in the closet, call the housekeeper, and she usually makes amends very quickly. If you want a newspaper sent up, try the hotel bell captain first. (He may refer you to room service.) If a bellman brings you that paper, or your pressing or medicines you ordered from the hotel drugstore, you should give him a fifty-cent tip for each errand.

Things to Remember If you are an avid in-bed reader like me, bring your own strong light bulb, for bedside lamps in hotels and motels are of notoriously low wattage. In the desk drawer you will usually find pieces of hotel stationery for letters you have to write, and a few commercial hotel postcards (the same holds true for motels). One of the things many constant travelers object to is the eye pollution—the clutter—of advertising gimmicks stacked up on every tabletop, touting the delights of the various restaurants, room service menus, and the like. All of that would fit nicely in the desk drawer, and anyone who needed this information would know where it was.

Remember, if your family takes advantage of the motel pool, they are not to saunter through the lobby in their latest bikinis. Everyone should be decently clad in slippers and full-length robes for their trip to and from the pool. Some of these pools require bathing caps for long hair, so come prepared.

If you are one of the lucky VIPs who receives a basket of fruit in your room, with the hotel or motel manager's card attached, you are supposed to write him a note of thanks, no matter how VIP you feel. The same goes for a complimentary vase of flowers. In a very competitive market, chains are constantly trying to outdo each other in extras, such as having big-name interior designers redo the public rooms and lounges. However, if management would spend more time on the basics, on polite, well-trained help, and on good clean air, frequent travelers would be grateful. Most of us could not care less who designed the color scheme of our bedroom, but we do care if the air is foul from disinfectant or cigar smoke or liquor that remains in the room from previous occupants and previous cleanings. If one can open one's windows to change the air, there is no problem. When the rooms are sealed, as they are nowadays in most new motels and hotels, one is a prisoner in what seems like endlessly recycled, tired air.

Inviting Guests   It is perfectly correct to receive someone of the opposite sex in your room for a meeting, or drinks or dinner with room service. Not too many years ago hostelries in this country frowned upon anyone visiting one's room who was not a member of one's family or someone of the same sex. Today nobody notices and nobody cares. However, this does not give license to throw raucous, rowdy parties in one's room. This is just as objectionable as it ever was. Hotels and motels are there to serve all their guests, not just you. If you want a party in your room, take everyone to the bar after 7 P.M. Be considerate of your neighbors, including those with children, who want to get to sleep. This requires attention, too, to the volume on your TV set. The importance of such consideration for others holds true in the humble motel in a country town just as it does in a big expensive hotel lodged in a skyscraper.

Security   When you are in your room, always double-lock the door, and slide the chain bolt across if there is one. Be sure the sliding glass doors that lead to the outside are locked, too. Be sure you place cash, jewels, and other valuables in a safe deposit box, usually located at the front desk. These items should never be left in your room, but the wisest thing, of course, is not to take them with you in the first place. One friend of mine who was late for a dinner party given by one of her traveling companions in the main restaurant decided she didn't have time to leave her jewels in the vault at the front desk. Instead she stuffed them into her cocktail bag and took them with her. She slung the bag over the arm of her high velvet chair in the dark, glamorous restaurant. By the time she had finished after-dinner coffee, the jewels had been carefully lifted from her bag. Her wallet was untouched; just the jewels were taken.

Speaking of thievery, you are not supposed to take hotel or motel property away with you. Some people have no sense of guilt about absconding with anything from towels to blankets, water pitchers, and shower curtains. The days of merely stealing the ash trays seem to be gone forever. This is not souvenir-collecting; it is robbing the hotel. There are often "freebies" supplied by the hotel or motel you are welcome to take away from the bathroom—things like little packets of laundry soap, plastic shower caps, and treated paper shoe cleaners.

Traveling with Children   Both hotels and motels, when notified ahead of time, will arrange to have a baby's crib put in the room for you at no charge. Some motels will accommodate all children under a certain age absolutely free. Most of them will put in extra cots or allow children to sleep in their parents' room at a lower rate. Some motels even provide two double beds in each double room, in order to accommodate families traveling together. And of course, these hotels and motels with resort-like advantages are great places for the business person to invite his or her family to come along for the weekend.

I chatted for over an hour recently with a lovely white-haired, intelligent Irishwoman who is a veteran of forty years' experience in cleaning rooms for one of America's most famous, prestigious hotels. She talked with great nostalgia about the "old days" when people who had domestic staffs of their own would stay in the hotel and always behave "like ladies and gentlemen." They would leave their hotel rooms behind them in much the same way they would leave their bedrooms at home before going out in the morning.

"What's so different today?" I asked her.

"The difference is only between ladies and gentlemen and animals in a zoo," she retorted. Then she went on to tell me how people leave their hotel rooms today, stories I could not possibly repeat. It was a sad commentary on today's society, to say the least.

"But what are we going to do?" I asked. "The days of having one's own domestic staff and the leisurely grand life are gone, perhaps forever."

"Oh, it wasn't the fact that people had staffs," she protested. "It was the fact that they cared about other people."

Her reason for the change of behavior was a very concise one.

Chapter 67

TAKING A CRUISE

Booking Passage

When you book your space either through a travel agent or directly with the line, you pay a deposit of up to 10 per cent of the total fare. Lines differ on their regulations for payment, but for some the entire fare has to be paid sixty days before sailing, and if you cancel after that, you forfeit 25 per cent of the fare. Usually, if they sell your space again, they will refund you the money they had kept as a penalty fee.

Your cruise fare includes ocean transportation, stateroom accommodations, meals, entertainment, use of the sports equipment, and other services. The fare does not include gratuities (a major expense, so budget for it), the cost of your on-shore excursions and meals, bar bills or the wines ordered at dinner, the port taxes, your laundry, deck chair, hair appointments, and naturally your purchases made in the shops aboard ship. Most cruise ships accept credit cards for such on-board expenses. It's wise to check in advance.

When you make your final payment on the cruise, this is a good time to make your appointments for services like massages and the beauty salon. (The hairdressing department, by the way, closes down in bad weather, so if you don't have a wig for emergencies, you might take along shampoo, setting lotion, and rollers.) These services can be overcrowded during the cruise, particularly before special parties, which is why it is a good idea to book your appointments ahead, if you can. If not, book them as soon as you are on board ship.

When booking passage, reserve your table in the dining room. A table for two is frequently difficult to obtain, because of the demand. Families with young children usually reserve for the first of the two sittings (dinner is from six to eight for the early sitting). If you're alone, the wise move is to ask to be seated at one of the large "miscellaneous" tables, so that you will always have someone to talk to and you can make friends. When you first arrive at this table, introduce yourself, which should encourage everyone else at the table to introduce himself. If your group table turns out to be a disaster, speak immediately to the dining room steward. He will try to change you to another table.

When You Leave

The cruise line will provide you with a mailing itinerary giving the schedule of all ports of call, stating the full address required for mail to reach you, how many days ahead of ship arrival mail for you must be posted, and how much postage is required for each foreign port. For emergency communications, you may be reached at sea twenty-four hours a day by radiogram or by telephone.

The cruise line furnishes you with baggage tags for each piece. There may be a large sign at the pier stating tipping is not allowed of the stevedores (porters) who help you with your baggage from the car to the ship. Don't believe it. They will usually *tell* you in advance what the price for the job will be—anywhere from five to fifteen dollars, depending on the number in the group and the amount of baggage. Be sure you take the number of the porter, so that if you can't find your baggage on ship, you know how to inquire about it.

Bon Voyage Parties Some ships won't permit bon voyage parties any more for security reasons. For those who do, you should arrange the party ahead of time with the line or your travel agent. Be on board an hour ahead of your guests' arrival to check with the cabin steward that everything is arranged. He will furnish you with ice, soda water, soft drinks, glasses, and hor d'oeuvres, for which you will be charged. You must bring your own liquor for this party, since the ship can't sell liquor while in port. Once you are out at sea and you want to give a cocktail party in your cabin or in part of one of the salons, you will be charged *only* for the liquor. When the signal comes for the guests to leave, you should do your part to help the ship get ready for departure by getting your friends off the ship without delay.

On the Ship

When you are on board, go immediately to the purser to reconfirm your dining room reservations made earlier. You will have been assigned your cabin, of course, when you booked passage, and like all things in life, the higher the price paid, the more luxurious the accommodations. The most expensive cabins (with private baths) are topside or on the next upper deck, with windows instead of portholes. If you are miserable in the cabin to which you have been assigned, whether because of a lack of air circulation, noise from the engines or overpartying neighbors, consult the purser. He may be able to change your accommodations. If he cannot, accept it graciously, and don't let it ruin your trip. In other words, don't become known to the other passengers as a complainer.

After you are actually on board is the time to reserve your deck chair, which includes cushions and a blanket. There is a minor charge for all of this. If your purpose in sitting in a deck chair a good part of the day is to gain a much-needed rest, and you find yourself in the midst of a group of nonstop talkers, ask the steward to change your chair location. There is no need to be miserable for the length of the cruise. Some people desperately need rest; some desperately need companionship.

It is up to the personnel of the ship to help you reach your goal. An important element of every cruise is the "cruise director" or the "social director," whose purpose is to see to it that everyone has a good time. He or she will find, or try to find, dancing partners for people, a fourth for bridge, a contemporary for a shy teen-ager, or an available widower for a lonely widow. (The latter far outnumber the former.)

Things to Remember   Make your children behave. Running, screaming children on board ship are a menace. Teach them not to rush along wet slippery decks, for they could have a serious accident. Most cruise ships do have a doctor and a nurse on board for emergencies.

Early in the trip there will be a fire and lifeboat drill, which you must attend, even if you have been on this same ship numerous times. Everyone should have an attitude of respect for the ship's officers; everyone should attend and pay attention to this drill.

Never throw a cigarette overboard. The wind can blow a lit cigarette right back onto the deck, or through a porthole into a stateroom.

Do not smoke in your berth—ever. You create a fire hazard for the entire ship if you do.

If someone buys a round of drinks in which you're included, you should offer to pay for the next round, even if you are a woman traveling alone. Don't acquire the reputation of being a "bar moocher," someone who hangs out in the bar, hoping someone will buy her a drink and offer companionship.

If you decide to order wine at your table, offer to share it with any other wine drinkers at your table. The easiest way is for each wine drinker at your table to buy the wine for everyone on a rotating basis. If you are the only wine drinker at your table, go ahead and treat yourself to the bottle all by yourself.

Consult the ship's paper that is slipped under your door each morning so that you won't miss any activities that might be of particular interest that day. These special events could be anything from an exercise clinic given by a famous beauty expert to a lecture by an internationally renowned economist, to lessons in needlework or the newest dances or transcendental meditation. Something will surely interest you. If you are alone, by attending the events that intrigue you, you will make friends with others who share the same interests. There is no excuse for anyone to return from a cruise saying, "I was lonely." If however, you come across someone who consistently shies away from conversation and joining activities, leave him or her alone. That person is on board *for a rest.*

Seasickness Carry your own seasickness pills with you. And don't mix drinking liquor with the pills, for it can be very dangerous. Remain out on deck, if you're feeling queasy, for the air inside can seem suffocatingly stale when you're afflicted with *mal de mer.* Stay away from liquids, but munch on plain bread, dry rolls, or crackers. (Some passengers follow the old Italian custom of downing a Fernet Branca in the bar.)

The Captain's Table

To be invited to eat at the captain's table is an honor that one must accept quickly and appreciatively. It is also extremely gauche to try to have yourself invited to sit at this table. The people who join the captain are VIPs, celebrities, people of official rank, or business people who have a lot to do with the line. On some cruises the captain invites different guests for each dinner; sometimes he gives one or two cocktail parties. (If you are invited to one of these parties and cannot go, be sure to inform the purser's office.) Sometimes the other ship's officers will give a cocktail party, to which you will be invited. Again, do not press for one of these invitations.

In addressing the captain, you call him "Captain" with his surname. The ship's doctor, of course, is called "Dr." with his surname, but all of the other ship's officers are addressed simply as "Mr." with their surnames. One of the last events given on board ship is the "captain's dinner," which is often a costume affair. You can bring a costume with you, or buy one on board in a shop, or improvise with your own possessions. If you hate costume parties as much as I do, you can wear evening clothes and suffer through your fellow passengers' accusations of being a poor sport!

Dress

Cruisewear is much more informal than it used to be. Also, one never dresses formally the first or the last night out at sea, or the night before putting into port or leaving it. But a woman should have two long things in her wardrobe (an evening dress, caftan, party pajamas, long skirts with interchangeable blouses). And a man still has to bring along his black-tie attire. Some men don't wear an all-black suit on southern cruises; rather, they pack a black tropical-weight dinner jacket and colorful trousers, or they bring black evening trousers and a colorful dinner jacket. White dinner jackets are also in evidence on these cruises. Men who don't own dinner suits are advised to rent them for the cruise.

At lunch in the dining room of a cruise ship men wear jackets and ties, but they dress informally if lunch is served buffet-style on deck. Women wear slacks or shorts with shirts on deck and simple summery dresses in the dining room. Swimming and sunbathing enthusiasts should bring along at least two swimsuits and a pair of sandals; some ships require bathing caps for long-haired people to use the pool. If you are going to wander around during the day in your swimsuit, you should wear a suitable cover-up, of course. Women should pack a light sweater or shawls to wear for the cool evening breezes, but forget about bringing along a fur. Don't forget to bring sunglasses, and everyone should have a really comfortable pair of shoes for walking during in-port excursions.

On-shore Excursions

One pays extra for all on-shore excursions. You can either sign up for one of the tours offered through the ship's services, or you can strike out on your own. You may decide to walk around the town by yourself or hire a taxi to take you around an island. Use one of the taxis parked at the dock or ask at the local tourist office for a reputable one. These taxi drivers are often wonderful experiences in themselves, but be sure you have either the total price of your tour or the price he charges by the hour all understood before you accept his enthusiastic offer. Tip him according to the service he renders you. If you keep the car all day, it is common courtesy to buy your driver lunch. He does not have to eat at your table, however. It's risky to rent your own car. It might not be a safe one; it might not carry insurance. If you get lost, you might miss the boat's departure, and if you have an accident, you might be detained there for several days.

Women tourists who wear short-shorts and bra tops are asking for derision and criticism from the local people. If the figure in the short-shorts is not perfect, the laugh grows louder. One cannot dress on these excursions with the same casualness one does at home. The same goes for the men, too. Remember to act in a quiet, dignified manner on shore. The local people have seen some really dreadful behavior shown by tourists, and it's up to each of us to comport ourselves in such a way that we will be thought of as "those nice Americans," and not "those ugly Americans."

Tipping

Many lines send prospective passengers printed advice on how to deal with tipping on board their ships. Actually, one should be somewhat flexible and tip according to the amount of service one receives, but there are various guidelines that may be followed. For example, if you charge your drinks in the bar, you should tip 15 to 20 per cent of your total bill. (It is easier to do this at the end of the trip than to do it each time you order a drink.) The wine steward in the dining room should also receive between 15 and 20 per cent. If you are on a ship where it is customary to leave your shoes outside the cabin door at night (and you find them the next morning beautifully shined), you should tip that person, even if you never see him. Leave an envelope with a five-dollar bill tucked into your shoes on the last day. You should tip your dining room steward and your room steward anywhere from a dollar and a half to two dollars per day.

The cabin boys who do odd jobs for you are usually tipped fifty cents per errand. The chief steward should be tipped ten dollars at the end of each week of long cruises, and his assistant five dollars. The deck steward should receive five dollars a week, too. Before you leave the cruise, it's nice to tip the lounge stewards two or three dollars apiece, if they have given you any special service. One tips hairdressers, barbers, and masseurs the same as one does on shore. If you budget 15 per cent of the price of the total cruise for tips, you will be doing just about right.

On a long cruise, you can do your tipping each week on board. If you're on a week-long or ten-day cruise, do all of your tipping your last night out at sea. Put each person's tip in an envelope and hand it to him. A note inside at the end of the voyage saying, "Thank you for all you've done for us," is also nice, for these wonderfully trained, polite people really knock themselves out trying to take care of you.

You *never*, of course, tip any of the ship's officers.

Travel by Freighter

Travel by cargo liner is much less expensive than cruise ship travel, and consequently much less luxurious. The main purpose of a freighter is to haul cargo, not to carry passengers, and therefore, the few passengers (often twelve in all) do not receive priority. The cargo does. Sailing dates, choice of ports, amount of time spent in ports—everything can fluctuate, according to the cargo requirements of the ship. This is why freighter traveling is such an adventure.

Travel by freighter is great for someone who needs a rest and does not have a time schedule to meet. It's a wonderful way for an entire family to travel (since children under twelve travel at reduced fares, and some freighters carry children under three free); and it's almost a guaranteed success if a group of four or more band together to make the trip. The drawback of travel by freighter is that there are so few passengers and so little place to escape from them (except for the small cabins). If you are uncomfortable with the other passengers, your trip will be very difficult.

Some freighters traveling in the northern seas do not have air conditioning. They don't really need it. Others offer the luxury of carpeted, air-conditioned cabins with full baths and outside windows.

Some freighters will not carry children. Since there is neither a doctor nor a nurse on board, pregnant women are not welcomed, nor are passengers who have passed their seventy-fifth birthdays. Anyone sixty-five years or older must show a doctor's certificate of good health before he is given space.

Cancellation fees of 25 per cent of the fare are levied if you cancel within thirty days of sailing.

Be sure to have your passport in order (you will need one on some trips), and find out from the line the inoculation requirements for the countries you will visit. Carry your own medicines, alarm clock, complete supply of film, hair care equipment, sunglasses, an extra pair of prescription glasses (if you wear them), and your own favorite soap. On most freighters there's a small "ship's store" for certain necessities, but it is better to bring everything with you.

Packing and Dressing   On some lines there's a maximum free baggage allowance of 500 pounds per adult, and 250 pounds per child. The line usually has very limited liability for damage or theft of your bags, so you should take out insurance coverage on the total amount of your possessions brought on board. You won't need "black-tie" attire for this kind of travel. In fact, men can eat in the dining room without jackets or ties, except for the captain's dinner. (Mealtime comes early on these ships: breakfast might be served at 7:30, lunch at 11:30, and dinner at 5:30. The passengers have to adjust to the crew's schedule.)

During the trip women wear sports separates, and in northern waters, even in summer, one should bring some heavy sweaters. No matter what the season, you should pack rain gear. The easiest to carry, of course, are drip-dry garments, but you will find on board some freighters washing machines, detergent, and electric irons for the use of passengers. When you put into a port for a couple of days, you can have your laundry or dry cleaning done on shore. You should pack conservative clothing for freighter life. This is no time for the haute couture, furs, and jewelry. It's a time for comfortable slacks, sneakers, and ponchos. Everything is relaxed and informal. Be sure to carry some sturdy walking shoes, because you will use them on the days you're in port. Most freighters do not have swimming pools, but if you are in a warm weather climate, bring a bathing suit for sunbathing. Some women "dress" for dinner on freighters by donning a long, packable jersey dress after bathing; it gives the rest of the passengers a lift, even if "the rest of the passengers" consist of one's family and a couple of friends.

Since there is so much free time and no organized activity, except for an occasional movie, you should bring lots of books on board. You will be able to accomplish vast amounts of handwork (one man I know did the needle-point chair seats for his dining room while going around the world on a freighter!); you can get articles written and pictures painted. The food on board is usually simple but good, requiring a certain amount of planned exercise in order not to gain weight from it.

Take traveler's checks (and cash) with you. You may not be able to cash your personal checks, even on board (although this can be arranged rather well in advance by following the procedures required by the line).

Your cruise fare does not include your shipboard "necessity" purchases, port taxes, liquor purchased on board, gratuities to personnel, or on-shore excursions. You buy your liquor, mixes, and soft drinks by the bottle on board; usually the bar is self-service, and you keep your name on your bottle.

Tipping is a flexible thing. You might think of 15 per cent of your passage cost as a reasonable sum to budget for gratuities, but in reality you will tip certain members of the crew handsomely, like the chief steward, because those particular people do the most for you.

The great thing about freighters is that you may stop over for a few days or weeks in a country and pick up a freighter of the same line continuing on with your itinerary when it suits you, and when that freighter has a bunk for you. Some freighter lines allow stopovers of up to a year's duration!

And as for good manners, again, the complimentary note to the captain about the "great trip" and his "wonderful crew" is a nice gesture. (You might also carbon the president of the line.)

INDEX

A

Abbot, correct forms of address for, 602–3
Acceptances. *See* Invitations
Accessories, 663–68. *See also specific accessories, occasions*
    gloves, 664–65
    handbags, 664–65
    hats, 664
    jewelry, 666–67
    shoes, 666
    wristwatches, 667–68
Accidents,
    with rental cars, 819
    skiing, 720
    at table, 415. *See also* Spillage
        dropping utensils in restaurant, 690
        ladle falls in sauce, 413–14
    tennis, and eye injury, 707
Accountants, single persons and, 68
Acolytes, at weddings, 221
Address, correct forms of, 563–629
    British officials and individuals, 604, 606–17
    French officials and nobility, 604, 618–23
    Italian officials and individuals, 604–5, 622–27
    Spanish officials and nobility, 605, 626–29
    U.S. government officials and individuals, 564–67, 568–81
    U.S. military personnel, 582–93
Addresses. *See also* Address, correct forms of; Invitations
    on at home cards, 152–53
    on calling cards, 548
    return. *See* Return addresses
    on social envelopes, 509–11
        change of, 510–11
        to children, 510
        to couples living together, 509–10
        to homosexual couples, 510
        with hyphenated names, 510
        and keeping married name, 509
Admirals
    abbreviation of rank, 585
    correct forms of address to, 590–91
    how to tell rank, 582, 583
Adolescents. *See* Teen-agers
Adopted children, 62–65
    adoptive parents' attitude and, 65
    announcing adoption, 63–64
    and engagement announcement, 126–27
    explaining another child's adoption, 65
    showers and presents for, 62–63
    talking to, about parents, 64–65
    and wedding invitations, 140
Age. *See also* Introductions; Old age
    as subject of conversation, 746

Air Force, U. S., 582
    abbreviations of rank, 585
    correct forms of address, 586–89
    Academy cadets, 592–93
        how to tell rank, 584
Airplane glue, inhaling, 55
Airplanes and plane travel, 799–807
    bottles on, 825
    checking in for flight, 801–2
    with children, 805
    clothes to wear, 805–6
    in flight, 803–5
    golden rule and, 806–7
    points to consider, 799–801
    using napkins on, 409
Alarm services, 824
Alcohol (liquor), 54, 56–58. *See also* Alcoholics; Drinks and drinking; *specific occasions*
    bachelor dinners and, 198
    on boats, 703
    cannot be sold on ships in port, 791, 835
    Christian Scientists and, 231
    college parties and, 402
    as depressant, 55
    and driving, 56ff., 817
        teen-agers and, 48
    and example for children at home, 57–58
    in executive dining room, 454
    as hostess gift, 788
    parents and education of children on, 56–57
    problem drinkers, 342–45. *See also* Alcoholics
    prohibited on naval vessels, 647
    and seasickness medication, 837
    and teen-agers,
        car manners, 48
        dating, 43
        parties, 46, 396
    when child drinks at home, 58
Alcoholics, 57, 58, 342–45
    entertaining recovered, 344–45
    handling, 343–44
    help for, 60, 344
Alcoholics Anonymous, 60, 344
Allowances, 34–36
    how much?, 34–35
    keeping records, 36
    teen-agers and, 38–39
    withholding, 35–36
Ambassadors
    American
        correct forms of address for, 574–75
        stationery, 506
    foreign, correct forms of address, 580–81
        British, 616–17
        French, 620–21

Italian, 624–25
Spanish, 628–29
American Automobile Association, 817
American Cancer Society, 60–61
American Lung Association, 61
American National Red Cross Lifesaving Book, 722
American Sign Language, 11, 12, 13
Amphetamines, 55
Amtrak, 807–8
"Angel dust," 55
Anniversaries
    of friend's death, 279
    wedding, 262–65
        children toasting at, 294
        gifts, 264–65, 783–84
        invitations and replies, 263–64
        photos, 265
        reaffirmation of vows, 265
Announcements
    of adoptions, 63–64
    of birth of baby, 107–8
    of business opening, 486–87
    change of address, 510–11
    engagement, 122–24, 131
    graduation, 115
    wedding, 132–33ff., 160–62. *See also*
        Invitations: wedding
        and elopement, 236
        heraldic devices on, 135, 557
        military forms, 161–62
        second marriage, 253–54
        variations of usual wording, 160–61
Annulment, marriage, 251
    and engagement announcement, 124
    and wedding gifts, 166
Answering machine, telephone-, 472
Answering services, dealing with, 471
Apartments
    children's parties in, 391–92
    dinners on balconies, 371
    and planning trip, 823–24
Apology, letters of, 522
    business, 477
Appearance, alcohol and, 57
Appetizers. *See also* First course
    table setting for, 330
    wines, 317
Apples, how to eat, 425
    stewed, 427
Application forms, job, 439–40
Apricots, how to eat, 425
Archbishops, correct forms of address for,
    Catholic, 602–3
    Eastern Orthodox, 594–95
Archdeacons, correct forms of address for,
    600–3
Archimandrite, Eastern Orthodox, correct
    forms of address for, 594–95
Army, U. S., 582. *See also* Military
    abbreviations of rank, 585
    correct forms of address, 586–89
        for Military Academy cadets, 592–93
    how to tell rank, 582–83
Artichokes, how to eat, 421–22
Artificial flowers,
    as gifts, 763
    for table setting, 328
Ascots, 675
    for riding, 711
Ash trays,

at cocktail parties, 338
at formal dinners, 361
at formal luncheons, 364
at restaurants, 689
in table settings, 330, 333–34
Asparagus,
    how to eat, 422
    serving, 296
Aspirin, 54
Assemblyman or assemblywoman, correct
    forms of address for, 576–77
Assistant secretary of the Cabinet, correct
    forms of address for, 570–71
Associate justice, correct forms of address
    for, 568–69
Association of Women Business Owners,
    490
Athletic shoes. *See* Sneakers
At Home cards, 152–53
    and foreign wedding procedures, 150
Attorney General, correct forms of address
    for, 570–71
Authority, children and respect for, 6
Automobiles. *See* Cars and driving
Avocado halves, how to eat, 425–26

B

Babies,
    alcohol and pregnancy, 57
    announcing birth of, 107
    Brith Milah, 113
    and car travel, 818–19
    choosing names, 106–7
    christening, 108–12
        at church, 110–11
        dressing for, 110
        gifts for, 109, 766–67
        godparents and responsibilities, 109
        at home, 111
        invitations to party, 109–10
        refreshments after celebration, 111–12
    elopers and, 236
    flying with, 800, 805
    gifts for, 105, 766–67
    showers, 105–6
    visiting, 108
Baby nurses, 83
    hiring, 85
    and time off, 86
    uniforms for, 85
Baby-sitters, 83, 90–93
    and proper working conditions, 92–93
    spelling out duties to, 91–92
    ways to locate, 91
Bachelor dinners, 198
Bachelors. *See also* Single life
    and announcing engagement of adopted
        child, 126–27
Bacon, how to eat, 422
Badges, at business social events, 462–63
Bad language (swearing), 743
    children and, 21–22
    teen-agers and, 50
Bad news, writing or calling after hearing,
        49, 477, 519. *See also* Condolence
        letters of
Baggage. *See also* Luggage
    and bus travel, 812
    and cruises, 835
        freighter, 840

and flying, 801, 802, 807
at hotel, 829
Balls. *See* Debutantes and debuts
Bananas
  how to eat, 426
  and teen-agers' table manners, 29
Bank accounts,
  children and, 34–35
  joint, 780
Bankers, single persons and, 68
Banquette seating, 681–82
Baptisms. *See* Christenings
Barbecues, 378–79
Barbiturates, 53, 55
Bar Mitzvah, 113–14
  Bat Mitzvah, 113–14
  gifts, 114, 769–70
Baronesses, correct forms of address for,
  British, 612–13
  French, 622–23
  Italian, 626–27
Baronets, correct forms of address for,
    612–13
  wives of, 614–15
Barons, correct forms of address for,
  British, 612–13
  French, 622–23
  Italian, 626–27
Bartenders
  catering services and, 82
  for cocktail parties, 339–40
  for college parties, 402
Baruch, Bernard, 292, 485
Bathing suits (swimsuits), 714–15
  on cruises, 838, 840
Bath linens,
  as shower gifts, 755
  in trousseau, 169–70
    basic needs, 176
Bathrooms. *See also* Lavatories; Toilets
  children and, 30
  in cleaning routine, 94
  guests and, 383–84, 387, 388
  teen-age manners and, 49
Bat Mitzvah, 113–14
  gifts for, 114, 769–70
Beach. *See* Swimming
Beach clubs, 716–17
Bedjackets, for hospital, 750
Bed linens,
  as shower gifts, 775
  in trousseau, 169
    basic needs, 176
Beds. *See also* Bed linens
  making, 94, 95–96
  smoking in, 59
Bedspreads,
  in bedmaking, 95
  in trousseau, 170
Bedtime, children and, 32
Beer
  alcoholic content of, 57
  on picnic, 373, 375
  service at buffet, 300
Bellmen, hotel, 829
Belts, packing for trip, 827
Bermuda shorts, men's, 675–76
Berries, how to eat, 426
Best man, 188–90, 218, 220, 221, 227, 228,
    232. *See also* Weddings: preparations;
    Weddings: pre-wedding parties
  dress of, 204

duties of, 189–90
gift to, 167
at reception, 241, 243ff.
and rehearsal, 212ff.
and wedding ring, 189, 205, 212
Beverages. *See* Drinks and drinking
Bikinis, 714, 715
Binoculars, as gift, 794
Birds,
  how to eat, 422, 423–24
  taking portions of, 412
Birthday gifts, 785–86. *See also* Birthday
    parties; Gifts
  jewelry, 785–86
Birthday parties, 391–96
  games, 393–94
  hiring entertainment, 394–95
  loot bags, 395
  manners of children at, 20, 395–96
  and ostentatious gifts, 765
  prizes for games, 395
  and thank-you notes, 19
  toasting at, 294
Birthstones, 785–86
Bishops, correct forms of address for
  Catholic, 602–3
  Eastern Orthodox, 594–95
  Episcopal, 598–99
  Mormon, 600–1
"Black Tie," 676. *See also specific occasions*
  on cruise, 837
  position of phrase on invitations, 534ff.
  studs for, as gift for man, 764
  and White House invitations, 635, 636
Blankets, in bedmaking, 95
Blazer buttons, as gift for man, 764
Blazers, men's, 674–75
Blind people (visually handicapped), 12–13
  and bus travel with dogs, 812
Bloody marys, 314
Blouses, packing for trip, 827
Blue jeans. *See* Jeans
Boater hats, men's, 674
Boating. *See* Yachting and sailing
Bonds, as gifts, 761, 781
Bon voyage gifts, 790–91
Bon voyage parties, 835
Bookplates, heraldic devices on, 556
Books. *See also* Reading
  children and respect for, 22
  on freighter cruises, 840–41
  gifts for ship travelers, 791
  gifts for sportspersons, 794
  teen-agers and respect for, 51
Booth seating, in restaurants, 682
Boots, 666
  for cross-country skiing, 721
  for hiking, 675
  for riding, 711, 714
  on trips, rubber, 825
Borrowing and lending
  in office, 484
  teen-agers and, 49
Bouquets, brides', 210
  and second weddings, 257
  throwing, 247
Bourbon, 341
Boutonnieres,
  for proms, 47
  for weddings, 210
    second, 257
Bowls, soup in handled, 409

Bow ties, 671
for formal wear, 676
tying, 672
Boy friends. *See also* Dating
baby-sitters and, 93
Bracelets, 667
first jewelry for girls, 764
identification, as gifts for men, 763
Brain damage, alcohol and, 57
Brandy, in restaurants, 684
Brandy snifters, holding, 410
Breads
at formal dinners, 359
how to eat hot, 432
as pusher and sopper, 414
at restaurants, hot, 690
Breakfast
for club speaker, 738–39
in executive conference room, 453
for guests, 384
in household routine, 93
wedding, 243
Breeches, riding, 711, 714
Bridal attendants. *See* Weddings
Bridal showers, 196–98. *See also specific
kinds*
gifts for, 197–98
Bridal teas, 196
Brides. *See* Weddings
Bridesmaid, 188, 194, 218, 223, 226, 227
dress for, 208
and mature bride, 203
gifts to, 167
party of, for bride, 195
at reception, 244, 247
in receiving line, 238, 239
at rehearsal, 213ff.
Bridge-playing, 352–54
afternoon, 354
serving dessert, 354
Brigadier generals
abbreviations of rank, 585
correct forms of address for, 588–89
how to tell rank, 582
Brith Milah, 113
British (English)
and coats of arms, 554
correct forms of address for, 604, 606–17
Brooches, as first jewelry for girls, 764
Brothers. *See also* Best man
use of "Messrs.," 511–12
and wedding invitations, 136
Brothers (religious), correct forms of
address for, 602–3
Bruce-White, Donald, 368ff.
Brunch menu, 314–15
Buffets. *See also specific occasions*
brunch menu, 314–15
cocktail, 312, 345
luncheon, 348
out of doors, 371–72
restaurant service, 691–92
sit-down dinners, 302–4
suppers, 298–301
table for, 300–1
taking token portions at, 410
teen-age parties, 26
Bugs (insects)
in food, 418

and patio entertaining, 372
picnic, 374
Bullshots, 314
Bumping into people, teen-age manners
and, 51
Burial (interment), 268, 276
clothing for, 268
Burping, 417–18
Bus boys, 679, 693
Buses, traveling on, 811–13
sneezing, coughing while, 51, 416
teen-age manners and, 51
Business (the office), 433–90
calls at White House, 637–38
change of address, 510
and Christmas cards, 532
do's and don'ts, 482–84
dressing for, 451–53
blazers, 675
shoes, 674
entertaining, 455–64. *See also*
Entertaining: business
executive facilities, 453–54
getting a job, 437–44
application forms, 439–40
employer's responsibility toward
applicants, 442
going on interview, 440–42
letters of reference, 442–44
writing a resumé, 437–39
gifts, 480–81
for openings, 487
for secretaries, 765
handling executive visitors and
appointments, 478–80
handling R.S.V.P.s from office, 541–42
men and women as colleagues, 447–54
and dress in office, 451–53
lighting and offering cigarettes, 450
and picking up tab, 448–50
and travel, 450–51
use of "Ms.," 447–48
women's raised consciousness, 447
opening own, 485–90
announcing opening, 486–87
budget check list, 486
free advice on, 489–90
gifts for opening, 487
and office image, 489
stationery for, 487–89
party behavior, 481–82
personal, letters for, 526–30
complaints, 527–28
making reservations, 527
ordering from stores, 526–27
sending memos, 528–30
single person and, 68
resignation from job, letter of, 444–46
secretaries, 474–76. *See also* Telephone
gifts for, 765
smoking in office, 482
stationery, 500–2
executive woman, 500–2
men's personal stationery, 502–4
telephone, 465–73
answering, 465–67
executives and own phones, 468–69
answering machine, 472
answering service, 471

conversations, 469–70
  long-distance calls, 470
  and messages, 467–68
  and recorded music, 472–73
  use of "ma'am" and "sir," 728
  use of "Ms.," 447–48
  use of "women" and "men" vs. "ladies"
    and "gentlemen," 728
  well-written notes, 476–78
Business cards, 548
  women's, 550
Business suits, 669–70
Butlers, 80–81
  catering services and, 82
  at formal meals, 357, 358, 361, 362, 365
Butter, 332
  adding to food, 413
  for toast and hot breads, 432
  using at restaurants, 690
Butter plates, 329–32
  at formal luncheons, 363, 364
  and teen-agers' table manners, 28
Buttons, blazer, as gift for man, 764

C

Cabin boys, tipping on cruise, 839
Cabinet members, correct forms of address
    for, 568–71
Cafeteria service, 692
Caffeine, 55
Cakes,
  christening, 111–12
  how to eat, 422
  on picnic, 373
  wedding, 245–46
    cutting, 246
    for double weddings, 224
    for second weddings, 258
Calling cards (visiting cards), 500, 547–52
  as gift enclosures, 550
  how names are used on, 547–50
    for a man, 547–48
    for a woman, 549–50
  joint, 550
Calls, making and receiving, 551–52
  business, at White House, 637–38
Cameras. *See* Photographs and
    photography
Campers. *See also* Recreational vehicles
  gifts for, 794
Canapés, how to eat, 429
Candle lighters, at weddings, 209–10
Candles,
  at formal tea, 365
  at patio dinners, 372
  in table settings, 334
Candlesticks, 328
Canons (religious), correct forms of
    address for, 600–1
Cantaloupe, how to eat, 426
Cantors, Jewish, correct forms of address
    for, 596–97
Capitani (butler), 81
Captains
  Army
    abbreviations of rank, 585
    correct forms of address for, 588–89
    how to tell rank, 583
  boat. *See* Yachting and sailing

in hotel dining rooms, 830
  Navy (*See also* Navy, U. S.)
    abbreviation of rank, 585
    correct forms of address for, 590–91
    how to tell rank, 583
  restaurant, 679, 680
  ship. *See* Cruise travel; Navy, U. S.
Captain's table, 837–38
Cardinals, Catholic, correct forms of
    address for, 602–3
Cars and driving, 816–20. *See also* Taxis
  alcohol and, 56, 57, 58, 343
    teen-agers and, 48
  chauffeurs, 81, 82–83
    with children, 817–19
  don't lend to employees, 86
  in funeral procession, 275
  rental, 819–20
    on cruise trips, 838
  sensible drivers, 816–17
  teen-agers and, 48–49
    a girl and her car, 48–49
    and parents' permission, 48
  wedding transportation
    attendants and, 188
    to church, 194
    to reception, 236, 248
Car-sickness. *See* Motion sickness
Carving, at informal dinners, 296
Cashiers, paying, at restaurants, 686
Casseroles, at picnics, 375
Cassettes. *See* Tapes and tape recorders
Castel Gandolfo, papal audiences at, 650
CATALYST, 490
Caterers, 82, 367–70
  and cancellation, 369
  caution regarding, 369–70
  cost of, 369
  making arrangements with, 368–69
  where to find, 367–68
Catholics,
  audience with Pope, 649–52
  and christenings, 108–9ff.
  confirmation, 112
  First Communion, 112, 768
  funerals, 272ff., 276–77
    mass cards, 272
  hierarchy, correct forms of address for,
    600–3
  naming children, 106
  and saying grace, 421
  weddings (marriage), 188, 225–26
    and choosing time for wedding, 181
    to divorced people, 180
    grouping at altar, 218, 220
    invitations, 138
    and "Kiss of Peace," 221
Cats, flying with, 800
Catsup, 413
Caviar, how to eat, 422–23
Celebrities. *See also* Prominent people
  speakers, 737–39
    what not to do for, 739
    talking to, 746–47
Celery, how to eat, 423, 428
Centerpieces,
  for formal dinners, 357
  for formal luncheons, 363
  gifts of flowers for, 762

and informal dinners, 334
for restaurant dinners, 687
Ceremonies, 101–281
  christenings and confirmations, 108–12
    gifts for, 109, 766–67, 769–70
  engagements, 121–31. *See also*
    Engagements
  funerals, 266–81
  graduations and debuts, 115–20. *See also*
    Debutantes and debuts; Graduations
  Jewish traditions, 113–14
  wedding anniversaries, 262–65
    gifts for, 264–65, 783–84
  weddings, 132–261. *See also* Weddings
Chairs. *See also* Sitting
  deck, 836
  do not tip, 420
  formal dinners, 357
  teen-agers and table manners, 26
Chambers of Deputies, correct forms of
    addresses for Presidents of
  French, 618–19
  Italian, 622–23
  Spanish, 626–27
Champagne, 318. *See also* Toasting; *specific
    ceremonies*
  children and, 58
  at formal dinners, 357, 361
  at formal luncheons, 364
  gift for ship travelers, 791
  glasses, 320ff.
  service, 322, 323–24
Change of address, 510–11
Chaperons, at teen parties, 46–47
Chaplains, correct forms of address for, 585
Chaps, riding, 711–12
Charge accounts, and change of address,
    511
Chargés d'affaires, American, correct forms
    of address for, 574–75
Charity. *See* Donations
Chauffeurs, 81, 82–83
Checkout lines, teen-age manners in, 51
Checkrooms. *See also* Restaurants
  hat-check person, women and tipping,
    149
  parcels in, 682
Checks
  and freighter cruise, 840
  as gifts, 761, 765, 780–81
  in hotels and motels, 828
  signing, 506
Cheese, and teen-agers' table manners, 28
Chefs, 81
Cherries, how to eat, 425
  stewed, 427
Chesterfield coats, 678
Chicken, how to eat, 423–24
Chief justices, correct forms of address for,
    568–69
Chiefs of naval operations, correct forms of
    address for, 586–87
Chiefs of staff, correct forms of address for,
  Air Force, 586–87
  Army, 586–87
Chief warrant officers, how to tell rank,
  Army, 583
  Navy, 583
Children, 3. *See also* Babies; Baby-sitters;
    Families; Teen-agers

addressing mail to, 510
adopted, 62–65. *See also* Adopted
    children
age to begin note-writing, 516
and alcohol, 56–58, 343
  and driving, 56ff.
  and example at home, 57–58
  parents need to educate, 56–57
  when child drinks at home, 58
allowances, 34–36
and audiences with Pope, 650
and bad language, 21–22
and baked potatoes, 428
and bathrooms, 30
bedtimes, 32
birthday parties, 391–96. *See also*
    Birthday parties
burial of, clothing for, 268
and bus travel, 812, 813
car travel with, 817–19
  babies, 818–19
  motion sickness, 818
  in rental cars, 820
caterers and, 369–70
and christening of siblings, 108, 111
classic presents for, 768
and clothes, 32–34. *See also specific
    occasions*
  choosing own, 33–34
  hand-me-downs, made-overs, 33
  laundresses and, 82
and cocktail parties, 338, 339, 342
and compliments, 19
confirmations, 112–13, 769
  Jewish (Bar and Bat Mitzvahs), 113,
    769–70
conversation about, 307, 745
on cruises, 834, 835, 839, 840
and dancing classes, 17, 20–21
and dinner-party help, 302
and division of labor, 98–99
and divorce of parents, 71, 72, 74–75
and drugs, 52–54
  major categories, 55
  marijuana and hashish, 54
  parents and alertness to change, 53
  preventing abuse, 53–54
  socially acceptable, 54
  why drugs are abused, 52–53
in family relationships, 5–13
  and communication, 7–9
  consideration for those who serve, 6–7
  and grandparents living at home, 15–16
  in-laws and care of, 14
  is it a child's world?, 5
  parents shoot too high, 5–6
  and people with special problems,
    10–13
  respect for authority, 6–7
  and rules, 10
  and self-control, 7
  and threats, 9
  and tone of voice of parents, 9
at fast-food restaurants, 692–93
first communion, 12
  gifts, 112, 768
first jewelry for girls, 764
flying with, 805
and funerals, 271, 273
at hotels and motels, 832–33

and ice-cream cones, 427
ice skating, 721
introducing to domestic help, 84
and introductions, good-bys, 18
and invitations, 19–20. *See also specific*
  occasions
Jewish ceremonies (Bar and Bat
  Mitzvahs), 113–14, 769–70
and making Christmas gifts, 778
making mind manners, 17–18
and "Nanny," 81–82
and national anthem, 642–43
organizing Christmas gifts for, 777
and ostentatious gifts, 765
party manners, 20. *See also* Birthday
  parties
and pets, 31–32
  don't give as gifts, 764
on picnics, 374
at reaffirmation of marriage vows, 265
and respect for others' property, 22
sailing classes, 704
and saying grace, 420–21
social behavior, 17–22. *See also specific*
  occasions
and soup, eating of, 409
stationery for, 504–5
stocks or bonds as gifts, 761
and swimming, 715
  pools, 376–77, 717
table manners, 22–29. *See also specific*
  foods
  choosing own foods, 23–24
  learning how to converse, 25–26
  playing with food, 22–23
  use of napkins, 409
  when to begin eating, 407
  young child at family table, 24–25
and taxis, 814
and teachers' presents, 774
and telephone, 30–31
at tennis matches, 707
and "thank you," 18–19
and tidiness, responsibility for, 29–30
and toasting, 294–95
and train travel, 809
use of "ma'am" and "sir," 728
and visiting a naval vessel, 645–46
and weddings,
  as bridal attendants, 208–10. *See also*
    specific attendants
  as bridesmaids, 188
  and invitations, 136, 150, 157
  and second weddings (remarriages), 256,
    258
  ushers and, 191–92
weekend guests and, 386, 387
widow, widower and, 69–70, 72
and woman living with someone, 130
Child-sitters. *See* Baby-sitters
China. *See also* Gifts: wedding; Table
  setting
  in trousseau, 170–71
Choking, 415–16
Chops, how to eat, 424
Chopsticks, use of, 411
Christenings, 108–12
  church, 110–11
  dressing baby for, 110
  gifts for, 109, 766–67

godparents' responsibilities, 109
  at home, 111
  invitation to party, 109–10
  refreshments after ceremony, 111–12
Christian ceremonies. *See* Ceremonies;
  specific ceremonies, sects
Christian Science wedding, 231
Christmas
  cards
    addressing, signing, 532
    after bereavement, 281
    business, 532
    to Jews, 531
  gifts, 776–78
    for answering service, 471
    children and thank-you notes, 19
    for club employees, 698
    godparents and, 109
    how much to spend and making it
      yourself, 778
    mail-order catalogues for, 778
    office, 481
    organizing list, 776–78
Churches. *See also* Houses of worship;
  specific ceremonies
  American flag in, 642
  domestic employees and, 86
  aid in finding baby-sitter, 91
  and making friends in new community,
    260
  pants suits, worn at, 662
  for reaffirmation of marriage vows, 265
Churchill, Sir Winston, 419
Church of Jesus Christ of Latter-day Saints.
  See Mormons
Cigarettes. *See also* Ash trays; Smoking
  at formal dinners, 361
  at formal luncheons, 364
  women and lighting or offering, 450
Cigars
  on airplanes, 804
  gifts for smokers, 793
  at informal dinners, 298
  in restaurants, 684, 689
  at White House dinners, 637
Circumcision, Jewish, 113
Civil marriage, 236, 237
Clams
  and finger bowls, 367
  how to eat, 429, 430
Cleaning routine, 94
Cleaning women, 82
  hiring, 84
  and uniform, 85
Cleanliness. *See also* Grooming; Litter and
  littering
  children and, 5–6
  and teen-age dating, 43
Clergy. *See also specific religious officials;*
  specific ceremonies
  gifts for, 772–73. *See also specific*
    occasions
  and saying grace, 421
  and weddings. *See also* Weddings
    best man and fee, 189
    and own weddings, 234–35
    preparations, 180
    at reception, 244
    at rehearsal dinner, 199
Cloakrooms. *See also* Checkrooms

tipping attendants at wedding receptions, 242
Clocks, alarm, on trips, 826
Clothing (attire; dress). *See also specific articles*
    accessories, 663–68
    for audience with Pope, 651–52
    as baby gift, 767
    for Bar, Bat Mitzvah, 114
    for boating, 701
        on big yachts, 704
    for buffet parties, 299
        outdoors, 372
    for burial, 268
    and business party invitations, 456
    for business trips, women's, 451
    and bus travel, 812
    children's, 32–34. *See also specific occasions*
        choosing own, 33–34
        hand-me-downs, made-overs, 33
    laundress and, 82
    for christenings, babies', 110
    for cocktail party servers, 339–40
    for confirmation, 112–13
    for cruises, 837–38
        freighter, 840
        for debuts, 118, 119
    dressing well and following fashion, 658–59
    embarrassing choice of, on teen-age date, 44
    for first communion, 112
    for flying, 805–6
    for golf, 710
    for hospital patients, 750
    of household staff, 80–82. *See also Uniforms; specific staff members*
    how well you move in, 661–62
    for hunting, 713–14
    for informal teas, 351
    invitations and telling guests what to wear, 544
    for job interviews, 440
        teen-agers', 41
    for jury duty, 633
    laundresses and, 82
    men's, 669–78. *See also specific articles, occasions*
        formal wear, 676–78
    for motel swimming pools, 83
    for mourning, 280–81
    for naval vessel visit, 646
    in the office, 451–53
    organizing woman's wardrobe, 657–58
    for poolside entertaining, 377, 378
    for public speaking, 736–37
    for restaurant dining, 688
    for riding, fox hunting, 711–12, 713–14
    skiing, 719–20
        après-ski, 720
        cross-country, 720–21
        style, 659–60
        swimsuits, 714–15
        on cruises, 838, 840
    tennis, 707–8
    for trip (packing), 826–28. *See also specific means of travel*
    valet service, 831
    wedding, 200–11. *See also Weddings*

civil marriages, 237
    second, 257
    weekend guests and, 381, 386
    and White House invitations
        dinners, 635–36
        luncheons, 635
        receptions, 635
    for White House tours, 639
    you and your wardrobe, 657–68
Clubs, 694–98
    beach or swimming, 716–17
    Christmas fund for employees, 698
    joining, 695–97
        letter of proposal for membership, 696
        letter of resignation, 696–97
    listing women's names, 507
    press relations for, 739–40
    special interest, 698
    staying overnight, 697
    using facilities for entertaining when not a member, 697–98
    women and picking up lunch tab, 448–49
    yacht, 703–4
        dress for, 701
Coast Guard, 582
    abbreviations of rank, 583
    correct forms of address for Academy cadets, 592–93
    how to tell rank, 584
Coast Guard Publication 340 (boating guide), 700
Coat racks, in cafeteria, 692
Coats. *See also* Business suits; Jackets
    checking in restaurant, 680
    fur, 663
        as gifts, 765
    men's formal wear, 677–78
    riding, 711, 714
Coats of arms. *See* Heraldic devices
Cocaine, 55
Cocktail parties, 337–46
    bar glasses, 338–39
    bartenders at, 339–40
    bringing a friend, 545
    buffet, 345
        menus, 312
    after christenings, 110
    on cruises, 835, 837
    ending, 342
    gift for ship travelers, 791
    logistics, 337–39
    menus, 340–42
        buffet, 312
        napkins, 339
        plastic glasses, 338–39
    problem drinkers, 342–45
    and "Regrets Only," 542–43
    special kinds, 345–46
    spouses and invitations, 456
Cocktails. *See also* Cocktail parties
    in executive dining room, 454
    at formal luncheon, 363
    at informal lunch, 347–48
    ordering in restaurant, 682–83
    on picnic, 375
    teen-agers and tasting, 58
Codeine, 55
Coffee
    as drug, 54, 55
    in executive conference room, 453

at formal dinners, 362
  White House, 637
at formal tea, 364, 365
at informal dinners, 298
at informal lunches, 348–49
parties, 352
in restaurant, 684
  iced, 690
secretaries and making, 475
service of demitasse, 333
testing hot, 410
and use of napkin, 409
Cola drinks, caffeine in, 55
Collectors, gifts for, 793
College (college students). *See also*
    Baby-sitters
  entertaining, 398–403
    activities, 402–3
    date for, 399
    first step in organizing, 398–99
    food and drinks, 401–2
    guest list, 400–1
    invitations, 400
    place for, 399–400
  graduations, 115–16
    gifts, 764, 772
  stocks or bonds as gifts, 761
  and supervision of teen-age parties, 46
College of Arms (Heralds' College), 553,
    554
Colonels
  abbreviations of rank, 583
  correct forms of address for, 588–89
  how to tell rank, 582
Colonial Dames of America, 698
Colors. *See also specific articles of clothing*
  hunt, 713, 714
  in woman's wardrobe, 658
Commandant of the Marine Corps, correct
    forms of address for, 586–87
Commanders, Navy,
  abbreviation of rank, 583
  correct forms of address for, 590–91
  how to tell rank, 583
Commodores, how to tell rank, 583
Communication. *See also* Conversation;
    Language
  baby-sitters and, 91–92
  and deafness, 11–12
  domestic help and foreign languages, 87,
    89
  parent-child, 7–9
    and drugs, 53
Communion
  First, 112, 768
  weddings and, 219
Community, teen-agers and, 50
Complaints
  to airlines, 807
  letters for, 527–28
  to restaurants, 690–91
Compliments
  acknowledging, 727
  children and, 19
  and conversation, 744–45
  to freighter captain, 841
  praising dinner-party hosts, 329
  and restaurants, 691
  teen-agers and, 49
Concert halls, teen-age manners in, 51

Condolence, letters of, 279, 519–21
  business, 477
Conference room, executive, 453–54
Confirmation, 112–13, 769
  Jewish (Bar and Bat Mitzvah), 113,
    769–70
Congratulations (good news), 49, 518–19.
    See also specific occasions
  business letter of, 478
Congregational weddings, 219, 220
Congressmen (representatives), correct
    forms of address for, 572–73
Consulates, and travel, 823
Consuls general, correct forms of address
    for
  American, 574–75
  French, 620–21
  Italian, 624–25
  Spanish, 628–29
Continental-style eating, 406, 407
  children and, 25
  teen-agers and, 27
Contributions. *See* Donations
Convents of the Sacred Heart, 18
Conversation, 742–47. *See also* Dinners and
    dinner parties
  after-dinner, 305–7
  appropriateness of subject, 744–46
  basis of good, 743–44
  and bus travel, 812
  divorce as subject, 71
  at family dinner table, children and,
    25–26
  on a flight, 803–4
  hospital visitors and, 749
  and leaving table, 418
  in receiving line, 240–41
  at table, 419–20. *See also* Dinners and
    dinner parties; Table manners
  talking to celebrities, 746–47
  taxi drivers and, 814–15
  telephone, 469–70. *See also* Telephone
  the way you talk, 742–43
Cooking, when disaster strikes in, 315
Cooks, 81
  gourmet, gifts for, 774–75, 791–92
Corkscrews, 323
Corn on the cob, 424
Correspondence. *See* Letters; *specific types*
Correspondence cards
  men's, 503, 504
  women's, 501
Corsages
  for debuts, 118
  for proms, 47
  for wedding party, 210
Coughing
  public speakers and, 737
  teen-age manners and, 51
Counseling, psychological, single person
    and, 67
Counters, teen-age manners and seats at, 51
Countesses, correct forms of address for
  British (earl's wife), 610–11
  British royal, 606–7
  French, 620–21
  Italian, 624–25
  Spanish, 628–29
Country clubs. *See* Clubs; Golf
Counts, correct forms of address for

French, 620–21
Italian, 624–25
Spanish, 628–29
Cousins, double wedding invitation to, 142
Crabs, how to eat, 429–30
Crayons, children and, 22
Credit, single person and, 68
Credit cards,
  and change of address, 511
  hotels and motels and, 828
  in purse, 665
  at restaurants, 686
Cremation, 275–76
Crepes, how to eat, 424
Crest, heraldic, 555, 557
Crippled persons (physically handicapped),
  11, 13
Criticism, and grandparents living with you,
  16
Cross-country skiing, 720–21
Crowds, teen-age manners in, 51
Crudités, 341
Cruise travel, 834–41. *See also* Yachting
      and sailing
  bon voyage gifts, 790–91
  bon voyage parties, 835
  booking passage, 834–35
  captain's table, 837
  doctor on board, 825
  dress for, 837–38
    freighter, 840–41
  freighter trips, 839–41
    packing and dressing for, 840–41
  on ship, 835–37
    seasickness, 837
    things to remember, 837
  on-shore excursions, 838
  tipping, 838–39
  when you leave, 835
    bon voyage parties, 835
Crumbs; crumbing table, 297
  at formal meals, 366
Crystal. *See* Gifts: wedding; Glassware
Cuff links, 671, 677
  gifts for men, 764, 765
Cummerbunds, 676, 677
Cups
  how to hold, 410
  soup in handled, 409
Curtains, in trousseau, 170
Curtsying, of little girls, 18
"Cutting in" at dances, 47

D

Dallas, debuts in, 118
Dances. *See also* Dancing; Debutantes and
      debuts
  invitations to formal, 534–35
    when guest may bring escort, 535
    when reply is sent to social secretary,
      535
  proms, 47
Dancing. *See also* Dances
  after-dinner, 308–9
  at college parties, 399
  newlyweds and, 260–61
  at teen-age parties, 397
  teen-agers and duty dances, 47
  at wedding receptions, 246–47
Dancing classes, 17, 18, 20–21

Dandruff, 660
Dating (dates; escorts)
  and business party invitations, 456
  formal invitations to dances when guest
      may bring escort, 535
  at graduation, 115
  and informal dinner parties, 288
  and social communication, 514–15
  teen-age, 42–49, 50
    adult supervision for, 46–47
    car manners in, 48–49
    and duty dances, 47
    embarrassing moments in, 44
    and going steady, 45–46
    how does boy ask for date?, 43–44
    and money, 44–45
    parents and, 45
    proms, 47
    refusing date, 45
    returning home, 45
  and wedding invitations, 133
  widow, widower and, 69–70
Daughters of the American Revolution
      National Society, 698
Deaf persons, 11–12
Deans (religious), correct forms of address
      for, 600–1
Deans (university), correct forms of
      address for, 578–79
Death. *See also* Condolence, letters of;
      Widows (and widowers)
  American flag and, 641
  anniversary of friend's, 279
  funerals, 266–81. *See also* Funerals
  infant, 106
  parents'
    and engagement announcement,
      124–25, 126
    godparents and, 109
  of public figures, 277
  terminally ill patients, 749
  wedding gifts and death of groom, 166
  wedding invitations to those in mourning,
      133–34
Death certificate, 267
Death notices, 269–70
Debutantes and debuts, 116–20
  attire for, 118
    gloves, 664
  bad manners at parties, 120
  flowers for, 118
  gifts for, 771–72
  group debuts, 117–18
  invitations, 116–17, 537
  responsibility of male escorts, 119–20
  small private dance, 119
  teas, 118–19
Deck chairs, on cruises, 836
Decorations, wearing with white tie, 678
Demerol, 55
Demitasse. *See* Coffee
Deodorants, 660
  as inhalants, 55
Depressants, 55
Derbies, as hunting attire, 714
Desserts. *See also* Cakes; Fruit; *specific
      occasions*
  and bridge playing, 354
  eating continental-style, 407
  ice cream, how to eat, 427
  at informal luncheon, 348, 349

on picnic, 375
in restaurants, 684
 dividing, 685
table setting for, 332. *See also* Table
 setting
taking portions from serving dish, 412
at teen-age parties, 397–98
teen-agers' table manners and, 28–29
Dessert wines, 318
 service of, 322
De Verdura, Fulco, 667
Diamond jewelry, 667
 rings. *See also* Wedding rings
 gifts for men, 763
Diapers, on airplanes, 805
Diaper service, 83
Diet pills, 55
Diets
 and flying, 801
 guests on, 316
 for hospital patients, 748
 and restaurant eating, 684, 687
Dill, how to eat, 428
Dining. *See* Hotels; Meals; Restaurants;
 specific meals, occasions
Dining rooms. *See also* Hotels; *specific
 meals*
 executive, 454
Dinners and dinner parties, 287–309. *See
 also* Buffets; Conversation; First
 course; Restaurants; Table manners;
 Table setting; *specific occasions*
 after-dinner activities, 305–9
 baby-sitters and, 92
 breaking engagements for, 546
 bringing a friend, 545
 on business trips,
 men, women and, 450
 women and, 451
 on city apartment balcony, 371
 flowers as gift for, 762. *See also* Flowers
 formal, 355–62
 arrival and introduction of guests,
 357–58
 catered, 367–70
 departing after, 362
 gloves at, 664–65
 guests at, 365–67
 invitations, 355, 534, 535–36
 leaving dining room, 362
 seating, 355–57
 service, 357, 361–62
 table setting, 358–61
 hotel, motel, 830. *See also* Hotels
 how many courses?, 316
 invitations, 287–89
 formal, 355, 534, 535–36
 nuances of accepting, 543
 White House, 634–35
 menus, 310–12. *See also* Menus
 newlyweds at, 261
 no-maid, sit-down, 301–5
 one-maid, 295–98
 picking up tab. *See also* Restaurants
 women and, 448–50
 playing bridge after, 352–54
 seating at, 290–93
 formal, 355–57
 smoking etiquette, 59. *See also* Smoking
 special needs of guests, 316–17. *See also*
 Diets

teen-agers and table manners, 26–29
velvet blazer worn to, 675
wedding anniversary, 262–65
wedding rehearsal, 198–99
White House, 635–36, 636–37
wine at, 317–26
 cellar, 318–19
 glasses, 319–22
 kinds to serve, 317–18
 service, 322–26
Dinner suits. *See* Formal wear
Dirty jokes, 746
Dishes. *See also* China; Table manners
 tipping of, 409
 washing, 97–98
Divers, scuba, gifts for, 794
Division of labor, in household tasks, 98–99
Divorce, 70–72. *See also* Single life
 and calling cards, 549
 children and, 8, 71, 72, 74–75
 and conversation, 71
 and engagement announcement, 124
 parents' divorce and, 125
 and funeral attendance, 271
 Greek Orthodox, and remarriage, 232
 and hyphenated names, 75, 510
 and invitations, 571–72
 of Jews, and remarriage, 226
 listing name in clubs, 507
 Mormons and, 233
 Quakers and, 233
 and name of woman, 74–75. *See also*
 Names
 and stationery, 74
 and weddings (remarriage), 180, 253,
 255, 258
 announcements and, 161, 252, 253–54
 and father's responsibility for
 daughter's wedding, 186
 and giving away bride, 220
 Greek Orthodox Church and, 232
 invitations and, 140, 141, 145, 151
 Jewish marriages, 226
 and receptions, 240, 243, 248
 seating couple's families, 193
Doctors, 752. *See also* Titles
 correct forms of address for medical
 officers, 584
 ships', 837
 and wedding invitations, 136
Doggie bags, 688
Dogs,
 flying with, 800
 Seeing Eye (guide dogs), 13
 and bus travel, 812
 and train travel, 809
Domestic help. *See* Household
 management; *specific occasions*
Domestic prelate, correct forms of address
 for, 602–3
Donations (charity), 761
 after a death, 277ff.
 writing for, 526
Doormen, hotel, 829–30
Doors
 car, and teen-age manners, 48
 closing, teen-agers and, 50
 elevator, and teen-age manners, 51
 knocking before entering, 49
Double weddings, 222–24
 gifts for, 781

invitations to, 142
"Dowager," use of, 607n
"Downers," 55
Draperies, in trousseau, 170
Dress. *See* Clothing
Dresses. *See also specific occasions*
  for cruise travel, 838, 840
  packing for trip, 827
Drinks and drinking. *See also* Alcohol;
    Cocktails; Toasting; *specific*
    occasions
  on airplanes, 804
  and bridge playing, 354
  and bus travel, 812
  caffeine in, 55
  on cruises, 836ff., 841
  for college parties, 401
  at debut, paying for, 120
  ordering in restaurants, 681
  at picnic, 373, 375
  for post-college entertaining, 403
  and table manners, 408
  for teen-age parties, 397
  women on business trips and, 457
Driving. *See* Cars and driving
Drugs, 52–55
  major categories of, 55
  marijuana and hashish, 54
  parents and alertness to changes in
    children, 53
  preventing abuse, 53–54
  socially acceptable, 54
  teen-age car manners and, 48
  and teen-age parties, 46, 396
  where to go for help, 60
  why drugs are abused, 52–53
Duchesses, correct forms of address for
  British (nonroyal), 608–9
  British royal, 608–9
  French, 620–21
  Italian, 624–25
  Spanish, 628–29
Duck, how to eat, 423
Duffel bags, for boating, 701
Duke(s), correct forms of address for
  British (nonroyal), 608–9
    daughter of, 608–9
    wife of, 608–9
    younger son of, 608–9
  British, of Edinburgh, 606–7
  British royal, 608–9
  French, 620–21
  Italian, 624–25
  Spanish, 628–29
Dutch treat
  restaurant dinners, 686–87
  and teen-age dating, 44
Duty dances, teen-agers and, 47

E

Earls, British, correct forms of address for,
  610–11
Earrings, 666
  first jewelry for girls, 764
  and playing tennis, 708
Eastern Orthodox Church
  confirmations, 112
  correct forms of address for officials,
    594–95
  weddings, 231–32

Eating. *See* Food and eating; Meals;
  specific occasions
Edgartown, Mass., 704
Education, single persons and, 67
Eggs, soft-boiled, how to eat, 424–25
Elbows on table, 420
Elderly. *See* Old age
Elevators
  doors of, teen-age manners and, 51
  sneezing, coughing in, 51, 416
Elopements, 236–37
  gifts for, 236–37
  parties for, 237
Enclosure cards,
  with wedding gifts, 782
  with wedding invitations, 150–53
Engagement rings, 127–28
  bride, wearing, 201
  widow's, widower's, and consideration for
    new spouse, 70
Engagements (engaged couples), 121–31
  announcing, 122–24, 131
  before second marriages, 251–52
  behavior of couples, 128
  breaking, 128
  bride on her own, 127
  complicated relationships and, 124–27
  and informal dinners, 292
    invitations to couples, 288–89
  legally changed names and, 127
  and premarital living together, 128–31
  parties, 122–23
  and rings. *See* Engagement rings
  telling the family, 121–22
  and wedding invitations, 133
  when engagement is not announced, 124
English. *See* British
English-style dinner service, 304, 362
Engraving. *See also* Invitations
  monogram on personal stationery, 495–96
  vs. printing, 495
Ensigns, Navy
  abbreviation of rank, 585
  correct forms of address for, 590–91
  how to tell rank, 583
Entertaining, 283–463. *See also* Invitations;
    specific ceremonies, occasions
  allergic guests, 316
  barbecues, 378
  bridge parties, 352–54
  buffet, 298–304. *See also* Buffets
  business, 455–64
    and badges, 462–63
    hosts and receiving lines, 462
    invitations, 455–61
      from business associates, 463–64
    office parties, 481–82
    opening parties, 487
    R.S.V.P. cards, 461
    thank-yous for, 462
  catering services, 82. *See also* Catering
  children's parties, 391–96
    party games and entertainment, 393–95
  club facilities for, 697–98
  cocktail parties, 337–46. *See also*
    Cocktail parties
  coffees, 352
  college parties, 398–403
    post-college entertaining, 403–4
  demitasse, 298
  dieting guests, 316

entertainment, after meal, 305–09
formal, 355–70. *See also* Invitations
  caterers and, 367–70
  dinners, 355–62. *See also* Dinners and
    dinner parties
  greeting guests, 298–90
  guests at meals, 365–67
  luncheons, 363–64. *See also* Luncheons
    and lunching
  teas, 364–65
house guests. *See also* House guests
  overnight, 388
  weekend, 381–90
housewarmings and open house, 345–46
informal, 287–309, 347–54. *See also*
  specific occasions
menu inspiration for, 310–26. *See also*
  Menus
out of doors, 371–80
  barbecues, 378–80
  buffets, 371–72
  dinner on city apartment balcony, 371
  patio, 372–73
  picnics, 373–76
  poolside, 376–78
philosophy of, 285
picnics, 373–76
  pool party, 376
problem drinkers, 342–44. *See also*
  Alcoholics
in restaurants. *See* Restaurants
seating, 290, 293
separation of sexes, 298
serving food, 295–305, 357–62. *See also*
  specific occasion
setting your table, 327–36. *See also* Table
  setting
single persons and, 67, 75–77
  "extra woman," 76
  host and hostess in one person, 76
  men and, 76–77
  transportation for single woman, 77
  widow, widower, 69
small space, dining in, 304–5, 371
smoking, 418–19
  service of cigarettes and cigars, 298
special types, 391–404
  children's birthday parties, 391–96
  college, 398–403
  post-college, 403–4
  special-event parties, 404
  teen-age parties, 396–98
teas, 349–52, 364–65. *See also* Teas;
  specific occasions
toasting, 293–95, 329
wines, 316–19. *See also* Wines
Entrées. *See also* Dinners and dinner parties
  table setting, 331
Envelopes. *See also* Stationery
  lined, 497
Episcopalians
  correct forms of address for bishops,
    598–99
  funerals, 272, 273
  weddings, 219, 220, 221
Equal Credit Opportunity Act, 68
Equal Employment Opportunity
  Commission, 490
Escorts. *See* Dating; *specific occasions*
"Esquire," use of, 566–67
Ethnic jokes, 746

Eulogies, funeral, 273
Executive facilities, special, 453–54
  conference room, 453–54
  dining room, 454
Executives. *See* Business
Exercise and exercising
  gifts for, 794
  for posture, 661
"Extra woman." *See* Single life
Eye injuries, tennis and, 707
Eyeliner, teen-agers and, 41
Eye shadow, teen-agers and, 41
Expertise. *See* Special interests

F

Families, 1–65. *See also* Children; Home;
  Parents; Teen-agers; *specific*
  ceremonies
  adopted child, 62–65. *See also* Adopted
    children
  and aged parents, 14–16
  children and, 5–13
  complicated relationships
    and engagements, 124–27
    and seating of wedding parties, 193
  and drugs, alcohol, tobacco, 52–61
  in-laws and grandparents, 13–14
  manners in, 17–36
    allowances, 34–36
    around the home, 29–32
    clothes for children, 32–34
    social behavior of children, 17–22
    at table, children's, 22–29. *See also*
      Children
  and news events, 740–41
  prominent. *See* Prominent people
  relationships in, 5–16
  teen-agers and courtesy to, 49–50
  widow, or widower, and late spouse's
    family, 70
Fast-food service, 692–93
Fathers. *See* Children; Parents; *specific*
  ceremonies
Fathers-in-law. *See also* Grandparents;
  specific occasions
  and family relations, 13–14
Feast of Weeks, 113
Federated Garden Clubs, 698
Fedora hats, 674
Feet, and teen-age manners
  on furniture, 50
  and public passageways, 50
Finances. *See also* Business: opening own
  engagements and income, 121–22
  single person's, 68
  support of parents, 15
Fine Arts Committee for the White House,
  639
Finger bowls, 333, 360
  presentation of, 366–67
  teen-agers' table manners and, 28
Fingers. *See also* Hands; Nails
  teen-agers and nervous habits, 50
Fire(s)
  at beach, 716
  drill on ship, 836
  and instructions for baby-sitters, 92
Firing household employees, 89–90

and letters of reference, 89–90
and references over telephone, 90
First Communion, 112
  gifts, 112, 768
First course, 305
  in restaurants, 684
  service with one maid, 295–96
  table setting for, 330
First lieutenants
  abbreviations of rank, 585
  correct forms of address for, 588–89
  how to tell rank, 583
Fish
  how to eat, 425
  taking portions from serving dish, 412
  teen-agers and dinner-party manners, 27
Fishermen, gifts for, 794
Flags
  American, 640–44
    and honors to civilians on naval vessel,
      646
    invocation and salute to, 642
    in synagogues, 644
  yacht club, 704
Flatware (silver). *See also* Silver; Table
      setting
  at restaurants, 689–90
  use of, 406, 407
    dessert, 408
    placement of used, 406, 407
  if utensil is missing, 409
Fleet admiral, how to tell rank, 583
Floors, cleaning routine and, 94
Flower girls, 208, 209, 218
  at Jewish weddings, 228
  at receptions, 238
  at rehearsals, 213, 215, 216
Flowers, 762–63. *See also* Boutonnieres;
      Corsages
  artificial, 763
    for table setting, 328
  for debuts, 118, 119
  for formal luncheons, 363
  for funerals, 271–72, 274
    acknowledgments for, 277
  for graves, 268, 274
  in hotel room, 831
  for men, 762
  in office, 483
  for opening of new business, 487
  for public speakers, 737
  at restaurant dinners, 687
  for weddings, 181–82, 210. *See also*
      Bouquets, brides'
    at receptions, 242
  weekend guests and, 390
  to White House, 637
Food and eating. *See also* Caterers; Cooks;
      Meals; Menus; Table manners;
      specific foods, meals
  baby-sitters and, 92
  at bridge party, 354
  children and. *See also* Table manners
    on airplanes, babies and, 805
    at birthday party, 392
    and car travel, 817, 818, 820
    choosing own, 23–24
    playing with, 22–23
  cocktail party, 341–42, 345, 346
  coffee party, 352
  college parties, 401–2

freighter cruises, 840
  after funerals, 279–80
  how to eat various foods, 421–32
  to hospital patients, 748
  hostess gifts, 788
  in office, 484
  on picnic, 373, 375
  speaking with food in mouth, 417
  tasting others' food in restaurants, 688
  for teen-age parties, 397
  on trains, 808, 809–10
Footmen, 81
  at formal dinners, 361
Foreign languages, 149–50, 743. *See also*
      Travel
  airplane flights and, 807
  domestics and, 87, 88
  on menu cards, 334
  government officials and nobility,
      addressing, 580–81, 604–29
    British, 604, 606–17
    French, 604, 618–23
    Italian, 604–5, 623–27
    Spanish, 605, 627–29
  national anthems of, 644
Foreign matter in food, 418
Foreign Policy Association, 698
Forgetting names, introductions and, 726
Forks, 406, 407. *See also* Flatware; Table
      manners; Table setting; *specific
      occasions*
  in continental- vs. American-style use, 25,
      27
  dessert, use of, 408
  serving, use of, 412
Formal entertaining. *See also* Debutantes
      and Debuts; Dinners and dinner
      parties; Formal wear; Luncheons and
      lunching
  invitations, 533–41. *See also specific
      meals*
    accepting, 538–40
    map enclosures, 541
    more than one person issuing, 538
    regrets, 540–41
    telling guests what to wear, 544
    when guest may bring escort, 535
    when not to send formal regret, 540–41
Formal wear, 676–78. *See also specific
      occasions*
  Black Tie, 676–78
    pastel or piped dinner suits, 678
    summer variations, 678
  White Tie, 678
Foster parents. *See also* Adopted children
      and wedding invitations, 140
Four-in-hand ties, 671
  tying, 673
Fox hunting, 712–14
  attire for, 713–14
  hunt colors, 713
  joining hunt, 713
  spectators, 713
Franchising businesses, 490
Freighter travel, 839–41
  packing and dressing for, 840–41
French officials and nobility, correct forms
      of address for, 618–23, 604
Friends (friendship). *See also* Eating;
      Entertaining; Houseguests; *specific
      occasions*

bringing to parties, 544–45
    cocktail parties, 545
    dinner parties, 545
    meals, 544–45
death of, 279
double wedding invitations to, 142
jealousy over, divorce and, 72
jury duty and, 634
letters of reference for travelers abroad,
    523–24
newlyweds and new, 260
notes to new neighbors, 551
single persons and, 67
    widows, widowers, 69
teen-agers and courtesies to, 49–50
weddings at home of, 146–47
    reception, 150
Frogs' legs, how to eat, 422
Fruit
    in hotel room, 831
    how to eat, 425–27
        with pits, 414–15
        stewed, 427
    teen-agers' table manners and, 29
Fund-raising. *See* Donations
Funerals, 266–81
    acknowledgments for flowers, donations,
        277–78
    acknowledgments to clergy, pallbearers,
        ushers, 278
    attending, 271
    calls, 272–73
    choosing someone to be in charge, 267–68
    clothing for burial, 268
    concept of mourning, 281
    contributions to charity, 279
    cremation, 274–75
    dealing with mortician, 268
    death notices, 269–70
    distributing family possessions, 280
    fees to clergymen, sexton, musicians,
        276–77
    food after, 279–80
    greeting cards after bereavement, 281
    hanging the bell, 269
    interment and grave marking, 276
    letters of condolence, 279. *See also*
        Condolence, letters of
    mass cards, 272
    mourning dress, 280–81
    obituaries for prominent people, 270
    sending flowers, 271–72
    services, 273–74
    what to do when death comes, 266–67
Furniture, teen-agers and feet on, 50
Furs, 663
    checking coats in restaurants, 680
    gifts of coats, 765
    men's hats, 674

G

Games
    after-dinner, 309
    children's party, 393–94
        prizes for, 395
    teen-age party, 397
    for wedding gifts, 783
Gaper's, 369
Garden Clubs of America, 698

Gardeners and gardening, 82
    gifts for, 792
    service industry and, 83
Garment bags, for trips, 825
Garnishes, how to eat, 428
Garters, brides', 247
Gasoline, as inhalant, 55
Gemstones, mixing, 667
General of the Army, how to tell rank, 582
Generals
    abbreviations of rank, 585
    correct forms of address for, 588–89
    how to tell rank, 582, 584
"Gentleman," use of, 728
Get-well cards, 531
Gift certificates, 761
Gifts, 755–94
    anniversary, 783–85
        pegged to the year, 784–85
    and audiences with Pope, 651
    baby, 766–67
        shower, 105
    Bar or Bat Mitzvah, 114, 769
    birthday, 785–86. *See also* Birthday
        parties
    for boating party, 703
    calling cards as enclosures, 550
    and car travel with children, 817–18
    certificates, 761
    to charitable organizations, 761. *See also*
        Donations
    christening, 109, 766–67
    Christmas, 776–78. *See also* Christmas
    classic
        for children ten and under, 768
        for teen-agers, 768–69
    for clergymen (priests, ministers, rabbis),
        772–73. *See also specific occasions*
    confirmation, 112–13, 769–70
    debutante, 771–72
    don't-gives, 764–65
    engagement, 122
    fine jewelry, 763–64
    First Communion, 112, 768
    flowers, 762–63. *See also* Flowers
    for gourmet cooks, 774–75
    graduation, 115
        college, 115, 764, 772
        high school, 115, 770–71
    house guests and, 386, 390, 787–88
        food and liquor, 788
    for hot-weather entertaining, 787–88
    housewarming, 346, 774–75, 786–87
    to hospital nurses, 751
    to hosptial patients, 748, 750, 789
    ideas for all occasions, 766–94
    and invitations from business associates,
        463
    for kitchen showers, 774
    for linen showers, 775
    from mail-order catalogs, 778
    money, 760–61. *See also* Money
    for nuns, 773
    office, 480–81
    for opening of new business, 487
    philosophy of giving, 759–65
    special-interest, 791–94
    for teachers, 774
    thank-you notes, 517–18. *See also*
        Thank-you notes
        for money, 518

and refusing gifts, 518
and retirement, 518
for travelers, 789–91
  bon voyage, 790–91
unexpected, 761–62
wedding, 163–68, 778–83. *See also*
    Showers; Trousseau
  for attendants, 167, 198
  bridal registry, 163
  bridal showers, 197–98. *See also*
      Showers
  choosing, 779–80
  couple's to each other, 168
  display of, 164
  double wedding, 781
  elopement and, 236–37
  enclosure cards, 782
  exchanging, 166
  money, 780–81
  monogramming, 781
  to official at civil marriage, 237
  one-of-a-kind, 780
  at receptions, 164
  register of, 163–64
  and remarriage (second wedding), 255,
      256, 782–83
  returning, 166–67
  suitable, 779
  thank-you letters for, 164–66
  timetable for sending, 781
  from wedding party, 168, 193
  where to send, 781–82
wedding anniversary, 264–65
  to clergy at reaffirmation of vows, 265
  to White House, 637
Gin, 341
Glassware (crystal)
  for cocktail party, 338–39
  for formal dinner, 361
  and how to drink at table, 408
  how to hold, 410
  as part of trousseau, 173–76
  on trips, 825
  washing, 97
  wine, 319–22
Gloves, 664–65
  golf, 710
  ice skating, 722
  men's formal-wear, 677
  removing for handshake, 665, 725. *See
      also* Receiving lines
  riding, 711, 714
  at weddings
    bride's, 201
    flower girls and, 208
    guests and, 202n
    men's, 205
    mothers', 210
  for White House meals, 635, 636
Glue, as inhalant, 55
Godparents, 109, 110
  and Brith Milah, 113
  and confirmation, 112–13
Gofer, secretary as, 475
Going steady, 45–46
Gold, 667. *See also* Jewelry; *specific
    occasions*
Golf, 708–10
  clothing, on course, 710

gifts for players, 794
handling cart, 709–10
Good-bys. *See also specific occasions*
  children and adults and, 18
  teen-age dates and, 45
Good news. *See* Congratulations
Gossip, 745
Gourmet cooks, gifts for, 774–75, 791–92
Governors
  calling cards of, 548
  correct forms of address for, 574–75
  stationery for, 506
Gown, bridal, 200–1
Grace, saying, 420–21
Graduations, 115–16
  gifts, 115
    college, 115, 764, 772
    high school, 115, 770–71
Grandparents
  and announcing adoption, 63
  and family relations, 14ff.
  at Jewish weddings, 226
  living with you, 15–16
  naming babies after, 106
  widow, widower, and late spouse's family,
      70
Grapefruit, how to eat, 426
Grapes
  how to eat, 426
  teen-agers' table manners and, 29
Grave marking, 276
Gravies, adding, 412
Greek Orthodox Church
  celibacy of clergymen, 594n
  and naming children, 106
Greeting cards, 530–31. *See also*
    Announcements
  after bereavement, 281
  and change of address, 511
  Christmas, 531–32
    addressing, signing, 532
    business, 532
    to Jews, 531
Greetings, 726–27. *See also* Guests; *specific
    occasions*
  teen-agers and, 51
Grooming, 660–61. *See also* Clothes
  and children at table, 24, 25
  for job interviews, 440
  for office, 452–53
  teen-agers and, 41
Guard rings, 201
Guest bathroom, 383–84
  necessities in, 383
  niceties in, 383–84
Guest book, wedding, 183–84, 242
Guest room, 381–83
  necessities in, 382
  niceties in, 382–83
Guests. *See* House guests; Introductions;
    Invitations; *specific occasions*
Guidebooks, 823
Guide dogs (Seeing Eye dogs), 13
  and bus travel, 812
Gum chewing,
  in office, 484
  and teen-agers' job interviews, 41
Gynecologists, for woman living with a
    man, 130

H

Hacking, 711
"Hail to the Chief," 637, 644
Hair, 660
　bride's hairdo, 203
　don't fix on job, 483
　teen-agers and, 41, 51
　　nervous habits with, 50
Hair spray, as inhalant, 55
Hallucinogens, 55
Hamburgers, on picnics, 375
Hamlet, quoted, 421
Handbags, 665–66
　packing for trip, 827
　in restaurants, 682
Handicapped persons, 10–13
　and guide dogs on buses, 812
　teen-agers and, 50
Handkerchieves, 670
　for formal wear, 677
　and sneezing, coughing, 51, 414
Hand-me-down clothes, 33
Hands. *See also* Fingers; Handshaking;
　　Nails
　children and table manners, 25
　in public speaking, 734–35
　at table, 420
Handshaking,
　children and, 18
　importance of, 724–25
　removing glove for, 665, 725. *See also*
　　Receiving line
Hanging the bell, 269
Hanukkah cards, 531
Hard of hearing, the, 11
Hat checking, 680
　women and tipping, 449
Hats (and head coverings), 664. *See also*
　　Head gear
　for boating, 701
　checking in restaurant, 680
　for cross-country skiing, 720
　for formal wear, 678
　at funerals, Jews and, 275
　with fur coats, 663
　for hunting, 714
　men's, 674. *See also specific occasions*
　　tipping, 674
　for public speaking, 736
　rain, on trips, 825
　riding, 711, 712
　　derby, 714
　for tennis, 707
　at weddings, 202n, 206n, 210
　　Jewish, 225, 231
　for White House luncheons, 635
Head gear. *See also* Hats
　for ice skating, 722
　for skiing, 719
Headwaiters (maîtres d'), 679, 680, 682,
　　683, 686, 690
　and check, 685–86
　on trains, 809
　women and tipping, 449
Health. *See also* Illness
　as subject of conversation, 745–46
Heimlich Maneuver, 415–16
Helmets, riding, 711
Heraldic devices (coats of arms), 553–57
　how used, 557

　by married woman, 557
　on wedding invitations and
　　announcements, 135, 557
　by women, 556–57
　lozenge, 555–56, 557
　silver marking and coat of arms, 557
Heralds' College (London), 553, 554
Herb teas, 351
Heroin, 55
High school students. *See* Graduations;
　　Teen-agers
Hikers, gifts for, 794
Hiring. *See also* Jobs
　of domestic employees, 83–87
　　continuous training, 86–87
　　helping employees start right, 85
　　interview, 83–85
　　living quarters, 85
　　and overwork, 87
　　and time off, 86
　　uniforms and, 85–86
Home (house). *See also* Families
　basic household needs, 176–78
　business calls at, 471
　expenses after marriage, 187
　funerals at, 269, 277
　household management, 80–99
　　baby- or child-sitter, 90–93
　　basic needs, 176–78
　　firing employees, 89–90
　　former "household staff," 80–82
　　handling of telephone, 88–89
　　hiring domestic help, 83–87
　　routine, 93–99
　　Social Security and withholding tax,
　　　87–88
　　in today's world, 82–83
　　unemployment tax, 88
　　workmen's compensation, 87
　manners around, 29–32
　　bathroom, 30
　　bedtime, 32
　　keeping things tidy, 29–30
　　pets, 31–32
　　telephone, 30–31
　newlyweds in new neighborhood, 260
　and planning trips, safety of, 386, 823–24
　single persons and, 67, 77–79
　and stationery, 505
　weddings at, 233–34
　　civil, 237
　　invitations to, 144–47
Homosexual couples
　addressing envelopes to, 510
　and wedding invitations, 133
Honeydew melon, how to eat, 426
Honeymoon, 259–60
　at destination, 260
　where to go, 259–60
Horseback riding, 710–14
　fox hunting, 712–14
　hacking, 711
　safety in, 712
　Western, 711–12
Hors d'oeuvres, for cocktail parties, 339,
　　341, 342, 345, 346
Hose. *See* Socks
Hospitals, 748–53
　doctors in, 752
　how a woman registers, 750
　nurses in, 751–52

psychiatric patients, 752–53
roommates, 751
services, 750–51
tips for patients, 750
visiting patients, 748–49
  gifts for patients, 748, 762, 789
  the terminally ill, 749
  visitors' manners, 748–49
Hostess, in restaurant dining room, 690
Hostess gifts. *See* House guests; *specific
  occasions*
Hotels, 828–33. *See also* Reservations
  checking in, 828–29
  with children, 832–33
  and inviting guests, 832
  security in, 832
  things to remember, 831–32
  tipping and room service, 829–31
  and wedding guests, 184
House. *See* Home
House guests
  bringing to party, 545
  and gifts, 390, 787–88
    food and liquor, 788
    for hot-weather entertaining, 787–88
  weekend, 381–90
    breakfast for, 384
    guest bathroom, 383–84
    for guest to remember, 385–88
    guest room, 381–83
    invitations, 381
    organizing the day, 385
    saying thank you, 389–90, 517
Household management, 80–99
  baby- or child-sitter, 90–93
  basic needs, 176–78
  firing employees, 89–90
  former "household staff," 80–82
  handling telephone, 88–89
  hiring domestic help, 83–87
  routine, 93–99
  Social Security and withholding tax,
    87–88
  in today's world, 82–83
  unemployment insurance, 88
  workmen's compensation, 87
Housekeepers, 81
  hiring, 84
  hotel, 831
  and uniform, 85
Housekeeping. *See also* Household
    management
  service industry and, 82
Housemaids. *See* Maids
Housemen, 81
  catering services and, 82
House of Commons, correct forms of
  address for member of, 614–15
House of Representatives, correct forms of
  address for members of, 572–73
Houses of worship. *See also* Churches;
    Synagogues; *specific ceremonies*
  single persons and, 67
  teen-agers and, 50
Housewarmings, 345–46
  gifts for, 346, 774–75, 786–87
Housework. *See also* Home; Household
    management
  baby-sitters and, 92
Hunters, gifts for, 794
Husbands. *See also* Marriage

and division of labor, in household tasks,
  98
Hyphenated names
  and addressing envelopes, 510
  and divorce, 75

I

Ice, at picnics, 374
Ice cream, how to eat, 427
Ice skating, 721–22
  dress for, 722
  on pond or lake, 722
Identification bracelets, for men, 763
Illness (sickness)
  and greeting cards, 531
  hospital patients, 748–53
    and doctors, 752
    how a woman registers, 750
    nurses and, 751–52
    psychiatric patients, 752–53
    roommates and, 751
    services for, 750–51
    tips for, 750
    visiting, 748–49
  and office gifts, 481
  and regrets. *See* Invitations
  teen-age manners and, 49
Impulse notes, 521
India, 564
Informal entertaining, 287–309. *See also
    specific meals, occasions*
  after-dinner activities, 305–9
  buffet supper, 298–301
  dinner with one maid, 295–98
  greeting guests, 289–90
  invitations, 287–89, 541–43. *See also
    specific meals*
    accepting, 541–43
    breaking engagements, 546
    bringing a friend, 544–45
    bringing house guests, 545
    canceling, 545–46
    handwritten notes, 541
    telling guests what to wear, 544
  protocol, 292–93
  seating at dinner, 290–92
  sit-down dinner, with no maid, 301–5
  toasting, 293–95
Inhalants, 55
Initials. *See also* Monograms
  in naming babies, 106
Injuries
  skiing, 720
  tennis and eye, 707
In-laws. *See also* Grandparents; *specific
    occasions*
  and family relations, 13–14
Insects. *See* Bugs
Insurance
  baggage, and flying, 802
  car
    sensible driver and, 816
    teen-agers and, 48
    and freighter travel, 840
  life, and couple living together, 130
  and planning trip, 824
  single persons and, 68
  unemployment, 88
  workmen's compensation, 87
Interment (burial), 268, 276
  clothing for, 268

Internal Revenue Service, and restaurant
    checks, 686
International Franchise Association, 490
Interviews
  going on job, 440–42
    teen-agers and, 41
  in hiring domestic help, 83–84
  with reporters, when family makes news,
    741
Introductions, 723–28. *See also* Address,
    correct forms of; *specific occasions*
  acknowledging compliments, 727
  children and adults, 18
    domestic help, 84
  forgetting names, 726
  husbands and wives introducing each
    other, 725
  importance of handshake, 724–25
  letters, 522–23
    for audience with Pope, 650
    to friends abroad, 523–24
  people greeting each other, 726–27
  receiving lines, 727. *See also* Receiving
    lines
  speakers, 731–32
  strangers at parties, 725–26
  and teen-age dating, of date to parents,
    45
    and car manners, 48
  use of "lady" and "gentleman" vs.
    "woman" and "man," 728
  use of "ma'am" and "sir," 728
  when woman keeps maiden name, 725
  who is introduced to whom, 723–24
Investment counselors, single persons and,
    68
Invitations (acceptances and regrets),
    533–52. *See also* Address, correct
    forms of; Dating; Letters
  accepting, 539, 541, 543
  baby shower, 105
  breaking an engagement, 546
  bringing a friend, 544–45
  bringing house guests, 545
  and business entertaining, 455–61
    from business associates, 463–64
    how to extend, 457–61
    when no R.S.V.P. card is enclosed, 461
  canceling party, 545–46
  from captain on ship, 837
  from child to child, 19–20
  christening, 109–10
  cocktail party, 337. *See also* Cocktail
    parties
  coffee party, 352
  college parties, 400
  on correspondence cards, 501
  to couple living together, 129–30
  debut, 116–17, 120
  to divorced people, 71–72
  fill-ins, 534
  formal, 533–41. *See also specific
    occasions*
  graduation, 115
  and handwriting, 535–36
  informal, 287–89, 541–43. *See also
    specific occasions*
  on informals, 498
  by mailgram, 539
  map enclosure, 541
  poolside entertaining, 376–77

  postage considerations, 543
  post-college entertaining, 403
  postponing or canceling, 545, 546
  regrets, 540, 542
  reminders, 501, 543–44
  teen-agers and, 41
  by telephone, 287, 460, 539
  telling guests what to wear, 544
  wedding, 132–62
    addressing envelopes, 135–37
    combining church ceremony and
      reception, 147–48
    enclosure cards, 150–53
    engraving and stationery, 134–35
    foreign procedures, 149–50, 158
    heraldic devices, 135, 557
    to informal weddings, 159
    late reception, 148–49
    military forms, 161–62
    postponing weddings, 154
    preparing list, 132–33
    recalling, 153–54
    recalling acceptances, 158
    replying to formal, 155–58
    replying to informal, 159–60
    second marriages, 252–53
    second receptions, 250
    separate reception, 148
    when to send, 134
    wording of formal, 137–47
  wedding anniversary, 262, 263–64
  weekend guests, 381
  when to send, 533
  White House, 635–36
Irish, and coats of arms, 554
Irish Genealogical Office, 554
Ironing, 98
Italian officials and individuals, correct
    forms of address for, 604–5, 622–27
Italy, audience with Pope, 649–52

                    J

Jackets. *See also* Business suits; Formal
    wear
  cruisewear, 837
  packing for trip, 827–28
  restaurant code, 676, 688
  riding, 712, 714
  sports, 674–75
Jeans, 662–63
  at restaurant dinner, 688
  riding, 711
Jellies, table manners with, 413
Jewelry, 666–67. *See also specific items,
    occasions*
  birthday gifts, 785–86
  bride's, 201
  christening or baby gifts, 766–67
  fine, gifts of, 763–64. *See also specific
    occasions*
  with gloves, 665
  men's
    for formal wear, 677
    for gifts, 763–64
    wedding, 207
  for public speaking, 736
  tennis playing with, 707–8
  on trip, 826
  widow, widower, and new spouse, 70
  with wristwatches, 667–68

Jews (Jewish ceremonies), 113–14. *See also*
　Synagogues
　Bar and Bat Mitzvahs, 113–14
　　gifts, 114, 769–70
　Brith Milah, 113
　and Christmas cards, 531
　correct forms of address for officials,
　　596–97
　and flag salute, national anthem, 644
　funerals, 272, 273, 275, 280
　　shrouds for burial, 268
　naming children, 106
　saying grace, 420, 421
　weddings, 225, 226–31
　　choosing time for, 181
　　long dresses at, 210
　　paying for pictures, 203
Job Resource Centers, 490
Jobs, 437–46. *See also* Business
　application forms, 439–40
　employer's responsibility toward
　　applicants, 442
　free advice on, 490
　going on interviews, 440–42
　　teen-agers and, 41
　letters of resignation, 444–46
　single persons and, 67, 72–73
　teen-agers and, 39–41. *See also*
　　Allowances
　　applying for summer, 40–41
　　and dating, 44
　writing résumé, 437–39
Jodhpurs, 711, 714
Johnson, Lyndon, 378, 379
Joint Chiefs of Staff, correct forms of
　address for, 586–87
Joint savings account, 780
Joint signatures, 507–8
Joint social cards, 550
Jokes, in conversation, 746
Judges, correct forms of address for,
　571–77
"Jr.," use of, 508
Junior bridesmaids, 188, 220
　dress for, 208
　at receptions, 238
　at rehearsals, 213
Jury duty, 633–34

K

Kennedy, President and Mrs. John F., 355,
　356, 639
　and thank-yous, 389
　White House menus, 310, 311–12
Keys
　men's carrying, 670
　to neighbor, when taking trip, 823–24
　in purse, 665
Kids and Alcohol, 60
King of Spain, correct forms of address for,
　626–27
Kitchen, 171. *See also* Cooks
　basic needs for, 177–78
　cleaning, 94
　dishwashing, 97–98
　shower gifts for, 774–75
Knights, British (and wives), correct forms
　of address for, 614–15
Knives. *See also* Flatwear; Table manners;
　Table setting; *specific occasions*

in continental- vs. American-style eating,
　25, 27
use of, 406, 407
　for dessert, 408
Kumquats, how to eat, 425

L

Labor, Department of, 73
"Lady," use of, 728
Lakes, skating on, 722
Lamb chops
　how to eat, 424
　taking portions, 412
Land, teen-agers and working with, 50
Language. *See also* Conversation; Foreign
　languages; *specific terms*
　children and bad, 21–22
　teen-agers and, 50
Latin America, and correct forms of
　address, 605
　presenting American ambassadors in,
　574n
Laundress, 82
Laundry, 82, 83, 98
Lavatories (rest rooms). *See also*
　Bathrooms
　on airplanes, 806, 807
　attendants at wedding receptions, and
　　tips, 242
　at work, keeping neat, 483
Lawyers
　correct forms of address for, 578–79
　and "Esquire," 567
　and personal business of single person, 68
　when family makes news, 741
　for woman living with a man, 130
Left-handed person, 414
Legal papers, signing, 506
Legs, crossing, 662
Leisure wear, men's, 674–76
　ascots, 675
　polo shirts, 676
　sports jackets and blazers, 674–75
　walking shorts, 675–76
Lemons, how to use, 428
Lending. *See* Borrowing and lending
Lent, weddings in, 181
Letters (letter writing), 513–32. *See also*
　Address, correct forms of;
　Invitations; Signatures; Stationery;
　specific uses
　age to begin note writing, 516
　business notes, personal, 476–78, 483
　forms for, 514–15
　　dating social communications, 514–15
　　handwriting vs. typing, 515
　　sequence of pages in informals, 515
　　sequence of pages in letters, 515
　　for social letters, 514
　greeting cards, 530–31. *See also* Greeting
　　cards
　personal business, 526–30
　postcards, 530
　to public figures, 524–26
Lettuce. *See* Salad
Libraries, public, 22
Librium, 55
Lieutenant colonels
　abbreviations of rank, 585

correct forms of address for, 588–89
how to tell rank, 583
Lieutenant commanders
abbreviation of rank, 585
correct forms of address for, 590–91
how to tell rank, 583
Lieutenant generals
abbreviations of rank, 585
correct forms of address for, 588–89
how to tell rank, 582
Lieutenants
Army
abbreviations of rank, 585
correct forms of address for, 588–89
how to tell rank, 583
Junior Grade
abbreviation of rank, 585
correct forms of address for, 590–91
how to tell rank, 583
Navy
abbreviation of rank, 585
correct forms of address for, 590–91
how to tell rank, 583
Lifeboat drill, on ship, 836
Lifeguards, 715
Life preservers, 700, 715
Lighting
bulbs for hotel use, 831
at formal tea, 365
poolside, 378
stage, 731
Linens
bed and bath, 169–70, 176
second wedding gift, 783
shower gifts, 775
table, 327
for picnics, 374, 375
for trousseau, 170
Lines, standing in, 51
Lingerie shower, gifts for, 775–76
Liqueurs
at formal dinners, 362
in restaurants, 684
service of, 322
Liquor. *See* Alcohol; Drinks and drinking;
specific occasions
Literary Guild, logo of, 458, 459
Litter and littering (trash)
beach, 715–16
on boats, 703
ice skating and, 722
and rental cars, 820
at restaurants, 688–89
in taxis, 815
on trains, 809
Liver, alcohol and the, 57
Living together, 128–31
addressing couple, 129–30, 509–10
announcing engagement when, 131
and At Home cards, 153
and informal dinner party invitations,
288–89
parents' attitude and, 129
as social entity, 129
and wedding invitations, 133, 136–37
what to call partner, 130
word to the woman, 131
Loafers, 674
with blazers, 675
Lobsters
how to eat, 429–30, 431

use of napkins with, 26, 409
Locks, safety, 824
Logo, for business stationery, 487–88
Long-distance telephoning, 470
Loot bags, at birthday parties, 395
Lord Lyon King of Arms, 554
Lovemaking, at restaurant dinner table, 688
Lozenge, heraldic, 555–56, 557
LSD, 55
Luce, Clare Boothe, 81
Luggage. *See also* Baggage
gifts for travelers, 789–90
packing suitcase, 826–28
and train travel, 809
weekend guests and, 385–86
Lunch counters, 692
Luncheons and lunching, 313–14, 347–49.
See also specific occasions
booth seating, 682
buffet, 348
cold-weather, 314
cruisewear for, 837–38
in executive dining room, 454
formal, 363–64
arranging table, 363–64
catered, 367–70
food, 364
greeting guests, 363
guests at, 365–67
place cards and menus, 363
hot-weather, 313
with maid, 349
official, invitations to, 538
poolside, 376–77
thank-you note for business, 476
White House, invitations to, 635
women and picking up tab, 448–50

M

"Ma'am," use of, 728
"Madame," use of, 563–64
Made-over clothes, 33
Magazines, in flight, 803
Maiden dinner, 198
Maiden name. *See also* Names
divorcée and, 74–75
and introductions, 725
Maiden of honor, 108. *See also* Junior
bridesmaid
Maids, 81
hotel, tipping, 830–31
and informal dinners, 289–90
service with one, 295–98
nursery, 82
and uniforms, 85
weekend guests and, 387–88
Maids of honor, 187–88, 218, 220ff., 226,
227
and bridal showers, 196
dress for, 208
gift to, 167
at receptions, 238, 239, 241, 243, 244
at rehearsal dinner, 199
and rehearsals, 212–14ff.
Mail. *See also* Addresses; Postcards;
Stationery; *specific uses*
and cruise travel, 835
and planning trip, 823–24
Mailbox (postbox)
holding lid for others, 51
and names of couple living together, 130

Mailgrams
  for accepting formal invitations, 539
  condolences by, 279
  for formal invitations, 538
  for invitations to business events, 460
  to recall wedding invitations, 153
  and replies to wedding invitations, 158,
    160
Mail-order catalogues for Christmas gifts,
    778
Maître d'. *See* Headwaiters
Major Generals
  abbreviations of rank, 585
  correct forms of address for, 588–89
  how to tell rank, 582
Majors
  abbreviations of rank, 585
  correct forms of address for, 588–89
  how to tell rank, 583
Make-up, 660
  bride's, 203
  don't fix on job, 483
  in purse, 665
  teen-agers and, 41–42
"Map," use of, 728
Mangoes, how to eat, 426
Maps, 541
  with wedding invitations, 151
Marchionesses, correct forms of address
    for
  British, 610–11
  French, 620–21
  Italian, 624–25
  Spanish, 628–29
Margarine, on dinner table, 332
Marijuana, 54
  teen-age parties and, 396
Marine Corps, 582
  abbreviations of rank, 585
  Band at White House, 636, 637
  correct forms of address for, 586–89
  how to tell rank, 584
Marquesses, correct forms of address for
  British, 610–11
  French, 620–21
  Italian, 624–25
  Spanish, 628–29
Marriage (spouses). *See also* Divorce;
    Engagements; Families; Weddings;
    Widows (and widowers)
  between people in military service, 584
  and introductions, 725
    husbands and wives introduce each
      other, 725
    when woman keeps maiden name, 725
  and invitations
    business associates', 463–64
    business party, 456
    nuances of accepting informal, 543
  and name of wife. *See* Names
  personal stationery of couple, 504
  reaffirmation of vows, 265
Marriage license, best man and, 189
Martinis, 341
Mascara, teen-agers and, 41
Mass cards, 272
"Master" use of, 510
Master of ceremonies, 732–33
Matrons of honor, 187–88, 218, 220ff., 226,
    227
  and bridal showers, 196

dress for, 208
gift to, 167
at reception, 238, 239, 241, 243, 244
at rehearsal dinner, 199
and rehearsals, 212–14ff.
Mayors
  and calling cards, 548
  correct forms of address for, 576–77
Meals. *See also* Food and eating; Menus;
    specific meals, occasions
  on airplanes, 799ff.
  bringing a friend to, 544–45
  and bus travel, 812
  on cruise, 834–35, 837–38
  on naval vessels, 647
  thank-you notes for, 517
Meat
  how to eat, 427–28
    chops, 424
  in restaurant, doggie bag for, 688
  taking portions of, 412
Medical officers, correct forms of address
    for, 584
Medications. *See also* Drugs; Motion
    sickness
  in travel preparation, 825
Melon, how to eat, 426
Memo pads, in women's staionery, 500
Memoranda, sending, 528–30
Memorial Day, American flag and, 641
Memorial services, 275
Mental health. *See* Psychiatric patients;
    Psychological counseling
Mental Health, Department of, 60
Mentally retarded people, 11, 13
Menu cards, 334–36
  for formal dinners, 358
  for formal luncheons, 363, 364
Menus, 310–26. *See also* Food and eating
  barbecue, 378–80
  brunch, easy Sunday, 314–15
  business social event, 459
  cocktail party, 340–42, 345, 346
    buffet, 312
  dinner, 310–11
  how many courses?, 316
  kinds of wine to serve, 317–18
  least expensive, 315
  lunch, 313–14, 348
  menu cards, 334–36
  picnics, 373–76
  poolside, 376
  special needs of guests, 316–17
  when disaster strikes in cooking, 315
  wine cellar, 318–19
  wineglasses, 319–22
  wine service, 322–26
Merchant Marine Academy, correct forms
    of address for midshipmen, 592–93
Mescaline, 55
"Mesdames," use of, 511
"Messrs." use of, 511–12
Methedrine, 55
Metropolitans (Eastern Orthodox), correct
    forms of address for, 594n
Microphones, in public speaking, 730–31,
    735
Military
  correct forms of address for, 584, 586–93
    academies 592–93
    Italian, 605
  how to tell rank, 582–84

Italian, correct forms of address for, 605
marriage between people in service, 584
and social card for officers, 550
visiting naval vessel, 645–48
wedding invitations and announcements, 161–62
White House social aides, 636
Milk, in tea, 351
Ministers (religious). *See* Clergy
Ministers of Foreign Affairs, correct forms of address for
French, 618–19
Italian, 624–25
Spanish, 626–27
Minnesota, and smoking in restaurants, 689
Mint, how to eat, 428
"Miss," use of, 448, 507
on calling cards, 549
on children's mail, 510
in formal invitations, 533, 537
Money. *See also* Allowances; Checks; Donations; Finances; *specific occasions*
gifts of, 760–61
thank-you notes for, 165, 518
wedding, 165, 196, 780–81
and teen-age dating, 44–45
for trip, 826
"Money Tree," 760
for bridal shower, 196
Monks (brothers), correct forms of address for, 602–3
Monograms
divorced woman and, 74
shirts with, 671
on stationery, 495–96, 498, 501
on trousseau linens, 169–70
on trousseau silver, 172–73
of wedding gifts, 781
for second wedding, 783
Mormons
correct forms of address for bishops, 600–1
weddings, 233
Morphine, 55
Morticians. *See* Funerals
Motels, 828–33
checking in, 828–29
with children, 818–19, 832–33
inviting guests, 832
security in, 832
things to remember, 831–32
tipping and room service, 829ff.
and wedding guests, 184
Mothers. *See* Children; Parents; *specific ceremonies*
Mothers-in-law. *See also* Grandparents; *specific occasions*
and family relations, 13–14
Motion sickness. *See also* Seasickness
bus travel and, 813
children and car travel, 818
Motorboats. *See* Yachting and sailing
Motor homes, 820–21
Motor vehicles, travel by, 814–21
with children, 817–19
recreational vehicles, 820–21
rental cars, 819–20
taxis, 815–16. *See also* Taxis
Moules marinières, 430
Mount Vernon dinner, 310, 356

Mourning, 69, 281
dress for, 280–81
Movie camera, use of, to see how you move, 661
"Mr.," use of, on calling cards, 547, 548
"Mrs.," use of, 448, 507
"Ms.," use of, 447–48
on calling cards, 549
for children's mail, 510
in formal invitations, 533, 537
Mufflers, for formal wear, 677
Mushrooms, "magic," 55
Music
after-dinner, 308
hiring musicians for, 307–8
funeral
fees to organist and vocalist, 277
memorial services, 275
national anthems, 642–44
in restaurants, strolling musicians and, 685
telephone hold, and recorded, 472–73
wedding, 182–83, 225, 226, 231, 234
at reception, 184, 246–47
at rehearsal, 212
second marriage and, 257
at White House, 636, 637
Mussels, how to eat, 430

N

Nagging, teen-agers and, 38
Nails, 660
don't take care of, at desk, 483
teen-age manners and, 41–42, 51
Names, 74–75, 509. *See also* Address; Addresses; At Home cards; Calling Cards; Introductions; Invitations
badges at business social events, 462–63
Brith Milah ceremony, 113
choosing baby's, 106–7
christening ceremony, 110
of domestic help, 84
engagement announcement and legally changed, 127
girl's same as mother's, and wedding invitations, 139
and hospital registration, 750
and hotel registration, 829
in return addresses, 496–97
signatures, 506
and women's raised consciousness in business, 447–48
on women's stationery, 496–97ff., 504
Nannies, 81–82, 83
Napkin rings, 409
Napkins, 327ff., 409
at cocktail parties, 339
at formal dinners, 358–59
at formal luncheons, 363
at informal luncheons, 347
for sneezing, 416
for spilled food, 415
teen-agers' table manners and, 26
in trousseau, 170
Narcotics, 53, 55
National anthems, 640–44
foreign, 644
National Audubon Society, 698
National Clearing House for Drug Abuse Information, 60

National Clearing House on Alcohol Information, 60
National Council on Alcoholism, 60, 344
National Federation of Business and Professional Women's Clubs, Inc., 698
National Guard officers, correct forms of address for, 585
National Ski Patrol, 720
National Trust for Historic Preservation, 698
Navy, U. S., 582
  abbreviations of rank, 585
  correct forms of address, 586–87, 590–91, 584–85
    Academy midshipmen, 592–93
    how to tell rank, 583
    visiting a vessel, 645–48
      boarding, 646
      embarking, 645–46
      honors to civilians, 646–47
      making call, 646
      nautical terms, 647–48
      officers' staterooms, 647
      prohibitions, 647
    wedding invitations and announcements and, 161–62
Necklaces, 666, 667
  chains as gifts for men, 763
  pearl, as graduation gifts, 764
Needleperson, gifts for, 792
Nervous mannerisms. *See also* Hands
  teen-agers and, 50
New England Historic Genealogical Society, 554
Newlyweds, 259–61
  behavior of, 260–61
  on honeymoon, 259–60
  at informal dinners, 292
  in new neighborhood, 260
Newspapers. *See also* Press relations
  adoption announcements, 64
  baby's birth announcement, 408
  and business-opening announcement, 487
  death notices, 269–70
  engagement announcements, 123–24ff.
  second marriage announcement, 254–55
  wedding publicity, 204
New York Yacht Club, 703, 704
Nightgowns, packing for trip, 828
Nobility, addressing. *See* Address, correct forms of
Noise, at restaurant dinner, 687
North American Center on Adoption, 62
North American College, 649, 650
North American Council on Adoptable Children, 62
Nose, blowing at table, 416
Notes. *See* Letters; *specific uses*
Nuns (sisters)
  correct forms of address for, 602–3
  gifts for, 773
Nursery maids, 82
Nurses, 751–52
  children's, 81–82. *See also* Baby nurses

O

Obituaries (death notices), 269–70
  for prominent people, 270
Obscenities. *See* Bad language

Ocean swimming, 715
Office of the Papal Audience, 649
Officers. *See* Military
Offices. *See* Business
Official luncheon, invitation to, 538
Official self, 559–652
  audience with Pope, 649–52
  correct forms of address, 563–629
  flag and national anthem, 640–44
  jury duty, 633–34
  parliamentary procedure, 630–32
  visiting naval vessel, 645–48
  White House visits, 635–39
Official stationery, 506
Old age (elderly, senior citizens), 14–16. *See also* Grandparents
  and baby-sitting, 91
  and drug-abuse prevention, 53–54
  and freighter travel, 839
  and wedding anniversary, 265
Olives, how to eat, 415, 423
Onassis, Aristotle, 704
"Opened by Mistake," use of, 511
Open house, 346
Opium, 55
Oranges, how to eat, 426
Orders, teen-agers and learning to take, 50
Outdoor entertaining, 371–80
  barbecues, 378–80
  buffets, 371–72
  dinner on city apartment balcony, 371
  patio, 372–73
  picnics, 373–76
  poolside, 376–78
Outdoor weddings, 146
Overnight guests, 388
Oyster fork, 360
Oysters, how to eat, 430

P

Paddle tennis, 705
Pages, bridal, 208, 209
  at Jewish wedding, 228
  at receptions, 238
  at rehearsals, 213, 215, 216
Pajamas
  dressy, 662
  packing for trip, 828
Pakistan, President of, 310, 356
Pallbearers, 273–74, 278
Panama hats, men's, 674
Pants. *See also* Business suits; *specific occasions*
  women's, 662–63
Papal chamberlain, correct forms of address, 602–3
Papayas, how to eat, 426
Paper litter. *See* Litter and littering
Parcels, checking in restaurants, 682
Parents. *See also* Children; Families; *specific problems*
  aged, 14–16
  and baby-sitters, 90–93
  and children's premarital living together, 129
  and children's prom dates, 47
  single, 72. *See also* Divorce; Widows (and widowers)
  and teen-agers. *See also* Teen-agers

and car manners, 48
and dating, 45, 47
Parents Without Partners, 72
Parliament, correct forms of address for
    members of British, 614–15
Parliamentary procedure, 630–32
Parsley, how to eat, 428
Parties. *See also* Christenings; Dating;
    Debutantes and debuts; Entertaining;
    Gifts; Introductions; Invitations;
    Showers; *specific occasions*
    children's manners at, 20
    inviting least popular person to teen-age,
        49
    teen-age manners and, 49
    to welcome adopted child, 63
Passageways, teen-agers and public, 50
Passports, 824–25, 840
Pasta, how to eat, 432
Patio entertaining, 372–73
Patriarchs, Eastern Orthodox, correct forms
    of address for, 594–95
PCP, 55
Peaches in wine or syrup, how to eat,
    426–27
Pearl necklaces
    cleaning, 667
    as graduation gifts, 764
Pears, how to eat, 425
    in wine or syrup, 426–27
Pediatrician, emergency number of, for
    baby-sitter, 92
Peerage, British, correct forms of address
    for members of, 606–15
Pendants, first jewelry for girls, 764
Penmanship, and wedding invitations, 137
Pens, ballpoint, on trips, 825
Pepper. *See* Salt: and pepper
Persian melon, how to eat, 426
Persimmons, how to eat, 427
"Personal," use of, 511
Pets, 31–32
    and bus travel, 812
    and cocktail parties, 338
    don't give as gifts, 764
    flying with dogs and cats, 800
    single persons and, 67
    weekend guests and, 386
Pew cards, 151
PFDs (personal flotation devices), for
    boating, 700
Pheasant, how to eat, 423
Photographs and photography (cameras,
    pictures)
    and baby announcements, 408
    and bus travel, 812–13
    on Christmas cards, 531
    with engagement announcements, 124
    at graduation, 116
    of house, before taking trip, 824
    movie camera, to see how you move, 661
    on naval vessels, 647
    as second wedding gift, 783
    on trip, 825
        bus, 812–13
    wedding, 183, 203
        Jewish, 231
        receptions, 241–42
    wedding anniversaries, 265
    at White House state dinner, 636–37
    and widow, widower, consideration for

new spouse, 70
Physical improvement, single persons and,
    67
Physically handicapped. *See* Handicapped
    persons
Pickles, how to eat, 428
Picnic baskets, as wedding gifts, 783
Picnics, 373–76
    check list for, 374–75
    cleaning up after, 376
    preparing area, 374
    preparing food ahead, 375
    table linens, plates, 373–74
    tailgate, 376
Picture-taking. *See* Photographs and
    photography
Pillows, in bedmaking, 95
Pineapple, how to eat, 427
Pipe smoking
    on airplanes, 804
    gifts for smokers, 793
    at restaurants, 689
    at White House dinners, 637
Pizza, how to eat, 428
Place cards. *See also* Address, correct forms
    of
    in executive dining rooms, 454
    at formal dinners, 358
    at formal luncheons, 363
    at informal dinner parties, 290–91
    at restaurant dinners, 687
Place mats, 328
    at formal luncheons, 363
    in trousseau, 170
Plants
    as gifts to men, 762
    in office, 483
Plastic bags, on trips, 825. *See also specific
    means of travel*
Platform tennis, 705
Playing cards, on airplanes, 806
"Please," children and, 18–19
"Please Forward," use of, 511
Pleasure principle, children and, 9
Plums, how to eat, 425
    stewed, 427
Police
    and cocktail party traffic, 337
    and driving to wedding, 194
    and planning trips, 821
Politics, single persons and, 67
Polo shirts, 676
Pomegranates, how to eat, 427
Ponchos, on trips, 825
Ponds, skating on, 722
Pools. *See* Swimming pools
Pope
    audience with, 649–52
        dressing for, 651–52
        general, 649–50
        private, 651
        semiprivate, 650–51
    correct forms of address for, 600–1
    in St. Peter's Basilica, 652
Pork chops, how to eat, 424
Porters. *See also* Redcaps
    stevedores and tipping, 835
Portuguese men-of-war, 715
Possessions. *See* property
Postage. *See* Stamps

Postbox (mailbox)
holding lid for others, 51
and names of couple living together, 130
Postcards, 530
change of address, 510
on trips, 825–26
in women's stationery, 499
Post-college entertaining, 403–4
Posture
how you move in clothes, 661–62
sitting, 661–62
in office, 484
at table, 420
Potatoes, how to eat, 428
Pots and pans, washing, 97
Pregnancy
elopement and expected babies, 236
and freighter cruises, 839
smoking and, 59
Presents. *See* Gifts
Presidents
French, correct forms of address for,
618–19
of Senate and Chamber of Deputies,
618–19
Italian, correct forms of address for,
622–23
of Senate and Chamber of Deputies,
622–23
Pakistani, visit of, 310, 356
Spanish, correct forms of address for,
626–27
Senate and Chamber of Deputies,
626–27
United States. *See also* White House
correct forms of address for, 568–69
music for, 644
university, correct forms of address for,
578–79
Press relations, 739–41
for club or volunteer activities, 739–40
when family makes news, 740–41
Priests. *See also* Clergy; *specific ceremonies*
Catholic. *See also specific ceremonies*
correct forms of address for, 602–3
Eastern Orthodox. *See also specific
ceremonies*
correct forms of address for, 594–95
Prime Ministers, correct forms of address
for
British, 616–17
French, 618–19
Italian, 622–23
Princes, correct forms of address for
British royal, 606–7
French, 620–21
Italian, 624–25
Spanish, 628–29
Princesses, correct forms of address for
British royal, 606–7
French, 620–21
Italian, 624–25
Spanish, 628–29
Printed stationery. *See also specific uses*
vs. engraved, 495
Privacy
and children's telephone manners, 31
and grandparents living with you, 16
Private clubs. *See* Clubs
Private collections, asking to see, 525–26
Privy counsellors, correct forms of address

for, 614–15
Professors, correct forms of address for,
578–81
Prominent people (families). *See also*
Celebrities; Public figures
and engagement announcements, 123
obituaries of, 270
weddings and newspaper publicity, 204
Proms, 47
Property (possessions)
children and respect for other people's, 22
and grandparents living with you, 16
office borrowing, 484
teen-age borrowing and lending, 49
Protestants
correct forms of address for clergy,
598–601
and christenings, 108ff.
and confirmations, 112
and funerals, 272, 274
and weddings
choosing time for, 181
divorced people and, 180
giving away bride, 217
grouping at altar, 218, 220
Prothonotary apostolic, correct forms of
address for, 602–3
Protocol, dinner-party, 292–93
Prunes, how to eat stewed, 427
Psychiatric patients, 752–53
Psychological counseling, single persons
and, 67
Psylotybin, 55
Public activities, 653–753
conversation, 742–47. *See also*
Conversation
hospitals and doctors, 748–53
importance of introductions, 723–28
men's apparel, 669–78
private clubs, 694–98
public speaking, 729–41
restaurant dining, 679–93
sports, 699–722
wardrobe and accessories, 657–58
Public behavior,
smoking on street, 59
teen-agers and, 50–51
Public figures, 524–26. *See also* Address,
correct forms of; Celebrities;
Prominent people
asking to see private collections of,
525–26
asking for donations, 526
death of, 277
persuading people in power, 525
White House, 525. *See also* White House
Public speaking, 729–41
American flag on platform, 641
handling press relations, 739–41
for club or volunteer work, 739–40
when your family makes news, 740–41
introducing speakers, 731–32
master of ceremonies, 732–33
microphones, 730–31
stage lighting, 731
taking care of celebrity speaker, 737–39
what not to do, 739
voice, 730
yourself as major speaker, 734–37
coughing or sneezing, 737
delivering your speech, 735

how to dress, 736–37
mannerisms to avoid, 734–35
slides, 735–36
Public transportation, 799–813
airplane, 799–807
bus, 811–13
train, 807–11
Punishment, children's allowances and, 35–36
Pursers, ships', 835
Purses. *See* Handbags

Q

Quail, how to eat, 422
Quaker weddings, 233
Queen Mother of Britain, correct forms of address for, 606–7
Queen of Great Britain, correct forms of address for, 606–7
Quilts, in bedmaking, 95

R

Rabbis. *See also* Jews; *specific ceremonies*
correct forms of address for, 596–97
Race, adopting child of different, 65
Racket sports, 705–8
proper attire for, 707–8
Radios
on airplanes, 806
at beach, 716
and bus travel, 812
public service spots, 740
teen-age manners with, 51
on trains, 809
on trips, 826. *See also specific transportation*
as wedding gifts, 783
Radishes, how to eat, 423, 428
Rain gear
on cruises, 840
rubber boots on trips, 825
for sports. *See specific sports*
Reading. *See also* Books; Magazines
in office, 484
single persons and, 67
Rear admirals
abbreviation of rank, 585
correct forms of address for, 590–91
how to tell rank, 583
Receiving lines, 664, 727
business hosts and, 462
wedding anniversary, 262–63
wedding receptions, 234, 238–41, 245
White House state dinner, 637
Receptionists
and eating at desk, 484
responsibilities of, 480
Receptions
debutante, invitations to, 537
wedding. *See* Weddings: receptions
White House, invitations to, 635
Recommendations. *See* References
Recordings. *See* Tapes and tape recorders
Recreational vehicles, 820–21
city ordinances and, 821
leaving on trip, 821
Redcaps, and tipping, 811
Red wines, 318
glasses for, 320, 321
at formal dinners, 357–61

ordering in restaurants, 683, 684
service, 322ff.
spillage, 325–26
References
in firing domestic employees, 89–90
social letters, 522–23
to friends abroad, 523–24
writing letters for job applicants, 442–44
in writing résumés, 439
Regrets. *See* Invitations
Relatives. *See* Families
Religion. *See also* Ceremonies; *specific ceremonies, sects,*
and condolence letters, 520–21
correct forms of address for chaplains, 585
correct forms of address for officials, 594–603
Remarriage (second marriage), 251–58. *See also* Divorce; Stepparents
announcements, 253–54
attendants at wedding, 255–56
cakes, 246
ceremony, 256
children and divorce, 71
children at wedding, 256
dress for, 256
elopement and, gifts for, 236
and engagement announcement, 123, 127
engagements before, 251–52
entertaining before, 256–57
gifts, 255, 782–83
elopement and, 236
invitations, 252–53
preparations, 255
receptions, 252–53, 258
what constitutes second marriage, 251
widow-widower and new spouse, 70
Reminder cards, 544
for informal dinners, 288
in women's stationery, 500, 501
Reminders, 543–44
Rental cars, 819–20
on cruise trips, 838
Representatives (congressmen, congresswomen), correct forms of address for, 572–73
state, 576–77
Reservations, making, 527
restaurant, 680
Resignation, letter of, 444–46
Response cards, with wedding invitations, 151–52
Restaurants, 679–93. *See also* Hotels; *specific meals*
bus boys, 679, 693
captains, 679, 680
complaints and compliments at, 690–91
entertaining large parties at, 687
fine restaurants, 679–82
coat checking, 680
greeting guests, 680
if guests arrive first, 681
making reservations, 680
seating, 681–82
staff, 679–80
informal, 691–93
buffet service, 691–92
cafeteria service, 692
fast-food service, 692–93

lunch counters, 692
jacket and tie code, 676, 688
manners at, 687–90
  functioning properly, 690
  table implements, 689–90
ordering at, 682–85
  cocktails, 682–83
  coffee, liqueurs, cigars, 684–85
  courses, 684
  meal, 683
  wine, 683–84
smoking in, 689
sommelier, 679
tipping and paying check at, 685–87
  calling for check, 685–86
  calling waiter, 685
  Dutch treat, 686–87
  paying cashier, 686
  strolling musicians, 685
waiters, 679, 685
women's hats in, 664
women and picking up tab in, 448–50
Rest rooms. *See* Lavatories; Toilets
Résumés, writing, 437–39
Retired military officers. *See also* Military
  and correct forms of address, 626
Retirement gifts, thank-yous for, 518
Return addresses, 496–97
  correct form for social letters, 514
  women's names in, 506
Riding, horseback, 710–14
  fox hunting, 712–14
  hacking, 711
  safety, 712
  Western, 711–12
Ring bearers (bridal), 208, 209, 221
  at receptions, 238
  at rehearsals, 213
Rings
  diamond, as gifts for men, 763
  engagement, 127–28
    if bride wears at wedding, 201
    widow's, and consideration for new
      husband, 70
  first jewelry for girls, 764
  wedding, 127, 201, 205, 220
    best man and, 189, 205, 212
    burial with, 268
    double-ring ceremonies, 222, 232
    Jewish, 230
    playing tennis with, 708
    at reaffirmation of marriage vows, 265
    at rehearsal, 212
Rising (standing up)
  and business appointments, 478–79
  children and introductions, good-bys, 18
  and introductions, 724
    children and, 18
  in parliamentary procedure, 630–31
Robert's Rules of Order, 630
Rock Cornish hens, how to eat, 423
Roman Catholics. *See* Catholics
Rome, audience with Pope in, 649–52
Room service, 830, 832
Rosé wines, 318
  service, 322
Royalty, addressing. *See* Address, correct
  forms of
R.S.V.P.s. *See* Invitations; *specific*

occasions
  cards, 539–40

S

Safety. *See also specific activities*
  teen-agers and, 50
Safety pin, in hunting attire, 714
Sailing. *See* Yachting and sailing
St. Peter's Basilica, Pope in, 652
Salad
  as first course in restaurants, 684
  how to eat, 428–29
  at picnics, 373, 375
  table setting for, 331, 332. *See also* Table
    setting
  and teen-agers' table manners, 28
Salad dressing, at restaurants, 690
Salaries, and job application forms, 440
Salt
  and pepper, 429
    adding at table, 413
    at formal dinners, 360–61
    and reaching across table, 418
    in table setting, 330, 332–33
  for wine spillage, 325–26
Sandwiches, how to eat, 429
Sauces
  barbecue, 380
  serving with food, 412–13, 413–14
Savings accounts
  children and, 35
  engaged couple's joint, 780
Scarves
  ascots, 675
  for boating, 701
  for formal wear, 677
  packing for trip, 827
  for riding, 712. *See also* Ascots
  skiing and, 719
  on trips, 825
Scotch whiskey, 341
Scottish, and coats of arms, 554
Scuba divers, gifts for, 794
Seafood, how to eat, 429–30, 431
Seasickness, 702, 837
Seasonings. *See also* Salt
  adding at table, 413
Seating. *See also* Seats
  formal dinners, 355–57
  informal dinners, 290–92
    protocol, 292–93
  in restaurants, 681–82
    banquette, 681–82
    booth, 682
Seats
  bus, 51
  at counters, 51
Second course. *See also* Dinners and dinner
    parties
  table setting, 331
Second lieutenants
  abbreviations of rank, 583
  correct forms of address for, 588–89
  how to tell rank, 583
Secretaries, 474–76
  and gifts, 765
  handling personal matters for boss and
    acting as gofer, 475
  in parliamentary procedure, 631
  responsibilities to visitors, 479–80

social. *See* Social secretaries
and telephone. *See* Telephone
traveling on business, 450
upward mobility for, 475–76
Securities. *Se also* Bonds; Stocks
wedding gifts of, 781
Sedatives, 55
Seeing Eye dogs (guide dogs), 13
and bus travel, 812
Self-control, teaching child, 7
Senate. *See also* Senators, U.S.
Presidents of foreign, correct forms of
address for
French, 618–19
Italian, 622–23
Spanish, 626–27
Senators, U.S.
correct forms of address for, 572–73
state, 576–77
and White House tours, 639
Senior citizens. *See* Old age
Separated parents
and engagement announcements, 126
and wedding invitations, announcements,
136, 139
and wedding receptions, 248
Servants. *See* Household management
Service industry, 82–83
Shaking hands. *See under* Hands
Sharks, 715
Shaving, teen-agers and, 41
Shavuoth, 113
Shawls, on cruises, 838
Sheets
in bedmaking, 95, 96
in trousseau, 169
Sherbet, how to eat, 427
Ships
cruise travel, 834–41
bon voyage gifts, 790–91
bon voyage parties, 835
booking passage, 834–35
captain's table, 837
doctor on board, 825
dress for, 837–38
freighter, 840–41
excursions on shore, 838
freighter trips, 839–41
seasickness, 837
on ship, 835–37
things to remember, 838
tipping, 838–39
when you leave, 835
visiting naval vessels, 645–48
boarding, 646
embarking, 645–46
honors to civilians, 646–47
making call, 646
nautical terms, 647–48
officers' staterooms, 647
prohibitions, 647
Shirts, 670–71
for formal wear, 677
packing for trip, 827
polo, 676
riding, 711
tennis, 707
for weddings, 206
"Shivah," 275
Shlumberger, Jean, 667

Shoes, 666
with blazers, 675
for boating, 701
on cruises, 838–39, 840
golf, 710
men's, 671–74. *See also specific occasions*
formal wear, 677
packing for trip, 827
removing in office, 484
tennis, 708
on trains, lockers for, 811
for weddings
bride's, 200
junior bridesmaids', 208
men's, 207
Shorts
on cruises, 838
men's walking, 675–76
tennis, 707
Showers
for adopted children, 62–63
baby, 105–6
bridal, 196–98
clergyman's wife and, 235
kitchen, gifts for, 774–75
linen, gifts for, 775
lingerie, gifts for, 775–76
Shrimp cocktail, how to eat, 430
Sickness. *See* Illness
Sierra Club, 698
Sight-impaired persons. *See* Blind persons
Signatures, 506–9. *See also* Letters
changing "Jr." and other suffixes, 508
common first name, 508
how woman signs letter, 506–7
illegible, 508
joint, 507–8
listing women's names in clubs and
organizations, 507
signing checks and legal papers, 506
use of "Sr.," 508–9
Signs
for businesses, 486
teen-agers and obeying, 50
Silver. *See also* Flatware; Gifts; Jewelry;
specific occasions
heraldic devices on, 557
in trousseau, 171–73
monogramming, 172–73
Single life (single persons), 66–79. *See also*
Dating
divorce and, 70–72, 74–75. *See also*
Divorce
extensive options, 66–67
going to work, 72–73
and home, 77–79
single man keeps house, 78–79
importance of entertaining, 75–77
host and hostess in one person, 76
"extra" woman, 76
men entertain, 76–77
transportation for single woman, 77
and making calls, 551–52
and new stationery, 74
personal business, 68
single parents, 72. *See also* Children;
Divorce; *specific occasions*
and travel, 67, 79
volunteer work, 73–74

widow and widower, 69–70. *See also*
　　Widows (and widowers)
"Sir," use of, 728
Sisters
　double wedding of, 142, 222–24
　and wedding invitation, 136, 141
Sisters (nuns)
　correct forms of address for, 602–3
　gifts for, 773
Sitting, 661–62. *See also* Chairs; Seating
　in office, 484
　at table, 420
Skating, 721–22
　dress for, 722
　on pond or lake, 722
Skiing, 718–21
　apparel, 719–20
　après-ski apparel, 720
　cross-country, 720–21
　equipment, 719
　injuries, 720
　water, 718
Skirts, 662
　packing for trip, 827
Slacks
　on cruises, 838
　packing for trip, 827
Sleeping cars, on trains, 810–11
Slickers, for riding, 712
Slides, presenting, at lecture, 735–36
Slippers
　for bus travel, 812
　for flying, 806
　for formal wear, 677
Small Business Administration, 489–90
Smoking. *See also* Ash trays; Cigarettes;
　　Cigars; Pipe smoking
　on boats, 702
　at bridge parties, 353
　domestic help and, 84, 85
　in executive conference room, 453
　in flight, 803, 804
　gifts for smokers, 793
　in hospital, 749
　marijuana, 54
　on naval vessels, 647
　in office, 482, 483
　at restaurants, 689
　and riding, 712
　on ships, 836
　at table, 418–19. *See also specific meals*
　in taxis, 815
　and teen-agers' job interviews, 41
　on trains, 808
　where to go for help, 60–61
　at White House dinners, 637
Snails, how to eat, 432
Sneakers (athletic shoes), 674
　for boating, 701
　for tennis, 707
Sneezing
　public speakers and, 737
　at table, 416–17
　teen-age manners and, 51
Soap
　and bathroom manners, 30
　on trip, 825
Social cards. *See* Calling cards
Social secretaries, 82, 86–87
　invitations to formal dance when reply is
　　sent to, 535

public, 82
Social Security, and use of "Jr.," 508
Society of Colonial Wars, 698
Socks (hose), 674
　and formal wear, 677
　with sports shoes, 675
　for tennis, 707
　weddings, 207
Soda, for picnics, 375
Soda water
　at cocktail party, 341
　for wine spillage, 326
Sofas, 661–62
Soft drinks. *See* Drinks and drinking;
　　specific occasions
Sommeliers, 679
Soup
　in handled bowls, 409
　table setting for, 330
　teen-agers and dinner party manners, 27
　testing hot, 410
Souvenirs, at White House dinners, 637
Spaghetti
　how to eat, 432
　use of napkin for, 26
Spanish officials and nobility, correct forms
　　of address for, 605, 626–29
Sparkling wines, 318. *See also* Champagne
Speaker of the House of Representatives,
　　correct forms of address for, 572–73
Speaking. *See also* Conversation
　with food in mouth, 417
　public. *See* Public speaking
Special diets. *See* Diets
Special-event parties, 404
Special interests
　gifts for, 791–94
　　cigar smokers, 793
　　collectors, 793
　　gardeners, 792
　　gourmet cooks, 774–75, 791–92
　　pipe smokers, 793
　　sportspersons, 793–94
　　wine lovers, 793
　single persons and, 67
"Speed" (amphetamines), 55
Spillage, of food or drink, 415
　at formal meals, 366
　on social letters, 514
Spitting, 51
Spoons. *See also* Flatware; Table manners;
　　Table setting; *specific occasions*
　dessert, use of, 407, 408
　serving, use of, 412
Sports, 699–722
　and conversation, 744
　gifts for enthusiasts, 793–94
　golf, 708–10
　　fashion on golf course, 710
　　handling cart, 709–10
　riding and fox hunting, 710–14
　skating, 721–22
　　dress for, 722
　　on ponds or lakes, 722
　skiing, 718–20
　swimming and water sports, 714–18. *See
　　also* Swimming
　tennis and racket sports, 705–8
　　proper attire for, 707–8
　winter, 718–22
　yachting and sailing, 700–5

Sports jackets, 674–75
Spouses. *See* Marriage
Squab, how to eat, 422
Squash, 705
"Sr.," use of, 508–9
Stage lighting, 731
Stairs, teen-age manners and, 50
Stamps (postage)
  and invitations, 543
    wedding, 137
  on trips, 825
Standing up (rising)
  and business appointments, 478–79
  children and introductions, good-bys, 18
  and introductions, 724
    children and, 18
  in parliamentary procedure, 630–31
"Star-Spangled Banner, The" (national
  anthem), 642–44
State legislators, correct forms of address
  for, 576–77
State unemployment insurance tax, 88
Stationery, 491–522, *See also* Letters;
  specific occasions
  addressing social envelopes, 509–11
  calling cards, 547–52
    as gift enclosures, 550
    how names are used on, 547–50
    joint, 550
  children's, 504–5
  heraldic devices, 553–57
  house, 505
  married couple's personal, 504
  men's personal, 502–4
  for new businesses, 487–89
  official paper, 506
  proper form of, 495–97
  signatures and, 506–9
  single life and, 74
  on trips, 825
  use of "Mesdames," 511
  use of "Messrs.," 511–12
  use of "personal," "please forward,"
    "opened by mistake," 511
  for wedding invitations, 134–35
  and women's names, 506
  women's personal, 497–502
Station wagon picnics, 376
Stepparents. *See also* Remarriage
  and announcing adoption, 63
  and communications about children, 8
  and engagement announcements, 126
  and wedding. *See also* Remarriage
    giving away bride, 217
    and invitations, 141
    and receptions, 240
Stevedores, tipping, 835
Stewards
  on big yachts, 704
  on ships, 839, 841
  on trains, 809, 810, 811
Stimulants (drugs), 55
Stocks (clothing), riding, 711, 714
Stocks (securities)
  as gifts, 761
  teen-agers and, 39
Stores
  charge accounts, and change of address,
    511
  checkout lines in supermarkets, teen-age
    manners and, 51

letters of complaint to, 528
memos to, 529
and notices for baby-sitters, 91
ordering from, 526–27
Strawberries, how to eat, 426
Students. *See also* College; Teen-agers
  and bus travel, 812
Studs and cuff links, 677
  gifts for men, 764
Subscriptions, and change of address, 510
Suitcases. *See* Luggage
Suits. *See also* Formal wear; *specific
  occasions*
  business, 669–70
  pants, women's, 663
Sunday brunch menu, 314–15
Sunglasses, 825
  on bus, 812
  on cruise, 838
  for tennis, 707
Supermarkets, checkout lines and teen-age
  manners, 51
Superstitions, wedding, 201
Suppers, buffet, 298–301
Supreme Court Justices, correct forms of
  address for, 568–69
Swearing. *See* Bad language
Sweaters
  on cruises, 838, 840
  for flying, 806
  for riding, 711
Sweets, children and, 23, 24
Swimming, 714–18
  beach manners, 715–16
  boating and, 702
  check list for beach day, 716
  children's safety and manners, 715
  clubs, 716–17
  gifts for swimmers, 794
  ocean, and lifeguards, 715
  pools, 376–78, 717–18
    entertaining at, 376–78
    motel, 831
Swimsuits (bathing suits), 714–15
  on cruises, 838, 840
Synagogues (temples). *See also* Jews;
  specific ceremonies
  domestic employees and, 86
  to find baby-sitters, 91
  and making friends in new community,
    260

T

Tablecloths, 327
  for formal dinners, 355
  for informal luncheons, 347
  for picnics, 374
  in trousseau, 170
Table-hopping, 688
Table linens, 327. *See also* Tablecloths
  at picnics, 374, 375
  in trousseau, 170
Table manners, 405–32
  accidents, 415. *See also* Spillage
  adding butter, 413
  adding gravies and sauces, 412–13
  bread as sopper and pusher, 414
  burping, 417–18
  children's, 22–29. *See also* Table
    manners: teen-agers'

choosing own food, 23–24
learning to converse, 25–26
playing with food, 22–23
young child at family table, 24–25
choking, 415–16
conversation, 419–20
children, and learning to make, 25–26
dessert silver, 408
drinking, 408
food in teeth, 414
foreign matter in food, 418
getting something out of mouth, 414–15
handled soup bowl or cup, 409
holding cups, 410
holding glasses, 410
how to eat various foods, 421–32
if silverware is lacking, 409
jellies and sauces, 413–14
leaving table, 418
left-handed persons, 414
napkins, 409
posture, 420
reaching across table, 418
rearranging seating, 414
saying grace, 420–21
and seasonings, 413
smoking, 418–19
sneezing, 416–17
speaking with food in mouth, 417
taking portions from serving dish, 412
teen-agers', 26–29, 50
testing liquids, 410
tipping of dishes, 409
token portions, 411
use of knife and fork, 406, 407
when to begin eating, 407
who is served first?, 405–7
Table setting, 327–36
buffet, 300–1
sit-down, 303
design revolution, 327–29
formal
dinners, 360–61
luncheons, 363
teas, 364–65
informal luncheons, 347, 348
logistics of, 329–34
menu cards, 334–36. *See also* Menu cards
outdoor entertaining, 371, 372
praising your hosts, 329
Talcum powder, for spots, 415
Talents, single persons and, 67
Talking. *See* Conversation; Speaking
Tapes and tape recorders
messages instead of letters, 521–22
for practice in public speaking, 730
teen-age manners and, 51
telephone hold and recorded music,
472–73
Taxes
domestic employees and, 87
restaurant checks and Internal Revenue
Service, 686
Taxis, 814–16
on business trips, men and women and
paying for, 450
hotel doormen and, 829–30
losing articles in, 815–16
and on-shore excursions during cruises,
838
for problem drinkers, 343–44

and protection, 814
for single woman, 77
and tipping, 816
you and driver, 814–15
Tea. *See also* Teas
caffeine in, 55
hot, serving of, 349, 351
iced, serving of, 348
at informal luncheons, 348, 349
kinds of, 351–52
making good, 351
at restaurants, iced, 690
testing hot, 410
service, in trousseau, 171
Teachers, presents for, 774
Tea-dances, 119
Teas
bridal, 196
debutante, 118–19
formal, 364–65
informal, 349–52
Teaspoons. *See* Flatware; Spoons
Teen-agers, 37–51. *See also* Alcohol; Drugs;
Smoking
and allowances, 38–39
as baby-sitters. *See* Baby-sitters
check list of common courtesies and
discourtesies, 49–51
and community, 50
public behavior, 50–51
and relatives and friends, 49–50
classic gifts for, 768–69
courtesy begins at home, 37–38
and dating, 42–49
adult supervision, 46–47
car manners, 48–49
duty dances, 47
embarrassing moments, 44
going steady, 45–46
how does boy ask for date?, 43–44
and money, 44–45
parents and, 45
proms, 47
refusing a date, 45
returning home, 45
and drinking, 343. *See also* Alcohol
at fast-food restaurants, 693
graduation, high school, 115–16
gifts for, 770–71
grooming, shaving, make-up, 41–42
manners, 38. *See also specific situations*
parties, 396–398
stocks or bonds as gifts, 761
table manners, 26–29
Teeth
food caught in, 417
picking. *See also* Toothpicks
and teen-age manners, 51
Telephone (telephone calls), 465–73
answering, 465
putting people on hold, 466
transferring calls, 466
when does executive come on line?, 466
when you are not there, 466–67
who do you say is calling?, 465–66
and appreciation for teen-agers' job
interview, 41
calling parents from honeymoon spot, 260
conversations, 469–70
give caller undivided attention, 469
if disconnected, 470

react while listening, 469
  and wrong numbers, 470
death notices over, 269–70
doctors and, 752
domestic employees and, 88–89
emergency numbers for baby-sitters, 92
executives answering own phones, 468–69
  dispensing with pests, 468–69
  and interruptions during appointments,
    469
  to give references for domestic
    employees, 90
  in hospital, 751
  and invitations, 287. *See also specific
    occasions*
  child to child, 19–20
jobs with telephone company, 39
on jury duty, 633
listings
  of couple living together, 130
  for single women, 74
messages, 467–68
  how to take, 467
  if you can't leave, 468
  leave, with secretary, 468
  secretary who won't take, 468
numbers
  on business letterheads, 489
  emergency, for baby-sitters, 92
  on house stationery, 505
  on personal stationery, 497
  wrong, 51, 470
secretary and business visitors, 479–80
teen-agers and courtesy, 50
  and wrong numbers, 51
weekend guests and, 388
  thank-yous by, 389
when family makes news, 741
wrong numbers, 51, 470
Television (TV)
  after-dinner "don't," 308
  in hospitals, 750, 751
  in hotels and motels, 832
  public service spots, 740
Temples. *See* Synagogues
Tennis, 705–8
  gifts for players, 794
  proper attire, 707–8
Terminally ill patients, 749
"Thank you," children and learning, 18–19
Thank-you letters (notes), 516–18
  age to begin writing, 516
  in business, 476–77
    for social events, 462
  children and, 19. *See also* Gifts
    age to begin writing, 516
  for fruit in hotel room, 831
  gifts and, 17. *See also* Gifts; *specific
    occasions*
    money, 518
    refusing, 518
  for job interviews, 442
    teen-agers and, 41
  for meal or weekend, 517. *See also* House
    guests; *specific meals*
  printed cards for, 518
  teen-agers and, 50
    for job interviews, 41
    parties and, 51
    proms and, 47
  from wedding guests, 249

weekend guests and, 389, 517
  for White House dinners, 637
  for White House tours, 639
Theaters
  sneezing in, 416–17
  teen-age manners in, 51
Threats, children and, 9
Ties, 670, 672–73
  cruisewear, 837
  restaurant code, 676, 688
  tying bow, 672
  tying four-in-hand, 673
  for weddings, 205, 206
Tiffany (N.Y.), 763
Tipping
  at beach clubs, 716
  and caterers, 369
  on cruises, 838–39
    freighters, 841
  hotel-motel, 829–31
  and plane flight, at checking in, 801
  in restaurants, 680, 686
    strolling musicians, 685
  stevedores, 835
  in taxis, 816
  on trains, 809, 810, 811
  at wedding receptions (gratuities), 242
  weekend guests and domestic staff,
    387–88
  women and picking up tab, 449
  on yachts, 704
Tisanes, 351
Titles. *See also* Address, correct forms of;
    Introductions
  on calling cards, 548
    women's, 550
  on place cards, 290–91
  in return addresses, 497
  in wedding invitations, 138, 139
Toast
  how to eat, 432
  in serving dish, 412
Toasting, 329
  at bachelor dinners, 198
  at christenings, 111
  at informal dinner parties, 293–95
  at wedding anniversaries, 262
  at wedding receptions, 244, 245
  at wedding rehearsal dinners, 199
Tobacco. *See* Smoking
Toilet articles, on trips, 825
Toilets. *See also* Bathrooms; Lavatories
  boys and seats, 30
  on boats, 702
  on buses, 812
  on trains, 810
Toothpicks, 417
  and eating corn, 424
Tortillas, how to eat, 432
Tourist bureaus, and travel, 823
Tourists. *See* Travel
Towels
  instead of finger bowls, 367
  in trousseau, 169, 170
Train travel, 807–11
  by coach or parlor car, 808–9
  eating on trains, 809–10
  planning trip, 807–8
  sleeping cars, 810–11
  in station, 811
  and tipping, 811

Transportation. *See also* Travel; *specific means*
　for domestic employees, 86
　for single women, 77
　for weekend guests, 385
Trash. *See* Litter and littering
Travel, 795–841. *See also* Address, correct forms of; Transportation; *specific means*
　business, 450–51
　　men and women on trips, 450
　　woman alone, 450
　gifts for travelers, 789–91
　　bon voyage, 790–91
　honeymoon trip, 259–60
　letters introducing tourists to friends abroad, 523–24
　making reservations, 527
　by motor vehicle, 814–21
　planning trip, 822–23
　　before you go, 823–24
　　check list, 825–26
　　hotels and motels, 828–33
　　packing suitcase, 826–28
　　preparations, 824–25
　　travel agents, 822–23
　public transportation, 799–813
　single person and, 67, 79
　　woman on business trip, 450
　taking cruise, 834–41
Travel agents, 822–23
Traveler's checks, 826
　on freighter cruises, 840
　as gifts, 761
Trips. *See* Travel
Trousers. *See* Business suits; Formal wear; Pants; Slacks; *specific occasions*
Trousseaus, 169–78
　basic household needs, 176–78
　bed and bath linens, 169–70, 176
　china, 170–71
　glassware, 173–76
　silver, 171–73
　table linens, 170
　tea service, 171
Twins, double wedding of, 224

U

Umbrellas, on trips, 825
Under secretaries of Cabinet, correct forms of address for, 570–71
Underwear. *See also* Lingerie
　for ice skating, 722
Unemployment insurance, 88
Uniform Anatomical Gift Act, 267
Uniforms
　of caterer's waiters and waitresses, 368
　for domestic help, 85–86
United Nations, correct forms of address
　for representatives, 572–73
　for Secretary General, 580–81
"United States Coast Guard Recreational Boating Guide," 700
United States Flag Foundation, 642
United States government officials and individuals, 564–67. *See also* White House
　correct forms of address for, 568–81
　unofficial ranking of, 564–66
　and use of "Esquire," 566–67

United States military personnel. *See* Military
United States Power Squadrons National Headquarters, 700
University officials, correct forms of address for, 578–81
"Uppers," 55
Ushers
　funeral, 274, 278
　wedding, 190–93, 218, 223ff., 227. *See also* Weddings
　　best man and, 189
　　and complicated seating for couple's families, 193
　　dress for, 205
　　duties of, 191–92
　　gifts to, 167
　　gifts to bride from, 193
　　at receptions, 193, 244, 247
　　at rehearsals, 212ff.
　　and seating mothers of couple, 192
Utensils. *See* Flatwear; Table manners; Table setting

V

Vacations. *See* Travel
Valet service, hotel, 831
Valium, 55
Vatican City, 649–52
Veal chops, how to eat, 424
Vegetables
　adding butter to, at table, 413
　how to eat various, 421ff.
　serving, 296
Veils, bridal, 200, 220
Vernon, René, 412
Vermouth, 341
Vicars general, correct forms of address for, 602–3
Vice admirals
　abbreviation of rank, 583
　correct forms of address for, 590–91
　how to tell rank, 583
Vice Presidents, correct forms of address for, 568–69
Visas, 824
Viscountesses, correct forms of address for, 612–13
Viscounts, correct forms of address for, 610–11
　families of, 612–13
Visiting cards. *See* Calling cards
Visually handicapped. *See* Blind persons
Vocabulary, good, as social asset, 743
Vodka, 341
Voice
　parents' tone of, 9
　and public speaking, 730
Volunteer work, 67, 73–74, 437–38
　press relations for, 740
Voting, in parliamentary procedure, 631–32

W

Waistcoats, 676–77
　for riding, 711, 714
Waiters (waitresses)
　catering services and, 82, 367, 368
　at cocktail parties, 339
　at formal meals, 365, 366
　　dinners, 357

luncheons, 363
hotel, 830
restaurant. *See also* Restaurants
 calling, 685
 women and tipping, 449
 on trains, 809–10, 811
Wakes, 269
Walking shorts, men's, 675–76
Wallets, carrying, 670
Walls, in cleaning routine, 94
Warrant officers
 correct forms of address for, 585
 how to tell rank
  Army, 583
  Navy, 583
Washcloths, on trips, 825
Washing. *See* Cleanliness; Dishwashing;
 Laundry
Washington, George, 638
Watches (wristwatches), 667–68
 for formal wear, 677
 in playing tennis, 708
 presents for men, 763–64
Water
 on boats, 702
 at cocktail parties, 341
 soda, for wine spillage, 326
Watercress, how to eat, 428
Water skiing, 718
Water sports, 714–18
 swimming, 714–18. *See also* Swimming
 water skiing, 718
Webb, David, 667
Wedding anniversaries, 262–65
 gifts, 264–65
 invitations and replies, 263–64
 photographs, 265
 reaffirmation of vows, 265
Wedding rings, 127, 201, 205, 220
 best man and, 189, 205, 212
 burial with, 268
 double-ring ceremonies, 222, 232
 Jewish ceremonies, 230
 and playing tennis, 708
 at reaffirmation of marriage vows, 265
 in rehearsals, 212
Weddings, 132–261. *See also* Marriage
 after, 259–61
 announcements, 132–33ff., 160–62. *See
  also* Weddings: invitations
  addressing envelopes, 135
  and elopement, 236
  divorcée, 254
  engraving and stationery, 134
  heraldic devices (coats of arms) on,
   135, 557
  mature bride, 160
  military forms, 161–62
  second marriage, 253–54
  variations in usual wording, 160–61
  when to send, 160
 attendants and duties, 187–94. *See also*
  Weddings: preparations; Weddings:
  pre-wedding parties
  best man, 188–90. *See also* Best man
  bridesmaids, 188. *See also* Bridesmaids
  clothes for, 204–8
  going to church, 194
  if one drops out, 194
  maids and matrons of honor, 187–88.

 See also Maids of honor; Matrons of
  honor
 receiving lines, 238, 240
 and receptions, 193, 247
 at second weddings, 255–56
 ushers, 190–94. *See also* Ushers
 ceremony, 217–37. *See also* Weddings:
  invitations
  at the altar, 218, 220–21
  clergyman's, 234–35
  differences in religion and, 225–33
  double-ring, 222, 232
  double-wedding, 222–24
  driving to reception, 236
  giving away bride, 217–20
  guests at church, 224–25
  at home, 233–34
  kissing parents during, 221–22
  if no reception, 236
  procedure during, 217
  second wedding, 257
  when does bride take groom's arm?,
   221
  when does groom kiss bride?, 221
 of couples living together, 131
 dress for, 200–11
  bridal attendants', 208–10
  bride's, 200–1ff.
  and bride's formal pictures, 203
  flowers, 210
  groom's and best man's, 204, 675
  men's, 206–7
  parents' and guests', 202, 206–7, 210–11
  publicity in papers, 204
  ring, 201. *See also* Wedding rings
  superstitions regarding, 201–3
  ushers', 205
  women's, 202
 elopements and civil ceremonies, 236
 gifts, 163–68, 778–83. *See also* Showers;
  Trousseaus
  for attendants, 167, 198
  bridal registry, 163
  bridal showers, 197–98. *See also*
   Showers
  choosing, 779–80
  couple's to each other, 168
  display of, 164
  at double weddings, 781
  elopement and, 236–37
  enclosure cards with, 782
  exchanging, 166
  money, 780–81
  monogramming, 781
  to official at civil marriage, 237
  one-of-a-kind, 780
  at receptions, 164
  register of, 163–64
  and remarriage (second weddings),
   255, 256, 782–83
  returning, 166–67
  suitable, 779
  thank-you letters for, 164–66
  timetable for sending, 781
  from wedding party, 168, 193
  where to send, 781–82
 home wedding, 233–34
 invitations, 132–62
  addressing envelopes, 135–37
  adopted child, 140
  at home cards, 152

by bride on her own, 143
to clergyman's wedding, 234
combining church ceremony and reception, 147–48
dinner following reception, 151
double wedding of cousins or friends, 142
double wedding of sisters, 142
enclosing maps with, 151
enclosure cards, 150–53
engraving and stationery, 134–35
by fathers and others, 140
foreign procedures, 149–50, 158
foster parent, 140
and girl with same name as mother, 139
by groom's family, 144
heraldic devices (coats of arms), 135, 557
to a house wedding, 144
to informal weddings, 159
late reception, 148–49
layout, different styles, 145
military forms, 161–62
to outdoor wedding, 146
pew cards, 151
postponing weddings, 154
preparing list, 132–33
recalling, 153–54
recalling acceptances, 158
remarried mother, 140
replying to formal, 155–58
replying to informal, 159–60
response cards, 151
second marriages, 145–46, 252–53
second receptions, 250
separated parents, 139
separate reception, 148
wedding at friend's home, 146
when bride keeps maiden name, 152
when names of bride's and groom's parents appear on invitation, 142
when to send, 134
woman with title, 139
wording of formal, 137–47
preparations, 179–86
arrangements with clergyman, 180
choosing place, 180–81
choosing time, 181
church preparations, 181–83
ex-husband's responsibility and, 186
expenses of bride's parents, 184–85
expenses of groom, 185–86
expenses of home, 186
guest book, 183–84
music, 184
photos, 183
putting up guests, 184
second marriage, 255
special problems, 180
pre-wedding parties, 195–99
bachelor dinner, 198
bridesmaids', 195
for out-of-town guests, 195–96
rehearsal dinner, 198–99
showers, 196–98. *See also* Showers
teas, 196
receptions, 238–50. *See also specific members of wedding party*
breakfast, 243
bride's table, 243–44

cake, 245–46. *See also* Cakes
after civil ceremonies, 237
clergyman's wedding, 234
congratulatory telegrams, 245
conversation in receiving line, 240–41
dancing, 247
driving to, 236
fathers in receiving line, 238
flowers at, 242
food at, 245
gifts at, 164
giving your own, 249
gratuities at, 242
guest book, 242
guests at, 248–49
if none, 236
invitations, 147, 148
Jewish, 230
Mormon, 233
music at, 246–47
parents' table, 243
photos at, 241–42
problems of divided house, 248
receiving line, 238–41
second or delayed, 249–50
second marriage, 256–57, 258
throwing bride's bouquet, 247
toasts at, 245
ushers and, 193
who receives in place of bride's mother, 240
rehearsals, 212–16
processional, 212–14
recessional, 214–16
when there are two main aisles, 214
which arm does bride take?, 212
second or subsequent, 251–58. *See also* Remarriage
trousseau, 169–70
Weekend guests, 381–90. *See also* House guests
breakfast for, 384
guest bathroom, 383–84
for guest to remember, 385–88
guest room, 381–83
invitations, 381
organizing the day, 385
saying thank you, 389–90, 517
Welsh, and coats of arms, 554
Western riding, 711–12
Wheel chairs, and flying, 801
White House, 635–39. *See also* Kennedy, President and Mrs. John F.
business calls, 637–38
dinners and menus, 310, 311–12, 355, 356, 636–37
gifts to, 638
and invitations, 635–36
letters to, 525, 638
stationery, 506
taking tour of, 639
and unofficial ranking of government officials, 564
"White Tie," 678. *See also specific occasions*
and White House invitations, 636
women and gloves, 664
White wine, 317–18
at cocktail parties, 340–41
at formal dinners, 357, 360

glasses for, 320, 321
ordering in restaurants, 683, 684
service of, 322ff.
spillage of, 326
Widows (and widowers), 69–70. *See also*
Funerals
and anniversary date, 262
calling cards of, 549
and consideration for late spouse's family,
70
and consideration for new spouse, 70
and dating, 69–70
and entertaining, 69
and personal stationery, 74, 498
and weddings (remarriage), 220, 255. *See
also* Remarriage
invitations, 136, 141, 145–46, 151
Wigs, on trips, 826
Wilderness Club, 698
Wine, 317–26. *See also* Champagne;
Dinners and dinner parties; Toasting
alcoholic content of, 57
cellar, 318–19
children and, 58, 343
on cruise, 836
at formal dinners, 357, 360, 361
at formal luncheons, 364
gifts for lovers of, 793
glasses for, 319–22
at informal luncheons, 348
for Jewish weddings, 230
kinds to serve, 317–18
appetizer, 317
dessert, 318
red table, 318. *See also* Red wine

sparkling, 318. *See also* Champagne
white table, 317–18. *See also* White
wine
men and women sharing on business trip,
450
ordering in restaurants, 683–84
on picnics, 373
service, 322–26
spillage, 325–26
Wine steward, 679
Withholding tax, 87
Wives. *See* Marriage
"Woman," use of, 728
Women for Sobriety, Inc., 60
Women's Bureau, 490
Woodwork, in cleaning routine, 94
Work. *See* Business; Jobs
Workmen's compensation, 87
Wranglers, in Western riding, 712
Wristwatches. *See* Watches

Y

Yacht clubs, 703–4
dress for, 701
Yachting and sailing, 700–5
before boarding sailboat, 700–1
clothes to take, 701
gifts, 703
guests' rules of behavior, 701–2
host's rules of behavior, 702–3
life on big yachts, 704
powerboats, 703
yacht clubs, 703–4